BICENTENNIAL
1807
WILEY
2007
BICENTENNIAL

THE WILEY BICENTENNIAL—KNOWLEDGE FOR GENERATIONS

*E*ach generation has its unique needs and aspirations. When Charles Wiley first opened his small printing shop in lower Manhattan in 1807, it was a generation of boundless potential searching for an identity. And we were there, helping to define a new American literary tradition. Over half a century later, in the midst of the Second Industrial Revolution, it was a generation focused on building the future. Once again, we were there, supplying the critical scientific, technical, and engineering knowledge that helped frame the world. Throughout the 20th Century, and into the new millennium, nations began to reach out beyond their own borders and a new international community was born. Wiley was there, expanding its operations around the world to enable a global exchange of ideas, opinions, and know-how.

For 200 years, Wiley has been an integral part of each generation's journey, enabling the flow of information and understanding necessary to meet their needs and fulfill their aspirations. Today, bold new technologies are changing the way we live and learn. Wiley will be there, providing you the must-have knowledge you need to imagine new worlds, new possibilities, and new opportunities.

Generations come and go, but you can always count on Wiley to provide you the knowledge you need, when and where you need it!

PRESIDENT AND CHIEF EXECUTIVE OFFICER   **CHAIRMAN OF THE BOARD**

Multicultural Education

Issues and Perspectives

SIXTH EDITION

Edited by

JAMES A. BANKS
University of Washington, Seattle

CHERRY A. McGEE BANKS
University of Washington, Bothell

BICENTENNIAL
1807
WILEY
2007
BICENTENNIAL

Photo Credits Part 1 PhotoDisc, Inc./Getty Images. PhotoDic, Inc./Getty Images. Dynamic Graphics, inc./Creatas. **Part 2** Corbis Digital Stock. Dynamic Graphics. Inc./Creatas. Corbis Digital Stock. **Part 3** Corbis Digital Stock. Digital Vision. PhotoDisc, Inc./Getty Images. **Part 4** Corbis Digital Stock. Dynamic Graphics, Inc./Creatas. PhotoDisc, Inc./Getty Images.

ACQUISITIONS EDITOR   Robert Johnston
SENIOR PRODUCTION EDITOR   Patricia McFadden
MARKETING MANAGER   Jeffrey Rucker
CREATIVE DIRECTOR   Harry Nolan
SENIOR DESIGNER   Kevin Murphy
SENIOR PHOTO EDITOR   Lisa Gee
EDITORIAL ASSISTANT   Katie Melega
MEDIA EDITOR   Sasha Giacoppo
PRODUCTION MANAGEMENT SERVICES   Ingrao Associates

This book was set in 10/12 New Times Roman by Techbooks and printed and bound by Malloy Lithographing. The cover was printed by Phoenix Color.

This book is printed on acid free paper.∞

To order books or for customer service please call 1-800-CALL WILEY (225-5945).

ISBN-13   978-0-471-78047-2
ISBN-10   0-471-78047-2

Printed in the United States of America

10 9 8 7 6 5 4 3 2 1

Chapter 9 is reprinted with the permission of the American Educational Research Association and Gloria Ladson-Billings. It was originally published as Gloria Ladson-Billings, G. Toward a Theory of Culturally Relevant Pedagogy. *American Educational Research Journal, 35*, 465–491(1995).

Chapter 11 is adapted from Janet Ward Schofield, *Prejudice, Discrimination, and Racism*, pp. 321–253. Copyright © 1986 by Academic Press Company and used with permission of the author and publisher.

Preface

World and national events since the publication of the fifth edition of this book have underscored the need to help students develop multicultural literacy, cosmopolitan attitudes and perspectives, and a commitment to act to promote social justice in the United States and the world. Worldwide immigration is increasing racial, ethnic, cultural, linguistic, and religious diversity throughout the United States as well as in other Western nations such as the United Kingdom, France, Germany, and Australia (Banks, 2004). The Western world is perplexed, exhausted, and fear ridden as it attempts to envision and implement viable and creative strategies to respond effectively to the intransigent conflicts in the Middle East (Barber, 2003). These events have resulted in bombings that have created a worldwide reign of terror—including the bombing of the Pentagon and the World Trade Center on September 11, 2001; the bombings of four commuter trains in Madrid, Spain, on March 11, 2004; the bombings in the London transportation system on July 7, 2005; and the bombing of a Red Sea resort at Sharm el-Sheikh in Egypt on July 23, 2005.

We are living in a dangerous, confused, and troubled world that demands leaders, educators, and classroom teachers who can bridge impermeable cultural, ethnic, and religious borders, envision new possibilities, invent novel paradigms, and engage in personal transformation and visionary action. The concepts, paradigms, and projects that facilitated the rise and triumph of the West between the sixteenth and the twentieth centuries are ineffective in the re-created world of the twenty-first century. The world is undergoing a transformation—and in the words of Thomas L. Friedman (2005), "The world is flat." In the flat world described by Friedman, scientific and technological workers educated in Asian nations such as India and China are competing successfully—and sometimes outperforming—scientific and technological workers in the United States. The United States can no longer take its scientific and technological superiority for granted because of the leap in scientific and technological education in Asian nations such as India and China. American students educated in Seattle, New York City, and Washington, D.C., must now be prepared to compete directly for jobs in the United States with students educated in India, Pakistan, and China. This is because technology allows U.S. firms to export many service jobs to other nations where they can be done as well as or better by foreign workers and for a fraction of the cost.

Effective teachers in a diverse and flat world need an education that enables them to attain new knowledge, paradigms, and perspectives on the United States and the world and to deal effectively with both the challenges and opportunities of diversity. There is increasing diversity as well as increasing recognition of diversity in nation-states throughout the world. Racial, cultural, ethnic, language, and religious diversity is also increasing in schools in the United States as well as within other nations.

The cultural, racial, ethnic, and religious diversity within the United States provides an excellent context for students to acquire the multicultural understandings and skills needed to function effectively in their local communities, the nation, and the world. Political upheaval, world migration, and transnational economic linkages are bringing peoples throughout the world into increased contact, cultural interaction, and conflict within national borders.

Racial, ethnic, language, class, and religious diversity is deepening within the United States as a consequence of worldwide population movements and the magnetic pull of the American Dream. Non-Hispanic Whites make up about 75 percent of the U.S. population (U.S. Census Bureau, 2001). However, the U.S. Census projects that the non-Hispanic White percentage of the nation's population will decrease in the coming years and that racial, ethnic, cultural, and language diversity will deepen. If current demographic trends continue, non-Hispanic Whites are expected to make up 50 percent of the U.S. population by 2050.

Diversity in the United States is becoming increasingly reflected in the nation's schools, colleges, and universities. In 2004, 41.3 percent of the students enrolled in grades 1–12 in the public schools were students of color (Hoffman & Sable, 2006). It is projected that students of color will make up about 48 percent of the nation's school-age youth by 2020. The KIDS COUNT Data Book (Anna E. Casey Foundation, 2005) indicates that 19 percent of school-age youth speak a language other than English at home. Consequently, large numbers of students in the nation's schools are English-language learners. It is projected that 20 to 25 percent of the students in U.S. public schools will be second-language learners by 2025.

Many of the nation's students are poor. In 2004, 36.9 million people in the United States were living in poverty, including one in five students (DeNavas-Walt, Proctor, & Lee, 2005). The gap between the rich and the poor is also widening. In 1976, the top 1 percent of Americans owned 20 percent of the nation's wealth. The top 1 percent owned 47 percent of U.S. wealth in 2001 (DeNavas-Walt, Proctor, & Lee).

These demographic, social, and economic trends have important implications for teaching and learning in today's schools. As the nation's students become increasingly diverse, most of the nation's teachers remain White, middle-class, and female. In 2002, approximately 87 percent of the nation's teachers were White and 74 percent were female. Consequently, a wide gap exists between the racial, cultural, and language characteristics of U.S. students and teachers.

The increasing diversity within the nation's schools provides both opportunities and challenges. Diverse classrooms and schools make it possible to teach students from many different cultures and groups how to live together cooperatively and productively. However, racial prejudice and discrimination are challenges that arise when people from diverse groups come together. Teachers need to acquire the knowledge and skills needed to maximize the opportunities that diversity offers and to minimize its challenges. Teacher education programs should help teachers attain the knowledge and behaviors needed to work effectively with students from diverse groups as well as help students from mainstream groups develop cross-cultural knowledge, values, and competencies.

Multicultural Education: Issues and Perspectives, Sixth Edition, is designed to help current and future educators acquire the concepts, paradigms, and explanations needed to become effective practitioners in culturally, racially, and linguistically diverse classrooms and schools. This Sixth Edition has been revised to reflect current and emerging research, concepts, and debates about the education of students from both genders and from different cultural, racial, ethnic, and language groups. Exceptionality is a part of our concept of diversity because there are exceptional students in each group discussed in this book.

Chapters 9 and 12 are new to this Sixth Edition. The new co-authors added to Chapters 6 and 8 have brought new information, insights, and perspectives to the revisions of these chapters. All of the chapters from the previous edition have been revised to reflect new research, theories, census data, statistics, interpretations, and developments. The Multicultural Resources in the appendix have been substantially revised and updated. The glossary has been revised to incorporate new census data and interpretations.

This book consists of six parts. The chapters in Part I discuss how race, gender, class, and exceptionality interact to influence student behavior. Social class and religion and their effects on education are discussed in Part II. Part III describes how educational opportunity differs for female and male students and how schools can foster gender equity. The issues, problems, and opportunities for educating students of color and students with language differences are discussed in Part IV. Chapter 11, on the colorblind perspective, highlights the importance of race even when it is unacknowledged by teachers. Part V focuses on exceptionality, describing the issues involved in creating equal educational opportunity for students who have disabilities and for those who are gifted. The final part, Part VI, discusses multicultural education as a process of school reform and ways to increase student academic achievement and to work more effectively with parents.

The appendix consists of a list of books for further reading. The glossary defines many of the key concepts and terms used throughout the book.

ACKNOWLEDGMENTS

We are grateful to the authors who revised their chapters for this Sixth Edition of *Multicultural Education* and to the authors who wrote new chapters. We thank Yuhshi Lee—a research assistant in the Center for Multicultural Education at the University of Washington—for helping to update the statistics in various parts of the book. We are grateful to Diane August and Kathryn Lindholm Leary for the thoughtful and helpful peer reviews they prepared on a draft of Chapter 13 that enabled the authors to strengthen it.

James A. Banks
Cherry A. McGee Banks

REFERENCES

Banks, J. A. (Ed.). (2004). *Diversity and Citizenship Education: Global Perspectives.* San Francisco: Jossey-Bass.

Barber, B. R. (2003). *Fear's Empire: War, Terrorism, and Democracy.* New York: Norton.

The Annie E. Casey Foundation. (2005). *2005 KIDS COUNT Data Book.* Retrieved January 30, 2006, from http://www.aecf.org/kidscount/sld/db05_pdfs/entire_db.pdf.

DeNavas-Walt, C., Proctor, B. D., and Lee, C. H. (2005). *U.S. Census Bureau, Current Population Reports, P60-229, Income, Poverty, and Health Insurance Coverage in the United States: 2004.* Washington, D.C.: U.S. Government Printing Office.

Friedman, T. L. (2005). *The World Is Flat: A Brief History of the Twenty-first Century*. New York: Farrar, Straus and Giroux.

Hoffman, L., and Sable, J. (2006). *Public Elementary and Secondary Students, Staff, Schools, and School Districts: School Year 2003–04* (NCES 2006–307). Washington, D.C.: National Center for Education Statistics.

U.S. Census Bureau. (2001) *Population Division and Housing and Household Economic Statistics Division*. Retrieved January 23, 2006, from http://www.census.gov/population/www/pop-profile/natproj.html.

Contents

7005 version
Chapter 9 Educationally Equality for students of color

Different

A major goal of multicultural education is to create schools in which students from diverse groups have an equal opportunity to learn.

Issues and Concepts

The three chapters in Part I define the major concepts and issues in multicultural education, describe the diverse meanings of culture, and describe the ways in which such variables as race, class, gender, and exceptionality influence student behavior. Various aspects and definitions of culture are discussed. Culture is conceptualized as a dynamic and complex process of construction; its invisible and implicit characteristics are emphasized. The problems that result when culture is essentialized are described.

Multicultural education is an idea, an educational reform movement, and a process whose major goal is to change the structure of educational institutions so that male and female students, exceptional students, and students who are members of diverse racial, ethnic, language, and cultural groups will have an equal chance to achieve academically in school. It is necessary to conceptualize the school as a social system in order to implement multicultural education successfully. Each major variable in the school, such as its culture, its power relationships, the curriculum and materials, and the attitudes and beliefs of the staff, must be changed in ways that will allow the school to promote educational equality for students from diverse groups.

To transform the schools, educators must be knowledgeable about the influence of particular groups on student behavior. The chapters in this part of the book describe the nature of culture and groups in the United States as well as the ways in which they interact to influence student behavior.

CHAPTER 1

Multicultural Education: Characteristics and Goals

James A. Banks

THE NATURE OF MULTICULTURAL EDUCATION

Multicultural education is at least three things: an idea or concept, an educational reform movement, and a process. Multicultural education incorporates the idea that all students— regardless of their gender and social class and their ethnic, racial, or cultural characteristics— should have an equal opportunity to learn in school. Another important idea in multicultural education is that some students, because of these characteristics, have a better chance to learn in schools as they are currently structured than do students who belong to other groups or who have different cultural characteristics.

Some institutional characteristics of schools systematically deny some groups of students equal educational opportunities. For example, in the early grades, girls and boys achieve equally in mathematics and science. However, the achievement test scores of girls fall considerably behind those of boys as children progress through the grades (Clewell, 2002; Francis, 2000). Girls are less likely than boys to participate in class discussions and to be encouraged by teachers to participate. Girls are more likely than boys to be silent in the classroom. However, not all school practices favor males. As Sadker and Zittleman point out in Chapter 6, boys are more likely to be disciplined than are girls, even when their behavior does not differ from that of girls. They are also more likely than girls to be classified as learning disabled (Donovan & Cross, 2002). Males of color, especially African American males, experience a highly disproportionate rate of disciplinary actions and suspensions in school. Some scholars, such as Noguera (2003), have described the serious problems that African American males experience in school and in the wider society.

In the early grades, the academic achievement of students of color such as African Americans, Latinos, and American Indians is close to parity with the achievement of White mainstream students (Steele, 2003). However, the longer these students of color remain in school, the more their achievement lags behind that of White mainstream students. Social-class status is also strongly related to academic achievement. Persell, in Chapter 4, describes how educational opportunities are much greater for middle- and upper-income students than for low-income students. Knapp and Woolverton (2004), as well as Oakes, Joseph, and Muir (2004), describe the powerful ways in which social class influences students' opportunities to learn.

Exceptional students, whether they are physically or mentally disabled or gifted and talented, often find that they do not experience equal educational opportunities in the schools. The chapters in Part V describe the problems that such exceptional students experience in schools and suggest ways that teachers and other educators can increase their chances for educational success.

Multicultural education is also a reform movement that is trying to change the schools and other educational institutions so that students from all social-class, gender, racial, language, and cultural groups will have an equal opportunity to learn. Multicultural education involves changes in the total school or educational environment; it is not limited to curricular changes (Banks & Banks, 2004). The variables in the school environment that multicultural education tries to transform are discussed later in this chapter and illustrated in Figure 1.5. Multicultural education is also a process whose goals will never be fully realized.

Educational equality, like liberty and justice, is an ideal toward which human beings work but never fully attain. Racism, sexism, and discrimination against people with disabilities will exist to some extent no matter how hard we work to eliminate these problems. When prejudice and discrimination are reduced toward one group, they are usually directed toward another group or they take new forms. Whenever groups are identified and labeled, *categorization* occurs. When categorization occurs, members of in-groups favor in-group members and discriminate against out-groups (Stephan, 1999). This process can occur without groups having a history of conflict, animosity, or competition, and without their having physical differences or any other kind of important difference. Social psychologists call this process *social identity theory* or the *minimal group paradigm* (Rothbart & John, 1993; Smith & Mackie, 1995). Because the goals of multicultural education can never be fully attained, we should work continuously to increase educational equality for all students. Multicultural education must be viewed as an ongoing process, not as something that we "do" and thereby solve the problems that are the targets of multicultural educational reform (Banks, 2006a).

HIGH-STAKES TESTING: A CHALLENGE FOR SOCIAL JUSTICE

The No Child Left Behind Act is being widely interpreted and implemented as a testing and assessment initiative. The emphasis on testing, standards, and accountability that is mandated in most states compels many teachers to focus on narrow and basic skills in reading, writing, and math (Sleeter, 2005). In too many classrooms, testing and test preparation are replacing teaching and learning. Research by Amrein and Berliner (2002) indicates that the emphasis on testing and accountability is having detrimental effects on student learning.

Because of the ways in which accountability is being conceptualized and implemented, the professional role of teachers is being fractured and minimized. However, some writers and researchers, such as Roderick, Jacob and Bryk (2002), have provided evidence that the focus on the underachievement of targeted groups of students that is required by the NCLB Act has in some cases resulted in higher achievement among these students.

The national focus on basic skills and testing is diverting attention from the broad liberal education that students need to live and function effectively in a multicultural nation and world. It is essential that all students acquire basic literacy and numeracy skills. However, students also need the knowledge, skills, and values that will enable them to live, interact, and make decisions with fellow citizens from different racial, ethnic, cultural, language, and religious groups.

The schools need to teach about social justice issues in addition to teaching basic skills. Teaching for social justice is very important because of the crises that the United States and the world face. An education that is narrowly defined as academic achievement and testing will not prepare students to become effective citizens who are committed to social justice. We should educate students to be reflective, moral, caring, and active citizens in a troubled world (Banks, 2004a). The world's greatest problems do not result from people being unable to read and write. They result from people in the world—from different cultures, races, religions, and nations—being unable to get along and to work together to solve the world's problems, such as global warming, the HIV/AIDS epidemic, poverty, racism, sexism, terrorism, international conflict, and war. Examples are the conflicts between the Western and Arab nations, North Korea and its neighbors, and the Israeli–Palestinian conflict.

MULTICULTURAL EDUCATION: AN INTERNATIONAL REFORM MOVEMENT

Since World War II, many immigrants and groups have settled in the United Kingdom and in nations on the European continent, including France, the Netherlands, Germany, Sweden, and Switzerland (Banks, 2004a; Figueroa, 2004). Some of these immigrants, such as the Asians and West Indians in England and the North Africans and Indochinese in France, have come from former colonies. Many Southern and Eastern European immigrants have settled in Western and Northern European nations in search of upward social mobility and other opportunities. Groups such as Italians, Greeks, and Turks have migrated to Northern and Western European nations in large numbers. Ethnic and immigrant populations have also increased significantly in Australia and Canada since World War II (Allan & Hill, 2004; Joshee, 2004).

Most of the immigrant and ethnic groups in Europe, Australia, and Canada face problems similar to those experienced by ethnic groups in the United States. Groups such as the Jamaicans in England, the Algerians in France, and the Aborigines in Australia experience achievement problems in the schools and prejudice and discrimination in both the schools and society at large. These groups also experience problems attaining full citizenship rights and recognition in their nation-states (Luchtenberg, 2005).

The United Kingdom, various nations on the European continent, and Australia and Canada have implemented a variety of programs to increase the achievement of ethnic and immigrant students and to help students and teachers develop more positive attitudes toward racial, cultural, ethnic, and language diversity (Banks, 2004a; Figueroa, 2004).

THE HISTORICAL DEVELOPMENT OF MULTICULTURAL EDUCATION

Multicultural education grew out of the ferment of the civil rights movement of the 1960s. During this decade, African Americans embarked on a quest for their rights that was unprecedented in the United States. A major goal of the civil rights movement of the 1960s was to eliminate discrimination in public accommodations, housing, employment, and education. The consequences of the civil rights movement had a significant influence on educational institutions as ethnic groups—first African Americans and then other groups—demanded that the schools and other educational institutions reform curricula to reflect their experiences, histories, cultures, and perspectives. Ethnic groups also demanded that the schools hire more Black and Brown teachers and administrators so that their children would have more successful role models. Ethnic groups pushed for community control of schools in their neighborhoods and for the revision of textbooks to make them reflect the diversity of peoples in the United States.

The first responses of schools and educators to the ethnic movements of the 1960s were hurried (Banks, 2006b). Courses and programs were developed without the thought and careful planning needed to make them educationally sound or to institutionalize them within the educational system. Holidays and other special days, ethnic celebrations, and courses that focused on one ethnic group were the dominant characteristics of school reforms related to ethnic and cultural diversity during the 1960s and early 1970s. Grant and Sleeter, in Chapter 3, call this approach "single-group studies." The ethnic studies courses developed and implemented during this period were usually electives and were taken primarily by students who were members of the group that was the subject of the course.

The visible success of the civil rights movement, plus growing rage and a liberal national atmosphere, stimulated other marginalized groups to take actions to eliminate discrimination against them and to demand that the educational system respond to their needs, aspirations, cultures, and histories. The women's rights movement emerged as one of the most significant social reform movements of the twentieth century (Schmitz, Butler, Rosenfelt, & Guy-Sheftal, 2004). During the 1960s and 1970s, discrimination against women in employment, income, and education was widespread and often blatant. The women's rights movement articulated and publicized how discrimination and institutionalized sexism limited the opportunities of women and adversely affected the nation. The leaders of this movement, such as Betty Friedan and Gloria Steinem, demanded that political, social, economic, and educational institutions act to eliminate sex discrimination and to provide opportunities for women to actualize their talents and realize their ambitions (Steinem, 1995). Major goals of the women's rights movement included equal pay for equal work, the elimination of laws that discriminated against women and made them second-class citizens, the hiring of more women in leadership positions, and greater participation of men in household work and child rearing.

When *feminists* (people who work for the political, social, and economic equality of the sexes) looked at educational institutions, they noted problems similar to those identified by ethnic groups of color. Textbooks and curricula were dominated by men; women were largely invisible. Feminists pointed out that history textbooks were dominated by political and military history—areas in which men had been the main participants (Trecker, 1973). Social and family history and the history of labor and of ordinary people were largely ignored. Feminists pushed for the revision of textbooks to include more history about the important roles of women in the development of the nation and the world. They also demanded that more women be hired for administrative positions in the schools. Although most teachers in the elementary schools were women, most administrators were men.

Other marginalized groups, stimulated by the social ferment and the quest for human rights during the 1970s, articulated their grievances and demanded that institutions be reformed so they would face less discrimination and acquire more human rights. People with disabilities, senior citizens, and gay rights advocates were among the groups that organized politically during this period and made significant inroads in changing institutions and laws. Advocates for citizens with disabilities attained significant legal victories during the 1970s. The Education for All Handicapped Children Act of 1975 (P.L. 94–142), which required that students with disabilities be educated in the least restricted environment and institutionalized the word *mainstreaming* in education, was perhaps the most significant legal victory of the movement for the rights of students with disabilities in education (see Chapters 13 and 14).

HOW MULTICULTURAL EDUCATION DEVELOPED

Multicultural education emerged from the diverse courses, programs, and practices that educational institutions devised to respond to the demands, needs, and aspirations of the various groups. Consequently, as Grant and Sleeter point out in Chapter 3, multicultural education is not in actual practice one identifiable course or educational program. Rather, practicing educators use the term *multicultural education* to describe a wide variety of programs and practices related to educational equity, women, ethnic groups, language minorities, low-income groups, and people with disabilities. In one school district, multicultural education may mean a curriculum that incorporates the experiences of ethnic groups of color; in another, a program may include the experiences of both ethnic groups and women. In a third school district, this term may be used the way it is by me and by other authors, such as Nieto (2004) and Sleeter and Grant (2006); that is, to mean a total school reform effort designed to increase educational equity for a range of cultural, ethnic, and economic groups. This broader and more comprehensive notion of multicultural education is discussed in the last part of this chapter. It differs from the limited concept of multicultural education, in which it is viewed as curriculum reform.

THE NATURE OF CULTURE IN THE UNITED STATES

The United States, like other Western nation-states such as the United Kingdom, Australia, and Canada, is a multicultural society. The United States consists of a shared core culture as well as many subcultures. In this book, we call the larger shared core culture the *macroculture*; the smaller cultures, which are a part of the core culture, are called *microcultures*. It is important to distinguish the macroculture from the various microcultures because the values, norms, and characteristics of the mainstream (macroculture) are frequently mediated by, as well as interpreted and expressed differently within, various microcultures. These differences often lead to cultural misunderstandings, conflicts, and institutionalized discrimination.

Students who are members of certain cultural, religious, and ethnic groups are sometimes socialized to act and think in certain ways at home but differently at school (Ogbu, 2003). In her study of African American students and families in Trackton, Heath (1983) found that the pattern of language use in school was very different from the pattern used at home. At home, most of the children's interaction with adults consisted of imperatives, or commands. At school, questions were the dominant form of interactions between teachers and students. A challenge that multicultural education faces is how to help students from diverse groups mediate between their home and community cultures and the school culture. Students should acquire the knowledge, attitudes, and skills needed to function effectively in each cultural setting. They should also be competent to function within and across other microcultures in their society, within the national macroculture, and within the world community (Banks, 2004a).

The Meaning of Culture

Bullivant (1993) defines culture as a group's program for survival in and adaptation to its environment. The cultural program consists of knowledge, concepts, and values shared by group members through systems of communication. Culture also consists of the shared beliefs, symbols, and interpretations within a human group. Most social scientists today view culture as consisting primarily of the symbolic, ideational, and intangible aspects of human societies. The essence of a culture is not its artifacts, tools, or other tangible cultural elements but how the members of the group interpret, use, and perceive them. It is the values, symbols, interpretations, and perspectives that distinguish one people from another in modernized societies; it is not material objects and other tangible aspects of human societies (Kuper, 1999). People in a culture usually interpret the meanings of symbols, artifacts, and behaviors in the same or in similar ways.

Identifying and Describing the U.S. Core Culture

The United States, like other nation-states, has a shared set of values, ideations, and symbols that constitute the core or overarching culture. This culture is shared to some extent by all the diverse cultural and ethnic groups that make up the nation-state. It is difficult to identify and describe the overarching culture in the United States because it is such a diverse and complex nation. It is easier to identify the core culture within an isolated premodern society, such as the Maoris before the Europeans came to New Zealand, than within highly pluralistic, modernized societies such as the United States, Canada, and Australia (Lisitzky, 1956).

When trying to identify the distinguishing characteristics of U.S. culture, one should realize that the political institutions in the United States, which reflect some of the nation's core values, were heavily influenced by the British. U.S. political ideals and institutions were also influenced by Native American political institutions and practices, especially those related to making group decisions, such as in the League of the Iroquois (Weatherford, 1988).

Equality

A key component in the U.S. core culture is the idea, expressed in the Declaration of Independence in 1776, that "all men are created equal, that they are endowed by their Creator with certain unalienable rights, that among these are life, liberty, and the pursuit of happiness." When this idea was expressed by the nation's founding fathers in 1776, it was considered radical. A common belief in the eighteenth century was that human beings were not born with equal rights—that some people had few rights and others, such as kings, had divine rights given by God. When considering the idea that "all men are created equal" is a key component of U.S. culture, one should remember to distinguish between a nation's ideals and its actual practices, as well as between the meaning of the idea when it was expressed in 1776 and its meaning today. When the nation's founding fathers expressed this idea in 1776, their conception of men was limited to White males who owned property (Foner, 1998; Ladson-Billings, 2004). White men without property, White women, and all African Americans and Indians were not included in their notion of people who were equal or who had "certain unalienable rights."

Although the idea of equality expressed by the founding fathers in 1776 had a very limited meaning at that time, it has proven to be a powerful and important idea in the quest for human rights in the United States. Throughout the nation's history since 1776, marginalized and excluded groups such as women, African Americans, Native Americans, and other cultural and ethnic groups have used this idea to justify and defend the extension of human rights to them and to end institutional discrimination, such as sexism, racism, and discrimination against people with disabilities (Branch, 2006). As a result, human rights have gradually been extended to various groups throughout U.S. history. The extension of these rights has been neither constant nor linear. Rather, periods of extension of rights have often been followed by periods of retrenchment and conservatism. Schlesinger (1986) calls these patterns "cycles of American history." The United States is still a long way from realizing the ideals expressed in the Declaration of Independence in 1776. However, these ideals remain an important part of U.S. culture and are still used by marginalized groups to justify their struggles for human rights and equality.

Individualism and Individual Opportunity

Two other important ideas in the common overarching U.S. culture are individualism and individual social mobility (Stewart & Bennett, 1991). Individualism as an ideal is extreme in the U.S. core culture. Individual success is more important than commitment to family, community, and nation-state. An individual is expected to achieve success solely by his or her own efforts. Many people in the United States believe that a person can go from rags to riches within a generation and that every American-born boy can, but not necessarily will, become president.

Individuals are expected to achieve success by hard work and to pull themselves up by their bootstraps. This idea was epitomized by fictional characters such as Ragged Dick, one of the heroes created by the popular writer Horatio Alger. Ragged Dick attained success by valiantly overcoming poverty and adversity. A related belief is that if you do not succeed, it is because of your own shortcomings, such as being lazy or unambitious; failure is consequently your own fault. These beliefs are taught in the schools with success stories and myths about such U.S. heroes as George Washington, Thomas Jefferson, and Abraham Lincoln. The beliefs about individualism in U.S. culture are related to the Protestant work ethic. This is the belief that hard work by the individual is morally good and that laziness is sinful. This belief is a legacy of the British Puritan settlers in colonial New England. It has had a powerful and significant influence on U.S. culture.

The belief in individual opportunity has proven tenacious in U.S. society. It remains strong in American culture despite the fact that individuals' chances for upward social, economic, and educational mobility in the United States are highly related to the social-class, ethnic, gender, and other ascribed groups to which they belong (Knapp & Woolverton, 2004). The findings of social science research, as well as the chapters in this book, document the extent of social-class stratification in the United States and the ways in which people's opportunities in life are strongly influenced by the groups to which they belong (Willis, 1977). Yet the belief in individual opportunity remains strong in the United States.

Individualism and Groupism

Although the groups to which people belong have a major influence on their life chances in the United States, Americans—particularly those in the mainstream—are highly individualistic in their value orientations and behaviors. The nuclear family reinforces individualism in U.S. culture. One result of the strong individualism is that married children usually expect their older parents to live independently or in homes for senior citizens rather than with them.

The strong individualism in U.S. culture contrasts sharply with the groupism and group commitment found in Asian nations, such as China and Japan (Butterfield, 1982; Reischauer, 1981). Individualism is viewed rather negatively in these societies. One is expected to be committed first to the family and group and then to oneself. Some U.S. social scientists, such as Lasch (1978) and Bellah, Madsen, Sullivan, Swidler, and Tipton (1985), lament the extent of individualism in U.S. society. They believe it is harmful to the common national culture. Some observers believe that groupism is too strong in China and Japan and that individualism should be more valued in those nations. Perhaps modernized, pluralistic nation-states can best benefit from a balance between individualism and groupism, with neither characteristic dominating.

Expansionism and Manifest Destiny

Other overarching U.S. values that social scientists have identified include the desire to conquer or exploit the natural environment, materialism and consumption, and the belief in the nation's inherent superiority. These beliefs justified Manifest Destiny and U.S. expansion to the West and into other nations and the annexation of one-third of Mexico's territory in 1848. These observations, which reveal the less positive side of U.S. national values, have been developed by social scientists interested in understanding the complex nature of U.S. society (Appleby, Hunt, & Jacob, 1994).

In his discussion of the nature of values in U.S. society, Myrdal (1944/1962) contends that a major ethical inconsistency exists in U.S. society. He calls this inconsistency "the American dilemma." He states that American creed values, such as equality and human dignity, exist in U.S. society as ideals. However, they exist alongside the institutionalized discriminatory treatment of African Americans and other ethnic and cultural groups in U.S. society. This variance creates a dilemma in the American mind because Americans try to reconcile their democratic ideals with their treatment of marginalized groups. Myrdal states that this dilemma has been an important factor that has enabled ethnic groups to fight discrimination effectively. In their efforts to resolve their dilemma when the inconsistencies between their ideals and actions are pointed out to them by human rights advocates, Americans, according to Myrdal, often support the elimination of practices that are inconsistent with their democratic ideals or the American creed. Some writers have refuted Myrdal's hypothesis and contend that most individuals in the United States do not experience such a dilemma (Ellison, 1995).

Microcultures in the United States

A nation as culturally diverse as the United States consists of a common overarching culture as well as a series of microcultures (see Figure 1.1). These microcultures share most of the core values of the nation-state, but these values are often mediated by the various microcultures

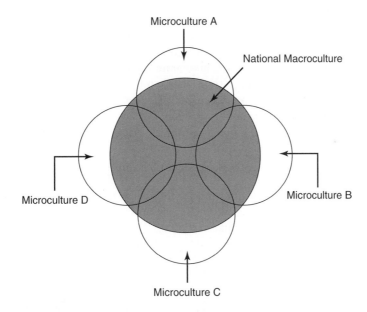

Figure 1.1   Microcultures and the National Macroculture

The shaded area represents the national macroculture. A, B, C, and D represent microcultures that consist of unique institutions, values, and cultural elements that are nonuniversalized and are shared primarily by members of specific cultural groups. A major goal of the school should be to help students acquire the knowledge, skills, and attitudes needed to function effectively within the national macroculture, their own microcultures, and within and across other microcultures.

Source: James A. Banks. *Cultural Diversity and Education: Foundations, Curriculum and Teaching*, 4th ed. (Boston: Allyn & Bacon), p. 73. Used with permission of the author.

and are interpreted differently within them. Microcultures sometimes have values that are some-what alien to the national core culture. Also, some of the core national values and behaviors may seem somewhat alien in certain microcultures or may take different forms.

The strong belief in individuality and individualism that exists within the national macro-culture is often much less endorsed by some ethnic communities and is somewhat alien within them. African Americans and Latinos who have not experienced high levels of cul-tural assimilation into the mainstream culture are much more group oriented than are main-stream Americans. Schools in the United States are highly individualistic in their learning and teaching styles, evaluation procedures, and norms. Many students, particularly African Americans, Latinos, and Native Americans, are group oriented (Irvine & York, 2001). These students experience problems in the highly individualistic learning environment of the school. Teachers can enhance the learning opportunities of these students, who are also called field dependent or field sensitive, by using cooperative teaching strategies that have been developed and field-tested by researchers such as Slavin (2001) and Cohen and Lotan (2004).

Some theories and research indicate that female students may have preferred ways of knowing, thinking, and learning that differ to some extent from those most often preferred by males (Goldberger, Tarule, Clinchy, & Belenky, 1996; Halpern, 1986; Taylor, Gilligan, & Sullivan, 1995). Maher (1987) describes the dominant inquiry model used in social science as male constructed and dominated. She contends that it strives for objectivity: "Personal feelings, biases, and prejudices are considered inevitable limitations" (p. 186). Feminist ped-agogy is based on different assumptions about the nature of knowledge and results in a dif-ferent teaching method. According to Maher and Tetreault (1994), feminist pedagogy enhances the learning of females and deepens the insight of males. In Chapter 7, Tetreault describes feminist pedagogy techniques she uses to motivate students and to enhance their understandings.

After completing a major research study on women's ways of knowing, Belenky, Clinchy, Goldberger, and Tarule (1986) concluded that conceptions of knowledge and truth in the core culture and in educational institutions "have been shaped throughout history by the male-dominated majority culture. Drawing on their own perspectives and visions, men have constructed the prevailing theories, written history, and set values that have become the guid-ing principles for men and women alike" (p. 5).

These researchers also found an inconsistency between the kind of knowledge most appealing to women and the kind that was emphasized in most educational institutions. Most of the women interviewed in their study considered personalized knowledge and knowledge that resulted from first-hand observation most appealing. However, most educational insti-tutions emphasize abstract, "out-of-context" knowledge (Belenky et al., 1986, p. 200). Ramírez and Castañeda (1974) found that Mexican American students who were socialized within traditional cultures also considered personalized and humanized knowledge more appealing than abstract knowledge. They also responded positively to knowledge that was presented in a humanized or story format.

Research by Gilligan (1982) provides some clues that help us better understand the find-ings by Belenky and her colleagues about the kind of knowledge women find most appealing. Gilligan describes caring, interconnection, and sensitivity to the needs of other people as dom-inant values among women and the female microculture in the United States. By contrast, she found that the values of men were more characterized by separation and individualism.

A major goal of multicultural education is to change teaching and learning approaches so that students of both genders and from diverse cultural, ethnic, and language groups will have equal opportunities to learn in educational institutions. This goal suggests that major changes ought to be made in the ways that educational programs are conceptualized, organized, and taught. Educational approaches need to be transformed.

In her research on identifying and labeling students with mental retardation, Mercer (1973) found that a disproportionate number of African American and Mexican American students were labeled mentally retarded because the testing procedures used in intelligence tests "reflect the abilities and skills valued by the American core culture" (p. 32), which Mercer describes as predominantly White, Anglo-Saxon, and middle and upper class. She also points out that measures of general intelligence consist primarily of items related to verbal skills and knowledge. Most African American and Latino students are socialized within microcultures that differ in significant ways from the U.S. core culture. These students often have not had an equal opportunity to learn the knowledge and skills that are measured in mental ability tests. Consequently, a disproportionate number of African American and Latino students are labeled mentally retarded and are placed in classes for slow learners (Donovan & Cross, 2002). Mental retardation, as Mercer points out, is a socially determined status. When students are placed in classes for the mentally retarded, the self-fulfilling prophecy develops. Students begin to act and think as though they *are* mentally retarded (Banks, 2000).

Groups and Group Identification

Thus far, this chapter has discussed the various microcultures that make up U.S. society. Individuals learn the values, symbols, and other components of their culture from their social group. The group is the social system that carries a culture. People belong to and live in social groups (Bullivant, 1993). A group is a collectivity of persons who share an identity, a feeling of unity. A group is also a social system that has a social structure of interrelated roles (Theodorson & Theodorson, 1969). The group's program for survival, values, ideations, and shared symbols constitutes its culture (Kuper, 1999).

The study of groups is the major focus in sociology. Sociologists believe that the group has a strong influence on the behavior of individuals, that behavior is shaped by group norms, and that the group equips individuals with the behavior patterns needed to adapt to their physical, social, and metaphysical environments. Sociologists also assume that groups have independent characteristics; they are more than aggregates of individuals. Groups possess a continuity that transcends the lives of individuals.

Sociologists also assume that knowledge about groups to which an individual belongs provides important clues to and explanations for the individual's behavior. Goodman and Marx (1982) write, "Such factors as shared religion, nationality, age, sex, marital status, and education have proved to be important determinants of what people believe, feel, and do" (p. 7). Although membership in a gender, racial, ethnic, social-class, or religious group can provide us with important clues about individuals' behavior, it cannot enable us to predict behavior. Knowing one's group affiliation can enable us to state that a certain type of behavior is probable. Membership in a particular group does not determine behavior but makes certain types of behavior more probable.

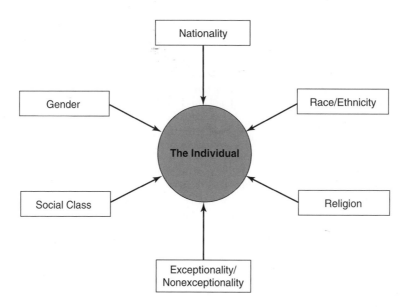

Figure 1.2 Multiple Group Memberships

An individual belongs to several different groups at the same time. This figure shows the major groups discussed in this book.

There are several important reasons that knowledge of group characteristics and modalities can enable us to predict the probability of an individual's behavior but not the precise behavior. This is, in part, because each individual belongs to several groups at the same time (see Figure 1.2). An individual may be White, Catholic, female, and middle class, all at the same time. She might have a strong identification with one of these groups and a very weak or almost nonexistent identification with another. A person can be a member of a particular group, such as the Catholic church, and have a weak identification with the group and a weak commitment to the tenets of the Catholic faith. Religious identification might be another individual's strongest group identification. Identification with and attachments to different groups may also conflict. A woman who has a strong Catholic identification but is also a feminist might find it difficult to reconcile her beliefs about equality for women with some positions of the Catholic church, such as its prohibiting women from being ordained as priests.

The more we know about a student's level of identification with a particular group and the extent to which socialization has taken place within that group, the more accurately we can predict, explain, and understand the student's behavior in the classroom. A knowledge of the importance of a group to a student at a particular time of life and within a particular social context will also help us understand the student's behavior. Ethnic identity may become more important to a person who becomes part of an ethnic minority when he or she previously belonged to the majority. Many Whites who have moved from the U.S. mainland to Hawaii have commented on how their sense of ethnic identity increased and they began to feel marginalized. Group identity may also increase when the group feels threatened, when a social movement arises to promote its rights, or when the group attempts to revitalize its culture.

The Teaching Implications of Group Identification

What are the implications of group membership and group identity for teaching? As you read the chapters in this book that describe the characteristics of the two gender groups and of social-class, racial, ethnic, religious, language, and exceptional groups, bear in mind that individuals within these groups manifest these behaviors to various degrees. Also remember that individual students are members of several of these groups at the same time. Above, the core U.S. culture is described as having highly individualistic values and beliefs. However, research by Gilligan (1982) indicates that the values of women, as compared with those of men, are more often characterized by caring, interconnection, and sensitivity to the needs of others. This observation indicates how core values within the macroculture are often mediated by microcultures within various gender, ethnic, and cultural groups.

As stated above, researchers have found that some students of color, such as African Americans and Mexican Americans, often have field-sensitive learning styles and therefore prefer more personalized learning approaches (Ramírez & Castañeda, 1974). Think about what this means. This research describes a group characteristic of these students, not the behavior of a particular African American or Mexican American student. It suggests that there is a higher probability that these students will have field-sensitive learning styles than will middle-class Anglo American students. However, students within all ethnic, racial, and social-class groups have different learning styles and characteristics (Irvine & York, 2001). Those groups influence students' behavior, such as their learning style, interactively, because they are members of several groups at the same time. Knowledge of the characteristics of groups to which students belong, of the importance of each of these groups to them, and of the extent to which individuals have been socialized within each group will give the teacher important clues to students' behavior.

The Interaction of Race, Class, and Gender

When using our knowledge of groups to understand student behavior, we should also consider the ways in which such variables as class, race, and gender interact and intersect to influence student behavior. Middle-class and more highly assimilated Mexican American students tend to be more field-independent than do lower-class and less-assimilated Mexican American students. African American students tend to be more field dependent (group oriented) than White students; females tend to be more field dependent than male students. Therefore, it can be hypothesized that African American females would be the most field dependent when compared to African American and White males and White females. This finding was made by Perney (1976).

Figure 1.3 illustrates how the major groups discussed in this book—gender, race or ethnicity, social class, religion, and exceptionality—influence student behavior, both singly and interactively. The figure also shows that other variables, such as geographic region and age, also influence an individual's behavior. The ways in which these variables influence selected student behaviors are described in Table 1.1.

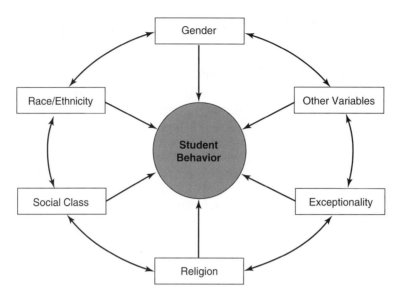

Figure 1.3   The Intersection of Variables

The major variables of gender, race or ethnicity, social class, religion, and exceptionality influence student behavior, both singly and interactively. Other variables, such as region and age, also influence student behavior.

Table 1.1   Singular and Combined Effects of Variables

Student Behavior	Gender Effects	Race/ Ethnicity Effects	Social- Class Effects	Religious Effects	Combined Effects
Learning Styles (Field Independent/Field Dependent)	X[a]	X			X
Internality/Externality			X		
Fear of Success	X	X			?
Self-Esteem	X	X			?
Individual vs. Group Orientation	X	X	X		?

[a]An X indicates that the variable influences the student behavior that is described in the far-left column. An X in the far-right column means that research indicates that two or more variables combine to influence the described behavior. A question mark indicates that the research is unclear about the combined effects of the variables.

THE SOCIAL CONSTRUCTION OF CATEGORIES

The major variables and categories discussed in this book, such as gender, race, ethnicity, class, and exceptionality, are social categories (Berger & Luckman, 1967; Mannheim, 1936). The criteria for whether an individual belongs to one of these categories are determined by human beings and consequently are socially constructed. Religion is also a social category. Religious institutions, symbols, and artifacts are created by human beings to satisfy their metaphysical needs.

These categories are usually related to the physical characteristics of individuals. In some cases, as when they are individuals with severe or obvious physical disabilities, the relationship between the labels given to individuals and their physical characteristics is direct and would be made in almost any culture or social system. The relationship between categories that are used to classify individuals and their physical characteristics, however, is usually indirect and complex. Even though one's sex is determined primarily by physical characteristics (genitalia, chromosome patterns, etc.), gender is a social construction created and shaped by the society in which individuals and groups function.

Gender

Gender consists of the socially and psychologically appropriate behavior for males and females sanctioned by and expected within a society. Gender-role expectations vary across cultures and at different times in a society and within microcultures in the same society. Traditionally, normative behavior for males and females has varied among mainstream Americans, African Americans, Native Americans, and Hispanic Americans. Gender-role expectations also vary somewhat across social classes within the same society. In the White mainstream society in the 1940s and 1950s, upper-middle-class women often received negative sanctions when they worked outside the home, whereas women in working-class families were frequently expected to become wage earners.

Sexual Orientation

The discussion of gender roles provides an appropriate context for the examination of issues related to sexual orientation. The quest by gays and lesbians for human and civil rights has been an important development within the United States and throughout the Western world within the last several decades. Sexual orientation deserves examination when human rights and social justice are discussed because it is an important identity for individuals and groups and because many gay youths are victims of discrimination and hate crimes (*Harvard Educational Review*, 1996; Lipkin, 1999). Sexual orientation is often a difficult issue for classroom discussion for both teachers and students. However, if done sensitively, it can help empower gay and lesbian students and enable them to experience social equality in the college and university classroom. Recognition is one important manifestation of social equality (Gutmann, 2004).

Race

Race is a socially determined category that is related to physical characteristics in a complex way (Jacobson, 1998; Roediger, 2002). Two individuals with nearly identical physical characteristics, or phenotypes, can be classified as members of different races in two different societies (Nash, 1999; Root, 2004). In the United States, where racial categories are well defined and highly inflexible, an individual with any acknowledged or publicly known African ancestry is considered Black (Davis, 1991). One who looks completely Caucasian but who acknowledges some African ancestry is classified as Black. Such an individual would be considered White in Puerto Rico. In Puerto Rico, hair texture, social status, and degree of eminence in the community are often as important as—if not more important than—physical characteristics in determining an individual's racial group or category. There is a saying in Puerto Rico that "money lightens," which means that upward social mobility considerably enhances an individual's opportunity to be classified as White. There is a strong relationship between race and social class in Puerto Rico and in most other Caribbean and Latin American nations.

Our discussion of race as a social category indicates that the criteria for determining the characteristics of a particular race vary across cultures, that an individual considered Black in one society may be considered White in another, and that racial categories reflect the social, economic, and political characteristics of a society.

Social Class

Social scientists find it difficult to agree on criteria for determining social class. The problem is complicated by the fact that societies are constantly in the throes of change. During the 1950s, social scientists often attributed characteristics to the lower class that are found in the middle class today, such as single-parent and female-headed households, high divorce rates, and substance abuse. Today, these characteristics are no longer rare among the middle class, even though their frequency is still higher among lower-class families. Variables such as income, education, occupation, lifestyle, and values are among the most frequently used indices to determine social-class status in the United States (Warner, 1949/1960). However, there is considerable disagreement among social scientists about which variables are the most important in determining the social-class status of an individual or family.

Social-class criteria also vary somewhat among various ethnic and racial groups in the United States. Teachers, preachers, and other service professionals were upper class in many rural African American communities in the South in the 1950s and 1960s but were considered middle class by mainstream White society. The systems of social stratification that exist in the mainstream society and in various microcultures are not necessarily identical.

Exceptionality

Exceptionality is also a social category. Whether a person is considered disabled or gifted is determined by criteria developed by society. As Shaver and Curtis (1981) point out, disabilities are not necessarily handicaps, and the two should be distinguished. They write, "A disability or combination of disabilities becomes a handicap only when the condition limits or impedes the person's ability to function normally" (p. 1). A person with a particular disability, such as having one arm, might have a successful college career, experience no barriers to his achievements in college, and graduate with honors. However, he may find that when he tries to enter the job market, his opportunities are severely limited because potential employers view him as unable to perform well in some situations in which, in fact, he could perform effectively (Shaver & Curtis, 1981). This individual has a disability but was viewed as handicapped in one situation (the job market) but not in another (his university).

Mercer (1973) has extensively studied the social process by which individuals become labeled as persons with mental retardation. She points out that even though their physical characteristics may increase their chance of being labeled persons with mental retardation, the two are not perfectly correlated. Two people with the same biological characteristics may be considered persons with mental retardation in one social system but not in another one. An individual may be considered a person with mental retardation at school but not at home. She writes, "Mental retardation is not a characteristic of the individual, nor a meaning inherent in behavior, but a socially determined status, which [people] may occupy in some social systems and not in others" (p. 31). She states that people can change their role by changing their social group.

The highly disproportionate number of African Americans, Latinos, and particularly males classified as learning disabled by the school indicates the extent to which exceptionality is a social category (Donovan & Cross, 2002). Mercer (1973) found that the school labeled more people mentally retarded than did any other institution. Many African American and Latino students who are labeled mentally retarded function normally and are considered normal in their homes and communities. Boys are more often classified as mentally retarded than are girls. The school, as Mercer and other researchers have pointed out, uses criteria to determine the mental ability of students of color that conflict with their home and community cultures. Some students in all ethnic and cultural groups are mentally retarded and deserve special instruction, programs, and services, as the authors in Part V of this book suggest. However, the percentage of students of color in these programs is too high. The percentage of students in each ethnic group labeled mentally retarded should be about the same as the total percentage of that group in school.

Giftedness is also a social category (Sapon-Shevin, 1994). Important results of the socially constructed nature of giftedness are the considerable disagreement among experts about how the concept should be defined and the often inconsistent views about how to identify gifted students (Ford & Harris, 1999). The highly disproportionate percentage of middle- and upper-middle-class mainstream students categorized as gifted compared to low-income students and students of color, such as African Americans, Latinos, and Native Americans, is also evidence of the social origin of the category.

Many students who are classified as gifted do have special talents and abilities and need special instruction. However, some students who are classified as gifted by school districts merely have parents with the knowledge, political skills, and power to force the school to classify their children as gifted, which will provide them with special instruction and educational enrichment (Sapon-Shevin, 1994).

Schools should try to satisfy the needs of students with special gifts and talents; however, they should also make sure that students from all social-class, cultural, language, and ethnic groups have an equal opportunity to participate in programs for academically and creatively talented students. If schools or districts do not have a population in their gifted programs that represents their various cultural, racial, language, and ethnic groups, steps should be taken to examine the criteria used to identify gifted students and to develop procedures to correct the disproportion. Both excellence and equality should be major goals of education in a pluralistic society.

THE DIMENSIONS OF MULTICULTURAL EDUCATION

When many teachers think of multicultural education, they think only or primarily of content related to ethnic, racial, and cultural groups. Conceptualizing multicultural education exclusively as content related to various ethnic and cultural groups is problematic for several reasons. Teachers who cannot easily see how their content is related to cultural issues will easily dismiss multicultural education with the argument that it is not relevant to their disciplines. This is done frequently by secondary math and science teachers.

The irrelevant-of-content argument can become a legitimized form of resistance to multicultural education when it is conceptualized primarily or exclusively as content. Math and science teachers often state, "Multicultural education is fine for social studies and literature teachers, but it has nothing to do with me. Math and science are the same, regardless of the culture or the kids." Multicultural education needs to be more broadly defined and understood so that teachers from a wide range of disciplines can respond to it in appropriate ways and resistance to it can be minimized.

Multicultural education is a broad concept with several different and important dimensions (Banks, 2004b). Practicing educators can use the dimensions as a guide to school reform when trying to implement multicultural education. The dimensions are (1) content integration, (2) the knowledge construction process, (3) prejudice reduction, (4) an equity pedagogy, and (5) an empowering school culture and social structure. Each dimension is defined and illustrated next.

Content Integration

Content integration deals with the extent to which teachers use examples and content from a variety of cultures and groups to illustrate key concepts, principles, generalizations, and theories in their subject area or discipline. The infusion of ethnic and cultural content into the subject area should be logical, not contrived.

More opportunities exist for the integration of ethnic and cultural content in some subject areas than in others. In the social studies, the language arts, and music, frequent and ample opportunities exist for teachers to use ethnic and cultural content to illustrate concepts, themes, and principles. There are also opportunities to integrate multicultural content into math and science. However, the opportunities are not as ample as they are in social studies, the language arts, and music.

The Knowledge Construction Process   *text book point of view*

The knowledge construction process relates to the extent to which teachers help students to understand, investigate, and determine how the implicit cultural assumptions, frames of reference, perspectives, and biases within a discipline influence the ways in which knowledge is constructed within it (Banks, 1996).

Students can analyze the knowledge construction process in science by studying how racism has been perpetuated in science by genetic theories of intelligence, Darwinism, and eugenics. In his important book *The Mismeasure of Man*, Gould (1996) describes how scientific racism developed and was influential in the nineteenth and twentieth centuries.

Scientific racism has had and continues to have a significant influence on the interpretations of mental ability tests in the United States.

The publication of *The Bell Curve* (Herrnstein & Murray, 1994), its widespread and enthusiastic public reception, and the social context out of which it emerged provide an excellent case study for discussion and analysis by students who are studying knowledge construction (Kincheloe, Steinberg, & Gresson, 1996). Herrnstein and Murray contend that low-income groups and African Americans have fewer intellectual abilities than do other groups and that these differences are inherited. Students can examine the arguments made by the authors, their major assumptions, and how their conclusions relate to the social and political context.

Gould (1994) contends that Herrnstein and Murray's arguments reflect the social context of the times, "a historical moment of unprecedented ungenerosity, when a mood for slashing social programs can be powerfully abetted by an argument that beneficiaries cannot be helped, owing to inborn cognitive limits expressed as low I.Q. scores" (p. 139). Students should also study counterarguments to *The Bell Curve* made by respected scientists. Two good sources are *The Bell Curve Debate: History, Documents, Opinions*, edited by Jacoby and Glauberman (1995), and *Measured Lies: The Bell Curve Examined*, edited by Kincheloe, Steinberg, and Gresson (1996).

Students can examine the knowledge construction process in the social studies when they study such units and topics as the European discovery of America and the westward movement. The teacher can ask the students the latent meanings of concepts such as the European discovery of America and the New World. The students can discuss what these concepts imply or suggest about the Native American cultures that had existed in the Americas for about 40,000 years before the Europeans arrived. When studying the westward movement, the teacher can ask the students, "Whose point of view or perspective does this concept reflect, that of the European Americans or the Lakota Sioux?" "Who was moving west?" "How might a Lakota Sioux historian describe this period in U.S. history?" "What are other ways of thinking about and describing the westward movement?"

Prejudice Reduction

Prejudice reduction describes lessons and activities teachers use to help students develop positive attitudes toward different racial, ethnic, and cultural groups. Research indicates that children come to school with many negative attitudes toward and misconceptions about different racial and ethnic groups (Banks, 2001b; Stephan & Vogt, 2004). Research also indicates that lessons, units, and teaching materials that include content about different racial and ethnic groups can help students to develop more positive intergroup attitudes if certain conditions exist in the teaching situation (Banks, 2001b). These conditions include positive images of the ethnic groups in the materials and the use of multiethnic materials in a consistent and sequential way.

Allport's (1954) *contact hypothesis* provides several useful guidelines for helping students to develop more positive interracial attitudes and actions in contact situations. He states that contact between groups will improve intergroup relations when the contact is characterized by these four conditions: (1) equal status, (2) cooperation rather than competition, (3) sanction by authorities such as teachers and administrators, and (4) interpersonal interactions in which students become acquainted as individuals.

An Equity Pedagogy

Teachers in each discipline can analyze their teaching procedures and styles to determine the extent to which they reflect multicultural issues and concerns. An equity pedagogy exists when teachers modify their teaching in ways that will facilitate the academic achievement of students from diverse racial, cultural, gender, and social-class groups. This includes using a variety of teaching styles and approaches that are consistent with the wide range of learning styles within various cultural and ethnic groups, being demanding but highly personalized when working with groups such as Native American and Alaskan students, and using cooperative learning techniques in math and science instruction in order to enhance the academic achievement of students of color (Cohen & Lotan, 2004; Slavin, 2001).

Several chapters in this book discuss ways in which teachers can modify their instruction in order to increase the academic achievement of students from different cultural groups and from both gender groups, including the chapters that constitute Parts III and IV.

An Empowering School Culture

Another important dimension of multicultural education is a school culture and organization that promotes gender, racial, and social-class equity. The culture and organization of the school must be examined by all members of the school staff. They all must also participate in restructuring it. Grouping and labeling practices, sports participation, disproportionality in achievement, disproportionality in enrollment in gifted and special education programs, and the interaction of the staff and the students across ethnic and racial lines are important variables that need to be examined in order to create a school culture that empowers students from diverse racial and ethnic groups and from both gender groups.

Figure 1.4 summarizes the dimensions of multicultural education described above. The next section identifies the major variables of the school that must be changed in order to institutionalize a school culture that empowers students from diverse cultural, racial, ethnic, and social-class groups.

THE SCHOOL AS A SOCIAL SYSTEM

To implement multicultural education successfully, we must think of the school as a social system in which all its major variables are closely interrelated. Thinking of the school as a social system suggests that we must formulate and initiate a change strategy that reforms the total school environment to implement multicultural education. The major school variables that must be reformed are presented in Figure 1.5.

Reforming any one of the variables in Figure 1.5, such as the formalized curriculum or curricular materials, is necessary but not sufficient. Multicultural and sensitive teaching materials are ineffective in the hands of teachers who have negative attitudes toward different racial, ethnic, and cultural groups. Such teachers are rarely likely to use multicultural materials or are likely to use them detrimentally. Thus, helping teachers and other members of the school staff to gain knowledge about diverse groups and democratic attitudes and values is essential when implementing multicultural programs.

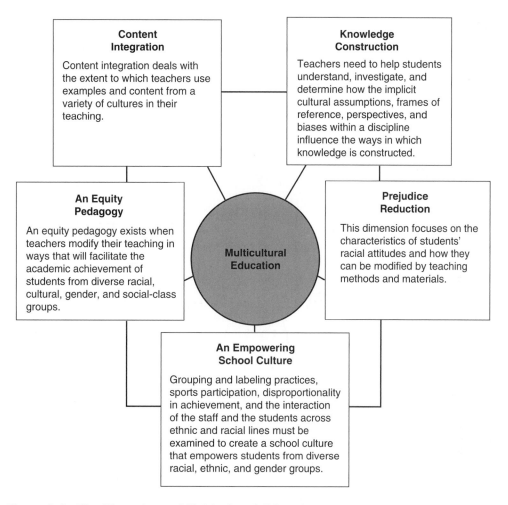

Content Integration

Content integration deals with the extent to which teachers use examples and content from a variety of cultures in their teaching.

Knowledge Construction

Teachers need to help students understand, investigate, and determine how the implicit cultural assumptions, frames of reference, perspectives, and biases within a discipline influence the ways in which knowledge is constructed.

An Equity Pedagogy

An equity pedagogy exists when teachers modify their teaching in ways that will facilitate the academic achievement of students from diverse racial, cultural, gender, and social-class groups.

Multicultural Education

Prejudice Reduction

This dimension focuses on the characteristics of students' racial attitudes and how they can be modified by teaching methods and materials.

An Empowering School Culture

Grouping and labeling practices, sports participation, disproportionality in achievement, and the interaction of the staff and the students across ethnic and racial lines must be examined to create a school culture that empowers students from diverse racial, ethnic, and gender groups.

Figure 1.4   The Dimensions of Multicultural Education

To implement multicultural education in a school, we must reform its power relationships, the verbal interaction between teachers and students, the culture of the school, the curriculum, extracurricular activities, attitudes toward minority languages (Beykont, 2000), the testing program, and grouping practices. The institutional norms, social structures, cause–belief statements, values, and goals of the school must be transformed and reconstructed.

Major attention should be focused on the school's hidden curriculum and its implicit norms and values. A school has both a manifest and a hidden curriculum. The manifest curriculum consists of such factors as guides, textbooks, bulletin boards, and lesson plans. These aspects of the school environment are important and must be reformed to create a school culture that promotes positive attitudes toward diverse cultural groups and helps students from these groups experience academic success. However, the school's hidden or latent curriculum is often more important than is its manifest or overt curriculum. The latent curriculum has been defined as

latent /
manifest

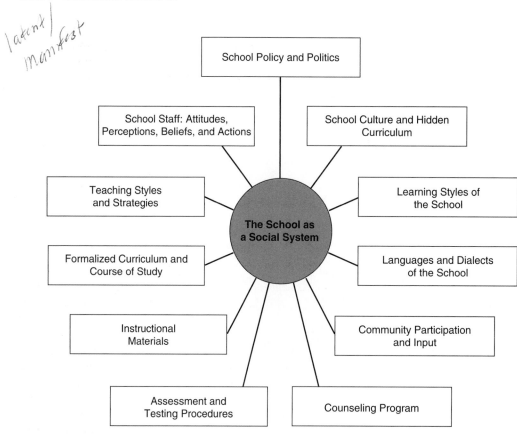

Figure 1.5   The School as a Social System

The total school environment is a system consisting of a number of major identifiable variables and factors, such as a school culture, school policy and politics, and the formalized curriculum and course of study. Any of these factors may be the focus of initial school reform, but changes must take place in each of them to create and sustain an effective multicultural school environment.

Source: Adapted with permission from James A. Banks (Ed.), *Education in the 80s: Multiethnic Education* (Washington, DC: National Education Association, 1981), Figure 2, p. 22.

the one that no teacher explicitly teaches but that all students learn. It is that powerful part of the school culture that communicates to students the school's attitudes toward a range of issues and problems, including how the school views them as human beings and its attitudes toward males, females, exceptional students, and students from various religious, cultural, racial, and ethnic groups. Jackson (1992) calls the latent curriculum the "untaught lessons."

When formulating plans for multicultural education, educators should conceptualize the school as a microculture that has norms, values, statuses, and goals like other social systems. The school has a dominant culture and a variety of microcultures. Almost all classrooms in the United States are multicultural because White students, as well as Black and Brown students, are socialized within diverse cultures. Teachers also come from many different groups.

Many teachers were socialized in cultures other than the Anglo mainstream, although these may be forgotten and repressed. Teachers can get in touch with their own cultures and use the perspectives and insights they acquired as vehicles for helping them relate to and understand the cultures of their students.

The school should be a cultural environment in which acculturation takes place; teachers and students should assimilate some of the views, perspectives, and ethos of each other as they interact. Teachers and students will be enriched by this process, and the academic achievement of students from diverse groups will be enhanced because their perspectives will be legitimized in the school. Both teachers and students will be enriched by this process of cultural sharing and interaction.

SUMMARY

Multicultural education is an idea stating that all students, regardless of the groups to which they belong, such as those related to gender, ethnicity, race, culture, language, social class, religion, or exceptionality, should experience educational equality in the schools. Some students, because of their particular characteristics, have a better chance to succeed in school as it is currently structured than students from other groups. Multicultural education is also a reform movement designed to bring about a transformation of the school so that students from both genders and from diverse cultural, language, and ethnic groups will have an equal chance to experience school success. Multicultural education views the school as a social system that consists of highly interrelated parts and variables. Therefore, in order to transform the school to bring about educational equality, all the major components of the school must be substantially changed. A focus on any one variable in the school, such as the formalized curriculum, will not implement multicultural education.

Multicultural education is a continuing process because the idealized goals it tries to actualize—such as educational equality and the eradication of all forms of discrimination—can never be fully achieved in human society. Multicultural education, which was born during the social protest of the 1960s and 1970s, is an international movement that exists in nations throughout the world (Banks, 2004a). A major goal of multicultural education is to help students to develop the knowledge, attitudes, and skills needed to function within their own microcultures, the U.S. macroculture, other microcultures, and the global community.

Questions and Activities

1. What are the three components or elements of multicultural education?
2. How does Banks define multicultural education?
3. Find other definitions of multicultural education in several books listed under the category "Issues and Concepts" in the Appendix. How are the definitions of multicultural education in these books alike and different from the one presented in this chapter?
4. In what ways did the civil rights and women's rights movements of the 1960s and 1970s influence the development of multicultural education?

5. Ask several teachers and other practicing educators to give you their views and definitions of multicultural education. What generalizations can you make about their responses?

6. Visit a local school and, by observing several classes as well as by interviewing several teachers and the principal, describe what curricular and other practices related to multicultural education have been implemented in the school. Share your report with your classmates or workshop colleagues.

7. What is a macroculture? A microculture?

8. How is culture defined? What are the most important components of culture in a modernized society?

9. List and define several core or overarching values and characteristics that make up the macroculture in the United States. To what extent are these values and characteristics consistent with practices in U.S. society? To what extent are they ideals that are inconsistent with realities in U.S. society?

10. How is individualism viewed differently in the United States and in nations such as China and Japan? Why? What are the behavioral consequences of these varying notions of individualism?

11. What is the American dilemma defined by Myrdal? To what extent is this concept an accurate description of values in U.S. society? Explain.

12. How do the preferred ways of learning and knowing among women and students of color often influence their experiences in the schools as they are currently structured? In what ways can school reform help make the school environment more consistent with the learning and cognitive styles of women and students of color?

13. In what ways does the process of identifying and labeling students with mental retardation discriminate against groups such as African Americans and Latinos?

14. In what ways can the characteristics of a group help us understand an individual's behavior? In what ways are group characteristics limited in explaining an individual's behavior?

15. How do such variables as race, class, and gender interact to influence the behavior of students? Give examples to support your response.

16. What is meant by the "social construction of categories"? In what ways are concepts such as gender, race, social class, and exceptionality social categories?

17. List and define the five dimensions of multicultural education. How can these dimensions be used to facilitate school reform?

References

Allan, R., & Hill, B. (2004). Multicultural Education in Australia: Historical Development and Current Status. In J. A. Banks & C. A. M. Banks (Eds.), *Handbook of Research on Multicultural Education* (2nd. ed., pp. 979–995). San Francisco: Jossey-Bass.

Allport, G. W. (1954). *The Nature of Prejudice*. Reading, MA: Addison-Wesley.

Amrein, A. L., & Berliner, D. C. (2002). High-Stakes Testing, Uncertainty, and Student Learning. *Education Policy Analysis Archives, 10*(8). Retrieved February 14, 2003, from http://eppa.asu.edu/eppa/v10n18/.

Appleby, J., Hunt, L., & Jacob, M. (1994). *Telling the Truth about History.* New York: Norton.

Banks, J. A. (Ed.). (1996). *Multicultural Education, Transformative Knowledge, and Action.* New York: Teachers College Press.

Banks, J. A. (2000). The Social Construction of Difference and the Quest for Educational Equality. In R. Brandt (Ed.), *Education in a New Era* (pp. 21–45). Arlington, VA: Association for Supervision and Curriculum Development.

Banks, J. A. (2001). Multicultural Education: Its Effects on Students' Racial and Gender Role Attitudes. In J. A. Banks & C. A. M. Banks (Eds.), *Handbook of Research on Multicultural Education* (pp. 617–627). San Francisco: Jossey-Bass.

Banks, J. A. (Ed.). (2004a). *Diversity and Citizenship Education: Global Perspectives.* San Francisco: Jossey-Bass.

Banks, J. A. (2004b). Multicultural Education: Historical Development, Dimensions, and Practice. In J. A. Banks & C. A. M. Banks (Eds.), *Handbook of Research on Multicultural Education* (2nd ed., pp. 3–29). San Francisco: Jossey-Bass.

Banks, J. A. (2006a). *Cultural Diversity and Education: Foundations, Curriculum, and Teaching* (4th ed.). Boston: Allyn & Bacon.

Banks, J. A. (2006b). *Race, Culture, and Education: The Selected Works of James A. Banks.* London & New York: Routledge.

Banks, J. A., & Banks, C. A. M. (Eds.). (2004). *Handbook of Research on Multicultural Education* (2nd ed.). San Francisco: Jossey-Bass.

Belenky, M. F., Clinchy, B. M., Goldberger, N. R., & Tarule, J. M. (1986). *Women's Ways of Knowing: The Development of Self, Voice, and Mind.* New York: Basic Books.

Bellah, R. N., Madsen, R., Sullivan, W. M., Swidler, A., & Tipton, S. M. (1985). *Habits of the Heart: Individualism and Commitment in American Life.* New York: Harper & Row.

Berger, P. L., & Luckman, T. (1967). *The Social Construction of Reality: A Treatise in the Sociology of Knowledge.* New York: Doubleday.

Beykont, Z. F. (Ed.). (2000). *Lifting Every Voice: Pedagogy and Politics of Bilingualism.* Cambridge, MA: Harvard Education Publishing Group.

Branch, T. (2006). *At Canaan's Edge: America in the King Years, 1965–68.* New York: Simon & Schuster.

Bullivant, B. (1993). Culture: Its Nature and Meaning for Educators. In J. A. Banks & C. A. M. Banks (Eds.), *Multicultural Education: Issues and Perspectives* (2nd ed., pp. 29–47). Boston: Allyn & Bacon.

Butterfield, F. (1982). *China: Alive in the Bitter Sea.* New York: Bantam.

Clewell, B. C. (2002). Breaking the Barriers: The Critical Middle School Years. In *The Jossey-Bass Reader on Gender in Education* (pp. 301–313). San Francisco: Jossey-Bass.

Cohen, E. G., & Lotan, R. (2004). Equity in Heterogeneous Classrooms. In J. A. Banks & C. A. M. Banks (Eds.), *Handbook of Research on Multicultural Education* (2nd ed., pp. 736–750). San Francisco: Jossey-Bass.

Davis, F. J. (1991). *Who Is Black? One Nation's Definition.* University Park: The Pennsylvania State University Press.

Donovan, M. S., & Cross, C. T. (Eds.). (2002). *Minority Students in Special and Gifted Education.* Washington, DC: National Academy Press.

Ellison, R. (1995). An American Dilemma: A Review. In J. F. Callahan (Ed.), *The Collected Essays of Ralph Ellison* (pp. 328–340). New York: The Modern Library.

Figueroa, P. (2004). Multicultural Education in the United Kingdom: Historical Development and Current Status. In J. A. Banks & C. A. M. Banks (Eds.), *Handbook of Research on Multicultural Education* (2nd ed., pp. 997–1026). San Francisco: Jossey-Bass.

Foner, E. (1998). *The Story of American Freedom.* New York: Norton.

Ford, D. Y., & Harris, J. J., III. (1999). *Multicultural Gifted Education.* New York: Teachers College Press.

Francis, B. (2000). *Boys, Girls and Achievement: Addressing the Classroom Issues.* London: RoutledgeFalmer.

Gilligan, C. (1982). *In a Different Voice: Psychological Theory and Women's Development.* Cambridge, MA: Harvard University Press.

Goldberger, N., Tarule, J., Clinchy, B., & Belenky, M. (Eds.). (1996). *Knowledge, Difference, and Power.* New York: Basic Books.

Goodman, N., & Marx, G. T. (1982). *Society Today* (4th ed.). New York: Random House.

Gould, S. J. (1994). Curveball. *The New Yorker,* 70(38), 139–149.

Gould, S. J. (1996). *The Mismeasure of Man* (rev. & exp. ed.). New York: Norton.

Gutmann, A. (2004). Unity and Diversity in Democratic Multicultural Education: Creative and Destructive Tensions. In J. A. Banks (Ed.), *Diversity and Citizenship Education: Global Perspectives* (pp. 71–98). San Francisco: Jossey-Bass.

Halpern, D. F. (1986). *Sex Differences in Cognitive Abilities.* Hillsdale, NJ: Erlbaum.

Harvard Educational Review. (1996). Lesbian, Gay, Bisexual, and Transgender People and Education. 66 (2). [Special issue].

Heath, S. B. (1983). *Ways with Words: Language, Life, and Work in Communities and Classrooms.* New York: Oxford University Press.

Herrnstein, R. J., & Murray, C. (1994). *The Bell Curve: Intelligence and Class Structure in American Life.* New York: Free Press.

Irvine, J. J., & York, E. D. (2001). Learning Styles and Culturally Diverse Students: A Literature Review. In J. A. Banks & C. A. M. Banks (Eds.), *Handbook of Research on Multicultural Education* (pp. 484–497). San Francisco: Jossey-Bass.

Jackson, P. W. (1992). *Untaught Lessons.* New York: Teachers College Press.

Jacobson, M. F. (1998). *Whiteness of a Different Color: European Immigrants and the Alchemy of Race.* Cambridge, MA: Harvard University Press.

Jacoby, R., & Glauberman, N. (Eds.). (1995). *The Bell Curve Debate: History, Documents, Opinions.* New York: Times Books/Random House.

Joshee, R. (2004). Citizenship and Multicultural Education in Canada: From Assimilation to Social Cohension. In J. A. Banks (Ed.), *Diversity and Citizenship Education: Global Perspectives* (pp. 127–156). San Francisco: Jossey-Bass.

Kincheloe, J. L., Steinberg, S. R., & Gresson, A. D., III (Eds.). (1996). *Measured Lies: The Bell Curve Examined.* New York: St. Martin's Press.

Knapp, M. S., & Woolverton, S. (2004). Social Class and Schooling. In J. A. Banks & C. A. M. Banks (Eds.), *Handbook of Research on Multicultural Education* (2nd ed., pp. 656–681). San Francisco: Jossey-Bass.

Kuper, A. (1999). *Culture: The Anthropologists' Account.* Cambridge, MA: Harvard University Press.

Ladson-Billings, G. (2004). Culture versus Citizenship: The Challenge of Racialized Citizenship in the United States. In J. A. Banks (Ed.), *Diversity and Citizenship Education: Global Perspectives* (pp. 99–126). San Francisco: Jossey-Bass.

Lasch, C. (1978). *The Culture of Narcissism.* New York: Norton.

Lipkin, A. (1999). *Understanding Homosexuality: Changing Schools.* Boulder, CO: Westview.

Lisitzky, G. (1956). *Four Ways of Being Human: An Introduction to Anthropology.* New York: Viking.

Luchtenberg, S. (Ed.) (2005). *Migration, Education and Change.* London: Routledge

Maher, F. A. (1987). Inquiry Teaching and Feminist Pedagogy. *Social Education, 51*(3), 186–192.

Maher, F. A., & Tetreault, M. K. (1994). *The Feminist Classroom.* New York: Basic Books.

Mannheim, K. (1936). *Ideology and Utopia: An Introduction to the Sociology of Knowledge.* New York: Harcourt Brace.

Meier, D. & Wood, G. H. (Eds.). (2005). *Many Children Left Behind: How the No Child Left Behind Act Is Damaging Our Children and Our Schools.* Boston: Beacon.

Mercer, J. R. (1973). *Labeling the Mentally Retarded: Clinical and Social System Perspectives on Mental Retardation.* Berkeley: University of California Press.

Myrdal, G., with Sterner, R., & Rose, A. (1944/1962). *An American Dilemma: The Negro Problem and Modern Democracy* (anniv. ed.). New York: Harper & Row. (Original work published 1944.)

Nash, G. B. (1999). *Forbidden Love: The Secret History of Mixed-Race America.* New York: Holt.

Nieto, S. (2004). *Affirming Diversity: The Sociopolitical Context of Multicultural Education* (4th ed.). Boston: Allyn and Bacon.

Noguera, P. A. (2003). The Trouble with Black Boys: The Role and Influence of Environmental and Cultural Factors on the Academic Performance of African American Males. *Urban Education,* 38, 411–459.

Oakes, J., Joseph, R., & Muir, K. (2004). Access and Achievement in Mathematics and Science: Inequalities That Endure and Change. In J. A. Banks & C. A. M. Banks (Eds.), *Handbook of Research on Multicultural Education* (2nd ed., pp. 69–90). San Francisco: Jossey-Bass.

Ogbu, J. U. (2003). *Black American Students in an Affluent Suburb: A Study of Academic Disengagement.* Mahwah, NJ: Earlbaum.

Perney, V. H. (1976). Effects of Race and Sex on Field Dependence–Independence in Children. *Perceptual and Motor Skills, 42,* 975–980.

Ramírez, M., & Castañeda, A. (1974). *Cultural Democracy, Bicognitive Development and Education.* New York: Academic Press.

Reischauer, E. O. (1981). *The Japanese.* Cambridge, MA: Harvard University Press.

Roderick, M., Jacob, B. A., & Bryk, A. S. (2002). The Impact of High-Stakes Testing in Chicago on Student Achievement in Promotional Gate Grades. *Educational Evaluation and Policy Analysis, 24* (4), 333–357.

Roediger, D. R. (2002). *Colored White: Transcending the Racial Past.* Berkeley: University of California Press.

Root, M. P. P. (2004). Multiracial Families and Children: Implications for Educational Research and Practice. In J. A. Banks & C. A. M. Banks (Eds.), *Handbook of Research on Multicultural Education* (2nd ed., pp. 110–124). San Francisco: Jossey-Bass.

Rothbart, M., & John, O. P. (1993). Intergroup Relations and Stereotype Change: A Social-Cognitive Analysis and Some Longitudinal Findings. In P. M. Sniderman, P. E. Telock, & E. G. Carmines (Eds.), *Prejudice, Politics, and the American Dilemma* (pp. 32–59). Stanford, CA: Stanford University Press.

Sapon-Shevin, M. (1994). *Playing Favorites: Gifted Education and the Disruption of Community.* Albany: State University of New York Press.

Schlesinger, A. M., Jr. (1986). *The Cycles of American History.* Boston: Houghton Mifflin.

Schmitz, B., Butler, J., Rosenfelt, D., & Guy-Sheftal, B. (2004). Women's Studies and Curriculum Transformation. In J. A. Banks & C. A. M. Banks (Eds.), *Handbook of Research on Multicultural Education* (2nd ed., pp. 882–905). San Francisco: Jossey-Bass.

Shaver, J. P., & Curtis, C. K. (1981). *Handicapism and Equal Opportunity: Teaching about the Disabled in Social Studies.* Reston, VA: Foundation for Exceptional Children.

Slavin, R. E. (2001). Cooperative Learning and Intergroup Relations. In J. A. Banks & C. A. M. Banks (Eds.), *Handbook of Research on Multicultural Education* (pp. 628–634). San Francisco: Jossey-Bass.

Sleeter, C. E. (2005). *Un-Standardizing Curriculum: Multicultural Teaching the Standards-Based Classroom.* New York: Teachers College Press.

Sleeter, C. E., & Grant, C. A. (2006). *Making Choices for Multicultural Education: Five Approaches to Race, Class, and Gender* (5th ed.). New York: Wiley.

Smith, E. R., & Mackie, D. M. (1995). *Social Psychology.* New York: Worth.

Steele, C. (2003). Stereotype Threat and African-American Student Achievement. In T. Perry, C. Steele, & A. Hilliard III, *Young, Gifted and Black: Promoting High Achievement among African-American Students* (pp. 109–130). Boston: Beacon.

Steinem, G. (1995). *Outrageous Acts and Everyday Rebellions.* New York: Holt.

Stephan, W. G. (1999). *Reducing Prejudice and Stereotyping in Schools.* New York: Teachers College Press.

Stephan, W. G. & Vogt, W. P. (Eds.). (2004). *Education Programs for Improving Intergroup Relations: Theory, Research, and Practice.* New York: Teachers College Press.

Stewart, E. C., & Bennett, M. J. (1991). *American Cultural Patterns: A Cross-Cultural Perspective.* Yarmouth, ME: Intercultural Press.

Taylor, J. M., Gilligan, C., & Sullivan, A. M. (1995). *Between Voice and Silence: Women and Girls, Race and Relationships.* Cambridge, MA: Harvard University Press.

Theodorson, G. A., & Theodorson, A. G. (1969). *A Modern Dictionary of Sociology.* New York: Barnes & Noble.

Trecker, J. L. (1973). Teaching the Role of Women in American History. In J. A. Banks (Ed.), *Teaching Ethnic Studies: Concepts and Strategies* (43rd Yearbook, pp. 279–297). Washington, DC: National Council for the Social Studies.

Warner, W. L., with Meeker, M., & Eells, K. (1960). *Social Class in America* (reissued ed.). New York: Harper Torchbooks. (Original work published 1949.)

Weatherford, J. (1988). *Indian Givers: How the Indians of the Americas Transformed the World.* New York: Fawcett Columbine.

Willis, P. (1977). *Learning to Labor.* New York: Columbia University Press.

Wills, J. S., Lintz, A., & Mehan, H. (2004). Ethnographic Studies of Multicultural Education in Classrom and Schools. In J. A. Banks & C. A. M. Banks (Eds.), *Handbook of Research on Multicultural Education* (2nd ed., pp. 163–183). New York: Macmillan.

CHAPTER 2

Culture in Society and in Educational Practices

Frederick Erickson

CULTURE: AN OVERVIEW

In a sense, everything in education relates to culture—to its acquisition, its transmission, and its invention. Culture is in us and all around us, just as is the air we breathe. In its scope and distribution it is personal, familial, communal, institutional, societal, and global.

Yet culture as a notion is often difficult to grasp. As we learn and use culture in daily life, it becomes habitual. Our habits become for the most part invisible to us. Thus, culture shifts inside and outside our reflective awareness. We do not think much about the structure and characteristics of culture as we use it, just as we do not think reflectively about any familiar tool in the midst of its use. If we hammer things a lot, we do not think about the precise weight or chemical composition of the steel of the hammer, especially as we are actually hammering; and when we speak to someone we know well, we are unlikely to think reflectively about the sound system, grammar, vocabulary, and rhetorical conventions of our language, especially as we are doing things in the midst of our speaking.

Just as hammers and languages are tools by which we get things done, so is culture; indeed, culture can be thought of as the primary human toolkit. Culture is a product of human creativity in action; once we have it, culture enables us to extend our activity still further. In the sense that culture is entirely the product of human activity, an artifact, it is not like the air we breathe. By analogy to computers, which are information tools, culture can be considered as the software—the coding systems for doing meaning and executing sequences of work—by which our human physiological and cognitive hardware is able to operate so that we can make sense and take action with others in daily life. Culture structures the "default" conditions of the everyday practices of being human.

Another way to think of culture is as a sedimentation of the historical experience of persons and social groupings of various kinds, such as nuclear family and kin, gender, ethnicity, race, and social class, all with differing access to power in society. We have become increasingly aware that the invention and sharing of culture (in other words, its production and reproduction) happen through processes that are profoundly political in nature, having to do with access to and distribution of social power. In these processes of cultural production and reproduction, the intimate politics of immediate social relations face to face are combined with a more public politics in the social forces and processes of economy and society writ large. How does the sedimentation of historical experience as culture take place? What are the micro- and macropolitical circumstances in which culture is learned and invented? How does culture get distributed, similarly and differently, within and across human groups and within and between human generations?

These are questions not only for social scientists or for social philosophers to address; they also are questions that raise issues that are essential for educators to consider. Culture, as it is more and less visible and invisible to its users, is profoundly involved in the processes and contents of education. Culture shapes and is shaped by the learning and teaching that happen during the practical conduct of daily life within all the educational settings we encounter as learning environments throughout the human life span—in families, in school classrooms, in community settings, and in the workplace. There is some evidence that we begin to learn culture in the womb, and we continue to learn new culture until we die. Yet people learn differing sets and subsets of culture, and they can unlearn culture—shedding it as well as adopting it. At the individual and the group level, some aspects of culture undergo change and other aspects stay the same within a single human life and across generations.

Educators address these issues every time they teach and every time they design curricula. Educators may address them explicitly and with conscious awareness, or they may be addressed implicitly and without conscious awareness. But at every moment in the conduct of educational practice, cultural issues and choices are at stake. This chapter makes some of those issues and choices more explicit.

Two final orienting assumptions are implicit in the previous discussion. First, everybody is cultural, and although there is no evidence base on which to decide that any particular cultural ways are intrinsically more valuable than others—more inherently superior or inferior— it is a plain political fact that not all cultural practices are equal in power and prestige in the United States or in any other country. Every person and social group possesses and uses culture as a tool for the conduct of human activity. This means that culture is not the possession or characteristic of an exotic other, but of all of us, the dominant and the dominated alike. In other words, and to put it more bluntly, within U.S. society White people are just as cultural as are people of color (indeed the terms *White* and *people of color* represent cultural categories that are socially constructed). Moreover, White Anglo-Saxon Protestants (WASPs) are just as cultural as are Jews or Catholics; men are just as cultural as women; adults are just as cultural as teenagers; Northerners are just as cultural as Southerners; English speakers are just as cultural as the speakers of other languages; and native-born Americans are just as cultural as immigrants or citizens who reside in other countries. This is to say Americans of African or European or Asian descent are just as cultural as people who live in Africa, Europe, or Asia. To reiterate, everybody in the world is cultural, even though not all cultures are equal in power or prestige.

The second orienting assumption is that everybody is multicultural. Every person and every human group possesses both culture and cultural diversity. For example, Americans of Mexican descent are not culturally identical to Puerto Ricans who live on the mainland, but not all Mexican Americans or Puerto Ricans (or White Episcopalians, for that matter) are culturally identical even if they live in the same neighborhood and attend the same school or church. Members of the same family also are culturally diverse. In fact, we often encounter cultural difference as individual difference, as well as encountering culture in its more institutionalized manifestations, such as school literacy, the legal system, or the broadcast media. An important way we meet culture is in the particular people with whom we interact daily.

It is not possible for individuals to grow up in a complex modern society without acquiring differing subsets of culture—differing software packages that are tools that can be used in differing kinds of human activity, tools that in part enable and frame the activities in which they are used. Through the nuclear family, through early and later schooling, through peer networks, and through life at work, we encounter, learn, and to some extent help create differing microcultures and subcultures. Just as everyone learns differing variants and styles of the various languages we speak, so that everybody is multilingual (even those of us who only speak English), so, too, is everybody multicultural. No matter how culturally isolated a person's life may appear, in large-scale modern societies (and even in small-scale traditional societies) each member carries a considerable amount of that society's cultural diversity inside. This insight is very clearly stated in an article by Goodenough (1976)—"Multiculturalism as the Normal Human Experience."

If it is true that every person and human group is both cultural and multicultural, then a multicultural perspective on the aims and conduct of education is of primary importance. That assumption guides this chapter. First, it considers a variety of definitions of culture. Then it discusses how culture is organized and distributed in society, and this raises issues that have special relevance for education. The discussion comments on teaching and learning in multicultural classrooms in the light of the conceptions of culture previously discussed. The chapter concludes with further discussion of the diversity of culture not only within society but also within the person and the implications of that diversity for multicultural education.

ALTERNATIVE DEFINITIONS AND CONCEPTIONS OF CULTURE

Attempts at formal definitions of culture have not been fruitful; even the experts have not been able to agree on what culture *really* is. Yet some ways of thinking about culture seem increasingly to be inadequate and misleading and others are more useful. Presented here is a range of definitions, emphasizing the differing conceptions of culture that underlie the various definitions. I begin with two initial definitions, the first of which was in use by the eighteenth century and the second of which became current in the nineteenth century. Then I consider five more contemporary conceptions of culture. Table 2.1 contains examples of each of the conceptions of culture.

1. Culture as Cultivation: Art and Fashion

All conceptions of culture imply a distinction between the cultural and the natural. Cultivation transforms the natural in a social sense just as agriculture transforms nature in a biological and chemical sense. Cultivating the soil makes for fewer weeds than in nature (indeed, the distinction between what is considered weed and what is considered plant is a cultural one). Cultivation requires effort and method—it evokes images of straight furrows, of working, and of planning for the future harvest.

The agricultural metaphor for culture bears a family resemblance to an artistic one. In the fine arts, cultivation also involves disciplining the natural—the fingers learn to find keys on the piano; the painter's eye and hand and the ballerina's feet are schooled by artistic convention. Thus, in ordinary use, culture has come to mean high culture—what we find in the museum, the symphony hall, the theater, and the library. In those institutions we find cultural products whose value is defined by elite tastes, which are defined and framed reflexively by those cultural products.

In contrast to prestigious high culture, there is also low culture—popular culture— which is another sense in which the term *culture* is used. Some artifacts of U.S. popular culture, such as blue jeans and popular music, have been adopted throughout the world. In the realm of popular culture, fashions change across time and across various social groups and social sectors, just as they do in the realm of high culture. We have diverse artifacts and practices of popular culture with differential appeal, such as classic rock'n'roll, rap, country, and Cajun music. We have Western cowboy boots, motorcycle boots, hiking boots, upland game hunting boots, and Nike basketball sneakers, each with a different resonance among subgroups within U.S. society and each potentially able to serve as badges of personal and group identity.

2. Emerging Understandings of Culture in Social Science

In the social sciences, the term *culture* refers to phenomena that are less mystifying than those of so-called high culture and less sensational than those of popular culture. In the social scientific sense, culture is seen as something everyone has and makes use of routinely, regardless of social position. It refers to the patterns for sense making and action that are part of the conduct of everyday life.

This egalitarian notion of culture arose among Western Europeans in the Enlightenment (Vico, 1744/1968), and it developed further in the early Romantic period, foreshadowed by Rousseau and continued by the brothers Grimm and von Humboldt. The Grimms collected folktales from German peasants whose language and folk knowledge had been made fun of by aristocrats in earlier times. This shift toward greater respect for the lifeways of ordinary people happened between the mid-eighteenth and the early nineteenth centuries.

By the early nineteenth century, culture was beginning to be seen as tradition that is handed down across generations. Within anthropology during the nineteenth century, culture was seen as a sum total of social inheritance. In 1871, the anthropologist Sir Edward Burnett Tylor (1871/1970) presented this broad definition: "Culture or Civilization . . . is that complex whole which includes knowledge, belief, art, morals, law, custom, and any other capabilities and habits acquired by man as a member of society" (p. 1).

As genetic theory was developing, culture came to be seen as a kind of gene pool existing at the level of social symbolism and meaning rather than biology. By 1917, a U.S. anthropologist called culture "superorganic," meaning that it had an ideational rather than material existence (Kroeber, 1917). Following Tylor and others, Kroeber assumed that culture was a whole system consisting of interrelated parts, not literally a living organism but metaphorically similar to one.

Yet the notion of culture remained fuzzy among social scientists. Near the end of his career, Kroeber collaborated with Kluckhohn in a review of the uses of the term *culture*. Their review of anthropology and sociology publications turned up hundreds of citations and differing shadings of meaning for the word (Kroeber & Kluckhohn, 1952). Since then, no scholar has tried to put forward a single, authoritative meaning of the term.

3. Culture as Information Bits

Let us turn now to contemporary definitions of culture. Currently, one conception of culture considers it analogous to information bits in a computer as well as to genetic information in a breeding population. According to this view, culture can be thought of as consisting of many small chunks of knowledge that are stored as a large pool of information within a bounded social group (see Goodenough, 1981). No single member of the group has learned all knowledge that is possessed by the group as a whole. The amounts and kinds of information known are seen as varying widely across individuals and subgroups within the total population.

This variation can be understood by analogy to language. What we call a *language* has a sound system (pronunciation), a syntax (grammar), and a lexicon (vocabulary). Those who understand the literal meaning of a sound system, a syntax, and a lexicon are termed members of the same *language community*. Subsets of the language are called dialects: they are spoken by members of subgroups within the overall language community. Dialects may vary in some aspects of pronunciation of vowels or consonants, or in some aspects of grammar, or in vocabulary, but any dialect is still intelligible overall to speakers of other dialects within the language. Each person within a language community speaks a unique form of that language, called an *idiolect* (i.e., no one individual actually speaks "English"; all individuals pronounce the language sounds in slightly differing ways and use grammar and vocabulary in individually distinct ways, in a kind of personal dialect). By this analogy, an overall general culture = language, while dialect = subculture, and idiolect = microculture, which can be thought of as a personal or immediately local variation on a subculture or general culture.

4. Culture as Symbol System

Another conception considers culture as a more limited set of large chunks of knowledge—conceptual structures that frame or constitute what is taken as "reality" by members of a social group (Geertz, 1973). These central organizing constructs—core symbols—are seen as being shared widely throughout the group. The routine ways of acting and making sense that are used by members of the group tend to repeat the major framing patterns again and again, just as within a musical composition many variations can be written on a few underlying thematic elements. This conception of culture emphasizes relatively tight organization of patterns, coherence in the overall meaning system, and identical (or at least closely shared) understandings of symbols and shared sentiments regarding those symbols among the members of the social group.

5. Culture as Models for Action and Emotion

Another current approach considers both the cognitive and emotional/motivational force of culture (Lutz, 1990). We learn customs, but why do we become emotionally attached to them? How do we come to desire and work for ends and to use means for reaching those ends that are culturally enjoined? We do not act on culturally defined goals simply because we are forced to do so, although in situations of unequal power subordinates may fake it— they may feign more allegiance to cultural norms, such as politeness or diligence, than they in fact are feeling. Still, culturally defined love objects are genuinely yearned for, culturally defined careers do become the objects of genuine aspiration and striving, and customs that are culturally defined as repulsive, such as eating sea slugs, evoke strong emotional reactions of disgust in some social groups, even though those same food practices are seen as normal or even highly desirable in other social groups.

Contemporary neuroscience shows that engaging in routine activities activates not only the neural networks that involve prior cognitive learning (i.e., neural connections to the cerebral cortex) but also the neural connections to our emotional states at the time of initial learning (i.e., neural connections to the limbic system). Thus, our repetition of certain customary activities evokes and reinforces emotional feelings as well as thoughts and skills (D'Andrade & Strauss, 1992). Through continued participation in daily life we thus acquire cultural models for its conduct that involve feeling in our knowing. In an important sense that went unrecognized in earlier cognitive psychology, all of our cognitions are "hot cognitions," and learning is a profoundly emotional activity as well as a cognitive one.

6. Culture as Distributed along Lines of Power in Society

A sixth conception treats the distribution of power and culture in modern societies as intertwined (Bourdieu, 1977; Bourdieu & Passeron, 1977; Williams, 1983). The fourth and fifth conceptions of culture could be applied to small-scale traditional societies as well as to large-scale modern ones. The sixth conception attempts to account for the production, distribution, and reproduction of culture as this distinctly happens in large-scale modern societies or in modernizing ones. It considers the basic social unit as the nation-state.

Some work within this stream of approaches emphasizes the diversity of cultural knowledge within a state (Barth, 1969, 1989). Cultural difference is seen as tracing lines of status, power, and political interest within and across the subgroups and institutions found in the nation-state as a total social unit. This variation in cultural difference within a whole modern society can be seen as analogous to the ways in which differences in air pressure or temperature are displayed on a weather map. There is variation in temperature in the earth's atmosphere, and it is nonrandomly distributed. There is variation in culture within a human society, and it, too, is nonrandomly distributed, closely related to the differential allocation of power and prestige within the society, across lines of social class, race, ethnicity, gender, language, and religious affiliation. For many who take this view of culture, the connections between social-class difference and cultural difference have been seen as primary.

One school of thought within this sixth mode sees culture not as being a cognitive template for the routine conduct of everyday life but as residing in the conduct of everyday life itself (Bourdieu, 1977; Ortner, 1984). This conduct is seen as practice, as routine activity that is habitual and goal directed (Connell, 1982). Practices are daily and customary, but they also tend toward a projected outcome, although the aims in such "projects" may not be entirely conscious. Thus, the person engaged in the practical conduct of everyday life can be seen as not simply following cultural "rules" (as in the second and third conceptions of culture listed previously) or as responding to cultural symbols always in the same ways (as is implied in the fourth conception of culture), but as being strategic—an active agent who uses culture as tools adaptively, employing novel means when necessary to achieve desired ends.

The second, third, fourth, and fifth conceptions of culture can be criticized as presuming that human actors are the passive recipients of shaping by their social circumstances and that once having acquired culture through learning they are on "automatic pilot," capable only of following general cultural rules or scripts and incapable of acting adaptively in unique local circumstances. These views consider the cultural actor as a robot or as a "social dope" (Garfinkel & Sacks, 1970); they leave no room for human agency. Practice theory, on the other hand, takes realistic account of how habitual and conservative our daily conduct is, but it leaves room for the assumption that individuals can make sense adaptively within their practices, rather than simply following cultural rules.

The schools of thought that see culture as inherently related to issues of social structure and power also tend to see culture as arising through social conflict, with the possibility of differing interest groups becoming progressively more culturally different across time even though the groups may be in continual contact.

Overall, the sixth conception of culture emphasizes three related points: (1) the systematic variation of culture in relation to the allocation of power in society; (2) social conflict as a fundamental process through which cultural variation is organized, through which traditional culture is being simultaneously forced on people and contested, and through which new culture is continually being invented; and (3) human agency in the use of cultural tools, both tools inherited through tradition and tools invented through their use in practice within changing circumstances (Giddens, 1984).

7. Culture as Residing in Local Communities of Practice

A seventh conception sees culture as the practices of specific sets of persons interacting within local communities of practice. In this view, not only is culture what persons do but it is what particular persons do in mutual influence upon one another as they associate regularly together. A particular family household group is one kind of local community of practice whose members possess distinct funds of knowledge (Moll, 1998; Moll & Greenberg, 1990). A particular school classroom is another local community of practice, a religious congregation is another, and a particular work setting is another—not the classroom or workplace considered abstractly as general social forms, but local gatherings of particular people considered as specific communities of practice. Individuals play roles of apprenticeship within such communities of practice, and those roles change over time as newcomers become more proficient in and centrally participatory in the sets of practices that are customary in a particular community of practice. Learning, from this perspective, can be defined as change over time in individuals' forms of participation within a local community of practice (see Lave & Wenger, 1990; Rogoff, 2003; Wenger, 1999).

The sources of the practices are in part nonlocal and in part local; that is, some practices may derive from the social-class, racial, ethnic, linguistic, and gender backgrounds of persons and groups in society at large (as in the sixth conception of culture), but the particular versions of these practices are locally distinct. They are partly the result of unique local invention. Thus, the class-based practices of one family are not identical to those of another family—there are subtle yet important differences between them. Moreover, across the life cycle individuals participate in multiple communities of practice, acquiring multiple microcultural repertoires as their own personal culture, and these repertoires differ from one individual to the next among persons within the "same" social category (e.g., class, race, gender). This seventh conception of culture, in other words, accounts for the acquisition of personal culture (the implications of distinctive diversity of culture within the individual will be explored later in this chapter). One's personal culture is acquired by showing up regularly in certain settings of practice rather than in others. Where one shows up, in which local communities of practice and how often, provides each individual with opportunities for cultural learning that are so distinct, so site specific and person specific, that they are literally unique.

This conception of culture also accounts for "bottom-up" cultural change, in the distinct local versions of practices that arise through invention and sharing within local communities of practice. Local communities of practice are thus seen as sites of cultural innovation. As a new member joins the group or as a current member begins to act differently within the group, this influences what other members do interactionally; the social ecology of the group changes as a result of the learning and/or the subtle cultural innovations that are continually taking place and are being manifested in the improvised actions of individual members. Some of this innovation may then be adopted by other local communities of practice in processes of social and cultural change within which the practices that originated locally come to influence the general society (Rogoff, 2003). Currently we do not understand well how the cultural innovation that initially takes place in local communities of practice comes to be adopted more widely within society. But bottom-up cultural change does happen, and cultural innovation is always occurring within local communities of cultural practice; that is, tactical innovation is inherent in the everyday conduct of work—of local practice (for a general argument along these lines, see Erickson, 2004).

From this perspective, the emphasis is not on culture as a general integrated system but on the content of cultural knowledge and practice within the specific life situations of the persons and groups by whom such knowledge is held and such practices are undertaken. This position assumes that new culture—whether conceived as small information bits or as larger structures of concept and activity—is being transformed continuously within the contradictions experienced by particular persons in their daily lives. These new cultural forms are either accepted, learned, and remembered, or rejected, ignored, and forgotten, depending on where one sits in the social order and depending on the particular circumstances in the situation in which the new culture is invented.

The seven conceptions of culture discussed above are summarized in Table 2.1.

Summary Discussion

Now, more than 40 years since Kroeber and Kluckhohn's review of social scientists' use of the term *culture*, formal definitions, while overlapping, still do not agree exactly (Kuper,

---

Table 2.1   Examples of Conceptions of Culture

Conception of Culture	Example of the Conception of Culture
Culture as Cultivation	Classical music, haut cuisine
Culture as Tradition	Ethnic foods and family recipes, folk tales, religion
Culture as Information Bits	How close to stand to someone else. What's too loud.
Culture as Symbol System	The national flag, the matador
Culture as Models for Action and Emotion	Letting the baby cry, and why you should. Not letting the baby cry, and why you should. Being a man. Being a woman.
Culture as Distributed along Lines of Power in Society	Cultural capital—insider knowledge and insider connections. What the plant manager knows how to do. What the assembly line worker knows how to do.
Culture as Residing in Local Communities of Practice	Families fixing cars and learning how to do that as a family member. Teenagers writing and playing popular songs and learning how to do that. Physicians practicing medicine and learning how to do that.

1999). Yet culture is generally seen as a product of human activity that is used as a tool. It is seen as being learned and transmitted from our elders and also as being invented (or incrementally transformed) through recurrent improvisation within current situations of practice. How much and in what ways culture is shared within and between identifiable human groups are issues on which there is much debate currently. Power and politics seem to be involved in the processes by which culture is learned, shared, and changed. Culture, in other words, takes shape in the weight of human history. Some aspects of culture are explicit, and others are implicit, learned, and shared outside conscious awareness. Our moods and desires as well as our thoughts are culturally constructed.

Culture can be thought of as a construction—it constructs us and we construct it. That is, all thoughts, feelings, and human activity are not simply natural but are the result of historical and personal experiences that become sedimented as culture in habit. Culture varies, somehow, from one person or group to another. Since our subjective world—what we see, know, and want—is culturally constructed, and since culture varies, persons really do not inhabit the same subjective worlds even though they may seem to do so. Even though some of us show up at what seems to be the same event, how we experience it is never quite the same across the various individuals who have joined together in interaction. Thus, no single or determinative human world is a fixed point of reference. Individually and collectively, we make cultural worlds and they are multiple. This point has profound implications for educators, as is discussed in the following sections.

As human beings, not only do we live in webs of meaning, caring, and desire that we ourselves create and that create us, but those webs also hang in social gravity (Geertz, 1973). Within the webs all our activity is vested in the weight of history; that is, in a social world of inequality all movement is up or down. Earlier conceptions of culture described it and

knowledge. Consider, for example, the political/cultural border between the United States and Mexico. On either side of the border are people who speak English and people who speak Spanish; that is, the boundaries of language community cross over the lines demarcating national citizenship. Yet on either side of the border, fluency in Spanish—which is an aspect of cultural knowledge—is differentially rewarded or punished. On the Mexican side of the border, fluency in Spanish is an advantage legally, educationally, and in the conduct of much daily life, while on the U.S. side, the same cultural knowledge is disadvantaged; indeed in parts of south Texas, speaking Spanish is still stigmatized.

When one arrives at a cultural border, one's cultural knowledge may be held up for scrutiny—stopped and frisked. An ancient example comes from the biblical Book of Judges. In approximately 800 B.C., the Hebrews were not yet fully unified politically under a monarch and they had not yet completely occupied the territory of Canaan. They were a loose federation of kinship groups or clans that periodically came together in an unstable, tense alliance against common enemies. A dispute broke out between soldiers of two of the clans, the men of Ephraim and the men of Gilead. After defeat in a battle with the Ammonites, the common enemy, the men of Ephraim were trying to escape across fords in the Jordan River. The fords were guarded on the Hebrew-occupied side of the river by Gileadites. The men of Gilead checked the clan identity of the retreating soldiers by testing their cultural knowledge: "When any of the fugitives of Ephraim said, 'Let me go over,' the men of Gilead said to him, 'Are you an Ephraimite?' When he said, 'No,' they said to him, 'Then say Shibboleth.' He said 'Sibboleth,' for he could not pronounce it correctly. Then they seized him and slew him at the fords of the Jordan" (Judges 12:5b-6a, RSV). The two clans of Hebrews differed in their pronunciation of the initial sibilant in the word *Shibboleth*. The Gileadites used the /sh/ phoneme for that consonant, while the Ephraimites used the /s/ phoneme. The Gileadite soldiers were aware of this cultural difference and made use of it to construct a sociolinguistic test at a geographic and political border, which, because of the test imposed, became a cultural border as well.

In modern societies the same thing can happen when one enters the emergency room of a hospital and speaks to an admitting clerk or when one speaks to the maitre d' at a restaurant. It also can happen in school classrooms. Yet cultural boundaries (the objective presence of cultural difference) need not necessarily be treated as cultural borders. This is a matter of socially constructed framing.

The framing of cultural difference as boundary or as border can change over time. Sometimes that change is very rapid, as in the following example (Fanon, 1963). In Algeria shortly before France gave up colonial rule, the pronunciation of the announcers on the state radio was made a cultural border issue by the independence movement. Complaints were voiced that Radio Algiers was not employing native Algerians. The independence movement saw this practice as another symbol of colonial oppression. Radio Algiers sent out a statement that its announcers were in fact Algerians. The independence movement then asked why the radio announcers spoke cosmopolitan French rather than the Algerian dialect. The complaints about the announcers became increasingly strident in the independence-oriented press, right up to Independence Day. After that day the announcers on Radio Algiers continued to speak cosmopolitan French but public complaint ended instantly. The reason for the complaint was gone, and so a small feature of cultural difference, which had been framed for a time as a cultural border, was reframed as a cultural boundary.

These two examples suggest that cultural difference, rather than being considered a cause of conflict in society (and in education), is more appropriately seen as a resource for conflict. If people have a reason to look for trouble, cultural difference—especially one that becomes a badge of social identity—can be used to start a fight. But the causes of the fight go beyond the cultural difference itself.

Cultural Differentiation as a Political Process

What happens over time when certain aspects of cultural difference get treated as border issues? Examples from language suggest that the differences become more extreme on either side. This suggests that political conflict, explicit and implicit, is a major engine of culture change. Such conflict generates cultural resistance. Labov (1963) found that on Martha's Vineyard, a small island off the coast of Massachusetts, certain sound features in the islanders' dialect became increasingly divergent from the more standard English spoken by summer tourists as the number of tourists staying on the island in the summer increased over time, although the islanders were not aware that this was happening. First-hand contacts with a standard model of American English had been increasing for the islanders, but across a generation their speech was becoming more different from that of the mainlanders.

A similar process of divergence was reported as taking place across the time span of half-hour interviews in experimental situations (Giles & Powesland, 1975). Speakers of differing British regional dialects were paired for two-person discussions. In some discussions, mild discomfort and conflict were experimentally introduced, while in other discussions conflict was not introduced. In the discussions with conflict and discomfort, by the end of a half-hour each person was speaking a broader form of his or her regional dialect than before the discussion began. In other words, if a Yorkshireman were talking to a person from Dorsetshire, he would become more distinctly Yorkshire in his pronunciation and the Dorset man would become more Dorsetshire in his pronunciation as the conversation between the two progressed. Conversely, when conflict was not introduced and the two parties spoke comfortably, pronunciation features that differed between their two dialects became less distinct—they were converging in speech style rather than diverging.

This example suggests that cultural divergence is a result rather than a cause of social conflict. Bateson, Jackson, Haley, and Weakland (1972) called the tendency of subsystems to evolve in increasingly differentiated ways *complementary schismogenesis*, which seems to be the process by which cultural resistance over time results in culture change. It should be emphasized, however, that such change can occur entirely outside the conscious awareness of those involved in it as well as in situations of more explicit, conscious awareness in which people are deliberate regarding the change they are struggling to produce.

The classic view of culture in social science was as a total system with integrated parts, the operation of which tended toward maintaining a steady state. As we have seen, culture now seems to be more labile than that—variable in the moment. This raises the question of how we conceive of culture change—as loss, as gain, as a mixture of both or less evaluatively as change. We must also consider how culture is shared within human groups. We usually think of ethnic and racial groups (and perhaps of gender categories as well) as necessarily identifying cultural boundaries. Such groups, we may assume, are defined by shared culture among their members. Barth (1969) contends, however, that culture sharing is not the crucial defining attribute of ethnic group membership. Rather, the ethnic or racial group is more appropriately considered as an economic and political interest group. Features of culture may be considered as identity badges, indicating group membership. But culture sharing is not essential for this, according to Barth. There may be much cultural diversity within the same named social category. He used as an example the Pathans (also called Pashtun), who live as a numerical minority on one side of the border between Pakistan and Afghanistan and as a majority on the other side. Some Pathans are herders—more so on the Afghan side of the border. Other Pathans are farmers—more so on the Pakistani side. Yet both herders and farmers will identify as Pathan and are so regarded by other ethnic groups on either side of the border. Their ethnic identification is at least as strong as is their identification with the nation-state within whose border they reside; that became apparent during the war in Afghanistan in 2002.

Culture Change as Culture Loss—or Not

When we think of ethnic/racial groups and cultural groups as having the same boundaries-the traditional view—we sometimes think of culture change as culture loss. Members of an ethnic group can blame themselves for losing a language, a religion, and a household practice. Native Americans, for example, have mourned the passing of old culture and have gone beyond mourning to self-blame, considering themselves less Indian than their forebears. Yet if a Koyukon Athabaskan now uses a snowmobile rather than a dog team and sled, does that mean he or she is any less Koyukon than before? Not necessarily, if we follow Barth's analysis. What is essential for the maintenance of ethnic groups and ethnic identities are not the specifics of culture traits practiced by the members; rather, being ethnic counts economically and politically in the larger society. Even the specific ways in which it counts to be ethnic can change; yet if there continue to be economic and political consequences of being identified as ethnic, especially if that is to the advantage of the members, then the ethnic group continues.

The classic view makes culture the defining attribute of ethnic identity. It becomes easy, then, to see culture change as culture loss. This can be thought of as the leaky bucket perspective on culture change—as if culture were held in a human group as water is contained in a bucket. Change then becomes the holes in the bucket. As one carries such a bucket over time and space, the water gradually drains out. Alternatively, we can conceive of the bucket of culture as always full. Air may replace the water, but the bucket is never empty. The contemporary Koyukon society, with its snowmobile practices, can be considered just as full culturally as the Koyukon society in the days of sled and dog team. What is in the bucket is different now, but the bucket is still not empty. During the summer, people in an Odawa community in northern Ontario wear T-shirts as they fish from aluminum boats powered by outboard motors. They no longer wear buckskin and use birchbark canoes. Yet they continue to fish, and they do so with differing fishing rights from those of White Canadians. Moreover, they still consider themselves Odawa, as distinct from White Canadians in neighboring villages who also fish from aluminum boats while wearing T-shirts.

Culture and Collective Identity Formation

To call something cultural has in itself political implications. Because so many aspects of culture are transparent to its users in their use, ordinarily we do not think about or notice them. Yet in complex and diverse modern societies, as ethnic, racial, religious, and gender identifications become self-aware among identification group members, they begin to notice their customary practices and to identify them as cultural. As with ethnic identification, cultural identification is always relational and comparative—with reference to an other. In the early nineteenth century, for example, German *Kultur* began to be invoked by German intellectuals in contrast and opposition to the French and Italians, whose tastes in literature and music, architecture, and clothing had previously set the standard of what was desirable in upper-class polite society. Without the presence of French and Italian models to compete with, Germans may not have become so aware of their own Germanness. This awareness progressed beyond rediscovery to invention, with German intellectuals such as Wagner helping to create a Germanic heritage with the support of the ruling interests in German society. With this rise in in-group awareness and solidarity came a heightened awareness of boundaries with non-Teutonic others. To the extent that this perception of out-groups was invidious, the boundaries became borders.

We see a similar phenomenon today with the rise of religious nationalism and of ethnic and racial nationalism. With in-group identification there is always the possibility for treating boundaries as borders. Especially when heightening of cultural awareness and identification is used as a political strategy for changing power relations in society, or for legitimating territorial or colonial expansion, in-group solidarity and identification can become demonic. As Said (1978) notes in commenting on the colonial relationship between Europe and a perceived Orient that was a cultural creation of Europeans themselves, when more powerful nations or interest groups identify some "other" as exotic and different, there can be a tendency for the more powerful to project their own flaws, contradictions, and hostilities on the constructed other. Such projections are reciprocated by those who have been "othered" in a process of mutual border framing. Through this process of projective "othering," negative cultural stereotypes result, making the fostering of intercultural and multicultural awareness a tricky business indeed.

Ethnic identification need not necessarily lead to othering in the negative sense, however—the comparisons with those who differ from "Us" need not be invidious. Cultural differences can be framed as boundaries rather than as borders even though such framing takes effort to maintain. It should be noted, however, that an increase in the deliberateness and intensity of cultural awareness necessarily involves a comparative awareness. The construction of in-group identity is a relational process through which a definition of Other as well as of Self, of Them as well as of Us—and in the case of subordinated groups a specific identification of aspects of oppression—becomes more focal in conscious awareness.

TEACHING AND LEARNING MULTICULTURALLY
Emphasizing Invisible as Well as Visible Culture

Schools can support or hinder the development of healthy identity and of intergroup awareness. The discussion now turns to teaching and learning in classrooms (see Wills, Lintz & Mehan, 2004). This chapter emphasizes the importance of culture and criticizes our tendencies to essentialize it. When we essentialize culture, assuming that all persons in a given social category are culturally similar and focusing on the unitary cultures of various Others without reflecting on our own cultures and their diversity, we open a Pandora's box of opportunity for negative attribution. Sometimes social scientific notions of culture, especially of culture as unified system and of group membership as culturally defined, have provided a justification for intergroup stereotypes. When these stereotypes come with social scientific warrant, we call them neostereotypes.

Teaching about the cultural practices of other people without stereotyping or misinterpreting them and teaching about one's own cultural practices without invidiously characterizing the practices of other people should be the aims of multicultural education. In situations of intergroup conflict these aims can be ideals that are difficult to attain. Educators should face such difficulty realistically.

One problem in multicultural curriculum and pedagogy is the overemphasis on visible (explicit) culture at the expense of the invisible and implicit. Focusing mainly on explicit culture can be misleading. Even when we do this respectfully of the lifeways of others, focus on visible culture easily slides into too comfortable a stance of cultural romance or cultural tourism.

Particular traits of visible culture, often treated in isolation, have become the basis for much of what we teach about cultural diversity in schools. Some educators speak critically of "piñata curriculum," "snowshoe curriculum," and "holidays and heroes" in characterizing this approach. By treating cultural practices as sets of static facts, we trivialize them in superficiality and we make it seem as if culture were necessarily unchanging. What if Mexican Americans were to have a party and not break a piñata? Would they be any less Mexican? They are only if we adopt an essentialist view of culture, with its accompanying leaky bucket image of culture change.

A way to teach about explicit culture without overgeneralizing about the lifeways of other people is to emphasize the variability of culture within social groups and the continual presence of cultural change as well as cultural continuity across time. Unfortunately, published multicultural materials that have an essentialist emphasis may not lend themselves well to this method. Yet in every classroom there is a resource for the study of within-group cultural diversity as well as between-group diversity. That resource is the everyday experience and cultural practices of the students and teachers themselves. (This is most easily done in a self-contained classroom, and so this discussion may seem most relevant for elementary school teaching, but many of the issues and approaches mentioned can be undertaken by high school and college teachers as well.)

Critical Autobiography as Curriculum and as Action Research

Critically reflective autobiographies by students and oral histories of their families—a form of community action research—can become important parts of a multicultural curriculum. Even in a classroom with a student population highly segregated by race or by social class, reflective investigation of their own lives and of family and local community histories by students will reveal diversity as well as similarity (hooks, 1993; Skilton Sylvester, 1994; Torres-Guzmán, 1992; Wiggington, 1986; Witherell & Noddings, 1991). Not all the Italian Americans in a classroom have had the same family experience of immigration. Not all the African American students whose forebears moved from the rural South to a large city have had the same experience of urbanization. As a result of differing life experiences, there are differences in cultural funds of knowledge between families who on the surface appear to be demographically similar—differences in family microcultures (see Moll, 1990, 1998).

Just as students can engage in critical autobiography, so their teachers need to identify the particular cultures of their individual students through observation of and dialogue with those students. An index for the individual student's distinctive cultural repertoire is that student's distinctive *daily round*—where the student shows up and what is happening there, in the specific sequences and ranges of engagement of the student in local communities of practice inside and outside school. By learning which particular communities of practice a student has had access to, and the kinds of participation in those communities that a student has engaged in, a teacher can come to understand the personal culture of each student—to see each student as "cultural" without stereotyping the student simplistically as "Anglo" or "African American," as "lower class" or "upper middle class," as "boy" or "girl." In order to develop this kind of nonstereotypical understanding of actual students, a teacher must spend time outside school in the school community(ies) from which the teacher's students come as well as pay attention to the communities of practice that are found during the school day in places beyond that teacher's own classroom. There is no substitute for this first-hand knowledge of the everyday interactional circumstances of the particular children one teaches—without it one adopts stereotypic, categorical "cultural" labels for students that are too general to be able to take accurate account of the actual lives, the personal cultures, that those specific children are developing.

A close look at particular families and at the daily rounds of individuals can reveal similarity as well as distinctiveness—as in variations on a common theme of life experience such as that of the experience of racism by African Americans or of language prejudice by those who grow up speaking Spanish in the United States. But not all the experiences, even of racism within a given racial group, are identical. Thus, diversity and similarity always accompany one another in the real stories of people in human groups. Those stories have involved struggles to change, to resist. Contemporary community issues, as students address them through local community study, also provide opportunities for students to take action to improve the circumstances of their lives and, in the process, come to see themselves and their families not simply as passive recipients of social and cultural influences, but as active agents who are making sense and making their lives.

Direct connections between the daily lives of students outside the classroom and the content of instruction in history, social studies, and literature can make the stated curriculum come alive. These connections also afford the teacher an opportunity to learn the cultural backgrounds and cultural diversity that he or she confronts with each set of students. As stated earlier, formal organizations in modern societies become collection sites for cultural diversity. This is true for every school classroom. Each new set of students represents a unique sampling from the universe of local cultural diversity present in the school area. Simply knowing that one has three Haitian students and four Cambodian students—or seventeen girls and eleven boys—in a certain classroom, for example, does not tell that teacher anything (necessarily) about the specific cultural backgrounds of those students and their families and their assumptions about ethnicity, race, or gender, given the cultural diversity that is possible within any social category. The teacher's tasks are to know not only about Haitians or Cambodians in general, or about girls and boys in general, but also about these students in particular. By making particular student culture and family history a deliberate object of study by all the students in the classroom, the teacher can learn much about what he or she needs to know in order to teach the particular students in ways that are sensitive and powerfully engaging, intellectually and emotionally.

As our standards for what students need to learn change from the lower-order mastery of facts and simple skills to higher-order reasoning and the construction of knowledge that is personally distinctive and meaningful (in other words, as we move from an essentialist understanding of curriculum, teaching, and learning to a more constructivist one), our conceptions of culture in multicultural education also need to become more constructivist and less essentialist. Teaching about culture as socially constructed and continually changing is thus consistent with contemporary definitions of good pedagogy as well as consistent with recent developments in culture theory and social theory.

Reframing Borders as Boundaries in the Classroom

This approach frames the cultural diversity to be found in the classroom in terms of cultural boundaries rather than cultural borders. Even when cultural difference and group identity are highly politicized in the wider society, by approaching the culture of students forthrightly in the classroom they can be depoliticized to a remarkable extent (or perhaps we might think of it as being repoliticized in a positive rather than negative frame).

A problem comes with teaching second-culture skills and knowledge as morality rather than as pragmatic skills for survival and success. Delpit (1995) observes that for students of color in the United States, the school's "second culture" often appears alien and dominating. Culturally mainstream ways of speaking and writing represent a "language and culture of power" that minority students need to master for success in the wider society. But this culture of power can be taught unsuccessfully in two ways. In the first, the teacher attempts to teach the second-culture skills in a moralizing way—the right way to act and to be. This approach is likely to stimulate student resistance and thus is a teaching strategy that risk student refusal to learn. (Consider the word *ain't*. Teachers for generations have been teaching working-class students not to say *ain't* as a moral lesson. Yet inside and outside the classroom the students still say *ain't*.)

Another unsuccessful way to teach a second-culture skill is implicitly, according to Delpit. She observes that among well-meaning middle-class White teachers, some aspects of the language of power are part of the teacher's own invisible culture. Taking it for granted themselves, they do not teach it explicitly to working-class African American students.

Delpit (1995) recommends an alternative approach to teach second-culture skills explicitly and carefully but without moralizing. The school's language and culture of power can be presented as a situational dialect to be used pragmatically for special situations, such as job interviews, formal writing, and college admissions interviews. When combined with reflective self-study of the student's own language use in the family, among peers, and in the neighborhood—study by which the student explores his or her own repertoire of differing speech styles used in differing situations—explicit teaching and learning of the language of power can be framed as a matter not of cultural borders but of cultural boundaries. This approach takes a critical and strategic view of multiculturalism for survival reasons.

Multicultural Pedagogy as Emancipatory

Other multicultural educators recommend a critical approach to cultures of domination and to the phenomenon of domination. Ladson-Billings (1994) describes African American and White teachers who are effective with African American students. They taught in a variety of styles, but one common approach was to deal directly and explicitly with issues of injustice and oppression and the privileging of mainstream knowledge and perspectives as they came up in the curriculum and in the reported daily experiences of their students. Trueba (1994), Nieto (1999), McCarthy (1993), Perry and Fraser (1993), Sleeter and Grant (1993), Apple (1996), and Giroux (1991) all recommend a similar approach, sometimes called critical pedagogy, counter-hegemonic pedagogy, or emancipatory pedagogy.

Cultural hegemony refers to the established view of things—a commonsense view of what is and why things happen that serves the interests of those people already privileged in a society. When the school presents a comfortable established view of the nature of U.S. society and of the goodness and inherent rightness of school knowledge and school literacy, that is hegemonic. Students whose lives are not affirmed by the establishment seem intuitively not to accept hegemonic content and methods of instruction. They often resist, consciously or unconsciously, covertly as well as overtly.

Multicultural education has an opportunity and a challenge to be counter-hegemonic. When such issues as racism, class privilege, and sexism are left silent in the classroom, the implicit message for students of color appears to be that the teacher and the school do not acknowledge that experiences of oppression exist. If only the standard language, the standard American history, and the voices and lives of White men appear in the curriculum, then the further implicit message (by what is left in and what is left out of the knowledge presented as legitimate by the school) seems to be that the real United States and real school are only about the cultural mainstream and its establishment ideology. This approach especially marginalizes the students of color who come to school already marginalized by life experience and by the historical experience of oppression in their ethnic or racial communities. Such a hegemonic approach also marginalizes female students (Sadker & Sadker, 1994). Marginalization is alienating, and one response to alienation is resistance—the very thing that makes teaching and learning more difficult for students and their teachers.

Ironically, for teachers to name and acknowledge tough social issues, rather than turning students against school and the teacher, makes it more possible for students who have experienced oppression to affiliate with the teacher and with school learning. By taking the moralizing that characterizes culturally hegemonic teaching out of the picture, reframing second-culture acquisition as strategically instrumental rather than inherently right, a teacher facilitates second-culture learning by students from nonmainstream backgrounds. Through such teaching, cultural borders are reframed as boundaries, and the politics of the dominant culture and cultures are, to some extent at least, depoliticized in the classroom. The cycles of resistance and schismogenesis that are stimulated by hegemonic curriculum and teaching do not get set off.

The role of resistance to cultures of domination in student disaffiliation from school learning is a fundamental issue in public education in the United States, Canada, and Australia, as well as Britain and the rest of Europe (Apple, 1996; Giroux, 1983; Willis, 1977). Ogbu (1987) has argued that for students of "caste-like" minority background in the United States (from groups with historic experiences of stigma and limitation of economic opportunity, such as African Americans, Mexican Americans, Puerto Ricans, and Native Americans), resistance to school is almost inevitable because of the effects of group history. Fordham (1996) has shown that African American high school students in Washington, D.C., defined achieving in school as "acting White." Other scholars (Erickson, 1987; Foley, 1991; Trueba, 1994) have acknowledged Ogbu's insight while observing that student resistance can result not only from a group history of oppression but also from oppressive and alienating circumstances surrounding teaching and learning within the school itself. Another difficulty with Ogbu's position is that it leaves no room for the possibility of school change.

A major theme here is that when business is done as usual in school, student resistance results from that, as well as from influences from the wider society on students. In the short run, we cannot change the wider society. But we can make school learning environments less alienating. Multicultural education, especially critical or antiracist multicultural education, is a way to change the business-as-usual of schools. When that happens, as Ladson-Billings (1994) and others have shown, minority students of backgrounds categorized as "caste-like" rise to the occasion. When treated with dignity and taught skillfully, such students affiliate with the school and achieve. As noted earlier, Moll and Greenberg (1990; see also Moll, 1998) show that minority students' families maintain *funds of knowledge* in their cultural practices that can be made use of in curriculum as teachers learn what those practices are and the kinds of knowledge and skill they entail. Gutierrez, in a series of compelling studies of classroom teaching (Gutierrez, Baquedano-López, Alvarez, & Chiu 1999; Gutierrez, Baquedano-López, & Tejeda 1999; Gutierrez, Rymes, & Larson 1995), shows that learning is enhanced (as is student morale—the will to learn) when teachers in classroom discourse make use of language and speech styles from students' homes and from popular culture. This bridging pedagogy between official school knowledge and unofficial knowledge creates an intermediate "third space"—a hybrid discourse that allows students to use the voices they bring to the classroom as they begin to affiliate with school voices and discourses and to appropriate them as their own. In such classrooms the price of school success is not that one gives up one's own self and voice to adopt a new and alien one. Rather, the student adds new voices and discourses to those already possessed, and the teacher through his or her own language use respects both the voices that are familiar to the student and those that are new.

A group history of oppression no doubt makes students and parents wary of school and its claims that the standard ways of teaching are good for you. That is, trust of a school's good intentions, especially by students and parents of color, is not automatic. But relationships of mutual trust and respect can be established between teachers and students in the classroom. Sensitive multicultural pedagogy is one foundation for such trust.

Conventional Teaching as Cultural Border Wars

If teachers treat the dominant culture in the curriculum as a matter of cultural borders rather than of boundaries, the classroom can become an unsafe place for students. It makes the classroom learning environment untrustable and can invite student resistance.

Aspects of invisible culture are often used as diagnostic indicators with clinical significance, especially in the early grades. For example, if a child comes from a home in which adults do not routinely ask him or her teacher-like questions to which the adults already know the answer, such questions by a teacher can initially seem confusing or intimidating (Heath, 1983). "What color is this?" the kindergarten teacher says on the first day of school, holding up a red piece of construction paper in front of an African American child whose mother is on welfare. "Aonh-oh' (I don't know)," the child replies, thinking there must be some trick, because anybody can see that the paper is red. "Lacking in reading readiness," the teacher thinks, writes this in the child's permanent record, and assigns the child to the bottom reading group.

Once again we find ourselves with the Ephraimites on the banks of the Jordan River, witnessing the consequences of a cultural border test. Yet because we do not recognize knowing about teacher-like questions as a distinct cultural skill, we may not see the teacher's informal readiness test as cultural or as culturally biased. Such framing of cultural difference as a border can be done inadvertently by teachers who are themselves members of the student's ethnic group and speech community as well as by teachers who are of majority background.

The cultural responsiveness or relevance of a classroom learning environment can differ in contradictory ways between the visible and the invisible aspects of culture. For example, in the same multiracial kindergarten or first-grade classroom in which a teacher uses informal tests of reading readiness that treat invisible cultural knowledge and skill as a cultural border (such as recognition of teacher questions and how to answer them), the teacher may have put a picture of Frederick Douglass on the wall, read a book about his life, presented information of West Africa in a positive light, and taught basic vocabulary in Yoruba or Swahili. Yet hanging a picture of Douglass, the African American abolitionist, on the wall next to a picture of George Washington, the White slave holder, or introducing students to an African language does not make that classroom fully multicultural if invisible aspects of the communicative cultural practices of African American students are still being treated in invidious ways.

Such contradictions between formal and informal culture must be confusing and alienating for students, even though that alienation may be experienced by them outside conscious awareness. This is why attention to issues of invisible informal culture as well as those of visible formal culture seems so important for the success of attempts at multicultural education. And in all this work we must critically investigate our notions of failure and success itself, for "school failure" and "school success" are themselves cultural constructions, generally within society and locally within each classroom (see Varenne & McDermott, 1998).

CONCLUSION: ON DIVERSITY OF TONGUES AND THEIR EDUCATIONAL POTENTIAL

The Russian literary critic Bakhtin (1981) provides us with a final way to consider culture in its continuity and in its diversity, as transmitted across generations and as invented in the present moment. He studied the novel as it emerged in the sixteenth and eighteenth centuries in Spain and France and in England, respectively, and as it developed in England, France, and Russia in the nineteenth century. Bakhtin noted that the classic novelists depicted a variety of ways of speaking across their various characters who differed in social class, gender, and region. That diversity he called *heteroglossia*, from the Greek, meaning "differing tongues." He believed that a fine novel encapsulated key aspects of the total diversity in speech styles found in the society at the historical moment in which that novel was written. To produce such a text convincingly, the author must have incorporated the diversity of tongues present in the society.

Bakhtin (1981) also observed a personal heteroglossia within the characters of the novel akin to that in its author. For example, in Cervantes's *Don Quixote* Bakhtin noticed that usually the good Don, of bourgeois background, spoke in an imitation of the literary romance. Thus, his speech style sounded like the Spanish of the nobility. Sancho Panza, the peasant, usually spoke in the speech style of the lower classes. Yet once in a while, when engaged with the Don, or when reflecting to himself on what he had been experiencing, Sancho's speech drifted slightly toward the more prestigious style of Spanish. This tendency, apparent from the beginning of the modern novel, was more pronounced in nineteenth-century French and Russian novels. Russian serfs, for example, were depicted as speaking in a variety of speech styles, what Bakhtin called "social languages"—some more elevated and agentive, some more subordinated and passive. Worldview, personal status, and agency seemed to shift, as did the characters' language style.

Bakhtin's insights suggest ways of understanding how cultural diversity is organized and distributed within a society and within persons. There is heteroglossia within a society. Members of distinct social categories and social networks speak more often than not in differing ways (reminiscent of the "speech community" notion discussed earlier). Men do tend to speak differently from women, African Americans from Whites, working-class people from upper-middle-class people, gay from straight, fundamentalist Christians from Unitarians, physicians from lawyers (and physicians from nurses). These ways of speaking are relatively continuously distributed within the various social groupings; they become badges of identity of such groupings; and for the most major social categories such as class, gender, race and ethnicity, and religion these social languages tend to persist across generations. In other words, social divisions and cultural and linguistic diversity appear to be consistently reproduced in society across time.

Moreover, the differing ways of speaking carry with them differing points of view that are the result of the differing life experiences of the speakers and, as the feminist slogan puts it, "the personal is political." Thus, the historical experience of a group and its particular political interests in assuming that things are really one way rather than some other—its ideology—come with the social language of the group, as uttered by a particular member of that group. Ways of speaking, then, are discourses—whole sets of assumptions about the world and roles for being in the world that are entailed in certain ways of creating oral and written texts (Foucault, 1979; Gee, 1990). Much more is involved than language style alone. To the extent that various group interests and their discourses are involved with the distribution of power in society, there can be conflict and contradiction between ways of speaking and thinking as well as between social groupings. A discourse is in a sense a social institution or a subculture.

Yet the consistency of cultural reproduction is not unitary or absolute. There is also heteroglossia within persons. Each person's life experiences differ somewhat from those of other people, and every person lives in a variety of social situations each day. Differing social situations provide differing ecologies of relationship with other people. They evoke differing aspects of the individual's overall repertoire of ways of speaking. One speaks differently to one's mother than to one's siblings, to one's teacher than to one's mother. Sometimes in complex relationships, such as that between an employee and supervisor who are also friends or between spouses who are simultaneously lovers, parents, and administrators of household resources, a variety of interrelated voices are evoked from moment to moment in what appears to be the same social situation. The utterances of persons in dialogue lean on one another in mutual influence, Bakhtin claimed. Thus, the phenomenon of ways of speaking (and of discourses) is inherently labile as well as stable. Culture at the group level varies in part because individuals differ among one another and within themselves as they find themselves in differing social circumstances. In other words, there is an inherent hybridity in cultural practices (see Arteaga, 1994; Gutierrez, Baquedano-López, & Tejeda, 1999; Valle & Torres, 1995)—a blending of sources and voices in which new combinations and recombinations of old elements with new ones are continually being made.

As diverse persons show up in the scenes of daily life, they bring their heteroglossia with them. There can be affiliation as well as conflict across those cultural differences. And discourses can be contested; they can be interrupted or interrogated. When that happens, the assumptions of the discourse become visible and available for criticism. If a person or a group were to change discourses in a conflict, that would be to take a different stance in the world. One may feel as if that is not permitted or as if that is one's right.

Since the discourses vary within persons as well as between groups, whatever conflict or affiliation there may be between the discourses in society is experienced within the personality. This means that the diversity of tongues and of voices within the person has profound emotional content and profound significance for personal identity and wholeness.

Schools are collection sites for a diversity of voices and identities. Schools ask of students that they try on new discourses, new ways of speaking and thinking, new ways of being a self, and to appropriate them as their own. At their best, schools ask this of teachers as well, in order that they may come into closer awareness of and engagement with the voices of their students and also develop intellectually within their careers, appropriating within themselves more of the various discourses and literacies of their society. That is personally risky business, for both students and teachers. When discourses, or cultures, are in conflict in society, then conflict can be experienced within the self over which discourses are being tried on.

As we have seen, students and teachers come to school already having appropriated multiple voices and cultures. One task of education can be reflection on the voices one already has. Multicultural education, especially that which considers invisible as well as visible culture, can assist in that process of personal and group reflection. Teachers and students, by looking within themselves, can come to see that everybody is cultural and multicultural, including themselves. By listening to the discourses around them and also within them and by testing how those discourses feel—more like self, more like other, owned or alienated—students and their teachers can valorize many discourses, treating them as inherently of equivalent worth, even though not all the discourses and cultures are treated as equal in power and prestige in the world outside the classroom. If school is a secure place to try on new cultures and voices, if cultural diversity is treated as boundaries rather than as borders, then students and their teachers can establish safe "third spaces" in which to explore growing relationships with new cultures and old ones. This third-space pedagogy (Gutierrez, Baquedano-López, Alvarez, & Chiu, 1999) makes legitimate within the walls of the classroom the cultural hybridity that students and teachers bring to it.

Ultimately, for persons in complex multicultural societies, growth into maturity involves coming to terms with the diversity of voices and cultures within. This is especially the case when the cultures and voices have been in conflict in the wider society and when the person is a member of a dominated group. Then, coming to terms with one's own diversity means making some kind of just peace with the voices within. For example, in every man there are the voices of women, and in every woman there are the voices of men. Are these voices alien and in conflict within the person, or have they been appropriated within the self? Can a woman come to terms with the male voices within without acquiescing to male hegemony and adopting an alienated self? In every White person in the United States, because of our historical experience, there are not only White voices but also Black ones. What do those voices sound more like—Amos and Andy or Frederick Douglass? Aunt Jemima or Alice Walker? How have those voices been appropriated within the person, and what role has the school played in facilitating that process? In every African American in the United States, there are not only Black voices but also White ones. How can the African American come to terms with the White voices within, forgiving and making peace with them, coming to own them while at the same time affirming and owning the Black voices, holding a continuing sense of the injustice of continuing racism? Doing all of that is necessary to mature into full adulthood as a African American (Cross, 1991; Helms, 1990).

To come to terms with the diversity of voices within is an educative task for society, for the individual, and for the school. It is what growing up means in a multicultural society and in a multicultural world. When the voices of the school curriculum and of its teaching and learning are fully multicultural, then the appropriation of multiple voices—in dignity and without coercion, keeping a critical stance without despair—becomes possible for all students. This is a noble aim for multicultural education. How difficult it is to achieve, yet how necessary. This becomes more apparent to educators as we become able to think more deeply about culture, its nuances, and its diversity in school and in society.

AFTERWORD

"What we are talking about is creating a new tradition, telling 'new stories' that are fundamentally different by virtue of the role that the lives of the historically oppressed have assumed in their construction. This is a matter of redefining American culture, not once and for all, but in the negotiated meanings that are always emerging out of a curricular process. It is in the day-to-day interactions of teachers and students, dealing with a transformed curriculum and attempting to create a transformed, democratic classroom, that the new common culture will be created and continually re-created." (Perry & Fraser, 1993, pp. 19–20)

Questions and Activities

1. The author describes seven conceptions of culture: (1) culture as cultivation, (2) culture as tradition, (3) culture as information bits, (4) culture as symbol system, (5) culture as motive and emotion, (6) culture as distributed along lines of power in society, and (7) culture as residing in local communities of practice. Form groups in your class or workshop to explore the diverse meanings of culture. Ask one student or workshop participant in each group to become an expert on one conception of culture given by the author. Discuss how the different conceptions of culture are both alike and different. Explain each definition by giving examples.

2. What does the author mean by "implicit and invisible aspects of culture"? In what ways are these aspects of culture important? Give some examples of invisible aspects of culture. What are some nonexamples of the concept?

3. In what ways might differences in invisible culture cause conflict? Give specific examples.

4. According to the author, what problems result when teachers focus on visible (explicit) culture at the expense of invisible (implicit) culture? What kinds of educational practices result when teachers focus on visible and tangible aspects of culture?

5. How does the author distinguish between a cultural boundary and a cultural border? Why is this distinction important? Is a cultural boundary always a cultural border? Explain.

6. According to the author, does cultural change necessarily mean cultural loss? Explain why or why not.

7. The author states that we sometime "essentialize" culture. What does he mean? What problems result, in his view, when culture is essentialized?

8. The author states that "our conceptions of culture in multicultural education need to become more constructivist and less essentialist." Explain what he means by this statement and its implications for educational practice.

9. The author states that "multicultural education has an opportunity and a challenge to be counter-hegemonic." Explain the meaning of this statement and give examples of how this might be done by classroom teachers.

References

Apple, M. W. (1996). *Cultural Politics and Education*. Buckingham, UK: Open University Press.

Arteaga, A. (1994). *An Other Tongue: Nation and Ethnicity in the Linguistic Borderlands*. Durham, NC: Duke University Press.

Bakhtin, M. M. (1981). *The Dialogic Imagination* (M. Holquist, Ed; C. Emerson & M. Holquist, Trans.). Austin: University of Texas Press.

Barth, F. (1969). *Ethnic Groups and Boundaries: The Social Organization of Culture Difference*. Boston: Little, Brown.

Barth, F. (1989). The Analysis of Culture in Complex Societies. *Ethnos, 54*, 120–142.

Bateson, G., Jackson, D., Haley, J., & Weakland, J. (1972). Toward a Theory of Schizophrenia. In G. Bateson, *Steps toward an Ecology of Mind* (pp. 201–227). New York: Ballantine.

Bourdieu, P. (1977). *Outline of a Theory of Practice* (Cambridge Studies in Social Anthropology No. 16). New York: Cambridge University Press.

Bourdieu, P., & Passeron, J. C. (1977). *Reproduction: In Education, Society and Culture*. Beverly Hills, CA: Sage.

Connell, R. (1982). *Making the Difference: Schools, Families, and Social Division*. Sydney, Australia: Allen & Unwin.

Cross, W. E. (1991). *Shades of Black: Diversity in African American Identity*. Philadelphia: Temple University Press.

D'Andrade, R. G., & Strauss, C. (Eds.). (1992). *Human Motives and Cultural Models*. New York: Cambridge University Press.

Delpit, L. (1995). *Other People's Children: Cultural Conflict in the Classroom*. New York: New Press.

Erickson, F. (1987). Transformation and School Success: The Politics and Culture of Educational Achievement. *Anthropology and Education Quarterly, 18*(4), 335–356. Reprinted in E. Jacob & C. Jordan (Eds.), *Minority Education: Anthropological Perspectives*. Norwood, NJ: Ablex, 1992.

Erickson, F. (2004). *Talk and Social Theory: Ecologies of Speaking and Listening in Everyday Life*. Cambridge, England: Polity Press.

Fanon, F. (1963). *The Wretched of the Earth* (C. Farrington, Trans.). New York: Grove.

Foley, D. E. (1991). Reconsidering Anthropological Explanations of Ethnic School Failure. *Anthropology and Education Quarterly, 22*(1), 60–86.

Fordham, S. (1996). *Blacked Out: Dilemmas of Race, Identity, and Success at Capital High*. Chicago: University of Chicago Press.

Foucault, M. (1979). *Discipline and Punish: The Birth of the Prison*. New York: Random House/Vintage.

Garfinkel, H., & Sacks, H. (1970). The Formal Properties of Practical Actions. In J. C. McKinney & E. A. Tiryakian (Eds.), *Theoretical Sociology* (pp. 331–336). New York: Appleton-Century-Crofts.

Gee, J. (1990). *Social Linguistics and Literacies: Ideology in Discourses*. Philadelphia: Falmer.

Geertz, C. (1973). *The Interpretation of Cultures*. New York: Basic Books.

Giddens, A. (1984). *The Constitution of Society: Outline of the Theory of Structuration*. Berkeley: University of California Press.

Giles, H., & Powesland, P. F. (1975). *Speech Style and Social Evaluation*. London: Academic Press.

Giroux, H. A. (1983). Theories of Reproduction and Resistance: A Critical Analysis. *Harvard Educational Review, 53*, 257–293.

Giroux, H. (1991). *Border Crossings: Cultural Workers and the Politics of Education*. New York: Routledge.

Goodenough, W. (1976). Multiculturalism as the Normal Human Experience. *Anthropology and Education Quarterly, 7*(4), 4–7.

Goodenough, W. (1981). *Culture, Language and Society*. Menlo Park, CA: Benjamin/Cummins.

Gumperz, J. J. (1982). *Discourse Strategies*. New York: Cambridge University Press.

Gutierrez, K., Baquedano-López, P., Alvarez, H., & Chiu, M. (1999). Building a Culture of Collaboration through Hybrid Language Practices. *Theory into Practice, 38*(2), 87–93.

Gutierrez, K., Baquedano-López, P., & Tejeda, C. (1999). Rethinking Diversity: Hybridity and Hybrid Language Practices in the Third Space. *Mind, Culture, and Activity, 6*(4) 286–303.

Gutierrez, K., Rymes, B., Larson, J. (1995). Script, Counterscript, and Underlife in the Classroom: James Brown versus *Brown* vs. *Board of Education*. *Harvard Educational Review, 65*(3), 445–471.

Hall, E. T. (1959). *The Silent Language*. New York: Doubleday.

Hall, E. T. (1976). *Beyond Culture*. New York: Doubleday.

Heath, S. B. (1983). *Ways with Words: Language, Life, and Work in Communities and Classrooms*. New York: Cambridge University Press.

Helms, J. (1990). *Black and White Racial Identity*. New York: Greenwood.

hooks, B. (1993). Transformative Pedagogy and Multiculturalism. In T. Perry & J. W. Fraser (Eds.), *Freedom's Plow: Teaching in the Multicultural Classroom* (pp. 91–98). New York: Routledge.

Hymes, D. H. (1974). *Foundations in Sociolinguistics: An Ethnographic Approach*. Philadelphia: University of Pennsylvania Press.

Kroeber, A. L. (1917). The Superorganic. *American Anthropologist, 19*, 163–213.

Kroeber, A. L., & Kluckhohn, C. (1952). *Culture: A Critical Review of Concepts and Definitions*, Vol. 47(1). Cambridge, MA: Peabody Museum of American Archaeology and Ethnology, Harvard University.

Kuper, A. (1999). *Culture: The Anthropologists' Account*. Cambridge, MA: Harvard University Press.

Labov, W. (1963). The Social Motivation of a Sound Change. *Word, 19*, 273–309.

Ladson-Billings, G. (1994). *The Dreamkeepers: Successful Teachers of African-American Children*. San Francisco: Jossey-Bass Publishers.

Lave, J., & Wenger, E. (1990). *Situated Learning: Legitimate Peripheral Participation*. Cambridge: Cambridge University Press.

Lutz, C. A. (1990). *Language and the Politics of Emotion*. New York: Cambridge University Press.

McCarthy, C. (1993). After the Canon: Knowledge and Ideological Representation in the Multicultural Discourse on Curriculum Reform. In C. McCarthy & W. Crichlow (Eds.), *Race, Identity, and Representation in Education* (pp. 289–305). New York: Routledge.

McDermott, R. P., & Gospodinoff, K. (1981). Social Contexts for Ethnic Borders and School Failure. In A. Wolfgang (Ed.), *Nonverbal Behavior: Applications and Cultural Implications* (pp. 175–195). New York: Academic Press.

Moll, L. C. (Ed.). (1990). *Vygotsky and Education: Instructional Implications and Applications of Sociohistorical Psychology.* New York: Cambridge University Press.

Moll, L. (1998, February). *Funds of Knowledge for Teaching: A New Approach to Culture in Education.* Keynote address delivered to the Illinois State Board of Education, 21st Annual Statewide Conference for Teachers of Linguistically and Culturally Diverse Students, Springfield, IL.

Moll, L., & Greenberg, J. (1990). Creating Zones of Possibilities: Combining Social Contexts for Instruction. In L. C. Moll (Ed.), *Vygotsky and Education* (pp. 319–348). New York: Cambridge University Press.

Nieto, S. (Ed.). (1999). *The Light in Their Eyes: Creating Multicultural Learning Communities.* New York: Teachers College Press.

Ogbu, J. U. (1987). Variability in Minority School Performance: A Problem in Search of an Explanation. *Anthropology and Education Quarterly, 18*(4), 312–334.

Ortner, S. B. (1984). Theory in Anthropology since the Sixties. *Comparative Studies in Society and History, 26*(1), 126–166.

Perry, T., & Fraser, J. W. (Eds.). (1993). *Freedom's Plow: Teaching in the Multicultural Classroom.* New York: Routledge.

Philips, S. U. (1983). *The Invisible Culture: Communication in School and Community on the Warm Springs Indian Reservation.* New York: Longman.

Rogoff, B. (2003). *The Cultural Nature of Human Development.* Oxford: Oxford University Press.

Sadker, M., & Sadker, D. (1994). *Failing at Fairness: How America's Schools Cheat Girls.* New York: Scribner's.

Said, E. W. (1978). *Orientalism.* New York: Pantheon.

Skilton Sylvester, P. (1994). Elementary School Curricula and Urban Transformation. *Harvard Educational Review, 64,* 309–331.

Sleeter, C. E., & Grant, C. A. (1993). *Making Choices for Multicultural Education.* New York: Merrill/Macmillan.

Torres-Guzmán, M. (1992). Stories of Hope in the Midst of Despair: Culturally Responsive Education for Latino Students in an Alternative High School in New York City. In M. Saravia-Shore & S. F. Arvizu (Eds.), *Cross-Cultural Literacy: Ethnographies of Communication in Multiethnic Classrooms* (pp. 477–490). New York: Garland.

Trueba, H. T. (1994). Reflections on Alternative Visions of Schooling. *Anthropology and Education Quarterly, 25*(3), 376–393.

Tylor, E. B. (1970). *Primitive Culture: Researches into the Development of Mythology, Philosophy, Religion, Language, Art, and Custom.* London: Murray. (Original work published 1871).

Valle, V., & Torres, R. (1995). The Idea of Mestizaje and the "Race" Problematic: Racialized Media Discourse in a Post-Fordist Landscape. In A. Darder (Ed.), *Culture and Difference: Critical Perspectives on the Bicultural Experience in the United States* (pp. 139–153). Westport, CT: Bergin & Garvey.

Varenne, H., & McDermott, R. (1998). *Successful Failure: The School America Builds.* Boulder, CO: Westview.

Vico, G. (1968). *The New Science of Giambattista Vico* (rev. ed.) (T. G. Bergin & M. H. Frisch, Trans.). Ithaca, NY: Cornell University Press. (3rd ed. published 1744).

Wenger, E. (1999). *Communities of Practice.* New York: Cambridge University Press.

Wiggington, S. (1986). *Sometimes a Shining Moment: The Foxfire Experience.* Garden City, NY: Anchor.

Williams, R. (1983). *Culture and Society.* New York: Columbia University Press.

Willis, P. E. (1977). *Learning to Labor: How Working-Class Kids Get Working-Class Jobs.* New York: Columbia University Press.

Wills, J. S., & Lintz, A., & Mehan, H. (2004). Ethnographic Studies of Multicultural Education in Classrooms and Schools. In J. A. Banks & C. A. M. Banks (Eds.), *Handbook of Research on Multicultural Education* (2nd ed., pp. 163–183). New York: Macmillan.

Witherell, C., & Noddings, N. (1991). *Stories Lives Tell: Narrative and Dialogue in Education.* New York: Teachers College Press.

CHAPTER 3

Race, Class, Gender, and Disability in the Classroom

Carl A. Grant and
Christine E. Sleeter

Schools have always been a focal point of debate. What should be taught? How should students be organized for instruction? How should teachers be prepared? What constitute acceptable standards, and who should set them? Developments and tensions in society continuously fuel debate about these questions.

First, over the past ten years or so, a rapidly growing standards and testing movement has been increasingly driving the work of schools. This movement began with the report *A Nation at Risk: The Imperative for Educational Reform* (National Commission on Excellence in Education, 1983), which warned that U.S. preeminence on the world stage was being eroded by the mediocre performance of its educational institutions. President George H. W. Bush and the nation's governors unveiled Goals 2000, declaring that every child in the United States would meet rigorous standards of academic achievement by the year 2000. After a brief attempt to develop national standards in the early 1990s, the task of standard writing quickly devolved to the states, where state standards for student and teacher performance and systems of testing were put into place. This system of setting standards and measuring student performance based on them was cemented by passage of the No Child Left Behind Act at the federal level in 2001. As a vice principal recently remarked to one of us, "Everything in our school is being driven by tests." Many advocates of multicultural education quickly found attention to diversity and equity being replaced by attention to standards and student test scores.

Second, at the same time, universities had become actively engaged in promoting diversity. The amount of multicultural research and curriculum mushroomed

(Banks & Banks, 2004), advancing perspectives that differed in some cases sharply from those of most political and economic leaders. This intellectual work supported the tremendous growth in ethnic and racial diversity the United States has been experiencing. By 2004, the population was roughly 68 percent non-Latino White, 13 percent Latino, 13 percent African American, 4 percent Asian and Pacific Islander, 1 percent Native American, 1 percent more than one race, and 6 percent some other race (U.S. Census Bureau, 2004). Whites were no longer the majority in many cities. In California and Hawaii, no racial or ethnic group was a majority in the public schools. The largest portion (about 45%) of immigrants, about 1.6 million, came from Latin America and the Caribbean, contributing to a social phenomenon being called "the hispanization of America" (U.S. Department of Homeland Security, 2003). Although Christianity is by far the largest religion, increasingly one finds "Islamic centers and mosques, Hindu and Buddhist temples," in addition to Jewish temples and more traditional churches (Eck, 2002). Of the U.S. population, 82 percent spoke only English at home, while 18 percent spoke a language other than English (U.S. Census Bureau, 2003).

Third, however, the United States can also be characterized as becoming increasingly polarized along several dimensions. The September 11 attacks and then the war against Iraq led to a strong wave of patriotism and reluctance on the part of many people to criticize any aspect of U.S. culture or policy. Public sentiment about diversity rapidly became more negative, particularly toward people of Arab descent. According to a Gallup poll, 58 percent of Americans thought Arab Americans should undergo more intense security checks than the rest of the population; 49 percent favored making Arab Americans have special ID cards. In another survey, 31 percent of respondents favored putting Arab Americans in detention camps (Sen, 2002). At the same time, anti-war protests and concern that the United States was engaging in imperialist actions in the Middle East grew. The American Council of Trustees and Alumni published a report charging university faculty with being the "weak link" in the U.S. response to terrorism because of questions many have raised about U.S. policies (Gonzalez, 2001). Figures such as Congresswoman Barbara Lee of California and actor Danny Glover were strongly criticized for questioning a loss of civil liberties and the U.S. war on terrorism. These tensions played out in the "red state–blue state" divide in the 2004 presidential election, and growing public disagreements about the role religion should play in public institutions.

Fourth, the United States had grown increasingly segregated by race and class (Orfield & Lee, 2005), with gaps between "haves" and "have-nots" continuing to widen. The gradually rising levels of educational attainment had not been accompanied by a rising quality of life. As transnational corporations exported jobs to Third World nations in order to cut wages, many middle-class and working-class people in the United States experienced an erosion of their lifestyles, and the poverty level rose, especially among women and children (Headley & Lowe, 2000; Ulrich, 2004). According to the Census Bureau (2004), while the wealthiest fifth of the U.S. population's share of income rose from 44 percent of the total in 1973 to 50 percent in 2002, everyone else's share fell.

While education is necessary for upward mobility and community uplift, education does not wipe away racial advantages. For example, African Americans and Latinos earn consistently less than their White counterparts with the same level of education. White high school graduates earn a median annual income of $30, 700, compared to $25,580 for Blacks and $25,500 for Latinos, a gap of 22 percent. White professionals with advanced degrees earn a median annual income of $60,320, while Blacks with the same educational level earn $51,220, and

Hispanics $51,740 (U.S. Department of Labor, 2005). At the same time, poverty and unemployment hit communities of color harder than White communities (U.S. Census Bureau, 2000). For most African Americans, the slow federal response to the Katrina disaster was confirming evidence that African Americans matter less to the national leadership than do Whites.

Prisons had become a growth industry. Many leaders of color view the explosion of prison populations as a new form of slavery, a warehousing of unemployed young men of color. Indeed, between 1977 and 1985, "when the prison population almost tripled, 70 percent of new inmates were African American, Latino, or other nonwhite minorities," a fact that had been downplayed by classifying Latinos as White (Chanse, 2002, p. 3).

Most adults with disabilities are either unemployed or underemployed, and their earnings are often below the poverty level. In 1998, only 31.2 percent of disabled high school graduates were employed—only a 2 percent increase since 1972 (U.S. Department of Labor, Bureau of Labor Statistics, 1998). While about 79 percent of non-disabled people work full-time, only about 29 percent of people with disabilities do so. Passage of the Americans with Disabilities Act was designed to protect people with disabilities from discrimination, and while it has helped, there are many issues that it cannot solve, such as lack of enough affordable housing.

A major thread running through the debates about schooling is the relative importance of preparing students for jobs versus preparing them for active citizenship. Schools have always done both, but recently much of the talk about what schools should do has emphasized job preparation; little has been said about citizenship. What kind of a nation do we want for ourselves and our children, given the challenges and problems we have been facing? How should limited resources be distributed, given our diversity and virtually everyone's desire for a good life? How can tomorrow's citizens who are in the schools now be prepared to build the kinds of institutions that support a diverse democracy in which people are truly equal? Who gets to decide the most effective ways of educating children from diverse backgrounds?

Students we teach usually give one of three reasons for wanting to become teachers: (1) they love kids, (2) they want to help students, (3) they want to make school more exciting than it was when they were students. If one of these is the reason you chose to enter the teaching profession, then we hope you will see the demographic and social trends described above as being challenging and will realize that your love and help are needed not just for some students but for all students.

This chapter discusses the importance of race, class, gender, language, and disability in classroom life and provides alternative approaches to dealing with these issues in the classroom.

RACE, CLASS, GENDER, LANGUAGE, DISABILITY, AND CLASSROOM LIFE

Ask yourself what you know about race, ethnicity, class, gender, language, and disability as they apply to classroom life. Could you write one or two good paragraphs about what these words mean? How similar or different would your meanings be from those of your classmates? How much do these dynamics of social organization influence the way you think about teaching? If you and your classmates organize into small discussion groups (try it) and listen closely to each other, you will probably notice some distinct differences in the ways you see the importance of these dynamics. The point of such an exercise is not to show that you have different ideas and interpretations, but to challenge you to think clearly about what your ideas and interpretations mean for working with your students: How will you teach with excellence and equity?

Race, social class, and gender are used to construct categories of people in society. On your college application form, you were probably asked to indicate your race, ethnicity, gender, disability, and parents' place of employment. Most institutions want to know such information. It provides the institution with the ability to analyze and report data related to any or all of your ascribed characteristics. Social scientists studying school practices often report results according to race, class, home language, or gender. You must understand how the dynamics of race, class, language, gender, and disability can influence your knowledge and understanding of your students. It is also important for you to consider these dynamics collectively, not separately. Each of your students is a member of multiple status groups, and these simultaneous memberships, in interaction with dynamics in the broader society, influence the students' perceptions and actions.

For example, a child in the classroom may be not just Asian American but also male, middle class, native–English-speaking, Buddhist, and not disabled. Thus, he is a member of a historically marginalized group—but also of a gender group and a social class that have historically oppressed others. Therefore, his view of reality and his actions based on that view will differ from those of a middle-class Asian American girl whose first language is Korean or a lower-class Asian American boy whose first language is Hmong and who has spina bifida. A teacher's failure to consider the integration of race, social class, and gender can lead to an over-simplified or inaccurate understanding of what occurs in schools and, therefore, to an inappropriate or simplistic prescription for educational equity and excellence. You may have noticed, for example, teachers assuming (often mistakenly) that Mexican American students identify strongly with each other and that they view issues in much the same way, or that African American male students have the same goals and views as African American female students.

We often begin working with teacher education students by having them take a self-inventory of the sociocultural groups they have been exposed to in their own schooling, religious, or work situations. The more honestly you examine your familiarity with the backgrounds of different children, the more readily you can begin to learn about people to whom you have had little exposure. It will be a much greater limitation on your ability to teach well if you assume you know more about different students than you actually know than if you recognize whose lives are unfamiliar to you, so that you can learn.

APPROACHES TO MULTICULTURAL EDUCATION

Educators often work with students of color, students from low-income backgrounds, and White female students according to one of five approaches to multicultural education. As we briefly explain these approaches, ask yourself which one you are most comfortable using in your teaching. Before we begin this discussion, you should understand two important points. First, space does not allow for a complete discussion of each approach; for a thorough discussion, please refer to *Making Choices for Multicultural Education: Five Approaches to Race, Class, and Gender* (Sleeter & Grant, 2005). Second, it is fine to discover that you are a true eclectic or that none of the approaches satisfy your teaching style as long as you are not straddling the fence. Indecision, dissatisfaction, and frustration in teaching style and technique may confuse your students. Also, to be the dynamic teacher you want to be, you need a teaching philosophy that is well thought out and makes learning exciting for your students. Good teaching requires that you have a comprehensive understanding of what you are doing in the classroom, why, and how you are doing it.

Teaching the Exceptional and the Culturally Different

If you believe that a teacher's chief responsibility is to prepare all students to fit into and achieve within the existing school and society, this approach may appeal to you. It may be especially appealing if categories of students, such as students of color, special education students, or language-minority students are behind in the main subject areas of the traditional curriculum. The goals of this approach are to equip students with the cognitive skills, concepts, information, language, and values traditionally required by U.S. society, and eventually to enable them to hold a job and function within society's institutions and culture. Teachers using this approach often begin by determining the achievement levels of students, comparing their achievement to grade-level norms, and then working diligently to help those who are behind to catch up.

A good deal of research documents learning strengths of students of different sociocultural groups, suggesting that if a teacher learns to identify and build on their strengths, students will learn much more effectively than if a teacher assumes the child cannot learn very well. For example, based on a study of high-performing Hispanic schools, Reyes, Scribner, and Scribner (1999) found that these schools share four characteristics: (1) The schools proactively involved families and communities, (2) The schools were organized around collaborative governance and leadership that was clearly focused on student success, (3) Culturally responsive pedagogy was widely used, Teachers viewed children as capable of high levels of achievement and viewed their cultural background as a valuable resource on which to build, and (4) The schools used advocacy-oriented assessment, which was used to support high achievement by giving information that could improve instruction and guide intervention on a day-to-day basis. Language sensitivity was part of this process. Teachers who understand how to build on the culture and language of students will read the classroom behavior of such children more accurately and adjust their instructional processes accordingly without lowering their expectations for learning.

As another example, Moses and Cobb (2001) taught algebra to inner-city middle school students by building on their experience. Students were having difficulty with numerical directionality—positive and negative numbers. So the teachers sent the students to the local subway and had them diagram the subway system in terms of directionality. The teachers then helped the students represent their experience with the subway numerically, in the process helping them to translate the familiar—subway routes—into the unfamiliar—positive and negative numbers.

Starting where the students are and using instructional techniques and content familiar to them are important. For example, one teacher who used this approach helped two African American students who had moved from a large urban area to a much smaller college town to catch up on their writing skills by having them write letters to the friends they had left behind in the city. A second teacher grouped the girls in her ninth-grade class who were having problems in algebra, allowing them to work together, support one another, and not be intimidated by the boys in the class who had received the kind of socialization that produces good math students. A third teacher provided two students with learning disabilities with materials written at their reading level that covered concepts comparable to those the rest of the class was reading about. A fourth teacher placed two Latino students with limited English-speaking abilities into a transitional bilingual program. A teacher may believe that only one or two students in the classroom need this approach or that all of them do, especially if the school is located in an inner-city community or barrio.

In sum, the heart of this approach is building bridges for students to help them acquire the cognitive skills and knowledge expected of the so-called average White middle-class student. This approach accepts that there is a body of knowledge all students should learn but proposes that teachers should teach that knowledge in whatever way works so students understand and learn it.

Human Relations Approach

If you believe that a major purpose of the school is to help students learn to live together harmoniously in a world that is becoming smaller and smaller, and if you believe that greater social equality will result if students learn to respect one another regardless of race, class, gender, or disability, then this approach may be of special interest to you. Its goal is to promote a feeling of unity, tolerance, and acceptance among people: "I am okay and you are okay."

The human relations approach engenders positive feelings among all students, promotes group identity and pride for students of color, reduces stereotypes, and works to eliminate prejudice and biases. For example, a teacher of a fourth-grade multiracial, mainstreamed classroom spends considerable time during the first two weeks of each semester, and some time thereafter, doing activities to promote good human relations in the class. Early in the semester he uses a sociogram to learn student friendship patterns and to make certain that every child has a buddy. He also uses this activity to discover how negative or positive the boy–girl relationships are. He uses sentence-completion activities to discover how students are feeling about themselves and their family members. Based on these data, he integrates into his curriculum concepts of social acceptance and humanness for all people, the reduction and elimination of stereotypes, and information to help students feel good about themselves and their people. Also, he regularly brings to his classroom speakers who represent the diversity in society to show all students that they, too, can be successful.

The curriculum for the human relations approach addresses individual differences and similarities. It includes contributions of the groups of which the students are members and provides accurate information about various ethnic, racial, disability, gender, or social-class groups about whom the students hold stereotypes. Instructional processes include a good deal of cooperative learning, role playing, and vicarious or real experiences to help the students develop appreciation of others. Advocates of this approach suggest that it should be comprehensive, integrated into several subject areas, and schoolwide. For example, a school attempting to promote gender equality is working at cross-purposes if lessons in language arts teach students to recognize sex stereotypes, while in the science class girls are not expected to perform as well as boys and thus are not pushed to do so. These contradictory practices simply reaffirm sex stereotypes.

While the teaching-the-exceptional-and-the-culturally-different approach emphasizes helping students acquire cognitive skills and knowledge in the traditional curriculum, the human relations approach focuses on attitudes and feelings students have about themselves and each other.

Single-Group Studies Approach

We use the phrase single-group studies to refer to the study of a particular group of people, for example, disability studies or Native American studies. The single-group studies approach seeks to raise the social status of the target group by helping young people examine how the group has been oppressed historically and what its capabilities and achievements have been. Unlike the two previous approaches, this one (as do the next two) views school knowledge as political rather than neutral and presents alternatives to the existing Eurocentric, male-dominant curriculum. It focuses on one specific group at a time so the history, perspectives, and worldview of that group can be developed coherently, rather than piecemeal. It also examines the current social status of the group and actions taken historically as well as contemporarily to further the interests of the group. Its advocates hope that students will develop more respect for the group and also the knowledge and commitment to work to improve the group's status in society.

Single-group studies are oriented toward political action and liberation. For example, in his discussion of the development of Asian American studies, Omatsu (1994) explains that

> the redefinition [of the Asian American experience] began with an
> analysis of power and domination in American society. It provided
> a way for understanding the historical forces surrounding us. And
> most importantly, it presented a strategy and challenge for
> changing our future. (p. 33)

Women's studies was created with a "vision of a world in which all persons can develop to their fullest potential and be free from all ideologies and structures that consciously and unconsciously oppress and exploit some for the advantage of others" (National Women's Studies Association, 2005). Gay and lesbian studies develop "an intellectual community for students and faculty that is ethnically diverse and committed to gender parity" (A National Survey, 1990/1991, p. 53). Ethnic studies helps "students develop the ability to make reflective decisions on issues related to ethnicity and to take personal, social, and civic actions to help solve the racial and ethnic problems in our national and world societies" (Banks, 2002, pp. 25–26).

Since the late 1960s and early 1970s, scholars have generated an enormous amount of research about various oppressed groups and have begun to map out new conceptual frameworks within various disciplines. For example, Afrocentric scholars redefined the starting point of African American history from slavery to ancient Africa, in the process rewriting story lines for African American history. Beginning history with a group other than European males enables one to view historical events very differently. A group's story may begin in Asia and move east, or begin in South or Central America and move north, or begin in Europe and move west, or begin right here on the North American continent thousands of years ago. Further, the story is different if one views the group as having started from a position of strength (e.g., African civilizations [Gates, 1999]), then having been subjugated, and now attempting to rebuild that strength, rather than starting from a position of weakness (such as slavery) and now attempting to rise.

A single-group studies curriculum includes units or courses about the history and culture of a group (e.g., African American history, Chicano literature, disability studies). It teaches how the group has been victimized and has struggled to gain respect as well as about current social issues facing the group. It is essential that such curricula be based on scholarship by people who have studied the group in depth, rather than on your own ideas about what you think might be important.

For example, in 2003, Tucson Unified School District's Mexican American/Raza Studies Department offered assistance to schools that were interested in incorporating Mexican American/Raza Studies into the curriculum. It also developed a Social Justice Education Project for high school Chicano students who were failing high school and considering dropping out. The curriculum, which met state standards, taught social studies from a Chicano/a perspective and involved students in reading college-level material and doing community research in which they developed "advanced, graduate-level skills in research, writing, and critical thinking" (VisionMark, 2005). By 2005, students who completed this program were graduating from high school and seeing themselves as capable learners, and over half were attending college. Similarly, Pinoy Teach is a social studies curriculum from a Filipino studies perspective. Halagao (2004), one of its authors, explains that Pinoy Teach "is my insider's attempt to write our people's perspective into social studies. It reflects the experiences of brown people who are not passive bystanders, but rather active figures who construct historical and important moments" (p. 464).

Although single-group studies focus mainly on the curriculum, they also give some attention to instructional processes that benefit the target group. Women's studies programs, for example, have developed what is known as "feminist pedagogy" (see Chapter 7). This is a teaching approach that attempts to empower students. The main idea is that in the traditional classroom, women are socialized to accept other people's ideas. By reading text materials that were written mainly by men and provide a male interpretation of the world, women learn not to interpret the world for themselves. In the feminist classroom, women learn to trust and develop their own insights. The feminist teacher may assign material to read and may encourage students to generate discussion and reflections about the material. The discussion and personal reflection are important parts of the process, during which "control shifts from me, the teacher, the arbiter of knowing, to the interactions of students and myself with the subject matter" (Tetreault, 1989, p. 137).

In summary, the single-group studies approach is aimed toward social change. It challenges the knowledge normally taught in schools, arguing that knowledge reinforces control by wealthy White men over everyone else. It offers an in-depth study of oppressed groups for the purpose of empowering group members, developing in them a sense of pride and group consciousness, and helping members of dominant groups understand where others are coming from.

Multicultural Education Approach

Multicultural education has become the most popular term used by educators to describe education for pluralism. We apply this term to a particular approach that multicultural education theorists discuss most often. As you will notice, this approach synthesizes many ideas from the previous three approaches.

The goals of this approach are to reduce prejudice and discrimination against oppressed groups, to work toward equal opportunity and social justice for all groups, and to effect an equitable distribution of power among members of the different cultural groups. These goals are worked toward by attempting to reform the total schooling process for all children, regardless of whether the school is an all-White suburban school or a multiracial urban school. Schools that are reformed around principles of pluralism and equality would then contribute to broader social reform.

Various practices and processes in the school are reconstructed so that the school models equality and pluralism. For example, the curriculum is organized around concepts basic to each discipline, but content elaborating on those concepts is drawn from the experiences and perspectives of several different U.S. groups. If you are teaching literature, you select literature written by members of different groups. This not only teaches students that groups other than Whites have produced literature; it also enriches the concept of literature because it enables students to experience different literature forms that are common to all writing. For example, the universal struggle for self-discovery and cultural connection within a White-dominant society can be examined by reading about a Puerto Rican girl in *Felita* (Mohr, 1990), a Chinese girl in *Dragonwings* (Yep, 1975), an African American boy in *Scorpions* (Myers, 1990), a European American girl in *The Great Gilly Hopkins* (Paterson, 1987), and Iranian youth in *Teenage Refugees from Iran Speak Out* (Strazzabosco, 1995).

It is also important that the contributions and perspectives you select depict each group as the group would depict itself and show the group as active and dynamic. This requires that you learn about various groups and become aware of what is important and meaningful to them. For example, Arab peoples are highly diverse. Further, in contrast to popular stereotypes, there is a long history of Arab feminism (Darraj, 2002) and Arab women in some countries working as well-educated professionals. Teachers wishing to teach about famous Native Americans should ask members of different Native American tribes whom they would like to see celebrated, instead of holding up to their students Pocahantas, Kateri Tekakwitha, or Sacajawea. These Native Americans are often thought among their people to have served White interests more than Native American interests. Additionally, African Americans are becoming increasingly concerned because the African American athlete or entertainer is often held up as the hero and heroine for the group, instead of African Americans who have done well in other areas of life, such as science or literature.

In this approach, instruction starts by assuming that students are capable of learning complex material and performing at a high level of skill. Each student has a personal, unique learning style that teachers discover and build on when teaching. The teacher draws on and uses the conceptual schemes (ways of thinking, knowledge about the world) that students bring to school. Cooperative learning is fostered, and both boys and girls are treated equally in a nonsexist manner. A staff as diverse as possible is hired and assigned responsibilities nonstereotypically. More than one language is taught; all students become at least bilingual. The multicultural education approach, more than the previous three, advocates total school reform to make the school reflect diversity. It also advocates giving equal attention to a variety of cultural groups regardless of whether specific groups are represented in the school's student population.

Multicultural Social Justice Education

Reflect back on the various forms of social inequality mentioned at the opening of this chapter. Multicultural social justice education deals more directly than the other approaches with oppression and social structural inequality based on race, social class, gender, and disability. Its purpose is to prepare future citizens to take action to change society so that it better serves the interests of all groups of people, especially those who are of color, poor, female, or have disabilities. The approach is rooted in social reconstructionism, which seeks to reconstruct society toward greater equity in race, class, gender, and disability. This approach also questions ethics and power relations embedded in the new global economy. It draws on the penetrating vision of George Bernard Shaw, who exclaimed, "You see things, and you say, 'Why?' But I dream things that never were, and I say, 'Why not?'"

As noted above, this approach extends the multicultural education approach, in that the curriculum and instruction of these two approaches are very similar. However, there are four practices unique to multicultural social justice education.

First, democracy is actively practiced in the schools. Reading the U.S. Constitution and hearing lectures on the three branches of government is a passive way to learn about democracy. For students to understand democracy, they must live it. They must practice politics, debate, social action, and the use of power. In the classroom this means that students will be given the opportunity to direct a good deal of their learning and to learn how to be responsible for that direction. This does not mean that teachers abdicate the running of their classroom to the students, but rather that they guide and direct students so they learn how to learn and develop skills for wise decision making. Shor (1980) describes this as helping students become subjects rather than objects in the classroom, and Freire (1985) says it will produce individuals "who organize themselves reflectively for action rather than men [and women] who are organized for passivity" (p. 82).

Second, students learn how to analyze institutional inequality within their own life circumstances. Freire (1973) distinguished among critical consciousness, magical consciousness, and naive consciousness:

> Critical consciousness represents things and facts as they exist
> empirically, in their causal and circumstantial correlations, naive
> consciousness considers itself superior to facts, in control of facts,
> and thus free to understand them as it pleases. Magic
> consciousness, in contrast, simply apprehends facts and attributes
> them to a superior power by which it is controlled and to which it
> must therefore submit. (p. 44)

To put it another way, a person with critical consciousness wants to know how the world actually works and is willing to analyze the world carefully for himself or herself. A person with naive or magic consciousness does not do that. If one sees the world through magic, one assumes that one cannot understand or affect the world; things just happen. If one sees the world naively, one assumes cause–effect relationships that one wants to assume or that one has been told exist, without investigating them or thinking critically for oneself.

In a stratified society, Freire (1973) argued, most ordinary people see the world naively or magically, as the elite would wish them to see it. Either they believe that they have no power to change the way the world works for them or they believe that their problems have no relationship to their position in the power hierarchy. For example, students are taught that education is the doorway to success and that if they obey the teacher and do their work, they will succeed. However, studies indicate that many students of color who comply with school rules and teachers' requests still do not receive the career guidance and schoolwork necessary for becoming successful (Grant & Sleeter, 1986). Earlier, we showed that education pays off better for Whites than for people of color. The earnings of full-time working women are only about 80 percent the earnings of full-time working men (U.S. Department of Labor, 2004), a gap that contributes heavily to the pauperization of women and children in female-headed households. This approach teaches students to question what they hear about how society works from other sources and to analyze the experiences of people like themselves in order to understand more fully what the problems actually are so they can prepare themselves to change unfair social processes.

Third, students learn to engage in social action. Parker (2003) explained that teaching for democracy should mean preparing young people for enlightened political engagement: "the action or participatory domain of citizenship" (p. 33), such as voting, contacting officials, deliberating, and engaging in boycotts, based on enlightenment, or the "knowledge, norms, values, and principles that shape this engagement" (p. 34). In other words, democracy is not a spectator sport.

For example, some stories that elementary school children read could deal with issues involving discrimination and oppression and could suggest ways to deal with such problems. Students of all ages can be taught to identify sexist advertising of products sold in their community and how to take action to encourage advertisers to stop these types of practices. Advocates of this approach do not expect children to reconstruct the world, but they do expect the schools to teach students how to do their part in helping the nation achieve excellence and equity in all areas of life.

Fourth, bridges are built across various oppressed groups (e.g., people who are poor, people of color, and White women) so they can work together to advance their common interests. This is important because it can energize and strengthen struggles against oppression. However, getting groups to work together is difficult because members often believe that they would have to place some of their goals second to those of other groups. Further, racial groups find themselves divided along gender and class lines to the extent that middle-class males of all colors fail to take seriously the concerns of women and of lower-class members of their own groups. Childs (1994) describes "transcommunal" organizations, such as the African American/Korean alliance in Los Angeles, which bring different groups together to identify and work on common concerns. Albrecht and Brewer's (1990) *Bridges of Power: Women's Multicultural Alliances* addresses concerns and issues women face in attempting to coalesce across racial and social-class lines.

You now have an idea of the approaches used to teach multicultural education. Which one best suits your teaching philosophy and style? An equally important question is, Which approach will best help to bring excellence and equity to education? This chapter next provides an example of how one teacher brings both excellence and equity to her classroom.

MS. JULIE WILSON AND HER APPROACH TO TEACHING

The following example describes a few days in the teaching life of Ms. Julie Wilson, a first-year teacher in a medium-large city. Which approach to multicultural education do you think Ms. Wilson is using? With which of her teaching actions do you agree or disagree? What would you do if assigned to her class?

May 23

Julie Wilson was both elated and sad that she had just completed her last exam at State U. As she walked back to her apartment, she wondered where she would be at this time next year. She had applied for 10 teaching positions and had been interviewed three times. As Julie entered her apartment building, she stopped to check the mail. A large, fat, white envelope addressed to her was stuffed into the small mailbox. She hurriedly tore it open and quickly read the first sentence. "We are pleased to offer you a teaching position." Julie leaped up the stairs three at a time. She burst into the apartment, waving the letter at her two roommates. "I've got a job! I got the job at Hoover Elementary. My first teaching job, a fifth-grade class!"

Hoover Elementary had been a part of a desegregation plan that brought together students from several different neighborhoods in the city. Hoover was situated in an urban-renewal area to which city officials were giving a lot of time and attention and on which they were spending a considerable amount of money. The city officials wanted to bring the Whites back into the city from suburbs and to encourage the middle-class people of color to remain in the city. They also wanted to improve the life chances for the poor. Julie had been hired because the principal was looking for teachers who had some record of success in working with diverse students. So far students were doing well enough on annual testing that the school was not on the list of schools needing improvement.

Julie had a 3.5 grade point average and had worked with a diverse student population in her practicum and student-teaching experience. She had strong letters of recommendation from her cooperating teacher and university supervisor. Julie also had spent her last two summers working as a counselor in a camp that enrolled a wide diversity of students.

August 25

Julie was very pleased with the way her classroom looked. She had spent the last three days getting it ready for the first day of school. Plants, posters, goldfish, and an old rocking chair added to the warmth of an attractive classroom. There was also a big sign across the room that said "Welcome Fifth Graders." Tomorrow was the big day.

August 26

Twenty-eight students entered Julie's classroom: fifteen girls and thirteen boys. There were ten White students, two Hmong students, six Latino students, nine African American students, and one Bosnian student. Three of the students were learning disabled, and one was in a wheelchair. Eleven of the students were from middle-class homes, nine were from working-class homes, and the remaining eight were from very poor homes. Julie greeted each student with a big smile and a friendly hello as they entered the room. She asked their names and told them hers. She then asked them to take the seat with their name on the desk.

After the school bell rang, Julie introduced herself to the whole class. She told them that she had spent most of her summer in England and that while she was there she had often thought about this day—her first day as a teacher. She talked briefly about some of the places she had visited in England as she pointed to them on a map. She concluded her introduction by telling them a few things about her family. Her mother and father owned a dairy farm in

Wisconsin, and she had one older brother, Wayne, and two younger sisters, Mary and Patricia. Julie asked if there were any students new to the school. Lester, an African American male, raised his hand, along with a female Hmong student, Mai-ka; a Bosnian female student, Dijana; and two Latino students, Maria and Jesus. Julie asked Mai-ka if she would like to tell the class her complete name, how she had spent her summer, and one favorite thing she liked to do. Then she asked the same of the other four. After all five had finished introducing themselves, Julie invited the other students to do the same. Julie then asked Lourdes, a returning student, to tell Mai-ka, Maria, Dijana, Jesus, and Lester about Hoover Elementary. As she listened to the students, she realized that Dijana and Jesus were both newcomers to the United States and neither spoke English fluently. To assist them, she asked two other students to buddy with them for the day. She realized that she would need to figure out a good buddy system, and she would also need help making her teaching accessible to these students while they learned English.

Once the opening greetings were completed, Julie began a discussion about the importance of the fifth grade and how special this grade was. She explained that this was a grade and class where a lot of learning would take place, along with a lot of fun. As Julie spoke, the students were listening intently. Julie radiated warmth and authority. Some of the students glanced at each other unsmilingly as she spoke of the hard work; however, when she mentioned "a lot of fun," the entire class perked up and looked at each other with big grins on their faces.

Julie had begun working on her educational philosophy in the Introduction to Education course at State U. Although she was continually modifying the way she thought about teaching, her basic philosophical beliefs had remained much the same. One of her major beliefs was that the students should actively participate in planning and shaping their own educational experiences. This, she believed, was as important for fifth graders as twelfth graders.

Julie asked the class if they were ready to take care of their classroom governance—deciding on rules, helpers, a discipline code, and time for classroom meetings. The class responded enthusiastically. The first thing the students wanted to do was to decide on the class rules. Several began to volunteer rules:

> "No stealing."
> "No rock throwing on the playground."
> "No sharpening pencils after the bell rings."
> "No fighting."

As the students offered suggestions, Julie wrote them on the chalkboard. After giving about sixteen suggestions, the class concluded. Julie commented, "All the rules seem very important"; she then asked the class what they should do with the rules. One student, Richard, suggested that they be written on poster board and placed in the upper corner of the room for all to see. Other class members said, "Yes, this is what we did last year in fourth grade." William, however, said, "Yes, we did do this, but we rarely followed the rules after the first day we made them." Julie assured the class this would not be the case this year and that they would have a weekly classroom meeting, run by an elected official of the class. She then asked if they thought it would be helpful if they wrote their rules using positive statements, instead of "no" or negative statements. The class said yes and began to change statements such as "no stealing" to "always ask before borrowing" and "no rock throwing" to "rock throwing can severely hurt a friend." Once the rules were completed, the class elected its officers.

After the classroom governance was taken care of, Julie asked the students if they would like her to read them a story. An enthusiastic "yes" followed her question. Julie glanced at the clock as she picked up *To Break the Silence* (Barrett, 1986) from the desk. The book is a varied collection of short stories, especially for young readers, written by authors of different racial backgrounds. It was 11:35. She could hardly believe the morning had gone by so quickly. She read for twenty minutes. All the students seemed to be enjoying the story, except Lester and Ben, two African American male students. Lester and Ben were drawing pictures, communicating nonverbally between themselves, and ignoring the rest of the class members. Julie decided that because they were quiet and not creating a disturbance, she would leave them alone.

After lunch, Julie had the class do two activities designed to help her learn about each student both socially and academically. She had the students do a self-concept activity, in which they did sentence completions that asked them to express how they felt about themselves. Then she had them play math and reading games to assess informally their math and reading skills. These activities took the entire afternoon, and Julie was as pleased as the students when the school day came to an end.

When Julie arrived at her apartment, she felt exhausted. She had a quick dinner and shower and then crawled into bed. She set the alarm for 7:00 P.M. and quickly fell asleep.

By 10:30 that night she had examined the students' self-concept activity and compared the information she had collected from the informal math and reading assessment with the official information from the students' cumulative record cards. She thought about each student's achievement record, social background, race, gender, and exceptionality. She said aloud, "I need to make plans soon to meet every parent. I need to find out about the students' lives at home, the parents' expectations, and if I can get some of them to volunteer."

Julie turned off her desk lamp at 11:45 to retire for the evening. She read a few pages from Anne Fadiman's (1997) *The Spirit Catches You and You Fall Down*, which tells the story of a Hmong child and the culture clash she experienced with American doctors. Then she turned out the light. Tonight she was going to sleep with less tension and nervousness than she had the night before. She felt good about the way things had gone today and was looking forward to tomorrow. As Julie slept, she dreamed of her class. Their faces and most of their names and backgrounds floated through her mind.

Eight of the ten White students were from Briar Creek, a middle-class single-unit housing community; these students were performing at grade level or above in all scholastic areas, and each of them was at least a year ahead in some core-area subject. Charles, who had used a wheelchair since being in an automobile accident three years ago, was three years ahead in both reading and math. However, Elaine and Bob had chosen a mixture of positive and negative adjectives when doing the self-concept activity, and this concerned Julie. She would keep her eye on them to try to determine the cause of their problems.

Estelle and Todd, the other two White students, were between six months and a year behind in most academic areas. Estelle had been diagnosed as learning disabled (LD), but the information in her personal cumulative folder seemed ambiguous about the cause of her problem. Julie wondered whether Estelle was classified as LD based on uncertain reasons. She recalled an article that discussed the learning-disability label as being a social construction rather than a medical condition.

Both of the Hmong students were at grade level or very close in their subjects. However, both of them, Mai-ka and Chee, were having some difficulty speaking English. Chee's family owned a restaurant in the neighborhood. The rumor mill reported that they were doing very well financially, so well that they had recently opened a restaurant in the downtown area of the city. Five of the six Latino students were Mexican American, born in the United States. Maria, José, and Lourdes were bilingual; Richard and Carmen were monolingual, with English being their primary language; and Jesus spoke mainly Spanish. Maria, José, and Lourdes were from working-class homes, and Richard, Jesus, and Carmen were from very poor homes. Lourdes, Carmen, and Richard's achievement scores were at least two years ahead of their grade level. José was working at grade level, and Maria and Jesus were one to two years behind. Jesus had immigrated to the U.S. only a year ago.

Five of the African American students—Lester, Ben, Gloria, Sharon, and Susan—were all performing two years behind grade level in all core-area subjects. All five lived in the Wendell Phillips low-rent projects. Two African American students—Shelly and Ernestine—lived in Briar Creek and were performing above grade level in all academic areas. Dolores and Gerard lived in Chatham, a working-class, predominantly African American neighborhood. Dolores was performing above grade level in all subjects; Gerard was behind in math. Gerard had also chosen several negative words when doing the self-concept activity.

Finally, Dijana, who had immigrated recently from Bosnia, did not know enough English to participate very well in any of the day's activities. Julie was glad that Shelley seemed to be taking an interest in helping her. Julie realized that she would need to think regularly about how to make sure Dijana was following along and would need to make sure both Dijana and Jesus were being tested for the English as a Second Language program.

All students in Julie's class were obedient and came from families that encouraged getting a good education.

May 25, 7:30 A.M.

Julie liked arriving early at school. The engineer, Mike, usually had a pot of coffee perking when she arrived. This was her time to get everything ready for the day. She had been teaching for almost one school year and was proud and pleased with how everything was going. The school principal, Mr. Griffin, had been in her class three times for formal visits and had told others, "Julie is an excellent teacher." He usually offered her one or two minor suggestions, such as "Don't call the roll every day; learn to take your attendance silently" and "The museum has an excellent exhibit on food and the human body your class may enjoy."

Julie had also been surprised by several things. She was surprised at how quickly most of the teachers left school at the end of the day. Out of a staff of twenty classroom teachers, only about five or six came early or stayed late. Even more surprising to her was how she and the other teachers who either came early or stayed late were chided about this behavior. She was surprised at the large number of worksheets and ditto sheets used and at how closely many teachers followed the outline in the books regardless of the needs of students. Also, she noticed, there was a common belief among the staff that her instructional style would not work.

Julie had made several changes in the curriculum. She studied the content standards she was expected to follow so that she would be sure to teach material that would be included on tests. But she carefully wove the standards into a project-based curriculum. She had incorporated tradebooks into reading and language arts, using them along with the language arts package her school had adopted. She made available to the students a wide assortment of books that featured different races, exceptionalities, and socioeconomic classes. In some stories, both males and females were featured doing traditional as well as nontraditional activities.

Stories were set in urban and rural settings, and some featured children with disabilities. It had taken Julie several months to acquire such a diverse collection of books for her students, and she had even spent some of her own money for the books, but the excitement the students had shown about the materials made the expense worthwhile. She made sure she was teaching the kinds of reading and language arts skills her students would be tested on but refused to sacrifice the richness of a literature-based curriculum for "test prep." Thankfully, her principal was supportive of her.

She also had several computers in her class. A computer lab was down the hall, but Julie wanted her students to use the computer on a regular basis. When she discovered that Richard's father owned a computer store, she convinced him to lend the class two iMacs, and she convinced Mr. Griffin to purchase six more at cost. Several of the students from Briar Creek had computers at home. Charles and Elaine, Julie discovered, were wizards at the computer. Julie encouraged them to help the other students (and herself—since she had taken only one computer course at State U). The two students enjoyed this assignment and often had a small group of students remain after school to receive their help. Julie was pleased at how well Charles and Elaine handled this responsibility. Lester and Ben were Charles's favorite classmates; they liked the computer, but Julie believed they liked Charles and his electric wheelchair even more. Julie had heard them say on several occasions that Charles was "cool." Lester's and Ben's work was showing a steady improvement, and Charles enjoyed having two good friends. This friendship, Julie believed, had excellent mutual benefits for all concerned, including herself.

Julie's mathematics pedagogy was built on two principles. First, she built on the thinking and life experiences of the students. Second, she sought to provide students with insights into the role of mathematics in the various contexts of society. These two principles of mathematics pedagogy guided her daily teaching. Julie often took her class to the supermarket, to the bank, and to engineering firms. She made certain that she selected firms that employed men and women of color and White women in positions of leadership. She often requested that a representative from these groups spend a few minutes with the students, explaining their roles and duties. On one occasion, Julie's students questioned a federal government official about the purpose and intent of the U.S. Census. One biracial student asked, "How are racial categories constructed?"

Julie took the students on field trips to supermarkets in different areas of town so the students could compare the prices and quality of products (e.g., fruit, meat, and vegetables) between the suburban area and the inner-city area. On two occasions this led to a letter-writing campaign to the owner of the food chain to explain their findings. The students also wondered why the cost of gas was cheaper in the suburban areas than in the inner-city area. This became a math, social studies, and language arts lesson. Letters were written and interviews conducted to ascertain the cost of delivering the gas to the inner city as compared to the suburban area of the city, and to ascertain the rental fee for service station property in the inner city in comparison to the suburban areas. Math skills were used to determine whether there needed to be a difference in gas prices between the areas after rental fees and delivery charges were taken into consideration.

Julie used advertisements and editorials from newspapers and magazines to help students see the real-life use of such concepts as sexism, justice, and equity. Julie supplemented her social studies curriculum on a regular basis. She found the text biased in several areas. She would integrate into the assigned curriculum information from the history and culture of different racial and ethnic groups. For example, when teaching about the settling of the local community years ago, she invited a Native American female historian and a White historian to give views on how the settling took place and on problems and issues associated with it. She invited an African American historian and a Latino historian to discuss what was presently happening in the area. She had her students identify toys that had been made in Third World countries, and she explored with them the child labor and low-wage work that many transnational corporations had put in place in order to maximize corporate profits.

Students were usually encouraged to undertake different projects in an effort to provide a comprehensive perspective on the social studies unit under study. Choices were up to the student, but Julie maintained high expectations and insisted that excellence in every phase of the work was always necessary for each student. She made certain that during the semester each student was a project leader. She also made certain that boys and girls worked together. For example, Julie knew that Ben, Lester, and Charles usually stayed close together and did not have a girl as a member of their project team. She also knew that Carmen was assertive and had useful knowledge about the project on which they were working. She put Carmen on the project team.

By the end of the year, her students were scoring well on the district-mandated achievement tests; on average, they compared with other fifth-grade students. Julie was especially pleased to see how well her new immigrant students, Jesus and Dijana, had learned to work with the curriculum and the rest of the class. Where they had been quiet and timid at the beginning of the semester, they were now talkative and inquisitive.

Julie did have two problems with her class that she could not figure out. Shelly and Ernestine did not get along well with any of the other African American students, especially Ben and Lester. George and Hank, two White boys from Briar Creek, had considerable difficulty getting along with José and went out of their way to be mean to Lourdes and Maria. Julie was puzzled by George's and Hank's behavior; she did not think it was racially motivated because both of the boys got along pretty well with Shelly. She labored over this problem and discussed it with the school counselor. She wondered whether she had a problem related to a combination of race, class, and gender in George's and Hank's relationship with José, Lourdes, and Maria. She also concluded that she might have a social-class problem among the African American students.

Julie decided to discuss her concerns with the students individually. After some discussion, she discovered that Shelly's and Ernestine's problem with Ben and Lester was related to social class and color. Both Shelly and Ernestine had very fair skin color. They had grown up in a predominantly White middle-class community and had spent very little time around other African American students. Ben and Lester were dark-skinned male students who lived in a very poor neighborhood. Julie felt that if her assumptions were true, she would need help with this problem. She was successful in getting an African American child psychiatrist to talk to her class. She did this in relationship to an art unit that examined "color, attitude, and feelings." His discussion enabled Julie to continue her discussion with Shelly and Ernestine and get them to examine their prejudice.

George and Hank admitted to Julie, after several discussions, that they did not care too much for any girls. But Hispanic girls who wore funny clothes and ate non-American foods were a big bore. It took Julie several months of talking with George and Hank, using different reading materials and having them all work on a group project under her direction, to get George and Hank to reduce some of their prejudices. At the end of the semester, Julie still believed this problem had not been completely resolved. Thus, she shared it with the sixth-grade teacher.

At the end of the school year, Julie felt very good about her first year. She knew she had grown as a teacher. She believed her professors at State U, her cooperating teacher, and her university supervisor would give her very high marks. They had encouraged her to become a reflective teacher—committed, responsible, and wholehearted in her teaching effort. Julie believed she was well on her way to becoming a reflective teacher, and she looked forward to her second year with enthusiasm.

She also realized that her sensitivity to things she did not know had grown, and she planned to engage in some learning over the summer. As she had become aware of resentments that students from low-income families felt toward students from upper-income families, she began to wonder what the city was doing to address poverty. She heard that the NAACP (National Association for the Advancement of Colored People), some Latino community leaders, and heads of homeless shelters were trying to work with the city council, and she wanted to find out more about how these groups viewed poverty in the city. She decided to join the NAACP so she could become more familiar with its activities. She also wanted to spend time with some Latino families, because before her teaching experience she had never talked directly with Latino adults; her principal suggested she should meet Luis Reyes, who directed a local community center and could help her do this. In addition, Julie felt somewhat overwhelmed by the amount of background information she had never learned about different groups in the United States and decided to start reading; because she enjoyed novels, she would start with some by Toni Morrison, Louise Erdrich, James Baldwin, and Maxine Hong Kingston. She would also read the novel *Reading Lolita in Tehran* by Azar Nafisi (2003).

From what you know of Julie, what is her approach to multicultural education? Would you be comfortable doing as Julie did? Discuss Julie's teaching with your classmates. How would you change it?

CONCLUSION

In Julie's classroom, as in yours, race, class, gender, and disability are ascribed characteristics students bring to school that cannot be ignored. To teach with excellence, Julie had to affirm her students' diversity. Why do we say this?

For one thing, Julie needed to pay attention to her students' identities in order to help them achieve. She needed to acknowledge the importance of African American males to American life to hold the interest of Lester and Ben; she needed to acknowledge Mai-ka's, Chee's, Jesus's, and Dijana's prior learning to help them learn English and school material; she needed to become familiar with her students' learning styles so her teaching would be most effective.

For another thing, Julie needed to pay attention to her students' personal and social needs to help them perceive school as a positive experience. Some of her students disliked other students because of prejudices and stereotypes. Some of her students did not know how to relate to people in wheelchairs or to people who looked or talked differently. Some of her students felt negative about their own abilities. These attitudes interfere not only with achievement but also with one's quality of life, both today as students and later as adults in a pluralistic society.

Julie realized over the year the extent to which schools are connected with their social context. She remembered having to take a course called School and Society and had not understood why it was required. She remembered reading about societal pressures on schools; during the year, she had come to see how societal pressures translated into funding, programs, and local debates that directly affected resources and guidelines in her classroom. Further, she realized the extent to which students are connected with their own cultural context. The African American students, for example, emphasized their African American identity and did not want to be regarded as White; teachers who tried to be colorblind regarded this as a problem, but teachers who found the community's diversity to be interesting saw it as a strength. On the other hand, immigrant students tried hard to fit in; Julie would not have understood why without considering why their families had immigrated and the pressures the children experienced.

Julie also knew that the future of the United States depends on its diverse children. Her students will all be U.S. adults one day, regardless of the quality of their education. But what kind of adults will they become? Julie wanted them all to be skilled in a variety of areas, to be clear and critical thinkers, and to have a sense of social justice and caring for others. Julie had some personal selfish motives for this: She knew her own well-being in old age would depend directly on the ability of today's children to care for older people when they become adults. She also knew her students of today would be shaping the society in which her own children would one day grow up. She wanted to make sure they were as well prepared as possible to be productive citizens who had a vision of a better society. She drew from all of the approaches, at one time or another, to address specific problems and needs she saw in the classroom. But the approach she emphasized, and the one that guided her planning, was multicultural social justice education.

How will you approach excellence and equity in your own classroom? We can guarantee that all your students will have their identities shaped partly by their race, social class, and gender; all of them will notice and respond in one way or another to people who differ from themselves; and all of them will grow up in a society that is still in many ways racist, sexist, and classist. You are the only one who can guarantee what you will do about that.

Questions and Activities

1. Why is it important for teachers to strive to attain both excellence and equity for their students? What can you do to try to achieve both goals in your teaching?

2. What does each of these terms mean to you in relationship to classroom life: race, ethnicity, language, class, gender, and disability? How are your notions of these concepts similar to and different from those of your classmates?

3. Give an example of how such variables as race, language, class, and gender interact to influence the behavior of a particular student.

4. Name the five approaches to multicultural education identified by Grant and Sleeter. What are the assumptions and instructional goals of each approach?

5. In what significant ways does the "multicultural social justice education" approach differ from the other four approaches? What problems might a teacher experience when trying to implement this approach in the classroom? How might these problems be reduced or solved?

6. Visit a school in your community and interview several teachers and the principal about how the school has responded to diversity and equity, both within the school and in the larger society. Using the typology of multicultural education described by the authors, determine what approach or combination of approaches to multicultural education are being used within the school. Share your findings with your classmates or fellow workshop participants.

7. Which approach to multicultural education is Julie using? Which aspects of her teaching do you especially like? Which aspects would you change?

8. Which approach to multicultural education described by the authors would you be the most comfortable using? Why?

References

A national survey of lesbian and gay college programs. (1990–1991). *Empathy*, 2(2), 53–56.

Albrecht, L., & Brewer, R. (1990). *Bridges of power: Women's Multicultural Alliances.* Philadelphia: New Society Publishers.

Banks, J. A. (2002). *Teaching Strategies For Ethnic Studies* (7th ed.). Boston: Allyn & Bacon.

Banks, J. A., & Banks, C. A. M., Eds. (2004). *Handbook of Research on Multicultural Education.* San Francisco: Jossey-Bass.

Barrett, P. A. (Ed.). (1986). *To Break the Silence.* New York: Dell.

Chanse, S. (2002). Racefile. *Colorlines*, 5(1), 3.

Childs, J. B. (1994). The Value of Transcommunal Identity Politics. *Z Magazine*, 7(7/8), 48–51.

Darraj, S. M. (2002). Understanding the Other Sister: The Case of Arab Feminism. *Monthly Review*, March, 15–25.

Eck, D. L. (2002). *A New Religious America.* San Francisco: Harper Collins.

Fadiman, A. (1997). *The Spirit Catches You and You Fall Down.* New York: Noonday.

Freire, P. (1973). *Education for Critical Consciousness.* New York: Seaburg.

Freire, P. (1985). *The Politics of Education: Culture, Power, and Liberation* (D. Macedo, Trans.). Boston: Bergin & Garvey.

Gates, H. L., Jr. (1999). *Wonders of the African World.* New York: Knopf.

Gonzalez, R. J. (2001, December 13). Lynne Cheney–Joe Lieberman Group Puts out a Blacklist. *San Jose Mercury News.* Retrieved May 29, 2003, from http://www.commondreams.org/views01/1213-05.htm.

Grant, C. A., & Sleeter, C. E. (1986). *After the School Bell Rings.* Philadelphia: Falmer.

Halagao, P. S. (2004). Holding up the Mirror: The Complexity of Seeing Your Ethnic Self in History. *Theory and Research in Social Education*, 32 (4): 459–483.

Headley, J., & Lowe, E. (2000). Mayors' 16th Annual Survey on "Hunger and Homelessness in America's Cities" Finds Increased Levels of Hunger, Increased Capacity to Meet Demand. Retrieved June 3, 2005, from http://www.usmayors.org/uscm/news/pree_releases/documents/ hunger_release.htm.

Mohr, N. (1990). *Felita.* New York: Bantam.

Moses, R. P., & Cobb, C. E., Jr. (2001). *Radical Equations.* Boston: Beacon Press.

Myers, W. D. (1990). *Scorpions.* New York: Harper Trophy.

Nafisi, A. (2003) *Reading Lolita in Tehran*. New York: Random House.

National Commission on Excellence in Education. (1983). *A Nation at risk: The Imperative for Educational Reform*. Washington, DC: U.S. Department of Education.

National Women's Studies Association. (2005). *NWSA Mission*. Retrieved May 11, 2005, from http://www.nwsa.org/about.html.

Omatsu, G. (1994). The "Four Prisons" and the Movements of Liberation: Asian American Activism From the 1960s to the 1990s. In K. Aguilar-San Juan (Ed.), *The State of Asian America* (pp. 19–70). Boston: South End Press.

Orfield, G., & Lee, C. (2005). *Why Segregation Matters: Poverty and Educational Inequality*. Cambridge, MA: Harvard University Civil Rights Project.

Parker, W. C. (2003). *Teaching Democracy*. New York: Teachers College Press.

Paterson, K. (1987). *The Great Gilly Hopkins*. New York: Harper Trophy.

Reyes, P., Scribner, J. D., & Scribner, A. P. (Eds.). (1999). *Lessons From High-Performing Hispanic Schools*. New York: Teachers College Press.

Sen, R. (2002). Durban and the War. *Colorlines*, 5(1): 7–9.

Shor, I. (1980). *Critical Teaching and Everyday Life*. Boston: South End Press.

Sleeter, C. E., & Grant, C. A. (2005). *Making Choices for Multicultural Education: Five Approaches to Race, Class, and Gender* (5th ed.). New York: Wiley.

Strazzabosco, G. (1995). *Teenage Refugees From Iran Speak Out*. New York: Rosen.

Tetreault, M. K. T. (1989). Integrating Content about Women and Gender into the Curriculum. In J. A. Banks & C. A. M. Banks (Eds.), *Multicultural Education: Issues and Perspectives* (pp. 124–144). Boston: Allyn & Bacon.

Ulrich, R. (2004). Taxing Proposals. *TomPaine.commonsense*. Retrieved June 3, 2005, from http://www.tompaine.com/articles.

U.S. Census Bureau (2000). *Statistical Abstract of the United States, 2000*. Washington, DC: U.S. Government Printing Office.

U.S. Census Bureau (2003). *Language Uses and English-Speaking Ability 2000*. Retrieved October 30, 2005, from http://www.census.gov/prod/2003pubs/c2kbr-29.pdf.

U.S. Census Bureau (2004). *Statistical Abstract of the United States, 2004–2005*. Washington, DC: U.S. Government Printing Office.

U.S. Department of Homeland Security (2003). *Yearbook of Immigration Statistics 2003*. Retrieved June 2, 2005, from http://uscis.gov/graphics/shared/statistics/yearbook/YrBk03Im.htm.

U.S. Department of Labor, Bureau of Labor Statistics. (1998). *Monthly Labor Review Online*. Washington, DC: U.S. Government Printing Office.

U.S. Department of Labor, Bureau of Labor Statistics. (2004). *Highlights of Women's Earnings in 2003*. Retrieved May 25, 2005, from http://www.bls.gov/cps/cpswom2003.pdf.

U.S. Department of Labor, Bureau of Labor Statistics. (2005). *Usual Weekly Earnings of Wage and Salary Workers: Fourth Quarter 2004*. Retrieved April 5, 2005, from http://www.bls.gov/cps/.

VisionMark (2005). *Students Speak out on Educational Inequalities*. Retrieved July 28, 2005, from http://www.visionmark.org/feature.php.

Yep, L. (1975). *Dragonwings*. New York: Harper & Row.

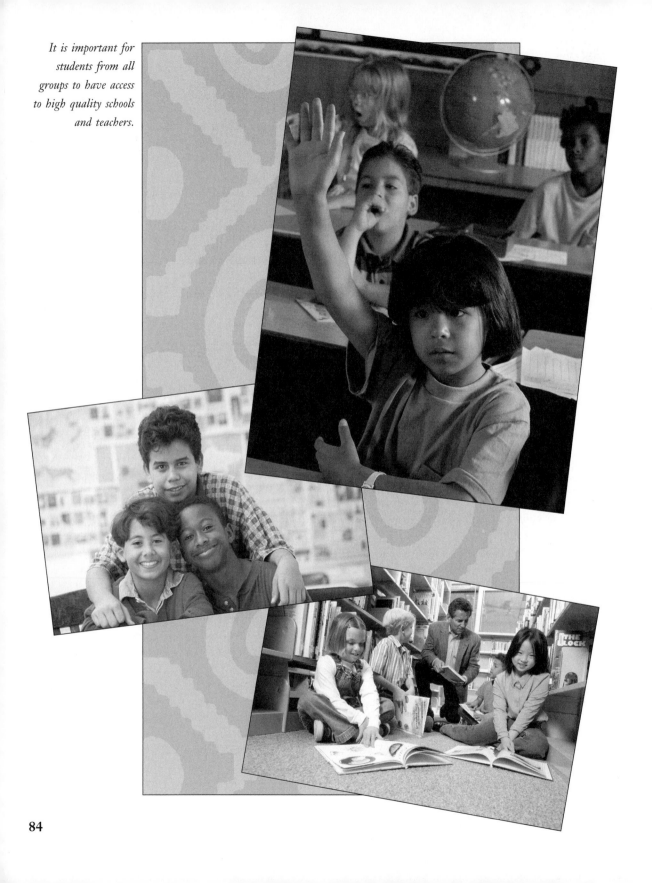

It is important for students from all groups to have access to high quality schools and teachers.

84

Social Class and Religion

The two chapters in Part II discuss the effects of two powerful variables on student behavior, beliefs, and achievement: social class and religion. Social class is a powerful variable in U.S. society despite entrenched beliefs about individual opportunity in the United States. As Persell points out in Chapter 4 and as Jonathon Kozol (2005) points out in his disturbing book, *The Shame of the Nation: The Restoration of Apartheid Schooling in America,* students who attend affluent middle- and upper-class schools have more resources, better teachers, and better educational opportunities than do students who attend low-income, inner-city schools. Students from the lower, middle, and upper classes usually attend different kinds of schools and have teachers who have different beliefs and expectations about their academic achievement. The structure of educational institutions also favors middle- and upper-class students. Structures such as tracking, IQ tests, and programs for gifted and mentally retarded students are highly biased in favor of middle- and upper-class students.

Students who are socialized within religious families and communities often have beliefs and behaviors that conflict with those of the school. Religious fundamentalists often challenge the scientific theories taught by schools about the origin of human beings. The controversy that occurred over intelligent design during the 2005–2006 school year epitomizes this phenomenon. Religious fundamentalists also attack textbooks and fictional books assigned by teachers that they believe violate or contradict their doctrines. Conflicts about the right to pray in the school sometimes divide communities. The school should help students mediate between their home culture and the school culture. Lippy, in Chapter 5, describes the religious diversity within the United States and some of its educational implications.

Reference

Kozol, J. (2005). *The Shame of the Nation: The Restoration of Apartheid Schooling in America.* New York: Random House.

CHAPTER 4

Social Class and Educational Equality

Caroline Hodges Persell

Picture three babies born at the same time, but to parents of different social-class backgrounds. The first baby is born into a wealthy, well-educated business or professional family. The second is born into a middle-class family in which both parents attended college and have middle-level managerial or social service jobs. The third is born into a poor family in which neither parent finished high school or has a steady job. Will these children receive the same education? Although the United States is based on the promise of equal opportunity for all people, the educational experiences of these three children are likely to be quite different.

Education in the United States is not a single, uniform system that is available to every child in the same way. Children of different social classes are likely to attend different types of schools, to receive different types of instruction, to study different curricula, and to leave school at different rates and times. As a result, when children end their schooling, they differ more than when they entered, and these differences may be used by society to legitimate adult inequalities. If we understand better how schools can help construct inequalities, we may be in a better position to try to change them.

The nature and meaning of social class are issues often debated by social scientists. U.S. researchers often measure social class by asking survey questions about a person's or a family's educational level, occupation, rank in an organization, and earnings. A few have tried to include measures of wealth such as home ownership or other assets. Several features of social class in the United States are worth special mention. Social-class inequality is greater in the United States than in any other industrial or postindustrial society in the world. Germany, Japan, Italy, France, Switzerland, England, Sweden, the Netherlands, you name it—all have considerably less social-class inequality than the United States. The countries with the least amount of class-based educational inequality are Sweden and the Netherlands, and they are also the countries where a family's social-class background is less related to their children's school achievement (Blossfeld & Shavit, 1993). Furthermore, income inequality has widened in the United States during the last 20 years, increasing inequality among children as well (Lichter & Eggebeen, 1993; Mayer, 2001).

The growing economic inequality in the United States affects how much education people receive. In states with bigger gaps between high- and low-income families (i.e., more income inequality), young people who grow up in high-income families obtain more education and children in low-income families obtain less education, compared to states with smaller gaps between high- and low-income families, where family income is not so strongly related to the amount of education children obtain (Mayer, 2001). The explanation for these differences seems to be more state spending for schooling and higher economic returns to schooling in states with greater income inequality (Mayer, 2001). At the same time, the United States has a historical belief in opportunity for all, regardless of their social origins.

This paradox of great and growing inequality and the belief in opportunity for all creates a special problem for the United States, namely, the "management of ambition" (Brint & Karabel, 1989, p. 7). Many more people aspire to high-paying careers than can actually enter them. One result has been the growth of educational credentialism, which means that more and more education is required for all jobs, especially professional and managerial occupations (Collins, 1979). This means that education is playing an ever-increasing role in the process of sorting people into their highly unequal adult positions. This sorting does not happen randomly, however.

Social class has been consistently related to educational success through time (Coleman et al., 1966; Gamoran, 2001; Goldstein, 1967; Grissmer, Kirby, Berends, & Williamson, 1994; Hanson, 1994; Mare, 1981; Mayeske & Wisler, 1972; Persell, 1977). Although there are a number of exceptions, students from higher social-class backgrounds tend to get better grades and to stay in school longer than do students from lower-class backgrounds. The question is, why does this happen? Does the educational system contribute to the widening of educational results over time? If so, what might change it—and how? I argue that three features of American education affect educational inequalities:

1. The structure of schooling in the United States.
2. The beliefs held by many members of U.S. society and hence by many educators.
3. Teachers, curricula, and teaching practices in U.S. schools.

The *structure of schooling* refers to such features as differences among urban, rural, and suburban schools as well as differences between public and private schools. *Educational beliefs* include beliefs about IQ (intelligence quotient) and testing. *Teachers, curricula, and teaching practices* include teacher training and recruitment, tracking of students into certain curricula, teachers' expectations about what different children can learn, and differences in the quantity and quality of what is taught.

This chapter reviews research showing differences in educational structures, beliefs, and practices; examines how these differences are related to the social-class backgrounds of students; considers the consequences they have for student achievement; and analyzes how they affect individuals' adult lives. Lest this be too depressing an account, at the end of the chapter I suggest some ways in which teachers, other educators, and parents might work to improve education.

EDUCATIONAL STRUCTURES

The three babies described above are not likely to attend the same school, even if they live in the same area. Most students in the United States attend schools that are relatively alike with respect to the social-class backgrounds of the other students. One reason this happens is that people in the United States tend to live in areas that are fairly similar with respect to class and race. If they attend their neighborhood school, they are with students from similar backgrounds. If children grow up in a fairly diverse area such as a large city, mixed suburb, or rural area, they are less likely to attend the same schools. The states with the most private schools, for example, are the states with the largest concentrations of urban areas (Coleman, Hoffer, & Kilgore, 1982). If, by chance, students of different backgrounds do attend the same school, they are very likely to experience different programs of study because of tracking and ability grouping.

In older suburbs or cities, children of higher-class families are more likely to attend homogeneous neighborhood schools, selective public schools, or private schools, and to be in higher tracks; lower-class children are also likely to attend school together. Middle-class families try to send their children to special public schools, parochial schools, or private schools if they can afford them.

Private day and boarding schools are also relatively similar with respect to social class, despite the fact that some scholarships are awarded. Researchers who studied elite boarding schools, for example, found that 46 percent of the families had incomes of more than $100,000 per year in the early 1980s (Cookson & Persell, 1985). This is undoubtedly true of many more than half the families today.

Let's look more closely at élite private schools and exclusive suburban schools, which are overwhelmingly attended by upper- and upper-middle-class students; at parochial schools, attended by middle-class and working-class students; and at large urban public schools, heavily attended by lower-class pupils. Although these descriptions gloss over many distinctions within each major type of school, they do convey some of the range of differences that exist under the overly broad umbrella we call U.S. education.

Schools of the Upper and Upper-Middle Classes

At most upper- and upper-middle-class high schools, the grounds are spacious and well kept; the computer, laboratory, language, and athletic facilities are extensive; the teachers are well educated and responsive to students and parents; classes are small; nearly every student studies a college preparatory curriculum; and considerable homework is assigned.

At private schools, these tendencies are often intensified. The schools are quite small, with few having more than 1200 students. Teachers do not have tenure or belong to unions, so they can be fired by the headmaster or headmistress if they are considered unresponsive to students or parents. Classes are small, often having no more than 15 students and sometimes fewer. Numerous advanced placement courses offer the possibility of college credit. Students remark that it is "not cool to be dumb around here" (Cookson & Persell, 1985, p. 95). Most students watch very little television during the school week and do a great deal of homework (Cookson & Persell, 1985). They have many opportunities for extracurricular activities, such as debate and drama clubs, publications and music, and the chance to learn sports that colleges value, such as crew, ice hockey, squash, and lacrosse. Research suggests that participating in one or more extracurricular activities increases students' desire to attend school. Students have both academic and personal advisers who monitor their progress, help them solve problems, and try to help them have a successful school experience.

Affluent suburban communities have a robust tax base to support annual costs, which in the 2000s often exceed $15,000 per pupil. School board members are elected by members of the community who are likely to know them. Private schools are run by self-perpetuating boards of trustees, many of whom are graduates of the school. The school head is chosen by the board of trustees and may be replaced by them if they are not satisfied.

Private Parochial Schools

Many differences exist among parochial schools, but in general these schools are also relatively small. More of the high school students in them study an academic program and do more homework than do their public school peers. They are also subjected to somewhat stricter discipline (Coleman et al., 1982). The classes, however, are often larger than élite private, suburban, or urban school classes, with sometimes as many as 40 or 50 pupils per class. Some non-Catholic middle- and working-class parents, especially those in urban areas, send their children to parochial schools (Coleman et al., 1982).

The costs at parochial schools are relatively low, especially compared to private schools, because these schools are subsidized by religious groups. These schools have relatively low teacher salaries and usually have no teachers' unions. Currently there are more lay teachers and fewer nuns, priests, and brothers as teachers. The schools are governed by the religious authority that runs them.

Urban Schools

Urban schools are usually quite large, and they are part of an even larger school system that is invariably highly bureaucratic. They usually offer varied courses of study, including academic, vocational, and general curricular tracks. The school systems of large cities and older, larger suburbs tend to lack both political and economic resources. These systems are generally highly centralized, with school board members generally elected on a city-wide basis. School board members are often concerned members of the community who may send their own children to private schools, and they may have little knowledge about or power over the daily operations of the public system. The authority of professional educators is often buttressed by bureaucratic procedures and by unionization of teachers and administrators (Persell, 2000). Some observers (Rogers, 1968; Rogers & Chung, 1983) have described the system as one of organizational paralysis rather than governance.

Economically, the large city school systems are also relatively powerless. Because schools are supported by local property taxes, and because there is a great deal of housing segregation by social class as well as race in the United States, students who live in low-income areas are very likely to attend schools with lower per-pupil expenditures. Some schools with very high per-pupil spending even raise additional private funds to supplement the generous tax monies used to support the school. Thus, they are able to provide additional educational enrichments to the students attending such schools.

Unequal educational expenditures have serious consequences for the condition of school buildings, libraries and laboratories, computer equipment, the richness of curricular offerings, the ability to hire experienced and certified teachers, class size, and the variety of extracurricular offerings. Such disparities in educational opportunities affect how much children learn, how long they stay in school, their graduation rates, and the rates at which they successfully pursue further education after high school. While the question of whether money makes a difference in educational achievement has long been debated (Coleman et al., 1966; Hanushek, 1989, 1996), more recent research has refined the question so as to see money as a threshold condition that is necessary but not always sufficient for achievement. How the money is spent certainly matters (Elliott, 1998; Gamoran, Secada, & Marret, 2000; Wenglinsky, 1997). Expenditures need to be connected to opportunities to learn effectively (Gamoran et al., 2000), to having good teachers (Darling-Hammond, 2001), to inquiry-based teaching methods (Elliott, 1998), and to good equipment, especially in the case of science (Elliott, 1998).

Because of the importance of funding equity, 20 states have faced court challenges, resulting in court decisions requiring them to provide all students with equal access to quality schools (Dively & Hickrod, 1992; "A Truce in New Jersey's School War," 2002). Perhaps the most extensive and bitterly contested of these suits is *Abbott v. Burke* in New Jersey, brought in 1981. This case produced eight court rulings, ordering equal funding in urban and suburban schools, a high-quality preschool program for poor districts, and standards-based reforms to close the achievement gap between rich and poor students. In January 2002, after years of delay, newly elected New Jersey Governor James McGreevey announced that he would abide by the court's rulings. This court case has been described by some as perhaps "the most significant education case since the Supreme Court's desegregation ruling nearly 50 years ago" ("A Truce in New Jersey's School War," 2002). It affects 30 underprivileged districts in the state and may have implications for other states facing such court challenges.

In general, then, a child's social-class background is related to the school attended, the size of the school, the political and economic resources available to the school, the curricula offered, and the ensuing educational opportunities (Persell, Cookson, & Catsambis, 1992).

EDUCATIONAL BELIEFS

Since the last century, ideas about testing students have permeated education. For decades the concept of measuring intelligence, or IQ testing, played a major role in education. The concept of IQ has been used to explain why some children learn more slowly than others, why African American children do less well in school than White children, and why lower-class children do less well than middle- and upper-middle-class children. The latest example of this argument is presented by Richard Herrnstein and Charles Murray (1994) in their highly controversial book. IQ tests are often used to justify variations in education, achievement, and rewards. The justification usually is that because some people are more intelligent than others, they are entitled to more opportunities and rewards, including curricular track placement and exposure to special educational programs and resources.

Critics of IQ tests have raised a number of good points about the accuracy of the tests. For example, IQ tests do not measure such important features of intelligence as creative or divergent thinking, logic, and critical reasoning. The idea of multiple intelligences is well developed by Howard Gardner (1983) in *Frames of Mind.* Stephen Jay Gould's (1981) *The Mismeasure of Man* may still be the single best critical analysis of IQ tests.

In the last several decades, increasing emphasis has been placed on the use of large-scale achievement tests. This so-called high-stakes testing has been used as the basis for deciding the educational track to which students are assigned, whether a student moves to the next grade in school, and whether a student graduates from high school. Such tests may also be used to hold educators, schools, and school districts accountable. The focus here is on how the use of tests affects individuals and whether they are discriminatory or unfair for students of certain social-class backgrounds.

The purposes of using such tests include setting high standards for student learning and raising student achievement. However, when some students do poorly on a test, schools and teachers can respond in several different ways. They can work harder with the students obtaining low scores, providing them with more personal attention, tutoring, and additional learning experiences in an effort to improve their achievement test scores. Such responses usually require additional resources, which many schools, especially ones that are already underfunded, may not have. Another possible response is that schools try to get rid of students with lower scores, by encouraging them to drop out or transfer, or through other means. This is clearly an unintended consequence of high-stakes testing and one that affects most severely the most educationally needy and vulnerable students. Many teachers, while not opposed to high standards, say that the existence of mandatory testing leads to "teaching in ways that contradicted their own ideas of sound educational practice" (Winter, 2003, p. B9).

Beliefs about high-stakes testing were institutionalized in 2002 when the No Child Left Behind Act (NCLB) was signed into law. The ostensible goals of NCLB are to reduce the achievement gap between low income and/or minority children and higher income and/or white children by holding educators accountable. Some of the key provisions of this federal law are state-level annual tests of third to eighth graders in reading and math, plus at least one test for students in grades 10–12. States and districts are required to report school-level data on students' test scores for various subgroups: African Americans, Latinos, Native Americans, Asian Americans, white non-Hispanic, special education, limited English proficiency (LEP), and/or low-income students. NCLB rewards or punishes school districts, schools, and teachers for the tested achievement of their students, but does not prescribe consequences for students (Dworkin, 2005).

However, in 26 states promotion and/or graduation is tied to the results of standardized tests. Under NCLB, states must set "adequate yearly progress" (AYP) goals for each school, and 100 percent of students must reach proficiency by 2014. Schools that fail to meet their AYP goals get labeled "in need of improvement" (INOI) and students in them must get the opportunity to transfer to other public schools and/or to get federally funded tutoring (Karen, 2005). Another feature of NCLB is the requirement that schools have "highly qualified teachers" in the "core academic subjects" of English, reading or language arts, math, science, foreign languages, civics and government, economics, arts, history, and geography by 2005–2006. There are also requirements for schools, districts, and states to organize programs of parental involvement and improved communication (Epstein, 2005).

However, the lack of federal resources to pay for mandated changes and the threat of losing a portion of existing state or local resources has led to a number of unintended consequences, including rising drop-out rates in some schools or systems, encouraging teachers to focus only on teaching for the test and hence narrowing the curriculum, and harming minority or low-income students (Dworkin, 2005; Heubert and Hauser, 1999; McNeil, 2000; Meier and Wood, 2004). In general, the law seems to assume that schools, teachers, and students operate in a vacuum rather than in socially structured contexts and organizations.

In 2005, a nation-wide test of 660,000 students taking the National Assessment of Educational Progress tests revealed mixed evidence about the possible effects of NCLB. Among both third and eighth graders, math scores rose slightly, but reading scores were flat among fourth graders and declined slightly among eighth graders. Moreover, the gap between white and minority students was unchanged since the early 1990s. Test scores actually rose more between 2000 and 2003, before NCLB had been fully implemented (Dillon, 2005).

TEACHERS, CURRICULUM, AND TEACHING PRACTICES

The relatively recent growth of high-stakes testing may deflect attention from essential features of schools that affect learning. Educational equity requires that we examine not only the educational funding but also what that funding is used for and how it affects education. Three features of schools highlight how students' educational experiences vary depending on their social class—specifically, the teachers they get, curricular tracking, and teachers' expectations.

Teachers

Schools with more low-income students are more likely to have teachers who are not certified at all or who are teaching out of their area of certification (Ingersoll, 2004). Large shortages of certified teachers in such major urban areas as New York City in recent years have led to several changes. The schools chancellor developed an alternative, abbreviated path to temporary certification, aimed at career-changers and recent college graduates with no teaching experience. The alternative path to provisional certification involves a month of intensive education courses. At the end of this time, these teachers are placed in the 100 lowest-performing schools from the prior year. About 30 percent of the new certified teachers in the fall of 2002 in New York City had this alternative certification. In addition, New York and other cities received recruits from Teach for America, a nonprofit organization that recruits college graduates, provides a summer of intensive training, and places them in troubled schools.

Like New York, many school districts around the country, including Los Angeles, Atlanta, and Washington, D.C., have alternative certification programs in an effort to address the shortage of qualified teachers. However, there is considerable debate over the abbreviated training that alternative-route certification involves. Arthur Levine, president of Teachers College at Columbia University, points out that the definition of a certified teacher has been changed, but the net result "is that we will still have large numbers of students this fall whose teachers are unprepared to teach them" (cited in Goodnough, 2002, p. 83). On the other hand, Rod Paige, the U.S. secretary of education, has "dismissed the pedagogical course work offered by schools of education—like Teachers College—as cumbersome and often ineffective" (Goodnough, 2002, p. B3). Research by Gomez and Grobe (1990, cited in Darling-Hammond, 2001, p. 472) finds that alternative-route teacher candidates had more uneven performance ratings compared to trained beginners, particularly in the area of classroom management and in their knowledge of instructional techniques. Their students, in turn, scored significantly lower in language arts, compared to students of fully prepared beginning teachers, when students' initial achievement levels were held constant (Gomez & Grobe, 1990, cited in Darling-Hammond, 2001, p. 472).

As Darling-Hammond (2001) notes, "policy makers have nearly always answered the problem of teacher shortages by lowering standards, so that people who have had little or no preparation for teaching can be hired" (p. 471). It is notable that this issue does not surface in more affluent suburban public schools, because they have very low percentages of teachers who are not certified or are teaching outside their areas of certification (Ingersoll, 2004). One reason that such areas can attract and retain certified teachers better than inner-city schools is that they pay higher salaries on the average. Teachers, however, work within educational structures that contribute to unequal learning opportunities. This is especially true of the educational practice of tracking.

Tracking

The first recorded instance of tracking was the Harris plan in St. Louis, begun in 1867. Since then, tracking has followed a curious pattern in the United States of alternate popularity and disuse. In the 1920s and 1930s, when many immigrants came to the United States, tracking increased greatly. Thereafter, it fell into decline until the late 1950s, when it was revived, apparently in response to the USSR's launching of *Sputnik* and the United States's competitive concern with identifying and educating the gifted (Conant, 1961; Oakes, 1985). That period was also marked by large migrations of rural southern African Americans to northern cities and by an influx of Puerto Rican and Mexican American migrants into the United States. Darling-Hammond (2001) points out that "tracking is much more extensive in U.S. schools than in most other countries" (p. 474). This observation prompts us to ask why this is the case. There are two differences between the United States and European countries that might account for the difference. The United States has more racial and economic inequality than European countries, and educational achievement and attainment are more important for a person's (more unequal) occupation, earnings, and other life chances in the United States than in European countries.

To understand tracking in elementary schools, we need to examine the distinction between ability grouping and curriculum differentiation. Proponents of ability grouping stress flexible subject-area assignments. By this they mean that students are assigned to learning groups on the basis of their background and achievement in a subject area at any given moment and that skills and knowledge are evaluated at relatively frequent intervals. Students showing gains can be shifted readily into another group. They might also be in different ability groups in different subjects, according to their own rate of growth in each subject.

This practice suggests a common curriculum shared by all students, with only the mix of student abilities being varied. It also assumes that, within that curriculum, all groups are taught the same material.

In fact, it seems that group placement becomes self-perpetuating, that students are often grouped at the same level in all subjects, and that even a shared curriculum may be taught differently to different groups. This is especially likely to happen in large, bureaucratic, urban public schools. Quite often, different ability groups are assigned to different courses of study, resulting in simultaneous grouping by curriculum and ability. Rosenbaum (1976) notes that although ability grouping and curriculum grouping may appear different to educators, in fact they share several social similarities: (1) students are placed with those defined as similar to themselves and are segregated from those deemed different, and (2) group placement is done on the basis of criteria such as ability or postgraduate plans that are unequally esteemed. Thus, group membership immediately ranks students in a status hierarchy, formally stating that some students are better than others (Rosenbaum, 1976). Following Rosenbaum's usage, the general term *tracking* is applied here to both types of grouping.

Tracking by academic level is widespread today, particularly in large, diverse school systems and in schools serving primarily lower-class students. It is less prevalent, and less rigid when it occurs, in upper-middle-class suburban and private schools and in parochial schools (Jones, Vanfossen, & Spade, 1985). Relatively few high schools now offer vocational programs. Instead, tracking has taken on a more subtle form, and it is not called "tracking" by school officials. High school courses now tend to be classified as Regular, College Prep, Honors, and Advanced Placement (AP), or something similar. Low-income students and parents, in particular, may be unaware of what the distinctions mean. They may not realize that decisions made in seventh or eighth grade or even earlier may affect what choices are possible in high school. They may be unaware that grades received in AP or Honors courses may be given greater weight when their grade point averages are computed, and thus may differentially affect their chances for college admission or scholarships. They also may not realize the importance of taking certain courses, e.g., calculus, for how they do on college entrance examinations. Many inner city and/or low-income schools do not offer even a single AP course, while many affluent suburban schools offer a dozen or more. Differences in the courses students take, especially in such areas as mathematics, science, and foreign language, go a long way toward explaining differences in achievement test scores (Darling-Hammond, 2001).

The social-class background of students is related to the prevalence of tracking in the schools, to the nature of the available tracks, and to the ways track assignments are made. Furthermore, while there is some relationship between tested ability and track placement, it is highly imperfect (Dreeben & Barr, 1988; Pallas, Entwisle, Alexander, & Stluka, 1994).

Once students are assigned to different tracks, what happens to them? Researchers suggest that tracking has effects through at least three mechanisms. These are instructional, social, and institutional in nature, and all three may operate together. The major *instructional processes* that have been observed to vary according to track placement include the unequal allocation of educational resources, the instruction offered, student–teacher interactions, and student–student interactions. Dreeben and Barr (1988) found variations in the content, pacing, and quantity of instruction in different tracks. Higher-ranked reading groups were taught more (and learned more) words than lower-ranked reading groups, according to Gamoran (1984, 1986).

Hallinan (1987) studied within-class ability grouping in 34 elementary school classes. She found that ability grouping affects the learning of students in higher and lower groups because it influences their opportunities for learning, the instructional climate, and the student aptitudes clustered in the different groups. High-ability groups spend more time on-task during class; that is, more class time is devoted to actual teaching activities. Also, teachers use more interesting teaching methods and materials. Finally, teachers hold higher expectations and the other students support learning more in the higher-ability groups. As a result, the aptitude of students in the higher groups tends to develop more than does the aptitude of students in the lower group (Hallinan).

In secondary schools, college-track students consistently receive better teachers, class materials, laboratory facilities, field trips, and visitors than their lower-track counterparts (Findley & Bryan, 1975; Oakes, 1985; Rosenbaum, 1976; Schafer, Olexa, & Polk, 1973). Oakes observed that teachers of high-track students set aside more time for student learning and devoted more class time to learning activities. Fewer students in these classes engaged in "off-task" activities (Oakes, 1985, p. 111). Oakes (1985) also found that "students are being exposed to knowledge and taught behaviors that differ not only educationally but also in socially important ways. Students at the top are exposed to the knowledge that is highly valued in our culture, knowledge that identifies its possessors as 'educated'" (pp. 91–92). Similarly, those students are taught critical thinking, creativity, and independence. Students at the bottom are denied access to these educationally and socially important experiences (Oakes, 1985).

Freiberg (1970) found that higher-track students received more empathy, praise, and use of their ideas, as well as less direction and criticism, than did lower-track students. Oakes (1985) observed that teachers spent more time in low-track classes on discipline and that students in those classes perceived their teachers as more punitive than did students in high-track classes.

Socially, tracks may create settings that shape students' self-esteem and expectations about academic performance. For example, Rosenbaum (1976) reported that more than one-third of lower-track (noncollege) students mentioned "blatant insults directed at them by teachers and administrators. 'Teachers are always telling us how dumb we are'" (p. 179). One articulate general-track student in that study reported that he sought academic help from a teacher but was told that he was not smart enough to learn the material. Several students reported that a lower-track student who asks a guidance counselor for a change of classes is not only prevented from changing but is also insulted for being so presumptuous as to make the request (Rosenbaum, 1976). Rosenbaum was told by one teacher, "You're wasting your time asking these kids for their opinions. There's not an idea in any of their heads." As the researcher notes, "This comment was not expressed in the privacy of the teacher's room; it was said at a normal volume in a quiet classroom full of students!" (p. 180).

Students have been observed to pick up on the negative evaluations associated with lower-track placement. They may make fun of lower-track students, call them unflattering names, or stop associating with them (Rosenbaum, 1976). Hence, a major result of tracking is differential respect from peers and teachers, with implications for both instruction and esteem.

Institutionally, tracking creates groups of students who are understood by teachers and parents as having certain qualities and capacities, above and beyond the actual skills they possess. The symbolic value of track placement thus creates expectations in teachers and parents, independent of student performance. These expectations affect placement in subsequent levels of the educational system (Gamoran, 1984). Ability groups limit teachers' perceptions of what grades are appropriate for students in different tracks (Reuman, 1989). Both parents and teachers rated children in higher reading groups as more competent and likely to do better in the future than children in low reading groups, even when children's initial performance levels and parents' prior beliefs about their children's abilities were held constant (Pallas et al., 1994, p. 41). Further consequences of tracking include segregation of students by social class and ethnicity (Esposito, 1973; *Hobson v. Hansen*, 1967; New York Education Department, 1969; Oakes, 1985), unequal learning by students in different tracks (Findley & Bryan, 1970; Oakes, 1985; Rosenbaum, 1976; Shafer et al., 1973), and unequal chances to attend college (Alexander, Cook, & McDill, 1978; Alexander & Eckland, 1975; Jaffe & Adams, 1970; Jones, Spade, & Vanfossen, 1987; Rosenbaum, 1976, 1980). The percentage of students in an academic curriculum may be the single most significant structural difference between different types of schools. Noncollege preparatory programs may foreclose future opportunities for young persons by failing to provide them with the courses or training necessary for admission to institutions of higher education or for pursuit of particular college majors (Hallinan, 1987; Oakes, Joseph, & Muir, 2004).

Darling-Hammond (2001) suggests that tracking persists because few teachers "are prepared to manage heterogeneous classrooms effectively" (p. 474). In the 1980s, tracking came under considerable attack, and a movement toward "detracking" gained support (Braddock & McParland, 1990; Oakes, 1985, 1992; Wheelock, 1992). But even when teachers have a strong ideology of detracking and have succeeded in ending tracking in some communities, they have encountered serious resistance and opposition from parents. In their three-year longitudinal case studies of ten racially and socioeconomically mixed secondary schools that were participating in detracking reform, Oakes, Wells, Jones, and Datnow (1997) found that detracking is a "highly normative and political endeavor that confronts deeply held cultural beliefs, ideologies, and fiercely protected arrangements of material and political advantage in local communities" (p. 507). For example, being in an honors course confers advantages in the competition for college admissions. Detracking was able to occur when politically savvy teachers were able to involve powerful parents in meaningful ways in the process of implementing it (Oakes et al., 1997).

Teachers' Expectations

Educational structures such as schools that are socioeconomically homogeneous, the growing use of standardized achievement tests, and practices such as tracking go a long way toward shaping the expectations teachers hold about students. Teacher training and textbooks have tended to attribute educational failures to deficiencies in the children. Often, such deficiencies are assumed to reside in the social characteristics of the pupils, such as their social-class background, ethnicity, language, or behavior, rather than in social structure. In a review of relevant research, Persell (1977) found that student social class was related to teacher expectations when other factors such as race were not more salient, when expectations were engendered by real children, or when teachers had a chance to draw inferences about a student's social class rather than simply being told his or her background. Sometimes social class was related to teacher expectations even when the children's current IQ and achievement were comparable. That is, teachers held lower expectations for lower-class children than for middle-class children even when those children had similar IQ scores and achievement.

Teachers' expectations may also be influenced by the behavior and physical appearance of the children (Ritts, Patterson, & Tubbs, 1992). Social class may influence teacher expectations directly or indirectly through test scores, appearance, language style, speed of task performance, and behavior. All of these traits are themselves culturally defined and are related to class position. Moreover, teacher expectations are influenced more by negative information about pupil characteristics than by positive data. It is important to know this because much of the information teachers gain about low-income children seems to be negative.

Another factor that may influence teacher expectations and pupil performance is the operation of the cultural capital possessed by families of higher social classes. As used here, the term *cultural capital* refers to the cultural resources and assets that families bring to their interactions with school personnel. By virtue of their own educational credentials and knowledge of educational institutions, parents, especially mothers, are able to help their children get the right teachers and courses and do extra work at home if necessary (Baker & Stevenson, 1986; Grissmer et al., 1994; Lareau, 1989; Useem, 1990). If teacher expectations are often influenced by the social class of students, do those expectations have significant consequences for students? Research on this question has produced seemingly contradictory results. The controversy began with the publication of *Pygmalion in the Classroom* (Rosenthal & Jacobson, 1968). That book suggested that the expectations of classroom teachers might powerfully influence the achievement of students. Hundreds of studies on the possibility of "expectancy effects" have been conducted since then (see Cooper & Good, 1983). One thing is clear: Only expectations that teachers truly believe are likely to affect their behaviors.

When teachers hold higher expectations for pupils, how does this affect their behavior? Their expectations seem to affect the frequency of interaction they have with their pupils and the kinds of behaviors they show toward different children. Teachers spend more time interacting with pupils for whom they have higher expectations (Persell, 1977). For example, Brophy and Good (1970) found that students for whom teachers held high expectations were praised more frequently when correct and were criticized less frequently when wrong or unresponsive than were pupils for whom teachers had low expectations.

Rosenthal (1974) believes that teachers convey their expectations in at least four related ways. He bases this judgment on his review of 285 studies of interpersonal influence, including at least 80 in classrooms or other settings. First, he sees a general climate factor, consisting of the overall warmth a teacher shows to children, with more shown to high-expectancy students. Second, he sees students for whom high expectations are held as receiving more praise for doing something right than do students for whom low expectations are held. Third, Rosenthal notes that high-expectancy students are taught more than are low-expectancy students. This is consistent with research by others and summarized by Persell (1977). Fourth, Rosenthal indicates that expectancy may be affected by a response-opportunity factor. That is, students for whom the teacher has higher expectations are called on more often and are given more chances to reply, as well as more frequent and more difficult questions.

A fifth way teachers convey their expectations, which Rosenthal does not mention but which has been observed by others, is the different type of curricula teachers may present to children for whom they have different expectations. One study found that teachers report that they present completely different types of economics to students of differently perceived abilities (Keddie, 1971). Another study reported that teachers use more reading texts and more difficult ones with the top reading group (Alpert, 1975). Clearly, there is evidence that at least some teachers behave differently toward students for whom they hold different expectations. The critical question remains: Do these expectations and behaviors actually affect students? Do the students think differently about themselves or learn more as a result of the expectations teachers hold? Therein lies the heart of the "Pygmalion effect" controversy.

Students report being aware of the different expectations teachers have for them, and they notice differences in the way teachers treat them. For example, students studied by Ferguson (2001) reported that when they asked the teacher a question, they received only a brief one-sentence reply, but when other students (for whom the teacher had higher expectations) asked the same question, the teacher spoke at length in response.

When teachers hold definite expectations and when those expectations are reflected in their behavior toward children, these expectations are related to student cognitive changes, even when pupil IQ and achievement are controlled. Moreover, negative expectations, which can be observed only in natural settings because it is unethical to induce negative expectations experimentally, appear to have even more powerful consequences than do positive expectations. Moreover, socially vulnerable children (i.e., younger, lower-class, and minority children) seem to be more susceptible to lower teacher expectations (Rosenthal & Jacobson, 1968).

CONSEQUENCES OF SOCIAL CLASS AND EDUCATIONAL INEQUALITY

This profile of social-class differences in education in the United States is oversimplified, but considerable evidence suggests that the general patterns described here do exist. Social-class backgrounds affect where students go to school and what happens to them once they are there. As a result, lower-class students tend to encounter less prepared teachers, are less likely to be exposed to valued curricula, are taught less of whatever curricula they do study, and are expected to do less work in the classroom and outside of it. Hence, they learn less and are less well prepared for the next level of education.

Although students have many reasons for dropping out of school or for failing to continue, their experiences in school may contribute to their desire to continue or to quit. Coleman et al. (1982) found that 24 percent of public high school students dropped out, compared to 12 percent of Catholic and 13 percent of other private school students. Social class is a more important cause of lost talent among U.S. youth in the late high school and post–high school years than gender or race, according to Hanson (1994).

Similarly, college attendance depends on a number of factors, including access to the necessary financial resources. Nevertheless, it is striking how differently students at different schools fare. Graduation from a private rather than a public high school is related to attending a four-year (rather than a two-year) college (Falsey & Heyns, 1984), attending a highly selective college (Persell et al., 1992), and earning higher income in adult life (Lewis & Wanner, 1979). Even within the same school, track placement is related to college attendance (Alexander et al., 1978; Alexander & McDill, 1976; Jaffe & Adams, 1970; Rosenbaum, 1976, 1980). College attendance, in turn, is related to the adult positions and earnings one attains (Kamens, 1974; Tinto, 1980; Useem, 1984; Useem & Karabel, 1986). In 2005, women with bachelor's degrees earned slightly more than $40,000 on average compared to women with high school degrees, who earned about $23,000, while men with bachelor's degrees earned $66,000 compared to men with high school degrees, who earned about $37,000 on average (U.S. Department of Commerce, 2005). Thus, educational inequalities help create and legitimate economic and social inequalities.

However, most educators do not want to enhance and legitimate social inequalities. Therefore, it seems reasonable to ask, What can they do to try to change these patterns?

RECOMMENDATIONS FOR ACTION

Teachers, educators, and concerned citizens might consider the following actions:

1. Working politically and legally to increase the educational resources available to all children, not just those in wealthy school districts, and not just the gifted and talented. Those concerned might do this by joining a political party that works to advance the interests of the less advantaged members of society, by attending political meetings, by holding candidates accountable for their positions on education, and by supporting class-action lawsuits for educational equity. We can join other people interested in scrutinizing candidates' records of support for education and contribute time, money, or both to the campaigns of candidates seeking to defeat incumbents who have not supported quality education for all children.

2. Working to reduce economic inequalities in society. This can be done by supporting income tax reforms at the national level that benefit hardworking low- and middle-income families, by opposing tax cuts for the rich, by supporting job programs at reasonable wages and health care programs for those who can work, and by providing aid for poor parents who are unable to work.

3. Working to build economically and racially integrated communities. This can be done by choosing to live in such a community, by supporting federal subsidies for low-income housing in mixed-income areas, and by opposing efforts to restrict access to certain communities by members of particular ethnic or income groups. Such restrictions might take the form of zoning that prohibits the construction of high-rise housing for low-income groups or limits housing lots to a large size, such as two acres, or of red-lining by banks that refuse to provide mortgages in certain neighborhoods.

4. Working to support prenatal care for all pregnant women. In 1989, about one-quarter of them received no prenatal care. Helping all pregnant women could reduce or eliminate perhaps one-third of all learning disorders (Hodgkinson, 1989).

5. Working to support Head Start programs for all eligible children. In 1988, only 16 percent of low-income children eligible for the preschool program for four-year-olds were enrolled in it, yet Head Start has a proven track record. Every dollar invested in quality preschool education yields $4.75 because of lower costs later on for special education, public assistance, and the incarceration of people who commit crimes (Children's Defense Fund, 1988; Weikart & Schweinhart, 1984).

6. Using tests for diagnosing rather than dismissing students. For example, instead of taking a low test score as evidence that a child cannot learn, we can examine what parts of a particular test were difficult for that child. If necessary, we can obtain further individual testing to identify and analyze what skills the child needs to develop and devise strategies for teaching those specific skills. We can try alternative teaching strategies with each child until we find one that works. If a child has difficulty learning to read phonetically, for example, we might try teaching that child a different way, perhaps visually. We can help children with various kinds of learning disabilities learn ways to compensate for their difficulties. For example, planning their work in advance, organizing it so that they have enough time to complete the necessary steps, and allowing time for someone else to check their spelling are all compensatory strategies that can be adopted to good effect by children trying to overcome various learning disabilities.

7. Working on finding the abilities students do have, rather than on deciding that they don't have any. For example, for students who have strong artistic, musical, athletic, or auditory talents, but are weaker in the verbal or mathematical areas, we can help them find ways into the academic subjects through their strengths.

8. Supporting efforts at detracking.

9. Learning about and using collaborative teaching techniques, such as those developed by Elizabeth Cohen and her colleagues at Stanford University, that work effectively in heterogeneous classes (Cohen, 1994, 2000; Cohen & Lotan 1997; Sharan, 1980).

10. Committing to the use of a variety of pedagogical techniques, curricular assignments, and projects that address the learning needs of individual children.

11. Expecting and demanding a lot from students in the way of effort, thought, and work. We can help students take pride in themselves and their work by teaching them what first-rate work should look like. The written materials students get from teachers and schools and the appearance of the classrooms and hallways should all convey a sense of care, quality, and value. We can carefully check the work students do, suggest constructive ways they might improve it, and expect them to do better the next time.

12. Teaching students content and subject matter. We can show students that we value them and their learning by devoting class time to pedagogically useful tasks, by refusing to waste class time on frivolous activities, and by trying to stick to an annual schedule of curricular coverage.

13. Helping students see how education is relevant and useful for their lives, perhaps by bringing back graduates who have used school as a springboard to better themselves and their worlds. Schools might keep a roster of successful graduates and post pictures and stories about them for current students to see. We can bring in examples that link learning with life accomplishments so students can begin to see connections between school and life. For example, we might invite people who run their own business to talk about how they use math or bring in people who work in social service organizations to show how they use writing in their daily work.

SUMMARY

This chapter explores how educational structures, beliefs, and practices contribute to unequal educational outcomes. To achieve greater educational equality, educators must understand what social-class differences presently exist in those structures, beliefs, and practices. If these differences are understood, then the educational experiences of students of all social classes might be made more similar.

The higher one's social-class background, the more likely one is to attend a smaller school with more resources, including better teachers, smaller classes, and an academic curriculum. Achieving greater educational equality means making such school experiences available to all students, regardless of their social-class backgrounds.

Widespread confidence in educational testing and the growing use of high-stakes testing runs the risk of blaming students for their failure and diverting attention from how the social organization of schools may help to create failures. Instead, we should be examining how teachers, curricula, and teaching practices of schools attended by children of different social classes influence their learning.

The educational process of tracking refers to the segregation of students into different learning or curriculum groups that are unequally ranked in a prestige hierarchy. Whether based on ability grouping or curricular grouping, such tracking tends to reduce learning opportunities for students in the lower groups, while increasing such opportunities for students in higher groups. As a result, this educational practice contributes to educational inequalities. The detracking movement represents an important effort toward achieving greater educational equality, but it has encountered some resistance from certain parents.

Teachers may unconsciously form different learning expectations about students of different social-class backgrounds. When teachers hold higher expectations for students, they tend to spend more time interacting with those students, praise them more, teach them more, call on them more often, and offer them a more socially valued curriculum. When teachers hold higher expectations, and when those expectations are evident in their behavior, they increase student learning. Thus, achieving greater educational equality means that teachers' expectations for lower-class students need to be raised.

Because the educational structures, beliefs, and practices examined here are related to unequal educational attainment, and because educational success is related to lifetime occupations and earnings, it is important that educational inequalities be reduced. This chapter recommends a number of steps that concerned educators and citizens can take to promote educational and social equality.

Questions and Activities

1. According to Persell, in what ways do schools contribute to inequality? What evidence does the author give to support her position?

2. Give examples of how each of the following factors contributes to educational inequality: (a) educational structures, (b) funding inequities, (c) testing practices, and (d) teachers and curriculum.

3. What are the major characteristics of each of the following types of schools: (a) élite private schools and exclusive suburban schools, (b) parochial schools, and (c) large urban public school systems?

4. Why do students from different social-class backgrounds often attend different schools or get assigned to different tracks when they attend the same schools? How does the social-class background of students influence the kind of education they often receive?

5. Visit and observe in (a) a local élite private school, (b) a school in an upper-middle-class suburb, and (c) an inner-city school. How are these schools alike? How are they different? Based on your visits and observations, what tentative generalizations can you make about education, social class, and inequality? To what extent are your generalizations similar to and different from those of Persell?

6. What cautions should teachers, principals, policy makers, and parents keep in mind when interpreting standardized achievement tests?

7. What is the self-fulfilling prophecy? How does it affect teacher expectations?

8. What is tracking? Why do you think tracking is more widespread in large, diverse school systems and in schools serving primarily lower-class students than in upper-middle-class suburban, private, and parochial schools?

9. How do the school experiences of students in lower and higher tracks differ? How does tracking contribute to educational inequality? What is detracking?

10. Why does tracking persist?

11. How do factors related to social class influence teacher expectations of students?

12. How do teacher expectations influence how teachers and pupils interact, what students are taught, and what students achieve?

References

Alexander, K. L., Cook, M., & McDill, E. L. (1978). Curriculum Tracking and Educational Stratification: Some Further Evidence. *American Sociological Review, 43*(1), 47–66.

Alexander, K. L., & Eckland, B. K. (1975). Contextual Effects in the High School Attainment Process. *American Sociological Review, 40*(3), 402–416.

Alexander, K. L., & McDill, E. L. (1976). Selection and Allocation within Schools: Some Causes and Consequences of Curriculum Placement. *American Sociological Review, 41*(6), 963–980.

Alpert, J. L. (1975). Do Teachers Adapt Methods and Materials to Ability Groups in Reading? *California Journal of Education Research, 26*(3), 120–123.

Baker, D. P., & Stevenson, D. L. (1986). Mothers' Strategies for Children's School Achievement: Managing the Transition to High School. *Sociology of Education, 59*(3), 156–166.

Blossfeld, H. P., & Shavit, Y. (1993). Persisting Barriers: Changes in Educational Opportunities in Thirteen Countries. In Y. Shavit & H. P. Blossfeld (Eds.), *Persistent Inequality: Changing Educational Attainment in Thirteen Countries* (pp. 1–23). Boulder, CO: Westview.

Braddock, J. H., II, & McPartland, J. M. (1990). Alternatives to Tracking. *Educational Leadership, 47*(7), 76–79.

Brint, S., & Karabel, J. (1989). *The Diverted Dream: Community Colleges and the Promise of Educational Opportunity in American, 1900–1985.* New York: Oxford University Press.

Brophy, J. E., & Good, T. L. (1970). Teachers' Communication of Differential Expectations for Children's Classroom Performance: Some Behavioral Data. *Journal of Educational Psychology, 61*(5), 365–374.

Children's Defense Fund. (1988). *A Call for Action.* Washington, DC: Author.

Cohen, E. G. (1994). Restructuring the Classroom: Conditions for Productive Small Groups. *Review of Educational Research, 64*(1), 1–35.

Cohen, E. G. (2000). Equitable Classrooms in a Changing Society. In M. T. Hallinan (Ed.), *Handbook of the Sociology of Education* (pp. 265–283). New York: Kluwer Academic/Plenum.

Cohen, E. G., & Lotan, R. A. (Eds.). (1997). *Working for Equity in Heterogeneous Classrooms: Sociological Theory in Practice.* New York: Teachers College Press.

Coleman, J. S., Campbell, E. Q., Hobson, C. J., McPartland, J., Alexander, M., Mood, A. M., Weinfeld, F. D., & York, R. L. (1966). *Equality of Educational Opportunity.* Washington, DC: U.S. Government Printing Office.

Coleman, J. S., Hoffer, T., & Kilgore, S. (1982). *High School Achievement.* New York: Basic Books.

Collins, R. (1979). *The Credential Society.* New York: Academic Press.

Conant, J. B. (1961). *Slums and Suburbs.* New York: McGraw Hill.

Cookson, P. W., Jr., & Persell, C. H. (1985). *Preparing for Power: America's Elite Boarding Schools.* New York: Basic Books.

Cooper, H. M., & Good, T. L. (1983). *Pygmalion Grows Up.* New York: Longman.

Darling-Hammond, L. (2001). Inequality and Access to Knowledge. In J. A. Banks & C. A. M. Banks (Eds.), *Handbook of Research on Multicultural Education* (pp. 465–483). San Francisco: Jossey-Bass.

Dillon, S. (2005). Bush Education Law Shows Mixed Results in First Test. *New York Times.* New York.

Dively, J. A., & Hickrod, G. A. (1992). Update of Selected States' School Equity Funding Litigation and the "Boxscore." *Journal of Education Finance, 17*(2), 352–363.

Dreeben, R., & Barr, R. (1988). Classroom Composition and the Design of Instruction. *Sociology of Education, 61*(3), 129–142.

Dworkin, A. G. (2005). The No Child Left Behind Act: Accountability, High-Stakes Testing, and Roles for Sociologists. *Sociology of Education* 78:170–174.

Elliott, M. (1998). School Finance and Opportunities to Learn: Does Money Well Spent Enhance Students' Achievement? *Sociology of Education, 71*(3), 223–245.

Epstein, J. L. (2005). Attainable Goals? The Spirit and Letter of the No Child Left Behind Act on Parental Involvement. *Sociology of Education* 78:179–182.

Esposito, D. (1973). Homogeneous and Heterogeneous Ability Grouping: Principal Findings and Implications for Evaluating and Designing More Effective Educational Environments. *Review of Educational Research, 43*(2), 163–179.

Falsey, B., & Heyns, B. (1984). The College Channel: Private and Public Schools Reconsidered. *Sociology of Education, 57*(2), 111–122.

Ferguson, R. F. (2001, December 13). Talk presented at New York University. "Closing the Achievement Gap: What Schools Can Do."

Findley, W. G., & Bryan, M. M. (1970). *Ability Grouping: 1970–1 The Impact of Ability Grouping on School Achievement, Affective Development, Ethnic Separation and Socioeconomic Separation.* Athens:

University of Georgia Center for Educational Improvement. (ERIC Document Reproduction Service No. ED 048382).

Findley, W. G., & Bryan, M. M. (1975). *The Pros and Cons of Ability Grouping*. Bloomington: Phi Delta Kappa.

Freiberg, J. (1970). *The Effects of Ability Grouping on Interactions in the Classroom*. (ERIC Document Reproduction Service No. ED 053194).

Gamoran, A. (1984). *Teaching, Grouping, and Learning: A Study of the Consequences of Educational Stratification*. Unpublished doctoral dissertation, Department of Sociology, University of Chicago.

Gamoran, A. (1986). Instructional and Institutional Effects of Ability Grouping. *Sociology of Education, 59*(4), 185–198.

Gamoran, A. (2001). American Schooling and Educational Inequality: A Forecast for the 21st Century. *Sociology of Education, 34*, 135–153.

Gamoran, A., Secada, W. G., & Marrett, C. B. (2000). The Organizational Context of Teaching and Learning. In M. T. Hallinan (Ed.), *Handbook of the Sociology of Education* (pp. 37–63). New York: Kluwer Academic/Plenum.

Gardner, H. (1983). *Frames of Mind*. New York: Basic Books.

Goldstein, B. (1967). *Low Income Youth in Urban Areas: A Critical Review of the Literature*. New York: Holt, Rinehart & Winston.

Goodnough, A. (2002, August 23). Shortage Ends as City Lures New Teachers. *New York Times*, pp. A1, B3.

Gould, S. J. (1981). *The Mismeasure of Man*. New York: Norton.

Grissmer, D. W., Kirby, S. N., Berends, M., & Williamson, S. (1994). *Student Achievement and the Changing American Family*. Santa Monica, CA: RAND.

Hallinan, M. T. (1987). Ability Grouping and Student Learning. In M. T. Hallinan (Ed.), *The Social Organization of Schools: New Conceptualizations of the Learning Process* (pp. 41–69). New York: Plenum.

Hanson, S. L. (1994). Lost Talent: Unrealized Educational Aspirations and Expectations among U.S. Youths. *Sociology of Education, 3*(3), 159–183.

Hanushek, E. A. (1989). The Impact of Differential Expenditures on School Performance. *Educational Researcher, 18*(4), 45–51.

Hanushek, E. A. (1996). School Resources and Student Performance. In G. Burtless (Ed.), *Does Money Matter?* (pp. 43–73). Washington, DC: Brookings Institution Press.

Herrnstein, R. J., & Murray, C. (1994). *The Bell Curve*. New York: Free Press.

Heubert, J. P., & Hauser, R. M. (Eds.). (1999). *High Stakes: Testing for Tracking, Promotion, and Graduation*. Washington, DC: National Academy Press.

Hobson v. Hansen. (1967, June 21). *Congressional Record* 6721–16766.

Hodgkinson, H. L. (1989). *The Same Client: The Demographics of Education and Service Delivery Systems*. Washington, DC: Institute for Educational Leadership.

Ingersoll, R. M. (2004). Why Some Schools Have More Underqualified Teachers than Others. In D. Ravitch (Ed.), *Brookings Papers on Education Policy* (pp. 45–88). Washington, DC: Brookings Institution Press.

Jaffe, A., & Adams, W. (1970). *Academic and Socio-Economic Factors Related to Entrance and Retention at Two- and Four-Year Colleges in the Late 1960's*. New York: Bureau of Applied Social Research, Columbia University.

Jones, J. D., Spade, J. N., & Vanfossen, B. E. (1987). Curriculum Tracking and Status Maintenance. *Sociology of Education, 60*(2), 104–122.

Jones, J. D., Vanfossen, B. E., & Spade, J. Z. (1985, August). *Curriculum Placement: Individual and School Effects Using the High School and Beyond Data.* Paper presented at the American Sociological Association Annual Meeting, Washington, DC.

Kamens, D. (1974). Colleges and Elite Formation: The Case of Prestigious American Colleges. *Sociology of Education, 47*(3), 354–378.

Karen, D. (2005). No Child Left Behind? Sociology Ignored! *Sociology of Education* 78:165–182.

Keddie, N. (1971). Classroom Knowledge. In M. F. D. Young (Ed.), *Knowledge and Control* (pp. 133–160). London: Collier-Macmillan.

Lareau, A. (1989). *Home Advantage.* Philadelphia: Falmer.

Lewis, L. S., & Wanner, R. A. (1979). Private Schooling and the Status Attainment Process. *Sociology of Education, 52*(2), 99–112.

Lichter, D. T., & Eggebeen, D. J. (1993). Rich Kids, Poor Kids: Changing Income Inequality among American Children. *Social Forces, 71*(3), 761–780.

Mare, R. (1981). Change and Stability in Educational Stratification. *American Sociological Review, 46*(1), 72–87.

Mayer, S. E. (2001). How Did the Increase in Economic Inequality between 1970 and 1990 Affect Children's Educational Attainment? *American Journal of Sociology, 107*(1), 1–32.

Mayeske, G. W., & Wisler, C. E. (1972). *A Study of Our Nation's Schools.* Washington, DC: U.S. Government Printing Office.

McNeil, L. M. (2000). *Contradictions of School Reform: Educational Costs of Standardized Testing.* New York: Routledge.

Meier, D., & Wood, G. (2004). *Many Children Left Behind: How the No Child Left Behind Act Is Damaging Our Children and Our Schools.* Boston, MA: Beacon.

New York Education Department. (1969). *Racial and Social Isolation in the Schools.* Albany: New York State Education Department.

Oakes, J. (1985). *Keeping Track: How Schools Structure Inequality.* New Haven, CT: Yale University Press.

Oakes, J. (1992). Can Tracking Research Inform Practice? Technical, Normative, and Political Considerations. *Educational Researcher, 21*, 12–21.

Oakes, J., Joseph, R., & Muir, K. (2004). Access and Achievement in Mathematics and Science: Inequalities That Endure and Change. In J. A. Banks & C. A. M. Banks (Eds.), *Handbook of Research on Multicultural Education* (2nd ed., pp. 69–90). San Francisco: Jossey-Bass.

Oakes, J., Wells, A. S., Jones, M., & Datnow, A. (1997). Detracking: The Social Construction of Ability, Cultural Politics, and Resistance to Reform. *Teachers College Record, 98*(3), 482–510.

Pallas, A. M., Entwisle, D. R., Alexander, K. L., & Stluka, M. F. (1994). Ability-Group Effects: Instructional, Social, or Institutional? *Sociology of Education, 67*(1), 27–46.

Persell, C. H. (1977). *Education and Inequality: The Roots and Results of Stratification in America's Schools.* New York: Free Press.

Persell, C. H. (2000). Values, Control, and Outcomes in Public and Private Schools. In M. T. Hallinan (Ed.), *Handbook of Sociology of Education* (pp. 387–407). New York: Kluwer Academic/Plenum.

Persell, C. H., Cookson, P. W., Jr., & Catsambis, S. (1992). Family Background, High School Type, and College Attendance: A Conjoint System of Cultural Capital Transmission. *Journal of Research on Adolescence, 2*(1), 1–23.

Reuman, D. A. (1989). How Social Comparison Mediates the Relation between Ability-Grouping Practices and Students' Achievement Expectancies in Mathematics. *Journal of Educational Psychology, 81*(1), 78–89.

Ritts, V., Patterson, M. L., & Tubbs, M. E. (1992). Expectations, Impressions, and Judgments of Physically Attractive Students: A Review. *Review of Educational Research, 62*(4), 413–426.

Rogers, D. (1968). *110 Livingston Street: Politics and Bureaucracy in the New York City School System.* New York: Random House.

Rogers, D., & Chung, N. H. (1983). *110 Livingston Street Revisited: Decentralization in Action.* New York: New York University Press.

Rosenbaum, J. E. (1976). *Making Inequality.* Hoboken: Wiley-Interscience.

Rosenbaum, J. E. (1980). Track Misperceptions and Frustrated College Plans: An Analysis of the Effects of Tracks and Track Perceptions in the National Longitudinal Survey. *Sociology of Education, 53*(2), 74–88.

Rosenthal, R. (1974). The Pygmalion Effect: What You Expect Is What You Get. *Psychology Today Library Cassette, #12.* New York: Ziff-Davis.

Rosenthal, R., & Jacobson, L. (1968). *Pygmalion in the Classroom.* New York: Holt, Rinehart & Winston.

Schafer, W. E., Olexa, C., & Polk, K. (1973). Programmed for Social Class: Tracking in American High Schools. In N. K. Denzin (Ed.), *Children and Their Caretakers* (pp. 220–226). New Brunswick, NJ: Transaction Books.

Sharan, S. (1980). Cooperative Learning in Small Groups: Recent Methods and Effects on Achievement, Attitudes, and Ethnic Relations. *Review of Educational Research, 50,* 241–271.

Tinto, V. (1980). College Origin and Patterns of Status Attainment. *Sociology of Work and Occupations, 7*(4), 457–486.

"A Truce in New Jersey's School War." (2002, February 9). *New York Times,* p. A18.

U.S. Department of Commerce, Bureau of the Census (2005). *U.S. Census Bureau, Housing and Household Economic Statistics Division,* Last Revised: October 4, 2005. Retrieved from http://pubdb3.census.gov/macro/023005/perinc/new03_127.htm.

Useem, E. L. (1990, April). *Social Class and Ability Group Placement in Mathematics in the Transition to Seventh Grade: The Role of Parental Involvement.* Paper presented at the annual meeting of the American Educational Research Association, Boston.

Useem, M. (1984). *The Inner Circle: Large Corporations and the Rise of Business Political Activity in the U.S. and U.K.* New York: Oxford University Press.

Useem, M., & Karabel, J. (1986). Educational Pathways to Top Corporate Management. *American Sociological Review, 51*(2), 184–200.

Weikart, D., & Schweinhart, L. J. (1984). *Changed Lives: The Effects of the Perry Preschool Program on Youths through Age 19.* Ypsilanti, MI: High Scope.

Wenglinsky, H. (1997). How Money Matters: The Effect of School District Spending on Academic Achievement. *Sociology of Education, 70,* 221–237.

Wheelock, A. (1992). *Crossing the Tracks: How "Untracking" Can Save America's Schools.* New York: New Press.

Winter, G. (2003, April 23). New Ammunition for Backers of Do-or-Die Exams. *New York Times,* p. B9.

CHAPTER 5

Christian Nation or Pluralistic Culture: Religion in American Life

Charles H. Lippy

Two threads in the tapestry representing American religious culture seem paradoxical, if not contradictory:

1. The United States is a Christian nation, founded on religious principles deriving from the Bible still embedded in the laws under which we live. Although other religious communities are tolerated, Christianity in its many forms has been and remains the dominant religious influence in our common life.

2. Religious freedom prevails in the United States because of the "separation of church and state." Hence Americans are free to believe whatever they want and to worship however they want. Consequently, many religious alternatives flourish side by side, with none dominating.

Both perceptions have long histories; both are vital to understanding the religious dynamics of American culture in the early twenty-first century.

EUROPEANS PLANT CHRISTIANITY IN NORTH AMERICA

When the thirteen colonies that became the United States broke away from Great Britain in 1776, European settlement in those areas stretched back less than 175 years. Most who came from England shared a religious consciousness shaped by Protestant Christianity (Lippy, Choquette, & Poole, 1992). In southern areas like Virginia, although there were some variations of belief, colonial arrangements included legal establishment of the Church of England. Establishment meant that Church of England parishes and the few clergy serving them were supported by public tax money and that all living there would in theory be part of a parish.

To the north, first to Plymouth and then to other areas of Massachusetts, came settlers who had deep ties to the Church of England. However, they were unhappy with what they saw as compromises the Church of England had made with Roman Catholic ways in trying to craft a religious establishment with broad appeal. These dissenters came to New England to set up churches reflecting their own understanding of religious truth. Generally, we label all of them Puritans, for all sought a more pure form of Protestant Christianity than they found in the Church of England. But there were important differences. The Pilgrims who came to Plymouth in 1620 believed that the Church of England was hopelessly engulfed in religious falsehood; therefore, the only way to assure their own salvation was to separate from the church by moving away and setting up their own religious institutions. The Puritans who settled much of the rest of New England still identified with the Church of England, but they thought that their abandoning a structure that relied on the authority of bishops and their simpler worship rendered them a more pure form of that church.

Regardless, both thought that relocating to North America would give them religious freedom, unwittingly giving birth to the idea that the United States was founded on the principle of religious freedom. In actuality, neither Plymouth Pilgrims nor other Puritans believed that those who disagreed with them should have any religious freedom; indeed, alternative points of view were seen as dangerous. For example, Massachusetts authorities banished Roger Williams in the 1630s because he was too much a religious seeker. Later acclaimed a bulwark of religious freedom whose perspective influenced Baptist developments, Williams then was regarded as a dangerous heretic. But all he needed to do was move a few miles away to what is now Rhode Island. There Massachusetts authorities had no control over him, and he was free to set up a church reflecting his own views.

Before the end of the seventeenth century, however, political changes in Britain mandated in the colonies a broader toleration of variant forms of Protestantism, so long as they did not disrupt public order and peace. Roman Catholics, however, were still not formally recognized, although they had carved a presence for themselves when Maryland was established. They later flourished, especially in Pennsylvania, where the Quaker-dominated government supported what the founder William Penn called a "holy experiment" of allowing persons of all religious persuasions to settle so long as they supported the commonweal.

EARLY SIGNS OF DIVERSITY

Even so, patterns of immigration generated a far greater diversity in many parts of the English colonies than public policy recognized. From the arrival of the first slave ships in Virginia in 1619, an African tribal substratum made most southern Christian life diverse, since many congregations in time became biracial. White Christians were at first reluctant to share their religion with the slaves, fearing that conversion would automatically bring freedom from the bonds of slavery. When more sustained efforts were made to preach Christianity to African Americans from the middle of the eighteenth century on, the result was a vibrant fusion of African ways with evangelical Protestantism. The chant, song, and dance central to much tribal religiosity fused with the enthusiastic and often emotional style of evangelicalism to give African American Christianity a distinctive expression that grew and developed alongside the churches with European roots. Those whose forced migration from Africa brought them first to the Caribbean added other twists that endured in practices popularly associated with voodoo once they planted those rituals on American soil. Both European Americans and African Americans were drawn to slaves with a gift for preaching. However, few Whites recognized how often the power of the slave preacher echoed that of the tribal conjurer, a blending that endured in the person of many African American clergy even after the abolition of slavery and the emergence of separate African American denominations. In addition, some of the first slaves were Muslims, although the conditions of slavery made it impossible for Muslim practice to last very long among the African population.

Ethnicity also contributed to other manifestations of diversity. The Dutch who had originally settled in New York (New Netherlands) generally espoused a Calvinistic Reformed faith; even after the English took control, they remained a strong presence. To what became New Jersey, clusters of Scandinavian immigrants brought their Lutheran religion with them. Various communities of German immigrants who came to Pennsylvania carried a variety of religious labels, most still within the orbit of Protestant Christianity. And almost from the inception of the colonies came Jewish immigrants, remaining on the margins of colonial religious life but establishing synagogues and communities in places such as Charleston, South Carolina; Savannah, Georgia; New York; and Newport, Rhode Island. Often unrecognized, because they were not understood even by well-intentioned Christian colonists as religious, were the practices of the Native American tribes on whose lands the Europeans settled. They, too, are part of the larger picture of diversity.

By the middle of the eighteenth century, Scots-Irish immigrants had planted their own form of Presbyterianism, especially in the middle colonies and then farther south as they settled along the eastern slopes of the Appalachian mountain chain. By midcentury, too, those inclined to Methodism, then a "new religion" in England, had made their way to North America. Even so, when the new United States conducted its first national census in 1790, statistics showed that only around 10 percent of the population were formal members of a religious group. But that figure is misleading, for it underestimates the influence of the churches in colonial and early national life and fails to take into account the conviction prevailing then that joining a church—actually becoming a member—was a serious, important step not to be taken lightly. Many who regularly attended worship and who tried to live by the moral codes of the churches never took that step.

English control did not extend to all areas of North America that eventually became part of the United States. The presence of Spanish settlements in areas from Florida through Texas and the Southwest to California adds another layer to the tale of diversity. The last of the Spanish missions, the one in San Francisco, was founded in 1776, the same year that the English colonies proclaimed their independence from Britain. In addition, a Catholicism reflecting the French experience flourished in areas along the Gulf of Mexico from Mobile to New Orleans and along the southern Mississippi River. When these areas became part of the United States, they intensified the story of diversity because of the long history of both Spanish and French Catholicism that had supported adjoining colonial empires.

COMMON THEMES

Presbyterians and Methodists, Lutherans and Dutch Reformed, Congregationalist Puritans and Baptists—all were part of the larger Protestant heritage in European Christianity since the Reformation of the sixteenth century. And although there were differences, there were also common features that became more evident in the first half-century or so after independence when the United States struggled with what it meant to be a republic, a representative democracy. Perhaps the most important feature was some sense that vital religion was based on personal experience, although there was considerable difference as to whether one had such experience of one's own volition or whether an experience of conversion, a sense of salvation, was something determined only by God. Congregationalists, Presbyterians, and Dutch Reformed, all looking back to the sixteenth-century reformer John Calvin, were more inclined to attribute all to the work of God, while Methodists were convinced that human beings had to accept God's gift of salvation of their own free will. Among Baptists, some emphasized free will and some believed that God alone determined who would be saved. Anglicans—those who were part of the Church of England—and Lutherans also showed some diversity, although many simply regarded the work of God in salvation as a mystery revealed to those who faithfully attended worship and accepted the doctrines of the church.

In the middle of the eighteenth century, the centrality of personal religious experience got a big boost when waves of revivals that historians call the Great Awakening swept through the colonies, although some debate whether historians invented both the phenomenon and the label. For about a decade or so after 1740, folks seemed to exhibit a renewed interest in religion. Many talked about being converted, some because they were convinced that God had given them signs that they were chosen for salvation and some because they believed they had willingly accepted God's gracious offer of salvation. The revival enriched the biracial character of Christianity in the southern colonies, for evangelical preachers, as already noted, were among the first who actively sought converts among enslaved African Americans.

Although church members remained a minority in the whole population, Protestant denominations emphasizing personal decision and free will in matters of religion saw their influence grow immensely in the first half of the nineteenth century. Even those who stressed election by God in salvation began to shed that idea. Free will and choice seemed consistent with the democratic ideas taking root in American political life, for in this approach, all persons were equal, whether as sinners or as those who chose salvation. Just as wealth and rank were not supposed to matter in the public order in a democracy, so, too, they had no clout in the evangelical denominations, like the Methodists and Baptists, that offered salvation to all. These groups—along with Presbyterians, who were gradually jettisoning the idea that God predestined some to salvation—were more aggressive in going where ordinary folk were to present their message.

As the American population grew and began to move westward, evangelicals were among the major proponents of the camp meeting, which brought together those who lived isolated lives on the frontier for times of preaching and fellowship. Then, as factory towns developed along the rivers and canals in the North (the Erie Canal in New York is a prime example), enterprising urban evangelists adapted the techniques of the frontier camp meeting and made revivalism a major device for spreading the influence of Protestant Christianity. Revivalists

Table 5.1   Number of Places of Worship in the United States

	1650	1750	1850	1950	1996
Baptist	2	132	9,375	77,000	98,228
Congregationalist	62	465	1,706	5,679	6,748
Episcopal	31	289	1,459	7,784	7,517
Presbyterian	4	233	4,824	13,200	14,214
Methodist	0	0	13,328	54,000	51,311
Roman Catholic	6	30	1,221	15,533	22,728
Jewish	0	5	30	2,000	3,975
Holiness/Pentecostal	0	0	0	21,705	52,868
Lutheran	4	138	1,217	16,403	19,077

Adapted from Gaustad and Barlow (2001), p. 390.

and itinerant evangelists earned their reputations because their preaching moved the minds and emotions of their audiences, not because of formal education in the rigors of theology once favored by New England Puritans. Denominations that still expected their clergy to have more formal training saw their influence dwindling; few had the time or the money to prepare for ministry in this way. Table 5.1 shows the relative growth of Christian groups from 1650 to 1996.

THE SPREAD OF EVANGELICAL PROTESTANTISM

These currents helped make a broad evangelical Protestantism the dominant style of Christianity in the United States by the time of the Civil War. Even the arrival of thousands of Roman Catholics from Ireland in the 1830s and 1840s did not diminish that influence, for Protestants were also the ones who ran the developing businesses and industries and usually the ones elected or appointed to political office. This Protestant Christian character became deeply etched into American culture more subtly as public education began to develop in the 1830s. The well-known *McGuffey Readers* (Westerhoff, 1978; Williams, 1980) were standard fare in primary education for generations of students. A quick look at the content of those readers reveals that they simply assumed that pupils shared a broad evangelical Protestant background, making the emerging public schools almost arms of the Protestant denominations in their fusion of Protestant beliefs, moral values, and sound learning. Hence, even though there were other groups present—Irish Catholics, German Catholics, Jews, and more—this broad evangelical Protestantism influenced every sector of common life, reinforcing the image of the United States as a Christian nation.

The decades between the close of the Civil War and the outbreak of World War I, when immigration from Europe reached its peak, brought challenges to that hegemony. Most of the millions who arrived on American shores in those decades came not from Protestant or even Catholic areas of Northern and Western Europe, but from Southern, Central, and Eastern Europe. Most were not Protestants, but Roman Catholics, Eastern Orthodox Christians, and Jews. Many Catholic parishes established parochial or parish schools, in part because Protestant assumptions pervaded public school curricula and instruction. But some of those in positions of social, economic, and political power recoiled not only at the religious orientation of these immigrants but also at their cultural and ethnic folkways. Calls to Americanize the immigrants, however, were also most often calls to Protestantize them, to force them into the dominant religious style and therefore perpetuate the image of the United States as a (Protestant) Christian nation.

The Congregationalist Josiah Strong, who worked for the interdenominational Evangelical Alliance, in his *Our Country* (1886/1964) of the mid-1880s, identified the religions of the immigrants, along with their concentration in the nation's cities and the rapid industrialization that their presence in the work force propelled, as major threats to American identity. But they were threats only if one assumed that an American identity was wedded to evangelical Protestant Christianity.

Adding another layer to the *de facto* diversity was the steady growth of African American Protestant denominations, most associated with the Methodist and Baptist traditions. By no means mirror images of their White counterparts, these groups played critical roles in allowing an indigenous leadership to develop, centered in the churches, that realized much of its potential in the civil rights movement of the twentieth century. In many areas of the South, where legal discrimination replaced slavery, churches were frequently the only property actually owned by African Americans, and the preachers who served them often the only ones with advanced education. The churches became more than religious centers; in the rural South especially they became broad social institutions, serving as centers for community life and offering numerous social welfare programs that remained essential as long as legal racism penetrated the larger society.

Nonetheless, Protestants from the mainline denominations continued to exert an influence in the business and political affairs of the nation that was increasingly out of proportion to their numbers in the whole population. Hence, after World War I, Congress enacted the first laws restricting immigration overall, expanding earlier legislation affecting primarily Chinese and Japanese immigration to California and other areas of the West. The new quotas assured that the bulk of those allowed to enter the United States each year would give at least tacit assent to Protestant Christian belief and thus preserve the image of the United States as a Christian nation. Table 5.2 presents data on religious affiliation from 1830 to 1990.

RELIGIOUS FREEDOM AND THE SEPARATION OF CHURCH AND STATE

Countervailing forces always challenged the reality of the image of the United States as a Christian nation and sustained the conviction that religious diversity and pluralism flourished in the culture. In this view, the United States has never been a Christian nation per se, but one where religious freedom prevailed and no one religious group or tradition, like Christianity,

Table 5.2   Percentage of Americans Claiming Religious Affiliation

	1830	1890	1990
Baptist	25.0%	18.0%	20.0%
Congregationalist	12.3	2.5	1.5
Episcopal	5.0	2.6	1.8
Presbyterian	17.0	6.2	2.7
Methodist	23.4	22.3	11.8
Roman Catholic	4.2	30.2	38.9
Jewish	*	*	4.4
Holiness/Pentecostal	*	*	4.4
Lutheran	3.4	6.0	6.0

*Less than 1 percent.
Adapted from Gaustad and Barlow (2001), p. 389.

dominated. Those who trumpet this religious freedom point to the First Amendment to the Constitution, which says simply that "Congress shall make no law respecting an establishment of religion, or prohibiting the free exercise thereof." Ever since the adoption of the Bill of Rights, courts and pundits have debated precisely what those words mean.

In the early Republic one reason not to have a nationally established religion was pragmatic. If most citizens of the new United States identified with one of the numerous Christian bodies, primarily Protestant ones, no one denomination or sect could count a majority as adherents, much less as members. Already Baptists, Methodists, Presbyterians, Quakers, Lutherans of many ethnic varieties, Episcopalians, and a host of others had learned to live in relative peace and harmony. This diversity, later celebrated by some as a kind of pluralism, meant that it would be unfair—undemocratic—to single out one group to receive governmental support. Another assumption undergirded this nod to diversity—namely, a conviction that regardless of label, all such groups inculcated the same values and morals that made their followers good citizens. Differences of theological doctrine paled in importance to this ethical bent.

At the same time, many leading political thinkers of the age embraced ideas of rationality and freedom of thought associated with the philosophical currents of the Enlightenment. The Age of the Revolution was also the Age of Reason. Thomas Jefferson, Benjamin Franklin, George Washington, and a host of others all subscribed to Enlightenment ideas. Contrary to later lore, they were not twenty-first-century fundamentalists disguised as eighteenth-century political leaders; nor were they what a later age would call secular humanists. Most accepted the idea that an overarching Providence worked through human affairs, a Providence that the more orthodox called God. All believed that religious doctrines, even if they did not subscribe to them individually, were useful because doctrines helped mold people into moral citizens and therefore supported peace and social order. All were suspicious of what could not be demonstrated on the basis of logic. Yet logic and reason also decreed that one had a right to think as one wished, to follow the truth given by one's own mind, without interference from others.

The rationalist emphasis on what the eighteenth-century Boston pastor Jonathan Mayhew (1749) called the "right of private judgment" and the more evangelical Protestant emphasis on a dynamic personal experience of conversion or election were actually two sides of the same coin. In different ways, both made the individual—not churches, ministers, priests, or even Scripture—the final authority in matters of personal belief and practice. Just as no one could have an experience of conversion for another person, so only the individual could determine what the mind saw as right and true. Most who accepted reason as a guide were confident—perhaps naively optimistic—that what was true would look pretty much the same to everyone. But there was no guarantee. Hence a democratic social order had no choice but to allow for latitude of belief among its citizens. If different minds arrived at different truths, so be it, so long as such difference did not disrupt civil order.

From the point of view of reason, the danger in having government endorse a particular belief system, no matter how worthy it was, or in giving official status to any one religious group or tradition, no matter how pervasive its influence, was the potential tyranny such a belief or group could exert over others. If a religious community could call on the coercive power of the state to force conformity to its beliefs and practices, it lost its legitimacy. It no longer had to persuade people of its truth on rational grounds or to move people to experience for themselves the reality of the salvation it offered.

Even before ratification of the Bill of Rights, the state of Virginia had adopted a statute providing for near-total religious freedom. Inspired by Thomas Jefferson, the Virginia statute became something of a model for other states, since the Constitution restricted only the Congress from establishing a religion. When the Bill of Rights was adopted, a few New England states still had constitutions that provided for the payment of salaries of teachers of religion and morals from public funds. The last state to drop such a provision was Massachusetts in 1833.

The phrase with which later generations are familiar, *separation of church and state*, is not strictly speaking part of the constitutional or legal heritage of the nation. Rather, it comes from a letter written in 1802 by President Thomas Jefferson to a group of Connecticut Baptists in which he referred to a "wall of separation between church and state." Jefferson noted that, like the Baptists who had written to him, he believed that "religion is a matter which lies solely between man and his God, that he owes account to none other for his faith or his worship" and "that the legislative powers of government reach actions only, and not opinions" (cited in Wilson, 1965, pp. 75–76). To be sure, Jefferson acknowledged the reality of God; what he wanted to avoid was government involvement in determining what individuals should believe and how they should put that belief into practice.

The legal provisions for religious freedom did not mean, however, that all sorts of fanatics made their way to the United States, although numerous individuals tried to drum up a following for their own particular points of view. In historical context, one result paralleled other Enlightenment-era shifts in Europe—namely, assuring that there were no political disabilities attached to Jewish identity. For centuries, Jews in much of Europe had been forced into ghettoes, prohibited from practicing certain occupations in the larger community, denied access to political life, and restricted in their educational opportunities. The idea of separation of church and state, a phrase that uses a Christian term (*church*) as a symbol for all religion, would make that impossible in the United States, although it did not eradicate either the overt or the covert anti-Semitism that ran through American culture.

This legal arrangement did mean that the United States became a nation where extraordinary religious experimentation and diversity prevailed just beneath the surface, even if a broadly evangelical Protestantism centered around a few denominations dominated public life. In the 1830s in upstate New York, for example, Joseph Smith reported having a vision that led to the founding of the Latter-day Saints, better known as the Mormons. Although the Mormons were not well received for a generation or so because their teachings seemed to undermine orthodox Protestant doctrine, they were able to move from one location to another. They garnered more followers as they went, finally winding up around the Great Salt Lake, ironically just before the Utah area was transferred from Mexican to U.S. control. The Saints represent what some historians regard as the first genuinely "new" religion to emerge in the American context.

Around the same time, John Humphrey Noyes relocated from Vermont to Oneida in upstate New York, where he preached his own version of the gospel and drew scores to his communitarian enterprise with its practice of complex marriage. In the 1830s as well, the Shakers, although planted on North American soil by their founder Ann Lee and a handful of adherents just before the American Revolution, also reached their peak. About 6000 men and women were leading the simple, celibate life in hopes of salvation in nearly two dozen different communities, several of them in upstate New York and New England. Countless other groups followed the lead of an inspired teacher, each carving a niche for itself because government would not interfere in matters of personal belief and practice. Many experimented with communal living. As in a marketplace, each group competed to gain a following, with those best able to convince men and women of their truth reaping the largest number of adherents.

Immigration in the first decades of the nineteenth century also assured that the United States would be home to a significant Jewish population. Although there had been several small Jewish communities in the English colonies, with synagogues early flourishing in places such as Newport, Rhode Island, and Charleston, South Carolina, the immigration of Jews from German cultures in Europe laid the foundation for diversity within the Hebrew tradition itself. Eager to seize the opportunities for fuller participation in public life that followed the Enlightenment and ended centuries of forced exclusion from society, many Jews were drawn to Reform Judaism. The Reform movement sought to abandon nonessential features of Jewish practice that were thought to be inextricably wedded to ancient Near Eastern culture and times and to take on a more modern appearance.

Later generations of Jewish immigrants pondered whether Reform was too radical, willing to yield too much. Those who resisted most strongly became known as Orthodox Jews, while in time the largest body became known as Conservative Jews. Conservative Jews were willing to make some modifications to traditional practice to accommodate life in a modern, religiously pluralistic culture but thought that Reform had jettisoned too much. Although various forms of Christianity continued to dominate American religious life, by the middle of the nineteenth century it was clear that a vibrant Jewish culture would remain a dynamic alternative.

The first half of the nineteenth century also saw other religious teachers who preached their own understanding of the truth at frontier camp meetings or who worked the lecture circuit, a form of popular entertainment, in the larger cities. Along the frontier, for example, several sought to restore what they believed to be the actual practice of first-century New Testament Christianity. That meant shedding denominational structure and, in some cases, even religious professionals like clergy. Out of that swirl of interest came groups that later coalesced into the Disciples of Christ and the Churches of Christ.

In cities like New York, individuals such as William Miller drew crowds to their presentations on biblical prophecy. Miller, renowned for predicting the imminent return of Christ to usher in the millennial age, even fixed a date when the Second Advent would transpire, more than once revising his calculations when the Second Advent did not occur on schedule. Although most of his followers scattered because of the "great disappointment" that ensued, his teaching formed part of the background for the Seventh-Day Adventists and the doctrines advocated by their early leader, Ellen G. Harmon White.

By the end of the nineteenth century, many other groups had emerged, some reflecting the religious styles of the continuing streams of immigrants and others arising from ideas offered by dynamic speakers and writers. Among the better-known immigrant communities are the Amish and their religious cousins, the Mennonites, who sought to live their version of a simple life without involvement in a larger society that they saw as hopelessly corrupted by modernity. Their major immigration to the United States and Canada came in the decades after the Civil War. That epoch was also a time of increasing interest in science and the application of scientific techniques to religious expression. Mary Baker Eddy, for example, called her approach to using mental power and faith to effect healing Christian Science, and her influence grew rapidly as she published summaries of her views and as practitioners of her way fanned out across the country, promoting her ideas.

These few examples demonstrate some of the diversity and pluralism beginning to color American religious life, a diversity and pluralism made possible in part because of the legal arrangements embedded in the First Amendment. Other factors aided this religious experimentation. The seemingly vast amount of land available in the expanding nation literally meant that there was room for various religious teachers and groups to go about their business without really interrupting or interfering with the lives of those around them. Consequently, the American experience helped demolish a myth that had helped buttress Western civilization from the days of the Roman Empire onward, namely, that some sort of religious uniformity—or at least tacit conformity to one religious tradition—was a necessary precondition for political stability and social harmony.

DIVERSITY, RELIGIOUS FREEDOM, AND THE COURTS

At the same time, some religious groups seemed to many Americans, primarily those identified with Protestant denominations, to push the limits of freedom too far. After all, they were minority groups on the margins of the larger religious culture. If their beliefs and practices were too far out of step with the majority, should they not be restrained or curtailed before they undermined the dominant religious style? In one sense, the basic issues were how much diversity free exercise allowed before it became dangerous and how much control government should wield to protect a presumed majority before it became tyrannical.

One example emerged when the Latter-day Saints founder Joseph Smith advocated the practice of plural marriage. A revelation he believed to be from God convinced him that the ancient Hebrew practice, recorded in the Bible, of men having more than one wife was appropriate for his own followers. However, most Americans were aghast at the idea of polygamy, and most states forbade polygamous practice when the Utah Territory was seeking admission to the Union. The situation was convoluted, and historians are not of a single mind as to exactly how subsequent Mormon teaching came to prohibit the practice. But until there were restrictions on polygamy, which the Saints once believed part of their free exercise of religion, Utah would not be admitted as a state. In the process, the U.S. Supreme Court heard two cases dealing with plural marriage, *Reynolds v. United States* in 1878 and *Davis v. Beason* in 1890 (Miller & Flowers, 1987). Even after the official position changed and Utah was admitted as a state with a constitution prohibiting plural marriage, some individuals who identified themselves as Mormons continued the practice. In the early twenty-first century, occasional cases still come to the attention of the media and the courts, although most are ignored since practitioners tend to live in remote rural areas where local folks often overlook what does not upset public order.

Laws protecting Sabbath observance go back to the colonial period. Among the earliest was a provision in Virginia, part of "Dale's Laws" issued in 1610, that not only required attendance at Christian worship but also prohibited "any gaming" in public or private on Sunday. As the Jewish population of the United States grew, those identified with Orthodox Judaism, with its emphasis on strict observance of the Sabbath from sundown Friday until sundown Saturday, found laws favoring Sunday as the Sabbath discriminatory. However, because the numbers of Jews were small and the Jewish population fairly scattered, there were few challenges to the status quo.

Sunday laws also affected Seventh-Day Adventists, who, as their name indicates, hold to the Hebrew practice of keeping the Sabbath, the seventh day or Saturday, as sacred. Most Christian groups, whether Protestant, Catholic, or Orthodox, that represented the majority of Americans believed that the Christian practice of keeping Sunday, the first day, as a sacred and holy day superseded seventh-day Sabbath observance. Well into the twentieth century, many states and local communities legally restricted what kinds of work could be done on Sunday, whether and what goods and products could be sold, and access to certain recreational activities. Popularly known as "blue laws," such regulations aroused little concern when the overwhelming majority of citizens in a town or area accepted the Christian practice for themselves. They tended to keep the day sacred even without such legal restraint. But what about those for whom the seventh day was holy?

Most legal challenges involving Seventh-Day Adventists and Orthodox Jews remained in local and state courts. Some early challenges to Sunday blue laws that reached the U.S. Supreme Court did not directly involve religious groups, although the issues at stake did. For example, the arrest of discount store employees for selling on Sunday products restricted by law propelled *McGowan v. Maryland* (1961), and in *Two Guys from Harrison-Allentown, Inc. v. McGinley* (1961), there was a similar situation, but with sufficient factual differences to require a separate decision. In both, the Court upheld Sunday blue laws on the grounds of "argument from history" and insisted that even if blue laws originally supported specifically Christian observance, they had come to promote the general welfare by mandating one day of rest in seven. But bringing such cases to the Supreme Court unwittingly set in motion moves to repeal most blue laws on a state and local level.

In times of war, court cases at every level have centered on those who refused to engage in military combat and sometimes in any activity that supported such combat. Although hundreds have been imprisoned, generally the courts concluded that persons who were members of religious groups such as the Quakers, the Mennonites, the Church of the Brethren, and other historic "peace churches" could refuse to serve, although most were required to perform alternative service. In the age of protest against the U.S. military presence in Vietnam, the protection of conscientious objection was extended to individuals who opposed all war on grounds of personal belief, regardless of whether they were formal members of any religious group.

Over the years, court cases involving groups that reject certain medical procedures (e.g., blood transfusions), like the Jehovah's Witnesses and the Church of Christ, Scientist, have also raised questions about free exercise. Generally, the courts have upheld the right of persons of legal age to refuse medical treatment on religious grounds, but the situation has been much more complex when it comes to parents who refuse to authorize medical procedures for their minor children on religious grounds. Here the issue has been whether the overriding responsibility of government to promote the welfare of minors could require treatments that the faith communities in which they were being raised opposed on religious grounds.

Where and how to draw the line between the duty of government to promote the welfare of the people and the right of free exercise also informed many of the cases, mostly on a state level, that concerned the ritual handling of serpents and ingesting of poisonous liquids such as strychnine. Serpent handlers claimed a biblical basis for the practice in the Gospel of Mark, Chapter 16, and insisted that they were doing what Scripture required. But did the possibility of death from a snake bite make serpent handling a practice that so undermined the general welfare that government was obligated to prohibit the practice? Since serpent-handling groups are concentrated in the mountains of central Appalachia, most of the laws making serpent handling illegal were passed by states in that region. But few of the laws were regularly enforced, and most of them had been rescinded before the end of the twentieth century.

Numerous cases wrestled with whether practices sanctioned by law resulted in a *de facto* establishment of religion, particularly in areas affecting education in public schools. Some of the earliest concerned children who were Jehovah's Witnesses. On religious grounds, Witnesses refuse to salute the flag, insisting that reciting the Pledge of Allegiance places a blasphemous loyalty to the state before their allegiance to God. Most cases brought by Witnesses came decades before the recent controversy over whether the phrase *under God* that was inserted into the Pledge of Allegiance by Congress in 1954 represented unconstitutional support for religion. Until the rights of the Witnesses received legal protection, episodes in several communities resulted in children who were Witnesses being expelled from school and their parents being prosecuted. At first, though, the Supreme Court was reluctant to see refusal to recite the Pledge of Allegiance as an exercise of religious freedom. In *Minersville School District v. Gobitis* (1940), the Court decreed that the social cohesion resulting from requiring students to recite the pledge superseded free exercise. But in *West Virginia State Board of Education v. Barnette*, which came just three years later, the court reversed its earlier opinion, setting a precedent that has prevailed since.

As noted above, when public education began to become the norm in the United States in the nineteenth century, a majority of students came from families with ties to mainline Protestant denominations, and curriculum materials often reflected the beliefs and practices of those groups. Christian holidays, such as Christmas and Holy Week before Easter, were times when classes were suspended; Jewish holy days did not as a rule receive such preferential treatment, although Jewish children were not penalized for absences on religious holidays. In some school districts school facilities were used, primarily by Protestant groups, for religious instruction, sometimes even during the regular class day. In 1948, in *McCollum v. Board of Education*, the Supreme Court ruled against using school facilities and class time for instruction in a particular faith tradition, even when participation was voluntary.

Some accommodation was reached in 1952 in *Zorach v. Clauson*, when the Court sanctioned dismissing children early from regular classes to attend voluntary off-site religious instruction. For a couple of decades after *Zorach v. Clauson*, there were a host of cooperative endeavors by Protestant churches as well as programs set up for Roman Catholic children not enrolled in parochial schools to be dismissed from school an hour early one day a week. By the end of the twentieth century, when it became difficult for groups to recruit volunteers to staff such programs and other extracurricular options expanded, most were dismantled.

The greatest controversy, however, has revolved around Bible reading and prayer in the public schools and whether such activities represent a tacit establishment or favoring of a particular religious tradition. In local communities there have been other cases, most notably those that challenged prayers at ceremonies preceding athletic events or at commencement exercises. The most famous cases to reach the Supreme Court came in the early 1960s. In 1962, the decision in *Engel v. Vitale* struck down a practice mandated by the New York State Board of Regents that required public school students to recite a presumably generic, nonsectarian prayer at the start of each school day. Before the furor over that judgment had abated, the Court announced its verdict the next year in *Abington v. Schempp*. It declared unconstitutional the reading of any portion of the Bible for devotional purposes and any recitation of the Lord's Prayer, even if those for whom the prayer was not an act of worship were not required to participate.

More than four decades later, school districts and state legislatures still wrangle with ways to get around these decisions. Subsequent cases, mostly in lower courts, have whittled away at the absolute prohibitions by allowing in some cases for student-initiated prayers at certain events and for use of facilities for voluntary student religious groups outside normal class hours on the same basis that they are available for other extracurricular programs. Frequently overlooked in the heat of controversy is the Supreme Court's insistence that prohibiting devotional practices associated with particular religions did not ban the academic study of religion in public schools, something rather different from instruction in the teachings of a particular faith tradition as ultimate truth. Nor did it mean that sacred texts such as the Bible could not be studied from literary and historical perspectives. That study, too, did not necessarily use the scriptures of any one religious tradition to promote personal belief and commitment. Yet most public school systems have been reluctant to offer the academic study of religion lest it be misconstrued, curriculum materials developed for such courses are limited but increasing, and few teachers are given the formal background to teach religion as an academic subject.

In the early twenty-first century, debates continued over what separation of church and state involved and how to assure the free exercise of religion. Some echoed earlier themes, such as a case involving whether Santeria was a religion and therefore its ritual of sacrificing chickens a protected religious practice. Others concerned dimensions of how religion and education might legally be linked, such as whether states or communities could provide vouchers that citizens could use to defray the cost of parochial or church-sponsored education.

Several focused on whether creationism was a science and should be included in biology text-books if theories of evolution were also presented. Because many saw creation science as a way to introduce a single religious perspective into public education, courts consistently rejected claims to include it in school curricula. However, when advocates began to speak of intelligent design as an explanation for the origins of the universe, a term some thought merely a new designation for creation science, a new round of court battles got underway. Emerging in school districts across the county, moves to introduce intelligent design challenged traditional teaching of science and appeared poised to open doors to introduce other matters of faith into public school curricula if they were successful. The few cases that had made their way through courts by 2005, however, generally refused to require teaching theories of intelligent design because they were construed as promoting religion, although in some instances, steps taken assured that even evolution would be presented as speculative theory, not as accepted scientific fact. The most widely publicized case centered in Dover, PA, where the school board had mandated the teaching of intelligent design in biology classes, along with statements that evolution was merely theory and not universally accepted scientific fact. In November 2005, while challenges to the board's policy were in the courts, voters soundly defeated for re-election school board candidates who supported teaching intelligent design, reaping criticism from religiously conservative evangelical pundits. But a ruling by Judge John E. Jones III issued the week before Christmas 2005 seemed likely to provide precedent around the country for similar cases. In his decree overturning the board's policy, Jones bluntly declared, "Intelligent design is not science" (Teepen, 2005). Efforts to provide opportunities to promulgate supernatural explanations in the classroom, however, seemed unlikely to disappear.

Several cases have emerged in the opening decade of this century that challenge not the recitation of the Pledge of Allegiance per se by public school students, but the words "under God" inserted into the pledge in 1954. In June 2004, the Supreme Court dismissed one such case coming from California, where a lower court had ruled that the phrase in question was unconstitutional, on the grounds that the parent who initiated the case, an avowed atheist, lacked standing since he did not have legal custody of his daughter who was the student required to recite the pledge. When California courts again ruled in a subsequent case involving different parties that the phrase was unconstitutional, the matter seemed more likely to come before the Supreme Court for a final ruling.

In retrospect, it seems that early cases concerned how to protect the rights of religious minorities, but some had come to believe that later cases imposed minority rule on the majority. Regardless, the array of legal cases concerning religion suggested that a deep and abiding diversity marked American life, even if in an earlier epoch a broadly based evangelical Protestantism had exercised dominant influence.

PLURALISM BECOMES THE NORM

The controversial court cases of the 1960s concerning prayer and Bible reading came at a time when the evangelical consensus that buttressed the image of the United States as a Christian nation was already unraveling. As early as 1955, Will Herberg, one-time labor union organizer and Jewish theologian who taught sociology of religion at Methodism's Drew

Theological Seminary, in his *Protestant, Catholic, Jew* (1960) argued that the vast majority of Americans regarded the many forms of Protestantism, Roman Catholicism, and Judaism as equally valid in molding adherents into responsible citizens. What mattered was that one had a religious label as a badge of social worth, not what that label was. For Herberg, the downside was the emergence of a culture of religion, what he called the "religion of the American Way of Life," that emphasized materialism and conspicuous consumption in place of the commitment and discipleship permeating biblical faith. That unconscious push to a common ground minimizing denominational particularities and even distinctions among faith traditions echoes in the oft-quoted statement attributed to President Eisenhower: The government of the United States "makes no sense unless it is founded on a deeply felt religious faith—and I don't care what it is" (cited in Herberg, 1960, p. 95).

Service in the military during World War II introduced thousands of Americans to persons of other religious persuasions; the shared experience of battle minimized faith differences. As veterans reentered civilian life at the close of World War II, employment opportunities frequently entailed relocation. The long-standing model of Americans going through childhood, coming to maturity, and ultimately dying in communities where they had been born or at least near to their places of birth quickly disappeared. Relocation for many meant finding a new church with which to affiliate, often chosen for reasons other than its denominational label. If the denomination of one's birth had no congregation nearby, it was a simple matter to affiliate with another one.

The suburban sprawl accompanying the rise in mobility also contributed to this gradual erosion of denominational loyalty. Mainline Protestant denominations raced to build new churches in rapidly growing suburban communities, often cooperating with each other so as not to "overchurch" a particular area. Church bureaucrats knew that families were likely to identify with a church, regardless of denomination, with programs oriented toward young families. Denominational switching became the norm. Denominations could no longer take for granted that those raised within the fold would retain a lifelong identification with a particular tradition. Individuals lost a sense of deep linkage to a particular heritage, relating only to the specific local congregation where they worshiped or held membership. Those not steeped in a certain tradition could hardly be expected to rear their own children with a firm bond to that heritage.

The rush to the nation's colleges and universities in the immediate postwar years, spurred by the famous G.I. Bill, in a different way undermined enduring denominational loyalty. The collegiate environment, like military experience, introduced many to a variety of ways of being religious. It was not, as some feared, that the colleges intentionally sought to destroy religious faith. Rather, those with sustained exposure to persons from other faiths or even from other Protestant denominations lost much of their apprehension of alternative religions. As a result, they began to see the various faith communities as functionally equivalent, with none having an exclusive claim to ultimate truth. Some Protestants did demur, believing this sort of exposure dangerous since it led to compromise with falsehood and contamination of authentic faith.

Mobility, military service, and collegiate experience were all catalysts for the sharp increase in interreligious marriage as the nation moved into the Cold War era. Marriage across Protestant denominational lines had long been common. Now there came a dramatic increase in marriages between Protestants and Roman Catholics and between Christians and Jews; the boundaries separating these larger faith traditions had previously proved far more unyielding than those between Protestant denominations. Then, too, hundreds of Protestant Americans who served in the Pacific during the war brought home spouses from various Asian or Pacific cultures, who, like other immigrants, sought to retain their religions of origin. As individual families carved out a religious identity of their own, ties to religious communities brought together in a single household varied. Some compromised by identifying with yet another religious group; sometimes husbands and wives went their separate ways in terms of religious affiliation, with children exposed to both, sometimes just to one, often to none. Many quietly dropped out of organized religion.

However families resolved the multiple religious heritages within the household, new dimensions of pluralism were taking on increasing importance in the daily lives of millions. The burgeoning ecumenical movement, primarily among Protestants, also contributed. Cooperative endeavors through various councils of churches, mergers of denominations within the same religious family such as the reunion of northern and southern Presbyterians in the 1980s, and talks of church union spearheaded by the Consultation on Church Union formed in the early 1960s all created the impression that all Protestant bodies were pretty much alike, that denominations per se made no difference and had no distinctive ways of determining what Christian faith was all about. If labels made no difference, then a passionate loyalty to a particular denomination made no difference. In promoting unity among Protestants, the ecumenical movement unwittingly eroded denominational loyalty.

In addition, social forces unleashed by the civil rights movement and then the antiwar efforts associated with U.S. military involvement in Vietnam challenged all forms of authority within American life, including the authority of religious groups and their leaders. The baby-boom generation, reaching adulthood during that turbulent epoch, tended more than earlier generations to shun commitment to all social institutions, including religious ones. Reared during a time when denominational loyalty was no longer paramount, they lacked a sense of identification with organized religion. Although earlier generations had drifted away from religious communities in late adolescence and early young adulthood, they had generally returned when they began to raise their own families, if only to provide some moral or religious anchor for their children. Boomers did not return in the same proportion. Many, however, identified themselves as spiritual, even if they shunned the designation of being religious.

Robert Wuthnow (1998) has argued that in the second half of the twentieth century, Americans exchanged the idea of a religious "home" or center, usually fixed around a religious tradition or group, for a religious "quest," something far more individualistic and idiosyncratic. An article in a popular journal captured the mood in its subtitle: "Design Your Own God" (Creedon, 1998). Women from the boomer generation, for example, have probed resources that take them well beyond the standard denominations to forge a spirituality that speaks to the female experience. Some draw on pagan and pre-Christian forms of religious expression, sparking panic in some Christian circles that feminist spirituality threatens the integrity of the churches. All of the following signal the dynamism of a spirituality that exists alongside and frequently outside organized religious institutions:

1. Those who gather in forest groves to celebrate rituals marking passages unique to women from childbirth to menopause.

2. Those who rarely attend worship but claim to be very spiritual because they occasionally read the Bible along with practicing Zen meditation techniques.

3. Those who fashion altars in their homes that may have a cross juxtaposed with New Age crystals.

4. Those who sport WWJD (What Would Jesus Do?) bracelets the way a previous generation took the cross and made it a piece of jewelry.

5. Those who walk the universal mandala, the labyrinth, in silence because organized religion has become too noisy.

At the same time, the Christian groups that have been growing have tended to be those that have resisted this privatization of spirituality. At the peak of the civil rights and antiwar movements, careful analysts recognized that among Protestants, those denominations and especially those independent congregations that were more orthodox in their religious teaching, more inclined to variations of fundamentalist and Pentecostal expression, were growing (Kelley, 1977). For generations, it had been easy to consign such forms of Christianity to the periphery. Scholars had mistakenly assumed that fundamentalism and Pentecostalism drew only from the economically disadvantaged and politically powerless.

Fundamentalists, Pentecostals, and other evangelicals had developed networks of association that forged enduring bonds and provided resources to build solid foundations for vital institutions during their time on the margins (Carpenter, 1997). They gathered strength from the abiding conviction that truth could not be questioned, thereby protecting the basis for belief and practice from the cultural attacks on authority that marked the larger culture in the last half of the twentieth century. If mainline Protestants and Catholics were torn apart by debates over civil rights, Vietnam, and feminism, these expressions of Christianity offered a refuge, a sense of direction, and a secure way of looking at the world, one not battered by social controversy but buttressed by a certainty that they still had a corner on the Truth. Their presence complicates efforts to discern any common religious base to American culture, and their leaders are often in the forefront of debates about public education, such as teaching intelligent design.

Some talk about a "Judeo-Christian tradition," an artificial construct at best, as reflecting the dominant religious mood. In the early twenty-first century, particularly in the wake of the terrorist attacks of September 2001, many of those who called for the posting of the Ten Commandments in courthouses, schools, and other public buildings reflected a hope that this amorphous amalgamation of traditions with roots in the biblical text could still provide a base for social cohesion. But their efforts were undercut by another facet of the religious pluralism that had become characteristic of American society—namely, the dramatic increase in the number of Americans who identified with religious traditions such as Islam, Buddhism, and Hinduism.

THE NEW FACES OF PLURALISM

Changes in immigration laws in 1965 have resulted in a dramatic increase in immigrants from both Latin America and Asia, and with them has come a burgeoning interest in the religions indigenous to those areas and fresh awareness of the links between ethnicity and religious style. In the last decade of the twentieth century, the greatest proportional growth in immigration from Latin America, the Near East, and Asia came in the Sun Belt. From

1990 to 2000, the percentage of those foreign born in North Carolina and Georgia (as well as in Nevada) increased by more than 200 percent, and in 2000, more than one-quarter of the population of California was foreign born (Malone et al., 2003). In Whitfield County, Georgia, the heart of the state's carpet industry, Hispanic Americans now constitute almost 50 percent of the population, and more than 50 percent of students in the lower grades of the public schools are Hispanic (Mahoney, 2002). Figures reported in the 2000 census indicate that 4.2 percent of the U.S. population was born in Asia (Reeves & Bennett, 2004), a percentage roughly equivalent to the number of residents and citizens in the United States born in Mexico, Cuba, and El Salvador and growing rapidly. By the early twenty-first century, many believed that those of Hispanic stock outnumbered African Americans and had come to constitute the largest single ethnic minority cluster in the nation.

In most urban areas across the nation, Roman Catholic parishes have added services in Spanish, recognizing that Hispanic Catholicism brings a rich blend of traditions to Catholic life, many reflecting the cultures of Central and South America. Cuban immigrants in the Miami area, for example, have erected a shrine to Our Lady of Charity that signals both a particular religious sensibility and a Cuban nationalism (Tweed, 1997). In a sense, these immigrants are simply doing what Italian and Irish Catholics and others did more than a century before—namely, bringing with them the festivals, patron saints, and fusion of religious and ethnic ways that give them a sense of identity and cultural cohesion.

Some Protestant denominations have launched special ministries to Spanish-speaking Americans, while many Pentecostal congregations, like their Roman Catholic counterparts, now provide services and programs designed to reflect the spirituality and concerns of Hispanic followers. Theologically, Hispanic Americans—both Protestant and Catholic—tend to be more traditional and conservative in their thinking, even as their practice reveals considerable syncretism in its expression. Even within the Christian tradition, it has become impossible to look at Anglo-American styles as normative.

Immigration from Asia swelled the ranks of Hindus, Buddhists, and Muslims in the United States. American interest in Asian religious cultures has a long history. In the nineteenth century, Transcendentalist writers such as Ralph Waldo Emerson were drawn to Asian religious philosophy, while thousands devoured reports of seemingly exotic religious practices in Asia through letters from missionaries published in popular religious magazines. But, except for a relatively small number of immigrants from China and Japan on the West Coast, few Americans had first-hand experience with these religions; even fewer were inclined to practice them.

A more direct exposure came with the World's Parliament of Religions, held in Chicago in 1893 in conjunction with the Columbian Exposition that marked the four-hundredth anniversary of Columbus's first voyage to America. Representatives from a number of religions, including Hindus and Buddhists, were invited to Chicago; some, like the Hindu philosopher Vivekananda, remained in the United States for an extended period, speaking in the nation's larger cities and attracting some interest, primarily among intellectuals, in the philosophy behind these religious approaches. With American involvement in military endeavors in Asia in World War II, the Korean War, and the Vietnam War, thousands had more direct exposure to Asian ways of being religious. Some brought spouses back to the United States who sought to continue the religious ways in which they had been nurtured.

The 1960s also witnessed a spate of Asian religious figures who sought to gain American converts, particularly from among those disenchanted with traditional American religious

Table 5.3   Estimates of Adherents of Asian Religions

	1900	1970	2000
Buddhists	30,000	200,000	2,000,000
Hindus	1,000	100,000	950,000
Muslims*	10,000	800,000	3,950,000

*Not including the Nation of Islam.

Figures based on data from the U.S. Bureau of the Census

life and who saw the dominant religious institutions as mired in racism and torn apart over government policy in Vietnam. The International Society of Krishna Consciousness, more popularly known as Hare Krishna, became a familiar presence in cities and college towns; thousands were drawn to practices like Transcendental Meditation, promoted by the Maharishi Mahesh Yogi and made fashionable by celebrities like the Beatles. A generation later, the Dalai Lama would become a symbol of American interest in Tibetan Buddhism, aided by the devotion of well-known figures like Richard Gere.

While some forms of Buddhism, such as that promoted by the Dalai Lama, and some popular forms of Hinduism, like Krishna Consciousness, have attracted primarily American devotees, the majority of American Buddhists, Hindus, and Muslims come from families who are doing what Americans have done for centuries—practicing the religion that the first generation of immigrants brought with them, albeit adapting it to the American context. What is changing the face of pluralism in the first decade of the twenty-first century is the steadily growing presence of immigrants for whom these traditions represent the heritages they bring with them when they come to the United States. Table 5.3 illustrates their relative growth.

Estimates suggest that the United States was home to only 30,000 Buddhists in 1900, but to two million a century later; to a mere 1000 Hindus in 1900, but 950,000 at century's end; to just 10,000 Muslims in 1900, but perhaps—and the estimates vary widely here—between two and one-half to four million a century later, not counting those affiliated with the Nation of Islam (U.S. Census Bureau, 2000). The Hindu tradition has never been inclined to proselytize; in other cultural contexts, Buddhists and Muslims have been more active in seeking converts. However, in the U.S. context, there is relatively little association among the various immigrant Buddhist communities and the centers that cater primarily to American converts to the various stands of Buddhism. American Muslims report that they are reticent to proselytize because popular perception links Muslims to international terrorism. Those Americans who have converted to Islam are more likely to be persons of African descent; they join a small but growing number of African immigrants who are also Muslim.

The growth of these groups signals the pluralism that marks American religious life and the impossibility of regarding a single tradition as normative or perhaps even culturally dominant in the twenty-first century. Alongside the mushrooming pluralism linked to immigration is the slow but steady increase in the number of Americans who eschew formal religious identity altogether and do not identify themselves as members of any religious body. Recent studies suggest that the proportion of those unaffiliated grew from one out of five Americans in 1991 to at least one of every three by 2004 ("Ratio," 2004). Add to that cluster the millions who called themselves "spiritual, but not religious" (Fuller, 2001), and it is clear that the very character of pluralism has expanded in such a way as to undermine any assumption that the nation now shares a common religious base.

SUMMARY AND EDUCATIONAL IMPLICATIONS

From the colonial period to the twenty-first century, the American landscape became ever more religiously diverse. If the first European invaders brought with them a range of Protestant sensibilities, their efforts to plant a Christian culture in America always faced challenges. These challenges came from the Native Americans whose tribal religions once flourished in the same places where Europeans settled as well as from enslaved Africans who managed to sustain an African religious consciousness despite the horrors of slavery. They also came from a variety of other groups who promoted alternative ways of being religious. Diversity was part of the American religious experience from the outset.

That diversity received acknowledgment when the Bill of Rights added an amendment to the U.S. Constitution guaranteeing the free exercise of religion. But the questions of what free exercise means and how to balance the religious sensibilities of the majority with those of many minorities have challenged the courts ever since. In the twentieth century, many of those challenges concerned the role of religion in public education. Today some of those challenges come from persons who wish to include religious theories such as intelligent design in the required curriculum.

Immigration has been a major force enhancing religious diversity over the centuries. Immigration helped cement a Roman Catholic and Jewish presence in American life in the nineteenth century. By the dawn of the twenty-first century, immigration was swelling the ranks of Buddhists, Hindus, Muslims, and a variety of others who called the United States home. At the same time, the number of Americans claiming no religious identity or formal affiliation was rising slowly, but steadily.

If public education in its early years in the middle third of the nineteenth century could assume that the bulk of students shared a broadly based evangelical Protestant background, by the end of that century those assumptions were no longer viable, although they had by no means vanished. By the end of the twentieth century, however, it was clear that religious pluralism rendered it impossible for education or any other dimension of the public sector to presume that a majority shared common beliefs and values—or even a common religious sensibility. As federal policy moved in the direction of funding "faith-based initiatives" to deal with ongoing social problems on a local level, it was increasingly difficult to determine how to distribute such funds without favoring any one, how to assure that recipients were not using funds to coerce those being helped into aligning with the religious group, and even how to ascertain which groups represented legitimate "faith-based" entities. Even more challenging is deciding how to study the religious mosaic that is the United States without either presuming allegiance to a particular faith tradition or granting any one faith community a privileged position.

RESOURCES

Jon Butler and Harry S. Stout (1998) have edited a seventeen-volume series of texts on religion in American life suitable for classroom use at the secondary level. Published by Oxford University Press, some are chronological in focus (colonial America, the nineteenth century, the twentieth century), some treat particular groups (Catholics, Jews, Mormons, Protestants, Muslims, Buddhists, Hindus, Sikhs), and others deal with specific topics (African American religion, church and state, immigration, women, Native American religion, alternative religions). The concluding volume is a biographical supplement and index. All are by leading scholars.

Also helpful is the nine-volume "Religion by Region" series (2004–2006) produced under the auspices of the Greenberg Center for the Study of Religion in Public Life at Trinity College, Hartford, CT. All are published by AltaMira Press. Eight focus on distinctive geographic regions of the country, examining how the particular religious cultures and history of a region have implications for the public policy, including education. The final volume looks at the role of region more generally in determining the interplay of religion and public policy.

Numerous materials appropriate for classroom use are identified in the several sections of the website for the Religion and Public Education Resource Center based at the California State University at Chico: www.csuchico.edu/rs/rperc.

Also specializing in teaching resources about American religious culture is the Wabash Center: www.wabashcenter.wabash.edu.

The Pluralism Project at Harvard University has focused primarily on the new diversity represented by the growth of Buddhism, Hinduism, and Islam in the last half-century. Its website includes not only state-by-state maps, but also a directory of religious centers, news summaries, profiles of groups, and teaching resources: http://www.pluralism.org.

There are also helpful websites on particular groups or topics that illustrate the diversity within American religious life. On African American religious history, for example, see: http://northstar.vassar.edu.

The Cushwa Center at Notre Dame University offers many resources on facets of U.S. Roman Catholic life and history: www.nd.edu/~cushwa.

Similarly, the American Jewish Historical Society identifies much that is useful to tracking the American Jewish experience: www.ajhs.org.

Questions and Activities

1. The principle of separation of church and state is a keystone of religious freedom in the United States. Investigate how closely church and state are tied together in the United States today. For example, can churches receive federal funding? If so, under what conditions? Can parochial and other religious schools receive support from public school districts? If so, what kind of support can they receive and what conditions do they need to meet in order to qualify for support?

2. Large numbers of African Americans and European Americans are members of Protestant churches and share religious traditions. However, services in African American and European American churches can be very different. Visit a Methodist

church service and an African Methodist Episcopal (AME) church service. Compare the services at the two churches by identifying factors such as the length of service, the music, and the enthusiasm of the minister. Discuss your findings with your classmates. An informative reference for this activity is *The Black Church in the African American Experience* (Lincoln & Mamiya, 1990).

3. The media have become a powerful force for disseminating religious messages that are tied to political positions. Form a group of approximately five students and identify five different religious television programs to watch over a one-month period. Record key themes that are embedded in the programs. Analyze the themes and ideas to determine whether they include political messages. Discuss the extent to which the paradox that Lippy discusses at the beginning of the chapter is being exacerbated by the media.

4. Most racial and ethnic groups in the United States are members of the major faith communities. However, most faith communities in the United States are segregated. Investigate churches, mosques, and temples in your community to find out the extent to which faith communities are segregated. Interview heads of religious communities. Ask them why they think faith communities tend to be predominately made up of one racial or ethnic group. Also ask them whether they have made efforts to desegregate their faith communities.

5. Revivals continue to play an important role in evangelical Protestant churches. Go to the Internet and investigate the types of revivals that are being held today, where they are being held, their goals, and their intended audience. To what extent do modern revivals reflect Lippy's discussion about the new faces of pluralism?

6. Religion in the United States is frequently associated with the roles that men have played in formulating religious ideas and institutions. However, women have made significant contributions to religious life in the United States. Read the biographies of women religious leaders such as Mary Baker Eddy and Ellen G. Harmon White. Also read *Righteous Discontent: The Women's Movement in the Black Church, 1880–1920* (Higginbotham, 1993). Discuss how gender has influenced the lives of women in the church.

7. How does social class intersect with religion? Are religious congregations primarily composed of people from the same social-class background? How do different religious organizations respond to low-income people? How do low-income people in your community feel about religious organizations? Study these questions by dividing the class into groups.

References

Butler, J., & Stout, H. S. (Eds.). (1998). *Religion in America: A Reader.* New York: Oxford University Press.

Carpenter, J. A. (1997). *Revive Us Again: The Reawakening of American Fundamentalism.* New York: Oxford University Press.

Creedon, J. (1998, July–August). God with a Million Faces: Design Your Own God. *Utne Reader,* pp. 42–48.

Fuller, R.C. (2001). *Spiritual but not Religious: Understanding Unchurched America*. New York: Oxford University Press.

Gaustad, E. S., & Barlow, P. L. (2001). *New Historical Atlas of Religion in America*. San Francisco: Harper.

Herberg, W. (1960). *Protestant, Catholic, Jew: An Essay in American Religious Sociology* (rev. ed.) Garden City, NY: Doubleday.

Higginbotham, E. B. (1993). *Righteous Discontent: The Women's Movement in the Black Church, 1880–1920*. Cambridge, MA: Harvard University Press.

Kelley, D. M. (1977). *Why Conservative Churches Are Growing* (2nd ed.). New York: Harper.

Lincoln, C. E., & Mamiya, L. M. (1990). *The Black Church in the African American Experience*. Durham, NC: Duke University Press.

Lippy, C. H., Choquette, R., & Poole, S. (1992). *Christianity Comes to the Americans, 1492–1776*. New York: Paragon House.

Mahony, P. (2002, July 26). Study Says Hispanic Buying Power Rising. *Chattanooga Times Free Press*. Retrieved May 16, 2003, from www.timesfreepress.com/2002/july/26jul/disposableincomehispanic._html.

Malone, N., Baluja, K. F., Costanzo, J. M., & Davis, C. J. (2003). "The Foreign-Born Population: 2000." *Census 2000 Brief* C2KBR-34. Washington, DC: U.S. Department of Commerce Census Bureau.

Mayhew, J. (1749). *Seven Sermons*. Boston: Rogers & Fowle.

Miller, R. T., & Flowers, R. B. (Eds.). (1987). *Toward Benevolent Neutrality: Church, State, and the Supreme Court* (3rd ed.). Waco, TX: Baylor University Press.

"Ratio of 'Unchurched' up Sharply Since 1991" (2004, June 1). *Christian Century*, p. 15.

Reeves, T. J., & Bennett, C. E. (2004). "We the People: Asians in the United States." *Census 2000 Special Reports* CENSR-17. Washington DC: U.S. Department of Commerce Bureau Census Bureau.

Strong, J. (1964). *Our Country* (J. Herbst, Ed.). Cambridge, MA: Harvard University Press. (Original work published 1886.)

Teepen, T. (2005, 30 December). Intelligent Design Lives On. *Chattanooga Times Free Press*, p. B6.

Tweed, T. A. (1997). *Our Lady of the Exile: Diasporic Religion at a Cuban Catholic Shrine in Miami*. New York: Oxford University Press.

U.S. Bureau of the Census. (2000). *Statistical Abstract of the United States*. Retrieved May 1, 2003, from www.census.gov/statab/www/.

Westerhoff, J. H. (1978). *McGuffey and His Readers: Piety, Morality, and Education in Nineteenth Century America*. Nashville, TN: Abingdon.

Williams, P. W. (1980). *Popular Religion in America: Symbolic Change and the Modernization Process in Historical Perspective*. Englewood Cliffs, NJ: Prentice Hall.

Wilson, J. F. (Ed.). (1965). *Church and State in American History*. Boston: Heath.

Wuthnow, R. (1998). *After Heaven: Spirituality in America Since the 1950s*. Berkeley: University of California Press.

Eliminating gender bias will increase learning opportunities for girls and boys from diverse racial, ethnic, social-class, and language groups.

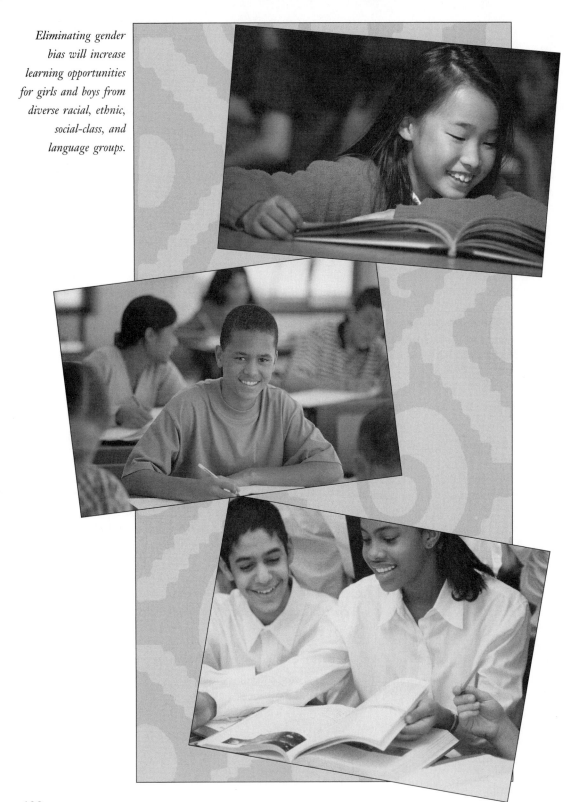

Gender

Social, economic, and political conditions for women have improved substantially since the women's rights movement emerged as part of the civil rights movement of the 1960s and 1970s. However, gender discrimination and inequality still exist in schools and in society at large. In 2004, the median earnings for women who were full-time workers were 77 percent of those for men, up from 73 percent in 1998 (DeNavas-Walt, Proctor, & Lee, 2005). The status of women in the United States within the last two decades has changed substantially. More women are now working outside the home than ever before, and more women are heads of households. In 2004, 59 percent of women worked outside the home, making up 49 percent of the total work force (Women in the Labor Force, 2005). In 2004, 22.5 percent of households in the United States were headed by women (Dalaker, Proctor, & Lee, 2000). A growing percentage of women and their dependents constitutes the nation's poor. Some writers use the term *feminization of poverty* to describe this development. In 2000, 53 percent of poor families in the United States were headed by women (Dalaker & Proctor, 2000).

The three chapters in Part III of this book describe the status of women in the United States, the ways in which schools perpetuate gender discrimination, and strategies that educators can use to create equal educational opportunities for both female and male students. As Sadker and Zittleman point out in Chapter 6, both males and females are harmed by sex stereotypes and gender discrimination. Tetreault, in Chapter 7, describes how school knowledge is dominated by male perspectives and how teachers can infuse their curricula with perspectives from both genders and thereby expand their students' thinking and insights. In Chapter 8, Butler and Raynor discuss how women of color have often been ignored by the women's movement, which is predominately a White, middle-class phenomenon. They describe perspectives and content that will enable teachers to integrate their curricula with the experiences and cultures of women of color.

References

Dalaker, J., & Proctor, B. D. (2000) *Poverty in the United States: 1999.* U.S. Census Bureau, Current Population Reports, Series P60-210. Washington, DC: U.S. Government Printing Office.

DeNavas-Walt, C., Proctor, B. D., & Lee, C. H. (2005). *U.S. Census Bureau, Current Population Reports, P60-229, Income, Poverty, and Health Insurance Coverage in the United States: 2004.* Washington, D.C.: U.S. Government Printing Office.

Women in the Labor Force: A Databook (2005). Retrieved January 30, 2006, from http://www.bls.gov/cps/wlf-databook2005.htm.

U.S. Census Bureau. (2001) *Population Division and Housing and Household Economic Statistics Division.* Retrieved January 23, 2006, from http://www.census.gov/population/www/pop-profile/natproj.html.

CHAPTER 6

Gender Bias: From Colonial America To Today's Classrooms

David Sadker and
Karen Zittleman*

A sage once remarked that if fish were anthropologists, the last thing they would discover would be the water. We are all like those fish, swimming in a sea of sexism, but few of us see the water, the gender bias that engulfs us. Sexism in schools is a major influence on children in urban, suburban and rural America, in wealthy and poor communities, in communities that are diverse as well as those that are homogeneous. In short, gender is a demographic that binds all schools and challenges all educators. Yet a cultural shortsightedness, coined "gender blindness," makes it difficult for educators to see how sexism influences virtually every aspect of how we teach and learn (Bailey, Scantlebury, & Letts, 1997).

In *Failing at Fairness* (1994), Myra and David Sadker referred to gender blindness in schools as "a syntax of sexism so elusive that most teachers and students were completely unaware of its influence" (p. 2). It is still elusive, and many teachers still miss it. Teacher education programs do little to prepare teachers to see, much less undo, subtle gender bias that shortchanges children (Zittleman, 2005). Students, on the other hand, view a very different world, a school filled with gender challenges. In a study of more than 400 middle schoolers, fighting, discipline, poor grades, fear of homophobia, and difficulty with friendships and emotions were readily identified as gender issues confronting males. For females, relational aggression (gossiping, spreading rumors, and inability to trust friends) topped the list. Students also noted girls' deliberate efforts to take easier courses, do poorly on tests and assignments, and "act dumb" in school to gain popularity or have a boyfriend (Zittleman, 2005).

---

*Myra Sadker co-authored earlier versions of this chapter. Myra died in 1995 while undergoing treatment for breast cancer. To learn more about her work, visit www.sadker.org.

Unfortunately, many of today's boys and girls are unaware of the historical struggle to gain even rudimentary educational rights for females. As a result, they—as well as their teachers—lack the perspective and tools necessary to challenge sexism in school.

This chapter provides a context for understanding gender bias in school. It includes (1) a brief historical overview of women's struggle for educational opportunity; (2) an update of the progress made and yet to be made in insuring gender equity in schools; (3) an analysis of gender bias in curriculum; (4) insights into gender bias in instruction; (5) a peek at some of today's trends and challenges concerning gender issues in school; and (6) a dozen suggestions for you on how to create gender-equitable classrooms.

THE HIDDEN CIVIL RIGHTS STRUGGLE

For centuries, women fought to open the schoolhouse door. The education of America's girls was so limited that less than one-third of the women in colonial America could even sign their names. Although a woman gave the first plot of ground for a free school in New England, female children were not allowed to attend the school. In fact, women were commonly viewed as being mentally and morally inferior to men, relegated to learning only domestic skills. Not until the 1970s and 1980s did they win the right to be admitted to previously all-male Ivy League colleges and universities, and not until the 1990s did they breach the walls of the Citadel and the Virginia Military Institute. It is rare indeed that such a monumental civil rights struggle—so long, so recent, and impacting so many—has remained so invisible. Let us take a brief look at this hidden civil rights struggle.

During the colonial period, dame schools educated very young boys and girls (with few exceptions, *White* boys and girls) in the homes of women who had the time and desire to teach. Girls lucky enough to attend such schools would learn domestic skills along with reading (so that they could one day read the Bible to their children). For the boys, such schools also taught them how to write and prepared them for further, more formal education. Girls graduated to the kitchen and the sewing area, focusing on their futures as wives and mothers.

With a new democracy came new ideas and the promise of greater educational opportunities for females. Elementary schools gradually opened their doors to females, and for the families financially able, secondary schools became possible in the form of female seminaries. Seminaries provided a protected and supervised climate melding religious and academic lessons. In New York, Emma Hart Willard battled to establish the Troy Female Seminary, and in Massachusetts, Mary Lyon created Mount Holyoke, a seminary that eventually became a noted women's college. Seminaries often emphasized self-denial and strict discipline, considered important elements in molding devout wives and Christian mothers. By the 1850s, with help from Quakers such as Harriet Beecher Stowe, Myrtilla Miner established the Miner Normal School for Colored Girls in the nation's capital, providing new educational opportunities for African American women. While these seminaries sometimes offered a superior education, they were also trapped in a paradox they could never fully resolve: They were educating girls for a world not ready to accept educated women. Seminaries sometimes went to extraordinary lengths to reconcile this conflict. Emma Willard's Troy Female Seminary was devoted to "professionalizing motherhood." (Who could not support motherhood?) But en route to reshaping motherhood, seminaries reshaped teaching.

For the teaching profession, seminaries became the source of new ideas and new recruits. Seminary leaders such as Emma Hart Willard and Catherine Beecher wrote textbooks on how to teach and how to teach more humanely than was the practice at the time. They denounced corporal punishment and promoted more cooperative educational practices. Since school was seen as an extension of the home and another arena for raising children, seminary graduates were allowed to become teachers—at least until they decided to marry. More than 80 percent of the graduates of Troy Female Seminary and Mount Holyoke became teachers. Female teachers were particularly attractive to school districts—not only because of their teaching effectiveness but also because they were typically paid one-third to one-half the salary of male teachers.

By the end of the Civil War, a number of colleges and universities, especially tax-supported ones, were desperate for dollars. Institutions of higher learning experienced a serious student shortage due to Civil War casualties, and women became the source of much-needed tuition dollars. But female wallets did not buy on-campus equality. Women often faced separate courses and hostility from male students and professors. At state universities, such as the University of Michigan, male students would stamp their feet in protest when a woman entered a classroom, a gesture some professors appreciated.

While an economic necessity for many colleges, educating women was not a popular idea, and some people even considered it dangerous. In *Sex in Education*, Dr. Edward Clarke (1873), a member of Harvard's medical faculty, argued that women attending high school and college were at medical risk. According to Dr. Clarke, the blood destined for the development and health of their ovaries would be redirected to their brains by the stress of study. Too much education would leave women with "monstrous brains and puny bodies . . . flowing thought and constipated bowels" (pp. 120–128). Clarke recommended that females be provided with a less demanding education, easier courses, no competition, and "rest" periods so that their reproductive organs could develop. The female brain was too small, and the female body too vulnerable, for such mental challenges. He maintained that allowing girls to attend places such as Harvard would pose a serious health threat to the women themselves, with sterility and hysteria potential outcomes. It would take another century before Harvard and other prestigious men's colleges would finally admit women.

Dr. Clarke's ideas constructed some powerful fears in women. M. Carey Thomas, future president of Bryn Mawr and one of the first women to earn a Ph.D. in the United States, wrote of the fears created by writers like Clarke. "I remember often praying about it, and begging God that if it were true that because I was a girl, I could not successfully master Greek and go to college, and understand things, to kill me for it" (cited in Sadker & Sadker, 2005, pp. 459–460). In 1895, the faculty of the University of Virginia concluded that "women were often physically unsexed by the strains of study" (cited in Sadker & Sadker, 2005, p. 460). Parents, fearing for the health of their daughters, would often place them in less demanding programs reserved for females or would keep them out of advanced education entirely. Even today, the echoes of Clarke's warnings resonate—some people still see well-educated women as less attractive, or view advanced education as "too stressful" for females, or believe that education is more important for males than for females.

There were clear racist overtones in Clarke's writing. The women attending college were overwhelmingly White, and education delayed marriage and decreased childbearing. As a result, while women of color were reproducing at "alarming" rates, wealthy White women were choosing college rather than motherhood. The dangers to the White establishment were clear.

By the twentieth century, women were winning greater access to educational programs at all levels, although well into the 1970s gender-segregated programs were the rule. Although females attended the same schools as males, they often received a less valuable education. Commercial courses prepared girls to become secretaries, while vocational programs channeled them into cosmetology and other low-paying occupations. After World War II it was not unusual for a university to require a married woman to submit a letter from her husband granting her permission to enroll in courses before she would be admitted. With the passage of Title IX of the Education Amendments of 1972, females saw significant progress toward gaining access to educational programs, but not equality.

Title IX of the 1972 Education Amendments Act became law as the women's movement gained momentum. The opening section of Title IX states:

> No person in the United States shall, on the basis of sex, be
> excluded from participation in, be denied the benefits of, or be
> subjected to discrimination under any education program or
> activity receiving federal financial assistance.

While most people have heard of Title IX in relation to sports, it reaches far beyond the athletic field. Every public school and most of the nation's colleges and universities are covered under Title IX, which prohibits discrimination in school admissions, in counseling and guidance, in competitive athletics, in student rules and regulations, and in access to programs and courses, including vocational education and physical education. Title IX also applies to sex discrimination in employment practices, including interviewing and recruitment, hiring and promotion, compensation, job assignments, and fringe benefits. Although enforcement remains sporadic, even this weakened entitlement of educational rights was targeted for elimination by the conservative political movement of the 1990s.

In *Backlash*, Susan Faludi (1991) documents the negative impact on women resulting from the conservative political gains of the 1980s and 1990s. Most of the federal educational programs designed to assist girls and women have been eliminated, and Title IX itself is often under attack. In high school and college, a "glass wall" still keeps women from entering the most lucrative careers and keeps men from entering traditionally female jobs. In certain vocational areas, such as engineering, physics, chemistry, and computer science, few women can be found. In nursing, teaching, library science, and social work, few men can be found. Even in high-status careers where tremendous progress has been made, like medicine and law, a second generation of bias persists. In both professions, women find themselves channeled into the least prestigious, least profitable specialties. Being aware of these historical threads, the channeling of females into certain specialties, and the devaluation of their worth as students or employees can help us to tease out the subtle (and not-so-subtle) biases that persist today.

By the mid-1990s, a militant cadre of political conservatives alleged that the feminist movement had gone too far and claimed that the real victims of sexism were males. After all, they point out, boys receive lower report card grades, are assigned in greater numbers to special education classes, are disciplined more, and are more likely to drop out of school. While many of their criticisms of educational research were politically motivated, they did remind us of the problems faced by males. As a result, some called for a return to separate schools for boys and girls, schools that could address the biological differences of each.

While some believe that gender bias is no longer a major problem, others see it as still virulent. Let's take a look at some of the salient statistics.

REPORT CARD: THE COST OF SEXISM IN SCHOOLS

Below is a report card you will not find in any elementary or secondary school, yet these statistics document the loss that both girls and boys suffer because of sex bias in society and in education. Decades after the passage of Title IX, gender inequities continue to permeate schools and shortchange our children (ACT, 2005; American Association of University Women [AAUW], 1998a, 2000, 2004; American Psychological Association, 1999; College Board, 2005; National Center of Educational Statistics [NCES], 2004a, 2004b, 2006; National Coalition for Women and Girls in Education [NCWGE], 2002; National Women's Law Center [NWLC], 2005b; Sadker & Sadker, 1994; Orfield, et al, 2004).

Academic

Girls

- In the early grades, girls score ahead of boys in verbal skills; their academic performance is equal to that of boys in math and almost equal to boys in science. However, as they progress through school, many of their high-stakes achievement test scores (such as the SATs) decline. Girls are the only group in our society to begin school with a testing advantage, yet they leave school with a testing disadvantage.

- Across all racial and ethnic groups, males outperform females on mathematics sections of the Scholastic Assessment Test (SAT). On the SAT verbal sections, males also continue to outperform females across all races and ethnicities, with one exception—Black females earn higher verbal scores than their Black male peers. Gender differences on the American College Testing Program Examination (ACT) are less pronounced, with females ahead in verbal scores and males in mathematics and science. On the majority of SAT IIs and GREs, males also score higher than females.

- Female enrollment in mathematics and science courses has increased dramatically in recent years. However, boys still take more advanced courses, such as calculus and physics, and score higher on competitive tests, such as the Advanced Placement tests.

- Although elementary school males and females like and do well in math and science, as they go through school, girls become less positive and do less well. By the third grade, 51 percent of males and 37 percent of females have used a microscope in class. And boys are far more likely to lead science demonstrations, while females assume note-taking responsibilities.

- Computer science and technology reflect continuing gender (and racial) disparities. Jobs requiring technology skills will increase by 5.6 million by 2008, yet girls are five times less likely than boys to consider technology-related careers. Girls from all ethnic groups rate themselves considerably lower than boys on technological ability, and boys account for 83 percent of all Advanced Placement computer science test-takers. One study found that 71 percent of male teachers are more likely to attribute boys' success in technology to talent, while dismissing girls' success as due solely to luck or diligence.

- In spite of the performance decline on many standardized achievement tests, girls frequently receive better grades in school. This may be one of the rewards they receive for more quiet and docile classroom behavior. However, their silence may be at the cost of achievement, independence, and self-reliance.

- Females experience fewer academic contacts in class. They are less likely to be called on by name, are asked fewer complex and abstract questions, receive less praise or constructive feedback, and are given less direction on how to do things for themselves. In short, girls are more likely to be invisible members of classrooms.

- Gifted girls, especially in math and science, are less likely to participate in special or accelerated programs to develop their talent, and this is particularly true for African American and Hispanic girls. Girls who suffer from learning disabilities are also less likely to be identified or enrolled in special education programs than are learning-disabled boys.

- The overall female dropout rate is in dispute but ranges from 8 to 28 percent. That dropout rate is approximately twice as high for African American girls than for white girls and still higher for Latinas.

- More women than men are college students and attain the majority of bachelor and master's degrees. Women earn the majority of degrees in education, psychology, biological sciences, and accounting. For professional degrees, women lag behind men in attaining medical (55%–45%), and dental (61%–39%) degrees. Women earn more degrees in pharmacy (65%–35%) and veterinary medicine (71%–29%) than do males. And in law, women and men have reached parity in degree attainment. Across all racial and ethnic groups, White and Asian females are more likely to attend college than are Hispanics and African Americans.

Boys

- Boys are more likely to be scolded and reprimanded in school, even when their misbehavior is equivalent to that of females. Males are more likely to be referred to school authorities for disciplinary action than are girls. They constitute 71 percent of school suspensions.

- Boys are far more likely to be identified as exhibiting learning disabilities, reading problems, and mental retardation. As a result, they are more likely to be enrolled in classes for the learning disabled and emotionally disturbed.

- Males receive lower report card grades from elementary school through college. In their elementary and high school years, they are more likely to be grade repeaters. Boys are also more likely to drop out of school than are girls.

The overall male dropout rate is elusive, ranging from 11 to 36 percent, with some reports putting the African American and Latino dropout rate as high as 50 percent or more.

- Males enroll in fewer English, sociology, psychology, foreign language, and fine arts courses than do females.

- African American males are about half as likely as African American females to take Advanced Placement exams.

- Males lag behind females in a variety of extracurricular areas, including school government, literary activities, and the performing arts.

- The National Assessment of Educational Progress indicates that males perform significantly below females in writing and reading achievement. Boys often regard reading and writing as "feminine" subjects that threaten their masculinity.

- Men are the minority (44 percent) of students enrolled in both undergraduate and graduate institutions, and they lag behind women in degree attainment at the associate, bachelor's, and master's, levels. Males dominate areas such as business, computer science, and engineering. Although White males and females attend college in fairly equal proportions, African American and Hispanic males are particularly underrepresented at all levels of education.

Psychological and Physical

Girls

- In sixth and seventh grades, girls rate popularity as more important than academic competence or independence.

- Sexual harassment—words and actions—begins in elementary school. Four out five girls, and almost as many boys, experience some form of sexual harassment during their schooling years, often negatively impacting school attendance and performance.

- More than 60 percent of adolescent girls report dieting, most in order to "look better." Frequent dieting in adolescence is linked to increased smoking. Females are less likely to engage in physical activity than their male peers.

- About 820,00 U.S. teenage girls get pregnant each year, a higher relative percentage than in most Western nations, and 35 percent of teens will become pregnant at least once. Teen pregnancy costs the United States at least $7 billion annually. Between 1991 and 2004, the overall teen birthrate declined by 33 percent, but this decrease is less pronounced among Latinas and African American females.

- Teenage pregnancy is related to a constellation of factors, including poverty, low self-esteem, academic failure, and the perception of few life options. One-third of the girls gave marriage or pregnancy as a reason for dropping out of school.

- Both girls and boys believe that girls will have a more difficult time achieving their aspirations than will boys, and adolescent girls report higher levels of stress and depression and a lower level of confidence. Females exhibit lower self-esteem than do males during secondary and higher education.

- Despite extraordinary strides made by females in high school athletic participation, female sports programs receive only about two-thirds the funding of male programs.

Boys

- Society socializes boys into an active, independent, and aggressive role. But such behavior is incongruent with school norms and rituals that stress quiet behavior and docility. This results in a pattern of role conflict for boys, particularly during the elementary years.
- Hyperactivity is estimated to be nine times more prevalent in boys than in girls. Boys are underdiagnosed for depression and are more likely to be involved in alcohol or drug abuse, and statistics indicate a higher suicide rate among males.
- Conforming to the male sex-role stereotype takes a psychological toll. Boys who score high on sex-appropriate behavior tests also score highest on anxiety tests.
- Males are less likely than females to be close friends with one another. When asked, most men identify women as their closest friends.
- While 1 in 20 students reports being victims of crime at school, males are far more likely to be involved with such violence. Three times as many boys as girls carry weapons, and twice as many have been threatened, injured with weapons, or hurt in physical fights. In general, African American and Latino boys are more likely than others to be involved with crime and violence on school property.
- At least 30 percent of students are victims of bullying, and 60 percent of students witness bullying at school every day. Males are more likely to bully others and be victims of physical bullying, while females frequently experience verbal and psychological bullying (through sexual comments or rumors).
- Males are more likely to succumb to serious disease and be victims of accidents or violence. The average life expectancy of men is approximately 5 years shorter than that of women, and 8 to 10 years shorter for African American and Hispanic men.

Career and Family Relationships

Women

- On average, a female college graduate of any racial, ethnic, socioeconomic, or ability group still earns less than a White male with a college degree.
- Women are half of the nation's workforce, two-thirds of minimum wage earners, and 70 percent of working women are mothers. Women overall earn 76 cents for every dollar earned by men; Latinas earn 54 cents, African American women earn 65 cents, White women earn seventy-six cents, and Asian American women earn eighty cents.
- The gender wage gap is apparent across occupations. For example, female physicians earn approximately two-thirds of what their male peers do, female lawyers earn about three-fourths as much as their male colleagues, and women who are public school elementary and secondary teachers earn approximately 80 percent as much as male teachers. Women are less than 10 percent of Fortune 500 top earners.

- In career and technical education programs, gender stereotypes still limit female employment options. Just as in the 1970s, high school girls are the vast majority of those enrolled in traditionally female courses, such as cosmetology and child care. And high school boys make up all but a tiny percentage of the students in traditionally male fields such as auto mechanics and construction. For example, in 2004 in the entire state of Maryland, only a single girl studied electrical engineering in a high school technical program. In Arizona, 98 percent of all cosmetology students were female. And girls represented only 2 percent of students studying to be automotive technicians in New Jersey. Nationally, the picture is little better: Girls make up 87 percent of students in traditionally female fields and only 15 percent of those in traditionally male fields. The leading occupational categories for women include receptionist, secretary, cashier, nursing aide, elementary school teacher, bookkeeper/accountant, and waitress.

- Within the few broad occupational categories in which women continue to be concentrated, further segregation also exists by race. For example, the occupations with the highest concentrations of African American women are nursing aides, cashiers, and secretaries; for Native American women, it is welfare aides, child-care workers, and teacher's aides; and for White women, it is administrative support workers, dental hygienists, and occupational therapists.

- Women are about three-quarters of the elementary and secondary school teachers but only 44 percent of the principals.

- A majority of women in their 20s and 30s believe that being a woman will hurt their chances of success. Almost 95 percent of women in business believe boys' networks still exist, and 86 percent are concerned about how to balance work with family.

Men

- Even well-meaning teachers and counselors often advise boys to enter sex-stereotyped careers and limit their potential in occupations such as kindergarten teacher, nurse, librarian, or social worker.

- Although males comprise 9 percent of elementary school teachers, they are almost half of elementary principals.

- Men dominate careers in politics, business, law, medicine, architecture, engineering, computer science, mathematical and physical science, as well as vocations such as plumbing, auto repair, construction, and firefighting.

- Current parenting patterns reinforce male stereotyping. Many families accept the notion that adolescent boys are naturally aggressive, withdrawn, and emotionally unexpressive, and they support these characteristics as normal development.

- As a result of the limited range of masculine role models, boys tend to define themselves in opposition to others, either as nonfemale, nonhomosexual, or anti-authority (e.g., schools, parents). Adolescent boys, in particular, see female qualities as unacceptable for males, contributing to an antigay and antifemale disposition.

- Both at school and at home, males are taught to hide or suppress their emotions; as husbands and fathers, they may find it difficult or impossible to show positive feelings toward their wives and children.

- Men and women vary in their beliefs about a father's role. Men emphasize the need for the father to earn a good income and to provide solutions to family problems. Women, on the other hand, stress the need for fathers to assist in caring for children and in responding to the emotional needs of the family. These differing perceptions of fatherhood increase family strain and anxiety, and many men become not so much parents as "transparents."

Research Summary

The report card reflects the volatile state of gender equity in and beyond school; while some gender barriers are crumbling, others seem impervious to change. During the past two decades, the gender gap has decreased in mathematics, biology, and chemistry, and in professional careers such as law and medicine. In fact, these rapid changes underscore the profound power of schools and society to radically alter age-old cultural norms (Duncan-Andrade, 2005; Grant & Sleeter, 2002; hooks, 2003). Yet other areas have been resistant to change: computer science, technology, physics, and engineering, for example, remain male domains, while elementary and preschool teachers are overwhelmingly female. To complicate matters further, an array of gender-related psychological and physical dynamics impact both males and females, in very different but often harmful ways. Gender equity has reached a new stage: just as the blatant bias and discrimination of the past have become less frequent, subtle and pervasive bias continues to plague schools and to shortchange both girls and boys.

For the typical classroom teacher, gender equity emerges as a continuing challenge on at least two levels. First, gender is often the invisible issue in the curriculum, with the contributions and experiences of women frequently absent. At other times, when the information is present, it is frightfully distorted. Second, female students typically receive less active instruction. Teachers focus more of their time and talent on male students for both academic and behavior reasons. As a result, in the pages of books and in the voices of the classroom, females struggle to be heard (Giordano, 2003; Hahn, 1996; Loewen, 1995). To help teachers tease out the subtle biases that persist in classrooms, we focus on two central areas of classroom life: student–teacher interaction and the curriculum.

GENDER BIAS IN TODAY'S CLASSROOMS: THE CURRICULUM

Today's curriculum, both low-tech books and high-tech computers, often sets the pace and the tone of classroom instruction. Studies suggest that students spend as much as 80 to 95 percent of classroom time using textbooks and that teachers make a majority of their instructional decisions based on the textbook (Fan & KaeLey, 2000; Starnes, 2004; Woodward & Elliot, 1990). In recent years, the Internet and enhanced media options, such as cable and satellite television broadcasting, have offered students a greater array of curricular resources than ever before. Both print and electronic resources typically determine what is taught and not taught in U.S. classrooms.

In the 1970s and 1980s, textbook companies and professional associations, such as the American Psychological Association and the National Council for Teachers of English, issued guidelines for nonracist and nonsexist books, suggesting how to include and fairly portray different groups in the curriculum. As a result, textbooks became more balanced in their description of underrepresented groups, but problems of biased instructional material persist. Newer history and science texts published in the 1990s continue to devote only 2 or 3 percent of book space to the contributions or experiences of women (Women's Educational Equity Act, 1999). Seventy percent of music-related figures found in school textbooks are male (Livingston, 1997), and male characters outnumber females two to one in current basal readers (Dutro 2001/2002; Evans & Davies, 2000). American Library Association book award winners and Caldecott selections also tell more male-centered stories (61%) than female (39%) (Gooden & Gooden, 2001; Davis & McDaniel, 1999). Although female characters do appear in newer roles such as doctors, lawyers, and scientists, stereotypes persist. Females are often the passive observers, watching their active brothers at work and at play and focusing on domestic life. Boys remain in the traditional role as well, unlikely to nurture or stray from typical male careers (Davis & McDaniel, 1999; Evans & Davies, 2000; Gooden & Gooden, 2001). Unfortunately, gender bias is alive and flourishing in today's curriculum.

How can teachers detect such bias? The first step is to be able to understand the different manifestations of bias. Following is a description of seven forms of bias that can be used to assess instructional materials. These forms of bias can be based not only on gender, race, or ethnicity, but they can also help identify prejudice against the elderly, people with disabilities, non-English speakers, gays and lesbians, and limited-English speakers. In short, any group can be inaccurately portrayed through one or more of these seven forms of bias.

Invisibility: *What You Don't See Makes a Lasting Impression*

When groups or events are not taught in schools, they become part of *the null curriculum*. Textbooks published prior to the 1960s largely omitted African Americans, Latinos, Asian Americans, and women. Many of today's textbooks continue to give minimal treatment to these groups and rarely include individuals with disabilities or gays and lesbians as examples, suggesting that they are neither mainstream nor important. When girls and women are systematically excluded from curricular material, students are deprived of information about half the nation's people. The result is that both boys and girls lower their opinions about the value of females. For example, when asked to name 20 famous women from American history, most students cannot do it. Typically, they list fewer than five (Sadker & Sadker, 1994). A similar case can be made for the invisibility of males in parenting and other roles nontraditional to their gender.

Stereotyping: *Glib Shortcuts*

Perhaps the most familiar form of bias is the stereotype, which assigns a rigid set of characteristics to all members of a group, denying individual attributes and differences. From traditional phonics reading texts to current computer software, boys have routinely been shown as active, creative, brave, athletic, achieving, and curious, and men are seen as the movers and shakers of history, scientists of achievement, and the political leaders. In striking contrast, girls are often stereotypically portrayed as dependent, passive, fearful, docile, and even as victims, with a limited role in or impact on the world. For example, a 1990s study of elementary mathematics software revealed that only 12 percent of the characters were female. Females were portrayed passively as mothers and princesses while male characters were shown as active and as "heavy equipment operators, factory workers, shopkeepers, mountain climbers, hang gliders, garage mechanics, and as a genie providing directions" (Hodes, 1995–1996).

Imbalance and Selectivity: *A Tale Half Told*

Sometimes a curriculum presents only one interpretation of an issue, event, or group of people. At other times, only one point of view is present to avoid potential controversy and to ensure that school board members, educational administrators, and teachers or parents are not offended.

The suffrage movement is one example of imbalance in history texts. The fight to enfranchise half the population and the efforts made by women like Elizabeth Cady Stanton are described as a time when women were "given" the vote. Few texts report the bravery and sacrifices of the suffrage leaders that eventually "won" the right to vote. The invention of the cotton gin is another example of textbook imbalance. Katherine Littlefield Greene was a co-inventor of this machine, but because societal norms inhibited women from registering for patents, Eli Whitney received the patent—and the sole credit in history textbooks ever after.

Unreality: *Rose-Colored Glasses*

Textbooks have gained a sort of notoriety for glossing over unpleasant facts and controversial events in favor of presenting noncontroversial views unlikely to offend potential adopters. When discussions of racial discrimination or sexual harassment are dismissed as remnants of a bygone day, or when the nuclear family is described only as a father, mother, and children, students are being treated to romanticized and sanitized narratives, an *unreality* that omits the information they will need to confront and resolve real social challenges.

Fragmentation: *An Interesting Sideshow*

Did you ever read a textbook that separates the discussion of women in a separate section or insert? For example, many of today's texts include special inserts highlighting certain gender topics, such as "What If He Has Two Mommies?" or "Ten Women Achievers in Science." This is called fragmentation (or isolation) and communicates to readers that while women and gender issues are an interesting diversion, their contributions do not constitute the mainstream of history, literature, or the sciences and are less important than the main narrative.

Linguistic Bias: *Words Count*

Language can be a powerful conveyor of bias, in both blatant and subtle forms. The exclusive use of masculine terms and pronouns, ranging from our *forefathers, mankind,* and *businessman* to the generic *he,* denies the full participation and recognition of women. More subtle examples include word orders and choices that place males in a primary role, like "men and their wives."

Selective adjectives also perpetuate linguistic bias. The conservative nineteenth-century diplomat Klemens von Metternich is described in one recent and popular high school history book as a man whose "charm" worked well with "elegant ladies"—words and facts of dubious historical import, but not without prurient interest (Beck, Black, Krieger, Naylor, & Shabaka, 2005). The German use of *fatherland* to describe Germany and the Russian use of *motherland* to describe Russia are examples of gendered nouns that offer insights into different national consciousness; such gender and linguistic insights are frequently left unexplained in texts.

Cosmetic Bias: *Pretty Wrapping*

Cosmetic bias offers an 'illusion of equity.' Beyond the attractive covers, photos, or posters that prominently feature an attractive multicultural America, bias persists. Examples include a science textbook that features a glossy pullout of female scientists, but precious little narrative of the scientific contributions of women. Another example is a music book with an eye-catching, multiethnic cover that projects a world of diverse songs and symphonies, yet behind the cover, traditional White male composers dominate. Cosmetic bias is a marketing strategy directed at potential adopters who flip through, but do not read, the pages, and might be lured into purchasing books that appear inclusive, but are not.

Until publishers and authors discuss relevant gender issues and the strategies needed to eliminate gender bias, it will be up to the creativity and commitment of teachers to fill in the missing pages. Educators who choose gender-fair materials can encourage positive growth in students. But gender-fair curricular materials by themselves are not sufficient to create a non-sexist educational environment. Attention must also be paid to the process of instruction.

GENDER BIAS IN TODAY'S CLASSROOMS: INSTRUCTION

The following scene, an updated general music class in action, reflects the subtle ways in which gender bias can permeate the instructional process (Carter, 1987).

As the bell rings, students take their seats. The girls are clustered in the front and on the right-hand side of the room, while the boys are predominantly on the other side of the room and in the back. This seating arrangement doesn't bother the students; they choose their own seats. It doesn't seem to bother their teacher, Mrs. Howe, who feels that students should have the right to sit where they choose (unless, of course, there is racial segregation; Mrs. Howe has little patience for that). Everyone seems comfortable with the boys and girls creating their own seating areas.

Mrs. Howe starts the lesson by playing part of Mozart's Symphony Concertante on the CD player. After about 5 minutes, she turns to the class with questions.

MRS. HOWE: Who can tell me the name of this composer?

(A few hands are raised when John shouts out, "Ricky Martin." After the laughter dies down, Mrs. Howe calls on Mitch.)

MITCH: Haydn.

MRS. HOWE: Why do you think so?

MITCH: Because yesterday you played Haydn.

MRS. HOWE: Close. Enrique, what do you think?

ENRIQUE: I don't know.

MRS. HOWE: Come on, Enrique. During the last two weeks we have been listening to various classical period composers. Out of those we've listened to, who wrote this piece? (Silence)

MRS. HOWE: John, can you help Enrique out?

JOHN: Beethoven.

MRS. HOWE: No, it's not Beethoven. Beethoven was more a Romantic period composer. Think!

(Mrs. Howe finally calls on Pam, who has had her hand half-raised during this discussion.)

PAM: I'm not sure, but is it Mozart?

MRS. HOWE: Uh-huh. Anyone else agree with Pam?

MITCH (calls out): It's Mozart. It's similar to the Mozart concerto you played yesterday.

MRS. HOWE: Very good. Can you tell us if this is another concerto he wrote?

MITCH: Yes, it's a violin concerto.

MRS. HOWE: That's almost right. It's a special concerto written for two instruments. To help you figure out the other instrument, let's listen to more of the piece.

(Mrs. Howe plays more of the piece and calls on Mitch.)

MITCH: Another violin.

MRS. HOWE: Peter?

PETER: A cello.

MRS. HOWE: You're all close. It's another string instrument, but it's not another violin or a cello.

RUTH (calls out): What about a viola?

MRS. HOWE: Ruth, you know I don't allow shouting out. Raise your hand next time. Peter?

PETER: A viola.

MRS. HOWE: Very good. This is a special kind of concerto Mozart wrote for both the violin and viola called Symphony Concertante. One reason why I want you to listen to it is to notice the difference between the violin and the viola. Let's listen to the melody as played first by the violin then the viola. Listen for the similarities and differences between the two.

This scenario demonstrates several important interaction patterns: in this gender-segregated classroom, Mrs. Howe called on the boys more often than on the girls and asked them more higher-order and lower-order questions. She gave male students more specific feedback, including praise, constructive criticism, and remediation. Research (Sadker & Sadker, 1985) shows that from grade school to graduate school, most classrooms demonstrate similar instructional patterns.

One large study (Sadker & Sadker, 1984) conducted in the fourth, sixth, and eighth grades in more than 100 classrooms in four states and the District of Columbia found that teachers gave boys more academic attention than they gave girls. They asked them more questions and gave them more precise and clear feedback concerning the quality of their responses. In contrast, girls were more likely to be ignored or given vague evaluation of the academic quality of their work (D'Ambrosio & Hammer, 1996; Sadker & Sadker, 1994a). Other research shows that these same patterns are prevalent at the secondary and postsecondary levels (Sadker, Sadker, & Klein, 1991).

One reason boys get more teacher attention is that they demand it (Altermatt, Jovanovic, & Perry, 1998; Spencer, Porche, & Tolman, 2003). More likely to shout out questions and answers, they dominate the classroom airwaves. However, when boys call out, teachers often accept their comments. In contrast, when girls call out, teachers usually reprimand them by saying things like, "In this class, we raise our hands before talking."

Another factor allowing boys to dominate interaction is the widespread gender segregation that characterizes classrooms. Occasionally teachers divide their classrooms along gender-segregated lines in groups, work and play areas, and seating. More frequently, students gender-segregate themselves. Drawn to the sections of the classroom where the more assertive boys are clustered, the teacher is positioned to keep interacting with male students.

The conclusion of many interaction studies is that teachers give more attention (positive, negative, and neutral) to male students. However, some researchers emphasize that low-achieving males get most of the negative attention, while high-achieving boys get more positive and constructive academic contacts (Babad, 1998). But no matter if they are high or low achievers, female students are more likely to be invisible and ignored (Brophy & Good, 1974; Francis, 2000; Jones & Gerig, 1994; Sadker & Sadker, 1994; Spencer, Porche, & Tolman, 2003).

The gender difference in classroom communications is more than a mere counting game of who gets the teacher's attention and who does not. Teacher attention is a vote of high expectations and commitment to a student. Decades of research show that students who are engaged are more likely to achieve and to express positive attitudes toward schools and learning (Flanders, 1970; Good & Brophy, 2003).

Most teachers are unaware of these biases, and when they are made aware, they want to adopt fairer strategies. Unfortunately, there are few resources available to help them become more equitable. National programs designed to eliminate classroom bias have been removed from the federal budget, and local and state teacher education programs do little to correct this problem. In a content analysis of twenty-three teacher education textbooks, Zittleman and Sadker (2002) found that introductory teacher education textbooks devote only about 7 percent of their content space to issues related to gender. Yet even this minimal treatment is problematic, since the stories of female pioneers are given far less coverage than those of males. Methods textbooks, those focusing on the skills and resources for teachers, devote only 1 percent of content space to gender concerns. Future teachers looking for information about the special problems boys encounter in reading, or girls encounter in science, will likely not even read that such problems exist. And if they should find the rare text that discusses such problems, it is unlikely that they will be given any ideas, strategies, or resources to untangle these puzzles. While most of today's teacher education textbooks voice support for gender-equity goals, they include precious few practical steps on how to achieve them. This is unfortunate because studies show that with resources, awareness, and training educators can eliminate gender bias in their teaching (Campbell & Sanders, 1997; Jones, Evans, Byrd, & Campbell, 2000; Sadker, Sadker, & Shakeshaft, 1992; Zittleman & Sadker, 2002).

TRENDS AND CHALLENGES

At both the beginning and the end of the twentieth century, gender in schools was center stage (Sadker, 1999). In the early 1900s, people believed that education could damage a girl's fragile health. Doctors argued that learning created detrimental stress on the female anatomy, a stress that could cause insanity as well as sterility. Girls were routinely kept out of school "for their own good" (Sadker & Sadker, 1994). In the 1990s, biology once again became an issue. Voices were heard advocating that girls' and boys' brain differences had educational consequences. Trying to educate girls and boys in the same classroom was now seen as a disservice to both, and single-sex schools and classrooms sprung up across the nation. Coeducation, once seen as a beacon of democracy and equality, was now seen as a barrier to effective teaching and learning. Are such single sex schools more effective? Are they even legal? Title IX, the law that banned sex discrimination in education, also prohibited most instances of sex segregation. Was the law being ignored?

The Perfect Storm: The Resurgence of Single-Sex Education

Sex-segregated schooling has existed in the United States for centuries. For many, it is a reminder of the unequal education afforded girls. Historically, girls received fewer resources, studied a sex-stereotyped curriculum, and were offered a clearly inferior education. Colonial dame schools, and later women's colleges and seminaries, had the primary mission of preparing young girls and women for their place at home as wives and mothers. Men's schools and colleges, on the other hand, were charged with preparing men to hold the reins of power in society. Separate schools and programs made perfect sense in preparing girls and boys for their separate domains (Tyack & Hansot, 1990).

Well into the mid-twentieth century, most private and public all-girls schools and colleges continued to offer a less-rigorous curriculum than their all-boys' counterparts. Not until Title IX was enacted (1972) did things begin to change. While Title IX prohibited discrimination based on gender, private schools, including many religious schools, were free to operate single-sex schools under the law. Single-sex programs in public schools also were permitted, but only under certain circumstances. For example, contact sports, classes in human sexuality, and remedial programs designed to help girls in the sciences or boys in the language arts were still legal under the new law. But change was in the air, and separating the sexes was now far less fashionable. Single-sex education—or gender segregation, as some saw it—was on the wane.

Public school districts began to abandon sex-segregated programs and schools. Viewed as an anachronism, most private single-sex schools and colleges also made the transition to coeducational institutions, or closed their doors. The number of women's colleges dwindled from almost 300 in the 1960s to fewer than 100 today, while only two male colleges and five single-sex public high schools survived. Some of the most striking changes were in career education. Formerly gender-segregated vocational programs, like home economics and cosmetology for girls or auto mechanics and carpentry for boys, became coeducational. So did traditionally male courses like physics and calculus.

The most prestigious Ivy League colleges and several military schools served as "speed bumps" on the road to coeducation, slowing down the integration of females. Some Ivies admitted women, but not for reasons of fairness. Finding families who could afford the very expensive tuition at these exclusive schools was challenging, and accepting females magically doubled their chances of attracting wealthy students. Also, Ivies like Yale and Princeton were discovering that many of their most desirable male applicants were going elsewhere because they wanted to attend colleges with women. So to attract the best men, the Ivies surrendered to the tide of coeducation and admitted women (Karabel, 2005). Columbia, the last Ivy to admit women, finally opened its doors in 1980. State-supported military schools, like the Citadel and Virginia Military Institute, held out even longer. Such schools had little interest in female students; they were committed to attracting men who desired a military education. They dug legal trenches, fighting skirmishes in the courts to retain their male only corps of cadets. The fact that military academies like West Point and Annapolis already had accepted women did not help their argument that women could not be superior cadets. Moreover, public funds supported these schools, and gender discrimination was not appreciated by the courts. By the mid-1990s, the Citadel and the Virginia Military Institute were forced to admit female students.

Ironically, even as these last holdouts began admitting women, a dramatic change was underway: Single-sex schools were increasingly seen not as a vestige of the past, but as a promise for the future. What accounted for such a dramatic reversal? Like the title of a popular book of the era, a "perfect storm" was forming. Several seemingly disparate events were coalescing to change public perceptions. During the next decade, this perfect storm would breathe new life into single-sex school movement. Let's build on this weather allusion and examine the different high pressure fronts that were converging to create this perfect storm.

Arguments for Single-Sex Schooling

High-Pressure Front #1: The Failures of Coeducation Schools

The perfect storm was fueled by reports and books published in the 1990s that documented the persistence of gender bias in coeducational schools. Coeducation was "failing at fairness," and girls were being "short-changed" in coed classrooms (AAUW, 1992; Sadker & Sadker, 1994; Sadker, 2005). Despite the feminist movement's best efforts, teachers continued to give boys more attention, to help them more, praise them more, and even criticize them more. Boys were more likely to shine on athletic teams and to receive higher SAT scores and eventually greater success and financial rewards after graduation. Teachers were repeating many of the sexist lessons of the past because teacher education institutions were doing little to incorporate gender into their training. While there were certainly exceptions, and some areas like law and medicine saw a dramatic increase in female students, girls continued to be rewarded for docile and compliant behaviors, the very behaviors that would undermine their success as adults. The wage gap between men and women persisted. Feminists and some educators argued that coeducation was failing girls and women, and they looked at the successes of women's colleges as a possible solution. They argued that a fair education for females could be achieved only in single-sex environments.

High-Pressure Front #2: The Backlash

By the mid-1990s, gender equity and feminism were fair game for ultraconservative commentators who not only attacked the movement, but suggested that girls had few if any problems in school. They argued that if gender bias exists at all, it was the boys who were the real victims. Gender equity research was now characterized as biased and political, and discounted as "advocacy research" (Sommers, 1995).

Despite many factual inaccuracies in the backlash argument (Sadker, 1996), the charge that schools were being run by feminists at the expense of boys resonated with many, particularly those who were familiar with the problems boys encountered in school. The crux of the backlash argument was that feminist educators were promoting an antimale agenda and that the resources spent on female achievement in school were coming at the expense of boys. These critics crusaded for changes that would better fit boys' learning styles: stronger discipline, more competitions, greater emphasis on physicality, and a curriculum that would feature male characters and war poetry (Sommers, 2000). Many of the recommendations advocated by the backlash critics were of dubious merit, but they did increase awareness of the problems faced by boys in school, and the solutions some believed existed in all male schools.

High-Pressure Front #3: Brain Differences and Biology

Research has resurrected the idea of biology as a kind of educational destiny, promoting the idea that female and male brains are so different that separate schools are necessary. The reason for boys' poor grades, high dropout rates, discipline dilemmas, and other school problems is easy to diagnose: Coed schools are simply unable to respond to the biological needs of boys. Since boys are genetically more competitive and active than girls, since boys need more discipline, since boys do better when they are "yelled at," school environments must change. Boys' schools should include physical games, tough competition, harsh discipline, and shorter lessons. Girls, on the other hand, have a very different biology. Girls are genetically more relational and collaborative in nature, placid and conforming, and prefer a calmer atmosphere, and they should have schools built around these characteristics. Simply put: Boys' brains and girls' brains are 'hard-wired' differently, and they must be taught in schools that reflect these genetic differences (Gurian & Stevens, 2005; Sax, 2005).

High-Pressure Front #4: Distraction Free Learning

Raging adolescent hormones provide another biological reason to separate the sexes. As adolescents go through puberty, they discover their sexuality and the sexuality of their peers, and spectacular changes occur. Social status and dating exert an extraordinary influence on their lives, and energy and attention better spent on academics are redirected to social and sexual concerns. Puberty and hormones can also spark sexual harassment, another common distraction in coed school life. Removing members of the opposite sex from the classroom will safeguard learning form the effects of powerful adolescent hormones.

High-Pressure Front #5: School Choice

Some argue that single-sex schools, like all school options, should be a matter of parental choice, available to all. This view, part of the broader school choice movement, is based on the idea that as schools compete, better schools will prosper as weaker ones decline. Charter schools, vouchers, and open enrollments have rapidly expanded public parental options beyond the neighborhood school. With the free market at work, consumers (i.e., parents) are free to choose the most appropriate school for their children. And one of these options should be single-sex schools, previously available only to wealthy parents who could afford private school tuition. The creation of several high-profile girls-only charter schools in Harlem, New York and in Chicago fueled the fire that choice would give poor families new options, and their children new hope.

High-Pressure Front #6: Creating a Legal Path

In 2001, Republican Senators Kay Bailey Hutchison and Susan Collins and Democratic Senators Hillary Rodham Clinton and Barbara Mikulski cosponsored an amendment to No Child Left Behind that allowed public school districts to create single-sex schools and classrooms, although they must do so under existing law. This amendment has created some confusion, since Title IX allows single-sex schooling under only special circumstances (e.g., classes in human reproduction, contact sports, remedial programs). Many public school districts viewed this amendment as federal encouragement to try single-sex education whenever they choose and for any reason, and so hundreds of single-sex classrooms and schools sprung up. Urban and suburban schools, short on answers for poor student performance on NCLB-mandated tests, were quick to jump on the new bandwagon. Separating the boys and girls, they believed, could be the key to improving both classroom management and test scores.

As the perfect storm gained strength, so did the single-sex school movement. Between 1998 and 1999, enrollments in all-girls' schools in the United States increased by 4.4 percent, and 32 new girls' schools opened their doors in the mid 1990s. Applications increased to girls' schools by more than a third and enrollment by almost a third between 1995 and 2000. To a lesser extent, boys' schools also saw an increase in attendance, by 16 percent in the decade of the 1990s, and applications for women's colleges increased (Salomone, 2003; Stabiner, 2002). While only five public single-sex high schools were still operating in 1996 (including Baltimore's Western High School, founded in 1844, and the Philadelphia High School for Girls, founded in 1846), a decade later that number had jumped to over 30 (Arms, in press). News reports of public school districts creating new single-sex schools and, even more frequently, single-sex classrooms became commonplace (Leach, 2005), although tracking specific numbers was difficult.

Has this been a positive development? Certainly there are a number of very strong and effective single-sex schools in the nation, and many alumnae speak forcefully about the power and effectiveness of single-sex schools (National Coalition of Girls School, 2005). But critics question whether these schools are successful because they are single sex or because they are strong schools that happen to be single sex. For each of the arguments above that support single-sex schools, competing arguments cast real doubts. To promote a balanced view, let's outline some of the counter-arguments, and then conclude this section with a brief overview of what research says.

Counter-arguments

1. *The Failures of Coeducation Schools:* There is no arguing that sexism remains a debilitating part of public school life. Research studies underscore the persistence of sexual harassment, curricular bias, and inequitable teacher interaction patterns. But creating a few single-sex schools may be a way of avoiding the issue, rather than responding to it. The vast majority of students and teachers continue to

teach and learn in coed schools. For them, creating some single-sex schools is not a solution. Sexist practices and behaviors remain a daily part of school life, and resources might better be spent in addressing sexism in coed schools, rather than leaving these problems to fester.

2. *The Backlash:* The backlash attack blamed feminists for the problems boys were encountering in school, yet failed to mention that boys had the very same school problems well before the women's movement began. Other arguments advanced in backlash publications were replete with factual errors. As an example, one of the coauthors of this chapter, David Sadker, was telephoned by one such backlash writer and asked to photocopy and mail hundreds of pages of a 15-year-old research report. When told this would be expensive and that the report was readily available in thousands of libraries, the backlash critic chose instead to write a number of articles claiming that because the report was not personally mailed, it never existed (Kleinfeld, 1999). That erroneous story of the "mysterious missing report" was repeated by others (Sommers, 2000) and soon found its way into publications ranging from the *Weekly Standard* to the *Atlantic Monthly*. Although many of these critical backlash stories were replete with similar errors and omissions, few media outlets ever pursued that line of inquiry (Sadker, 1996).

3. *Brain Differences and Biology:* Research on the psychology of gender differences has long argued that males and females are ultimately more alike than different (Maccoby, 1998), and the small sex differences that do exist are malleable and increased or decreased by socialization and education (Sadker & Sadker, 1994). Even proponents of the "brain research" such as Leonard Sax (2005) and Jo Ann Deak (2002) concede that there is considerable variability within genders (Arms, in press). Generalizing a pedagogy based on sex is sure to miss many students who do not fit the gender mold. Some believe that such gender-directed practices would reinforce traditional gender stereotypes. Others worry that single-sex schooling is a step back, a return to the separate and unequal education of the past. Researchers in the United Kingdom, after studying single-sex schooling for years, are adamant that there is no gender-specific pedagogy (Warrington & Younger, 2003).

4. *Distraction-Free Learning:* While this argument for choosing single-sex schooling is quite popular (Heather, 2002), it completely discounts the fact that students are quite capable of distracting each other in many creative ways. A British study of single-sex classes that found all-boys classes had a "macho, male culture" that boys used to distract each other (Jackson, 2002). Same-sex bullying may be as prevalent in single-sex schools as sexual harassment is in coed schools. Campbell and Sanders (2002) argue that the distraction argument assumes everyone is heterosexual, ignoring the issues confronting lesbian, gay, bisexual, or transgender students would encounter in single-sex environments. Rather than accepting distractions such as bullying and sexual harassment in school, educators and parents might be better advised to work to eliminate these problems, to create true learning communities, and to invest "in the real equity needs of coeducational schools" (Sadker, 2004, p. 8).

5. *School Choice:* The free market argument that all parents should be able to choose the school that best meets their child's needs and that competition among students will eventually lead to a satisfactory resolution has been criticized by many as simplistic. Others see darker forces at play and believe that school choice is little more than a plan to move public monies into the private sector (Apple, 2001; Molnar, 1996). How can parents be expected to make such choices? Will they believe that single-sex schools are better than coed schools? How will advertising influence parental choices? Since researchers and educators disagree over the effectiveness of such schools, is it reasonable that parents and children will make such choices on sound evidence, or on hype and hearsay? Might these resources be better spent improving current school practices?

6. *Creating a Legal Path:* Although senators representing different political leanings found common ground in promoting single-sex schools, legal issues persist. Some scholars believe that single-sex public schools would be legal under the Title IX regulations; others are less certain (Salomone, 2002). The courts may be called on to determine if these single-sex public schools are in compliance with Title IX or represent a violation of the law. Does this new momentum for gender segregation mark the beginning of the end for the landmark civil rights law, Title IX?

   There is also legal confusion about single-sex schools and the No Child Left Behind Act (2002). This act calls for schools to implement only "educational programs or practices that have been proven effective through rigorous scientific research" (http://www.ed.gov/policy/elsec/leg/esea02/index.html). The federal government asks for strong evidence of effectiveness before allowing new schools to be created. But as the next section illustrates, for single-sex schools, such evidence is lacking.

What the Research Says

What does research say about single-sex education? The findings, unfortunately, are neither uniform nor clear. Most of the studies have been done not in the United States but in countries with long traditions of public single-sex schools (e.g., the United Kingdom, New Zealand, Australia), and so those findings are not as relevant for U.S. schools (Warrington & Younger, 2003; Jackson, 2002; Sanford & Blair, 2002; Harker, 2000; Daly & Shuttleworth 1997). But even looking at studies done in the United States creates problems (Arms, in press). Many single-sex schools in this country are Catholic, and because of their religious orientation, selection of students, and parental commitment, generalizing these findings to other schools is not possible. At the college level, there has been a small body of positive research on the effectiveness of private women's colleges (Astin, 1993; Smith, 1990; Tidball & Kistiakowsky, 1976), but these findings are difficult to transfer to the K-12 context. Some argue that the successes of single-sex women's colleges are less a reflection of the single-sex college education, and more a reflection of the high admission standards of these colleges and the wealth of their students (Stoecker & Pascarella, 1991).

   Some advocates of single-sex education were encouraged by studies suggesting that females in single-sex schools demonstrate increased academic achievement, self-esteem, and career salience, as well as a decrease in sex-role stereotyping (Cairns, 1990; Tyack &

Hansot, 1990). One study found that girls' students in schools in the United States expressed greater interest in both mathematics and English, took more mathematics courses, did more homework, and had more positive attitudes toward academic achievement than girls attending coeducational institutions (Lee & Bryk, 1986). Girls in single-sex schools also showed more interest in the feminist movement and were less sex-role stereotyped than were their peers in coeducational schools (Lee & Marks, 1990; Riordan, 1990, 2002; Sadker & Sadker, 1994). Several educators called for caution with such findings, arguing that the effectiveness of single-sex schools might have little or nothing to do with the gender nature of these schools. Rather, these schools might have been successful because they modeled effective school practices, including small class size, skilled teachers, academically oriented learning communities, and committed and involved parents (Datnow & Hubbard, 2002). LePore and Warren (1997) found no significant academic differences between girls in all-girls' Catholic schools and girls in coeducational Catholic schools. Lee and her colleagues, after analyzing a national sample of private (not Catholic) secondary schools, found "no consistent pattern of effects for attending either single-sex or coeducational independent schools for either girls or boys" (Lee, 1998, p. 43). Other studies found unconvincing findings about the effectiveness of single-sex education (Moore, Piper, & Schaefer, 1992; Lee, 1997).

Even fewer studies exist showing that single-sex schooling works for boys. One exception was Riesman (1990), who found that boys, disadvantaged in the elementary years, felt more comfortable in fields and activities traditionally attended to by females in the single-sex environment. And Riordan (2002) found that social-economic class may make a difference: Poorer girls and boys attending single-sex schools had higher test scores in reading, math, science and civics, greater leadership skills, more homework being done, and higher academic expectations. But Riordan also found that single-sex schools had little or no effect on middle-class or wealthier children. Meanwhile, other studies have shown little or no benefits for boys regardless of social class (AAUW, 1998b).

Some studies suggest coeducation may be more effective than single-sex schooling. Shmurak (1994) examined records of nearly 13,000 graduates from 13 private schools recording the number of women pursuing careers in 10 fields, from medicine to architecture. She found that women graduating from coeducational schools were more likely to be in four fields: law, computers, scientific research, and psychology. There was no significant difference in other fields (including architecture, medicine, engineering, dentistry, veterinary medicine, and finance), and surprisingly none of the graduates from girls' schools had a higher proportion of graduates in any of these fields.

Despite lack of supportive research, single-sex education is on the rise, and this has created problems. Public school districts often lack a clear purpose for making the transition to single-sex education: Some do it to raise test scores, others to control discipline problems, and others to meet the "different needs" of girls and boys, reasons not supported by the research. Training is another forgotten chapter, as schools become single sex but provide little or no meaningful teacher training related to this new approach (Campbell & Sanders, 2002; Sadker, 2002). And sometimes, gender stereotyping is increased in these poorly designed experiments. In late 1990s, California funded several local single-gender schools. However, because of few resources, little training, lack of a clear purpose, and outside pressures, boys were soon stereotyped as troublemakers, and most of these schools closed their doors within a few years (Herr & Arms, 2002).

The perfect storm has been seeded by assumptions and events, not by a clear vision or persuasive research. Is single-sex schooling a good idea? The jury is out. What is needed is fairly obvious: a thoughtful plan to prepare selected schools to try single-sex education, and then a second plan to fairly evaluate them. Until this happens, failures, like the one in California, will continue (Woody, 2002).

Title IX

Title IX is the nation's educational promise that the talents of all its citizens—women and men, girls and boys—will not be restricted by sex discrimination. Widely known for its application to athletics, Title IX (of the 1972 Educational Amendments) prohibits sex discrimination in many arenas that have little to do with sports: counseling, discipline, testing, admissions, medical facilities, treatment of students, financial aid, and a host of educational activities. Today, Title IX provides legal protection for approximately 70 million students and employees in all educational institutions receiving federal financial assistance (NCWGE, 2002; U.S. Department of Education, 2002). The law also covers institutions such as vocational training centers, public libraries, and museums, wherever federally funded educational programs exist.

Before Title IX became law, girls were routinely discouraged or prohibited from taking science classes or joining the math club, while boys were excluded from home economics and cooking classes. Law schools and medical schools used quotas to keep the number of women students to just a few percent, or would refuse to admit women by claiming they would get pregnant and waste their education (Fischer, Schimmel, Stellman, & Kelly, 2002; NCWGE, 2002).

While Title IX bars sex discrimination in most educational areas, it is best known for creating dramatic increases in the numbers of girls and women participating in high school and college athletics. Title IX reminds us of the film *Field of Dreams*—if you build it, they will come. Title IX made it possible for girls and women to compete in athletics, and compete they did. Since Title IX's passage in 1972, women's participation in sports has increased by more than 400 percent at the college level and more than 800 percent in high schools (NCWGE, 2002; U.S. Department of Education, 2002). Despite this striking progress, females are just slightly more than 40 percent of all athletes. Yet for some male coaches, athletes, and administrators, 40 percent is too much. The National Wrestling Coaches Association filed a federal lawsuit alleging that Title IX is a quota system, requiring equal participation by male and females. Furthermore, the wrestlers charged that increased participation of females in sports causes men's teams to be unfairly eliminated or underfunded. In an important victory to support Title IX's civil rights protections, a federal court affirmed that Title IX is far from a quota system, and instead requires equitable opportunities and funding based on male and female enrollments (*National Wrestling Coaches Association v. United States Department of Education*, 2003). In fact, under Title IX, schools have *three* methods through which to provide fair athletic opportunities. School can show that organized sports participation roughly reflects the proportion of male and female students in the school; that the athletic interests and needs of female students are fulfilled; *or* that they are expanding to meet those needs. Schools are not required to offer identical sports, but they need to provide an equal opportunity for females to play in sports of interest. Title IX does not require equal expenditures, equal participation, or quotas. But for some, even this is too much. A new Title IX policy may make it easier for schools to ignore the interests of its female athletes.

Did you ever imagine that protection of your civil rights might be determined by a mass email? The U.S. Department of Education deems it a good idea. In March 2005, the Department decided that schools can claim compliance with Title IX based solely on the results of an online survey of female students' interest in sports. Moreover, schools are allowed to declare that lack of survey response means lack of interest (U.S. Department of Education, 2005). So a school can send out an email to all its students about athletic interests, and if females do not respond, then it is assumed they are not interested. Given the low response rates to email surveys (it's rather easy to hit the delete button) and the glitches with electronic communications, this policy is likely to lead schools to significantly underestimate females' interests in athletic participation. This is particularly damaging to middle and high school students who, rather than being encouraged to try a variety of sports, may be limited by lack of exposure to athletics. Additionally, to rely exclusively on self-assessment of ability shortchanges students who do not recognize their own potential until a coach, parent, teacher, or friend encourages them to try. This email interest survey is yet another attempt to weaken Title IX protections.

But even if no changes are made to the law, the reality is that Title IX has never been well enforced and even current requirements are often ignored (NCWGE, 2002; Zittleman, 2005). Too often, sexist school practices persist because teachers, parents, and students are unaware of their rights under the law, school administrators are unresponsive or uninformed, or the Office of Civil Rights is less than vigorous in enforcement. When nearly 100 middle school teachers and more than 400 middle school students were asked about their knowledge of Title IX, almost half of the teachers and over 98 percent of the students volunteered that they had no knowledge of the law. If these teachers and students had heard of Title IX at all, it was most often for creating more athletic opportunities for women and girls. Less than 10 percent of teachers and no students knew that the Department of Education was responsible enforcing the law, and fewer than 5 percent of teachers and not one student could name the Title IX coordinator for their school or district. Since schools are required to share such enforcement information with students and teachers, their lack of such information is itself a violation of Title IX. Obviously, ignorance of how to identify and report Title IX violations reduces the chances that such violations will be stopped (Zittleman, 2005).

In those rare cases where educators and students knew about their rights under Title IX, they have taken extraordinary actions to challenge unfairness: A valedictorian successfully overturned her school's decision forbidding her from giving a high school graduation speech because she was pregnant; a fourth-grade teacher and her students challenged a hospital-supported advertisement depicting girls sick due to math class; and a high school football coach lobbied his school board to fund equitable sports facilities for female and male athletes (NCWGE, 2002). In *Jackson v. Birmingham Board of Education*, a coach of a high school girls' basketball team alerted school authorities that girls were not getting the same funding, equipment, uniforms, and access to facilities that were provided to the boys' team. Instead of rectifying the injustice, school administrators fired Jackson from his coaching job. The coach sued the school board for retaliation, and the U.S. Supreme Court ruled in his favor. Because of Coach Jackson's courage, citizens filing a Title IX complaint are protected from retaliation (NWLC, 2005a).

Unfortunately, with little funding provided to promote awareness or enforcement of Title IX, gender bias continues to be a daily part of the school life for both students and teachers.

Despite 30 years of Title IX, we still fall short of the elimination of the "corrosive and unjustified sex discrimination" in education as described by the late Representative Edith Green and former Senator Birch Bayh when they sponsored Title IX (Congressional Record, 1971).

Gendered Aggression

It is no secret that teachers—new and seasoned—regularly cite classroom management as the most challenging aspect of their job. For many, it is the reason they leave teaching (Emmer, Evertson, & Worsham, 2006). Teacher–student discipline problems, steeped in gendered expectations, can lead to harsh punishments for males, especially males of color, too many of whom drop out of school. So for both teachers and students, understanding aggressive behavior is central to effective teaching and learning. Yet the gendered nature of student aggression is one of the least examined areas of classroom life.

Picture a disruptive classroom and you are likely to envision a few boys as troublemakers. Why boys? Many link male aggression with the male stereotype, the role boys are expected to play in society. William Pollack (1998) calls it the "boy code" and the "mask of masculinity"—a kind of swaggering posture that boys embrace to hide their fears, suppress dependency and vulnerability, and present a stoic, impervious front. What is that "boy code"? Thirty years ago, the psychologist Robert Brannon described the four basic rules of manhood (Brannon & David, 1976), characteristics echoed today by students:

1. *No sissy stuff.* Masculinity is the repudiation of the feminine.
2. *Be a big wheel.* Masculinity is measured by wealth, power, and status.
3. *Be a sturdy oak.* Masculinity requires emotional imperviousness.
4. *Give 'em hell.* Masculinity requires daring, aggression, and risk-taking in our society.

Boys' stereotypic expectations often lead to physical confrontations in the classroom, including harassment and bullying. Typically, boys targeted by such behaviors also respond physically, feeding the cycle of violence while underscoring a pervasive homophobia. Males adhering to traditional sex-role stereotypes are more likely to harass and be violent, more likely to see such acts as normal, and less likely to take responsibility for their actions (Perry, Schmidtke, & Kulik, 1998; Pollack, 1998).

Homophobia, an irrational fear of homosexuals, has been described as a universal experience for males, a "force stronger than gravity in the lives of adolescent boys" (Kindlon & Thompson, 1999, p. 89). Whether it is the fear of being called a "wuss," "fag" or "sissy" or the threat of being identified as feminine, boys of all ages are keenly aware of the strict behavioral boundaries set by the masculine ideal and the high price that is exacted from them for playing "out of bounds." Boys often project an outward appearance of strength, confidence, and security even when all are lacking. Homophobia encourages the disparity between outward appearance and inner self, further paving the way toward much of the disrespectful and violent behavior we are seeking to prevent in our schools.

For the teacher, the management lesson seems clear: Control the boys and all problems will be resolved. Since boys are usually more physically aggressive than girls, and more difficult to control, the teacher is advised to closely monitor males in the classroom, to ensure that things do not get out of control.

While male misbehavior captures teacher attention, girls' gendered behavioral problems typically fly below the radar screen of teachers. Relational aggression—spreading rumors, forming cliques, and even fighting—is harder to see than the physical male aggression, and can be delivered in a whisper. But such behavior is a form of aggression, readily seen and felt daily by students (Zittleman, 2005). Relational aggression harms healthy female relationships and distracts from academics. Research suggests that children find this form of aggression as painful as the more physical type (Brown, 2001; Merten, 1997). While teachers rarely react to relational aggression, they may overreact to even the potential of male misbehavior. Such disparities are readily detected by students who report that innocent boys are often targeted unfairly by teachers, and girls are able "to get away" with inappropriate and hurtful behavior (Zittleman, 2005). Such inequities detract from learning and a sense of security for all students.

Students are not the only ones able to detect relational aggression: The popular press reports on it often. Stories about "cruel and nasty girls" have been the subject of magazine articles, television shows, and popular books, such as *Mean Chicks, Cliques, and Dirty Tricks*, by Erika Karres, 2003; *Odd Girl Out: The Hidden Culture of Aggression in Girls*, by Rachel Simmons, 2003; and *Queen Bees and Wannabes*, by Rosalind Wiseman, 2001. How ironic that even as the media popularizes "mean" girls, educators remain unable to respond to them.

Is relational aggression important? A review of the psychological literature concerning girls reveals that relationship issues are central for girls. First, girls depend on close, intimate friendships to get them through life. The trust and support of these relationships provide girls with emotional and psychological safety nets; with their friends behind them, girls will do and say things that are remarkably creative and brave and "out of character." Second, girls, particularly in early adolescence, are excruciatingly tough on other girls. They talk behind each others' backs, they tease and torture one another; they police each others' clothing and body size and fight over real or imagined relationships with boys. In so doing they participate in and help to reproduce largely negative views of female relationships as untrustworthy, deceitful, manipulative, bitchy, and catty (Brown, 2003; Crick & Grotpeter, 1995; DeAngelis, 2003). Educators committed to creating fair and effective classrooms would be wise to listen to girls'—and boys'— voices, to address and correct damaging classroom aggression, both physical and relational.

A DOZEN STRATEGIES FOR CREATING GENDER-FAIR CLASSROOMS

Although some of these recent trends are discouraging, teachers have the power to make an enormous difference in the lives of students. The following suggestions consist of ways to make your own classroom nonsexist (AAUW, 1998a; Sadker, Sadker, & Klein, 1986, 1991; Sadker & Zittleman, 2005).

1. If the textbooks and software that you are given are biased, you may wish to confront this bias rather than ignore it. Discuss the issue directly with your students. It is entirely appropriate to acknowledge that instructional materials are

not always perfect. By engaging your students in a conversation about curricular omission and stereotyping, you can introduce them to important social issues and help them to develop critical literacy skills as well.

2. Supplementary materials can offset the influence of limited textbooks. School, university, and local libraries, as well as the Internet, can offer information on the lives and contributions of women and other underrepresented groups.

3. Have your students help you assemble bulletin boards, websites, and other instructional displays. Teach them about the forms of curricula bias and make sure that the displays, projects, and products are bias-free.

4. Analyze your seating chart to determine whether there are pockets of race, ethnic, class, or gender segregation in your classroom. Make certain that you do not teach from one area of the room, investing your time and attention on one group of students while ignoring others. When your students work in groups, construct the groups to reflect diversity. Monitor student groups for equitable participation and decision making.

5. Role modeling is central to learning. Students are taught less by what adults say and more by what adults do. This is particularly true in the classroom, where teachers' words are measured against their actions. A male teacher who cooks or weaves, or a female teacher active on the athletic fields or skillful with machines, teaches students believable and powerful lessons about the range of gender behaviors.

   Educators can extend these lessons by inviting multicultural guest speakers to the classroom, speakers who can address interests and competencies that break stereotypic boundaries. For younger children, inviting male nurses and female physicians to the classroom widens the career horizons of both genders. Even for older children, an engineer or a graphic artist who describes the exact tasks involved in their jobs (specifics that often elude even adults!) can enlighten both girls and boys to the amazing possibilities of the workplace.

6. Technology's promise can be short-circuited by curricular and instructional biases. Teachers should schedule computer time equally for all students. A schedule is better than the democratic-sounding phrase *free time*, which can result in the very undemocratic domination of the keyboard by a few of the more aggressive students. Schedules create more equitable access. In addition to creating rules for computer access, software needs to be analyzed. Newer technologies are no guarantee that old and destructive biases will not reappear. Teachers and students need to make certain that new technology does not reinforce racial, ethnic, gender, or any other form of destructive bias.

7. Peer tutoring and cooperative learning can encourage positive gender and racial relationships. Moreover, these techniques increase achievement not only for the students being helped but for those doing the helping. Both peer tutoring and cooperative learning are much more powerful when students receive training in how to work constructively with others. Where such training is not given, boys tend to dominate cooperative learning groups.

8. Positive reinforcement can be effective for increasing the amount of time boys and girls work and play in coeducational arrangements. In some studies (Holden, 1993; Petersen, Johnson, & Johnson, 1991; Schmuck & Schmuck, 1992) teachers made a consistent effort to praise girls and boys who were working and playing cooperatively together. When teachers praised in this way, the amount of time girls and boys spent working and playing cooperatively increased.

9. Most teachers find it difficult to track their own questioning patterns while they are teaching. Try to have someone do this for you. Make arrangements to have a professional whose feedback you value (a supervisor, your principal, another teacher) come into your classroom and observe. Your observer can tally how many questions you ask boys and how many you ask girls as well as how many questions you ask students of different racial and ethnic groups. Then you can consider the race and sex of the active students and silent students in your class. Determine whether one group is receiving more than its fair share of your time and attention.

10. Because teachers may find it difficult to have professional observers come into their classrooms on a regular basis, many have found it helpful to have students track interaction patterns, counting who gets questions and who is likely to be left out. Before you do this, you may want to explain to the class how important it is for all students to become involved in classroom discussion. Sharing your commitment to equity with your students is itself an important and genuine technique for promoting fairness in and beyond the classroom.

11. Do not tolerate harmful words, bullying, or harassment in your classroom. Do not say "Boys will be boys" to excuse sexist comments or behaviors. Nor are racist or antigay comments to be ignored, laughed at, or tolerated. As a teacher, you are the model and the norm setter: If you do not tolerate hurtful prejudice, your students will learn to honor and respect each other.

12. Because research on gender equity in education is occurring at a rapid pace, it is important to continue your reading and professional development in this area. Be alert for articles and other publications on the topic, and be careful that your own rights are not denied because of sex discrimination. Also, be discerning as you read related topics. Remember that research publications are less susceptible to political agendas than are the popular press or politically funded organizations.

Questions and Activities

1. The authors of this chapter list seven forms of gender bias that you can use when evaluating instructional materials: (1) invisibility, (2) stereotyping, (3) linguistic bias, (4) imbalance, (5) unreality, (6) fragmentation, and (7) cosmetic bias. In your own words, define each form of bias. Examine a sample K–12 textbook in your teaching

area and determine whether it contains any of these forms of gender bias. Are there forms of bias reflected against any other groups? Share your findings with your classmates or workshop participants.

2. Give three examples of how teachers can supplement textbooks to eliminate the seven forms of gender bias identified in item 1 (above). Now go online and search for equity websites that provide supplementary resources.

3. Why have centuries of female efforts to gain educational access gone almost unnoticed and unrecognized? How has that experience differed from civil rights efforts undertaken by African Americans, Latinos, and other groups? How has it been similar?

4. In what ways do Mrs. Howe's interactions with the boys and girls during the music lesson indicate gender bias? How might you help Mrs. Howe change her behavior and make it more gender-fair?

5. Observe lessons being taught in several classrooms that include boys and girls and students from different racial and ethnic groups. Create a seating chart and count the interactions between the teacher and each student. Did the ways in which the teachers interacted with males and female students differ? If so, in what ways? Did the teachers interact with students from various ethnic groups differently? If so, in what ways? Did you notice any ways in which gender and ethnicity combined to influence the ways the teachers interacted with particular students? If so, explain.

6. How can you use technology to supplement classroom materials and promote gender equity? Can you find some useful equity websites for your students that provide information missing from textbooks?

7. Girls start out in school ahead of boys in speaking, reading, and counting. Boys surpass girls in math performance by junior high school. Why do you think this happens? Recent research indicates that the disparities in the academic achievement of boys and girls are declining. Why do you think this achievement gap is shrinking?

8. In what ways, according to the authors, are single-sex schools beneficial for females? Why do you think all-girl schools are making a comeback? Why is the research on the effectiveness of boys' schools less persuasive? Do you think this trend toward single-sex schooling should be halted or supported? Why or why not?

9. After reading this chapter, do you think there are some ways in which you can change your behavior to make it more gender-fair? If yes, in what ways? If no, why not?

10. How are the rights of gay and lesbian students related to gender-equity issues? How does homophobia endanger the rights of all students? What can teachers do to create safe and effective classroom climates for all students?

11. Check out the requirements of Title IX. Prepare a brief list to remind yourself of some of the ways in which the law is designed to ensure gender equity. (The Internet is a good source for this information. Try http://www.titleix.info/index.jsp.)

12. Consider how gender bias affects males by creating questions based on the report card findings in this chapter. Interview boys of various ages and collect their insights about male and female roles. How aware are your interviewees about the dangers of the male stereotype? How do they describe their roles as adult men?

References

ACT. (2005). *ACT High School Profile Report 2005.* Retrieved on November 19, 2005, from http://www.act.org/news/data/05/.

Altermatt, E. R., Jovanovic, J., & Perry, M. (1998). Bias or Responsivity? Sex and Achievement-Level Effects on Teachers' Classroom Questioning Practices. *Journal of Educational Psychology, 90*(3), 516–527.

American Association of University Women (AAUW). (2004). *Hostile Hallways: Bullying, Teasing, and Sexual Harassment in School.* Washington, DC: AAUW.

American Association of University Women (AAUW). (2000). *Tech-Savvy: Educating Girls in the New Computer Age.* Washington, DC.

American Association of University Women (AAUW) Educational Foundation. (1998a). *Gender Gaps: Where Schools Still Fail Our Children.* Washington, DC: Author.

American Association of University Women (AAUW) Educational Foundation. (1998b). *Separated by Sex: A Critical Look at Single-Sex Education for Girls.* Washington, DC: Author.

American Association of University Women (AAUW) Educational Foundation. (1992). *How Schools Shortchane Girls.* Washington, DC: Author.

American Psychological Association, APA Public Policy Office. (1999). Is Youth Violence Just Another Fact of Life? In *Raising Children to Resist Violence: What You Can Do.* Washington, DC: Author.

Apple, M. W. (2001) *Educating the "Right Way": Market, Standards, God and Inequality.* New York: RoutledgeFalmer.

Arms, E. (in progress). Gender Equity in Coeducational and Single Sex Environments. In S. Klein (Ed.), *Handbook for Achieving Gender Equity through Education.* Mahwah, NJ: Erlbaum Associates.

Astin, A. (1993). *What Matters in College: Four Critical Years Revisited.* San Francisco: Jossey Bass.

Babad, E. (1998). Preferential Affect: The Crux of the Teacher Expectancy Issue. In J. Brophy (Ed.), *Advances in Research on Teaching: Expectations in the Classroom* (pp. 183–214). Greenwich, CT: JAI Press.

Bailey, B. L., Scantlebury, K., & Letts, W. J. (1997). It's Not My Style: Using Disclaimers to Ignore Issues in Science. *Journal of Teacher Education, 48*(1), 29–35.

Beck, R., Black, L., Krieger, L., Naylor, P., & Shabaka, D. (2005). *World History: Patterns of Interaction.* Evanston, IL: McDougal Littell.

Brannon, R., & David, D. (1976). *The Forty-Nine Percent Majority.* Reading, PA: Addison Wesley.

Brophy, J., & Good, T. (1974). *Teacher–Student Relationships: Causes and Consequences.* New York: Holt, Rinehart & Winston.

Brown, L. M. (2003). *Girlfighting: Betrayal and Rejection among Girls.* New York: New York University Press.

Cairns, E. (1990). The Relationship between Adolescent Perceived Self-Competence and Attendance at Single-Sex Secondary School. *British Journal of Educational Psychology, 60*(3), 207–211.

Campbell, P. B., & Sanders, J. (1997). Uninformed, but Interested: Findings of a National Survey on Gender Equity in Preservice Teacher Education. *Journal of Teacher Education, 48*(1), 69–75.

Campbell, P. B., & Sanders, J. (2002). Challenging the System: Assumptions and Data behind the Push for Single-Sex Schools. In A. Datnow & L. Hubbard (Eds.), *Gender in Policy and Practice: Perspectives on Single-Sex and Coeducational Schooling* (pp. 31–46). New York: Routledge/Falmer.

Carter, R. (1987). Unpublished class paper. American University, Washington, DC. Used with permission.

Clarke, E. H. (1873). *Sex in Education; Or, a Fair Chance for Girls.* Boston: Houghton Mifflin.

College Board. (2005). *College-Bound Seniors 2005, Total Group Profile Report.* Retrieved on November 19, 2005 from http://www.collegeboard.com/prod_downloads/about/news_info/cbsenior/yr2005/2005-college-bound-seniors.pdf.

Congressional Record 117 2658 (1971).

Crick N. R., & Grotpeter, J. K. (1995). Relational Aggression, Gender and Social Psychological Adjustment. *Child Development, 66,* 710–722.

D'Ambrosio, M., & Hammer, P. S. (1996, April). *Gender Equity in the Catholic Elementary Schools.* Paper presented at the annual convention and exposition of the National Catholic Education Association, Philadelphia.

Daly, P., & Shuttleworth, I. (1997). Determinants of Public Examination Entry and Attainment in Mathematics: Evidence on Gender and Gender-Type of School from the 1980's and 1990's in Northern Ireland. *Evaluation and Research in Education, 11*(2), 91–101.

Datnow, A., & Hubbard, L. (Eds.). (2002). *Gender in Policy and Practice: Perspectives on Single-Sex and Coeducational Schooling.* New York: Routledge/Falmer.

Davis, A., & McDaniel, T. (1999). You've Come a Long Way, Baby—or Have You? Research Evaluating Gender Portrayal in Recent Caldecott-winning books. *Reading Teacher, 52,* 532–536.

DeAngelis, T. (2003). Girls Use a Different Kind of Weapon. *Monitor on Psychology, 34* (7). Washington, DC: American Psychological Association. Retrieved on August 10, 2005, from http://www.apa.org/monitor/julaug03/girls.html.

Deak, J. (2002). *Girls Will Be Girls: Raising Confident and Courageous Daughters.* New York: Hyperion.

Duncan-Andrade, J. (2005). Developing Social Justice Educators. *Educational Leadership, 62*(6), 70–73.

Dutro, E. (2001/2002). "But That's a Girls' Book!" Exploring Gender Boundaries in Children's Reading Practices. *Reading Teacher, 55,* 376–384.

Emmer, E. Evertson, C., & Worsham, M. (2006). *Classroom Management for Secondary Teachers.* Boston: Allyn & Bacon.

Evans, L., & Davies, K. (2000). No Sissy Boys Here: A Content Analysis of the Representation of Masculinity in Elementary School Reading Textbooks. *Sex Roles, 42,* 255–270.

Faludi, S. (1991). *Backlash: The Undeclared War Against American Women.* New York: Crown.

Fan, L., & Kaeley, G. (2000). The Influence of Textbooks on Teaching Strategies. *Mid-Western Educational Researcher, 13*(4), 2–9.

Fischer, L., Schimmel, D., Stellman, L., & Kelly, C. (2002). *Teachers and the Law* (6th ed.). Boston: Allyn & Bacon.

Flanders, N. (1970). *Analyzing Teaching Behaviors.* Reading, MA: Addison-Wesley.

Francis, B. (2000). *Boys, Girls, and Achievement: Addressing the Classroom Issues.* London: Routledge/Falmer.

Giordano, G. (2003). *Twentieth-Century Textbook Wars: A History of Advocacy and Opposition.* New York: Peter Lang.

Good, T., & Brophy, J. (2003). *Looking in Classrooms* (9th ed.). New York: Longman.

Gooden, A., & Gooden, M. (2001). Gender Representation in Notable Children's Picture Books: 1995–1999. *Sex Roles: A Journal of Research, 45*(1–2), 89–101.

Grant, C., & Sleeter, C. (2002). *Turning on Learning: Five Approaches for Multicultural Teaching Plans for Race, Class, Gender, and Disability.* (3rd edition). Hoboken, NJ: Wiley.

Gurian, M., & Stevens, K. (2005) *The Minds of Boys: Saving Our Sons from Falling behind in School and Life.* San Francisco: Jossey Bass

Hahn, C. L. (1996). Gender and Political Learning. *Theory and Research in Education, 24*(1), 8–35.

Harker, R. (2000). Achievement, Gender, and the Single Sex/Coed Debate. *British Journal of Sociology of Education.* 21: 203–218.

Heather, B. (2002). Constructions of Gender in Parents' Choice of a Single Sex School for Their Daughters. In A. Datnow & L. Hubbard (Eds.), *Gender in policy and practice: Perspectives on Single-Sex and Coeducational Schooling.* New York: Routledge/Falmer.

Herr, K., & Arms, E. (2002). The Intersection of Educational Reforms: Single-Gender Academies in a Public Middle School. In A. Datnow & L. Hubbard (Eds.), *Gender in Policy and Practice: Perspectives on Single-Sex and Coeducational Schooling* (pp. 31–46). New York: Routledge/Falmer.

Hodes, C. L. (1995–1996). Gender Representations in Mathematics Software. *Journal of Educational Technology Systems, 24*, 67–73.

Holden, C. (1993). Giving Girls a Chance: Patterns of Talk in Co-Operative Group Work. *Gender & Education, 5*, 179–89.

hooks, B. (2003). *Teaching Community: A Pedagogy of Hope.* New York: Routledge.

Jackson, C. (2002). Can Single-Sex Classes in Co-Educational Schools Enhance the Learning Experiences of Girls and/or Boys? An Exploration of Pupils' Perceptions. *British Educational Research Journal, 28*(1), 37–48.

Jones, K., Evans, C., Byrd, R., & Campbell, K. (2000). Gender Equity Training and Teacher Behavior. *Journal of Instructional Psychology, 27*(3), 173–178.

Jones, G. M., & Gerig, T. M. (1994). Silent Sixth-Grade Students: Characteristics, Achievement, and Teacher Expectations. *The Elementary School Journal, 95*(2), 169–182.

Karabel, J. (2005). The *Chosen: The Hidden History of Admission and Exclusion at Harvard, Yale, and Princeton.* Boston: Houghton Mifflin.

Karres, E. (2003). *Mean Chicks, Cliques, and Dirty Tricks.* Avon, MA: Adams Media Corporation.

Kindlon, D., & Thompson, M. (1999). *Raising Cain.* New York: Ballantine.

Kleinfeld, J. (1999). Student Performance: Males versus Females. *The Public Interest, 134*, 3–20.

Leach, M. (2005). Shelby Considers Same-Sex Classes. *The Birmingham News*, November 21, 2005, retrieved on November 24, 2005, http://www.al.com/news/birminghamnews/.

Lee, V. E. (1998) "Is Single Sex Schooling a Solution to the Problem of Gender Inequity?" In *Separate Sex: A Critical look at Single Sex Education for Girls.* Washington, DC: AAUW Educational Foundation, 41–52.

Lee, V. E. (1997). Gender Equity and the Organization of Schools. In B. J. Bank & P. M. Hall (Eds.), *Gender, Equity, and Schooling: Policy and Practice* (pp. 135–158). New York: Garland Publishing.

Lee, V., & Bryk, A. (1986). Effects of Single-Sex Secondary Schools on Student Achievement and Attitudes. *Journal of Educational Psychology, 78*(5), 381–395.

Lee, V., & Marks, H. (1990). Sustained Effects of the Single-Sex Secondary School Movement on Attitudes, Behaviors, and Values in College. *Journal of Educational Psychology, 82*(3), 578–592.

LePore, P. C., & Wareren, J. R. (1997). A Comparison of Single-Sex and Coeducational Catholic Secondary Schooling: Evidence from the National Educational Longitudinal Study of 1988. *American Educational Research Journal, 34*(3), 485–511.

Livingston, C. (1997). Women in Music Education in the United States: Names Mentioned in History Books. *Journal of Research in Music Education, 45*(1), 130–144.

Loewen, J. (1995). *Lies My Teacher Told Me.* New York: New Press.

Maccoby, E. (1998). *The Two Sexes: Growing up Apart, Coming Together.* Cambridge: Harvard University Press.

Merten, D. (1997).The Meaning of Meanness: Popularity, Competition, and Conflict among Junior High School Girls. *Sociology of Education, 70,* 175–191.

Molnar, A. (1996). *Giving Kids the Business: The Commercialization of America's Schools.* Boulder, CO: Westview Press.

Moore, M., Piper, V., & Schaefer, E. (1992), Single-Sex Schooling and Educational Effectiveness: A Research Overview. In D. Hollinger & R. Adamson (Eds.), *Single-Sex Schooling: Proponents Speak.* Washington, DC: U.S. Department of Education, 7–67.

National Center for Education Statistics (NCES). (2004a) *Digest of Education Statistics, 2003.* Washington, DC: U.S. Government Printing Office.

National Center for Education Statistics (NCES). (2004b). *Trends in Educational Equity for Girls and Women.* Washington, DC: U.S. Government Printing Office.

National Center for Education Statistics (NCES). (2006). *Indicators of School Crime and Safety: 2005.* Retrieved on November 20, 2005, from http://nces.ed.gov/pubs2006/2006001.pdf.

National Coalition of Girls Schools (2005, October) *Report on Single-Sex Education Finds High Satisfaction Levels: 90% of Alumnae Would Choose Girls' School Again.* Retrieved on November 25, 2005, fromhttp://www.ncgs.org/pressview.php?aid=52.

National Coalition for Women and Girls in Education. (2002, June). *Title IX at 30: Report Card on Gender Equity.* Washington, DC: Author.

National Women's Law Center (2005a). *Supreme Court's Decision in Jackson v. Birmingham Board of Education Enhance Protections of Title IX.* Retrieved on November 9, 2005, from http://www.nwlc.org/pdf/FactSheet_JacksonSupremeCourt.pdf.

National Women's Law Center (2005b). *Tools of the Trade.* Retrieved on November 21, 2005, from http://www.nwlc.org/pdf/NWLCToolsoftheTrade05.pdf.

National Wrestling Coaches Association v. United States Department of Education. (2003). Civ. No. 02-0072, US. District Court.

Orfield, G., *Losen,* D., Wald, J., *Swanson,* C., (2004). Losing our Future; How Minority Youths Are Being by the Graduation Rate Crises, Washington, DC: Urban Institute. Retrieved online May 2006 at www.urban.org

Perry, E. L., Schmidtke, J. M., & Kulik, C. T. (1998). Propensity to Sexually Harass: An Exploration of Gender Differences. *Sex Roles: A Journal of Research, 38*(5–6), 443–460.

Petersen, R., Johnson, D., & Johnson, R. (1991). Effects of Cooperative Learning on Perceived Status of Male and Female Pupils. *Journal of Social Psychology, 131,* 717–735.

Pollack, W. (1998). *Real Boys: Rescuing Our Sons from the Myths of Boyhood.* New York: Random House.

Reisman, D. (1990). A Margin of Difference: The Case for Single-Sex Education. In J. R. Blau (Ed.), *Social Roles and Social Institutions,* pp. 243–244. Boulder, CO: Westview Press.

Riordan, C. (1990). *Girls and Boys in School: Together or Separate?* New York: Teachers College Press.

Riordan, C. (2002). What Do We Know About the Effects of Single-Sex Schools in the Private Sector? Implications for Public Schools. In A. Datnow & L. Hubbard (Eds.), *Doing Gender in*

Policy and Practice: Perspectives on Single-Sex and Coeducational Schooling (pp. 10–30). New York: Routledge/Falmer.

Sadker, D. (1996, September 4). Where the Girls Are? *Education Week*, Commentary, pp. 49–50.

Sadker, D. (1999). Gender Equity: Still Knocking at the Classroom Door. *Educational Leadership*, *56*(7), 22–26.

Sadker, D. (2002). At Issue: Should Federal Regulations Make It Easier for School Districts to Establish Single-Sex Schools or Classes? *Congressional Quarterly Researcher, 12*(25), 585.

Sadker, D. (2004). *Single-Sex Versus Coeducation: The False Debate.* Paper presented at the First International Conference on Gender Equity Education in the Asia Pacific Region, Taipei, Taiwan, November 25, 2004.

Sadker, D. (2005). Riding the Tiger: The Press, Myra and Me. In *Social Studies and the Press: Keeping the Tiger at Bay*, M. Crocco (Ed.) Greenwich, CT: Information Age Publishers.

Sadker, D., & Zittleman, K. (March/April 2005). "Closing the Gender Gap—Again!" *Principal Magazine, 84*, 18–22.

Sadker, M., & Sadker, D. (1984). *Year 3: Final Report: Promoting Effectiveness in Classroom Instruction.* Washington, DC: National Institute of Education. ED257819.

Sadker, M., & Sadker, D. (1985, March). Sexism in the Classroom of the 80s. *Psychology Today*, 54–57.

Sadker, M., & Sadker, D. (1994). *Failing at Fairness: How America's Schools Cheat Girls.* New York: Scribners.

Sadker, M., & Sadker, D. (2005). *Teachers, Schools, and Society* (7th ed.). Boston: McGraw-Hill.

Sadker, M., Sadker, D., & Klein, S. (1986). Abolishing Misperceptions About Sex Equity in Education. *Theory into Practice, 25*, 220–226.

Sadker, M., Sadker, D., & Klein, S. (1991). The Issue of Gender in Elementary and Secondary Education. In G. Grant (Ed.), *Review of Research in Education*, 17, 269–334. Washington, DC: American Educational Research Association.

Sadker, M., Sadker, D., & Shakeshaft, C. (1992). Sexuality and Sexism in School: How Should Educators Be Prepared? In S. S. Klein (Ed.), *Sex Equity and Sexuality in Education* (pp. 363–375). Albany: State University of New York Press.

Salomone, R. (2002). The Legality of Single-Sex Education in the United States: Sometimes "Equal" Means "Different." In A. Datnow & L. Hubbard (Eds.), *Doing Gender in Policy and Practice: Perspectives on Single-Sex and Coeducational Schooling* (pp. 47–72). New York: Routledge/Falmer.

Salomone, R. C. (2003). *Same, Different, Equal.* New Haven: Yale University Press.

Sanford, K., & Blair, H. (2002). Engendering Public Education: Single-Sex Schooling in Western Canada. In A. Datnow & L. Hubbard (Eds.), *Gender in Policy and Practice: Perspectives on Single-Sex and Coeducational Schooling.* New York: Routledge/Falmer.

Sax, L. (2005) *Why Gender Matters: What Parents and Teachers Need to Know About the Emerging Science of Sex Differences.* New York: Doubleday.

Schmuck, R., & Schmuck, P. (1992). *Group Processes in the Classroom* (6th ed.). Dubuque, IA: Brown.

Shmurak, C. B. (1994). What Will She Be When She Grows up? Career Paths of Independent School Alumnae. *Independent School, 55*(1), 36–42.

Simmons, R. (2003). *Odd Girl Out: The Hidden Culture of Aggression in Girls.* New York: Harcourt.

Smith, D. (1990). Women's Colleges and Coed Colleges: Is There a Difference for Women? *Journal of Higher Education, 61*(2), 181–197.

Sommers, C. H. (1995). *Who Stole Feminism? How Women Have Betrayed Women.* New York: Simon & Schuster.

Sommers, C. H. (2000). *The War against Boys: How Misguided Feminism Is Harming Our Young Men.* New York: Simon & Schuster.

Spencer, R., Porche, M., & Toman, D. (2003). We've Come a Long Way—Maybe. New Challenges for Gender Equity Education. *Teachers College Record, 105,* (9), 1774–1807. Retrieved on July 12, 2005, from http://www.tcrecord.org.

Stabiner, K. (2002). *All Girls: Single-Sex Education and Why It Matters.* New York: Riverhead.

Starnes, B. A. (2004). Textbooks, School Reform, and the Silver Lining. *Phi Delta Kappan, 86*(2), 170–171.

Stoecker, J. L., & Pascarella, E. T. (1991). Women's Colleges and Women's Career Attainments Revisited. *Journal of Higher Education, 62*(4), 394–406.

Tidball, E., & Kistiakowsky, V. (1976). Baccalaureate Origins of American Scientists and Scholars. *Science, 193,* 646–652.

Tyack, D., & Hansot, E. (1990). *Learning Together: A History of Coeducation in American Schools.* New Haven, CT: Yale University Press.

United States Department of Education, Office for Civil Rights. (2005). *Additional Clarification of Intercollegiate Athletics Policy: Three Part Test—Part Three.* Retrieved on June 30, 2005, from http://www.ed.gov/about/offices/list/ocr/docs/title9guidanceadditional.html.

United States Department of Education, Office for Civil Rights. (2002). *OCR Annual Report to Congress, 2001.* Washington, DC: U.S. Government Printing Office.

United States Department of Education. (2005). Principals in Public and Private Elementary and Secondary Schools by Selected Characteristics, *Digest of Educational Statistics 2000,* Washington, D.C.: U.S. Government Printing Office.

Warrington, M., & Younger, M. (2003). We Decided to Give It a Twirl: Single-Sex Teaching in English Comprehensive Schools. *Gender and Education, 15*(4): 339–350.

Wiseman, R. (2002). *Queen Bees and Wannabes.* New York: Crown.

Woodward, A., & Elliot, D. L. (1990). Textbook Use and Teacher Professionalism. In D. L. Elliot & A. Woodward (Eds.), *Textbooks and Schooling in the United States,* 89th Yearbook of the National Society for the Study of Education (pp. 178–193). Chicago: University of Chicago Press.

Woody, E. (2002). Constructions of Masculinity in California's Single Gender Academies. In A. Datnow & L. Hubbard (Eds.), *Doing Gender in Policy and Practice: Perspectives on Single-Sex and Coeducational Schooling* (pp. 280–303). New York: Routledge/Falmer.

Zittleman, K. (2005). Title IX and Gender: A Study of the Knowledge, Perceptions, and Experiences of Middle and Junior High School Teachers and Students. *Dissertation Abstracts International 66*(11), (UMI No. 3194815).

Zittleman, K., & Sadker, D. (2002). Gender Bias in Teacher Education Texts: New (and Old) Lessons. *Journal of Teacher Education, 53*(2), 168–179.

CHAPTER 7

Classrooms for Diversity: Rethinking Curriculum and Pedagogy

Mary Kay Thompson Tetreault

> It's time to start learning about things they told you you didn't
> need to know . . . learning about me, instead of learning about
> them, starting to learn about her instead of learning about him. It's
> a connection that makes education education. (A student of
> European and African American ancestry.)

This student's reflection on her education signals a twin transformation that is pushing us to rethink our traditional ways of teaching. The first is that students in our classrooms are increasingly more diverse and the second is that traditional course content has been enriched by the new scholarship on women, cultural studies, and multiculturalism. It is in the classroom that these transformations intersect, and it rests on the teacher to make education "education" for this student and for the majority who feel their education was not made for them—women of all backgrounds, people of color, and men who lack privilege because of their social class—by bringing the two together. The current challenges to classroom teachers are not only to incorporate multiple perspectives into the curriculum but also to engage in pedagogical practices that bring in the voices of students as a source for learning rather than managing or controlling them.

FEMINIST PHASE THEORY

One of the most effective ways I have found to set a frame for envisioning a gender-balanced, multicultural curriculum, while at the same time capturing the reforms that have occurred over the past thirty-five years, is feminist phase theory. Conceptually rooted in the scholarship on women, feminist phase theory is a classification system of the evolution in thought about the incorporation of women's traditions, history, and experiences into selected disciplines. The model I have developed identifies five common phases of thinking about women: *male-defined curriculum, contribution curriculum, bifocal curriculum, women's curriculum,* and *gender-balanced curriculum.* A gender-balanced perspective, one that is rooted in feminist scholarship, takes into account the experiences, perspectives, and voices of women as well as men. It examines the similarities and differences between women and men and also considers how gender interacts with such factors as ethnicity, race, culture, and class.

The language of this system or schema, particularly the word *phase,* and the description of one phase and then another suggest a sequential hierarchy in which one phase supplants another. Before reviewing the schema, please refrain from thinking of these phases in a linear fashion; envision them as a series of intersecting circles, or patches on a quilt, or threads in a tapestry, which interact and undergo changes in response to one another. It is more accurate to view the phases as different emphases that coexist in feminist research. The important thing is that teachers, scholars, and curriculum developers ask and answer certain questions at each phase.

The following section identifies key concepts and questions articulated initially at each phase, using examples from history, literature, and science; it then discusses how the phases interact and undergo changes in response to one another. The final part of this chapter shows teachers grappling with the intersection of changes in the disciplines and changes in the student population and presents four themes of analysis: mastery, voice, authority, and positionality. The chapter concludes with specific objectives, practices, and teaching suggestions for incorporating content about women into the K–12 curriculum in social studies, language arts, and science.

Male-Defined Curriculum

Male-defined curricula rest on the assumption that the male experience is universal, that it is representative of humanity, and that it constitutes a basis for generalizing about all human beings. The knowledge that is researched and taught, the substance of learning, is knowledge articulated by and about men. There is little or no consciousness that the existence of women as a group is an anomaly calling for a broader definition of knowledge. The female experience is subsumed under the male experience. For example, feminist scientists have cited methodological problems in some research about sex differences that draws conclusions about females based on experiments done only on males or that uses limited (usually White, middle-class) experimental populations from which scientists draw conclusions about all males and females.

The incorporation of women into the curriculum has not only taught us about women's lives but has also led to questions about our lopsided rendition of men's lives, wherein we pay attention primarily to men in the public world and conceal their lives in the private world. Historians, for example, are posing a series of interesting questions about men's history: What do we need to unlearn about men's history? What are the taken-for-granted truths about men's history that we need to rethink? How do we get at the significant masculine truths? Is man's primary sense of self defined in relation to the public sphere only? How does it relate to boyhood, adolescence, family life, recreation, and love? What do the answers to these questions imply about the teaching of history?

Feminist scholarship, like African American, Native American, Chicano/Latino, and Asian American scholarship, reveals the systematic and contestable exclusions in the male-defined curriculum. When we examine it through the lens of this scholarship, we are forced to reconsider our understanding of the most fundamental conceptualization of knowledge and social relations within our society. We understand in a new way that knowledge is a social construction, written by individual human beings who live and think at a particular time and within a particular social framework. All works in literature, science, and history, for example, have an author, male or female, White or ethnic or racial minority, elite or middle class or occasionally poor, with motivations and beliefs. The scientist's questions and activities, for instance, are shaped, often unconsciously, by the great social issues of the day (see Table 7.1). Different perspectives on the same subject will change the patterns discerned.

Table 7.1   Male-Defined Curriculum

Characteristics of Phase	Questions Commonly Asked about Women in History*	Questions Commonly Asked about Women in Literature*	Questions Commonly Asked about Women in Science*
The absence of women is not noted. There is no consciousness that the male experience is a "particular knowledge" selected from a wider universe of possible knowledge and experience. It is valued, emphasized, and viewed as the knowledge most worth having.	Who is the author of a particular history? What is her or his race, ethnicity, religion, ideological orientation, social class, place of origin, and historical period? How does incorporating women's experiences lead to new understandings of the most fundamental ordering of social relations, institutions, and power arrangements? How can we define the content and methodology of history so it will be a history of us all?	How is traditional humanism, with an integrated self at its center and an authentic view of life, in effect part of patriarchal ideology? How can the objectivist illusion be dismantled? How can the idea of a literary canon of "great literature" be challenged? How are writing and reading political acts? How do race, class, and gender relate to the conflict, sufferings, and passions that attend these realities? How can we study language as specific *discourse*, that is, specific linguistic strategies in specific situations, rather than as universal language?	How do scientific studies reveal cultural values? What cultural, historical, and gender values are projected onto the physical and natural world? How might gender be a bias that influences choice of questions, hypotheses, subjects, experimental design, or theory formation in science? What is the underlying philosophy of an andocentric science that values objectivity, rationality, and dominance? How can the distance between the subject and the scientific observer be shortened so that the scientist has some feeling for or empathy with the organism? How can gender play a crucial role in transforming science?

*New questions generated by feminist scholars.

Contribution Curriculum

Early efforts to reclaim women's rightful place in the curriculum were a search for missing women within a male framework. Although there was the recognition that women were missing, men continued to serve as the norm, the representative, the universal human being. Outstanding women emerged who fit this male norm of excellence or greatness or conformed to implicit assumptions about appropriate roles for women outside the home. In literature, female authors were added who performed well within the masculine tradition, internalizing its standards of art and its views on social roles. Great women of science who made it in the male scientific world, most frequently Marie Curie, for example, were added.

Examples of contribution history can be seen in U.S. history textbooks. They now include the contributions of notable American women who were outstanding in the public sphere as rulers or as contributors to wars or reform movements to a remarkable degree. Queen Liliuokalani, Hawaii's first reigning queen and a nationalist, is included in the story of the kingdom's annexation. Molly Pitcher and Deborah Sampson are depicted as contributors to the Revolutionary War, as is Clara Barton to the Civil War effort. Some authors have also included women who conform to the assumption that it is acceptable for women to engage in activities outside the home if they are an extension of women's nurturing role within the family. Examples of this are Dorothea Dix, Jane Addams, Eleanor Roosevelt, and Mary McLeod Bethune (Tetreault, 1986).

The lesson to be learned from understanding these limitations of early contribution history is not to disregard the study of notable women but to include those who worked to reshape the world according to a feminist reordering of values. This includes efforts to increase women's self-determination through a feminist transformation of the home, to increase education, political rights, and women's rights to control their bodies, and also to improve their economic status. A history with women at the center moves beyond paying attention to caring for the unfortunate in the public sphere to how exceptional women influenced the lives of women in general (see Table 7.2). Just as Mary McLeod Bethune's role in the New Deal is worth teaching to our students, so is her aggressive work to project a positive image of Black women to the nation through her work in Black women's clubs and the launching of the *Afro-American Woman's Journal*.

Bifocal Curriculum

In bifocal curricula, feminist scholars have made an important shift from a perspective that views men as the norm to one that opens up the possibility of seeing the world through women's eyes. This dual vision, or bifocal perspective, generated global questions about women and about the differences between women and men. Historians investigated the separation between the public and the private sphere and asked, for example, how the division between them explains women's lives. Some elaborated on the construct by identifying arenas of female power in the domestic sphere. Literary critics aimed to provide a new understanding of a distinctively female literary tradition and a theory of women's literary creativity. They sought to provide models for understanding the dynamics of female literary response to male literary assertion and coercion. Scientists grapple with definitions of woman's and man's nature by asking how the public and private, biology

Table 7.2   Contribution Curriculum

Characteristics of Phase	Questions Commonly Asked about Women in History	Questions Commonly Asked about Women in Literature	Questions Commonly Asked about Women in Science
The absence of women is noted. There is a search for missing women according to a male norm of greatness, excellence, or humanness. Women are considered exceptional, deviant, or other. Women are added into history, but the content and notions of historical significance are not challenged.	Who are the notable women missing from history and what did they and ordinary women contribute in areas or movements traditionally dominated by men, for example, during major wars or during reform movements, like abolitionism or the labor movement? What did notable and ordinary women contribute in areas that are an extension of women's traditional roles, for example, caring for the poor and the sick? How have major economic and political changes like industrialization or extension of the franchise affected women in the public sphere? How did notable and ordinary women respond to their oppression, particularly through women's rights organizations? *Who were outstanding women who advocated a feminist transformation of the home, who contributed to women's greater self-determination through increased education, the right to control their bodies, an increase in their political rights, and the improvement of their economic status? *What did women contribute through the settlement house and labor movements?	Who are the missing female authors whose subject matter and use of language and form meet the male norm of "masterpiece"? What primary biological facts and interpretations are missing about major female authors?	Who are the notable women scientists who have made contributions to mainstream science? How is women's different (and inferior) nature related to hormones, brain lateralization, and sociobiology? Where are the missing females in scientific experiments? What is the current status of women within the scientific profession? *How does adding minority women into the history of science reveal patterns of exclusion and recast definitions of what it means to practice science and to be a scientist? *How is the exclusion of women from science related to the way science is done and thought? *What is the usual pattern of women working in science? How is it the same as or different from the pattern of notable women? *How do our definitions of science need to be broadened to evaluate women's contributions to science? Do institutions of science need to be reshaped to accommodate women? If so, how?

*New questions generated by feminist scholars.

and culture, and personal and impersonal inform each other and affect men and women, science, and nature.

Scholars have pointed out some of the problems with bifocal knowledge. Thinking about women and men is dualistic and dichotomized. Women and men are thought of as having different spheres, different notions of what is of value in life, different ways of imagining the human condition, and different associations with nature and culture. But both views are valued. In short, women are thought of as a group that is complementary but equal to men; there are some truths for men and there are some truths for women. General analyses of men's and women's experiences often come dangerously close to reiterating the sexual stereotypes scholars are trying to overcome. Because many people believe that the public sphere is more valuable than the private sphere, there is a tendency to slip back into thinking of women as inferior and subordinate.

The generalized view of women and men that predominates in the bifocal curriculum often does not allow for distinctions within groups as large and as complex as women and men. Important factors like historical period, geographic location, structural barriers, race, paternity, sexual orientation, and social class, to name a few, clearly make a difference.

Other common emphases in the bifocal curriculum are the oppression of women and the exploration of that oppression. Exposés of woman-hating in history and literature are common. The emphasis is on the misogyny (the hatred of women) of the human experience, particularly the means men have used to advance their authority and to assert or imply female inferiority. The paradoxes of women's existence are sometimes overlooked with this emphasis on oppression. For example, although women have been excluded from positions of power, a few of them as wives and daughters in powerful families were often closer to actual power than were men. If some women were dissatisfied with their status and role, most women adjusted and resisted efforts to improve women's lot. Too much emphasis on women's oppression perpetuates a patriarchal framework presenting women as primarily passive, reacting only to the pressures of a sexist society. In the main, it emphasizes men thinking and women being thought about.

Women's scholarship from the 1970s through the present (Collins, 2000; Goldberger, Tarule, Clinchy, & Belenky, 1996; Schmitz, Butler, Guy-Sheftall, & Rosenfelt, 2004) has helped us see that understanding women's oppression is more complex than we initially thought. We do not yet have adequate concepts to explain gender systems founded on a division of labor and sexual asymmetry. To understand gender systems, it is necessary to take a structural and experiential perspective that asks from a woman's point of view where we are agents and where we are not, where our relations with men are egalitarian and where they are not. This questioning may lead to explanations of why women's experiences and interpretations of their world can differ significantly from men's.

Further, the concepts with which we approach our analysis need to be questioned. Anthropologists have pointed out that our way of seeing the world—for instance, the idea of complementary spheres for women (the private sphere) and men (the public sphere)—is a product of our experience in a Western, modern, industrial, capitalistic state with a specific history. We distort our understanding of other social systems by imposing our worldview on them. Feminist critics are calling for rethinking not only of categories like the domestic versus the public sphere, and production and reproduction, but also even of categories like gender itself.

Feminist scholars have helped us see the urgency of probing and analyzing the interactive nature of the oppressions of race, ethnicity, class, and gender (Collins, 2000; Hune & Nomura; Saldivar-Hull, 2000). We are reminded that we can no longer take a liberal reformist approach that does not probe the needs of the system that are being satisfied by oppression. We have to take seriously the model of feminist scholarship that analyzes women's status within the social, cultural, historical, political, and economic contexts. Only then will issues of gender be understood in relation to the economic needs of both male dominance and capitalism that undergird such oppressions.

One of the most important things we have learned about a bifocal perspective is the danger of generalizing too much, of longing for women's history instead of writing histories about women. We must guard against establishing a feminist version of great literature and then resisting any modifications or additions to it. We have also learned that the traditional disciplines are limited in their ability to shed light on gender complexities, and it becomes apparent that there is a need for an interdisciplinary perspective (see Table 7.3).

Women's Curriculum

The most important idea to emerge in women's scholarship is that women's activities, not men's, are the measure of significance. What was formerly devalued, the content of women's everyday lives, assumes new value as scholars investigate female rituals, housework, childbearing, child rearing, female sexuality, female friendship, and studies of the life cycle. For instance, scientists investigate how research on areas of interest primarily to women—menstruation, childbirth, and menopause—challenge existing scientific theories. Historians document women's efforts to break out of their traditional sphere of the home in a way that uses women's activities, not men's, as the measure of historical significance. These activities include women's education, women's paid work, and volunteer work outside the home, particularly in women's clubs and associations. Of equal importance is the development of a collective feminist consciousness, that is, of women's consciousness of their own distinct role in society. Analyses begun in the bifocal phase continue to explore what sex and gender have meant for the majority of women.

As scholars look more closely at the complex patterns of women's lives, they see the need for a pluralistic conceptualization of women. Although thinking of women as a monolithic group provides valuable information about patterns of continuity and change in those areas most central to women's lives, generalizing about a group as vast and diverse as women leads to inaccuracies. The subtle interactions among gender and other variables are investigated. Historians ask how the particulars of race, ethnicity, social class, marital status, and sexual orientation challenge the homogeneity of women's experiences. Third World feminists critique hegemonic "Western" feminisms and formulate autonomous, geographically, historically, and culturally grounded feminist concerns and strategies (Mohanty, 2003).

Questions about sex and gender are set within historical, ideological, and cultural contexts, including the culture's definition of the facts of biological development and what they mean for individuals. Researchers ask, for example, Why are these attitudes toward sexuality prevalent at this time in history? What are the ways in which sexual words, categories, and ideology mirror the organization of society as a whole? What are the socioeconomic

Table 7.3   Bifocal Curriculum

Characteristics of Phase	Questions Commonly Asked about Women in History	Questions Commonly Asked about Women in Literature	Questions Commonly Asked about Women in Science
Human experience is conceptualized primarily in dualist categories: male and female, private and public, agency and communion. Emphasis is on a complementary but equal conceptualization of men's and women's spheres and personal qualities. There is a focus on women's oppression and on misogyny. Women's efforts to overcome the oppression are presented. Efforts to include women lead to the insight that the traditional content, structure, and methodology of the disciplines are more appropriate to the male experience.	How does the division between the public and the private sphere explain women's lives? Who oppressed women, and how were they oppressed? *What are forms of power and value in women's world? *How have women been excluded from and deprived of power and value in men's sphere? *How do gender systems create divisions between the sexes such that experience and interpretations of their world can differ significantly from men's? *How can we rethink categories like public and private, productive and reproductive, sex and gender?	Who are the missing minor female authors whose books are unobtainable, whose lives have never been written, and whose works have been studied casually, if at all? How is literature a record of the collective consciousness of patriarchy? What myths and stereotypes about women are present in male literature? How can we critique the meritocratic pretensions of traditional literary history? How can we pair opposite-sex texts in literature as a way of understanding the differences between women's and men's experiences? How is literature one of the expressive modes of a female subculture that developed with the distinction of separate spheres for women and men? *How can feminist literary critics resist establishing their own great canon of literature and any additions to it?	How have the sciences defined (and misdefined) the nature of women? Why are there so few women scientists? What social and psychological forces have kept women in the lower ranks or out of science entirely? How do women fit into the study of history of science and health care? How do scientific findings, originally carried out on males of a species, change when carried out on the females of the same species? How do the theories and interpretations of sociobiology require constant testing and change to fit the theory for males and females with regard to competition, sexual selection, and infanticide? How does the science/gender system—the network of associations and disjunctions between public and private, personal and impersonal, and masculine and feminine—inform each other and affect men and women, science and nature? *What are the structural barriers to women in science?

*New questions generated by feminist scholars.

factors contributing to them? How do current conceptions of the body reflect social experiences and professional needs?

Life histories and autobiographies shed light on societies' perceptions of women and women's perceptions of themselves. Women's individual experiences are revealed through these stories and contribute to the fashioning of the human experience from the perspective of women.

Scholars find it necessary to draw on other disciplines for a clearer vision of the social structure and culture of societies as individuals encounter them in their daily life. Likewise, there are calls for new unifying frameworks and different ways to think of periods in history and literature to identify concepts that accommodate women's history and traditions. There is also a more complex conceptualization of historical time. The emphases in much history are on events, a unit of time too brief to afford a sense of structural change, changes in the way people think about their own reality, and the possibilities for other realities. L'Ecole des Annales in France (a group of historians who pioneered the use of such public records as birth, marriage, and death certificates in historical analysis) has distinguished between events and what they call the *longue durée* (Letters to the Editor, 1982). By the *longue durée* they mean the slow, glacial changes, requiring hundreds of years to complete, that represent significant shifts in the way people think.

Examples of areas of women's history that lend themselves to this concept are the structural change from a male-dominated to an egalitarian perspective and the transformation of women's traditional role in the family to their present roles as wives, mothers, and paid workers outside the home. Also important is the demographic change in the average number of children per woman of childbearing age from seven to fewer than two children between 1800 and 1990 (see Table 7.4).

Gender-Balanced Curriculum

This phase continues many of the inquiries begun in the women's curriculum phase, but it articulates questions about how women and men relate to and complement one another. Conscious of the limitations of seeing women in isolation and aware of the relational character of gender, researchers search for the nodal points at which women's and men's experiences intersect. Historians and literary critics ask if the private, as well as the public, aspects of life are presented as a continuum in women's and men's experience.

The pluralistic and multifocal conception of women that emerged in the women's curriculum phase is extended to human beings. A central idea in this phase is *positionality* (Alcoff, 2003; Haraway, 1997; Harding, 2004). Positionality means that important aspects of our identity (for example, our gender, our race, our class, and our age) are markers of relational positions rather than essential qualities. Their effects and implications change according to context. Recently, feminist thinkers have seen knowledge as valid when it comes from an acknowledgment of the knower's specific position in any context, one always defined by gender, race, class, and other variables.

Scientists ask explicit questions about the invention and reinvention of nature. For example, they ask questions about the meanings of the behavior and social lives of monkeys and

Table 7.4 Women's Curriculum

Characteristics of Phase	Questions Commonly Asked about Women in History	Questions Commonly Asked about Women in Literature	Questions Commonly Asked about Women in Science
Scholarly inquiry pursues new questions, new categories, and new notions of significance that illuminate women's traditions, history, culture, values, visions, and perspectives.

A pluralistic conception of women emerges that acknowledges diversity and recognizes that variables besides gender shape women's lives—for example, race, ethnicity, and social class.

Women's experience is allowed to speak for itself. Feminist history is rooted in the personal and the specific; it builds from that to the general.

The public and the private are seen as a continuum in women's experiences.

Women's experience is analyzed within the social, cultural, historical, political, and economic contexts.

Efforts are made to reconceptualize knowledge to encompass the female experience. The conceptualization of knowledge is not characterized by disciplinary thinking but becomes multidisciplinary. | What were the majority of women doing at a particular time in history? What was the significance of these activities?

How can female friendship between kin, mothers, daughters, and friends be analyzed as one aspect of women's overall relations with others?

What kind of productive work, paid and unpaid, did women do and under what conditions?

What were the reproductive activities of women? How did they reproduce the American family?

How did the variables of race, ethnicity, social class, marital status, and sexual preference affect women's experience?

What new categories need to be added to the study of history, for instance, romance, housework, childbearing, and child rearing?

How have women of different races and classes interacted throughout history?

What are appropriate ways of organizing or periodizing women's history? For example, how will examining women's experiences at each stage of the lifespan help us to understand women's experiences on their own terms? | What does women's sphere—for example, domesticity and family, education, marriage, sexuality, and love—reveal about our culture?

How can we contrast the fictional image of women in literature with the complexity and variety of the roles of individual women in real life as workers, housewives, revolutionaries, mothers, lovers, and so on?

How do the particulars of race, ethnicity, social class, marital status, and sexual orientation, as revealed in literature, challenge the thematic homogeneity of women's experiences?

How does literature portray what binds women together and what separates them because of race, ethnicity, social class, marital status, and sexual orientation?

How does the social and historical context of a work of literature shed light on it? | How do the cultural dualisms associated with masculinity and femininity permeate scientific thought and discourse?

How do women's actual experiences, as compared to the physician's analysis or scientific theory, challenge the traditional paradigms of science and of the health care systems?

How does research on areas of primary interest to women, for instance, menopause, childbirth, and menstruation/estrus, challenge existing scientific theories?

How do variables other than sex and gender, such as age, species, and individual variation, challenge current theories?

How do the experience of female primates and the variation among species of primates—for example, competition among females, female agency in sexuality, and infanticide—test the traditional paradigms? |

apes and male–female relations in animals and inquire about how such variables as age, species, and individual variation challenge current theories. They also explore contemporary technoscience—its stories and dreams, its facts and delusions, its institutions and politics, and its scientific advances (Haraway, 1991, 1997).

Accompanying this particularistic perspective is attention to the larger context, for example, the interplay among situation, meaning, economic systems, family organization, and political systems. Thus, historians ask how gender inequities are linked to economics, family organization, marriage, ritual, and politics. Research scientists probe how differences between the male and female body have been used to justify a social agenda that privileges men economically, socially, and politically. In this phase, a revolutionary relationship comes to exist between things traditionally treated as serious, primarily the activities of men in the public sphere, and those things formerly perceived as trivial, namely the activities of women in the private sphere.

This new relationship leads to a recentering of knowledge in the disciplines, a shift from a male-centered perspective to one that includes both females and males. This reconceptualization of knowledge works toward a more holistic view of the human experience. As in the previous stage, the conceptualization of knowledge is characterized by interdisciplinary thinking.

Feminist scholars have cautioned against moving too quickly from women's curricula to gender-balanced curricula. As the historian Gerda Lerner observed in the 1980s, our decade-and-a-half-old investigation of women's history is only a speck on the horizon compared to the centuries-old tradition of male-defined history. By turning too quickly to studies of gender, we risk short-circuiting important directions in women's studies and again having women's history and experiences subsumed under those of men. It remains politically important for feminists to defend women as women in order to counteract the male domination that continues to exist. The French philosopher Julia Kristeva (cited in Moi, 1985) and, more recently, Judith Butler (2004) push us to new considerations when they urge women (and men) to recognize the falsifying nature of masculinity and femininity, to explore how the fact of being born male or female determines one's position in relation to power, and to envision more fluid gender identities that have the potential to liberate both women and men to a fuller personhood (see Table 7.5). Of particular interest to teachers is the work of Barry Thorne (1993), who draws upon her daily observations in the classroom and on the playground to show how children construct gender and experience gender in the school.

Changing Traditional Ways of Teaching

Feminist scholarship has helped us understand that all knowledge, and therefore all classroom knowledge, is a social construction. This insight affirms the evolving nature of knowledge and the role of teachers and students in its ongoing construction. For me, the term *pedagogy* applies not just to teaching techniques but also to the whole classroom production of knowledge; it encompasses the full range of relationships among course materials, teachers, and students. Such broadened conceptualizations of pedagogy challenge the commonly held assumptions of the professor as a disinterested expert, the content as inherently

Table 7.5   Gender-Balanced Curriculum

Characteristics of Phase	Questions Commonly Asked about Women in History	Questions Commonly Asked about Women in Literature	Questions Commonly Asked about Women in Science
A multifocal, gender-balanced perspective is sought that weaves together women's and men's experiences into multilayered composites of human experience. At this stage, scholars are conscious of positionality. Positionality represents the insight that all women and men are located in historical contexts, contexts defined in terms of race, class, culture, and age, as well as gender, and that they gain their knowledge and their power from the specifics of their situations. Scholars begin to define what binds together and what separates the various segments of humanity. Scholars have a deepened understanding of how the private as well as public form a continuum in individual experience. They search for the nodal points at which comparative treatment of men's and women's experience is possible. Efforts are made to reconceptualize knowledge to reflect this multilayered composite of women's and men's experience. The conceptualization of knowledge is not characterized by disciplinary thinking but becomes multidisciplinary.	What is the knower's specific position in this historical context? How is gender asymmetry linked to economic systems, family organizations, marriage, ritual, and political systems? How can we compare women and men in all aspects of their lives to reveal gender as a crucial historical determinant? Are the private, as well as the public, aspects of history presented as a continuum in women's and men's experiences? How is gender a social construction? What does the particular construction of gender in a society tell us about the society that so constructed gender? What is the intricate relation between the construction of gender and the structure of power? How can we expand our conceptualization of historical time to a pluralistic one that conceives of three levels of history: structures, trends, and events? How can we unify approaches and types of knowledge of all social sciences and history as a means of investigating specific problems in relational history?	How does the author's specific position, as defined by gender, race, and class, affect this literary work? How can we validate the full range of human expression by selecting literature according to its insight into any aspect of human experience rather than according to how it measures up to a predetermined canon? Is the private as well as the public sphere presented as a continuum in women's and men's experiences? How can we pair opposite-sex texts in literature as a way of understanding how female and male characters experience "maleness" and "femaleness" as a continuum of "humanness"? How do the variables of race, ethnicity, social class, marital status, and sexual orientation affect the experience of female and male literary characters? How can we rethink the concept of periodicity to accentuate the continuity of life and to contain the multitude of previously ignored literary works, for example, instead of Puritanism, the contexts for and consequences of sexuality? How can we deconstruct the opposition between masculinity and femininity?	What explicit questions need to be raised about the invention and reinvention of nature? What is the meaning of male–female relations in animals? How do variables such as age, species, and individual variation challenge current theories? What are the limits to generalizing beyond the data collected on limited samples to other genders, species, and conditions not sampled in the experimental protocol? How have sex differences been used to assign men and women to particular roles in the social hierarchy? How have differences between the male and female body been used to justify a social agenda that privileges men economically, socially, and politically?

"objective," and the method of delivery as irrelevant to the message (hooks, 1994). To educate students for a complex, multicultural, multiracial world, we need to include the perspectives and voices of those who have not been traditionally included—women of all backgrounds, people of color, and females and males who perceive their education as not made for them. The anthropologist Renato Rosaldo (1994) has captured well how diverse classrooms contribute to new constructions of knowledge and change relationships among teachers and students:

> The question before us now is . . . how to teach more effectively
> in changed classroom environments. The new classrooms are not
> like the old ones. . . . In diverse classrooms, the question of
> "The Other" begins to dissolve. Who gets to be the we and who
> gets to be the other rotates from one day to the next, depending
> on the topic of discussion. And before long the stable us/them
> dividing line evaporates into a larger mix of differences and
> solidarity.

Feminist teachers are demonstrating how they transform courses through their attention to cultural, ethnic, and gender diversity and give concrete form to the complexity of the struggles over knowledge, access, and power (hooks, 1994; Maher & Tetreault, 1994, 2001; Weiler, 1988). In *The Feminist Classroom*, Frances Maher and I (Maher & Tetreault, 2001) show how all students may benefit from, and how some are even inspired by, college courses transformed by their professor's attention to cultural, ethnic, and gender diversity. We have found that the themes we used to analyze teaching and learning in seventeen classrooms on six campuses across the country apply to elementary and secondary classrooms as well. The four themes—*mastery, authority, voice,* and *positionality*—all relate to issues present in today's classroom. Although all four deal with reconstituted relationships between new students and new disciplinary frameworks, the themes of mastery and authority focus on knowledge and its sources; voice and positionality of the students themselves.

Mastery has traditionally meant the goal of an individual student's rational comprehension of the material on the teacher's and expert's terms. Women (and other marginalized groups) must often give up their voices when they seek mastery on the terms of the dominant culture. We found classrooms undergoing a shift away from unidimensional sources of expertise to a multiplicity of new information and insights. Students were no longer mastering a specific body of material, nor were they emphasizing subjective experiences that risk excluding students from a wealth of knowledge. Rather, they were struggling through or integrating often widely various interpretations of texts, scientific research, and social problems. These teachers redefined mastery as interpretation, as increasingly sophisticated handling of the topics at hand, informed by but not limited to the students' links to the material from their own experience. For example, a Japanese American student reread an Emily Dickinson poem about silences and invisibilities to comment on her gender and ethnic marginality:

> I couldn't help thinking of the idea of a mute culture within a
> dominant culture. A "nobody" knowing she's different from the
> dominant culture keeps silent. . . . But to be somebody! How

dreary! How public! So when you become a somebody and buy
into the dominant culture, you have to live in their roles.

A silly example: It's like watching a Walt Disney movie as a
child where Hayley Mills and these other girls dance and primp
before a party singing "Femininity," how being a woman is all
about looking pretty and smiling pretty and acting stupid to attract
men. As a child I ate it up, at least it seemed benign. But once
your eye gets put out and you realize how this vision has warped
you, it would split your heart to try and believe that again, it
would strike you dead.

Students were stretched by such broadenings of interpretative frameworks and indeed
became authorities for one another. A White male student in the same class said:

I could read Dickinson a thousand times and probably never try to
relate to that because it just would never make an impression on
me, but having the girls in that class interested in that particular
topic, "How does that relate to me as a woman?" then I sit back
and I think that's a really good question. Although I'm male I can
learn how women react to women's texts as opposed to maybe the
way I react to it or the teacher reacts to it.

The teachers in our study consciously used their *authority* to give students responsibility for their own learning (Finke, 1993). Students and professors became authorities for one
another to the extent that they were explicit about themselves as social and political actors
with respect to a text or an issue (Tetreault, 1991). The teachers also struggled with recon-
ceptualizing the grounds for their own authority, both over the subject matter and with students, because their traditional positions as the sole representatives of expertise were called
into question by these multiple new sources of knowledge. These professors shared a sense
of their authority as being grounded in their own experiences and in their intellectual engagement with feminist scholarship and other relevant fields.

As important as the rethinking of the disciplines is the power of expression that these
new forms of knowledge, coming from the students' questions as well as from new topics,
give to women and to other previously silenced groups. We explored the effects on students
through our theme of voice. *Voice* is frequently defined as the awakening of the students' own
responses. However, we came to think of these classrooms as arenas where teachers and students fashion their voices rather than "find" them, as they produce relevant experiences to
shape a narrative of an emerging self.

Our fourth theme is *positionality*, which is defined in the section on gender-balanced
curriculum. Positionality helps us to see the multiple ways in which the complex dynamics of difference and inequality, which come from outside society, also operate powerfully inside the classroom itself. Much of our emphasis in the past three decades has
been on the consequences of sexism and racism on females and on students of color. We
have learned much about how universalizing the position of maleness leads to intellectual
domination.

Some educators and theorists are arguing that we need to become conscious in similar ways about the effects of universalizing the position of Whiteness (Frankenberg, 1993, 1997; Mclntosh, 1990; Morrison, 1993; Tatum, 1992). For example, how does the norm of Whiteness or maleness shape the construction of knowledge in classrooms? How do those assumptions contribute to the intellectual domination of groups? Why is it that when we think of the development of racial identity in our students, we think primarily of students of color rather than of White students? What happens in classrooms where Whiteness is marked, revealed as a position? In our culture, the presumptions of Whiteness or maleness act to constrict voice by universalizing the dominant positions, by letting them float free of "position."

Frances Maher and I revisited data presented in *The Feminist Classroom* to examine how assumptions of Whiteness shape the construction of knowledge as it is produced and resisted in the classroom (Maher & Tetreault, 1997). We saw how the dominant voices continue to call the tune—that is, to maintain the conceptual and ideological frameworks through which suppressed voices are distorted or not fully heard. We saw more clearly the ways in which a thorough pedagogy of positionality must entail an excavation of Whiteness in its many dimensions and complexities. Understanding all the ways in which positionality shapes learning is a long, interactive process.

The lessons that follow attempt to model teaching that is constructed to reveal the particular and the common denominators of human experience. These sample lessons are organized by the subject areas of language arts, science, and social studies, but they can be adapted to other subject areas as well.

Language Arts

Analyzing Children's Literature
Suggested Activities

Ask students to locate five of their favorite children's books, to read or reread them, and to keep a written record of their reactions to the books. Either on the chalkboard or on a sheet of newsprint, keep a record of the students' (and your) book choices. Divide the class into small groups according to the same or similar favorite books and have students share their written reactions to the books. Ask the groups to keep a record of the most noteworthy ideas that emerge from their small-group discussions. When you bring the small groups together, ask each group to present its noteworthy ideas. Ideas that emerge may be as follows:

> How differently they read the book now than at the time of their first reading
>
> The differences and similarities in so-called girls' books and boys' books
>
> The importance of multicultural or international perspectives
>
> What the stories reveal about the culture in which the stories are set

A follow-up activity could be to interview grandparents, parents, teachers, and other adults about characters and stories they remember from childhood. Questions to ask include, How do they recall feeling about those stories? Have images of female and male behavior or expectations in children's stories changed? Is race or ethnicity treated similarly or differently?

Pairing Female and Male Autobiographies
Suggested Activities

Pairings of autobiographies and fiction by male and female authors can contribute greatly to students' multifocal, relational understanding of the human experience. Two pairings I have found to be particularly illuminating are *Black Boy*, by Richard Wright (1945/2000), and *Woman Warrior*, by Maxine Hong Kingston (1976). Other interesting pairings are Maya Angelou's *I Know Why the Caged Bird Sings* (1969) and Mark Twain's *The Adventures of Huckleberry Finn* (Twain, 1912/1985); *The Autobiography of Frederick Douglass* (Douglass, 1855/1994) and *Incidents in the Life of a Slave Girl* (Jacobs, 1861/1988); *The Adventures of Tom Sawyer* (Twain, 1910/1996) and *Little Women* (Alcott, 1880/1995).

One professor we observed at Lewis and Clark College, Dorothy Berkson, uses teaching logs to demystify the process of interpretation by linking the students' emotional connections to texts with their intellectual analysis. She asks her students to select a passage that puzzles or engages them or triggers a strong emotional reaction. Believing that some of the best criticism starts with such reactions, she asks the students next to paraphrase the passage they have chosen, to understand what it means, or, in a sense, to master it. They are then asked to look at it again, to become conscious of what cannot be captured by paraphrase as well as any concerns or questions that escaped them before. They finally place the passage in the context of the entire text, using the following questions: Where does it happen? Are there other passages that relate to it? That contradict it? That confirm it? That raise more questions about it? Concluding with a summary of where this procedure has taken them, they turn in these logs at the end of each class. Returned to the students with Berkson's comments, the logs then become the basis for the students' formal paper. This process forces students to reengage with the text over and over again, to engage in continuous reinterpretation of the text rather than to think they have arrived at some final mastery.

Science

Fear of Science: Fact or Fantasy?
Suggested Activities

Fear of science and math and the stereotyping of scientists contribute to the limited participation of some students, most often female, in math and science classes. Their inadequate participation limits their choice of most undergraduate majors that depend on a minimum of three years of high school mathematics. In *Aptitude Revisited: Rethinking Math and Science Education for America's Next Century*, David E. Drew (1996) argues that the people least encouraged to study mathematics and science in our society are those who have the least power—especially students from poverty, minority students, and young women. Policy makers, teachers, and even parents often steer certain students away from math and science for completely erroneous reasons. The result, Drew contends, is not simply an inadequately trained work force: This educational discrepancy is widening the gap between the haves and the have-nots in our society. He challenges the conventional view that science and math are too boring or too hard for many students to argue that virtually all students are capable of mastering these subjects.

The following exercise was designed by the Math and Science Education for Women Project at the Lawrence Hall of Science (Fraser, 1982).[1] The purpose of the exercise is to decrease female and male students' fear of science by enabling them to function as researchers who define the problem and generate solutions to it.

Ask students to complete the following sentence by writing for about 15 minutes:

> When I think about science, I . . .

When they are finished, divide students into groups of five or six to discuss their responses to the cue. Ask each group to state the most important things it has learned. Discuss fear of science with the class and whether there is a difference in how girls and boys feel about science. What could be some reasons for these differences or similarities? When the findings from this exercise are clear, suggest to students that they broaden their research to include other students and teachers in the school. Have each group brainstorm questions that might appear on a science attitude questionnaire. Put the questions on the chalkboard. Analyze the questions and decide on the ten best questions.

Decide with the class what group of students and teachers you will research and how you will do it, for example, other science classes, all ninth-grade science classes, or the entire school during second period. Obtain permission to conduct the survey from the administration and other teachers or classes involved in your research project. Have the class do the survey or questionnaire as a pilot activity. Analyze the questions for sex differences and make minor revisions before giving the survey and questionnaire to your research group. Distribute the survey or conduct interviews. Have the students decide how to analyze the information. Let each group decide how it will display findings and information. Current statistics of male and female scientists in biology, chemistry, physics, and other sciences can be found in the NSF Science and Engineering Indicators on the World Wide Web at www.nsf.gov/sbe/srs/seind98/start.htm. Another valuable resource is *Re-Engineering Female Friendly Science*, by Sue Rosser (1997).

Have each group give (1) a report to the class on what it found, using graph displays to convey the information, and (2) recommendations for decreasing science anxiety in the school. Place the entire student research project in the school library, main office, or gymnasium, where the rest of the school population can see the results. Have a student summarize and write an article for the school paper.

---

[1]Adapted from *Fact or Fantasy* (adapted from *Spaces: Solving Problems of Access to Careers in Engineering and Science*). Sherry Fraser, Project Director. Lawrence Hall of Science, Regents of Science, Regents of the University of California. Used with permission.

Doing Science

Suggested Activities

Evelyn Fox Keller's (1983) biography of Barbara McClintoch, *A Feeling for the Organism*, allows students to explore the conditions under which dissent in science arises, the function it serves, and the plurality of values and goals it reflects. Questions her story prompts are: What role do interests, individual and collective, play in the evolution of scientific knowledge? Do all scientists seek the same kinds of explanations? Are the kinds of questions they ask the same? Do differences in methodology between different subdisciplines ever permit the same kinds of answers? Do female and male scientists approach their research differently? This book is difficult reading for high school or college students, but it is manageable if they read carefully and thoroughly. The best way I have found to help them manage is to ask them to read a chapter or section and to come to class with their questions about the reading and to propose some answers.

Social Studies

My Family's Work History
Suggested Activities

Women and men of different social classes, ethnic groups, and geographic locations have done various kinds of work inside and outside their homes in agricultural, industrial, and postindustrial economies. Before introducing students to the history of work, I pique their interest by asking them to complete a Family Work Chart (see Table 7.6). When their charts are complete, the students and I build a work chronology from 1890 to the present. Our work chronology contains information gleaned from the textbook and library sources about important inventions, laws, demographics, and labor history.

I then reproduce the work chronology on a chart so they can compare their family's history with key historical events. By seeing their families' histories alongside major events in our collective work history, students can see how their family was related to society. A sample of items from our chart looks like this (Chapman, 1979):

Students conclude this unit by writing about a major theme in their family's work history. They might focus on how the lives of the women in the family differed from the lives of the men. They might focus on how their family's race or ethnicity shaped their work history.

Integrating the Public and Private Spheres

Suggested Activities

Human life is lived in both the public and the private spheres in wartime as well as in peacetime. By asking students consciously to examine individuals' lives as citizens, workers, family members, friends, members of social groups, and individuals, they learn more about the interaction of these roles in both spheres. War is an extraordinary

Table 7.6   Family Work Chart

| | | | Work Experience | |
| | | | AFTER MARRIAGE | |
	YEAR OF BIRTH	BEFORE MARRIAGE	WHILE CHILDREN WERE YOUNG	WHEN CHILDREN WERE GROWN
Your maternal side				
Mother				
Grandmother				
Grandfather				
Great-grandmother				
Great-grandfather				
Great-great-grandmother				
Great-great-grandfather				
Your paternal side				
Father				
Grandmother				
Grandfather				
Great-grandmother				
Great-grandfather				
Great-great-grandmother				
Great-great-grandfather				

This activity was developed by Carol Frenier. Reprinted with permission from the Education Development Center from Adeline Naiman, Project Director, *Sally Garcia and Family Resource Guide,* Unit 3 of *The Role of Women in American Society* (Newton, Mass.: Education Development Center, Inc., 1978), p. 62.

Historical Events	*Your Family History*
1890 Women are 17 percent of the paid labor force	
1915 Telephone connects New York and San Francisco	
1924 Restriction of immigration	

time when the nation's underlying assumptions about these roles are often put to the test. By having students examine the interaction of these roles in wartime, they can see some of our underlying assumptions about the roles and how they are manipulated for the purposes of war. Through researching the histories of their families, and by reading primary source accounts, viewing films, and reading their textbook, they will see the complexity and variety of human experiences in the United States during World War II.

Students research their family's history during World War II by gathering family documents and artifacts and by interviewing at least one relative who was an adult during World War II. Students draw up questions beforehand to find out how the individual's social roles were affected by the war. During the two weeks they are researching their family's history, two class periods are spent on this project. During the first period, students give oral reports to a small group of fellow students in read-around groups.

Appropriate readings and films on World War II are widely available. Studs Terkel's (1984) *The Good War* is particularly useful because of the variety of people the author interviewed. For instance, students can read about the internment of Japanese Americans and can role-play an account read. Their textbook may provide good background information. A moving account written by an author who was interned is *Desert Exile: The Uprooting of a Japanese-American Family*, by Yoshiko Uchida (1982). My students answer two questions in this unit: World War II has been described as a "good war." From the materials you have examined, was it a good war for individuals' lives as citizens, workers, family members, friends, and members of social groups? How were their experiences similar to or different from those of your relatives?

SUMMARY

This chapter has illustrated how women's studies is challenging male domination over curricular content. The evolution of that challenge is illuminated by understanding the different emphases that coexist in male-defined, contribution, bifocal, women's, and gender-balanced curricula. We now have a conceptual framework for a curriculum that interweaves issues of gender with ethnicity, culture, and class. This framework acknowledges and celebrates a multifocal, relational view of the human experience.

The idea of the phases of feminist scholarship as a series of intersecting circles, or patches on a quilt, or threads on a tapestry, suggests parallel ways to think about a class of students. Each student brings to your classroom a particular positionality that shapes his or her way of knowing. Your challenge as a teacher is to interweave the individual truths with course content into complex understandings that legitimize students' voices.

This relational knowledge, with the authority of the school behind it, has the potential to help students analyze their own social, cultural, historical, political, and economic contexts. The goal of relational knowledge is to build a world in which the oppressions of race, gender, and class, on which capitalism and patriarchy depend, are challenged by critical citizens in a democratic society.

Questions and Activities

1. What is a gender-balanced, multicultural curriculum?

2. What is feminist phase theory?

3. Define and give an example of each of the following phases of the feminist phase theory developed and described by the author: (a) male-defined curriculum, (b) contribution curriculum, (c) bifocal curriculum, (d) women's curriculum, (e) gender-balanced curriculum.

4. What problems do the contribution and bifocal phases have? How do the women's curriculum and gender-balanced curriculum phases help solve these problems?

5. The author states that "knowledge is a social construction." What does this mean? In what ways is the new scholarship on women and ethnic groups alike? In what ways does the new scholarship on women and ethnic groups challenge the dominant knowledge established in society and presented in textbooks? Give examples.

6. Examine the treatment of women in a sample of social studies, language arts, mathematics, or science textbooks (or a combination of two types of textbooks). Which phase or phases of the feminist phase theory presented by the author best describe the treatment of women in the textbooks you examined?

7. What is the *longue durée?* Why is it important in the study of social history, particularly women's history?

8. Research your family history, paying particular attention to the roles, careers, and influence of women in your family's saga. Also describe your ethnic heritage and the influence of ethnicity on your family's past and present. Share your family history with a group of your classmates or workshop participants.

References

Alcoff, L. (2003). *Identities: Race, Class, Gender and Nationality.* London: Blackwell.

Alcott, L. M. (1880/1995). *Little Women.* New York: Scholastic.

Angelou, M. (1969). *I Know Why the Caged Bird Sings.* New York: Bantam.

Butler, J. (2004). *Undoing Gender.* New York: Routledge.

Chapman, A. (Ed.). (1979). *Approaches to Women's History.* Washington, DC: American Historical Association.

Collins, P. H. (2000). *Black Feminist Thought.* New York and London: Routledge.

Douglass, F. (1855/1994). *The Autobiography of Frederick Douglass.* New York: Penguin.

Drew, D. E. (1996). *Aptitude Revisited: Rethinking Math and Science Education for America's Next Century.* Baltimore: John Hopkins University Press.

Finke, L. (1993). Knowledge as Bait: Feminism, Voice, and the Pedagogical Unconscious. *College English, 55*(1), 7–27.

Frankenberg, R. (1993). *White Women, Race Matters: The Social Construction of Whiteness*. Minneapolis: University of Minnesota Press.

Frankenberg, R. (Ed.). (1997). *Displacing Whiteness: Essays in Social and Cultural Criticism*. Durham, NC: Duke University Press.

Fraser, S. (1982). *Spaces: Solving Problems of Access to Careers in Engineering and Science*. Berkeley: University of California, Lawrence Hall of Science.

Goldberger, N., Tarule, J., Clinchy, B., & Belenky, M. (Eds.). (1996). *Knowledge, Difference, and Power*. New York: Basic Books.

Haraway, D. J. (1991). *Simians, Cyborgs, and Women*. New York: Routledge.

Haraway, D. J. (1997). *Modest-Witness@ Second-Millennium*. New York: Routledge.

Harding, S. (2004). *The Feminist Standpoint Theory Reader: Intellectual and Political Controversies*. New York and London: Routledge.

hooks, B. (1994). *Teaching to Transgress: Education as the Practice of Freedom*. New York: Routledge.

Hune, S., & Nomura, G. (2003). *Asian/Pacific Islander American Women: A Historical Anthology*. New York: New York University Press.

Jacobs, H. (1861/1988). *Incidents in the Life of a Slave Girl*. New York: Oxford University Press.

Kingston, M. H. (1976). *Woman Warrior*. New York: Knopf.

Letters to the Editor. (1982). *Social Education, 46*(6), 378–380.

Maher, F., & Tetreault, M. K. (1994). *The Feminist Classroom*. New York: Basic Books.

Maher, F., & Tetreault, M. K. (1997). Learning in the Dark: How Assumptions of Whiteness Shape Classroom Knowledge. *Harvard Educational Review, 67*(2), 321–349.

Maher, F., & Tetreault, M. K. (2001). *The Feminist Classroom* (2nd ed.). New York: Rowman & Littlefield.

McIntosh, P. (1990). White Privilege and Male Privilege. In M. L. Andersen & P. J. Collins (Eds.), *Race, Class and Gender* (pp. 70–81). Boston: Wadsworth.

Mohanty, C. (2003). *Feminism without Borders: Decolonizing Theory, Practicing Solidarity*. Durham, NC: Duke University Press.

Moi, T. (1985). *Sexual/Textual Politics*. New York: Methuen.

Morrison, T. (1993). *Playing in the Dark: Whiteness and the Literary Imagination*. New York: Vintage.

Rosaldo, R. (1994). Cultural Citizenship and Educational Democracy. *Cultural Anthropology, 9*(3), 405.

Rosser, S. V. (1997). *Re-Engineering Female Friendly Science*. New York: Teachers College Press.

Saldivar-Hull, S. (2000). *Feminism on the Border: Chicana Gender Politics and Literature*. Berkeley: University of California Press.

Schmitz, B., Butler, J. E., Guy-Sheftall, B., & Rosenfelt, D. (2004). Women's Studies and Curriculum Transformation in the United States. In J. A. Banks & C. A. M. Banks (Eds.), *Handbook of Research on Multicultural Education* (2nd ed.) (pp. 882–905). San Francisco: Jossey-Bass.

Tatum, B. (1997). *"Why Are All the Black Kids Sitting Together in the Cafeteria?" and Other Conversations about Race*. New York: Basic Books.

Terkel, S. (1984). *The Good War: An Oral History of World War II*. New York: Pantheon.

Tetreault, C. (1991). *Metacommunication in a Women's Studies Classroom.* Unpublished senior honors thesis, Vassar College, Poughkeepsie, NY.

Tetreault, M. K. T. (1986). Integrating Women's History: The Case of United States History Textbooks. *The History Teacher, 19*(2), 211–262.

Thorne, B. (1993). *Gender Play: Girls and Boys in School.* New Brunswick, NJ: Rutgers University Press.

Twain, M. (1910/1996). *The Adventures of Tom Sawyer.* New York: Oxford University Press.

Twain, M. (1912/1985). *The Adventures of Huckleberry Finn.* New York: Collier.

Uchida, Y. (1982). *Desert Exile: The Uprooting of a Japanese-American Family.* Seattle: University of Washington Press.

Weiler, K. (1988). *Women Teaching for Change: Gender, Class, and Power.* South Hadley, MA: Bergin & Garvey.

Wright, R. (1945/1983). *Black Boy.* New York: Harper & Brothers.

194

CHAPTER 8

Transforming the Curriculum: Teaching about Women of Color

Johnnella E. Butler and
Deirdre J. Raynor

Many efforts to include women and issues of gender into what is called the mainstream curriculum focus on White, middle-class women from the United States or on women from other nations and cultures. The question arises as to why educators should also teach about women of color in the United States and consider issues related to the construction and reality of race in the curriculum. After the publication of Toni Morrison's *Paradise*, Ed Bradley asked her during a January 31, 1999, interview on *60 Minutes* about the uses of race in her writing. She responded with the question: What do we know when we know an individual's race? Morrison, similar to other writers such as Zora Neale Hurston (1970) and Alice Walker (1997), contends that race reveals little about an individual except the "baggage" associated with the clearly delineated racial markers that exist in U.S. society. Teaching about women of color provides us with the opportunity to engage students in a dialogue about the lived experiences of groups that are racialized by others and who may define themselves by the social constructions of race, class, and gender as these categories intersect.

THE PRIMACY OF RACE IN THE UNITED STATES

The media coverage and political response to the 2005 tragedy associated with Hurricane Katrina provides a powerful example of social inequity in U.S. society and how this inequity is raced and classed. What is conspicuously missing from discussions of race and class in the aftermath of Hurricane Katrina are the day-to-day lived experiences of the invisible and poor African American women in the hurricane-ravaged Ninth Ward in New Orleans. The media presented a number of photographs focused on African American women and children on the streets of New Orleans and in the domes in both New Orleans and Houston. Although these photographs show real people who have become displaced by the hurricane, the photographs do not tell us about their day-to-day lived experiences. The observer must construct meaning and a narrative to explain the lives of the women depicted in these photographs. This narrative more often than not is informed by the social meanings assigned to individuals based on race, class, and gender. Often the social meanings assigned to race are based on stereotypes. Consequently, we often have an incomplete story about the individuals and groups that are racialized by outsiders.

Generally, we have taken the White, middle-class woman's experience as the norm when examining and talking about women's lives. When we want to know about women's lives that differ from that norm, we generally have explored the global experience (Gross, 1987), despite the large number of texts both by and about women of color in the United States across disciplines (Collins, 1998). When we have studied the experiences of women of color in the United States, these experiences are often examined without considering the differences between them based on their racial/ethnic categorization and socioeconomic class. Studying about women of color allows us to explore issues of race, class, and gender and the intersections of these categories, as they relate to White men, White women, and men of color.

When teaching about the intersections of race, class, and gender categories, we should avoid perpetuating binary oppositions, which occurs when two terms are differentiated in such a way that they become polarized. Perpetuating binary oppositions reinforces the oppressor/oppressed dichotomy and results in all groups of students resisting a diverse curriculum. Teaching about the intersections of race, class, and gender in the lives of women—by focusing specifically on women of color—requires paying attention to sameness and difference between women of color and White women and women of specific racial and ethnic groups. As Crenshaw (1995) points out, there is "social power" in "delineating difference," and this social power "need not be the power of domination; it can instead be the source of social empowerment and reconstruction" (p. 357). Teaching about women of color opens up the curriculum. Emphasizing empowerment and reconstruction in talking about the lives of women of color makes courses more attractive and meaningful to students and helps them begin to understand the multiplicity of identity.

IDENTITY, KNOWLEDGE, AND EXPERIENCE

Paula Moya (2000), in *Realist Theory and the Predicament of the Postmodern*, expresses succinctly the predicament we find ourselves in today regarding identity:

> "Identity" remains one of the most urgent—as well as hotly disputed—topics in literary and cultural studies. For nearly two decades, it has been a central focus of debate for psychoanalytic, poststructuralist, and cultural materialist criticism in areas ranging from postcolonial and ethnic studies to feminism and queer theory. Oddly enough, much of what has been written about identity during this period seeks to delegitimize, and in some cases eliminate, the concept itself by revealing its ontological, epistemological, and political limitations. Activists and academics alike have . . . conclud[ed] that (social or cultural) identity, as a basis for political action, is theoretically incoherent and politically pernicious. (pp. 1–2)

>The first problem with essentialist conceptions of identity,
>according to critics, is the tendency to posit one aspect of identity
>(say, gender) as the sole cause or determinant constituting the
>social meanings of an individual's experience. The difficulty, critics
>of identity point out, is that identities are constituted differently in
>different historical contexts. . . . They remind us that insofar as
>every woman differs from every other woman in more or less
>significant ways, it is impossible to determine the (racial, class,
>cultural, etc.) identity of the "authentic woman" and thus to unify
>different women under the signifier "woman." (p. 3)

Within the context of the United States, identity formation is informed by social stratification and the race, gender, and class consciousness that develop as a result of this stratification.

Simon Woolley, a British activist and head of Operation Black Vote, commented during a 2003 luncheon discussion about identity at the London U.S. Embassy that such an approach to identity obscured its salience and made it "impossible to move from A to B" in bringing people together in coalition. The very term *women of color* derives from and points to the possibility of coalition, of cultural and aesthetic expression, and social and political action based on shared experience and shared values. It is important to clarify, then, the approach to identity in this chapter, for simply invoking the term *women of color* may to some appear, at first glance, reductionist or essentialist, that is, characterizing women and women of color as one-dimensional or monologic.

Identities are not fixed essences. One is not a woman or a man, or a Latina or a Baptist, in a unified, homogeneous way that does not change over time. Rather, identities matter enormously, reflecting and revealing knowledge about the world. As Hames-García demonstrates (2000), identity is multiple:

>Memberships in various social groups combine with and
>mutually constitute one another. Membership in one group
>(e.g., "femaleness") thus means something different in the
>context of some simultaneous group memberships (e.g.,
>"blackness") than in others (e.g., "motherhood"). The totality of
>these relations in their mutual constitution comprises the self.
>One important consequence of this fact is that one cannot
>understand a self as the sum of so many discrete parts, that is
>femaleness + blackness + motherhood. The whole self is
>constituted by the mutual interaction and relation of its parts to
>one another. Politically salient aspects of the self, such as race,
>ethnicity, sexuality, gender and class, link and imbricate
>themselves in fundamental ways. (p.103)

This chapter is intended to show how teaching about women of color can transform our understanding of how identity functions in experience and in producing knowledge. Women of color reflect most directly the multiplicity Hames-García (2000) describes and therefore, in their individual and collective complex experiences, can shed light on concepts key to a curriculum that not only recognizes sociocultural diversity but also engages, produces knowledge about, and learns from that diversity in ways that certainly move us from A to B.

WHY WOMEN OF COLOR?

The term *women of color* came into use gradually during the 1970s. It immediately brings to mind differences of race and culture. It also makes clear that African American women are not the only women of color in a nation where the Black racial experience historically and legally operates both to define and to obscure racial dynamics between Whites and other racialized ethnic groups (see, e.g., Brodkin, 1998). Moreover, in a democratically structured society with a great power imbalance signified by race and class privilege, labels representative of reality for people outside the realm of power are difficult to determine. The form of that power is both cultural and political and consequently further complicates labeling. Selecting the phrase *women of color* by many women of U.S. ethnic groups of color is part of their struggle to be recognized with dignity for their humanity, racial heritage, and cultural heritage as they work within the women's movement in the United States. The effort of women of color to name themselves is similar to attempts by African Americans and other ethnic groups to define with dignity their race and ethnicity and to counter the many stereotypical names bestowed on them. Because we tend to use the word *women* to be all-inclusive and general, we usually obscure both the inter-group and intra-group differences and the similarities among women.

With the decline of the civil rights movement of the 1960s, the women's movement in the second half of the twentieth century got under way. Not long after, African American women began to articulate the differences they experienced as African American women, not only because of the racism within the women's movement or the sexism within the African American community, but also because of their vastly differing historical reality. A major question posed by Toni Cade Bambara's (1970) pioneering anthology, *The Black Woman*, remains applicable: How relevant are the truths, the experiences, and the findings of White women to Black women? Are women after all, simply women? Bambara answers the question then as it might still be answered today:

> I don't know that our priorities are the same, that our
> concerns and methods are the same, or even similar enough so
> that we can afford to depend on this new field of experts (White,
> female). It is rather obvious that we do not. It is obvious that we
> are turning to each other. (p. 9)

This anthology served as a turning point in the experience of the African American woman.

Previously, White males, for the most part, had interpreted her realities, her activities, and her contributions. *The Negro Family: The Case for National Action* (1965), whose primary author was the Harvard professor and later U.S. Senator Daniel Patrick Moynihan, was the most notable example of this scholarship. It was widely publicized and well received by most U.S. readers. Blaming African American social and economic problems on the Black family, Moynihan argued that Black families, dominated by women, are generally pathological and pathogenic. Moynihan's scholarship directly opposed the scholarship of Andrew Billingsley (1968) and others, which demonstrates the organizational differences between Black and White family units, the existence of a vital African American cultural experience on which to base solutions to the problems, and the effects of racism, sexism, classism, and ethnocentrism in shaping the Black reality and government policy and societal attitudes toward that reality (Billingsley, 1968; Ladner, 1973; McAdoo, 1981; Moynihan, 1965).

Moynihan's depiction of the Black matriarch and the implicit claim that Black women are responsible for the problems Black families face deflect blame from American public policy and law, racial discrimination, and the historical precedent established during slavery that devalues not only Black womanhood but Black motherhood as well. The photographs of African American women and children displaced by Hurricane Katrina in 2005 mentioned at the beginning of this chapter without a discussion of the real people, their history in the context of the United States, and how their experiences are shaped by the intersections of race, class, and gender can be misconstrued as visual evidence of the dysfunctional single mother-headed Black families described by Moynihan in 1965. Ivy Kennelly's (1999) study illustrates the pervasiveness of Moynihan's stereotype of the Black female matriarch and the dangerous effects of this stereotype on contemporary working-class African American women when they enter the labor force.

Bambara's (1970) anthology responded directly to racist, sexist, and classist attacks leveled against Black women and resulting policy, and called for Black women's direct involvement in both defining the problems and fashioning the solutions. Although we are beyond the point of the complete invisibility and distortion of women of color in women's studies, African American women must still demand to be heard and insist on being dealt with from the perspective of the experiences of women of color, just as they did in 1970, as the blurb on the paperback edition of *The Black Woman* (Bambara, 1970) implies: "Black Women Speak Out. A Brilliant and Challenging Assembly of Voices That Demand to Be Heard." By the latter part of the 1970s, the logic of a dialogue among women of color became a matter of course (*Conditions, Five,* 1979; Moraga & Anzaldúa, 1981).

The academic community began to recognize U.S. women of color who identify with the Third World, both for ancestral heritage and for related conditions of colonization. In 1980, for example, we saw the publication of Dexter Fisher's (1980) anthology *The Third Woman: Minority Women Writers of the United States,* another milestone giving greater access to the voices of U.S. women of color. Unfortunately, this dialogue has waned considerably due to the postmodern critiques of identity, discussed above, and to the political fragility of coalition that is constantly undermined by racism. Yet, late twentieth- and early twenty-first-century interest in topics including mixed-race identity, multicultural education, multicultural women's literature, reproductive rights, and feminism serve as points of focus in a number of publications that are keeping the dialogue alive (Brock, 2005; Dowdy, 2005; Duncan, 2004; Avila, 2005; Silliman, 2004; Anzaldúa & Keating, 2002; Anzaldúa, 1987; Madison, 1994).

The most familiar ethnic groups of color are the Asian Americans, African Americans, Hispanic Americans, and Native Americans. Yet within each group there are cultural, class, and racial distinctions. These ethnic groups can be further delineated: Asian Americans include Chinese Americans, Japanese Americans, Filipino Americans, Korean Americans, and the more recent immigrants from Southeast Asia and East India. African Americans consist of U.S. African Americans, West Indian, or African Caribbean immigrant, and a growing number of African immigrants. Hispanic Americans or Latino Americans include U.S. Hispanic Americans and immigrants from Puerto Rico, Mexico, Central and Latin America, Cuba, and other Caribbean nations. The Native American are made up of many idigenous nations, such as Sioux, Apache, Navajo, and Creek.

The number of individuals who identify themselves as mixed race or biracial has increased significantly in recent years (Root, 2004). The increase in people categorizing themselves as mixed race or biracial has led to discussions about how to incorporate mixed-race identity into the curriculum. Within this newly developed space for examining mixed-race identity are rich opportunities for discussing sameness and difference in teaching about women of color of mixed race because the mixed-race individual is the literal embodiment of "sameness" and "difference." Layli Phillips (2004) argues that media representations and public discourse around issues of race have been transformed in recent years as a result of multiculturalism and globalization. The American public embraces mixed-race individuals who self-identify in a variety of ways such as Halle Berry who identifies herself as a Black woman although she has a White mother, and Mariah Carey, who identifies as biracial. Music industry moguls, however, downplayed Carey's Blackness in order to increase her appeal within American pop music circles. As a result of the shifting discourse and the influence of media, Phillips claims that U.S. attitudes have changed about "racial, ethnic, and cultural blending and the social value of the blended individual" (p. 224).

The phrase *women of color* helps women of all these groups acknowledge both their individual ethnicity and their racial solidarity as members of groups that are racial minorities in the United States, as well as a majority as people of color in the world. The concept also acknowledges similarity in historical experiences and position in relation to the White American. In addition, *women of color* implies the existence of the race and ethnicity of White women, for whom the word *women* most often is used to indicate an assumed norm for all women or to exclude other women.

WHAT WE LEARN FROM STUDYING WOMEN OF COLOR

When we study women of color, we raise our awareness and understanding of the experiences of all women either implicitly or directly. Quite significantly, because of the imbalanced power relationship between White women and women of color, information about one group tends to make more apparent the experiences of the other group. It is well known, for example, that ideals of beauty in the United States are based on the blond, blue-eyed model. Dialogue about the reactions to that model in the experience of women of color, both within their ethnic groups and as they relate to White women, ultimately reveals that White women often judge themselves by that model of beauty. White women also serve simultaneously as reminders or representatives of that ideal to women of color and, most frequently, to themselves as failures to meet the ideal.

Many girls and women of color also judge themselves by the mainstream model of beauty that excludes them. This exclusion and sense of not fitting the ideal wreaks havoc on the psyche of some women of color. Phillips's (2004) study of biracial adolescent females shows that mixed race Black/White and Asian/White adolescent girls who identify themselves as White have lower self-esteem than adolescent girls who identify with the race of the parent of color when asked questions about their physical attractiveness. Phillips concludes that these girls have lower self-esteem and that their self-esteem is tied in large part to perceptions of what constitutes physical attractiveness, which is in turn tied to social acceptance. When we teach about women of color we have the opportunity to help students develop critical analysis skills that will allow them to uncover the myths associated with the feminine ideal. Teachers can also present students with other models of womanhood as early as elementary school when students begin to develop a sense of self tied to groups outside their families.

We come to another level of awareness and understanding when we study women of color. We develop an understanding of both the oppressor and the oppressed. We see clearly that White women function both as women who share certain similar experiences with women of color and as oppressors of women of color. This is one of the most difficult realities to cope with and still maintain productive, generative dialogue among women while teaching and conducting scholarship. White women who justifiably see themselves as oppressed by White men find it difficult to separate themselves from the effects of and power shared with White men. White women share with White men an ethnicity, an ancestral heritage, racial dominance, and certain powers and privileges by virtue of White skin privilege (Brodkin, 1998; Frye, 1983; Lipsitz, 1998; McIntosh, 1987; Roediger, 1991, 1994, 2005).

Studying women of color also illustrates how women of color are always raced subjects regardless of class, although depending on the context, one's socioeconomic class may influence how a woman's race is interpreted. Condoleeza Rice, Oprah Winfrey, and the anonymous Black women in photographs depicting the aftermath of Hurricane Katrina are all seen first and foremost as Black women, but their Blackness is interpreted in different ways and represents different things. Oprah Winfrey and Condoleeza Rice represent equality and how far we have come as a society in the minds of some Americans. Moreover, Oprah Winfrey and Condolezza Rice represent economic and political success respectively. The Black women depicted in the photographs from the hurricane-ravished Ninth Ward in New Orleans reveal stark inequality. Some people would rather not see these women because of the questions their visibility raises about racism, classism, and sexism as these "isms" affect Black women.

When we study women of color, we raise our awareness and understanding of the experiences of all women either explicity or implicitly. Once we realize that all women are not White, and once we understand the implications of this realization, we can see immediately the importance of race, ethnicity, and class when considering gender. Interestingly, much scholarship that intends to illustrate and analyze class dynamics is blind to racial and ethnic dynamics. In similar fashion, much scholarship that illustrates and analyzes racial dynamics and class dynamics fails to examine ethnic dynamics. Other scholarship gives short shrift to, or even ignores, class. We have, however, begun to grapple with the connectedness of the four big isms—racism, sexism, classism, and ethnocentrism.

Much scholarship in women's studies, however, fails to work within the context of race, class, ethnicity, and gender and their related isms, which modulate each other to a greater or lesser extent. Spelman (1982) illustrates how the racist equating of Blackness with lust-fulness in Western culture modulates sexism toward African American women. One result-ing stereotype is that the African American woman has a bestial sexuality and, as such, deserves or expects to be raped. This racism is also modulated by an ethnocentrism that fur-ther devalues the African American woman, thereby justifying sexism.

WOMEN OF COLOR: THE AGENT OF TRANSFORMATION

In dealing with the commonalities and differences among women (a necessity in teaching about women of color), we are reminded that the title of Paula Giddings's (1984) work on African American women is taken from Anna J. Cooper's observation: "When and where I enter, then and there the whole . . . race enters with me" (p. 82). Repeated in many forms by women of color, from the nineteenth-century struggle for the vote to present-day women's organizing, this truth ultimately contains the goal of transformation of the curriculum: a cur-riculum that reflects all of us, egalitarian, communal, nonhierarchical, and pluralistic. Women of color are inextricably related to men of color by virtue of ethnicity and traditions as well as by common conditions of oppression. Therefore, at minimum, their struggle against sex-ism and racism is waged simultaneously. The experiences and destinies of women and men of color are linked. This reality poses a special problem in the relationship between White women and women of color. Moreover, in emphasizing the commonalities of privilege between White men and women, the oppressive relationship between men of color and White men, women of color and White men, and men of color and White women—all implied in Anna J. Cooper's observation—the teaching about women of color provides the naturally pluralistic, multidimensional catalyst for transformation. As such, women of color are agents of transformation.

This section of this chapter defines transformation and provides the theoretical frame-work for the pedagogy and methodology of transformation. The final section discusses aspects of the process of teaching about women of color, which, though closely related to the theoretical framework, manifest themselves in very concrete ways.

A review of feminist pedagogy over the past twenty years or so reveals a call for teach-ing from multifocal, multidimensional, multicultural, pluralistic, interdisciplinary perspec-tives. This call, largely consistent with the pedagogy and methodology implied thus far in this chapter, can be accomplished only through *transformation*. Although many theorists and teachers now see this point, the terminology has still to be corrected to illustrate the process. In fact, we often use the words *mainstreaming*, *balancing*, *integration*, and *transformation* inter-changeably. Mainstreaming, balancing, and integration imply adding women to an estab-lished, accepted, and unchangeable body of knowledge. The experience of White, middle-class women has provided a norm in a way that White Anglo American male ethnicity provides a norm. The experiences of all other women are added to and measured by those racial, class, ethnic, and gender roles and experiences.

Transformation, which emphasizes the multiplicity of identity, allows us to see the many aspects of women's lives. Understanding the significance of naming the action of treating women's lives through a pluralistic process—transformation—leads naturally to a conver-gence between women's studies and ethnic studies. This convergence is necessary to give us the information that illuminates the function and content of race, class, and ethnicity in women's lives and in relation to gender. In similar fashion, treating the lives of people of color through a pluralistic process leads to the same convergence, illuminating the functions and content of race, class, and gender in relation to the lives of ethnic Americans and in relation to ethnicity.

We still need to understand exactly what is meant by this pluralistic, multidimensional, interdisciplinary scholarship and pedagogy. Much of the scholarship on, about, and even frequently by women of color renders them systematically invisible, erasing their experience or part of it. White, middle-class, male, and Anglo American are the imposed norms corresponding to race, class, gender, and ethnicity. In contrasting and comparing experiences of pioneers, White males and females when dealing with Native Americans, for example, we often speak of "the male," "the female," and "the Indian." Somehow, those of a different ethnicity and race are assumed to be male. Therefore, both the female and the male Indian experiences are observed and distorted. They must be viewed both separately and together to get a more complete view, just as to have a more complete view of the pioneer experience the White male and White female experiences must be studied both separately and together. Thus, even in our attempts to correct misinformation resulting from measurement by one norm, we can reinforce measurement by other norms if we do not see the interaction of the categories, the interaction of the isms, as explained in the previous section of this chapter. This pluralistic process and eye are demanded in order to understand both the particulars and the generalities of people's lives.

Why is it so easy to impose these norms effectively to erase the experience of others? Although erasing these experiences is not always intentional, this erasure results from the dominance of the Western cultural norms of individuality, singularity, rationality, masculinity, and Whiteness at the expense of the communal, the plural, the intuitive, the feminine, and people of color. A brief look at Elizabeth Spelman's (1982) seminal work, "Theories of Race and Gender: The Erasure of Black Women," explains the important aspects of how this erasure comes about. Then a consideration of the philosophical makeup of transformation tells us both how our thinking makes it happen and how we can think to prevent it from happening.

Spelman (1982) gives examples of erasure of the Black woman, similar to the examples provided in this chapter. She analyzes concepts that assume primacy of sexism over racism. Furthermore, she rejects the additive approach to analyzing sexism, an approach that assumes a sameness of women modeled on the White, middle-class, Anglo-oriented woman. Spelman shows that it is premature to argue that sexism and racism are either mutually exclusive, totally dependent on one another, or in a causal relationship with one another. She discusses how women differ by race, class, and culture or ethnicity. Most important, she demonstrates that Black does not simply indicate victim. Black signifies African diasporic cultural identity—in the United States, African American identity. She suggests, then, that we present women's studies in a way that makes it a given that women are diverse, that their diversity is apparent in their experiences with oppression and in their participation in U.S. culture. To teach about women in this manner, our process must not be additive, that is, integrating, mainstreaming, or balancing the curriculum. Rather, transformation is the process that leads to this goal.

Essentially, *transformation* is the process of revealing unity among human beings and the world, as well as revealing important differences. Transformation implies acknowledging and benefitting from the interaction among sameness and diversity, groups and individuals. The maxim on which transformation rests may be stated as an essential affirmation of the West African proverb "I am because we are. We are because I am." The communality, the human unity implicit in the proverb, operates in African traditional (philosophical) thought in regard to human beings and to other categories of life—categories of knowledge and ways of thinking and being (Davidson, 1969; Mbiti, 1975). Traditional African thought is in opposition to the European, Western pivotal axiom, on which integration, balancing, and mainstreaming rest (as expressed through the White, middle-class, Anglo norm in the United States)—"I think; therefore, I am," as expressed by Descartes.

Traditional African thought is in tune with a pluralistic, multidimensional process; the European Western axiom with a monolithic, one-dimensional process. Stated succinctly as "I am we," the West African proverb provides the rationale for the interaction and modulation of the categories of race, class, gender, and ethnicity; for the interaction and modulation of their respective isms; for the interaction and modulation of the objective and subjective, the rational and the intuitive, the feminine and the masculine—all those things that we, as Westerners, see as either opposite or as standing rigidly alone. This view is the breakdown of what is called feminist pedagogy, or multifocal teaching, when the ends are the comprehension of and involvement with cultural, class, racial, and gender diversity toward an egalitarian world based on communal relationships within humanity. It also indicates the multiplicity and complexity of identity that evolves from dialogue among individuals and community. Elsa Barkley Brown (1989) gives us an insightful and useful discussion of teaching African American women's history in a way consistent with transformation as described here. This way of teaching creates "a polyrhythmic, 'nonsymmetrical,' nonlinear structure in which individual and community are not competing entities" (p. 926).

To realize this transformation, we must redefine categories and displace criteria that have served as norms in order to bring about the life context (norms and values) as follows:

1. Nonhierarchical terms and contexts for human institutions, rituals, and action.
2. A respect for the interaction and existence of both diversity and sameness (a removal of measurement by norms perpetuating otherness, silence, and erasure).
3. A balancing of and interaction between the individual and the group.
4. A concept of humanity emanating from interdependence of human beings on one another and on the world environment, both natural and human-created.
5. A concept of humanity emanating from a sense of self that is not totally abstract and totally individually defined (I think; therefore, I am), but that is both abstract and concrete, individually and communally defined (I am we; I am because we are; we are because I am).
6. A concept of individuals being multifaceted and identity being defined and shifting based on context.
7. A concept of how society uses race, class, and gender to construct a narrative of its history.

Such a context applies to pedagogy and scholarship in the dissemination and ordering of knowledge in all disciplines and fields. Within this context (the context in which the world does operate and against which the Western individualistic, singular concept of humanity militates), it becomes possible for us to understand the popular music form rap as an Americanized, Westernized version of African praise singing, functioning, obviously, for decidedly different cultural and social reasons. It becomes possible to understand the syncretization of cultures that produced Haitian voodoo, Cuban Santería, and Brazilian Candomblé from Catholicism and the religion of the Yoruba. It becomes possible to understand what is happening when a Japanese American student is finding it difficult to reconcile traditional Buddhist values with her American life. It becomes possible to understand that Maxine Hong Kingston's (1976) *Woman Warrior* is at one level about the struggle to syncretize Chinese ways within the United States, whose dominant culture devalues and coerces against syncretization, seeking to impose White, middle-class conformity.

TEACHING USING HERESIES

Thinking in this manner is foreign to the mainstream of thought in the United States, although it is alive and well in Native American traditional philosophy, in Taoist philosophy, in African traditional philosophy, and in African American folklore. It is so foreign, in fact, that in order to bring about this context, we must commit certain so-called sins. The philosopher Elizabeth Minnich (1990) suggested that these sins might be more aptly characterized as heresies, because they are strongly at variance with established modes of thought and values.

The following heresies challenge and ultimately displace the ways in which the Western mind orders the world (for related discussions, see Freire, 1969, 1973; Hord & Lee, 1995; Yancy, 1998; Young, 1990; 2005). These heresies emanate from the experiences of people of color, the nature of their oppression, and the way the world operates. Adopting them is a necessity for teaching about women of color. Using the heresies to teach women's studies and about the lives of all women becomes natural when we study women of color, and it leads to a transformation of the curriculum that makes pluralistic, egalitarian, and multidimensional.

- **Heresy #1** The goal of interaction among human beings, action, and ideas must be seen not only as synthesis but also as the identification of opposites and differences. These opposites and differences may or may not be resolved; they may function together by virtue of the similarities identified and the tensions they generate as they move ultimately toward resolution.

- **Heresy #2** We *can* address a multiplicity of concerns, approaches, and subjects without a neutral or dominant center. Reality reflects opposites as well as overlaps in what are perceived as opposites. There exist no pure, distinct opposites. Human experience has multiple, interconnected centerings.

- **Heresy #3** It is not reductive to look at gender, race, class, and culture as mutually interactive and related parts of a multiply constituted, complex whole. The more different voices we have, the closer we are to the whole.

- **Heresy #4** Transformation demands an understanding of ethnicity that takes into account the differing cultural continua (in the United States, Western European, Anglo American, African, Asian, Native American) and their similarities.

- **Heresy #5** Transformation demands a relinquishing of the primary definitiveness of gender, race, class or culture, and ethnicity as they interact with theory, methodology, pedagogy, institutionalization, and action, both in synthesis and in a dynamic that functions as opposite and same simultaneously. A variation on this heresy is that although all isms are not the same, they are connected and operate as such; likewise, their correctives.

- **Heresy #6** Transformation depends upon transgressive teaching which allows women of color to "speak up" and "speak out" about gender, race, and class as these classifications intersect and shape their identity and experiences. (For a discussion of "speaking up" and "speaking out" in connection with Black female students, specifically African Caribbean, middle school students, see "'Speaking Up' and "Speaking Out': Examining Voice in a Reading Writing Program with Adolescent Caribbean Girls" by Annette Henry (1998). Also see "The Occult of True Black Womanhood: Critical Demeanor and Black Feminist Studies" by Ann duCille (1994).

- **Heresy #7** The Anglo-American, and ultimately the Western, norm must be seen as only one of many norms, and also as one that enjoys privilege and power that has colonized, and may continue to colonize, other norms.

- **Heresy #8** Feelings are direct lines to better thinking. The intuitive as well as the rational is part of the process of engaging experience and moving from the familiar to the unfamiliar in acquiring knowledge.

- **Heresy #9** Knowledge is identity and identity is knowledge. All knowledge is explicitly and implicitly related to who we are, both as individuals and as groups. [For an extended discussion of this heresy, see Mohanty (2000).]

Engaging transformation through these nine heresies means addressing the connections among human beings and the environment, among experiences, and categories of identity. It means using the intuitive and the cognitive, displacing dominating norms, exploring the comparative and relational aspects of various norms as well as the conflictual aspects, and acknowledging the power of knowledge to define self, others, and experience. Transformation, then, provides the basis of a pedagogy that stems from teaching about the experience of women of color in a way that engages both how women of color are constructed as subject and an implicit understanding of how the student is constructed as subject.

Such an approach may prove helpful in teaching other content to today's postmodern youth, whom Henry Giroux (1994) describes as "border youth," that is, youth for whom "plurality and contingency—whether mediated through the media or through the dislocations spurned by the economic system, the rise of new social movements or the crisis of representation—have resulted in a world with few secure psychological, economic, or intellectual markers. . . . [They] increasingly inhabit shifting cultural and social spheres marked by a plurality of languages and cultures" (p. 355). The content, context of, and pedagogy for teaching about women of color in the United States is part of the needed dialogue between modernism and postmodernism. The fragmentation and dislocation of women of color in relation to what and how we teach frequently reflect and refract the objectification of the student when we teach as if we are filling empty repositories, fulfilling Freire's (1969) banking concept.

As the agent of transformation, women of color as subject content in the humanities and social sciences provide an excellent point for engaging our modern/postmodern conflict. It also provides a philosophical perspective-transformation-for a generative pedagogy that fosters students as subjects, generates knowledge and understanding through building on the interconnections among student, teacher, and content, and engages the conflictive from the strength of the multiply-centered, relational context.

TEACHING ABOUT WOMEN OF COLOR

The first seven heresies cited above address content and methodology for gathering and interpreting content. They inform decisions such as the following:

1. Not teaching Linda Brent's *Incidents in the Life of a Slave Girl* (1861/1973) as the single example of the slave experience of African American women in the nineteenth century, but rather presenting it as a representative example of the slave experience of African American women that occurs within a contradictory, paradoxical world that had free Black women such as Charlotte Forten Grimke and African American abolitionist women such as Sojourner Truth. The picture of Black women that emerges then becomes one that illuminates the complexity of their experiences and their differing interactions with White people rather than an aberrant or unidimensional experience.

2. Not simply teaching about pioneer women in the West, but teaching about Native American women, perhaps through their stories, which they have passed on to their children and their children's children, using their word to advance those concepts crucial to cultural survival. The picture of settling the West becomes more balanced, suggesting clearly to students the different perspectives and power relationships. The Native American becomes a subject—one who acts and interacts—rather than an object of Whites, portrayed as the only subjects.

3. Not choosing a single biography each for children to read of a White American woman, an Asian American woman, and an African American woman, but rather finding ways through biography, poetry, and storytelling to introduce children to different women's experiences—different according to race, class, ethnicity, and gender roles and sexual identity—as well as ways to discuss women's lives comparatively.

The last two heresies directly address process. After accurate content, process is the most important part of teaching. Students who learn in an environment that is sensitive to their feelings and that supports and encourages the pursuit of knowledge will consistently meet new knowledge and new situations with the necessary openness and understanding for human development and progress. If this sounds moralistic, we must remember that the stated and implied goal of critical pedagogy and feminist pedagogy, as well as of efforts to transform the curriculum with content about women and ethnicity, is to provide an education that more accurately reflects the history and composition of the world, that demonstrates the relationship of what we learn to how we live, and that implicitly and explicitly reveals the relationship between knowledge and social action. Process is most important, then, in helping students develop ways throughout their education to reach the closest approximation of truth toward the end of a better, more democratic human condition.

The key to understanding the teaching process in any classroom in which teaching about women of color from the perspective of transformation is a goal is recognizing that the content alters all students' perceptions of themselves. First, they begin to realize that we can never say *women* to mean all women, that we must particularize the word as appropriate to context and understanding (e.g., White, middle-class women; Chinese American, lower-class women; Mexican American, middle-class women). Second, students begin to understand that using White, middle-class women as the norm will seem distortingly reductive. White women's ethnic, regional, class, and gender commonalities and differences soon become apparent, and the role in oppression of the imposed Anglo-American ethnic conformity stands out. Third, students begin to see that experience shapes identity and that identity shapes experience (Hames-García 2000; Mohanty, 2000).

Student reactions may range from surprise, to excitement about learning more, to hostility and anger. In *Gendered Subjects*, Margo Culley (1985) details much of what happens. Her opening paragraph summarizes her main thesis:

> Teaching about gender and race can create classrooms that are charged arenas. Students enter these classrooms imbued with the values of the dominant culture: they believe that success in conventional terms is largely a matter of will and that those who do not have it all have experienced a failure of will. Closer and closer ties between corporate America and higher education, as well as the "upscaling" of the student body, make it even harder to hear the voices from the margin within the academy. Bringing those voices to the center of the classroom means disorganizing ideology and disorienting individuals. Sometimes, as suddenly as the fragments in a kaleidoscope rearrange to totally change the picture, our work alters the ground of being for our students (and perhaps even for ourselves). When this happens, classrooms can become explosive, but potentially transformative arenas of dialogue. (p. 209)

Even though Culley's observation is more than 20 years old, reports from graduate students and faculty in various workshops we conduct nationwide suggest that it still holds.

"Altering the ground of being" happens to some extent on all levels. The White girl kindergarten pupil's sense of the world is frequently challenged when she discovers that heroines do not necessarily look like her. Awareness of the ways in which the world around children is ordered occurs earlier than most of us may imagine. The niece of one of the authors, barely four years old, told her grandfather in a definitive tone as they entered a church farther from her home than the church to which she belongs, "Gramps, this is the Black church." The family had not referred to the church as such, yet clearly that Catholic congregation was predominantly Black and the girl's home congregation predominantly White. Her younger sister, at age three, told her mother that the kids in the day school she attended were "not like me." She then pointed to the brown back of her hand. Young children notice difference. We direct what they do with and think of that difference.

Teaching young children about women of color gives male and female children of all backgrounds a sense of the diversity of people, of the various roles in which women function in U.S. culture, and of the various joys and sorrows, triumphs, and struggles they encounter. Seeds of awareness of the power relationships between male and female, and among racial, ethnic, and class groups are sown and nurtured.

Teaching about women of color early in students' academic experience allows the voices of the margin to be heard and to become a part of the matrix of reality. Teaching about women of color reveals race, ethnicity, gender, and class as essential components of human identity and also questions ideology and ways of being. It encourages an openness to understanding, to difference and similarity, and to the foreign and the commonplace necessary to the mind-set of curiosity about and fascination for knowledge that we want to inspire in our students no matter what the subject. Moreover, it highlights connections among human beings and human experiences and reveals relationships among actions.

Culley (1985) also observes that "anger is the energy mediating the transformation from damage to wholeness," the damage being the values and perspectives of the dominant culture that have shaped opinions based on a seriously flawed and skewed American history and interpretation of the present (p. 212). Certain reactions occur and are part of the process of teaching about women of color. Because they can occur at all levels to a greater or lesser extent, it is useful to look for variations on their themes.

It is important to recognize that these reactions occur within the context of student and teacher expectations. Students are concerned about grading; teachers, about evaluations by superiors and students. Frequently, fear of, disdain for, or hesitancy about feminist perspectives by some students may create a tense, hostile atmosphere. Similarly, fear of, disdain for, or hesitancy about studying people different from you (particularly by the White student) or people similar to you (particularly by the student of color or of a culture related to people of color) may also create a tense, hostile atmosphere. Student expectations of teachers, expectations modulated by the ethnicity, race, class, and gender of the teacher, may encourage students to presume that a teacher will take a certain position. The teacher's need to inspire students to perform with excellence may become a teacher's priority at the expense of presenting material that may at first confuse the students or challenge their opinions. It is important to treat these reactions as though they are as much a part of the process of teaching as are the form of presentation, the exams, and the content, for, indeed, they are. Moreover, they can affect the success of the teaching of the material about women of color.

Specifically, these reactions are part of the overall process of moving from the familiar to the unfamiliar. As Heresy #8 guides us, "Feelings are direct lines to better thinking." Affective reactions to content, such as anger, guilt, and feelings of displacement, when recognized for what they are, lead to the desired cognitive reaction—the conceptualization of the facts so that knowledge becomes useful as the closest approximation to the truth. As Japanese American female students first read accounts by Issei (first-generation) women about their picture-bride experiences, the students' reactions might at first be mixed. Raising the issue of Japanese immigration to the United States during the late nineteenth century may not only challenge the exotic stereotype of the Japanese woman, but it may also engender anger toward Japanese males because of students' incomplete access to history. White students may respond with guilt or indifference because of the policy of a government whose composition is essentially White and Anglo-oriented and with which they identify. Japanese American male students may become defensive, desirous of hearing Japanese American men's stories about picture-bride marriages. African American male and female students may draw analogies between the Japanese American experience and the African American experience. Such analogies may be welcomed or resented by other students. Of course, students from varied backgrounds may respond to learning about Issei women with a reinforced or instilled pride in Japanese ancestry or with a newfound interest in immigration history.

Teacher presentation of Issei women's experience as picture brides should include, of course, lectures, readings, films, and videos about the experience of male Issei immigrants to the United States during the first quarter of the twentieth century—the cheap labor they provided, the impossibility of return to Japan due to low wages, the male–female ratio of Japanese Americans at the turn of the century, and the tradition of arranged marriage in Japan. Presentations should also anticipate, however, student reaction based on their generally ill-informed or limited knowledge about the subject. Discussion and analysis of the students' initial perspectives on Issei women, of how those perspectives have changed given the historical, cultural, and sociological information, allow for learning about and reading Issei women's accounts to become an occasion, then, for expressing feelings of guilt, shame, anger, pride, interest, and curiosity, and for uncovering the reasons for those feelings.

Understanding those feelings and working with them to move the student from a familiar that may be composed of damaging misinformation and even bigotry to a balanced understanding sometimes becomes a major portion of the content, especially when anger or guilt is directed toward a specific group—other students, the teacher, or perhaps even the self. Then it becomes necessary for the teacher to use pressure-release sessions. The need for such sessions may be revealed in many ways. For example,

> the fear of being regarded by peers or by the professor as racist, sexist or "politically incorrect" can polarize a classroom. If the [teacher] participates unconsciously in this fear and emotional self-protection, the classroom experience will degenerate to hopeless polarization, and even overt hostility. He or she must constantly stand outside the classroom experience and anticipate such dynamics. . . . "Pressure release" discussions work best when the teacher directly acknowledges and calls attention to the tension in the classroom. The teacher may initiate the discussion or allow it to come about in whatever way he or she feels most comfortable. (Butler, 1985, p. 236)

The hostility, fear, and hesitancy "can be converted to fertile ground for profound academic experiences . . . 'profound' because the students' knowledge is challenged, expanded, or reinforced" by a subject matter that is simultaneously affective and cognitive, resonant with the humanness of life in both form and content (Butler, 1985, p. 236). Students learn from these pressure-release sessions, as they must learn in life to achieve balance and harmony in whatever pursuits, that paradoxes and contradictions are sometimes resolved and sometimes stand separately yet function together (recall Heresy #1).

Teaching about women of color can often spark resistance to the teacher or cause students to question subject veracity. For example, students usually are taught that the latter part of the nineteenth century and the turn of the twentieth century was a time of expansion for the United States—the Progressive Era. Learning of the experiences of Native American and Mexican women who were subjected to particular horrors as the United States pushed westward, or reading about restrictions on Chinese immigrant women who were not allowed to enter the United States with the Chinese men who provided what was tantamount to slave labor for the building of the railroads, students begin to realize that this time was anything but progressive or expansive.

Teaching about Ida Wells-Barnett (2002/1892), the African American woman who waged the anti-lynching campaigns at the end of the nineteenth century and well into the twentieth century, also belies the progress of that time. Ida Wells-Barnett describes the fore the horror of lynchings of African American men, women, and children; the shameful and inhuman practice of castration that was part of the lynching of Black males; the stereotyped ideas of African American men and women, ideas that were, as Giddings (1984) reminds us, "older than the Republic itself—for they were rooted in the European minds that shaped America" (p. 31). Furthermore, Wells-Barnett's life work reveals the racism of White women in the suffragist movement of the early twentieth century, a reflection of the racism in that movement's nineteenth-century manifestation.

The ever-present interaction of racism and sexism, the stereotyping of African American men and women as bestial, the unfounded labeling of African American men as rapists in search of White women, and the horrid participation in all of this by White men and women in all stations of life make for difficult history for any teacher to teach and for any student to study. The threat to the perfect founding fathers and Miss Liberty versions is apparent. Such content is often resisted by African American and White students alike, perhaps for different reasons, including rage, anger, or shame that such atrocities were endured by people like them; indifference in the face of reality because "nothing like that will happen again;" and anger, guilt, or shame that people of their race were responsible for such hideous atrocities. Furthermore, all students may resent the upsetting of their neatly packaged understandings of U.S. history and of their world.

The teacher must know the content and be willing to facilitate the pressure-release sessions that undoubtedly will be needed. Pressure-release sessions should help students sort out facts from feelings and, most of all, must clarify the relevance of the material to understanding the world in which we live and to preventing such atrocities from recurring. Also, in teaching about the Issei women and about the life of Ida Wells-Barnett, teachers must never let the class lose sight of the vision these women had, how they dealt with joy and sorrow, the triumphs and struggles of their lives, and the contributions to both their own people and to U.S. life at large. It is most important, also, to remind students of the contributions of many Whites such as John Brown, the militant, hanged abolitionist; or Viola Liuzzo, the murdered Italian American civil rights worker; or the persistent civil rights lawyer Morris Dees. The possibility of coalition among people from different, and even conflicting experiences, should always be modeled as we examine the often brutal failures of humanity.

In addition to variations on anger, guilt, and challenges to credibility in learning about women of color, students become more aware of the positive aspects of race and ethnicity and frequently begin to take pride in their identities. As Heresy #9 states, "Knowledge is identity and identity is knowledge. All knowledge is explicitly and implicitly related to who we are, both as individuals and as groups." The teacher, however, must watch for overzealous pride as well as for unadmitted uneasiness with one's ethnic or racial identity. White students, in particular, may react in a generally unexpected manner. Some may predictably claim their Irish ancestry; others may be confused as to their ethnicity, for they may come from German and Scottish ancestry, which early on assumed Anglo-American identity. Students of Anglo-American ancestry, however, may hesitate to embrace that terminology, for it might suggest to them, in the context of the experiences of women and men of color, an abuse of power and "all things horrible in this country," as one upset student once complained to one of the authors. Here, teachers must be adept not only at conveying facts but also at explaining the effects of culture, race, gender, and ethnicity in recording and interpreting historical facts.

Teachers also must be able to convey to students both the beautiful and the ugly in all of us. Thus, the African American teacher may find himself or herself explaining the cultural value of Anglo-American or Yankee humor, of Yankee precision in gardening, of Yankee thriftiness, of the conflicting values of the founding fathers, and how we all share, in some way, that heritage. At whatever age this occurs, students must be helped to understand the dichotomous, hierarchical past of that identity and to move toward expressing their awareness in a pluralistic context.

Now that we have explored the why of the phrase *women of color*, identified the essence of what we learn when we study women of color, discussed the theory of transformation and its heresies, and identified and discussed the most frequent reactions of students to the subject matter, in conclusion we focus on the teacher.

Conclusion

Teaching about women of color should result in conveying information about a group of people largely invisible in our curricula in a way that encourages students to seek further knowledge and ultimately to begin to correct and reorder the flawed perception of the world based on racism, sexism, classism, and ethnocentrism. To do so is no mean feat. Redefining one's world involves not only the inclusion of previously ignored content but also the revision, deletion, and correction of accepted content in light of missing and ignored content. As such, it might require a redesignation of historical periods, a renaming of literary periods, and a complete reworking of sociological methodology to reflect the ethnic and cultural standards at work. Fundamentally, it demands a rethinking about and a reclaiming of identity and its multiple, complex, and vital role in theorizing about the world and in the development of knowledge.

Women of color in the academy have paved the way for transforming the curriculum so that it includes women of color in more than an additive way. For instance, African American female literary scholars have uncovered the "lost" works of African American writers such as Zora Neale Hurston, Nella Larsen, and Ann Petry [See Alice Walker's "Looking for Zora" in *In Search of Our Mother's Gardens: Womanist Prose* (1983), Thadious Davis's *Nella Larsen, Novelist of the Harlem Renaissance: A Woman's Life Unveiled* (1994), Ann

Petry's *Short Fiction* (2004), and *The Critical Response to Ann Petry* (2005)]. Not only have female scholars of color "found" lost works, but they have also constructed criticism and theory that places these works within a tradition of American literature as well as within the African American literacy canon [See Barbara Christian's *Black Feminist Criticism: Perspectives on Black Women Writers* (1985), Mary Helen Washington's *Invented Lives: Narratives of Black Women 1860–1960* (1987), Hazel Carby's *Reconstructing Womanhood: The Emergence of the Afro-American Novelist* (1987), Ann duCille's *The Coupling Convention: Sex, Text, and Tradition in Black Women's Fiction* (1993), and Toni Cade Bambara's *The Black Woman: An Anthology* (2005)].

Another example of female scholars of color transforming the academic landscape with their groundbreaking work can be seen in the work of African American historians, including Nell Irvin Painter's *Sojourner Truth: A Life, A Symbol* (1996), Debra Grey White's *Ar'n't I a Woman: Female Slaves in the Plantation South* (1999) and Stephanie Camp's *Closer to Freedom: Enslaved Women and Everyday Resistance in the Plantation South* (2004).

The work of Gloria Anzaldúa, Cherrie Moraga, and Carla Trujillo are examples of scholarship that examines the lives of women of color, especially Latinas and provides a theoretical frame for others to teach the work of women of color and add to the scholarship. Joy Harjo, Gloria Bird, Leslie Marmon Silko, and Louise Erdrich through their art, criticism, and essays are among the women of color who have paved the way for studies of Native American women. Maxine Hong Kinston, Amy Tan, Jeanne Wakatsuki Houston, and Nora Okja Keller are among the women of color who have brought issues concerning Asian American women to the forefront through their literary works. Beverly Guy-Sheftall (1995) and Chandra Talpade Mohanty (2003) bring pedagogy, scholarship, and activism together in their work on women of color. Teachers and scholars interested in transforming the curriculum and teaching and writing about women of color serve themselves well by examining the groundwork laid by female scholars of color, acknowledging the work of these women and building on it. There is a wealth of information for teachers to use as they develop and teach a curriculum that examines the experiences of women of color and how these experiences are informed by the intersections of race, class, and gender.

This chapter is an introduction to the journey that teachers must embark on to begin providing students with a curriculum that reflects the reality of the past, prepares them to deal with and understand the present, and creates the basis for a more humane, productive, and caring future. The implications of teaching about women of color are far-reaching, involving many people in many different capacities. New texts need to be written for college-level students. Teacher education must be restructured to include not only the transformed content but also the pedagogy that reflects how our nation and the world are multicultural, multiethnic, multiracial, multifocal, and multidimensional. College texts, children's books, and other materials need to be devised to help teach this curriculum. School administrators, school boards, parents, and teachers need to participate in and contribute to this transformation in all ways that influence what our children learn.

The immediate implications of a transformed curriculum may seem overwhelming, because transformation is a long-term project. Presently, we are in the formative stages of understanding what must be done to correct the damage in order to lead to wholeness. We can begin small, that is, decide to include women of color in your classes this year. Begin adding some aspect of that topic to every unit. Pay close attention to how that addition relates to what you already teach. Does it expand the topic? Does it present material you already cover within that expansion? Can you delete some accepted, repetitive material and still meet your objectives? Does the new material conflict with the old? How? Is that conflict a valuable learning resource for your students? Answering such questions will move you quickly from simply adding to revisioning and transforming. Continue to do this each year. Gradually, other central topics will emerge about men of color, White men, White women, class, race, ethnicity, and gender. By beginning with studying women of color, the curriculum then will evolve to be truly pluralistic.

Another important task of the teacher is changing how, in our attempts to change the construction of the student as object, a receptacle of information, we have constructed the student as a distant, theoretical, abstract subject. Shilb (1992) cogently describes what it means to change how we construct the student as subject:

> Changing how the student is constructed as subject entails a number of related teaching practices. It means considering how social differences can affect the interests, backgrounds, learning styles, and degrees of confidence that students bring to the classroom. It means examining how authority operates there as well as in the larger society, analyzing how traditional power relations might be rethought or merely reinforced when teachers and students meet. It means taking students' accounts of their own experiences as at least potentially legitimate avenues to knowledge. It means recognizing that learning can involve intuition and emotion, not just cold, hard logic. Overall, it means taking as a central classroom aim the empowerment of students as conscious, active subjects in the learning process, thereby enhancing their capacity to develop a more democratic world. (p. 65)

The difficulty of the process of transformation is one factor contributing to the maintenance of the status quo. Often, we look for the easiest way out. It is easier to work with students who are not puzzled, concerned, or bothered by what they are studying. We, as teachers, must be willing to admit that we do not know everything but that we do know how to go about learning in a way that reaches the closest approximation of the truth. Our reach must always exceed our grasp, and, in doing so, we will encourage the excellence, the passion, the curiosity, the respect, and the love needed to create superb scholarship and encourage thinking, open-minded, caring, and knowledgeable students.

Questions and Activities

1. When Butler and Raynor use the phrase *women of color*, to what specific ethnic groups are they referring? Why did this phrase emerge, and what purpose does it serve?

2. How can a study of women of color help broaden our understanding of White women? Of women in general? Of White men, men of color?

3. In what ways, according to the authors, is ethnicity an important variable in women's lives? Give specific examples from this chapter to support your response.

4. How does racism, combined with sexism, influence the ways in which people view and respond to women of color?

5. What do the authors mean by *transformation* and a *transformed curriculum?* How does a transformed curriculum differ from a mainstream or balanced curriculum?

6. How can content about women of color serve as a vehicle for transforming the school curriculum?

7. The authors lists nine heresies, or assumptions, about reality that differ fundamentally from dominant modes of thought and values. Why do they believe these heresies are essential when teaching about women of color?

8. The authors state that teaching about women of color may spark resistance to the teacher, the subject, or both. What examples of content do they describe that may evoke student resistance? Why, according to the authors, might students resist this content? What tips do the authors give teachers for handling student resistance?

9. Develop a teaching unit in which you incorporate content about women of color, using the transformation approach described in this chapter. Useful references on women of color are found in the Appendix ("Gender" section).

References

Anzaldúa, G. E. (1987). *Borderlands/La Frontera*. San Francisco: Spinsters, Aunt Lute.

Anzaldúa, G. E., & Keating, A. (Eds.). (2002). *The Bridge We Call Home: Radical Visions of Transformation*. New York: Routledge.

Avila, I. H. (Ed.). (2005). *Reading Native American Women: Critical/Creative Representations*. Lanham, MD: Altamira Press.

Bambara, T. C. (Ed.). (1970). *The Black Woman: An Anthology*. New York: New American Library.

Billinglsey, A. (1968). *Black Families in White America*. Englewood Cliffs, NJ: Prentice-Hall.

Brent, L. (1861/1973). *Incidents in the Life of a Slave Girl* (L. M. Child, Ed.). New York: Harcourt.

Brock, R. (2005) *Sista Talk: the Personal and the Pedagogical*. New York: Peter Lang.

Brodkin, K. (1998). *How Jews Became White Folks and What That Says about Race in America*. New Brunswick, NJ: Rutgers University Press.

Brown, E. B. (1989). African American Women's Quilting: A Framework for Conceptualizing and Teaching African American Women's History. *Signs: Journal of Women in Culture and Society, 14*(4), 921–929.

Butler, J. E. (1985). Toward a Pedagogy of Everywoman's Studies. In M. Culley & C. Portuges (Eds.), *Gendered Subjects: The Dynamics of Feminist Teaching* (pp. 230–239). Boston: Routledge & Kegan Paul.

Collins, P. H. (1998). *Fighting Words: Black Women and the Search for Justice*. Minneapolis: University of Minnesota Press.

Conditions, Five. (1979). The Black Woman's Issue, *2*(3).

Crenshaw, K. W. (1995). Mapping the Margins: Intersectionality, Identity Politics, and Violence Against Women of Color. In K. Crenshaw (Ed.), *Critical Race Theory: The Key Writings That Framed the Movement* (pp. 357–384). The New Press: New York.

Culley, M. (1985). Anger and Authority in the Introductory Women's Studies Classroom. In M. Culley & C. Portuges (Eds.), *Gendered Subjects: The Dynamics of Feminist Teaching* (pp. 209–217). Boston: Routledge & Kegan Paul.

Davidson, B. (1969). *The African Genius.* Boston: Little, Brown.

Dowdy, J. K. (Ed). (2005). *Readers of the Quilt: Essays on Being Black, Female, and Literate.* Cresskill, NJ: Hampton Press.

duCille, A. (1994). The Occult of True Black Womanhood: Critical Demeanor and Black Feminist Studies. *Signs, 19*(3), 591–629.

Duncan, Patti. (Ed). (2004). *Tell This Silence: Asian American Women Writers and the Politics of Speech.* Iowa City: University of Iowa Press.

Fisher, D. (Ed.). (1980). *The Third Woman: Minority Women Writers of the United States.* Boston: Houghton Mifflin.

Freire, P. (1969). *Pedagogy of the Oppressed.* New York: Seabury.

Freire, P. (1973). *Education for Critical Consciousness.* New York: Seabury.

Frye, M. (1983). On Being White: Toward a Feminist Understanding of Race and Race Supremacy. In M. Frye (Ed.), *The Politics of Reality: Essays in Feminist Theory* (pp. 110–127). Trumansburg, NY: Crossing Press.

Giddings, P. (1984). *When and Where I Enter: The Impact of Black Women on Race and Sex in America.* New York: Morrow.

Giroux, H. (1994). Slacking Off: Border Youth and Postmodern Education. *Journal of Advanced Composition, 14*(2), 347–366.

Gross, S. H. (1987). Women's History for Global Learning. *Social Education, 51*(3), 194–198.

Guy-Sheftall, Beverly (Ed). (1995) *Words of Fire: An Anthology of African American Feminist Thought.* New York: New Press.

Hames-García, M. (2000). "Who Are Our Own People?" Challenges for a Theory of Identity. In P. Moya & M. Hames-García (Eds.), *Reclaiming Identity: Realist Theory and the Predicament of Postmodernism* (pp. 102–129). Berkeley: University of California Press.

Henry A. (1998). "Speaking Up" and "Speaking Out" Examining Voice in a Reading/Writing Program with Adolescent African Caribbean Girls." *Journal of Literacy Research, 30*(2), 233–252.

Hord, F. L., & Lee, J. (1995). *I Am Because We Are: Readings in Black Philosophy.* Amherst: University of Massachusetts Press.

Hurston, Z. N. (1970). *Dust Tracks on a Road: An Autobiography.* Edited and with an introduction by R. Hemenway. Urbana: University of Illinois Press.

Kennelly, Ivy. (1999). That Single Mother Element: How White Employers Typify Black Women. *Gender and Society, 13*(2), 168–192.

Kingston, M. H. (1976). *The Woman Warrior: Memories of a Girlhood among Ghosts.* New York: Random House.

Ladner, J. (Ed.). (1973). *The Death of White Sociology.* New York: Vintage.

Lipsitz, G. (1998). *The Possessive Investment in Whiteness: How White People Profit from Identity Politics.* Philadelphia: Temple University Press.

Madison, D. S. (1994). *The Woman That I Am: The Literature and Culture of Contemporary Women of Color.* New York: St. Martin's.

Mbiti, J. (1975). *Introduction to African Religion.* London: Heinemann.

McAdoo, H. (Ed.). (1981). *Black Families.* Beverly Hills, CA: Sage.

McIntosh, P. (1987, June). *Understanding Correspondence between White Privilege and Male Privilege through Women's Studies Work*. Paper presented at the annual meeting of the National Women's Studies Association, Atlanta, GA.

Minnich, E. (1990). *Transforming Knowledge*. Philadelphia: Temple University Press.

Morrison, T. (1998). *Paradise*. New York: Knopf.

Mohanty, C. T. (2003). *Feminism Without Borders: Decolonizing Theory, Practicing Solidarity*. Duke University Press.

Mohanty, S. P. (2000). The Epistemic Status of Cultural Identity: On *Beloved* and the Postcolonial Condition. In P. Moya and M. Hames-García (Eds.) *Reclaiming Identity: Realist Theory and the Predicament of Postmodernism* (pp. 29–66). Berkeley: University of California Press.

Moraga, C., & Anzaldúa, G. E. (Eds.) (1981). *This Bridge Called My Back: Writings by Radical Women of Color*. Watertown, MA: Persephone Press.

Moya, P. (2000). Introduction: Reclaiming Identity. In P. Moya & M. Hames-García (Eds.), *Reclaiming Identity: Realist Theory and the Predicament of Postmodernism* (pp. 1–26). Berkeley: University of California Press.

Moynihan, D. P. et. al., (1965). *The Negro Family, the Case for National Action*. Washington, DC: U.S. Government Printing Office.

Phillips, Layli. (2004). Fitting in and Feeling Good: Patterns of Self-Evaluation and Psychological Stress Among Biracial Adolescent Girls. *Women and Therapy*, 2004, January–February 27(2), 217–236.

Roediger, D. R. (1991). *The Wages of Whiteness: Race and the Making of the American Working-Class*. London: Verso.

Roediger, D. R. (1994). *Towards the Abolition of Whiteness: Essays on Race, Politics, and Working-Class History*. London: Verso.

Roediger, D. R. (2005). *Working Toward Whiteness: How America's Immigrants Became White: The Strange Journey from Ellis Island to the Suburbs*. New York: Basic Books.

Root, M. P. P. (2004). Multiracial Families and Children: Implications for Educational Research and Practice. In J. A. Banks & C. A. M. Banks (Eds.), *Handbook of Research on Multicultural Education* (pp. 110–124). San Francisco: Jossey-Bass.

Shilb, J. (1992). Poststructuralism, Politics, and the Subject of Pedagogy. In M. Kecht (Ed.), *Pedagogy Is Politics: Literary Theory and Critical Teaching* (pp. 62–85). Urbana: University of Illinois Press.

Silliman, J. (2004). *Undivided Rights: Women of Color Organize for Reproductive Justice*. Cambridge, MA: South End Press.

Spelman, E. V. (1982). Theories of Gender and Race: The Erasure of Black Women. *Quest: A Feminist Quarterly*, 5(4), 36–62.

Walker, A. (1997). *Anything We Love Can Be Saved: A Writer's Activitism*. New York: Random House.

Yancy, G. (Ed.). (1998). *African American Philosophers: 17 Conversations*. New York: Routledge.

Young, I. M. (2005). Five Faces of Oppression. In A. Cudd and R. Andreasen (Eds.), *Feminist Theory: A Philosophical Anthology*. Blackwell Publishing, Ltd.

Young, R. (1990). *White Mythologies: Writing History and the West*. New York: Routledge.

Wells-Barnett I. B. (2002/1892). *On Lynchings*. Amherst, NY: Humanity Books. (Original work published 1892.)

All students benefit when teachers create culturally responsive learning experiences for students from diverse diverse racial, ethnic, language, and social-class groups.

Race, Ethnicity, and Language

The drastic increase in the percentage of students of color and of language-minority students in the nation's schools is one of the most significant developments in education in the last several decades. The growth in the percentage of students of color and of language-minority students in the nation's schools results from several factors, including the new wave of immigration that began after 1968 and the aging of the White population. The nation's classrooms are experiencing the largest influx of immigrant students since the beginning of the twentieth century. The United States receives nearly 1 million immigrants annually, most of whom come from nations in Asia and Latin America. However, the Immigration and Naturalization Service reported that in 2001, 16.5 percent of all legal immigrants came from Europe, many of them from nations in the Russian Federation. Between 1990 and 1996, nearly 1 million immigrants entered the United States each year. Another 3.3 million arrived between January 2000 and March 2002.

Demographers predict that if current trends continue, about 46 percent of the nation's school-age youths will be of color by the year 2020. In 2004, 41.2 percent of students in grades 1 to 12 in public schools were members of a minority group, an increase of about 8 percent since 1994. They were a majority of the students in the state of California as well as in many major cities, such as Seattle, San Francisco, Chicago, and Washington, D.C. Another important characteristic of today's students is the large percentage who low-income poor and who live in female-headed households. Today, about one out of every five students lives in a low-income family.

While the nation's students are becoming increasingly diverse, most of the nation's teachers remain White (87 percent), female (74 percent), and middle-class. The percentage of teachers of color remains low. In 2002 teachers of color made up only 13 percent of the nation's teachers. The growing racial, cultural, and income gap between teachers and students underscores the need for all teachers to develop the knowledge, attitudes, and skills needed to work effectively with students from diverse racial, ethnic, social-class, and language groups. The four chapters in this part of the book present concepts, knowledge, and strategies that all teachers will find helpful in working with students from diverse groups.

CHAPTER 9

Culturally Relevant Teaching: Theory and Practice

Gloria Ladson-Billings

Teacher education programs throughout the nation have coupled their efforts at reform with revised programs committed to social justice and equity. Thus, their focus has become the preparation of prospective teachers in ways that support equitable and just educational experiences for all students. Examples of such efforts include work in Alaska (Kleinfeld, 1992; Noordhoff, 1990; Noordhoff & Kleinfeld, 1991), California (King & Ladson-Billings, 1990), Illinois (Beyer, 1991), and Wisconsin (Murrell, 1990, 1991).

Currently, there are debates in the educational research literature concerning both locating efforts at social reform in schools (Popkewitz, 1991) and the possibilities of "re-educating" typical teacher candidates for the variety of student populations in U.S. public schools (Grant, 1989; Haberman, 1991a, 1991b). Rather than looking at programmatic reform, this chapter considers educational theorizing about teaching itself and proposes a theory of culturally focused pedagogy that might be considered in the reformation of teacher education.

Shulman's often cited article, "Knowledge and Teaching: Foundations of the New Reform" (1987), considers philosophical and psychological perspectives, underscored by case knowledge of novice and experienced practitioners. Although Shulman's work mentions the importance of both the knowledge of learners and their characteristics and knowledge of educational contexts, it generally minimizes the culturally based analyses of teaching that have preceded it. In this chapter I attempt to build on the educational anthropological literature and suggest a new theoretical perspective to address the specific concerns of educating teachers for success with African American students.

TEACHING AND CULTURE

For more than a decade, anthropologists have examined ways that teaching can better match the home and community cultures of students of color who have previously not had academic success in schools. Au and Jordan (1981, p. 139) termed "culturally appropriate" the pedagogy of teachers in a Hawaiian school who incorporated aspects of students' cultural backgrounds into their reading instruction. By permitting students to use *talk-story*, a language interaction style common among Native Hawaiian children, teachers were able to help students achieve at higher than predicted levels on standardized reading tests.

Mohatt and Erickson (1981) conducted similar work with Native American students. As they observed teacher–student interactions and participation structures, they found teachers who used language interaction patterns that approximated the students' home cultural patterns were more successful in improving student academic performance. Improved student achievement also was evident among teachers who used what they termed "mixed forms" (p. 117)—a combination of Native American and Anglo language interaction patterns. They termed this instruction "culturally congruent" (p. 110). Cazden and Leggett (1981) and Erickson and Mohatt (1982) used the term "culturally responsive" (p. 167) to describe similar language interactions of teachers with linguistically diverse and Native American students, respectively. Later, Jordan (1985, p. 110) and Vogt, Jordan, and Tharp (1987, p. 281) began using the term "culturally compatible" to explain the success of classroom teachers with Hawaiian children.

By observing the students in their home/community environment, teachers were able to include aspects of the students' cultural environment in the organization and instruction of the classroom. More specifically, Jordan (1985) discusses cultural compatibility in this way:

> Educational practices must match with the children's culture in
> ways which ensure the generation of academically important
> behaviors. It does not mean that all school practices need be
> completely congruent with natal cultural practices, in the sense of
> exactly or even closely matching or agreeing with them. The point
> of cultural compatibility is that the natal culture is used as a guide
> in the selection of educational program elements so that
> academically desired behaviors are produced and undesired
> behaviors are avoided. (p. 110)

These studies have several common features. Each locates the source of student failure and subsequent achievement within the nexus of speech and language interaction patterns of the teacher and the students. Each suggests that student "success" is represented in achievement within the current social structures of schools. Thus, the goal of education becomes how to "fit" students constructed as "other" by virtue of their race/ethnicity, language, or social class into a hierarchical structure that is defined as a *meritocracy*. However, it is unclear how these conceptions do more than reproduce the current inequities. Singer (1988) suggests that "cultural congruence is an inherently moderate pedagogical strategy thats accepts that the goal of educating minority students is to train individuals in those skills needed to succeed in mainstream society" (p. 1).

Three of the terms employed by studies on cultural mismatch between school and home—*culturally appropriate, culturally congruent,* and *culturally compatible*—seem to connote accommodation of student culture to mainstream culture. Only the term *culturally responsive* appears to refer to a more dynamic or synergistic relationship between home/community culture and school culture. Erickson and Mohatt (1982) suggest their notion of culturally responsive teaching can be seen as a beginning step for bridging the gap between home and school:

> It may well be that, by discovering the small differences in social
> relations which make a big difference in the interactional ways
> children engage the content of the school curriculum,
> anthropologists can make practical contributions to the
> improvement of minority children's school achievement and to the
> improvement of the everyday school life for such children and
> their teachers. Making small changes in everyday participation
> structures may be one of the means by which more culturally
> responsive pedagogy can be developed. (p. 170)

For the most part, studies of cultural appropriateness, congruence, or compatibility have been conducted within small-scale communities—for example, Native Hawaiian and Native Americans. However, an earlier generation of work considered the mismatch between the language patterns of African Americans and the school in larger, urban settings (Gay & Abrahamson, 1972; Labov, 1969; Piestrup, 1973).

Villegas (1988) challenged the microsocial explanations advanced by sociolinguists by suggesting that the source of cultural mismatch is located in larger social structures and that schools as institutions serve to reproduce social inequalities. She argued that:

> . . . as long as school performs this sorting function in society, it
> must necessarily produce winners and losers. . . . Therefore,
> culturally sensitive remedies to educational problems of oppressed
> minority students that ignore the political aspect of schooling are
> doomed to failure. (pp. 262–263)

Although I would agree with Villegas's attention to the larger social structure, other scholars in the cultural ecological paradigm (Ogbu, 1981, 1983) are ahistorical and limited, particularly in their ability to explain African American student success (Perry, 1993).[1] The long history of African American educational struggle and achievement is well documented (Anderson, 1988; Billingsley, 1992; Bond, 1969; Bullock, 1967; Clark, 1983; Harding, 1981; Harris, 1992; Johnson, 1936; Rury, 1983; Woodson, 1919; Weinberg, 1977). This historical record contradicts the glib pronouncements that "Black people don't value education."

---

[1]Although issues of culturally relevant teaching can and should be considered cross-culturally, this chapter looks specifically at the case of African American students.

Second, more recent analyses of successful schooling for African American students (King, 1991a; Ladson-Billings, 1992a, 1994; Siddle-Walker, 1993) challenge the explanatory power of the cultural ecologists' caste-like category and raise questions about what schools can and should be doing to promote academic success for African American students.[2]

Despite their limitations, the microanalytic work of sociolinguists and the macrostructural analysis of cultural ecologists both are important in helping scholars think about their intersections and consider possible classroom/instructional adjustments. For scholars interested in the success of students of color in complex, urban environments, this work provides some important theoretical and conceptual groundwork.

Irvine (1990) developed the concept of *cultural synchronization* to describe the necessary interpersonal context that must exist between the teacher and African American students to maximize learning. Rather than focus solely on speech and language interactions, Irvine's work describes the acceptance of students' communication patterns, along with a constellation of African American cultural mores such as mutuality, reciprocity, spirituality, deference, and responsibility (King & Mitchell, 1990).

Irvine's work on African American students and school failure considers both micro- and macro-analyses, including teacher-student interpersonal contexts, teacher and student expectations, institutional contexts, and the societal context. This work is important for its break with the cultural deficit or cultural disadvantage explanations which led to compensatory educational interventions.[3] A next step for positing effective pedagogical practice is a theoretical model that not only addresses student achievement but also helps students to accept and affirm their cultural identity while developing critical perspectives that challenge inequities that schools (and other institutions) perpetuate. I term this pedagogy *culturally relevant pedagogy*.

Several questions, some of which are beyond the scope of this discussion, drive this attempt to formulate a theoretical model of culturally relevant pedagogy. What constitutes student success? How can academic success and cultural success complement each other in settings where student alienation and hostility characterize the school experience? How can pedagogy promote the kind of student success that engages larger social structural issues in a critical way? How do researchers recognize that pedagogy in action? And, what are the implications for teacher preparation generated by this pedagogy?

---

[2]It is interesting to note that a number of trade books have emerged that detail the rage and frustration of academically successful, professional, middle-class, African American adults, which suggests that, even with the proper educational credentials, their lives continue to be plagued by racism and a questioning of their competence. Among the more recent books are Jill Nelson's *Volunteer Slavery* (1993), Brent Staples's *Parallel Time* (1994), and Ellis Cose's *The Rage of a Privileged Class* (1993).

[3]It should be noted that the "cultural deficit" notion has been reinscribed under the rubric of "at-risk" (Cuban, 1989). Initially, the U.S. Commission on Excellence in Education defined the nation as at risk. Now, almost 10 years later, it appears that only some children are at risk. Too often, in the case of African American students, their racial/cultural group membership defines them as at risk.

THE ILLUSION OF A THEORETICAL INQUIRY

Educational research is greeted with suspicion both within and outside of the academy. Among practitioners, it is regarded as *too theoretical* (Kaestle, 1993). For many academicians, it is regarded as *atheoretical* (Katzer, Cook, & Crouch, 1978). It is the latter notion that I address in this section of the chapter.

Clearly, much of educational research fails to make explicit its theoretical underpinnings (Argyris, 1980; Amundson, Serlin, & Lehrer, 1992). However, I want to suggest that, even without explicating a theoretical framework, researchers do have explanations for why things "work the way they do." These theories may be partial, poorly articulated, conflated, or contradictory, but they exist. What is regarded as traditional educational theory—theories of reproduction (as described by Apple & Weis, 1983; Bowles, 1977; Weiler, 1988) or neoconservative traditional theory (as described in Young, 1990)—may actually be a *default* theory that researchers feel no need to make explicit. Thus, the theory's objectivity is unquestioned, and studies undergirded by these theories are regarded as truth or objective reality.

Citing the *ranking*, or privileging, of theoretical knowledge, Code (1991) observes:

> Even when empiricist *theories* of knowledge prevail, knowledgeable
> *practice* constructs positions of power and privilege that are by no
> means as impartially ordered as strict empiricism would require.
> Knowledge gained from practical (untheorized) experience is
> commonly regarded as inferior to theoretically derived or theory-
> confirming knowledge, and theory is elevated above practice. (p. 243)

In education, work that recognizes the import of practical experience owes an intellectual debt to scholars such as Smith (1978), Atkin (1973), Glaser and Strauss (1967), and Lutz and Ramsey (1974) who explored notions of grounded theory as an important tool for educational research. Additionally, work by scholars in teacher education such as Stenhouse (1983), Elliott (1991), Carr and Kemmis (1986), Zeichner (1990), and Cochran-Smith and Lytle (1992) illuminates the action research tradition where teachers look reflexively at their practice to solve pedagogical problems and assist colleagues and researchers interested in improving their teaching. Even some scholars in the logical positivist tradition acknowledge the value of a more experientially grounded research approach in education (Cronbach, 1975). More fundamental than arguing the merits of quantitative versus qualitative methodology (Gage, 1989) have been calls for broader understanding about the limits of any research methodology (Rist, 1990). In using selected citations from Kuhn, Patton, Becker, and Gouldner, Rist (1990) helps researchers understand the significance of research paradigms in education. For example:

> Since no paradigm ever solves all of the problems it defines and
> since no two paradigms leave all the same problems unsolved,
> paradigm debates always involve the question: Which problems is
> it more significant to have solved? (Kuhn, 1970, p. 46)

> A paradigm is a world view, a general perspective, a way of
> breaking down the complexity of the real world. As such,
> paradigms are deeply embedded in the socialization of adherents

> and practitioners, telling them what is important, what is reasonable. (Patton, 1975, p. 9)

> The issue is not research strategies, per se. Rather, the adherence to one paradigm as opposed to another predisposes one to view the world and the events within it in profoundly differing ways. (Rist, 1990, p. 83)

> The power and pull of a paradigm is more than simply a methodological orientation. It is a means by which to grasp reality and give it meaning and predictability. (Rist, 1990, p. 83)

It is with this orientation toward the inherent subjectivity of educational research that I have approached my work. In this next section, I discuss some of the specific perspectives that have informed my work.

THE PARTICIPANT–OBSERVER ROLE FOR RESEARCHERS WHO ARE "OTHER"

Increasingly, researchers have a story to tell about themselves as well as their work (Carter, 1993; Peterson & Neumann, 1995). I, too, share a concern for situating myself as a researcher—who I am, what I believe, what experiences I have had all impact what, how, and why I research. What may make these research revelations more problematic for me is my own membership in a marginalized racial/cultural group.

One possible problem I face is the presumption of a "native" perspective (Banks, 1992; Narayan, 1993; Padilla, 1994; Rosaldo, 1989) as I study effective practice for African American students. To this end, the questions raised by Narayan seem relevant:

> "Native" anthropologists, then, are perceived as insiders regardless of their complex backgrounds. The differences between kinds of "native" anthropologists are also obviously passed over. Can a person from an impoverished American minority background who, despite all prejudices, manages to get an education and study her own community be equated with a member of a Third World elite group who, backed by excellent schooling and parental funds, studies anthropology abroad yet returns home for fieldwork among the less privileged? Is it not insensitive to suppress the issue of location, acknowledging that a scholar who chooses an institutional base in the Third World might have a different engagement with Western-based theories, books, political stances, and technologies of written production? Is a middle-class white professional researching aspects of her own society also a "native" anthropologist? (p. 677)

This location of myself as native can work against me (Banks, 1992; Padilla, 1994). My work may be perceived as biased or, at the least, skewed, because of my vested interests in the African American community. Thus, I have attempted to search for theoretical grounding that acknowledges my standpoint and simultaneously forces me to problematize it. The work of Patricia Hill Collins (1991) on Black feminist thought has been most helpful.

Briefly, Collins's work is based on four propositions: (1) concrete experiences as a criterion of meaning, (2) the use of dialogue in assessing knowledge claims, (3) the ethic of caring, and (4) the ethic of personal accountability. Below, I briefly describe the context and methodology of my study and then attempt to link each of these propositions to a 3-year study I conducted with successful teachers of African American students.

ISSUES OF CONTEXT AND METHODOLOGY

While it is not possible to fully explicate the context and method of this study in this chapter, it is necessary to provide readers with some sense of both for better continuity. I have provided more elaborate explanations of these aspects of the work in other writings (Ladson-Billings, 1990, 1992a, 1992b, 1994). Included here is a brief explanation of the research context and method.

In 1988, I began working as a lone investigator with a group of eight teachers in a small (fewer than 3,000 students) predominantly African American, low-income elementary school district in Northern California. The teachers were identified through a process of *community nomination* (Foster, 1991), with African American parents (in this case, all mothers) who attended local churches suggesting who they thought were outstanding teachers. The parents' criteria for teaching excellence included being accorded respect by the teacher, student enthusiasm toward school and academic tasks, and student attitudes toward themselves and others. The parents' selections were cross-checked by an independent list of excellent teachers generated by principals and some teaching colleagues. Principals' criteria for teaching excellence included excellent classroom management skills, student achievement (as measured by standardized test scores), and personal observations of teaching practice. Nine teachers' names appeared on both the parents' and principals' lists and were selected to be in the study. One teacher declined to participate because of the time commitment. The teachers were all females: five were African American and three were White.

The study was composed of four phases. During the first phase, each teacher participated in an ethnographic interview (Spradley, 1979) to discuss her background, philosophy of teaching, and ideas about curriculum, classroom management, and parent and community involvement. In the second phase of the study, teachers agreed to be observed by me. This agreement meant that the teachers gave me carte blanche to visit their classrooms. These visits were not scheduled beforehand. I visited the classrooms regularly for almost 2 years, an average of 3 days a week. During each visit, I took field notes, audiotaped the class, and talked with the teacher after the visit, either on-site or by telephone. The third phase of the study, which overlapped the second phase, involved videotaping the teachers. I made decisions about what to videotape as a result of my having become familiar with the teachers' styles and classroom routines.

The fourth and final phase of the study required that the teachers work together as a research collective or collaborative to view segments of one another's videotapes. In a series of ten 2–3-hour meetings, the teachers participated in analysis and interpretation of their own and one another's practice. It was during this phase of the study that formulations about culturally relevant pedagogy that had emerged in the initial interviews were confirmed by teaching practice.

My own interest in these issues of teaching excellence for African-American students came as a result of my desire to challenge deficit paradigms (Bloom, Davis, & Hess, 1965) that prevailed in the literature on African American learners. Partly as a result of my own experiences as a learner, a teacher, and a parent, I was convinced that, despite the literature, there were teachers who were capable of excellent teaching for African American students. Thus, my work required a paradigmatic shift toward looking in the classrooms of excellent teachers, *through* the reality of those teachers. In the next section, I discuss how my understanding of my own theoretical grounding connected with the study.

CONCRETE EXPERIENCES AS A CRITERION OF MEANING

According to Collins, "Individuals who have lived through the experiences about which they claim to be experts are more believable and credible than those who have merely read and thought about such experience" (p. 209). My work with successful teachers of African American students began with a search for "expert" assessment of good teachers. The experts I chose were parents who had children attending the schools where I planned to conduct the research. The parents were willing to talk openly about who they thought were excellent teachers for their children, citing examples of teachers' respect for them as parents, their children's enthusiasm and changed attitudes toward learning, and improved academics in conjunction with support for the students' home culture. In most cases, the basis for their assessments were comparative, both from the standpoint of having had experiences with many teachers (for each individual child) and having had several school-age children. Thus, they could talk about how an individual child fared in different classrooms and how their children collectively performed at specific grade levels with specific teachers.

The second area where concrete experiences as a criterion of meaning was evident was with the teachers themselves. The eight teachers who participated in this study had from 12 to 40 years of teaching experience, most of it with African American students. Their reflections on what was important in teaching African American students were undergirded by their daily teaching experiences.

THE USE OF DIALOGUE IN ASSESSING KNOWLEDGE CLAIMS

This second criterion suggests that knowledge emerges in dialectical relationships. Rather than the voice of one authority, meaning is made as a product of dialogue between and among individuals. In the case of my study, dialogue was critical in assessing knowledge claims. Early in the study, each teacher participated in an ethnographic interview (Spradley, 1979). Although I had specific areas I wanted to broach with each teacher, the teachers' own life histories and interests determined how much time was spent on the various areas. In some cases the interviews reflect a teacher's belief in the salience of his or her family background and education. In other instances, teachers talked more about their pedagogical, philosophical, and political perspectives. Even after I began collecting data via classroom observations, it was the teachers' explanations and clarifications that helped to construct the meaning of what transpired in the classrooms.

Additionally, after I collected data from classroom observations and classroom videotaping, the teachers convened as a research collaborative to examine both their own and one anothers' pedagogy.[4] In these meetings, meaning was constructed through reciprocal dialogue. Instead of merely accepting Berliner's (1988) notions that "experts" operate on a level of automaticity and intuition that does not allow for accurate individual critique and interpretation—that is, they cannot explain how they do what they do—together the teachers were able to make sense of their own and their colleagues' practices. The ongoing dialogue allowed them the opportunity to reexamine and rethink their practices.

THE ETHIC OF CARING

Much has been discussed in feminist literature about women and *caring* (Gilligan, 1982; Noddings, 1984, 1991). Other feminists have been critical of any essentialized notion of women (Weiler, 1988) and suggest that no empirical evidence exists to support the notion that women care in ways different from men or that any such caring informs their scholarship and work. I argue that Collins's use of caring refers not merely to affective connections between and among people but to the articulation of a greater sense of commitment to what scholarship and/or pedagogy can mean in people's lives.

For example, in this study, the teachers were not all demonstrative and affectionate toward the students. Instead, their common thread of caring was their concern for the implications their work had on their students' lives, the welfare of the community, and unjust social arrangements. Thus, rather than the idiosyncratic caring for individual students (for whom they did seem to care), the teachers spoke of the import of their work for preparing the students for confronting inequitable and undemocratic social structures.

THE ETHIC OF PERSONAL ACCOUNTABILITY

In this final dimension, Collins (1991) addresses the notion that *who* makes knowledge claims is as important as *what* those knowledge claims are. Thus, the idea that individuals can "objectively" argue a position whether they themselves agree with the position, as in public debating, is foreign. Individuals' commitments to ideological and/or value positions are important in understanding knowledge claims.

In this study, the teachers demonstrated this ethic of personal accountability in the kind of pedagogical stands they took. Several of the teachers spoke of defying administrative mandates in order to do what they believed was right for students. Others gave examples of proactive actions they took to engage in pedagogical practices more consistent with their beliefs and values. For example, one teacher was convinced that the school district's

---

[4]The research collaborative met to view portions of the classroom videotapes that I, as researcher, selected for common viewing.

mandated reading program was inconsistent with what she was learning about literacy teaching/learning from a critical perspective. She decided to write a proposal to the school board asking for experimental status for a literacy approach she wanted to use in her classroom. Her proposal was buttressed by current research in literacy and would not cost the district any more than the proposed program. Ultimately, she was granted permission to conduct her experiment, and its success allowed other teachers to attempt it in subsequent years.

Although Collins's work provided me with a way to think about my work as a researcher, it did not provide me with a way to theorize about the teachers' practices. Ultimately, it was my responsibility to generate theory as I practiced theory. As previously mentioned, this work builds on earlier anthropological and sociolinguistic attempts at a cultural "fit" between students' home culture and school culture. However, by situating it in a more critical paradigm, a theory of culturally relevant pedagogy would necessarily propose to do three things: produce students who can achieve academically, produce students who demonstrate cultural competence, and develop students who can both understand and critique the existing social order. The next section discusses each element of culturally relevant pedagogy.

CULTURALLY RELEVANT PEDAGOGY AND STUDENT ACHIEVEMENT

Much has been written about the school failure of African American students (see, e.g., African American Male Task Force, 1990; Clark, 1983; Comer, 1984; Irvine, 1990; Ogbu, 1981; Slaughter & Kuehne, 1988). However, explanations for this failure have varied widely. One often-cited explanation situates African American students' failure in their "caste-like minority" (p. 169) or "involuntary immigrant" status (Ogbu, 1983, p. 171). Other explanations posit *cultural difference* (Erickson, 1987, 1993; Piestrup, 1973) as the reason for this failure and, as previously mentioned, locate student failure in the cultural mismatch between students and the school.

Regardless of these failure explanations, little research has been done to examine academic success among African American students. The *effective schools* literature (Brookover, 1985; Brookover, Beady, Flood, Schweitzer, & Wisenbaker, 1979; Edmonds, 1979) argued that a group of schoolwide correlates were a reliable predictor of student success.[5] The basis for determining a school "effective" in this literature was how far above predicted levels students performed on standardized achievement tests. Whether or not scholars can agree on the significance of standardized tests, their meaning in the real world serves to rank and characterize both schools and individuals. Thus, teachers in urban schools are compelled to demonstrate that their students can achieve literacy and numeracy (Delpit, 1992). No matter how good a fit develops between home and school culture, students must achieve. No theory of pedagogy can escape this reality.

---

[5]These correlates include: a clear and focused mission, instructional leadership, a safe and orderly environment, regular monitoring of student progress, high expectations, and positive home-school relations.

Students in the eight classrooms I observed did achieve. Despite the low ranking of the school district, the teachers were able to help students perform at higher levels than their district counterparts. In general, compared to students in middle-class communities, the students still lagged behind. But, more students in these classrooms were at or above grade level on standardized achievement tests.[6] Fortunately, academic achievement in these classrooms was not limited to standardized assessments. Classroom observations revealed a variety of demonstrated student achievements too numerous to list here. Briefly, students demonstrated an ability to read, write, speak, compute, pose, and solve problems at sophisticated levels— that is, pose their own questions about the nature of teacher- or text-posed problems and engage in peer review of problem solutions. Each teacher felt that helping the students become academically successful was a primary responsibility.

CULTURALLY RELEVANT TEACHING AND CULTURAL COMPETENCE

Among the scholarship that has examined academically successful African American students, a disturbing finding has emerged—the students' academic success came at the expense of their cultural and psychosocial well-being (Fine, 1986; Fordham, 1988). Fordham and Ogbu (1986) identified a phenomenon they called "acting White" (p. 176), where African American students who were academically successful were ostracized by their peers. Bacon (1981) found that, among African American high school students identified as gifted in their elementary grades, only about half were continuing to do well at the high school level. A closer examination of the successful students' progress indicated that they were social isolates, with neither African American nor White friends. The students believed that it was necessary for them to stand apart from other African American students so that teachers would not attribute to them the negative characteristics they may have attributed to African American students in general.

The dilemma for African American students becomes one of negotiating the academic demands of school while demonstrating cultural competence.[7] Thus, culturally relevant pedagogy must provide a way for students to maintain their cultural integrity while succeeding academically. One teacher in the study used the lyrics of rap songs as a way to teach elements

---

[6]Students in this district took the California Achievement Test (CAT) in October and May of each school year. Growth scores in the classrooms of the teachers in the study were significantly above those of others in the district.

[7]This is not to suggest that cultural competence for African American students means being a failure. The problem that African American students face is the constant devaluation of their culture both in school and in the larger society. Thus, the styles apparent in African-American youth culture—e.g., dress, music, walk, language—are equated with poor academic performance. The student who identifies with "hip-hop" culture may be regarded as dangerous and/or a gang member for whom academic success is not expected. He (and usually it is a male) is perceived as not having the *cultural* capital (Bourdieu, 1984) necessary for academic success.

of poetry.[8] From the rap lyrics, she went on to more conventional poetry. Students who were more skilled at creating and improvising raps were encouraged and reinforced. Another teacher worked to channel the peer group leadership of her students into classroom and school-wide leadership. One of her African American male students who had experienced multiple suspensions and other school problems before coming to her classroom demonstrated some obvious leadership abilities. He could be described as culturally competent in his language and interaction styles and demonstrated pride in himself and his cultural heritage. Rather than attempt to minimize his influence, the teacher encouraged him to run for sixth-grade president and mobilized the entire class to organize and help run his campaign. To the young man's surprise, he was elected. His position as president provided the teacher with many opportunities to respond to potential behavior problems. This same teacher made a point of encouraging the African American males in her classroom to assume the role of academic leaders. Their academic leadership allowed their cultural values and styles to be appreciated and affirmed. Because these African American male students were permitted, indeed encouraged, to be themselves in dress, language style, and interaction styles while achieving in school, the other students, who regarded them highly (because of their popularity), were able to see academic engagement as "cool."

Many of the self-described African-centered public schools have focused on this notion of cultural competence.[9] To date, minimal data have been reported on the academic success of students in these programs. However, the work of African American scholars such as Ratteray (1994), Lee (1994), Hilliard (1992), Murrell (1993), Asante (1991), and others indicates that African-centered education does develop students who maintain cultural competence and demonstrate academic achievement.

CULTURALLY RELEVANT TEACHING AND CULTURAL CRITIQUE

Not only must teachers encourage academic success and cultural competence, they must help students to recognize, understand, and critique current social inequities. This notion presumes that teachers themselves recognize social inequities and their causes. However, teacher educators (Grant, 1989; Haberman, 1991b; King, 1991b; King & Ladson-Billings, 1990; Zeichner, 1992) have demonstrated that many prospective teachers not only lack these understandings but reject information regarding social inequity. This suggests that more work on recruiting particular kinds of students into teaching must be done. Also, we are fortunate to

---

[8]An examination of rap music reveals a wide variety of messages. Despite the high profile of "gangsta rap," which seems to glorify violence, particularly against the police and Whites, and the misogynistic messages found in some of this music, there is a segment of rap music that serves as cultural critique and urges African Americans to educate themselves because schools fail to do so. Prominent rap artists in this tradition are Arrested Development, Diggable Planets, KRS-1, and Queen Latifah.

[9]I am indebted to Mwalimu Shujaa for sharing his working paper, "Afrikan-Centered Education in Afrikan-Centered Schools: The Need for Consensus Building," which elaborates the multiplicity of thinking on this issue extant in the African-centered movement.

have models for this kind of cultural critique emanating from the work of civil rights work-ers in the United States (Aaronsohn, 1992; Morris, 1984; Clark, 1964; Clark, with Brown, 1990) and the international work of Freire (1973, 1974) that has been incorporated into the critical and feminist work currently being done by numerous scholars (see, e.g., Ellsworth, 1989; Giroux, 1983; hooks, 1989; Lather, 1986; McLaren, 1989). Teachers who meet the cul-tural critique criteria must be engaged in a critical pedagogy which is

> a deliberate attempt to influence how and what knowledge and
> identities are produced within and among particular sets of social
> relations. It can be understood as a practice through which people
> are incited to acquire a particular "moral character." As both a
> political and practical activity, it attempts to influence the occurrence
> and qualities of experiences. (Giroux & Simon, 1989, p. 239)

Thus, the teachers in this study were not reluctant to identify political underpinnings of the students' community and social world. One teacher worked with her students to identify poorly utilized space in the community, examine heretofore inaccessible archival records about the early history of the community, plan alternative uses for a vacant shopping mall, and write urban plans which they presented before the city council.

In a description of similar political activity, a class of African American, middle-school students in Dallas identified the problem of their school being surrounded by liquor stores (Robinson, 1993). Zoning regulations in the city made some areas dry while the students' school was in a wet area. The students identified the fact that schools serving White, upper-middle-class students were located in dry areas, while schools in poor communities were in wet areas. The students, assisted by their teacher, planned a strategy for exposing this inequity. By using mathematics, literacy, social, and political skills, the students were able to prove their points with reports, editorials, charts, maps, and graphs. In both of these exam-ples, teachers allowed students to use their community circumstances as official knowledge (Apple, 1993). Their pedagogy and the students' learning became a form of cultural critique.

THEORETICAL UNDERPINNINGS OF CULTURALLY RELEVANT PEDAGOGY

As I looked (and listened) to exemplary teachers of African American students, I began to develop a grounded theory of culturally relevant pedagogy. The teachers in the study met the aforementioned criteria of helping their students to be academically successful, cultur-ally competent, and sociopolitically critical. However, the ways in which they met these cri-teria seemed to differ markedly on the surface. Some teachers seemed more structured or rigid in their pedagogy. Others seemed to adopt more progressive teaching strategies. What theoretical perspective(s) held them together and allowed them to meet the criteria of cul-turally relevant teaching?

One of the places I began to look for these commonalities was in teachers' beliefs and ideologies. Lipman (1993) has suggested that, despite massive attempts at school reform and restructuring, teacher ideologies and beliefs often remain unchanged, particularly toward African American children and their intellectual potential. Thus, in the analysis of the teacher interviews, classroom observations, and group analysis of videotaped segments of their teaching, I was able to deduce some broad propositions (or characteristics) that serve as theoretical underpinnings of culturally relevant pedagogy.

I approach the following propositions tentatively to avoid an essentialized and/or dichotomized notion of the pedagogy of excellent teachers. What I propose represents a range or continuum of teaching behaviors, not fixed or rigid behaviors that teachers must adhere to in order to merit the designation "culturally relevant." The need for these theoretical understandings may be more academic than pragmatic. The teachers themselves feel no need to name their practice culturally relevant. However, as a researcher and teacher educator, I am compelled to try to make this practice more accessible, particularly for those prospective teachers who do not share the cultural knowledge, experiences, and understandings of their students (Haberman, 1994).

The three broad propositions that have emerged from this research center around the following:[10]

- The conceptions of self and others held by culturally relevant teachers.
- The manner in which social relations are structured by culturally relevant teachers.
- The conceptions of knowledge held by culturally relevant teachers.

CONCEPTIONS OF SELF AND OTHERS

The sociology of teaching literature suggests that, despite the increasing professionalization of teaching (Strike, 1993), the status of teaching as a profession continues to decline. The feeling of low status is exacerbated when teachers work with what they perceive to be low-status students (Foster, 1986). However, as I acted as a participant–observer in the classrooms of exemplary teachers of African American students, both what they said and did challenged this notion. In brief, the teachers:

- Believed that all the students were capable of academic success.
- Saw their pedagogy as art—unpredictable, always in the process of becoming.
- Saw themselves as members of the community.
- Saw teaching as a way to give back to the community.
- Believed in a Freirean notion of "teaching as mining" (1974, p. 76) or pulling knowledge out.

The teachers demonstrated their commitment to these conceptions of self and others in a consistent and deliberate manner. Students were not permitted to choose failure in their classrooms. They cajoled, nagged, pestered, and bribed the students to work at high

---

[10]Readers should note that I have listed these as separate and distinct categories for analytical purposes. In practice, they intersect and overlap, continuously.

intellectual levels. Absent from their discourse about students was the "language of lacking." Students were never referred to as being from a single-parent household, being on AFDC (welfare), or needing psychological evaluation. Instead, teachers talked about their own shortcomings and limitations and ways they needed to change to ensure student success.

As I observed them teach, I witnessed spontaneity and energy that came from experience and their willingness to be risk takers. In the midst of a lesson, one teacher, seemingly bewildered by her students' expressed belief that every princess had long blond hair, swiftly went to her book shelf, pulled down an African folk tale about a princess, and shared the story with the students to challenge their assertion. In our conference afterward, she commented:

> I didn't plan to insert that book, but I just couldn't let them go on
> thinking that only blond-haired, White women were eligible for
> royalty. I know where they get those ideas, but I have a responsibility
> to contradict some of that. The consequences of that kind of
> thinking are more devastating for *our* children, (sp-6, Field notes)[11]

The teachers made conscious decisions to be a part of the community from which their students come. Three of the eight teachers in this study live in the school community. The others made deliberate efforts to come to the community for goods, services, and leisure activities, demonstrating their belief in the community as an important and worthwhile place in both their lives and the lives of the students.

A final example is an elaboration of a point made earlier. It reflects the teachers' attempt to support and instill community pride in the students. One teacher used the community as the basis of her curriculum. Her students searched the county historical archives, interviewed long-term residents, constructed and administered surveys and a questionnaire, and invited and listened to guest speakers to get a sense of the historical development of their community. Their ultimate goal was to develop a land-use proposal for an abandoned shopping center that was a magnet for illegal drug use and other dangerous activities. The project ended with the students' making a presentation before the city council and urban planning commission. One of the students remarked to me, "This [community] is not such a bad place. There are a lot of good things that happened here, and some of that is still going on." The teacher told me that she was concerned that too many of the students believed that their only option for success involved moving out of the community, rather than participating in its reclamation.

SOCIAL RELATIONS

Much has been written about classroom social interactions (see, e.g., Brophy & Good, 1970; Rist, 1970; Wilcox, 1982). Perhaps the strength of some of the research in this area is evidenced by its impact on classroom practices. For example, teachers throughout the nation have either heard of or implemented various forms of cooperative learning (Cohen & Benton, 1988; Slavin, 1987): cross-aged, multi-aged, and heterogeneous ability groupings. While

---

[11]"These letters and numbers represent codes I employed to distinguish among the interview data and field notes I collected during the study.

these classroom arrangements may be designed to improve student achievement, culturally relevant teachers consciously create social interactions to help them meet the three previously mentioned criteria of academic success, cultural competence, and critical consciousness. Briefly, the teachers:

- maintain fluid student–teacher relationships,
- demonstrate a connectedness with all of the students,
- develop a community of learners, and
- encourage students to learn collaboratively and be responsible for another.

In these teachers' classrooms, the teacher–student relationships are equitable and reciprocal. All of the teachers gave students opportunities to act as teachers. In one class, the teacher regularly sat at a student's desk, while the student stood at the front of the room and explained a concept or some aspect of student culture. Another teacher highlighted the expertise of various students and required other students to consult those students before coming to her for help: "Did you ask Jamal how to do those math problems?" "Make sure you check with Latasha before you turn in your reading." Because she acknowledged a wide range of expertise, the individual students were not isolated from their peers as teacher's pets. Instead, all of the students were made aware that they were expected to excel at something and that the teacher would call on them to share that expertise with classmates.

The culturally relevant teachers encouraged a community of learners rather than competitive, individual achievement. By demanding a higher level of academic success for the entire class, individual success did not suffer. However, rather than lifting individuals (and, perhaps, contributing to feelings of peer alienation), the teachers made it clear that they were working with smart classes. For many of the students, this identification with academic success was a new experience. "Calvin was a bad student last year," said one student. "And that was last year," replied the teacher, as she designated Calvin to lead a discussion group. Another example of this community of learners was exemplified by a teacher who, herself, was a graduate student. She made a conscious decision to share what she was learning with her sixth graders. Every Friday, after her Thursday evening class, the students queried her about what she had learned.

A demonstration of the students' understanding of what she was learning occurred during the principal's observation of her teaching. A few minutes into a discussion where students were required to come up with questions they wanted answered about the book they were reading, a young man seated at a table near the rear of the class remarked with seeming disgust, "We're never gonna learn anything if y'all don't stop asking all of these low-level questions!" His comment was evidence of the fact that the teacher had shared Bloom's *Taxonomy of Educational Objectives* (1956) with the class. At another time, two African American boys were arguing over a notebook. "What seems to be the problem?" asked the teacher. "He's got my meta-cognitive journal!" replied one of the boys. By using the language of the teacher's graduate class, the students demonstrated their ability to assimilate her language with their own experiences.

To solidify the social relationships in their classes, the teachers encouraged the students to learn collaboratively, teach each other, and be responsible for the academic success of others. These collaborative arrangements were not necessarily structured like those of cooperative learning. Instead, the teachers used a combination of formal and informal peer collaborations.

One teacher used a buddy system, where each student was paired with another. The buddies checked each other's homework and class assignments. Buddies quizzed each other for tests, and, if one buddy was absent, it was the responsibility of the other to call to see why and to help with makeup work. The teachers used this ethos of reciprocity and mutuality to insist that one person's success was the success of all and one person's failure was the failure of all. These feelings were exemplified by the teacher who insisted, "We're a family. We have to care for one another as if our very survival depended on it. . . . Actually, it does!"

CONCEPTIONS OF KNOWLEDGE

The third proposition that emerged from this study was one that indicated how the teachers thought about knowledge—the curriculum or content they taught—and the assessment of that knowledge. Once again, I will summarize their conceptions or beliefs about knowledge:

- Knowledge is not static; it is shared, recycled, and constructed.
- Knowledge must be viewed critically.
- Teachers must be passionate about knowledge and learning.
- Teachers must *scaffold*, or build bridges, to facilitate learning.
- Assessment must be multifaceted, incorporating multiple forms of excellence.

For the teachers in this study, knowledge was about doing. The students listened and learned from one another as well as the teacher. Early in the school year, one teacher asked the students to identify one area in which they believed they had expertise. She then compiled a list of "classroom experts" for distribution to the class. Later, she developed a calendar and asked students to select a date that they would like to make a presentation in their area of expertise. When students made their presentations, their knowledge and expertise was a given. Their classmates were expected to be an attentive audience and to take seriously the knowledge that was being shared by taking notes and/or asking relevant questions. The variety of topics the students offered included rap music, basketball, gospel singing, cooking, hair braiding, and baby-sitting. Other students listed more school-like areas of expertise such as reading, writing, and mathematics. However, all students were required to share their expertise.

Another example of the teachers' conceptions of knowledge was demonstrated in the critical stance the teachers took toward the school curriculum. Although cognizant of the need to teach certain things because of a districtwide testing policy, the teachers helped their students engage in a variety of forms of critical analyses. For one teacher, this meant critique of the social studies textbooks that were under consideration by a state evaluation panel. For two of the other teachers, critique came in the form of resistance to district-approved reading materials. Both teachers showed the students what it was they were supposed to be using along with what they were going to use and why. They both trusted the students with this information and enlisted them as allies against the school district's policies.

A final example in this category concerns the teachers' use of complex assessment strategies. Several of the teachers actively fought the students' *right-answer* approach to school tasks without putting the students down. They provided them with problems and situations and helped the students to say aloud the kinds of questions they had in their minds but had been taught to suppress in most other classrooms. For one teacher, it was simply requiring students to always be prepared to ask, "Why?" Thus, when she posed a mathematical word problem, the first question usually went something like this: "Why are we interested in knowing this?" Or, someone would simply ask, "Why are we doing this problem?" The teacher's response was sometimes another question: "Who thinks they can respond to that question?" Other times, the teacher would offer an explanation and then ask, "Are you satisfied with that answer?" If a student said "Yes," she might say, "You shouldn't be. Just because I'm the teacher doesn't mean I'm always right." The teacher was careful to help students to understand the difference between an intellectual challenge and a challenge to the authority of their parents. Thus, just as the students were affirmed in their ability to code-switch, or move with facility, in language between African American and a standard form of English, they were supported in the attempts at role-switching between school and home.

Another teacher helped her students choose both the standards by which they were to be evaluated and the pieces of evidence they wanted to use as proof of their mastery of particular concepts and skills. None of the teachers or their students seemed to have test anxiety about the school district's standardized tests. Instead, they viewed the tests as necessary irritations, took them, scored better than their age-grade mates at their school, and quickly returned to the rhythm of learning in their classroom.

Conclusion

I began this chapter arguing for a theory of culturally relevant pedagogy. I also suggested that the tensions that surround my position as a native in the research field forced me to face the theoretical and philosophical biases I bring to my work in overt and explicit ways. Thus, I situated my work in the context of Black feminist thought. I suggested that culturally relevant teaching must meet three criteria: an ability to develop students academically, a willingness to nurture and support cultural competence, and the development of a sociopolitical or critical consciousness. Next, I argued that culturally relevant teaching is distinguishable by three broad propositions or conceptions regarding self and other, social relations, and knowledge. With this theoretical perspective, I attempted to broaden notions of pedagogy beyond strictly psychological models. I also have argued that earlier sociolinguistic explanations have failed to include the larger social and cultural contexts of students and the cultural ecologists have failed to explain student success. I predicated the need for a culturally relevant theoretical perspective on the growing disparity between the racial, ethnic, and cultural characteristics of teachers and students along with the continued academic failure of African American, Native American, and Latino students.

Although I agree with Haberman's (1991b) assertion that teacher educators are unlikely to make much of a difference in the preparation of teachers to work with students in urban poverty unless they are able to recruit "better" teacher candidates, I still believe researchers are obligated to re-educate the candidates we currently attract toward a more expansive view of pedagogy (Bartolome, 1994). This can be accomplished partly by helping prospective teachers understand culture (their own and others) and the ways it functions in education. Rather than add on versions of multicultural education or human relations courses (Zeichner, 1992) that serve to exoticize diverse students as "other," a culturally relevant pedagogy is designed to problematize teaching and encourage teachers to ask about the nature of the student-teacher relationship, the curriculum, schooling, and society.

This study represents a beginning look at ways that teachers might systematically include student culture in the classroom as authorized or official knowledge. It also is a way to encourage praxis as an important aspect of research (Lather, 1986). This kind of research needs to continue in order to support new conceptions of collaboration between teachers and researchers (practitioners and theoreticians). We need research that proposes alternate models of pedagogy, coupled with exemplars of successful pedagogues. More importantly, we need to be willing to look for exemplary practice in those classrooms and communities that too many of us are ready to dismiss as incapable of producing excellence.

The implication of continuing this kind of work means that research grounded in the practice of exemplary teachers will form a significant part of the knowledge base on which we build teacher preparation. It means that the research community will have to be willing to listen to and heed the "wisdom of practice" (Shulman, 1987, p. 12) of these excellent practitioners. Additionally, we need to consider methodologies that present more robust portraits of teaching. Meaningful combinations of quantitative and qualitative inquiries must be employed to help us understand the deeply textured, multilayered enterprise of teaching.

I presume that the work I have been doing raises more questions than it answers. A common question asked by practitioners is, "Isn't what you described just 'good teaching?'" And, while I do not deny that it is good teaching, I pose a counter question: Why does so little of it seem to occur in classrooms populated by African American students? Another question that arises is whether or not this pedagogy is so idiosyncratic that only "certain" teachers can engage in it. I would argue that the diversity of these teachers and the variety of teaching strategies they employed challenge that notion. The common feature they shared was a classroom practice grounded in what they believed about the educability of the students. Unfortunately, this raises troubling thoughts about those teachers who are not successful, but we cannot assume that they do not believe that some students are incapable (or unworthy) of being educated. The reasons for their lack of success are far too complex for this discussion.

Ultimately, my responsibility as a teacher educator who works primarily with young, middle-class, White women is to provide them with the examples of culturally relevant teaching in both theory and practice. My responsibility as a researcher is to continue to inquire in order to move toward a theory of culturally relevant pedagogy.

References

Aaronsohn, L. (1992). Learning to Teach for Empowerment. *Radical Teacher, 40,* 44–46.

African American Male Task Force. (1990). *Educating African American Males: A Dream Deferred* (Report). Washington, D.C.: Author.

Amundson, R., Serlin, R. C., & Lehrer, R. (1992). On the Threats That Do Not Face Educational Research. *Educational Researcher, 21*(9), 19–24.

Anderson, J. (1988). *The Education of Blacks in the South, 1860–1935.* Chapel Hill, NC: University of North Carolina Press.

Apple, M. (1993). *Official Knowledge.* New York: Routledge.

Apple, M., & Weiss, L. (1983). *Ideology and Practice in Schooling.* Philadelphia: Temple University Press.

Argyris, C. (1980). *Inner Contradictions of Rigorous Research.* New York: Academic.

Asante, M. K. (1991). The Afrocentric Idea in Education. *The Journal of Negro Education, 60,* 170–180.

Atkin, J. M. (1973). Practice-Oriented Inquiry: A Third Approach to Research in Education. *Educational Researcher, 2*(7), 3–4.

Au, K., & Jordan, C. (1981). Teaching Reading to Hawaiian Children: Finding a Culturally Appropriate Solution. In H. Trueba, G. Guthrie, & K. Au (Eds.), *Culture and the Bilingual Classroom: Studies in Classroom Ethnography* (pp. 139–152). Rowley, MA: Newbury.

Bacon, M. (1981, May). *High Potential Children from Ravenswood Elementary School District* (Follow-up study). Redwood City, CA: Sequoia Union High School District.

Banks, J. A. (1992). African American Scholarship and the Evolution of Multicultural Education. *The Journal of Negro Education, 61,* 273–286.

Bartolome, L. (1994). Beyond the Methods Fetish: Toward a Humanizing Pedagogy. *Harvard Educational Review, 64,* 173–194.

Becker, H. S. (1967). Whose Side Are We On? *Social Problems, 14,* 239–247.

Berliner, D. (1988, October). *Implications of Studies of Expertise in Pedagogy for Teacher Education and Evaluation. New Directions for Teacher Assessment.* Conference proceedings of the ETS Invitational Conference. Princeton, NJ: Educational Testing Service.

Beyer, L. E. (1991). Teacher Education, Reflective Inquiry, and Moral Action. In B. R. Tabachnick & K. M. Zeichner (Eds.), *Inquiry-Oriented Practice Teacher Education* (pp. 112–129). London: Falmer.

Billingsley, A. (1992). *Climbing Jacob's Ladder: The Enduring Legacy of African American Families.* New York: Simon & Schuster.

Bloom, B. (1956). *Taxonomy of Educational Objectives* (1st ed.). New York: Longman, Green.

Bloom, B. S., Davis, A., & Hess, R. (1965). *Compensatory Education for Cultural Deprivation.* New York: Holt.

Bond, H. M. (1969). *Negro Education: A Study in Cotton and Steel.* NY: Octagon.

Bourdieu, P. (1984). *Distinctions: The Social Critique of the Judgment of Taste.* Cambridge, MA: Harvard University Press.

Bowles, S. (1977). Unequal Education and the Reproduction of the Social Division of Labor. In J. Karabel & A. H. Halsey (Eds.), *Power and Ideology in Education* (pp. 137–153) New York: Oxford University Press.

Brookover, W. (1985). Can We Make Schools Effective for Minority Students? *The Journal of Negro Education, 54,* 257–268.

Brookover, W., Beady, C, Flood, P., Schweitzer, J., & Wisenbaker, J. (1979). *School Social Systems and Student Achievement: Schools Can Make a Difference.* New York: Praeger.

Brophy, J., & Good, T. (1970). Teachers' Communication of Differential Expectations for Children's Classroom Performance. *Journal of Educational Psychology, 61,* 365–374.

Bullock, H. A. (1967). *A History of Negro Education in the South from 1614 to the Present.* Cambridge, MA: Harvard University Press.

Carr, W., & Kemmis, S. (1986). *Becoming Critical: Education, Knowledge and Action Research* (Rev. ed.). Victoria, Australia: Deakin University Press.

Carter, K. (1993). The Place of Story in the Study of Teaching and Teacher Education. *Educational Researcher, 22*(1), 5–12, 18.

Cazden, C., & Leggett, E. (1981). Culturally Responsive Education: Recommendations for Achieving Lau Remedies II. In H. Trueba, G. Guthrie, & K. Au (Eds.), *Culture and the Bilingual Classroom: Studies in Classroom Ethnography* (pp. 69–86). Rowley, MA: Newbury.

Clark, R. (1983). *Family Life and School Achievement: Why Poor Black Children Succeed or Fail.* Chicago: Chicago University Press.

Clark, S. (1964, First Quarter). Literacy and Liberation. *Freedomways,* pp. 113–124.

Clark, S., with Brown, C. (1990). *Ready from Within: A First Person Narrative.* Trenton, NJ: Africa World Press.

Cochran-Smith, M., & Lytle, S. (1992). *Inside/outside: Teachers, Research, and Knowledge.* NY: Teachers College Press.

Code, L. (1991). *What Can She Know? Feminist Theory and the Construction of Knowledge.* Ithaca, NY: Cornell University Press.

Cohen, E., & Benton, J. (1988, Fall). Making Groupwork Work. *American Educator,* pp. 10–17, 45–46.

Collins, P. H. (1991). *Black Feminist Thought.* New York: Routledge.

Comer, J. (1984). Home School Relationships as They Affect the Academic Success of Children. *Education and Urban Society, 16,* 323–337.

Cose, E. (1993). *The Rage of a Privileged Class.* New York: HarperCollins.

Cronbach, L. J. (1975). Beyond the Two Disciplines of Scientific Psychology. *American Psychologist, 30,* 116–127.

Cuban, L. (1989). The "At-Risk" Label and the Problem of Urban School Reform. *Phi Delta Kappan, 70,* 264–271.

Delpit, L. (1992). Acquisition of Literate Discourse: Bowing before the Master? *Theory into Practice, 31,* 296–271.

Edmonds, R. (1979). Effective Schools for the Urban Poor. *Educational Leadership, 37,* 15–24.

Elliot, J. (1991). *Action Research for Educational Change.* Philadelphia: Open University Press.

Ellsworth, E. (1989). Why Doesn't This Feel Empowering? Working through the Repressive Myths of Critical Pedagogy. *Harvard Educational Review, 59,* 297–324.

Erickson, F. (1987). Transformation and School Success: The Politics and Culture of Educational Achievement. *Anthropology and Education, 18,* 335–356.

Erickson, F. (1993). Transformation and School Success: The Politics and Culture of Educational Achievement. In E. Jacob & C. Jordan (Eds.), *Minority Education-Anthropological Perspectives* (pp. 27–51). Norwood, NJ: Ablex.

Erickson, F., & Mohatt, G. (1982). Cultural Organization and Participation Structures in Two Classrooms of Indian Students. In G. Spindler (Ed.), *Doing the Ethnography of Schooling* (pp. 131–174). New York: Holt, Rinehart & Winston.

Fine, M. (1986). Why Urban Adolescents Drop into and out of High School. *Teachers College Record, 87,* 393–409.

Fordham, S. (1988). Racelessness as a Factor in Black Students' School Success: Pragmatic Strategy or Pyrrhic Victory? *Harvard Educational Review, 58,* 54–84.

Fordham, S., & Ogbu, J. (1986). Black Students' School Success: Coping with the Burden of "Acting White." *The Urban Review, 18,* 176–206.

Foster, H. L. (1986). *Ribbin', Jivin' and Playin' the Dozens.* Cambridge, MA: Ballinger.

Foster, M. (1991). Constancy, Connectedness, and Constraints in the Lives of African American Teachers. *National Women's Studies Journal, 3,* 233–261.

Freire, P. (1973). *Education for Critical Consciousness.* New York: Seabury.

Freire, P. (1974). *Pedagogy of the Oppressed.* New York: Seabury.

Gage, N. L. (1989). The Paradigm Wars and Their Aftermath. *Educational Researcher, 18*(7), 4–10.

Gay, G., & Abrahamson, R. D. (1972). Talking Black in the Classroom. In R. D. Abrahamson & R. Troike (Eds.), *Language and Cultural Diversity in Education* (pp. 200–208). Englewood Cliffs, NJ: Prentice-Hall.

Gilligan, C. (1982). *In a Different Voice.* Cambridge, MA: Harvard University Press.

Giroux, H. (1983). *Theory and Resistance: A Pedagogy for the Opposition.* Hadley, MA: Bergin & Garvey.

Giroux, H., & Simon, R. (1989). Popular Culture and Critical Pedagogy: Everyday Life as a Basis for Curriculum Knowledge. In H. Giroux & P. McLaren (Eds.), *Critical Pedagogy, the State, and Cultural Struggle* (pp. 236–252). Albany, NY: State University of New York Press.

Glaser, B. G., & Strauss, A. L. (1967). *The Discovery of Grounded Theory: Strategies for Qualitative Research.* Chicago: Aldine.

Gouldner, A. (1970). *The Coming Crisis in Western Sociology.* New York: Basic.

Grant, C. A. (1989). Urban Teachers: Their New Colleagues and Curriculum. *Phi Delta Kappan, 70,* 764-770.

Haberman, M. (1991a). The Rationale for Training Adults as Teachers. In C. E. Sleeter (Ed.), *Empowerment through Multicultural Education* (pp. 275-286). Albany, NY: State University of New York Press.

Haberman, M. (1991b). Can Cultural Awareness Be Taught in Teacher Education Programs? *Teaching Education, 4,* 25–32.

Haberman, M. (1994, January 24). Redefining the "Best and the Brightest." *In These Times,* pp. 17–18.

Harding, V. (1981). *There Is a River: The Black Struggle for Freedom in America.* New York: Harcourt Brace Jovanovich.

Harris, V. (1992). African American Conceptions of Literacy: A Historical Perspective. *Theory into Practice, 31,* 276–286.

Hilliard, A. (1992). Behavioral Style, Culture, and Teaching and Learning. *The Journal of Negro Education, 61,* 370–377.

hooks, B. (1989). *Talking Back: Thinking Feminist, Thinking Black.* Boston: South End Press.

Irvine, J. (1990). *Black Students and School Failure.* Westport, CT: Greenwood. Johnson, C. (1936).

Johnson, C. (1936). The Education of the Negro Child. *American Sociological Review, 1*, 264–272.

Jordan, C. (1985). Translating Culture: From Ethnographic Information to Educational Program. *Anthropology and Education Quarterly, 16*, 105–123.

Kaestle, C. (1993). The Awful Reputation of Educational Research. *Educational Researcher, 22*(1), 23, 26–31.

Katzer, J., Cook, K., & Crouch, W. (1978). *Evaluating Information.* Menlo Park, CA: Addison-Wesley.

King, J. (1991a). Unfinished Business: Black Student Alienation and Black Teachers' Emancipatory Pedagogy. In M. Foster (Ed.), *Readings on Equal Education* (Vol. II, pp. 245–271). New York: AMS.

King, J. (1991b). Dysconscious Racism: Ideology, Identity, and the Miseducation of Teachers. *The Journal of Negro Education, 60*, 133–146.

King, J., & Ladson-Billings, G. (1990). The Teacher Education Challenge in Elite University Settings: Developing Critical Perspectives for Teaching in a Democratic and Multicultural Society. *European Journal of Intercultural Studies, 1*, 15–30.

King, J., & Mitchell, C A. (1990). *Black Mothers to Sons: Juxtaposing African American Literature with Social Practice.* New York: Peter Lang.

Kleinfeld, J. (1992). Learning to Think Like a Teacher: The Study of Cases. In J. Shulman (Ed.), *Case Methods in Teacher Education* (pp. 33–49). New York: Teachers College Press.

Kuhn, T. S. (1970). *The Origins of Scientific Revolutions.* Chicago: University of Chicago Press.

Labov, W. (1969). The Logic of Non-standard Negro English. In J. E. Alatis (Ed.), *Linguistics and the Teaching of Standard English* (Monograph Series on Language and Linguistics, No. 22). Washington, DC: Georgetown University Press.

Ladson-Billings, G. (1990). Like Lightning in a Bottle: Attempting to Capture the Pedagogical Excellence of Successful Teachers of Black Students. *International Journal of Qualitative Studies in Education, 3*, 335–344.

Ladson-Billings, G. (1992a). Liberatory Consequences of Literacy: A Case of Culturally Relevant Instruction for African American Students. *The Journal of Negro Education, 61*, 378–391.

Ladson-Billings, G. (1992b). Reading between the Lines and Beyond the Pages: A Culturally Relevant Approach to Literacy Teaching. *Theory into Practice, 31*, 312–320.

Ladson-Billings, G. (1994). *The Dreamkeepers: Successful Teaching for African American Students.* San Francisco: Jossey-Bass.

Lather, P. (1986). Research as Praxis. *Harvard Educational Review, 56*, 257–277.

Lee, C. (1994). African-Centered Pedagogy: Complexities and Possibilities. In M. J. Shujaa (Ed.), *Too Much Schooling, Too Little Education* (pp. 295–318). Trenton, NJ: Africa World Press.

Lipman, P. (1993). *The Influence of Restructuring on Teachers' Beliefs about and Practices with African American Students.* Unpublished doctoral dissertation, University of Wisconsin, Madison.

Lutz, R., & Ramsey, M. (1974). The Use of Anthropological Field Methods in Education. *Educational Researcher, 3*(10), 5–9.

McLaren, P. (1989). *Life in Schools.* White Plains, NY: Longman.

Mohatt, G., & Erickson, F. (1981). Cultural Differences in Teaching Styles in an Odawa School: A Sociolinguistic Approach. In H. Trueba, G. Guthrie, & K. Au (Eds.), *Culture and the Bilingual Classroom: Studies in Classroom Ethnography* (pp. 105–119). Rowley, MA: Newbury.

Morris, A. (1984). *The Origins of the Civil Rights Movement.* New York: The Free Press.

Murrell, P. (1990, April). *Cultural Politics in Teacher Education: What's Missing in the Preparation of African American Teachers?* Paper presented at the Annual Meeting of the American Educational Research Association, Boston.

Murrell, P. (1991, April). *Deconstructing Informal Knowledge of Exemplary Teaching in Diverse Urban Communities: Apprenticing Preservice Teachers as Case Study Researchers in Cultural Sites.* Paper presented at the Annual Meeting of the American Educational Research Association, Chicago.

Murrell, P. (1993). Afrocentric Immersion: Academic and Personal Development of African American Males in Public Schools. In T. Perry & J. Fraser (Eds.), *Freedom f, plow: Teaching in the Multicultural Classroom* (pp. 231–259). New York: Routledge.

Narayan, K. (1993). How Native is a "Native" *Anthropologist? American Anthropologist, 95,* 671–686.

Nelson, J. (1993). *Volunteer Slavery.* Chicago: Noble.

Noddings, N. (1984). *Caring.* Berkeley: University of California Press.

Noddings, N. (1991). Stories in Dialogue: Caring and Interpersonal Reasoning. In C. Witherell & N. Noddings (Eds.), *Stories Lives Tell: Narrative and Dialogue in Education* (pp. 157–170). New York: Teachers College Press.

Noordhoff, K. (1990). Shaping the Rhetoric of Reflection for Multicultural Settings. In R. T. Cliff, W. R. Houston, & M. C. Pugach (Eds.), *Encouraging Reflective Practice in Education* (pp. 163–185). New York: Teachers College Press.

Noordhoff, K., & Kleinfeld, J. (1991, April). *Preparing Teachers for Multicultural Classrooms: A Case Study in Rural Alaska.* Paper presented at the Annual Meeting of the American Educational Research Association, Chicago.

Ogbu, J. (1981). Black Education: A Cultural-Ecological Perspective. In H. P. McAdoo (Ed.), *Black Families* (pp. 139–154). Beverly Hills: Sage.

Ogbu, J. (1983). Minority Status and Schooling in Plural Societies. *Comparative Education Review, 27,* 168–190.

Padilla, A. (1994). Ethnic Minority Scholars, Research, and Mentoring: Current and Future Issues. *Educational Researcher, 23*(4), 24–27.

Patton, M. Q. (1975). *Alternative Evaluation Research Paradigm.* Grand Forks, ND: University of North Dakota Press.

Perry, T. (1993). *Toward a Theory of African American School Achievement* (Report No. 16). Wheelock College, Boston, MA: Center on Families, Communities, Schools, and Children's Learning.

Peterson, P., & Neumann, A. (Eds.). (1995). *Research and Everyday Life: The Personal Sources of Educational Inquiry.* New York: Teachers College Press.

Piestrup, A. (1973). *Black Dialect Interference and Accommodation of Reading Instruction in First Grade* (Monograph No. 4). Berkeley: Language Behavior Research Laboratory.

Popkewitz, T. S. (1991). *A Political Sociology of Educational Reform.* New York: Teachers College Press.

Ratteray, J. D. (1994). The Search for Access and Content in the Education of African Americans. In M. J. Shujaa (Ed.), *Too Much Schooling, Too Little Education* (pp. 123–142). Trenton, NJ: Africa World Press.

Rist, R. (1970). Student Social Class and Teacher Expectations: The Self-fulfilling Prophecy in Ghetto Schools. *Harvard Educational Review, 40,* 411–450.

Rist, R. (1990). On the Relations among Educational Research Paradigms: From Disdain to d'Etentes. In K. Dougherty & F. Hammack (Eds.), *Education and Society: A Reader* (pp. 81–95). New York: Harcourt Brace Javanovich.

Robinson, R. (1993, February 25). P. C. Anderson Students Try Hand at Problem-Solving. *Dallas Examiner*, pp. 1, 8.

Rosaldo, R. (1989). *Culture and Truth: The Remaking of Social Analysis.* Boston: Beacon.

Rury, J. (1983). The New York African Free School, 1827–1836: Conflict over Community Control of Black Education. *Phylon, 44,* 187, 198.

Shulman, L. (1987). Knowledge and Teaching: Foundations of the New Reform. *Harvard Educational Review, 63,* 161–182.

Siddle-Walker, V. (1993). Caswell County Training School, 1933–1969: Relationships between Community and School. *Harvard Educational Review, 63,* 161–182.

Singer, E. (1988). *What Is Cultural Congruence, and Why Are They Saying Such Terrible Things about It?* (Occasional paper). East Lansing, MI: Institute for Research on Teaching.

Slaughter, D., & Kuehne, V. (1988). Improving Black Education: Perspectives on Parent Involvement. *Urban League Review, 11,* 59–75.

Slavin, R. (1987). Cooperative Learning and the Cooperative School. *Educational Leadership, 45,* 7–13.

Smith, L. M. (1978). An Evolving Logic of Participant Observation, Education Ethnography, and other case studies. In L. Shulman (Ed.), *Review of Research in Education* (pp. 316–377). Itasca, IL: Peacock/AERA.

Spradley, J. (1979). *The Ethnographic Interview.* New York: Holt, Rinehart & Winston.

Staples, B. (1994). *Parallel Time: Growing up in Black And White.* New York: Pantheon.

Stenhouse, L. (1983). The Relevance of Practice to Theory. *Theory into Practice, 22,* 211–215.

Strike, K. (1993). Professionalism, Democracy, and Discursive Communities: Normative Reflections on Restructuring. *American Educational Research Journal, 30,* 255–275.

Villegas, A. (1988). School Failure and Cultural Mismatch: Another View. *The Urban Review, 20,* 253–265.

Vogt, L., Jordan, C., & Tharp, R. (1987). Explaining School Failure, Producing School Success: Two Cases. *Anthropology and Education Quarterly, 18,* 276–286.

Weiler, K. (1988). *Women Teaching for Change.* New York: Bergin & Garvey.

Weinberg, M. (1977). *A Chance to Learn: A History of Race and Education in the United States.* Cambridge, MA: Cambridge University Press.

Wilcox, K. (1982). Differential Socialization in the Classroom: Implications for Equal Opportunity. In G. Spindler (Ed.), *Doing the Ethnography of Schooling* (pp. 268–309). Prospect Heights, IL: Waveland.

Woodson, C. G. (1919). *The Education of the Negro Prior to 1861.* Washington, DC: Associated Publishers.

Young R. (1990). *A Critical Theory of Education.* New York: Teachers College Press.

Zeichner, K. (1990). Preparing Teachers for Democratic Schools. *Action in Teacher Education, 11,* 5–10.

Zeichner, K. (1992). *Educating Teachers for Cultural Diversity* (Special report). East Lansing, MI: National Center for Research on Teacher Learning.

CHAPTER 10

Approaches to Multicultural Curriculum Reform

James A. Banks

THE MAINSTREAM-CENTRIC CURRICULUM

The United States is made up of many different racial, ethnic, religious, language, and cultural groups. In 2000, people of color—such as African Americans, Latinos, and Asian Americans—made up 28 percent of the U.S. population. These groups are projected to make up 48 percent of the U.S. population by 2050 (Martin & Midgley, 1999). Despite the deepening ethnic texture within the United States, the U.S. school, college, and university mainstream curriculum is organized around concepts, paradigms, and events that reflect the experiences of mainstream Americans (Banks, 1996, 2004b). The dominant, mainstream curriculum has been challenged and fractured within the last 35 years, beginning with the civil rights movement of the 1960s and 1970s. Consequently, the mainstream curriculum and textbooks today are much more multicultural than they were when the civil rights movement began. Progress has been made, and it should be acknowledged. However, the reforms have been neither as extensive nor as institutionalized as is needed, and the process of curriculum transformation needs to continue. Curriculum transformation is a process that never ends because of the changes that are continuing within the United States and throughout the world (Banks, 2004a).

A curriculum that focuses on the experiences of mainstream Americans and largely ignores the experiences, cultures, and histories of other ethnic, racial, cultural, language, and religious groups has negative consequences for both mainstream students and students of color. A mainstream-centric curriculum is one major way in which racism and ethnocentrism are reinforced and perpetuated in the schools, in colleges and universities, and in society at large.

A mainstream-centric curriculum has negative consequences for mainstream students because it reinforces their false sense of superiority, gives them a misleading conception of their relationship with other racial and ethnic groups, and denies them the opportunity to benefit from the knowledge, perspectives, and frames of reference that can be gained from studying and experiencing other cultures and groups. A mainstream-centric curriculum also denies mainstream U.S. students the opportunity to view their culture from the perspectives of other cultures and groups. When people view their culture from the point of view of another culture, they are able to understand their own culture more fully, to see how it is unique and distinct from other cultures, and to understand better how it relates to and interacts with other cultures.

A mainstream-centric curriculum negatively influences students of color such as African Americans, Latinos, and Asian Americans. It marginalizes their experiences and cultures and does not reflect their dreams, hopes, and perspectives. It does not provide them social equality within the school, an essential characteristic of democratic institutions (Gutmann, 2004). Students learn best and are more highly motivated when the school curriculum reflects their cultures, experiences, and perspectives. Many students of color are alienated in the school in part because they experience cultural conflict and discontinuities that result from the cultural differences between their school and community (Au, 2006). The school can help students of color mediate between their home and school cultures by implementing a curriculum that reflects the culture of their ethnic groups and communities. The school can and should make effective use of the community cultures of students of color when teaching them such subjects as writing, language arts, science, and mathematics (Gordon, Bridglall, & Meroe, 2005; Mahiri, 2004).

In the mainstream-centric curriculum, events, themes, concepts, and issues are viewed primarily from the perspective of mainstream Americans and Europeans. Events and cultural developments such as the European explorations in the Americas and the development of American music are viewed from Anglo and European perspectives and are evaluated using mainstream-centric criteria and points of view (Bigelow & Peterson, 1998).

When the European explorations of the Americas are viewed from a Eurocentric perspective, the Americas are perceived as having been "discovered" by the European explorers such as Columbus and Cortés (Loewen, 1995; Zinn, 1999). The view that Native peoples in the Americas were discovered by the Europeans subtly suggests that Indian cultures did not exist until they were "discovered" by the Europeans and that the lands occupied by the American Indians were rightfully owned by the Europeans after they settled on and claimed them.

When the formation and nature of U.S. cultural developments, such as music and dance, are viewed from mainstream-centric perspectives, these art forms become important and significant only when they are recognized or legitimized by mainstream critics and artists. The music of African American musicians such as Chuck Berry and Little Richard was not viewed as significant by the mainstream society until White singers such as the Beatles and Rod Stewart publicly acknowledged the significant ways in which their own music had been heavily influenced by these African American musicians. It often takes White artists to legitimize ethnic cultural forms and innovations created by Asian Americans, African Americans, Latinos, and Native Americans.

Public Sites and Popular History

Anglocentric history is not only taught in the nation's schools, colleges, and universities but is also perpetuated in popular knowledge in the nation's parks, museums, and other public sites. Loewen (1999) describes the ways in which public history in the nation's historic sites often distort history in order to present a positive image of Anglo Americans. The title of his book is *Lies across America: What Our Historic Sites Get Wrong.*

I have seen several examples of markers in public sites that perpetuate Anglocentric views of American history. The first appears on a marker in a federal park on the site where a U.S. Army post once stood in Fort Townsend in the state of Washington. With the choice of words such as *settlers* (instead of *invaders*), *restive*, and *rebelled*, the author justifies the taking of the Indians' lands and depicts their resistance as unreasonable.

Fort Townsend

> A U.S. Army Post was established on this site in 1856. In [the] mid–nineteenth century the growth of Port Townsend caused the Indians to become *restive*. *Settlers* started a home guard, campaigned wherever called, and defeated the Indians in the Battle of Seattle. Indians *rebelled* as the government began enforcing the Indian Treaty of 1854, by which the Indians had ceded most of their territory. Port Townsend, a prosperous port of entry on Puget Sound, then asked protection of the U.S. army. (emphasis added)

The second example is in Marianna, Arkansas, my hometown, which is the city center for Lee County. The site commemorates the life and achievements of Confederate soldiers from Lee County and the life of Robert E. Lee, a general of the Confederate Army and a southern hero. The marker reads in part, "In loving memory of Lee County's Confederate soldiers. No braver bled for a brighter land. No brighter land had a cause so grand." The final example is from a marker in the Confederate Park in Memphis, Tennessee, which commemorates the life of Jefferson Davis, president of the Confederate States of America. The marker reads, in part: "Before the war between the States, he served with distinction as a United States Congressman and twice as a United States Senator. He also served as Secretary of War of the U.S. He was a true American patriot." Describing Davis as a "true American patriot" is arguable.

Another interesting and revealing book by Loewen (2005) is *Sundown Towns: A Hidden Dimension of Racism in America.* In this informative book, Lowewen describes communities that kept out groups such as African Americans, Chinese Americans, and Jewish Americans by force, law, or custom. These towns are called "sundown towns" because specific minorities had to be out of the towns before the sunset. Loewen reports that he found more than 440 of these towns that existed across the United States.

EFFORTS TO ESTABLISH A MULTICULTURAL CURRICULUM

Since the civil rights movement of the 1960s, educators have been trying, in various ways, to better integrate the school curriculum with multicultural content and to move away from a mainstream-centric and Eurocentric curriculum (Banks, 2002). These have proven to be difficult goals for schools to attain for many complex reasons. The strong assimilationist ideology embraced by most U.S. educators is one major reason (Banks, 2006). The assimilationist ideology makes it difficult for educators to think differently about how U.S. society

not to be mainstream-centric

and culture developed and to acquire a commitment to make the curriculum multicultural. Individuals who have a strong assimilationist ideology believe that most important events and developments in U.S. society are related to the nation's British heritage and that the contributions of other ethnic and cultural groups are not very significant by comparison. When educators acquire a multicultural ideology and conception of U.S. culture, they are then able to view the experiences and contributions of a wide range of cultural, ethnic, language, and religious groups as significant to the development of the United States.

Ideological resistance is a major factor that has slowed and is still slowing the development of a multicultural curriculum, but other factors have also affected its growth and development. Political resistance to a multicultural curriculum is closely related to ideological resistance. Many people who resist a multicultural curriculum believe that knowledge is power and that a multicultural perspective on U.S. society challenges the existing power structure. They believe that the dominant mainstream-centric curriculum supports, reinforces, and justifies the existing social, economic, and political structure. Multicultural perspectives and points of view, in the opinion of many observers, legitimize and promote social change and social reconstruction.

During the 1980s and 1990s a heated debate occurred about how much the curriculum should be Western and European-centric or reflect the cultural, ethnic, and racial diversity in the United States. At least three major positions in this debate can be identified. The Western traditionalists argue that the West, as defined and conceptualized in the past, should be the focus in school and college curricula because of the major influence of Western civilization and culture in the United States and throughout the world (Ravitch, 1990; Schlesinger, 1991). Afrocentric scholars contend that the contributions of Africa and of African peoples should receive major emphasis in the curriculum (Asante, 1998; Asante & Ravitch, 1991). The multiculturalists argue that although the West should receive a major emphasis in the curriculum, the West should be reconceptualized so that it reflects the contributions that people of color have made to the West (Zinn & Kirschner, 1995). In addition to teaching about Western ideals, the gap between the ideals of the West and its realities of racism, sexism, and discrimination should be taught (Dilg, 2003). Multiculturalists also believe that in addition to learning about the West, students should study other world cultures, such as those in Africa, Asia, the Middle East, and the Americas as they were before the Europeans arrived (Gates, 1999).

Other factors that have slowed the institutionalization of a multicultural curriculum include the focus on high-stakes testing and accountability that has emerged within the last decade, the low level of knowledge about ethnic cultures that most educators have, and the heavy reliance on textbooks for teaching. Many studies have revealed that the textbook is still the main source for teaching, especially in such subjects as the social studies, reading, and language arts (Sleeter, 2005).

Teachers need in-depth knowledge about ethnic cultures and experiences to integrate ethnic content, experiences, and points of view into the curriculum. Many teachers tell their students that Columbus discovered America and that America is a "new world" because they know little about the diverse Native American cultures that existed in the Americas more than 40,000 years before the Europeans began to settle in the Americas in significant numbers in the sixteenth century. As Gary Howard (2006) states in the title of his cogent and informative book, *We Can't Teach What We Don't Know*.

LEVELS OF INTEGRATION OF MULTICULTURAL CONTENT

The Contributions Approach

I have identified four approaches to the integration of multicultural content into the curriculum (see Figure 10.1). The contributions approach to integration (Level 1) is frequently used when a school or district first attempts to integrate multicultural content into the mainstream curriculum.

The contributions approach is characterized by the insertion of ethnic heroes/heroines and discrete cultural artifacts into the curriculum, selected using criteria similar to those used to select mainstream heroes/heroines and cultural artifacts. Thus, individuals such as Crispus Attucks, Benjamin Bannaker, Pocahontas, Martin Luther King, Jr., and Cesar Chavez are added to the curriculum. They are discussed when mainstream American heroes/heroines such as Patrick Henry, George Washington, Thomas Jefferson, Betsy Ross, and Eleanor Roosevelt are studied in the mainstream curriculum. Discrete cultural elements such as the foods, dances, music, and artifacts of ethnic groups are studied, but little attention is given to their meanings and importance within ethnic communities.

An important characteristic of the contributions approach is that the mainstream curriculum remains unchanged in its basic structure, goals, and salient characteristics. Prerequisites for the implementation of this approach are minimal. They include basic knowledge

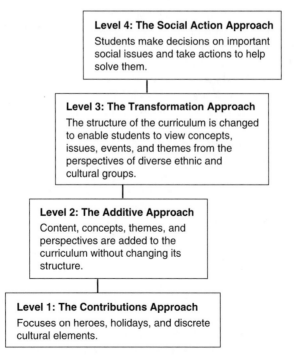

Figure 10.1   Banks's Four Levels of Integration of Multicultural Content

about U.S. society and knowledge about ethnic heroes/heroines and their roles and contributions to U.S. society and culture.

Individuals who challenged the dominant society's ideologies, values, and conceptions and advocated radical social, political, and economic reform are seldom included in the contributions approach. Thus, Booker T. Washington is more likely to be chosen for study than is W. E. B. Du Bois, and Pocahontas is more likely to be chosen than is Geronimo. The criteria used to select ethnic heroes/heroines for study and to judge them for success are derived from the mainstream society, not from the ethnic community. Consequently, use of the contributions approach usually results in the study of ethnic heroes/heroines who represent only one important perspective within ethnic communities. The more radical and less conformist individuals who are heroes/heroines only to the ethnic community are often invisible in textbooks, teaching materials, and activities used in the contributions approach.

The heroes/heroines and holidays approach is a variant of the contributions approach. In this approach, ethnic content is limited primarily to special days, weeks, and months related to ethnic events and celebrations. Cinco de Mayo, Martin Luther King, Jr.'s birthday, and African American History Week are examples of ethnic days and weeks celebrated in the schools. During these celebrations, teachers involve students in lessons, experiences, and pageants related to the ethnic group being commemorated. When this approach is used, the class studies little or nothing about the ethnic or cultural group before or after the special event or occasion.

The contributions approach (Level 1 in Figure 10.1) provides teachers with a way to integrate ethnic content into the curriculum quickly, thus giving some recognition to ethnic contributions to U.S. society and culture. Many teachers who are committed to integrating their curricula with ethnic content have little knowledge about ethnic groups and curriculum revision. Consequently, they use the contributions approach when teaching about ethnic groups. These teachers should be encouraged, supported, and given the opportunity to acquire the knowledge and skills needed to reform their curricula by using one of the more effective approaches described later in this chapter.

There are often strong political demands from ethnic communities for the school to put their heroes/heroines, contributions, and cultures into the school curriculum. These political forces may take the form of demands for heroes and contributions because mainstream heroes, such as Washington, Jefferson, and Lincoln, are highly visible in the school curriculum. Ethnic communities of color want to see their own heroes/heroines and contributions alongside those of the mainstream society. Such contributions may help give them a sense of structural inclusion, validation, and social equality. Curriculum inclusion also facilitates the quests of marginalized ethnic and cultural groups for a sense of empowerment, efficacy, and social equality. The school should help ethnic group students acquire a sense of empowerment and efficacy. These factors are positively correlated with academic achievement (Coleman et al., 1966).

The contributions approach is also the easiest approach for teachers to use to integrate the curriculum with multicultural content. However, this approach has several serious limitations. When the integration of the curriculum is accomplished primarily through the infusion of ethnic heroes/heroines and contributions, students do not attain a global view of the role of ethnic and cultural groups in U.S. society. Rather, they see ethnic issues and events primarily as an addition to the curriculum and consequently as an appendage to the main story of the development of the nation and to the core curriculum in the language arts, the social studies, the arts, and other subject areas.

Teaching ethnic issues with the use of heroes/heroines and contributions also tends to gloss over important concepts and issues related to the victimization and oppression of ethnic groups and their struggles against racism and for power. Issues such as racism, poverty, and oppression tend to be avoided in the contributions approach to curriculum integration. The focus tends to be on success and the validation of the Horatio Alger myth that all Americans who are willing to work hard can go from rags to riches and "pull themselves up by their bootstraps."

The success stories of ethnic heroes such as Booker T. Washington, George Washington Carver, and Jackie Robinson are usually told with a focus on their success, with little attention to racism and other barriers they encountered and how they succeeded despite the hurdles they faced. Little attention is also devoted to the *process* by which they become heroes/heroines. Students should learn about the process by which people become heroes/heroines as well as about their status and role as heroes/heroines. Only when students learn the process by which individuals become heroes/heroines will they understand fully how individuals, particularly individuals of color, achieve and maintain hero/heroine status and what the process of becoming a hero/heroine means for their own lives.

The contributions approach often results in the trivialization of ethnic cultures, the study of their strange and exotic characteristics, and the reinforcement of stereotypes and misconceptions. When the focus is on the contributions and unique aspects of ethnic cultures, students are not helped to view them as complete and dynamic wholes. The contributions approach also tends to focus on the *lifestyles* of ethnic groups rather than on the *institutional structures*, such as racism and discrimination, that significantly affect their life chances and keep them powerless and marginalized.

The contributions approach to content integration may provide students with a memorable one-time experience with an ethnic hero/heroine, but it often fails to help them understand the role and influence of the hero/heroine in the total context of U.S. history and society. When ethnic heroes/heroines are studied apart from the social and political context in which they lived and worked, students attain only a partial understanding of their roles and significance in society. When Martin Luther King, Jr., and Rosa Parks are studied outside the social and political context of institutionalized racism in the U.S. South in the 1940s and 1950s, and without attention to the more subtle forms of institutionalized racism in the North during this period, their full significance as social reformers and activists is neither revealed nor understood by students.

The Additive Approach

Another important approach to the integration of ethnic content into the curriculum is the addition of content, concepts, themes, and perspectives to the curriculum without changing its basic structure, purposes, and characteristics. The additive approach (Level 2 in Figure 10.1) is often accomplished by the addition of a book, a unit, or a course to the curriculum without changing it substantially. Examples of this approach include adding a book such as *The Color Purple* to a unit on the twentieth century in an English class, the use of the film *Miss Jane Pittman* during a unit on the 1960s, and the addition of a videotape on the internment of the Japanese Americans, such as *Rabbit in the Moon*, during a study of World War II in a class on U.S. history.

The additive approach allows the teacher to put ethnic content into the curriculum without restructuring it, a process that would take substantial time, effort, and training as well as a rethinking of the curriculum and its purposes, nature, and goals. The additive approach can be the first phase in a transformative curriculum reform effort designed to restructure the total curriculum and to integrate it with ethnic content, perspectives, and frames of reference.

However, this approach shares several disadvantages with the contributions approach. Its most important shortcoming is that it usually results in the viewing of ethnic content from the perspectives of mainstream historians, writers, artists, and scientists because it does not involve a restructuring of the curriculum. The events, concepts, issues, and problems selected for study are selected using mainstream-centric and Eurocentric criteria and perspectives. When teaching a unit entitled "The Westward Movement" in a fifth-grade U.S. history class, the teacher may integrate the unit by adding content about the Oglala Sioux Indians. However, the unit remains mainstream-centric and focused because of its perspective and point of view.

A unit called "The Westward Movement" is mainstream and Eurocentric because it focuses on the movement of European Americans from the eastern to the western part of the United States. The Oglala Sioux were already in the West and consequently were not moving westward. The unit might be called "The Invasion from the East" from the point of view of the Oglala Sioux. Black Elk, an Oglala Sioux holy man, lamented the conquering of his people, which culminated in their defeat at Wounded Knee Creek on December 29, 1890. Approximately 200 Sioux men, women, and children were killed by U.S. troops. Black Elk said, "The [Sioux] nation's hoop is broken and scattered. There is no center any longer, and the sacred tree is dead" (Neihardt, 1972, p. 230).

Black Elk did not consider his homeland "the West," but rather the center of the world. He viewed the cardinal directions metaphysically. The Great Spirit sent him the cup of living water and the sacred bow from the West. The daybreak star and the sacred pipe originated from the East. The Sioux nation's sacred hoop and the tree that was to bloom came from the South (Black Elk's Prayer, 1964). When teaching about the movement of the Europeans across North America, teachers should help students understand that different cultural, racial, and ethnic groups often have varying and conflicting conceptions and points of view about the same historical events, concepts, issues, and developments. The victors and the vanquished, especially, often have conflicting conceptions of the same historical event (Limerick, 1987). However, it is usually the point of view of the victors that becomes institutionalized within the schools and the mainstream society. This happens because history and textbooks are usually written by the people who won the wars and gained control of the society, not by the losers—the victimized and the powerless. The perspectives of both groups are needed to help us fully understand our history, culture, and society.

The people who are conquered and the people who conquered them have histories and cultures that are intricately interwoven and interconnected. They have to learn each others' histories and cultures to understand their own fully. White Americans cannot fully understand their own history in the western United States and in America without understanding the history of the American Indians and the ways their histories and the histories of the Indians are interconnected.

James Baldwin (1985) insightfully pointed out that when White Americans distort African American history they do not learn the truth about their own history because the history of Blacks and Whites in the United States is tightly bound together. This is also true for African American history and Indian history. The history of African Americans and Indians in the United States is closely interconnected, as Katz (1986) documents in *Black Indians: A Hidden Heritage.*

The histories of African Americans and Whites in the United States are tightly connected, both culturally and biologically, as Ball (1998) points out when he describes the African Americans ancestors in his White family and as Gordon-Reed (1997) reveals when she describes the relationship between Thomas Jefferson and Sally Hemings, his slave mistress. The additive approach fails to help students view society from diverse cultural and ethnic perspectives and to understand the ways in which the histories and cultures of the nation's diverse ethnic, racial, cultural, and religious groups are interconnected.

Multicultural history enables students and teachers to understand America's complexity and the ways in which various groups within the United States are interconnected (Takaki, 1993). Sam Hamod (cited in Reed, 1997) describes the way in which diverse ethnic perspectives enrich our understandings and lead to more accurate versions of U.S. society: "Our dual vision of 'ethnic' and American allows us to see aspects of the United States that mainstream writers often miss; thus, our perspectives often allow us a diversity of visions that, ironically, may lead us to larger truth—it's just that we were raised with different eyes" (p. xxii).

Content, materials, and issues that are added to a curriculum as appendages instead of being integral parts of a unit of instruction can become problematic. Problems might result when a book such as *The Color Purple* or a film like *Miss Jane Pittman* is added to a unit when the students lack the concepts, content background, and emotional maturity to deal with the issues and problems in these materials. The effective use of such emotion-laden and complex materials usually requires that the teacher help students acquire, in a sequential and developmental fashion, the content background and attitudinal maturity to deal with them effectively. The use of both of these materials in different classes and schools has resulted in major problems for the teachers using them. A community controversy arose in each case. The problems developed because the material was used with students who had neither the content background nor the attitudinal sophistication to respond to them appropriately. Adding ethnic content to the curriculum in a sporadic and segmented way can result in pedagogical problems, trouble for the teacher, student confusion, and community controversy.

The Transformation Approach

The transformation approach differs fundamentally from the contributions and additive approaches. In those two approaches, ethnic content is added to the mainstream core curriculum without changing its basic assumptions, nature, and structure. The fundamental goals, structure, and perspectives of the curriculum are changed in the transformation approach.

The transformation approach (Level 3 in Figure 10.1) changes the basic assumptions of the curriculum and enables students to view concepts, issues, themes, and problems from several ethnic perspectives and points of view. The mainstream-centric perspective is one of only several perspectives from which problems, concepts, and issues are viewed. Richard White (1991), a historian of the American West, indicates how viewing the American West from a transformative perspective can provide new insights into U.S. history. He writes, "The first Europeans to penetrate the West arrived neither as conquerors nor as explorers. Like so many others history has treated as discoverers, they were merely lost" (p. 5).

It is neither possible nor desirable to view every issue, concept, event, or problem from the point of view of every U.S. ethnic and cultural group. Rather, the goal should be to enable students to view concepts and issues from more than one perspective and from the point of view of the cultural, ethnic, and racial groups that were the most active participants in, or were most cogently influenced by, the event, issue, or concept being studied.

The key curriculum issues involved in multicultural curriculum reform is not the addition of a long list of ethnic groups, heroes, and contributions but the infusion of various perspectives, frames of references, and content from different groups that will extend students' understandings of the nature, development, and complexity of U.S. society. When students are studying the revolution in the British colonies, the perspectives of the Anglo revolutionaries, the Anglo loyalists, African Americans, Indians, and the British are essential for them to attain a thorough understanding of this significant event in U.S. history (see Figure 10.2). Students must study the various and sometimes divergent meanings of the revolution to these diverse groups to understand it fully (Gay & Banks, 1975).

In the language arts, when students are studying the nature of U.S. English and proper language use, they should be helped to understand the rich linguistic and language diversity in the United States and the ways in which a wide range of regional, cultural, and ethnic groups have influenced the development of U.S. English. Students should also examine how normative language use varies with the social context, the region, and the situation. The use of Black English is appropriate in some social and cultural contexts and inappropriate in others. This is also true of standard U.S. English. The United States is rich in languages and dialects. The nation had more than 35 million Latino citizens in 2000; Spanish is the first language for most of them. Most of the nation's approximately 34.6 million African Americans speak both standard English as well as some form of Black English or Ebonics. The rich language diversity in the United States includes more than twenty-five European languages; Asian, African, and Middle Eastern languages; and American Indian languages. Since the 1970s, languages from Indochina, spoken by groups such as the Hmong, Vietnamese, Laotians, and Cambodians, have further enriched language diversity in the United States (Ovando & McLaren, 2000).

When subjects such as music, dance, and literature are studied, the teacher should acquaint students with the ways these art forms among U.S. ethnic groups have greatly influenced and enriched the nation's artistic and literary traditions. The ways in which African American musicians such as Bessie Smith, W. C. Handy, and Leontyne Price have influenced the nature and development of U.S. music should be examined when the development of U.S. music is studied (Burnim & Maultsby, 2006). African Americans and Puerto Ricans have significantly influenced the development of American dance. Writers of color, such as Langston Hughes, Toni Morrison, N. Scott Momaday, Carlos Bulosan, Maxine Hong Kingston, Rudolfo A. Anaya, and Piri Thomas, have not only significantly influenced the development of American literature but have also provided unique and revealing perspectives on U.S. society and culture (Gillan & Gillan, 1994; Rico & Mano, 1995).

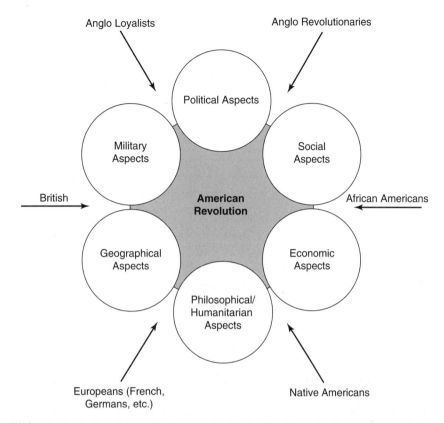

Figure 10.2   A Multicultural Interdisciplinary Model for Teaching the American Revolution

Source: James A. Banks and Geneva Gay. "Teaching the American Revolution: A Multiethnic Approach," *Social Education,* Vol. 39, No. 7 (November-December 1975); 462. Used with permission of the National Council for the Social Studies.

When studying U.S. history, language, music, arts, science, and mathematics, the empha-sis should not be on the ways in which various ethnic and cultural groups have contributed to mainstream U.S. society and culture. *The emphasis should be on how the common U.S. cul-ture and society emerged from a complex synthesis and interaction of the diverse cultural elements that originated within the various cultural, racial, ethnic, and religious groups that make up U.S. society.* I call this process *multiple acculturation* and argue that even though Anglo Americans are the dominant group in the United States—culturally, politically, and economically—it is misleading and inaccurate to describe U.S. culture and society as an Anglo-Saxon Protestant culture (Banks, 2006). Other U.S. ethnic and cultural groups have deeply influenced, shaped, and participated in the development and formation of U.S. society and culture. African Americans, for example, profoundly influenced the development of the southern culture, even though they had very little political and economic power. One irony of conquest is that those who are conquered often deeply influence the cultures of the conquerors.

A multiple acculturation conception of U.S. society and culture leads to a perspective that views ethnic events, literature, music, and art as integral parts of the common, shared U.S. culture. Anglo American Protestant culture is viewed as only a part of this larger cultural whole. Thus, to teach American literature without including significant writers of color, such as Maxine Hong Kingston, Carlos Bulosan, and Toni Morrison, gives a partial and incomplete view of U.S. literature, culture, and society.

The Social Action Approach

The social action approach (Level 4 in Figure 10.1) includes all the elements of the transformation approach but adds components that require students to make decisions and take actions related to the concept, issue, or problem studied in the unit (Banks & Banks, with Clegg, 1999). Major goals of instruction in this approach are to educate students for social criticism and social change and to teach them decision-making skills. To empower students and help them acquire *political efficacy*, the school must help them become reflective social critics and skilled participants in social change. The traditional goal of schooling has been to socialize students so they would accept unquestioningly the existing ideologies, institutions, and practices within society and the nation-state (Banks, 2004a; Hahn, 1998).

Political education in the United States has traditionally fostered political passivity rather than political action. A major goal of the social action approach is to help students acquire the knowledge, values, and skills they need to participate in social change so that marginalized and excluded racial, ethnic, and cultural groups can become full participants in U.S. society and the nation will move closer to attaining its democratic ideals (Banks, 2004a). To participate effectively in democratic social change, students must be taught social criticism and helped to understand the inconsistency between our ideals and social realities, the work that must be done to close this gap, and how students can, as individuals and groups, influence the social and political systems in U.S. society. In this approach, teachers are agents of social change who promote democratic values and the empowerment of students. Teaching units organized using the social action approach have the components described below.

1. *A decision problem or question.* An example of a question is: What actions should we take to reduce prejudice and discrimination in our school?

2. *An inquiry that provides data related to the decision problem.* The inquiry might consist of these kinds of questions:
   a. What is prejudice?
   b. What is discrimination?
   c. What causes prejudice?
   d. What causes people to discriminate?
   e. What are examples of prejudice and discrimination in our school, community, nation, and the world?
   f. How do prejudice and discrimination affect the groups below? How does each group view prejudice? Discrimination? To what extent is each group a victim or a perpetuator of prejudice and discrimination?

g. How has each group dealt with prejudice and discrimination? (Groups: White mainstream Americans, African Americans, Asian Americans, Hispanic Americans, Native Americans)

The inquiry into the nature of prejudice and discrimination would be interdisciplinary and would include readings and data sources in the various social sciences, biography, fiction, poetry, and drama. Scientific and statistical data would be used when students investigated how discrimination affects the income, occupations, frequency of diseases, and health care within these various groups.

3. *Value inquiry and moral analysis.* Students are given opportunities to examine, clarify, and reflect on their values, attitudes, beliefs, and feelings related to racial prejudice and discrimination. The teacher can provide the students with case studies from various sources, such as newspapers and magazines. The case studies can be used to involve the students in discussions and role-playing situations that enable them to express and to examine their attitudes, beliefs, and feelings about prejudice and discrimination.

Poetry, biography, and powerful fiction are excellent sources for case studies that can be used for both discussion and role playing. Countee Cullen's powerful poem "Incident" describes the painful memories of a child who was called "nigger" on a trip to Baltimore. Langston Hughes's poem "I, too" poignantly tells how the "darker brother" is sent into the kitchen when company comes. The teacher and the students can describe verbally or write about incidents related to prejudice and discrimination they have observed or in which they have participated. The following case, based on a real-life situation, was written by the author for use with his students. After reading the case, the students discuss the questions at the end of it.

Trying to Buy a Home in Lakewood Island[1]

About a year ago, Joan and Henry Green, a young African American couple, moved from the West Coast to a large city in the Midwest. They moved because Henry finished his Ph.D. in chemistry and took a job at a big university in Midwestern City. Since they have been in Midwestern City, the Greens have rented an apartment in the central area of the city. However, they have decided that they want to buy a house. Their apartment has become too small for the many books and other things they have accumulated during the year. In addition to wanting more space, they also want a house so that they can receive breaks on their income tax, which they do not receive living in an apartment.

---

[1]Reprinted with permission from James A. Banks (2003). *Teaching Strategies for Ethnic Studies* (7th ed.). Boston: Allyn and Bacon, pp. 217, 219.

The Greens also think that a house will be a good financial investment.

The Greens have decided to move into a suburban community. They want a new house and most of the houses within the city limits are rather old. They also feel that they can obtain a larger house for their money in the suburbs than in the city. They have looked at several suburban communities and decided that they like Lakewood Island better than any of the others. Lakewood Island is a predominantly White community, which is comprised primarily of lower-middle-class and middle-class residents. There are a few wealthy families in Lakewood Island, but they are exceptions rather than the rule.

Joan and Henry Green have become frustrated because of the problems they have experienced trying to buy a home in Lakewood Island. Before they go out to look at a house, they carefully study the newspaper ads. When they arrived at the first house in which they were interested, the owner told them that his house had just been sold. A week later they decided to work with a realtor. When they tried to close the deal on the next house they wanted, the realtor told them that the owner had raised the price $10,000 because he had the house appraised since he put it on the market and had discovered that his selling price was much too low. When the Greens tried to buy a third house in Lakewood Island, the owner told them that he had decided not to sell because he had not received the job in another city that he was almost sure he would receive when he had put his house up for sale. He explained that the realtor had not removed the ad about his house from the newspaper even though he had told him that he had decided not to sell a week earlier. The realtor the owner had been working with had left the real estate company a few days ago. Henry is bitter and feels that he and his wife are victims of racism and discrimination. Joan believes that Henry is too sensitive and that they have been the victims of a series of events that could have happened to anyone, regardless of their race.

Questions: What should the Greens do? Why?

4. *Decision making and social action* (synthesis of knowledge and values). Students acquire knowledge about their decision problem from the activities in item 2 above. This interdisciplinary knowledge provides them with the information they need to make reflective decisions about prejudice and discrimination in their communities and schools. The activities in item 3 enable them to identify, clarify, and analyze their values, feelings, and beliefs about prejudice and discrimination. The decision-making process enables the students to synthesize their knowledge and values to determine what actions, if any, they should take to reduce prejudice and discrimination in their school. They can develop a chart in

which they list possible actions to take and their possible consequences. They can then decide on a course of action to take and implement it.

Mixing and Blending Approaches

The four approaches for the integration of multicultural content into the curriculum (see Table 10.1) are often mixed and blended in actual teaching situations. One approach, such as the contributions approach, can be used as a vehicle to move to other, more intellectually challenging approaches, such as the transformation and social action approaches. It is unrealistic to expect a teacher to move directly from a highly mainstream-centric curriculum to one that focuses on decision making and social action. Rather, the move from the first to higher levels of multicultural content integration is likely to be gradual and cumulative.

A teacher who has a mainstream-centric curriculum might use the school's Martin Luther King, Jr., birthday celebration as an opportunity to integrate the curriculum with ethnic content about King as well as to think seriously about how content about African Americans and other ethnic groups can be integrated into the curriculum in an ongoing fashion. The teacher could explore with the students these kinds of questions during the celebration:

1. What were the conditions of other ethnic groups during the time that King was a civil rights leader?
2. How did other ethnic groups participate in and respond to the civil rights movement?
3. How did these groups respond to Martin Luther King, Jr.?
4. What can we do today to improve the civil rights of groups of color?
5. What can we do to develop more positive racial and ethnic attitudes?

The students will be unable to answer all the questions they have raised about ethnic groups during the celebration of Martin Luther King, Jr.'s, birthday. Rather, the questions will enable the students to integrate content about ethnic groups throughout the year as they study such topics as the family, the school, the neighborhood, and the city. As the students study these topics, they can use the questions they have formulated to investigate ethnic families, the ethnic groups in their school and in schools in other parts of the city, ethnic neighborhoods, and various ethnic institutions in the city such as churches, temples, synagogues, mosques, schools, restaurants, and community centers.

As a culminating activity for the year, the teacher can take the students on a tour of an ethnic community in the city. However, such a tour should be both preceded and followed by activities that enable the students to develop perceptive and compassionate lenses for seeing ethnic and cultural differences and for responding to them with sensitivity. A field trip to an ethnic community or neighborhood might reinforce stereotypes and misconceptions if students lack the knowledge and insights needed to view ethnic cultures in an understanding and caring way. Theory and research indicate that contact with an ethnic group does not necessarily lead to more positive racial and ethnic attitudes (Allport, 1979; Schofield, 2004). Rather, the conditions under which the contact occurs and the quality of the interaction in the contact situation are the important variables.

Table 10.1 Banks's Approaches for the Integration of Multicultural Content

Approach	Description	Examples	Strengths	Problems
Contributions	Heroes, cultural components, holidays, and other discrete elements related to ethnic groups are added to the curriculum on special days, occasions, and celebrations.	Famous Mexican Americans are studied only during the week of Cinco de Mayo (May 5). African Americans are studied during African American History Month in February but rarely during the rest of the year. Ethnic foods are studied in the first grade with little attention devoted to the cultures in which the foods are embedded.	Provides a quick and relatively easy way to put ethnic content into the curriculum. Gives ethnic heroes visibility in the curriculum alongside mainstream heroes. Is a popular approach among teachers and educators.	Results in a superficial understanding of ethnic cultures. Focuses on the lifestyles and artifacts of ethnic groups and reinforces stereotypes and misconceptions. Mainstream criteria are used to select heroes and cultural elements for inclusion in the curriculum.
Additive	This approach consists of the addition of content, concepts, themes, and perspectives to the curriculum without changing its structure.	Adding the book *The Color Purple* to a literature unit without reconceptualizing the unit or giving the students the background knowledge to understand the book. Adding a unit on the Japanese American internment to a U.S. history course without treating the Japanese in any other unit. Leaving the core curriculum intact but adding an ethnic studies course, as an elective, that focuses on a specific ethnic group.	Makes it possible to add ethnic content to the curriculum without changing its structure, which requires substantial curriculum changes and staff development. Can be implemented within the existing curriculum structure.	Reinforces the idea that ethnic history and culture are not integral parts of U.S. mainstream culture. Students view ethnic groups from Anglocentric and Eurocentric perspectives. Fails to help students understand how the dominant culture and ethnic cultures are interconnected and interrelated.

GUIDELINES FOR TEACHING MULTICULTURAL CONTENT

The following fourteen guidelines are designed to help you better integrate content about racial, ethnic, cultural, and language groups into the school curriculum and to teach effectively in multicultural environments.

   1. You, the teacher, are an extremely important variable in the teaching of multicultural content. If you have the necessary knowledge, attitudes, and skills,

Table 10.1   Continued

Approach	Description	Examples	Strengths	Problems
Transformation	The basic goals, structure, and nature of the curriculum are changed to enable students to view concepts, events, issues, problems, and themes from the perspectives of diverse cultural, ethnic, and racial groups.	A unit on the American Revolution describes the meaning of the revolution to Anglo revolutionaries, Anglo loyalists, African Americans, Indians, and the British. A unit on 20th-century U.S. literature includes works by William Faulkner, Joyce Carol Oates, Langston Hughes, N. Scott Momaday, Saul Bellow, Maxine Hong Kingston, Rudolfo A. Anaya, and Piri Thomas.	Enables students to understand the complex ways in which diverse racial and cultural groups participated in the formation of U.S. society and culture. Helps reduce racial and ethnic encapsulation. Enables diverse ethnic, racial, and religious groups to see their cultures, ethos, and perspectives in the school curriculum. Gives students a balanced view of the nature and development of U.S. culture and society. Helps to empower victimized racial, ethnic, and cultural groups.	The implementation of this approach requires substantial curriculum revision, inservice training, and the identification and development of materials written from the perspectives of various racial and cultural groups. Staff development for the institutionalization of this approach must be continual and ongoing.
Social Action	In this approach, students identify important social problems and issues, gather pertinent data, clarify their values on the issues, make decisions, and take reflective actions to help resolve the issue or problem.	A class studies prejudice and discrimination in their school and decides to take actions to improve race relations in the school. A class studies the treatment of ethnic groups in a local newspaper and writes a letter to the newspaper publisher suggesting ways that the treatment of ethnic groups in the newspaper should be improved.	Enables students to improve their thinking, value analysis, decision-making, and social action skills. Enables students to improve their data-gathering skills. Helps students develop a sense of political efficacy. Helps students improve their skills to work in groups.	Requires a considerable amount of curriculum planning and materials identification. May be longer in duration than more traditional teaching units. May focus on problems and issues considered controversial by some members of the school staff and citizens of the community. Students may be able to take few meaningful actions that contribute to the resolution of the social issue or problem.

when you encounter racist content in materials or observe racism in the statements and behavior of students, you can use these situations to teach important lessons about the experiences of ethnic, racial, and cultural groups in the United States. An informative source on racism is Gary Howard (2006), *We Can't Teach What We Don't Know: White Teachers, Multiracial Schools*, Second Edition. Another helpful source on this topic is Chapter 11 in this book.

2. Knowledge about ethnic groups is needed to teach ethnic content effectively. Read at least one major book that surveys the histories and cultures of U.S. ethnic groups. One book that includes historical overviews of U.S. ethnic groups is James A. Banks (2003), *Teaching Strategies for Ethnic Studies*.

3. Be sensitive to your own racial attitudes, behaviors, and the statements you make about ethnic groups in the classroom. A statement such as "Sit like an Indian" stereotypes Native Americans.

4. Make sure that your classroom conveys positive and complex images of various ethnic groups. You can do this by displaying bulletin boards, posters, and calendars that show the racial, ethnic, and religious diversity within U.S. society.

5. Be sensitive to the racial and ethnic attitudes of your students and do not accept the belief, which has been refuted by research, that "kids do not see colors." Since the pioneering research by Lasker (1929), researchers have known that very young children are aware of racial differences and that they tend to accept the evaluations of various racial groups that are normative within the wider society (Van Ausdale & Feagin, 2001). Do not try to ignore the racial and ethnic differences that you see; try to respond to these differences positively and sensitively. Chapter 11 of this book provides thoughtful guidelines for avoiding the "colorblind" stance. Also see Walter Stephan (1999), *Reducing Prejudice and Stereotyping in Schools*.

6. Be judicious in your choice and use of teaching materials. Some materials contain both subtle and blatant stereotypes of groups. Point out to the students when an ethnic, racial, cultural, or language group is stereotyped, omitted from, or described in materials from Anglocentric and Eurocentric points of view.

7. Use trade books, films, videotapes, CD's and recordings to supplement the textbook treatment of ethnic, cultural, and language groups and to present the perspectives of these groups to your students. Many of these sources contain rich and powerful images of the experience of being a person of color in the United States. Numerous books and videotapes are annotated in James A. Banks (2003), *Teaching Strategies for Ethnic Studies*.

8. Get in touch with your own cultural and ethnic heritage. Sharing your ethnic and cultural story with your students will create a climate for sharing in the classroom, will help motivate students to dig into their own ethnic and cultural roots, and will result in powerful learning for your students.

9. Be sensitive to the possibly controversial nature of some ethnic studies materials. If you are clear about the teaching objectives you have in mind, you can often use a less controversial book or reading to attain the same objectives. *The Color Purple,* by Alice Walker (1982), for example, can be a controversial book. A teacher, however, who wants his or her students to gain insights about African Americans in the South can use *Roll of Thunder, Hear My Cry,* by Mildred D. Taylor (1976), instead of *The Color Purple.*

10. Be sensitive to the developmental levels of your students when you select concepts, content, and activities related to racial, ethnic, cultural, and language groups. Concepts and learning activities for students in kindergarten and the primary grades should be specific and concrete. Students in these grades should study such concepts as *similarities, differences, prejudice,* and *discrimination* rather than higher-level concepts such as *racism and oppression.* Fiction and biographies are excellent vehicles for introducing these concepts to students in kindergarten and the primary grades. As students progress through the grades, they can be introduced to more complex concepts, examples, and activities.

    (*If you teach in a racially or ethnically integrated classroom or school, you should keep the following guidelines in mind.*)

11. View your students of color as winners. Many students of color have high academic and career goals. They need teachers who believe they can be successful and are willing to help them succeed. Both research and theory indicate that students are more likely to achieve highly when their teachers have high academic expectations for them.

12. Keep in mind that most parents of color are very interested in education and want their children to be successful academically even though the parents may be alienated from the school. Do not equate education with schooling. Many parents who want their children to succeed have mixed feelings about the schools. Try to gain the support of these parents and enlist them as partners in the education of their children.

13. Use cooperative learning techniques and group work to promote racial and ethnic integration in the school and classroom. Research indicates that when learning groups are racially integrated, students develop more friends from other racial groups and race relations in the school improve. A helpful guide is Elizabeth G. Cohen's (1994) *Designing Groupwork: Strategies for the Heterogeneous Classroom.*

14. Make sure that school plays, pageants, cheerleading squads, publications, and other formal and informal groups are racially integrated. Also make sure that various ethnic and racial groups have equal status in school performances and presentations. In a multiracial school, if all of the leading roles in a school play are filled by White actors, an important message is sent to students and parents of color whether such a message was intended or not.

SUMMARY

This chapter describes the nature of the mainstream-centric curriculum and the negative consequences it has for both mainstream students and students of color. This curriculum reinforces the false sense of superiority of mainstream students and fails to reflect, validate, and celebrate the cultures of students of color. Many factors have slowed the institutionalization of a multicultural curriculum in the schools, including ideological resistance, lack of teacher knowledge of ethnic groups, the heavy reliance of teachers on textbooks, and the focus on high-stakes testing and accountability. However, the institutionalization of ethnic content into the school, college, and university curriculum has made significant progress within the last thirty years. This process needs to continue because curriculum transformation is a development that never ends.

Four approaches to the integration of ethnic content into the curriculum are identified in this chapter. In the *contributions approach*, heroes/heroines, cultural components, holidays, and other discrete elements related to ethnic groups are added to the curriculum without changing its structure. The *additive approach* consists of the addition of content, concepts, themes, and perspectives to the curriculum with its structure remaining unchanged. In the *transformation approach*, the structure, goals, and nature of the curriculum are changed to enable students to view concepts, issues, and problems from diverse ethnic perspectives.

The *social action approach* includes all elements of the transformation approach, as well as elements that enable students to identify important social issues, gather data related to them, clarify their values, make reflective decisions, and take actions to implement their decisions. This approach seeks to make students social critics and reflective agents of change. The final part of this chapter presents guidelines to help you teach multicultural content and to function more effectively in multicultural classrooms and schools.

Questions and Activities

1. What is a mainstream-centric curriculum? What are its major assumptions and goals?

2. Examine several textbooks and find examples of the mainstream-centric approach. Share these examples with colleagues in your class or workshop.

3. How does a mainstream-centric curriculum influence mainstream students and students of color?

4. According to Banks, what factors have slowed the development of a multicultural curriculum in the schools? What is the best way to overcome these factors?

5. What are the major characteristics of the following approaches to curriculum reform: the contributions approach, the additive approach, the transformation approach, the social action approach?

6. Why do you think the contributions approach to curriculum reform is so popular and widespread within schools, especially in the primary and elementary grades?

7. In what fundamental ways do the transformation and social action approaches differ from the other two approaches identified above?

8. What are the problems and promises of each of the four approaches?

9. What problems might a teacher encounter when trying to implement the transformation and social action approaches? How might these problems be overcome?

10. Assume that you are teaching a social studies lesson about the westward movement in U.S. history and a student makes a racist, stereotypic, or misleading statement about Native Americans, such as, "The Indians were hostile to the White settlers." How would you handle this situation? Give reasons to explain why you would handle it in a particular way.

11. Since September 11, 2001, and the United States/British–Iraq War in 2003, there has been an increased emphasis on patriotism in U.S. society. Some groups have called for more emphasis on the teaching of patriotism in the schools. What is patriotism? Describe ways in which multicultural content can be used to teach reflective patriotism. A useful reference for this exercise is *A Patriot's Handbook: Songs, Poems, Stories and Speeches Celebrating the Land We Love,* edited by Caroline Kennedy (2003). It contains selections by authors from diverse racial, ethnic, and cultural groups. Gwendolyn Brooks, Thomas Jefferson, Langston Hughes, Gloria Anzaldúa, E. B. White, and Paul Lawrence Dunbar are among the writers included in this comprehensive and useful collection.

References

Allport, G. W. (1979). *The Nature of Prejudice* (25th anniversary ed.). Reading, MA: Addison-Wesley.

Asante, M. K., & Ravitch, D. (1991). Multiculturalism: An Exchange. *The American Scholar, 60*(2), 267–276.

Asante, M. K. (1998). *The Afrocentric Idea* (Rev. ed.). Philadelphia: Temple University Press.

Au, K. (2006). *Multicultural Issues and Literacy Achievement.* Mahwah, NJ: Earlbaum Associates.

Baldwin, J. (1985). *The Price of the Ticket: Collected Nonfiction, 1948–1985.* New York: St. Martin's.

Ball, E. (1998). *Slaves in the Family.* New York: Farrar, Straus & Giroux.

Banks, J. A. (Ed.). (1996). *Multicultural Education, Transformative Knowledge, and Action: Historical and Contemporary Perspectives.* New York: Teachers College Press.

Banks, J. A. (2002). *An Introduction to Multicultural Education* (3rd ed.). Boston: Allyn & Bacon.

Banks, J. A. (2003). *Teaching Strategies for Ethnic Studies* (7th ed.). Boston: Allyn & Bacon.

Banks, J. A. (Ed.). (2004a). *Diversity and Citizenship Education: Global Perspectives.* San Francisco: Jossey-Bass.

Banks, J. A. (2004b). Race, Knowledge Construction, and Education in the United States: Lessons from History. In J. A. Banks & C. A. M. Banks (Eds.), *Handbook of Research on Multicultural Education* (2nd ed., pp. 228–239). San Francisco: Jossey-Bass.

Banks, J. A. (2006). *Cultural Diversity and Education: Foundations, Curriculum, and Teaching* (5th ed.). Boston: Allyn & Bacon.

Banks, J. A., & Banks, C. A. M., with Clegg, A. A., Jr. (1999). *Teaching Strategies for the Social Studies* (5th ed.). New York: Longman.

Bigelow, B., & Peterson, B. (1998). *Rethinking Columbus: The Next 500 Years*. Milwaukee, WI: Rethinking Schools.

Black Elk's Prayer from a Mountaintop in the Black Hills, 1931. (1964). In J. D. Forbes (Ed.), *The Indian in America's Past* (p. 69). Englewood Cliffs, NJ: Prentice-Hall.

Burnim, M. V., & Maultsby, P. K. (2006). *African American: An Introduction*. New York: Routledge.

Cohen, E. G. (1994). *Designing Groupwork: Strategies for the Heterogeneous Classroom* (2nd ed.). New York: Teachers College Press.

Coleman, J. S., Campbell, E. Q., Hobson, C. J., McPartland, J., Mood, A. M., Weinfeld, F. D., & York, R. L. (1966). *Equality of Educational Opportunity*. Washington, DC: U.S. Government Printing Office.

Dilg, M. (2003). *Thriving in the Multicultural Classroom: Principles and Practices for Effective Teaching*. New York: Teachers College Press.

Gates, H. L., Jr. (1999). *Wonders of the African World*. New York: Knopf.

Gay, G., & Banks, J. A. (1975). Teaching the American Revolution: A Multiethnic Approach. *Social Education, 39*, 461–465.

Gillan, M. M., & Gillan, J. (Eds.). (1994). *An Anthology of Contemporary Multicultural Poetry*. New York: Penguin.

Gordon, E. W., Bridglall, B. L., & Meroe, A. S. (Eds.). (2005). *Supplementary Education: The Hidden Curriculum of High Academic Achievement*. Lanham, MD: Rowman and Littlefield.

Gordon-Reed, A. (1997). *Thomas Jefferson and Sally Hemings: An American Controversy*. Charlottesville: University Press of Virgina.

Gutmann, A. (2004). Unity and Diversity in Democratic Multicultural Education: Creative and Destructive Tensions. In J. A. Banks (Ed.), *Diversity and Citizenship Education: Global Perspectives* (pp. 71–96). San Francisco: Jossey-Bass.

Hahn, C. L. (1998). *Becoming Political: Comparative Perspectives on Citizenship Education*. Albany: State University of New York Press.

Howard, G. (2006). *We Can't Teach What We Don't Know: White Teachers, Multiracial Schools* (2nd ed.). New York: Teachers College Press.

Katz, W. L. (1986). *Black Indians: A Hidden Heritage*. New York: Atheneum.

Kennedy, C. (Ed.). (2003). *A Patriot's Handbook: Songs, Poems, Stories, and Speeches Celebrating the Land We Love*. New York: Hyperion.

Lasker, B. (1929). *Race Attitudes in Children*. New York: Holt.

Limerick, P. N. (1987). *The Legacy of Conquest: The Unbroken Past of the American West*. New York: Norton.

Loewen, J. W. (1995). *Lies My Teacher Taught Me: Everything Your American History Textbook Got Wrong*. New York: New Press.

Loewen, J. W. (1999). *Lies across America: What Our Historic Sites Get Wrong*. New York: New Press.

Loewen, J. S. (2005). *Sundown Towns: A Hidden Dimension of Racism in America*. New York: New Press.

Mahiri, J. (2004). *Why They Don't Learn in School: Literacy in the Lives of Urban Youth*. New York: Peter Lang.

Martin, P., & Midgley, E. (1999). Immigration to the United States. *Population Bulletin, 54*(2), 1–44. Washington, DC: Population Reference Bureau.

Neihardt, J. G. (1972). *Black Elk Speaks*. New York: Pocket Books.

Ovando, C. J., & McLaren, P. (Eds.). (2000). *The Politics of Multiculturalism and Bilingual Education*. Boston: McGraw-Hill.

Ravitch, D. (1990, Spring). Diversity and Democracy: Multicultural Education in America. *American Educator*, pp. 16–48.

Reed, I. (Ed.). (1997). *MultiAmerica: Essays on Cultural Wars and Cultural Peace*. New York: Viking.

Rico, B. R., & Mano, S. (Eds.). (1995). *American Mosaic: Multicultural Readings in Context* (2nd ed.). Boston: Houghton Mifflin.

Schlesinger, A. M., Jr. (1991). *The Disuniting of America: Reflections on a Multicultural Society*. Knoxville: Whittle Direct Books.

Schofield, J. W. (2004). Improving Intergroup Relations among Students. In J. A. Banks & C. A. M. Banks (Eds.), *Handbook of Research on Multicultural Education* (2nd ed., pp. 799–812). San Francisco: Jossey-Bass.

Sleeter, C. E. (2005). *Un-Standardizing Curriculum: Multicultural Teaching in the Standards-Based Classroom*. New York: Teachers College Press.

Stephan, W. (1999). *Reducing Prejudice and Stereotyping in Schools*. New York: Teachers College Press.

Takaki, R. (1993). *A Different Mirror: A History of Multicultural America*. New York: Little, Brown.

Taylor, M. (1976). *Roll of Thunder, Hear My Cry*. New York: Dial.

Walker, A. (1982). *The Color Purple*. New York: Harcourt Brace.

White, R. (1991). *"It's Your Misfortune and None of My Own:" A New History of the American West*. Norman: University of Oklahoma Press.

Van Ausdale, D., & Feagin, J. R. (2001). *The First R: How Children Learn Race and Racism*. Lanham: Rowman & Littlefield.

Zinn, H. (1999). *A People's History of the United States* (20th anniversary ed.). New York: HarperCollins.

Zinn, H., & Kirschner, G. (1995). *A People's History of the United States: The Wall Charts*. New York: New Press.

CHAPTER 11

The Colorblind Perspective in School: Causes and Consequences

Janet Ward Schofield

INTRODUCTION

Race matters, or at least it has historically in the United States, although it is a scientifically imprecise construct the meaning of which is heavily influenced by social context (Jones, 1997). Racial group membership is the basis on which individuals were treated as the property of others. It is also the basis on which the basic rights of citizenship were denied to individuals even after the formal abolition of slavery. The civil rights laws passed in the middle of the twentieth century were designed to do away with such group-based discrimination—to dismantle dual school systems, to ensure political rights, and to prevent discrimination in employment and housing, among other things. However, the passage of these laws created a situation that Jones (1998) has called the "New American Dilemma"— a conflict between "the values embodied in the democratic principles of freedom and equality without regard to race, and . . . the belief that current as well as cumulative racial biases persist making it necessary to take race into account in order to realize the principles of freedom and equality" (p. 645). The first of these perspectives was given voice by Supreme Court Justice John Marshall Harlan in his famous call for a colorblind society in his dissenting opinion in *Plessy v. Ferguson*. A colorblind society is one in which racial or ethnic group membership is irrelevant to the way individuals are treated (Rist, 1974). People in favor of colorblind approaches to policy argue that taking cognizance of group membership in decision making is illegitimate since it is likely to lead either to discrimination against minority groups or to reverse discrimination in their favor. Neither of these is viewed as desirable. The people aligned with this side of the debate argue that, because the laws that systematically disadvantaged African Americans were overturned decades ago, a fair system is now in place and this system can only be truly fair to the extent that it completely ignores group membership—treating individuals solely as individuals and striving to ignore race or ethnicity completely.

Yet others (Bonilla-Silva, 2003; Levin, 2003; Guinier & Torres, 2002) argue that such an approach is the antithesis of fairness—that it is akin to a race between a well-nourished and well-trained athlete whom most of the spectators are rooting for and an individual who has just been released from an unjust prison term during which food was sparse and opportunities for exercise and training were denied. People taking this perspective agree with Justice Harry Blackmun, who wrote in the *Regents of the University of California v. Bakke* (1978) case that "in order to get beyond racism, we must first take account of race. In order to treat persons equally, we must treat them differently" (pp. 2806–2808). They contend that the reality of continuing racism (Jones, 1997; Sidanius & Pratto, 1999; Trent et al., 2003) as well as the continuing impact of prior discrimination, such as the striking difference in net worth among African Americans and Whites with similar incomes due at least in part to larger inheritances received by Whites (Jaynes & Williams, 1989), make policies designed specifically to promote the inclusion of African Americans in the economic and political life of the country both just and wise. Thus, they tend to support affirmative action and other related policies designed to do this by explicitly taking account of the relative participation rates of various groups—an approach at direct odds with the colorblind perspective. From this perspective, colorblindness stands in the way of achieving fairness because it justifies moving away from race-based policies designed to promote fairness (Gotanda, 1991).

This tension between views that see taking cognizance of racial or ethnic group membership positively and those that see it negatively is strongly reflected in controversy over how our educational system should function (Wolsko, Park, Judd, & Wittenbrink, 2000). Specifically, one approach to education in our increasingly diverse society calls for redoubling efforts to teach all students core information and values in an attempt to strengthen a unified American identity (Bennett, 1987; Hirsch, 1996; Schlesinger, 1992). This approach, which typically decries bilingual and multicultural approaches to education, is quite consistent with the colorblind perspective in that it seeks to ignore or deemphasize subgroup identities and differences in an effort to create a unified citizenry. In contrast, another approach, typically endorsed by proponents of multicultural education, argues that responding to diversity by including material about many groups and using approaches to teaching that recognize cultural differences is needed to serve students well and to build harmony and respect between those from different backgrounds (Banks, 2005; Nieto, 2004; Takaki, 1993; Yinger, 1994).

Interestingly, this tension between ignoring or focusing on group membership is reflected in theoretical stances with sharply differing implications even in social-psychological research on improving intergroup relations, as Wolsko et al. (2000) point out. Specifically, one major line of theorizing and research suggests that it is the categorization of individuals into groups that lays the basis for stereotyping and discrimination (Brewer & Miller, 1984, 1988; Tajfel, 1978). From this perspective, the logical solution to the problem is to minimize the salience of the group or to redefine the in-group in a more inclusive way so that old out-groups join together in assuming a new, more expansive shared identity (Gaertner, Dovidio, Anastasio, Bachman, & Rust, 1993). Another perspective, clearly much less common, suggests that intergroup relations can be improved by careful and explicit focus on group differences (Lee & Duenas, 1995; Randolph, Landis, & Tzeng, 1977; Triandis, 1976).

The issues raised by the New American Dilemma are complex and unlikely to be easily resolved. Full consideration of them would of necessity involve work from fields as disparate as philosophy, history, psychology, law, ethics, economics, and politics. Thus, this chapter does not try to solve this dilemma. Rather, it has a more modest but nonetheless important goal: to provide a glimpse of how the colorblind perspective works in reality in one of the most important institutions in our society—its schools.

I did not set out initially to explore this question. Rather, as a scholar deeply interested in the potential of interracial school settings for improving intergroup relations, I embarked on a longitudinal ethnographic study designed to illuminate the nature of peer relations in a desegregated school and the impact that school policies, structures, and culture have on those relations (Schofield, 1989). It just so happened that having chosen a particular school for study, as described below, I found myself in an environment that strongly endorsed the colorblind perspective. Furthermore, over time, it became apparent that the institution's endorsement of this perspective had important consequences that educators at the school did not anticipate and often did not recognize. Thus, the causes and consequences of this perspective became the focus of the part of my research reported here.

I argue that two basic factors make understanding the implications of the colorblind perspective important. First, evidence suggests that this perspective is widespread in schools both within the United States and elsewhere, either as part of official policy or as an informal but nonetheless powerful social norm that applies in many situations (Eaton, 2001; Gillborn, 1992; Goetz & Breneman, 1988; Jervis, 1996; Pollock, 2004; Rist, 1978; Sagar & Schofield, 1984; Sleeter, 1993). Second, the colorblind approach is also frequently espoused as a goal to be sought in many other realms, including employment practices and judicial proceedings. This research led me to conclude that although in many ways the colorblind perspective is appealing because it is consistent with a long-standing American emphasis on the importance of the individual, it easily leads to a misrepresentation of reality in ways that allow and sometimes even encourage discrimination against minority group members, as later parts of this chapter demonstrate.

THE RESEARCH SITE: WEXLER MIDDLE SCHOOL

In choosing a site for the research, I adopted a strategy that Cook and Campbell (1976) call "generalizing to target instances." The aim was not to study what happens in a typical racially-mixed school, if such an entity can even be said to exist. Rather, it was to explore peer relations between African American and White students under conditions that theory suggests should be relatively conducive to the development of positive relations between them.

In his classic book *The Nature of Prejudice*, Allport (1954) proposed that intergroup contact may reinforce previously held stereotypes and increase intergroup hostility unless the contact situation is structured in a way that (1) provides equal status for minority and majority group members, (2) encourages cooperation toward shared, strongly desired goals, and (3) provides the support of law, authority, and customs for positive relations. These ideas, as elaborated and refined by subsequent theoretical and empirical work (Amir, 1976; Cook, 1969, 1985; Gaertner, Rust, Dovidio, Bachman, & Anastasio, 1994; Hewstone & Brown, 1986; Pettigrew, 1986, 1998, 2004; Pettigrew & Tropp, 2000; Schofield, 2001; Schofield & Eurich-Fulcer, 2001; Stephan & Stephan, 1996), constitute a useful foundation for understanding the likely outcomes of interracial contact. Although equal status may be neither a necessary prerequisite nor a sufficient condition for change, it does appear to be very helpful (Amir, 1969, 1976; Brewer & Brown, 1998; Brown, 1995; Cohen, 1975, 1997; Cohen, Lockheed, & Lohman, 1976; Cook, 1978, 1985; Norvell & Worchel, 1981; Pettigrew, 1998; Riordan, 1978; Schofield & Eurich-Fulcer, 2001; Stephan & Stephan, 1996, 2001). In addition, a substantial body of research suggests that cooperation toward mutually desired goals is indeed generally conducive to improved intergroup relations (Aronson & Patnoe, 1997; Bossert, 1988/89; Cook, 1978, 1985; Johnson & Johnson, 1982; Johnson, Johnson, & Maruyama, 1984; Johnson, Maruyama, Johnson, Nelson, & Skon, 1981; Schofield, 2001; Sharan, 1980; Sherif, 1979; Slavin, 1995; Slavin & Cooper, 1999; Stephan & Stephan, 1996, 2001).

Wexler Middle School was constructed in a large northeastern city to serve as a model of high-quality integrated education. When it first opened, Wexler had a student body almost precisely 50 percent African American and 50 percent White, mirroring closely the proportion of Black and White students in the city's public schools. This school, which serves 1200 children in sixth through eighth grades, was chosen for study because the decisions made in planning for it suggested that it would come reasonably close to meeting the conditions specified by Allport and the more recent theorists who have built on his work. The school's strong efforts to provide an environment conducive to improving intergroup relations can be illustrated by examination of its staffing policy. The top four administrative positions are filled by two African Americans and two Whites, clearly symbolizing the school's commitment to providing equal status for members of both groups. About 25 percent of the faculty are African-American, a proportion below that of the student body but markedly higher than the proportion of African American teachers in the school district in which Wexler was embedded.

The extent to which Wexler met the conditions specified by Allport and his intellectual heirs as conducive to the development of improved intergroup relations has been discussed at length elsewhere (Schofield, 1989). Here, I merely report the conclusion drawn in that discussion—that Wexler came considerably closer to these criteria than did most desegregated public schools. Yet it fell seriously short of meeting them completely in a number of ways, many of which were the direct result of societal conditions over which Wexler had little or no control. For example, in spite of Wexler's commitment to a staffing pattern that would provide equal formal status for African Americans and Whites, the proportion of African-American teachers on its staff was considerably lower than the proportion of Black students in the school because the school system did not want to put too high a proportion of its Black teachers in one school.

In addition, a large majority of Wexler's White students came from middle- or upper-middle-class homes. Although some of the African American children were middle class, the majority came from either poor or working-class families. These social-class differences had implications for the status of African American and White students within the school. For example, in the eighth grade, which divided students into a "regular" and a "gifted" track, a much higher proportion of the White than African American students achieved scores on standardized tests that led to their placement in the gifted track. Even in the sixth and seventh grades, which had academically heterogenous classes, this difference influenced students' status (Schofield, 1980), although not in a way emphasized and formalized by a tracking policy. In sum, Wexler made stronger than usual efforts to foster positive relations between

African American and White students but fell markedly short of being a theoretically ideal milieu for the accomplishment of this goal.

DATA GATHERING

The analysis that follows is based on an intensive four-year study of peer relations at Wexler. The basic data-gathering strategy was intensive and extensive observation in Wexler's classrooms, hallways, playgrounds, and cafeteria. Observers used the full field-note method for recording the events they witnessed (Olson, 1976). A large number of events were observed because they were representative of the events that filled most of the school day at Wexler. However, an important subgroup of events was oversampled in relation to their frequency of occurrence because of their direct relevance to the study's focus. This strategy, which Strauss (1987) calls theoretical sampling, led to oversampling certain activities, such as affective education classes, designed to help students get to know each other, and meetings of Wexler's interracial student advisory group set up to handle the special problems students might face in a desegregated school. Over the course of the study, more than 500 hours were devoted to the observation of students and staff at Wexler.

A wide variety of other data-gathering techniques ranging from sociometric questionnaires to experimental work to quantitative observational approaches were also used (Sagar & Schofield, 1980; Sagar, Schofield, & Snyder, 1983; Schofield, 1979; Schofield & Francis, 1982; Schofield & Sagar, 1977; Schofield & Whitley, 1983; Whitley & Schofield, 1984). Interviews were employed extensively. For example, randomly selected students participated in open-ended interviews twice a year. Teachers and administrators were also interviewed repeatedly. In addition, graffiti in the bathrooms and on the school walls were routinely recorded, school bulletins were collected, and careful note was taken of such things as wall decorations and public address system announcements.

Space does not allow full discussion of the many varied techniques used in collecting and analyzing the data on which this chapter is based. However, two general principles that guided the research must be mentioned. First, both data gathering and analysis were as rigorous and systematic as possible. For example, sampling techniques were employed where appropriate; trained coders, who were unaware of the race and sex of particular respondents, coded the open-ended interviews using reliable systems developed for this research; and field notes were carefully indexed so that all notes relevant to a given topic could be examined.

Second, because it is often impossible to achieve high levels of precision and control in field research, strong efforts were made to triangulate the data (Webb, Campbell, Schwartz, & Sechrest, 1966). Great care was taken to gather many different types of information bearing on the same issue, to minimize the potential problems with each data source, and to be sensitive in analyzing and interpreting data that might reflect biases in the data set that could not be completely eliminated. The basic approach used in the analysis of the qualitative data is outlined in works such as Bogdan and Taylor (1975), Campbell (1975), Miles and Huberman (1984), and Strauss and Corbin (1990). Fuller details on data gathering and analysis are presented elsewhere, as is information on the strategies used to minimize observer reactivity and bias (Schofield, 1989; Schofield & Sagar, 1979).

THE COLORBLIND PERSPECTIVE AND ITS COROLLARIES

Wexler's faculty clearly tended to subscribe to the colorblind view of interracial schooling. Interviews with both African American and White teachers suggested that the majority of both groups tended to see Wexler as an institution that could help impart middle-class values and modes of behavior to lower-class students so that they could break out of the cycle of poverty and become middle-class persons themselves. Even though most of these lower-class students were African American, race was seen as quite incidental to the anticipated class assimilation process.

An African-American administrator, with perhaps more candor than many similarly oriented White administrators and teachers, made her class assimilation goals explicit and, at the same time, made it clear just which students needed to be so assimilated:

> I really don't address myself to group differences when I am dealing with youngsters. . . . I try to treat youngsters, I don't care who they are, as youngsters and not as Black, White, green or yellow. . . . Many of the Black youngsters who have difficulty are the ones who . . . have come from communities where they had to put up certain defenses and these defenses are the antithesis of the normal situation . . . like they find in school. It is therefore [difficult] getting them to become aware that they have to follow these rules because [they] are here . . . not over there in their community. . . . I think that many of the youngsters [from the] larger community have a more normal set of values that people generally want to see, and therefore do not have [as] much difficulty in coping with their school situation. . . . [The Black children] do have difficulty in adjusting because they are just not used to it. Until we can adjustively counsel them into the right types of behavior . . . I think we're going to continue to have these types of problems.

The only thing atypical in the preceding remarks is the frank acknowledgment that the children perceived as lacking the "normal set of values that people generally want to see" are typically African American. More usually, this was implicit in remarks emphasizing the negative effects of growing up in a poor family or a low-income neighborhood.

As a reaction to the invidious distinctions that have traditionally been made in the United States on the basis of race, the colorblind perspective is understandable, even laudable. However, this orientation was accompanied at Wexler by a number of other logically related beliefs, which taken together with it had some important though largely unrecognized negative consequences. These beliefs and their basis in the ongoing social reality at Wexler are discussed individually. Then the consequences of this belief system are discussed in some detail.

Race as an Invisible Characteristic

It is not a very great leap from the colorblind perspective, which says that race is a social category of no relevance to one's behaviors and decisions, to a belief that individuals should not or perhaps even do not notice each other's racial group membership. At Wexler, acknowledging that one was aware of another's race was viewed by many people as a possible sign of prejudice, as illustrated by the following excerpt from project field notes:

> When I was arranging the student interviews, I mentioned to
> Mr. Little [White] that I thought there was only one White girl in
> one of his classes. I asked if I was right about this and he said,
> "Well, just a minute. Let me check." After looking through the
> class roster in his roll book he said, "You know, you're right. I
> never noticed that. . . . I guess that's a good thing." Our data
> suggest that teachers not only denied that they noticed children's
> race when the researchers were present, but also did so among
> themselves. For example, when complying with a request to mark
> down the race of his students on a class roster for research
> purposes, a White teacher remarked, "Did you ever notice those
> teachers who say, 'I never notice what they are'?"

Although there was less unanimity on the issue of whether students noticed the race of others than of whether teachers did, a substantial proportion of Wexler's faculty asserted that the students rarely noticed race. This point of view is exemplified by the following excerpt from an interview with an African American science teacher:

MS. MONROE: You know, I hear the things the students usually fight about. As I said before, it's stupid things like someone taking a pencil. It's not because [the other person] is Black or White. . . . At this age level . . . I don't think it's Black or White.

INTERVIEWER: There's something I'm wondering about. It is hard to believe, given the way our society is, that you can just bring kids together and they won't be very much aware.

MS. MONROE: They just go about their daily things and don't . . . I don't think they think about it really. . . . I see them interacting with one another on an adult basis. . . . They are not really aware of color . . . or race or whatever.

INTERVIEWER: You really don't see that as a factor . . . in their relationships?

MS. MONROE: No.

Although the faculty at Wexler saw themselves, and to a lesser extent their students, as oblivious to the race of others, a wide variety of data suggest that this view was not accurate. Most removed from the specific situation at Wexler, but nonetheless pertinent, is a substantial body of data from research on stereotyping and person perception. This work suggests that individuals tend to use preexisting categories in perceiving and responding to others (Brewer & Brown, 1998; Brown, 1995; Fiske & Neuberg, 1990). More specifically, research suggests that individuals spontaneously use the physical appearance of other people as a basis for categorizing them by race. Further, this categorization has an impact on how individuals are perceived and on how others respond to them (Devine, 1989; Dovidio et al., 1997; Duncan, 1976; Fazio, Jackson, Dunton, & Williams, 1995; Katz, Wackenhut, & Hass, 1986; Katz, 1976; Malpass & Kravitz, 1969; Sagar & Schofield, 1980; Taylor, Fiske, Etcoff, & Ruderman, 1978).

The teachers and students at Wexler were to some extent self-selected members of an interracial institution and thus might conceivably be less prone to use race as a category for processing information about others than would the college student populations used in most studies on person perception cited above. However, given the importance of race as a social category in many aspects of life in the United States, it seems highly unlikely that the prevailing tendency at Wexler was for individuals not even to notice each other's race.

Interviews with students made it clear that many of them were very conscious of their race or of the race of other students, which is hardly surprising given the fact that interracial schooling was a new and somewhat threatening experience for many of them. The following excerpt from an interview in which the interviewer had not herself previously mentioned race suggests just how salient racial categories were to the children.

INTERVIEWER: Can you tell me who some of your friends are?

BEVERLY [AFRICAN AMERICAN]: Well, Stacey and Lydia and Amy, even though she's White.

Similarly, students' awareness of racial group membership is seen in an excerpt from field notes taken in a seventh-grade class with a higher-than-average proportion of African American students because the teachers had decided to put many lower-achieving children in a class by themselves.

Howard, a White male, leaned over to me (a White female observer) and said, "You know, it just wasn't fair the way they set up this class. There are sixteen Black kids and only nine White kids. I can't learn in here." I said, "Why is that?" Howard replied, "They copy and they pick on you. It just isn't fair."

Race as a Taboo Topic

Before discussing why the view that they and their students tended not even to notice race gained considerable popularity among Wexler's teachers in spite of everyday indications that this was often not the case, this section discusses two other phenomena closely related to the development of the colorblind perspective. The first was the development of a norm strong enough to be labeled a virtual taboo against the use of the words *White* and *Black* in a context in which they referred to racial group membership. Thus, for example, in almost 200 hours of observations in classrooms, hallways, and teachers' meetings during Wexler's first year, fewer than 25 direct references to race were made by school staff or students (Schofield, 1989). Any use of the words *black* and *white* in a context in which they referred to an individual or group was classified as a reference to race, as were racial epithets and words and phrases used almost exclusively within one group to express solidarity (e.g., "Hey, Brother") or the like. As mentioned previously, this reluctance to talk about race has been noted in many other racially mixed schools (Eaton, 2001; Gillborn, 1992; Goetz & Breneman,1988; Jervis, 1996; Larson & Ovando, 2001; Pollock, 2004; Rist, 1978; Sagar & Schofield, 1984; Sleeter, 1993). Recently, this reluctance to speak about race has been characterized as color muteness by Pollock (2004), who found it especially prevelant in situations in which certain kinds of problems are discussed.

The extremely infrequent reference to race at Wexler was all the more surprising when one considers that our observations included a wide variety of formal and informal situations, ranging from workshops funded by the Emergency School Assistance Act, federal legislation that provided funds to desegregating schools to help them handle special problems that might arise as a result of desegregation, to informal student interactions on the playgrounds and in the hallways.

Students' awareness of the taboo is shown clearly in the following field notes, which recount a conversation with a White social worker whose work at Wexler on the extracurricular program was funded by a local foundation concerned with race relations. Perhaps not surprisingly under these circumstances, she showed much less reluctance than did most staff to deal in a straightforward manner with the issue of race.

> Ms. Fowler said that a short while ago she had heard from Martin [Black] that another child had done something wrong. The offense was serious enough so that she wanted to track down this individual. She asked Martin to describe the child who had committed the offense. Martin said, "He has black hair and he's fairly tall." He didn't give the race of the other person even though he went on to give a fairly complete description otherwise. Finally, Ms. Fowler asked, "Is he Black or White?" Martin replied, "Is it all right for me to say?" Ms. Fowler said that it was all right. Martin then said, "Well, the boy was White."

Students were well aware that making references to race displeased many of their teachers and might also offend peers.

INTERVIEWER: You know, the other day I was walking around the school and heard a sixth-grade student describing a student from the seventh grade to a teacher who needed to find this student in order to return something she had lost. The sixth grader said the seventh grader was tall and thin. She described what the girl had been wearing and said her hair was dark, but she didn't say whether the girl was Black or White. . . . Why do you think she didn't mention that?

SYLVIA [AFRICAN AMERICAN]: The teacher might have got mad if she said whether she was White or Black.

INTERVIEWER: Do some teachers get mad about things like that?

SYLVIA: Some do . . . they holler. . . .

INTERVIEWER: Now, when you talk to kids who are Black, do you ever mention that someone is White or Black?

SYLVIA: No.

INTERVIEWER: What about when you're talking with kids who are White?

SYLVIA: Nope.

INTERVIEWER: You never mention race? Why not?

SYLVIA: They might think I'm prejudiced.

Social Life as a Web of Purely Interpersonal Relations

Consistent with the view that race is not, or at least should not be, a salient aspect of other individuals and with the practice of not speaking about race were tendencies to conceptualize social life as a web of interpersonal rather than intergroup relations and to assume that interpersonal relations are not much influenced by group membership. As one teacher put it:

> Peer-group identity here in middle school . . . has nothing to
> do with race. There's a strong tendency to group that exists
> independent of . . . racial boundaries. . . . We started in September
> with these students letting them know we weren't going to fool
> around with that. . . . You're a student and we don't care what
> color you are.

This tendency to minimize the potential importance of intergroup processes was illustrated clearly during an inservice training session, the stated purpose of which was to help teachers deal effectively with the racially-mixed student body. The facilitator, a White clinical psychologist employed by a local foundation, began by making some general statements about the importance of understanding cultural differences between students. Although the facilitator kept trying to nudge and finally to push the group to discuss ways in which the racially-mixed nature of the student body influenced peer relations, appropriate curricular materials, and the like, the group ended up discussing issues such as the problems caused by individual children who acted out aggressively in the classroom, the difficulty that overweight children have in gaining peer acceptance, and the fact that children with disabilities were sometimes taunted by their classmates.

Contrasting sharply with the teachers' tendency to insist that they and their students reacted to each other exclusively as individuals and to deemphasize the importance of intergroup as opposed to interpersonal processes was the students' willingness to discuss with interviewers the important role race played in Wexler's social life.

> INTERVIEWER: I have noticed . . . that [in the cafeteria] very often White kids sit with White kids and Black kids sit with Black kids. Why do you think that this is?
>
> MARY [WHITE]: 'Cause the White kids have White friends and the Black kids have Black friends. . . . I don't think integration is working. . . . Blacks still associate with Blacks and Whites still associate with Whites. . . .
>
> INTERVIEWER: Can you think of any White kids that have quite a few Black friends or of any Black kids who have quite a few White friends?
>
> MARY: Not really.

The tendency for students to group themselves by race in a variety of settings was very marked. For example, on a fairly typical day at the end of the school's second year of operation 119 White and 90 African American students attended the seventh-grade lunch period. Of these more than 200 children, only six sat next to someone of the other race (Schofield & Sagar, 1977).

Of course, it is possible that race itself was not a factor in producing such interaction patterns, but something correlated with race such as socioeconomic status, academic achievement, or the opportunity for previous contact with each other. Such factors did appear to reinforce the tendency to prefer intragroup interactions and were often cited by teachers as the actual cause of the visually apparent tendency of students to cluster with those of their own race. Yet the results of an experiment conducted at Wexler demonstrate that race itself was a real factor in peer relations. In this study, eighty male sixth graders were presented with carefully drawn pictures of a number of ambiguously aggressive types of peer interactions that were quite common at Wexler, such as poking another student with a pencil. For each type of interaction, some students were shown pictures in which both students were African American, others saw pictures in which both students were White, and others saw mixed-race dyads with the Black student shown as either the initiator of the behavior or as the student to whom it was directed.

The results suggested that the race of the person initiating the behavior influenced how mean and threatening the behavior was interpreted as being (Sagar & Schofield, 1980) (see Table 11.1). Such a finding is, of course, inconsistent with the notion that students take no notice of others' race. It is also incompatible with the idea that intergroup processes have no influence on students' reactions to their peers because the data suggest that the perception of an individual's behavior is influenced by the group membership of the person performing it.

Table 11.1   Mean Ratings of Both White and Black Actors' Ambiguously Aggressive Behaviors by White and Black Participants

Subject Group	Actor Race	Rating Scale: Mean/Threatening
White	White	8.28
	Black	8.99
Black	White	7.38
	Black	8.40

Note. Means are based on sums of paired 7-point scales indicating how well the given adjective described the behaviors, from 1 (not at all) to 7 (exactly). N = 40 in each group. Each Participants rated two White and two Black actors (e.g., the perpetrator of the ambiguously aggressive act) and two White and Black targets. The 4 × 4 nature of the Latin square required treating the race permutations as four levels of a single factor. Significant F values on this factor provided justification for testing actor race, target race, and interaction effects with simple contrasts, using the error variance estimate generated by the ANOVA. The significant main effect of race permutations on the summed mean/threatening scales, $F(3,192) = 3.02$, $p < .05$, was found to reflect, as predicted, a tendency for subjects to rate the behaviors by Black actors more mean/threatening than identical behaviors by White actors, $t(144) = 2.90$, $p < .01$. Means are not broken down by target race because no statistically significant main effects or interactions were found for this variable.

Source: From Sagar, H. A., and Schofield, J. W. (1980). Racial and Behavioral Cues in Black and White Children's Perceptions of Ambiguously Aggressive Acts. *Journal of Personality and Social Psychology, 39*(4) 590–598. Copyright 1980 by the American Psychological Association. Adapted with permission.

THE FUNCTIONS AND CONSEQUENCES OF THE COLORBLIND PERSPECTIVE AND ITS COROLLARIES

Regardless of the fact that the colorblind perspective and its corollaries were not completely accurate views of the social processes occurring at Wexler, they appeared to influence the development of the social fabric at Wexler in ways that had a number of important consequences, some positive and some negative. The following discussion of the functions of this set of beliefs suggests why the colorblind perspective was attractive to teachers and how it affected both the education and social experiences of Wexler's students.

Reducing the Potential for Overt Conflict

One concern that typifies many schools with diverse student bodies is a desire to avoid dissension and conflict that are or could appear to be race related (Sagar & Schofield, 1984). The adoption of colorblind policies is often seen as useful in achieving this goal, because if such policies are implemented fully, they can help protect the institution and people in positions of responsibility in it from charges of discrimination. Furthermore, a colorblind approach may be seen, especially by White educators, as keeping the school focussed on issues of interest to all groups, rather than on issues of differential interest to different stakeholders in the school (Larson & Ovando, 2001) This is not to say that such an approach leads to equal outcomes for members of all groups. Indeed, when there are initial group differences on criteria relevant to success in a given institution, such policies are likely to lead to differential outcomes, a situation that some people would characterize as institutional racism (Jones, 1997). However, as noted earlier, the colorblind perspective is consistent with notions of fairness that have long held sway in the United States and thus can be relatively easily defended. Policies that give obvious preference to either minority or majority group members are much more likely to spark controversy and conflict.

An example from Wexler illustrates how the operation of the colorblind perspective helps to minimize overt conflict in situations in which the outcomes for African Americans and Whites as a whole are extremely different. The suspension rate for African American students at Wexler was roughly four times that for White students. The strong correlation between race and socioeconomic background at Wexler made it predictable that the African American students' behavior would be less consistent than that of White students with the basically middle-class norms prevailing in the school. However, the colorblind perspective appeared instrumental in helping to keep Wexler's discipline policies from becoming a focus of contention. To my knowledge, the disparity in suspension rates was never treated as a serious issue that needed attention. When researchers asked faculty and administrators about it, some, perhaps not altogether candidly, denied having noticed it. Others argued that it was not a problem in the sense that individual students were generally treated fairly. In fact, teachers often emphasized strongly the effort they made to treat discipline problems with White and African American students in exactly the same way.

On the relatively rare occasions when charges of discrimination were raised by students unhappy with the way a teacher had dealt with them, teachers tended to discount the complaints by reiterating their commitment to the colorblind perspective:

> MS. WILSON [WHITE]: I try not to let myself listen to it [the charge of discrimination].
> Maybe once in a while I ask myself, "Well, why would he make that statement?"
> But I know in my mind that I do not discriminate on the basis of race. . . . And
> I will not have someone create an issue like that when I know I have done my best
> not to create it.

Only an occasional teacher, more often than not African American, suggested that the colorblind perspective actually worked to help create the disparity in suspension rates; this issue is addressed later in this chapter. Be that as it may, the colorblind perspective clearly fostered an atmosphere that minimized the chances that the disparity itself was likely to become the focus of either overt discontent or constructive action.

Minimizing of Discomfort and Embarrassment

Many of the faculty and students at Wexler had little prior experience in desegregated schools. Also, most of them lived in neighborhoods that were either heavily White or heavily African American. Thus, for many, there was an initial sense of awkwardness and anxiety, like the intergroup anxiety Stephan and Stephan (1985) discuss. Under such circumstances, avoiding mention of race and contending that it rarely influenced relations between individuals seemed to minimize the potential for awkward or embarrassing social situations. This is related to the aforementioned conflict-avoidance function of these beliefs, but it can be distinguished conceptually because feelings of awkwardness and embarrassment can but do not always lead to conflict. In fact, the colorblind perspective and the related norms against mention of race seemed to help maintain the veneer of politeness that Clement, Eisenhart, and Harding (1979) have argued is part of the etiquette of race relations in some desegregated situations.

Consistent with the idea that teachers avoided talk of race in order to avoid discomfort and personal embarrassment, Pollock (2004) concluded that although teachers in the school she studied made reference to race in describing conflicts between students of different backgrounds, they very rarely mentioned race when describing their own conflicts with students. This phenomenom suggests that although teachers in that school were willing to entertain the idea that problems between students might have a racial element, they were not willing to raise the specter of race-related problems in their own interactions with students, a much more personally threatening possibility.

One way to illustrate the ways in which the colorblind perspective and the associated beliefs and norms helped smooth social relations between Blacks and Whites is to compare the situation at Wexler to another sort of interaction that is often rather strained, at least initially—interaction between individuals who have visible disabilities and those who do not. In a fascinating analysis of this latter situation, Davis (1961) argues that the emotion aroused in the person without disabilities by the sight of a person with disabilities creates tension and an uncertainty about what is appropriate behavior; this tension interferes with normal interaction patterns. There is a tendency for the disability to become the focus of attention and to foster ambiguity about appropriate behavior. Davis argues that the initial reaction to this situation is often a fictional denial of the disability and of its potential effect on the relationship, that is, a tendency to pretend to ignore the existence of the disability, which at least temporarily relieves the interactants of the necessity of dealing with its implications.

Analogously, one can think of the racial group membership of individuals in an intergroup interaction, be they Black or White, as a sort of visually apparent disability. Like a disability, group membership may provoke an affective response in others that predisposes them to avoidance or at least raises questions about appropriate behavior. Of course, just as some individuals feel more awkward than will others when interacting with a person with a disability, so some individuals are more likely to be more affected by interacting with someone of the other race. However, to the extent that race is perceived as a potential threat to a smooth, relaxed, and pleasant interaction, one way of handling that threat is to pretend to be unaware of the attribute that creates it.

Although Davis (1961) argues that initial interactions between people with disabilities and others are characterized by a fictional denial of the disability, he also suggests that with time this fiction is discarded because, being based on an obvious falsehood, it is inherently unstable and in the long run dysfunctional. Similarly, I argue that although the colorblind perspective and the accompanying taboo may have made the initial adjustment to Wexler easier, in the long run they tended to inhibit the development of positive relations between African American and White students. These students were vividly aware of differences and of tensions between them that were related to their group membership. Yet such issues could not be dealt with in a straightforward manner in the colorblind climate in which race functioned as a public secret, as Williams (1998) suggests it often does. Thus, anger sometimes festered and stereotypes built when fuller discussion of the situation might have made it easier for individuals to see each other's perspectives.

This is not to suggest that schools have the responsibility to function as giant T-groups or as therapeutic institutions. Rather, it is to say that the refusal of many of Wexler's faculty to recognize the fundamental role that race played in peer relationships meant that they played a less constructive role than they might have in guiding students through a new and sometimes threatening experience. Jervis (1996) observed a similar phenomenon with similar results in her study of a multiethnic middle school. Furthermore, the norms discouraging discussion of race not only undercut potentially constructive teacher–student interactions related to this topic; they discouraged student discussion of this topic with peers as well. This clearly minimized the potential for conflict. But it also minimized the potentially constructive impact of such discussions, suggested by research demonstrating that discussion of race between more and less prejudiced students can actually reduce prejudice in the former without increasing it in the latter (Aboud & Doyle, 1996; Aboud & Fenwick, 1999).

Increasing Educators' Freedom of Action

The colorblind perspective and its corollaries undoubtedly gained some of their appeal because they tended to simplify life for Wexler's staff and to increase their freedom of action. An example can illustrate both points. After being asked by one member of the research team about the outcome of a closely contested student council election, a White teacher disclosed that she had purposely miscounted votes so that a "responsible child" (a White boy) was declared the winner rather than the "unstable child" (an African American girl) who had actually received a few more votes. The teacher seemed ambivalent about and somewhat embarrassed by her action, but the focus of her concern was her subversion of the democratic process. She reported that she had looked at the two children as individuals and decided that one was a more desirable student council representative than the other. As far as I could tell from an extended discussion with her, she did not consciously consider the race of the students involved. Further, she did not appear to consider the fact that her action had changed the racial composition of the student council.

The failure to consider such issues clearly simplifies the decision-making process because there is one less item, and an affect-laden one at that, to be factored into it. Related to this, such a colorblind approach increases educators' freedom of action because policies or actions that sometimes appear acceptable if one thinks about them in a colorblind way often appear much less acceptable from a perspective that is not colorblind. For example, Goetz and Breneman (1988) point out how avoiding discussion of the fact that school policies will affect Black and White students in different ways made it easier to adopt policies that worked to Black students' disadvantage in two Southern elementary schools. In addition, Pollock (2004) describes how colormuteness, the avoidance of reference to race, can actually increase the role that race plays in schooling and its outcomes. Indeed, the colorblind perspective and its corollaries foster an environment that research suggests is conducive to discriminatory behavior, at least on the part of certain types of individuals. Specifically, work by Snyder, Kleck, Strenta, and Mentzer (1979) demonstrates that people are more likely to act in accordance with feelings they prefer not to reveal when they can appear to be acting on some other basis than when no other obvious explanation for their behavior is available. More directly pertinent to this discussion are several decades of work on a phenomenon called aversive racism, which suggests that many Whites tend to discriminate against African Americans in situations in which the basis for their actions is ambiguous and their behavior can be attributed to something other than prejudice. Failure to explicitly consider race in making decisions seems very conducive to producing such discrimination by minimizing the possibility that actions and decisions are likely to be seen as influenced by racial considerations.

However, when the situation did not provide this sort of rationale for avoidance behavior, the tendency to avoid people with physical disabilities disappeared. Thus, by analogy, one might expect that an environment that minimizes the importance of race and even forbids overt consideration or discussion of the topic would free individuals whose basic tendency is to discriminate (a normatively unacceptable orientation at Wexler) to do so. The vast majority of Wexler's faculty espoused basically egalitarian racial attitudes and would quite rightly be insulted by the idea that they would intentionally discriminate against their African American students. Yet the work of Gaertner and Dovidio (1986, 2005) demonstrates that one need not be an old-fashioned racist to discriminate against African Americans when the conditions are conducive to doing so.

Specifically, Gaertner and Dovidio (1986, 2005) argue that a great many liberal Whites are highly motivated to maintain an image of themselves as egalitarian individuals who neither discriminate against others on the basis of race nor are prejudiced. However, the desire to maintain such an image is coupled with some negative affect and with certain beliefs that predispose them to react negatively to African Americans. This predisposition is expressed primarily in circumstances that do not threaten an egalitarian self-concept. One important relevant circumstance is the availability of non–race-related rationales for the behavior in question (Dovidio & Gaertner, 1998; Gaertner & Dovidio, 1986). It is precisely this aspect of the situation that is influenced by the colorblind perspective and its corollaries. To the extent that they help remove awareness of race from conscious consideration, they make other explanations for one's behavior relatively more salient. Thus, they free the aversive racist to act in a discriminatory fashion. Further, to the extent that the taboo at Wexler inhibited individuals from challenging the behavior of other people as racist in outcome or intent, it removed a potential barrier to racist behavior because it minimized the probability that such behavior would pose a threat to an eqalitarian self-concept. Furthermore, it is important to note that the colorblind perspective may negatively affect racial attitudes as well. Specifically, experimental research suggests that being in an environment that advocates this approach increases both explicit and implicit bias in racial attitudes compared to being in one that advocates a multicultural approach (Richeson & Nussbaum, 2003).

Ignoring the Reality of Cultural Differences between Students

Although the colorblind perspective and its corollaries served some useful purposes, they also had several unrecognized negative effects, as indicated. One important negative consequence of this mind-set was a predisposition to ignore or deny the possibility of cultural differences between White and Black children that influenced how they functioned in school. For example, the differential suspension rate for African American and White children may have stemmed partially from differences between these students in what Triandis and his colleagues (Triandis, 1994; Triandis, Vassiliou, Vassiliou, Tanaka, & Shanmugam, 1972) call their "subjective culture." Specifically, data from the Sagar and Schofield (1980) experiment described earlier suggested that African American boys saw certain types of ambiguously aggressive acts as less mean and threatening and as more playful and friendly than did their White peers. These behaviors were ones that sometimes began conflicts between students that resulted in suspensions. Awareness of the differential meaning of such behaviors to White and African American students might at least have suggested ways of trying to reduce the disproportionate suspension of Black students.

Other research suggests that Black-White differences in culture relevant to education are not limited to this one area (Hill, 1971; Irvine, 1990; Jones, 1986, 1997; Lee & Slaughter-Defoe, 2004). For example, Kochman (1981) has argued convincingly that Black and White students use widely differing styles in classroom discussion and that misunderstanding the cultural context from which students come can lead peers and teachers to misinterpret involvement for belligerence. Heath's (1982) research suggests that the types of questions teachers typically pose in elementary school classrooms are quite similar to those asked in White middle-class homes but differ substantially from those typically addressed to young children in poor African American homes. Thus, there is reason to think that in assuming a completely colorblind perspective teachers may rule out awareness and use of information that would be helpful in deciding how best to structure materials in ways that work well for the range of students they teach as well as in interpreting many aspects of their students' behavior.

Failing to Respond to and Capitalize on Diversity

There were numerous less subtle ways in which the colorblind perspective and the accompanying deemphasis on the biracial nature of the school worked to the disadvantage of Wexler's students—and more often to the disadvantage of African American than of White students. One of the more obvious of these concerned the extent to which efforts were made to use instructional materials and pedagogical approaches that were likely to reflect the interests and life experiences of Wexler's African American students, an approach that has been called "using culturally responsive pedagogy" (Carter & Goodwin, 1994; Irvine, 1991; Nieto, 2004; Ramsey, 1987). Wexler operated as part of a school system that made some effort to use multicultural texts. In addition, some teachers, a disproportionate number of whom were African American, took special care to relate class work to the concerns and interests likely to be found in their Black students as well as their White ones. The prevailing tendency, however, was to abjure responsibility for making sure instructional materials reflected the diversity of the student body. Interviews with teachers suggested that many saw no reason to try to locate or develop instructional materials that reflected African Americans' participation in and contributions to our society. For example, one math teacher who used a book in which all individuals in the illustrations were White contended that "math is math" and that an interview question about the use of multicultural materials was irrelevant to his subject matter. Perhaps more surprisingly, similar claims were made by other teachers, including some who taught reading, language arts, and social studies.

The colorblind perspective and its corollaries not only made it more likely that individual teachers would ignore the challenge of trying to present all students with materials that related in motivating ways to their own experiences, but they actually led to a constriction of the education provided to students. For example, in a lesson on the social organization of ancient Rome, one social studies teacher discussed at length the various classes in Roman society, including the patricians and plebeians, but avoided all reference to slaves. Another teacher included George Washington Carver on a list of great Americans from whom students could pick individuals to learn about but specifically decided not to mention that Carver was African American for fear of raising racial issues. In the best of all worlds, there would be no need to make such mention because the students would have had no preconception that famous people are generally White. However, in a school in which a White child was surprised to learn from a member of my research team that Martin Luther King, Jr., was African American, not White, highlighting the accomplishments of African Americans and encouraging students not to assume famous figures are White are reasonable practices.

Such constriction based on a desire to avoid racial problems is not unique at Wexler. For example, Scherer and Slawski (1979) report that a desegregated high school they studied eliminated the lunch hour and study halls to minimize the sort of loosely supervised contact between students that seemed to be likely to lead to conflict. However, the nature of the constriction at Wexler was influenced by the colorblind perspective and its corollaries. At Wexler, the tendency was to ignore or avoid certain topics. Such a tendency, while undeniably a low-risk one, failed to take advantage of the diversity of experiences and perspectives of Wexler's students as a resource for the educational process. Furthermore, in some cases, it literally distorted the education all students received as teachers attempted to avoid potentially controversial facts or issues.

CONCLUSIONS

Since Supreme Court Justice Harlan first spoke of a colorblind society as a goal to be striven for more than 100 years ago, the colorblind approach has often been held up as a needed antidote to the virulent racism in our society that traditionally consigned certain individuals to subordinate positions on the basis of their color and their color alone. However, this chapter takes the position that the colorblind perspective is not without some dangers. It may ease initial tensions and minimize the frequency of overt conflict. Nonetheless, it can also foster such phenomena as the taboo against ever mentioning race or connected issues and the refusal to recognize and deal with the existence of intergroup tensions. Thus, it fosters an environment in which aversive racists, who are basically well intentioned, are prone to act in a discriminatory manner. In addition, it can foster lack of recognition of problems that might be dealt with constructively if they were acknowledged. Further, the colorblind perspective makes it unlikely that the opportunities inherent in a pluralistic institution will be fully realized and that the challenge facing such an institution of providing all its students with an engaging and effective education will be met.

Although the colorblind approach clearly has many disadvantages, this finding does not lead to the conclusion that it is best to constantly call students' attention to group membership. There are several reasons to be wary of an unrelenting emphasis on group membership, and especially on group differences. First, there is substantial evidence that liking of others is enhanced by the perception of similarity (Berscheid & Reis, 1998), so a constant emphasis on difference is likely to be unproductive. Second, an emerging body of research about a phenomenon called stereotype threat also suggests that it may be unwise to make race constantly salient (Alexander & Schofield, in press; Aronson & Good, 2002; Aronson & Steele, 2005). For example, researchers studying this phenomenon have found that merely raising the issue of race by having students indicate their group membership before completing a task can lead to markedly decreased performance by African American students on tasks relevant to existing negative stereotypes about their ability (Steele & Aronson, 1995). Further, a large body of social psychological research mentioned earlier in this chapter has demonstrated that categorization of individuals into in-groups and out-groups tends to promote stereotyping and biased behavior.

What, then, is likely to be the most effective stance for schools to take? A full answer to this question would be an entire chapter in itself. However, I would suggest that at least three things are highly desirable. First, the education system needs to make a concerted effort to be responsive to our society's diversity in planning curriculum, in making staffing choices, and in thinking about how best to serve students. This seems likely to help make schools institutions that students from different backgrounds can feel engaged with and connected to, in addition to providing them with the breadth of information and perspectives necessary to function effectively in our increasingly diverse society. Second, schools need to help students and teachers see that groups are composed of individuals with their own unique characteristics who may be both similar to and different from those in both their in-group and in out-groups, which should help undercut the tendency to stereotype and to see group membership as defining an individual's characteristics. Finally, schools should provide students with opportunities to build meaningful shared identities as members of the school, the community, and the nation that complement and supplement, rather than replace or undermine, their identities as members of specific social groups.

Acknowledgments

The author expresses her deep appreciation to the students and staff of Wexler School. The research on which this chapter is based was funded by the author's contract with the National Institute of Education (Contract 400–76–0011). Other expenses relating to the chapter's preparation were covered by the Learning Research and Development Center, which was partly funded by the NIE when this research was conducted. However, all opinions expressed herein are solely those of the author, and no endorsement of the ideas by the NIE is implied or intended.

Questions and Activities

1. According to the author, how does the social context influence the expression of racism and discrimination?

2. What is the *colorblind perspective?* Give some examples of it. On what major beliefs and assumptions is it based?

3. In what ways does the colorblind perspective contribute to racial discrimination and institutionalized racism in schools? Give specific examples.

4. How does the colorblind perspective often lead to what the author calls a "misrepresentation of reality"? Which realities are often misrepresented by the colorblind perspective?

5. Why did the teachers at Wexler deny that they were aware of the race of their students? What were some consequences of their denial? How was their denial inconsistent with many realities related to race in the school?

6. What did the interviews with Wexler students reveal about their conceptions of race? How did their conceptions of race differ from those of the teachers? Why?

7. Why do teachers often embrace the colorblind perspective? According to the author, what are its benefits and costs?

8. How does the colorblind perspective make it easier for liberal White teachers to discriminate? Give specific examples from this chapter and from your own observations and experiences in schools and in other settings and contexts.

9. How does the colorblind perspective negatively affect the development of a multicultural curriculum? What are the most promising ways to counteract the colorblind perspective? Give specific examples.

References

Aboud, F. E., & Doyle, A. B. (1996). Does Talk of Race Foster Prejudice or Tolerance in Children? *Canadian Journal of Behavioral Science, 28*(3), 161–170.

Aboud, F. E., & Fenwick, V. (1999). Exploring and Evaluating School-Based Interventions to Reduce Prejudice. *Journal of Social Issues, 55*(4), 767–785.

Alexander, K., & Schofield, J. W. (in press). Stereotype Threat and the Achievement Gap. In J. W. Schofield, *Minority-group Membership, Migration Background and Academic Achievement: Research Evidence from Social, Developmental and Educational Psychology*. Berlin: Wissenschaftszentrum Berlin für Sozialforschung.

Allport, G. W. (1954). *The Nature of Prejudice*. Cambridge, MA: Addison-Wesley.

Amir, Y. (1976). The Role of Intergroup Contact in Change of Prejudice and Ethnic Relations. In P. A. Katz (Ed.), *Towards the Elimination of Racism* (pp. 245–308). New York: Pergamon.

Aronson, J. A., & Good, C. (2002). The Development and Consequences of Stereotype Vulnerability in Adolescents. In F. Pajares & T. Urdan (Eds.), *Academic Motivation of Adolescents* (pp. 299–330). Greenwich, CT: Information Age Publishing.

Aronson, E., & Patnoe, S. (1997). *The Jigsaw Classroom* (2nd ed.). New York: Longman.

Aronson, J., & Steele, C. M. (2005). Stereotypes and the Fragility of Academic Competence, Motivation, and Self-Concept. In A. J. Elliot & C. S. Dweck (Eds.), *Handbook of Competence and Motivation* (pp. 436–460). New York: The Guilford Press.

Banks, J. A. (2005). Multicultural Education: Characteristics and Goals. In J. A. Banks & C. A. M. Banks (Eds.), *Multicultural Education: Issues & Perspectives* (5th ed., pp. 3–30). New York: Wiley.

Bennett, W. (1987). *James Madison High School: A Curriculum for American Students*. Washington, DC: U.S. Department of Education.

Berscheid, E., & Reis, H. T. (1998). Attraction and Close Relationships. In D. T. Gilbert, S. T. Fiske, & G. Lindzey (Eds.), *The Handbook of Social Psychology* (4th ed., pp. 193–281). New York: McGraw-Hill.

Bogdan, R. C., & Taylor, S. J. (1975). *Introduction to Qualitative Research Methods: A Phenomenological Approach to the Social Sciences*. New York: Wiley.

Bonilla-Silva, E. (2003). *Racism Without Racists: Color-blind Racism and the Persistence of Racial Inequality in the United States*. New York: Rowman and Littlefield.

Bossert, S. T. (1988/89). Cooperative Activities in the Classroom. In E. Z. Rothkopt (Ed.), *Review of Research in Education* (Vol. 15, pp. 225–250). Washington, DC: American Educational Research Association.

Brewer, M. B., & Brown, R. J. (1998). Intergroup Relations. In D. T. Gilbert, S. T. Fiske, & G. Lindzey (Eds.), *The Handbook of Social Psychology* (4th ed., pp. 554–594). New York: McGraw-Hill.

Brewer, M. B., & Miller, N. (1984). Beyond the Contact Hypothesis: Theoretical Perspectives on Desegregation. In N. Miller & M. B. Brewer (Eds.), *Groups in Contact: The Psychology of Desegregation* (pp. 281–302). Orlando, FL: Academic Press.

Brewer, M. B., & Miller, N. (1988). Contact and Cooperation: When Do They Work? In P. A. Katz & D. A. Taylor (Eds.), *Eliminating Racism: Profiles in Controversy* (pp. 315–328). New York: Plenum.

Brown, R. (1995). *Prejudice: Its Social Psychology*. Oxford, UK: Blackwell.

Campbell, D. T. (1975). Degrees of Freedom and the Case Study. *Comparative Political Studies, 8*(2), 178–193.

Carter, R. T., & Goodwin, A. L. (1994). Racial Identity and Education. In L. Darling-Hammond (Ed.), *Review of Research in Education* (pp. 291–336). Washington, DC: American Educational Research Association.

Clement, D. C., Eisenhart, M., & Harding, J. R. (1979). The Veneer of Harmony: Social-Race Relations in a Southern Desegregated School. In R. C. Rist (Ed.), *Desegregated Schools* (pp. 15–62). New York: Academic Press.

Cohen, E. G. (1975). The Effects of Desegregation on Race Relations. *Law and Contemporary Problems, 39*(2), 271–299.

Cohen, E. G. (1997). Understanding Status Problems: Sources and Consequences. In E. G. Cohen & R. A. Lotan (Eds.), *Working for Equity in Heterogeneous Classrooms: Sociological Theory in Practice* (pp. 61–76). New York: Teachers College Press.

Cohen, E., Lockheed, M., & Lohman, M. (1976). The Center for Interracial Cooperation: A Field Experiment. *Sociology of Education, 49*, 47–58.

Cook, S. W. (1969). Motives in the Conceptual Analysis of Attitude-Related Behavior. In W. J. Arnold & D. Levine (Eds.), *Nebraska Symposium on Motivation* (Vol. 17, pp. 179–235). Lincoln: University of Nebraska Press.

Cook, S. W. (1978). Interpersonal and Attitudinal Outcomes in Cooperating Interracial Groups. *Journal of Research and Development in Education, 12*(1), 97–113.

Cook, S. W. (1985). Experimenting on Social Issues: The Case of School Desegregation. *American Psychologist, 40*, 452–460.

Cook, T., & Campbell, D. (1976). The Design and Conduct of Quasi-Experiments and True Experiments in Field Settings. In M. Dunnette (Ed.), *Handbook of Organizational Psychology* (pp. 223–281). Chicago: Rand McNally.

Davis, F. (1961). Deviance Disavowal: The Management of Strained Interaction by the Visibly Handicapped. In H. S. Becker (Ed.), *The Other Side: Perspectives on Deviance* (pp. 119–137). New York: Free Press.

Devine, P. G. (1989). Stereotyping and Prejudice: Their Automatic and Controlled Components. *Journal of Personality and Social Psychology, 56*, 5–18.

Dovidio, J. F., & Gaertner, S. L. (1998). On the Nature of Contemporary Prejudice: The Causes, Consequences, and Challenges of Aversive Racism. In J. L. Eberhardt & S. T. Fiske (Eds.), *Confronting Racism: The Problem and the Response* (pp. 3–32). Thousand Oaks, CA: Sage.

Dovidio, J. F., Gaertner, S. L., Voulidzic, A., Matoka, A., Johnson, B., & Frazier, S. (1997). Extending the Benefits of Recategorization: Evaluations, Self-Disclosure, and Helping. *Journal of Experimental Social Psychology, 33*, 401–420.

Duncan, B. L. (1976). Differential Racial Perception and Attribution of Intergroup Violence. *Journal of Personality and Social Psychology, 35*, 590–598.

Eaton, S. E. (2001). *The Other Boston Busing Story*. New Haven, CT: Yale University Press.

Fazio, R. H., Jackson, J. R., Dunton, B. C., & Williams, C. J. (1995). Variability in Automatic Activation as Unobtrusive Measure of Racial Attitudes: A Bona Fide Pipeline? *Journal of Personality and Social Psychology, 69*, 1013–1027.

Fiske, S. T., & Neuberg, S. L. (1990). A Continuum of Impression Formation, from Category-Based to Individuating Processes: Influences of Information and Motivation on Attention and Interpretation. In M. P. Zanna (Ed.), *Advances in Experimental Social Psychology* (Vol. 23, pp. 1–74). New York: Academic Press.

Gaertner, S. L., & Dovidio, J. F. (1986). The Aversive Form of Racism. In J. F. Dovidio & S. L. Gaertner (Eds.), *Prejudice, Discrimination, and Racism* (pp. 61–89). Orlando, FL: Academic Press.

Gaertner, S. L., & Dovidio, J. F. (2005). Understanding and Addressing Contemporary Racism: From Adversive Racism to the Common Ingroup Identity Model. *Journal of Social Issues, 61*(3), 615–639.

Gaertner, S. L., Dovidio, J. F., Anastasio, P. A., Bachman, B. A., & Rust, M. C. (1993). The Common Ingroup Identity Model: Recategorization and the Reduction of Intergroup Bias. In W. Stroebe & M. Hewstone (Eds.), *European Review of Social Psychology* (pp. 1–26). Chichester, UK: Wiley.

Gaertner, S. L., Rust, M. C., Dovidio, J. F., Bachman, B. A., & Anastasio, P. A. (1994). The Contact Hypothesis: The Role of a Common Ingroup Identity on Reducing Intergroup Bias. *Small Group Research, 25*(2), 224–249.

Gillborn, D. (1992). Citizenship, Race, and the Hidden Curriculum. *International Studies in Sociology of Education, 2*(1), 57–73.

Goetz, J. P., & Breneman, E. (1988). Desegregation and Black Students' Experiences in Two Rural Southern Elementary Schools. *The Elementary School Journal, 88*(3), 489–502.

Gotanda, N. (1991). A Critique of "Our Constitution is Color-blind." *Stanford Law Review, 44*, 1–68.

Guinier, L., & Torres, G. (2002). *The Miner's Canary: Enlisting Race, Resisting Power, Transforming Democracy.* Cambridge, MA: Harvard University Press.

Heath, S. B. (1982). Questioning at Home and at School: A Comparative Study. In G. Spindler (Ed.), *Doing the Ethnography of Schooling: Educational Anthropology in Action* (pp. 102–131). New York: Holt, Rinehart & Winston.

Hewstone, M., & Brown, R. (Eds.). (1986). *Contact and Conflict in Intergroup Encounters.* Oxford, UK: Blackwell.

Hill, J. (1971). *Personalized Education Programs Utilizing Cognitive Style Mapping.* Bloomfield Hills, MI: Oakland Community College Press.

Hirsch, E. D. (1996). *The Schools We Need, and Why We Don't Have Them.* New York: Doubleday.

Irvine, J. J. (1990). *Black Students and School Failure: Policies, Practices, and Prescriptions.* Westport, CT: Greenwood.

Irvine, J. J. (1991, January). Culturally Responsive and Responsible Pedagogy: The Inclusion of Culture, Research, and Reflection in the Knowledge Base of Teacher Education. Paper presented at the annual meeting of the American Association of Colleges for Teacher Education, Atlanta.

Jaynes, G. D., & Williams, R. M., Jr. (1989). *A Common Destiny: Blacks and the American Society.* Washington, D.C.: National Academy Press.

Jervis, K. (1996). How Come There Are No Brothers on That List? Hearing the Hard Questions All Children Ask. *Harvard Educational Review, 66*(3), 546–576.

Johnson, D. W., & Johnson, R. T. (1982). The Study of Cooperative, Competitive, and Individualistic Situations: State of the Area and Two Recent Contributions. *Contemporary Education: A Journal of Reviews, 1*(1), 7–13.

Johnson, D. W., Johnson, R. T., & Maruyama, G. (1984). Goal Interdependence and Interpersonal Attraction in Heterogeneous Classrooms: A Meta-Analysis. In N. Miller & M. B. Brewer (Eds.), *Groups in Contact: The Psychology of Desegregation* (pp. 187–212). Orlando, FL: Academic Press.

Johnson, D. W., Maruyama, G., Johnson, R. T., Nelson, D., & Skon, L., (1981). Effects of Cooperative, Competitive, and Individualistic Goal Structures on Achievement: A Meta-Analysis. *Psychological Bulletin, 89*, 47–62.

Jones, J. M. (1986). Racism: A Cultural Analysis of the Problem. In J. F. Dovidio & S. L. Gaertner (Eds.), *Prejudice, Discrimination, and Racism* (pp. 279–313). Orlando, FL: Academic Press.

Jones, J. M. (1997). *Prejudice and Racism* (2nd ed.). New York: McGraw-Hill.

Jones, J. M. (1998). Psychological Knowledge and the New American Dilemma of Race. *Journal of Social Issues, 54*(4), 645.

Katz, I., Wackenhut, J., & Hass, R. G. (1986). Racial Ambivalence, Value Duality, and Behavior. In J. F. Dovidio & S. L. Gaertner (Eds.), *Prejudice, Discrimination, and Racism* (pp. 35–59). Orlando, FL: Academic Press.

Katz, P. A. (1976). The Acquisition of Racial Attitudes. In P. Katz (Ed.), *Toward the Elimination of Racism* (pp. 125–156). New York: Pergamon.

Kochman, T. (1981). *Black and White Styles of Conflict*. Chicago: University of Chicago Press.

Larson, C. L., & Ovando, C. J. (2001). The Color of Bureaucracy: The Politics of Equity in Multicultural School Communities. Belmont, CA: Wadsworth/Thomson Learning.

Lee, C. D., & Slaughter-Defoe, D. T. (2004). Historical and Sociocultural Influences on African American Education. In J. A. Banks & C. A. M. Banks (Eds.), *Handbook of Research on Multicultural Education* (2nd ed., pp. 462–490). San Francisco: Jossey-Bass.

Lee, Y. T., & Duenas, G. (1995). Stereotype Accuracy in Multicultural Business. In Y. T. Lee, L. J. Jussim, & C. R. McCauley (Eds.), *Stereotype Accuracy: Toward Appreciating Group Differences* (pp. 157–188). Washington, DC: American Psychological Association.

Levin, S. (2003). Social Psychological Evidence on Race and Racism. In M. J. Chang, D. Witt, J. Jones, & K. Hakuta (Eds.), *Compelling Interest: Examining the Evidence on Racial Dynamics in Colleges and Universities* (pp. 97–125). Stanford, CA: Stanford University Press.

Malpass, R. S., & Kravitz, J. (1969). Recognition for Faces of Own and Other Races. *Journal of Personality and Social Psychology, 13,* 330–334.

Miles, M. B., & Huberman, A. M. (1984). *Qualitative Data Analysis: A Sourcebook of New Methods.* Newbury Park, CA: Sage.

Nieto, S. (2004). *Affirming Diversity: The Sociopolitical Context of Multicultural Education* (4th ed.). Boston: Allyn & Bacon.

Norvell, N., & Worchel, S. (1981). A Reexamination of the Relation between Equal Status Contact and Intergroup Attraction. *Journal of Personality and Social Psychology, 41,* 902–908.

Olson, S. (1976). *Ideas and Data: Process and Practice of Social Research.* Homewood, IL: Dorsey.

Pettigrew, T. (1986). The Intergroup Contact Hypothesis Reconsidered. In M. Hewstone & R. Brown (Eds.), *Contact and Conflict in Intergroup Encounters* (pp. 169–195). Oxford, UK: Blackwell.

Pettigrew, T. F. (1998). Intergroup Contact Theory. *Annual Review of Psychology, 49,* 65–85.

Pettigrew, T. F., & Tropp, L. R. (2000). Does Intergroup Contact Reduce Prejudice: Recent Meta-Analytic Findings. In S. Oskamp (Ed.), *The Claremont Symposium on Applied Social Psychology* (pp. 93–114). Mahwah, NJ: Erlbaum.

Pettigrew, T. F. (2004). Intergroup Contact. In J. A. Banks & C. A. M. Banks (Eds.), *Handbook of Research on Multicultural Education* (2nd ed., pp. 770–781). San Francisco: Jossey-Bass.

Pollock, M. (2004). *Colormute: Race Talk Dilemmas in an American School.* Princeton, NJ: Princeton University Press.

Ramsey, P. G. (1987). *Teaching and Learning in a Diverse World.* New York: Teachers College Press.

Randolph, G., Landis, D., & Tzeng, O. C. S. (1977). The Effects of Time and Practice on Cultural Assimilator Training. *International Journal of Intercultural Relations, 1,* 105–119.

Regents of the University of California *vs.* Baake, 76–811 U.S. (1978).

Richeson, J. A., & Nussbaum, R. J. (2003). The Impact of Multiculturalism versus Colorblindness on Racial Bias. *Journal of Experimental Social Psychology, 40,* 417–423.

Riordan, C. (1978). Equal-Status Interracial Contact: A Review and Revision of the Concept. *International Journal of Intercultural Relations, 2*(2), 161–185.

Rist, R. C. (1974). Race, Policy, and Schooling. *Society, 12*(1), 59–63.

Rist, R. C. (1978). *The Invisible Children: School Integration in American Society*. Cambridge, MA: Harvard University Press.

Sagar, H. A., & Schofield, J. W. (1980). Racial and Behavioral Cues in Black and White Children's Perceptions of Ambiguously Aggressive Acts. *Journal of Personality and Social Psychology*, *39*(4), 590–598.

Sagar, H. A., & Schofield, J. W. (1984). Integrating the Desegregated School: Problems and Possibilities. In M. Maehr & D. Bartz (Eds.), *Advances in Motivation and Achievement: A Research Annual* (pp. 203–241). Greenwich, CT: JAI Press.

Sagar, H. A., Schofield, J. W., & Snyder, H. N. (1983). Race and Gender Barriers: Preadolescent Peer Behavior in Academic Classrooms. *Child Development*, *54*, 1032–1040.

Scherer, J., & Slawski, E. J. (1979). Color, Class, and Social Control in an Urban Desegregated School. In R. C. Rist (Ed.), *Desegregated Schools* (pp. 117–153). New York: Academic Press.

Schlesinger, A. M. (1992). *The Disuniting of America: Reflections on a Multicultural Society*. New York: Norton.

Schofield, J. W. (1979). The Impact of Positively Structured Contact on Intergroup Behavior: Does It Last under Adverse Conditions? *Social Psychology Quarterly*, *42*(3), 280–284.

Schofield, J. W. (1980). Cooperation as Social Exchange: Resource Gaps and Reciprocity in Academic Work. In S. Sharon, P. Hare, C. Webb, & R. Hertz-Lazarowitz (Eds.), *Cooperation in Education* (pp. 160–181). Provo, UT: Brigham Young University Press.

Schofield, J. W. (1989). *Black and White in School: Trust, Tension or Tolerance?* New York: Teachers College Press.

Schofield, J. W. (2001). Improving Intergroup Relations among Students. In J. A. Banks & C. A. M. Banks (Eds.), *Handbook of Research on Multicultural Education* (pp. 635–645). San Francisco: Jossey-Bass.

Schofield, J. W., & Eurich-Fulcer, R. (2001). When and How School Desegregation Improves Intergroup Relations. In R. Brown & S. Gaertner (Eds.), *Handbook of Social Psychology* (Vol. 4, pp. 474–494). New York: Blackwell.

Schofield, J. W., & Francis, W. D. (1982). An Observational Study of Peer Interaction in Racially-Mixed "Accelerated" Classrooms. *Journal of Educational Psychology*, *74*(5), 722–732.

Schofield, J. W., & Sagar, H. A. (1977). Peer Interaction Patterns in an Integrated Middle School. *Sociometry*, *40*(2), 130–138.

Schofield, J. W., & Sagar, H. A. (1979). The Social Context of Learning in an Interracial School. In R. Rist (Ed.), *Inside Desegregated Schools: Appraisals of an American Experiment* (pp. 155–199). San Francisco: Academic Press.

Schofield, J. W., & Whitley, B. E. (1983), Peer Nomination versus Rating Scale Measurement of Children's Peer Preferences. *Social Psychology Quarterly*, *46*(3), 242–251.

Sharan, S. (1980). Cooperative Learning in Teams: Recent Methods and Effects on Achievement, Attitudes and Ethnic Relations. *Review of Educational Research*, *50*(2), 241–272.

Sherif, M. (1979). Superordinate Goals in the Reduction of Intergroup Conflict: An Experimental Evaluation. In W. G. Austin & S. Worchel (Eds.), *The Social Psychology of Intergroup Relations* (pp. 257–261). Monterey, CA: Brooks/Cole.

Sidanius, J., & Pratto, F. (1999). *Social Dominance: An Intergroup Theory of Social Hierarchy and Oppression*. Port Chester, NY: Cambridge University Press.

Slavin, R. E. (1995). *Cooperative Learning: Theory, Research, and Practice* (2nd ed.). Boston: Allyn & Bacon.

Slavin, R. E., & Cooper, R. (1999). Improving Intergroup Relations: Lessons Learned from Cooperative Learning Programs. *Journal of Social Issues, 55*(4), 647–663.

Sleeter, C. E. (1993). How White Teachers Construct Race. In C. McCarthy & W. Crichlow (Eds.), *Race Identity and Representation in Education* (pp. 157–171). New York: Routledge.

Snyder, M. L., Kleck, R. E., Strenta, A., & Mentzer, S. J. (1979). Avoidance of the Handicapped: An Attributional Ambiguity Analysis. *Journal of Personality and Social Psychology, 12,* 2297–2306.

Steele, C. M., & Aronson, J. (1995). Stereotype Threat and the Intellectual Test Performance of African Americans. *Journal of Personality and Social Psychology, 69*(5), 797–811.

Stephan, W. G., & Stephan, C. W. (1985). Intergroup Anxiety. *Journal of Social Issues, 41*(3), 157–175.

Stephan, W. G., & Stephan, C. W. (1996). *Intergroup Relations.* Boulder, CO: Westview.

Stephan, W. G., & Stephan, C. W. (2001). *Improving Intergroup Relations.* Thousand Oaks, CA: Sage.

Strauss, A. (1987). *Qualitative Analysis for Social Scientists.* New York: Cambridge University Press.

Strauss, A., & Corbin, J. (1990). *Basics of Qualitative Research.* Newbury Park, CA: Sage.

Tajfel, H. (1978). *Differentiation between Social Groups: Studies in the Social Psychology of Intergroup Relations.* New York: Academic Press.

Takaki, R. (1993). *A Different Mirror: A History of Multicultural America.* Boston: Little, Brown.

Taylor, S., Fiske, S., Etcoff, N., & Ruderman, A. (1978). Categorical and Contextual Basis of Person Memory and Stereotyping. *Journal of Personality and Social Psychology, 36*(7), 778–793.

Trent, W., Owens-Nicholson, D., Eatman, T., Burke, M., Daugherty, J., & Norman, K. (2003). Justice, Equality of Educational Opportunity, and Affirmative Action in Higher Education. In M. J. Chang, D. Witt, J. Jones, & K. Hakuta (Eds.), *Compelling Interest: Examining the Evidence on Racial Dynamics in Colleges and Universities* (pp. 22–48). Stanford, CA: Stanford University Press.

Triandis, H. C. (Ed.). (1976). *Variations in Black and White Perceptions of the Social Environment.* Urbana: University of Illinois Press.

Triandis, H. C. (1994). *Culture and Social Behavior.* New York: McGraw-Hill.

Triandis, H. C., Vassiliou, V., Vassiliou, G., Tanaka, Y., & Shanmugam, A. (Eds.). (1972). *The Analysis of Subjective Culture.* Hoboken': Wiley.

Webb, E. J., Campbell, D. T., Schwartz, R. D., & Sechrest, L. (1966). *Unobtrusive Measures: Nonreactive Research in the Social Sciences.* Chicago: Rand McNally.

Whitley, B. E., & Schofield, J. W. (1984). Peer Preference in Desegregated Classrooms: A Round Robin Analysis. *Journal of Personality and Social Psychology, 46*(4), 799–810.

Williams, P. J. (1998). *Seeing a Colorblind Future: The Paradox of Race.* New York: Noonday Press.

Wolsko, C., Park, B., Judd, C., & Wittenbrink, B. (2000). Framing Interethnic Ideology: Effects of Multicultural and Color-Blind Perspectives on Judgments of Groups and Individuals. *Journal of Personality and Social Psychology, 78*(4), 635–654.

Yinger, J. M. (1994). *Ethnicity: Source of Strength? Source of Conflict?* Albany: State University of New York Press.

CHAPTER 12

Language Diversity and Schooling

Tom T. Stritikus
Manka M. Varghese

Cuando eres un inmigrante, muchas puertas están cerradas. Pues, si, algunas, algunas, están abiertas—pero están escondidas. Sin ayuda, no puedo encontrarlas.

When you are an immigrant, many doors are closed. Well, yes, some, some are open—but they are hidden. Without help, I can't find them.

Edgar
(Stritikus, 2004)

Edgar is a 15-year-old immigrant student from Mexico. He had been in the United States for five months when he was asked by a researcher to talk about what he hoped to accomplish by attending school in the United States (Stritikus, 2004). Rather than focus on his career goals or his educational plans after high school, Edgar highlighted the limited educational opportunities he believed characterized his new life in the United States. Although Edgar had only been in the United States for a limited time, he had already developed a keen sense of the social, cultural, and linguistic barriers to his success. Unfortunately, Edgar's reality is shared by many immigrant students for whom the doors of educational opportunity remain obscured and closed. In this chapter, we consider what schools and teachers can do to better assist linguistically diverse students like Edgar.

As typical teachers look at the students in their classrooms, they see dramatic differences from the classrooms of their youth. Today two in five students in the United States are from an ethnically or racially diverse group; one in seven speaks a language other than English at home, and one in fifteen is born outside of the United States (National Center for Education Statistics [NCES], 2002). Linguistic and cultural diversity are now standard facets of our schools. By 2026, demographers estimate that one in four students will come from homes in which English is not the primary language spoken (Garcia, 1999).

When considering linguistic diversity, it is also important to take into consideration cultural and linguistic groups who do not immediately come to mind; these include African Americans and indigenous populations. Many African Americans are 'bidialectal'—that is, they are speakers of Ebonics and Standard English, and issues of language diversity have shaped their school experience in important ways (Baugh, 1999; Smitherman, 2000). Indigenous groups, such as American Indian, Alaskan Native, and Native Hawaiian contribute significantly to linguistic diversity, representing speakers of about 175 indigenous languages and various varieties of English (Krauss, 1998). In this chapter, we briefly examine some of the legal, linguistic, and programmatic issues surrounding the education of these groups. Space considerations do not allow us to present a full discussion of their experiences in U.S. schools.

Unfortunately, schools have fallen short in meeting the needs of linguistically diverse students. In key academic indicators such as standardized test scores, graduation rates, and retention, immigrant students are trailing their native English-speaking peers (Rumberger & Gandara, 2004; Garcia, 1999; Kindler, 2002). To understand how schools can better meet the needs of linguistically diverse students, we begin this chapter by taking a closer look at the linguistically diverse population in the United States. Then, to understand the legal obligations of schools in meeting the needs of linguistically diverse students, we examine important events in the legal, policy, and judicial history of linguistically diverse students in the United States. Next, we consider various programmatic responses to linguistic diversity and their efficacy in meeting the needs of linguistically diverse students. We conclude the chapter with a discussion of how teachers might better respond to the needs of immigrant students. We now turn to an examination of one of the primary sources of linguistic diversity, immigration, and consider how increased immigration influences U.S. schools.

THE IMMIGRANT POPULATION IN THE UNITED STATES

Immigration continues to be one of the primary sources for linguistic diversity in the United States. Foreign-born residents now make up a larger percentage of the U.S. population than any other time since the great waves of immigration in the early 1900s (U.S. Census Bureau, 2001). Because of restrictive immigration laws, most immigrants who came to the United States between 1880 and 1930 were from Europe. Changes to immigration law during the 1960s resulted in a steady increase of immigrants from Latin America, Southeast Asia, the Caribbean, and Africa. While immigration has a tremendous impact on all of American life, nowhere has this been more keenly felt than in U.S. public schools.

Historical immigration to the United States has played a significant role in shaping current perceptions of today's immigrants. The opinions that Americans have about the current wave of immigrants are shaped in part by their views of the earlier waves of immigrants—perceptions influenced by both fact and fiction. Several key differences and similarities exist between the experiences of the immigrants who came at the turn of the 20th century and those who are coming today. Understanding these differences is an important way for teachers working with linguistically diverse students to fully understand the reality faced by immigrant populations.

Despite the common perception to the contrary, the immigrants who came at the turn of the last century did not experience universal success in school. In major cities like Boston,

Chicago, and New York, the graduation and school continuation rates of Southern Italian, Polish, and Russian Jewish children lagged far behind native-born "White" students (Olneck & Lazerson, 1974). Newcomers to the United States have always been marked in someway by the existing population. Many of the same negative discourses about today's immigrants took place when older groups of immigrants came to the United States. The Italians, Jewish, and Irish immigrants of the early twentieth century faced significant social, political, and cultural barriers (Jacobson, 1998). Despite these realities, today's immigration debates are often cast in terms of how the older immigrants were more easily absorbed and more beneficial to American society than the Latin American, Asian, and African immigrants today. A helpful concept for understanding the tensions faced by immigrant groups is the concept of ethnic succession, which explains that new immigrants are rarely viewed as positively as the groups that came before them (Banks, 2005).

While there are similarities between the issues faced by "old" and "new" immigrants, there are important differences as well. The current wave of immigration draws immigrants from several regions of the world which were not a major part of the last wave of immigration. In recent years, scholars from various disciplines have claimed that world economies and societies have become increasingly interconnected through advances in technology, media, and mass transit, all of which facilitate the movement of people, goods, services, and ideas. This new phenomena has been called globalization, borderless economies, and/or the transnational era (Castles, 2003). One of the characteristics of globalization is the increased flow of people across the planet. While some people voluntarily migrate in order to improve their lives, others are forced to migrate in order to survive (Suarez-Orozco & Suarez-Orozco, 2003). Social scientists (Portes, 1996; Suarez-Orozco, 1997) have argued that immigration and its role in providing both cheap unskilled labor and highly technically skilled labor are key components of the new transnational era that the world's societies have entered.

The back-and-forth movement of ideas and goods that characterizes the current transitional period also parallels the experience of many immigrant students. The experience of immigrant students has often been cast in terms of assimilation whereby immigrants eventually lose contact with their home communities and are slowly absorbed into their new locality. Departing from the traditional model of assimilation, scholars have argued that immigrants negotiate more complex patterns of social interaction in their new countries (Itzigsohn et al., 1999; Rose, 1997; Suarez-Orozco & Suarez-Orozco, 2003). In the current transnational era, some immigrant groups continue to have strong ties with their countries of origin once they reside in their receiving community. These ties influence immigrant children's socialization patterns and create social and cultural experiences that span transnational lines (Mahler, 1998; Portes, 1999; Smith & Guarnizo, 1998).

The mass movement of people and ideas has major consequences for educational issues in the United States. The current back-and-forth movement of ideas and people serves to replenish social and cultural practices (Garcia, 1999). While previous generations of immigrants did have some contact with their home countries, this was limited by the difficulty of travel and the lack of efficient communication. For current immigrant communities, ethnic media, telecommunications, and ease of travel can significantly change the nature of the communities in which they settle. This is often very difficult for the native-born population to accept, but the impact of current immigration on host communities is undeniable (Garcia, 1999). Thus, immigration must be viewed as a dynamic social phenomenon. Immigrants are both significantly changing the social context of new communities while simultaneously shaping the social realities in their home countries.

A second important factor shaping the immigrant experience is related to the current nature of U.S. society. The immigrant family enters a country that is economically, socially, and culturally distinct from the one faced by early waves of immigrants. Previous waves of immigrants arrived on the eve of a great expansion of the industrial economy. The manufacturing jobs which were created during the transition to a fully industrialized economy provided a possible entrée for immigrants to the middle class. However, not all immigrants had equal access to the economy and society. Gordon (1964) explains that earlier waves of immigrants who were members of racially diverse groups did not experience the same structural assimilation into U.S. society as did European immigrants.

Today's immigrants face many of the same issues related to structural assimilation as did older waves of immigrants. However, as Suarez-Orozco and Suarez-Orozco (2003) argue, today's economy—characterized by an hourglass shape—presents unique challenges for immigrant populations. At the top of the hourglass, highly skilled immigrants are moving into well-compensated, knowledge-based industries at an extremely high rate. At the other end of the hourglass, immigrant workers occupy the jobs that many U.S.-born workers are unwilling to take. Immigrants occupy a large part of the low-skilled, low-paid workers in the service, labor, and agriculture sectors. Unlike the jobs that were available to previous waves of immigrants, these jobs offer limited prospects for upward mobility (Suarez-Orozco & Suarez-Orozco, 2003).

Immigrants today are more diverse than ever, exhibiting a dramatic range in educational level, social class, and economic capital. Present immigrants are more likely than native-born populations to have family members who have graduated from college. At the same time, immigrant populations are more likely to have not graduated from high school than native-born populations (Rumbaut, 1997; Suarez-Orozco & Suarez-Orozco, 2003). This pattern of potential outcomes for immigrant students is further examined in Portes and Rambaut's (2001) discussion of *segmented assimilation*. Segmented assimilation explains three possible outcomes for immigrant families: (1) economic success with integration into the middle class; (2) permanent poverty and integration into the underclass; and (3) economic advancement with the deliberate maintenance of community values and practice. Each outcome is currently at work in the immigrant community. While a full discussion of the factors contributing to segmented assimilation is beyond the scope of this chapter, it is important for teachers to know that immigrant groups are demonstrating each outcome.

Socially, immigrants find themselves in a tenuous position. Opinion polls on immigration indicate that the native-born population sees recent immigrants as weakening the fabric of American society because they refuse to become Americanized like previous waves of immigrants. Many native-born Americans believe that immigrants take jobs away from them and represent a drain on social services and schools (Suarez-Orozco & Suarez-Orozco, 2003). Many scholars of immigration argue that the most salient difference between today's immigrants and the older waves of immigration is that they are people of color (Garcia, 1999; Olsen, 1997; Portes, 1996; Suarez-Orozco & Suarez-Orozco, 2003). Moreover, in the United States an "anti-immigrant" ideology exists that affects the way immigrants and refugees are perceived (Behdad, 1997; Castles & Davidson, 2000). Today's culturally and ethnically diverse immigrants enter a very racialized society that has historically sorted, classified, and excluded people based on the color of their skin. It is not as easy to eventually blend into "White America" as did the mostly European immigrants of the 1900s. Racial tensions in the United States make assimilation a problematic process for linguistically and ethnically diverse immigrants.

The social, political, and economic difficulties faced by immigrants make relocation to a new country an incredibly taxing experience. The culture and worldviews of individuals are often challenged or threatened when they come in contact with U.S. culture (Portes & Rumbaut, 1996). The dislocation and upheaval caused by immigration can be especially challenging for immigrant children. Lucas (1997) describes the experiences of immigrant students in U.S. schools as characterized by a number of critical transitions. She points out that all children experience important transitions in life: childhood to adolescence; home to school; middle to high school. However, as she correctly notes, immigrant students undergo these critical issues while adapting to a new language and culture.

The social context in which immigrant students begin their new lives must be considered to understand the experience of linguistically diverse students in schools. Suarez-Orozco and Suarez-Orozco (2003) argue that the "ethos of reception" —the social and cultural climate students experience in schools—is strongly influenced by society's views about immigration. Thus, the strongly negative attitudes toward immigrant students in U.S. society influence students' perceptions of U.S. schooling. These negative attitudes also significantly influence teacher and institutional expectations of immigrant students. Thus, the political, economic, and historical factors shaping immigration have a dramatic influence on the opportunities and experiences that immigrant students have in public schools.

Dramatic Growth in Linguistic Diversity in Schools

Federal government and state educational statistics reveal the number of immigrants in the United States who are receiving special services to learn English. The federal government uses the term *Limited English Proficient (LEP)* students to classify students who qualify for special services to learn English. However, many states and schools use the more positive designation of *English Language Learners (ELLs)*, which we use in this chapter. In the past decade, there has been a dramatic rise in the students classified as ELL. In 1999–2000, State Educational Agencies reported that 9.3 percent (4.5 million) of all U.S. schoolchildren were classified as ELL students. Since 1990, the growth rate for linguisticly diverse students has hovered at 10 percent per year. During the late 1990s, Kindler (2002) reports that the ELL student enrollment grew by 27 percent per year. The total number of ELL students in the United States is probably double the number reported by federal statistics, which have traditionally undercounted the total number of ELL students.

In school districts throughout the United States, immigrants from most nations in the world can be found. It is common for school districts to have 50–60 languages represented in their immigrant population. Despite this range of immigrants, nearly 90 percent of all immigrant students are from the following language groups: Spanish, Tagalog, Vietnamese, Chinese, and Hmong. Students from Latin America now represent nearly 85 percent of all ELL students in the United States (Kindler, 2002).

The languages listed above do not represent the vast diversity within the immigrant population. Students who speak Spanish as a first language come from countries throughout

Central and South America; to categorize them into one group is a simplification of their distinct characteristics. Even immigrants from within the same country exhibit immense degrees of diversity. Immigrants from Mexico might be speakers of indigenous languages from rural areas or élite educated individuals from large cities (Valdés, 2000). The diversity within Spanish speakers also exists among Asian immigrants. The above figures combine speakers of Chinese languages, which actually represent several distinct language groups. Chinese immigrants have enormous heterogeneity in education and socioeconomic status (Wong & Lopez, 2000). Students from Southeast Asia are often viewed as a group, which ignores the distinct cultural, social, and ethnic differences of students from Vietnam, Cambodia, and Laos (Chung, 2000; Lopez, 2000).

While linguistic diversity is a reality throughout the United States, the highest populations of ELL students are concentrated in a few states: California (1,480,527), Texas (554,949), Florida (235,181), New York (228,730), Illinois (143,855), and Arizona (125,311). While these states are currently and historically the most common places for immigrants to settle, almost all states have been affected by immigration. In fact, the largest increase in percentages of ELL students has been in what have been considered unlikely destinations for immigrants: South Carolina, Minnesota, Michigan, and Arkansas (Kindler, 2002).

Additional Sources of Linguistic Diversity—Dialect Variation and Indigenous Languages

Immigration is not the sole contributor to linguistic diversity. Along with multiple languages in the United States, dialect variation contributes to our diverse tapestry of language use. A *dialect* is a variation of a language characterized by distinct pronunciation, grammar, and vocabulary. Many linguists have posited that the distinction between a *language* and a *dialect* is often more political than linguistic. The famed M.I.T. linguist Noam Chomsky (2000) has often repeated the bon mot coined by Max Weinreich that a language is a dialect with an army and a navy. A common but less than perfect way of distinguishing a language from a dialect is the standard of mutual intelligibility.

Speakers of a different dialects are said to be able to understand each other while speakers of the different languages are not. However, what are considered dialects of some languages are so distinct that speakers cannot understand each other. Chinese has two major dialects—Cantonese and Mandarin—whose speakers have great difficulty in understanding each other. In contrast, speakers of the Scandinavian languages Danish, Norwegian, and Swedish are cable of understanding a great deal of each other's languages. Thus, it is important to note that the distinction between dialect and languages has more to do with political, social, and cultural factors than specific linguistic distinctions between the two.

Political and social factors surrounding dialect variation play out in language use in U.S. schools. Educational practices in the United States embrace the idea that Standard English should be the dominant variety of language used in all written and oral communication. Many linguists dispute the idea that a pure or standard form of a language exists in any other form but writing. Thus, standard English often is a term associated with the groups within a society that possess social or political power (Wolfram, Adger, & Christian, 1998). Because dialect variation tends to be associated with race, social class, and geographic region, the dialects of groups with less social power tend to be viewed as inferior or incorrect versions of standard

English. This is the case with Black English (BE), also referred to as African American Vernacular English, Ebonics (this term was coined by putting together the word "ebony" and "phonics"), and Black Dialect. Most linguists and sociolinguists recognize that however Black English is defined, it is a rule-governed language system linked to the identity of a specific community (Baugh, 1999; Labov, 1972; Smitherman, 2000). As Delpit (1998, p. 17) powerfully writes, "I can be neither for Ebonics or against Ebonics any more than I can be for or against air. It exists." Speakers of BE are also most likely speakers of other varieties of English, including Standard English. Thus, speakers of BE, like other speakers of dialects, are often bidialectal. Some of these students' educational experiences as speakers of Ebonics are discussed with regards to the Oakland school district case later in this chapter.

Another major source of linguistic diversity in the United States is indigenous populations. Although fewer and fewer of the 175 indigenous languages spoken by over 550 tribes are spoken by children, the heritage language is still the primary language for a large number of indigenous students (McCarty, 2002). Indigenous students do not have another homeland from which to garner support for learning and maintaining their language. The 1990 U.S. Census reported that more than one-third of American Indian and Alaskan Native languages have fewer than 100 speakers. Therefore, bilingual/bicultural schooling is critical for indigenous language maintenance, as it is for other linguistic and cultural groups. Most of the efforts in formal language maintenance for indigenous language groups have been directed at Hawaiian dialects and the languages of the Navajo and Pueblo nations in the U.S. Southwest. Attempts to use bilingual education to revitalize these languages have met with modest but important results (McCarty, 2002).

HISTORICAL AND LEGAL OVERVIEW OF LANGUAGE POLICY IN THE UNITED STATES

The next section of this chapter describes the legal and historical developments of linguistic diversity and language education. Understanding the historical evolution of language policy in the United States as well as the legal milestones for language minority students will help teachers understand the legal protections for these students and the ambivalent stance that the United States has had toward language policy historically. Overall, language policy in the United States has leaned toward supporting a transition into English. However, there has also been support of other languages and the rights of those speakers. In fact, there have been periods in U.S. history that have been more supportive of multilingualism than others.

Earlier History

In a society of immigrants, such as the United States, the school has always been the primary medium for acculturation and for unifying individuals of diverse cultures and backgrounds. Language has been perceived both as an important mechanism for achieving unity among Americans and a vehicle for the expression of individual rights (Del Valle, 2003). This ambivalence toward language policy can be found close to the inception of the nation state, when John Adams wanted to establish an American language academy "for refining, correcting, improving and ascertaining" (cited in Crawford, 1999, p. 20) the English language and establish it as the official language. Some leaders viewed Adams's position as an infringement of individual rights and opposed them.

As we stated earlier, it is impossible to discuss language policy and language education without examining the surrounding political and economic context (Skutnabb-Kangas, 1988). Language is integrally related to issues of identity, politics, and economics. Ricento (2003) contends that ethnic politics rather than the psychological benefits of bilingual education have always driven immigrant language policies. In order to demonstrate the links between language and politics in the United States, historians and linguists have referred most commonly to the case of German Americans and how the support for the German language decreased over time.

Numerically, Germans constituted the largest non–English-speaking population until the 1930s. Perlmann (1990) states that language preservation by Germans was tolerated by many politicians. This was because public officials had a need for their votes in local elections and for their numbers in the newly constituted public school system. However, there was widespread fear that German could supplant the dominance of the English language. The beginning of World War I provoked a larger anti-German sentiment that signaled an end of the support for maintenance of the German language. All states prohibited teaching in languages other than English from 1917 to 1923.

German citizen groups petitioned these laws in the courts, but found no remedy until the Supreme Court intervened in *Meyer vs. Nebraska* (1923). The circumstances of the case involved a private school teacher who had been convicted for teaching in German under the Nebraska law. The court ruled that the rights of the parents and the teachers were protected by the Fourteenth Amendment and overturned the teacher's conviction and the state ruling. Testifying to the ambivalent stance held by the United States on the language issue, the Supreme Court decided in subsequent court cases of the 1920s that requiring English to be the language of instruction in state schools and institutions was constitutional although impeding groups in their attempts to promote their native language was not.

Although the *Meyer (1923)* ruling offered some protection of language rights, many other policies in the United States provide examples of ethnic language suppression in the name of Americanization. These include: the policies following the Spanish-American War that prohibited the use of Spanish in the Philippines and Puerto Rico; the land and mining squabbles in California between Mexicanos and Anglos that set the grounds for suppressing Spanish; and the campaign to "civilize" indigenous tribes in the United States through the establishment of restrictive and racist boarding schools that contributed largely to the death of many indigenous languages and a loss of many of the rights of these groups (Crawford, 1999; Freeman, 1998).

Implementation of Federal Policy

The Bilingual Education Act (BEA), Title VII, signed into law by Lyndon Johnson, acted as legislation which sought to provide compensatory education for students who were both economically and linguistically disadvantaged in schools. From 1968 until 2002, Title VII provided funds for different types of programs for ELLs throughout the nation, including Transitional Bilingual Education (TBE) programs and two-way immersion programs; it also provided funding for program evaluators and researchers investigating these different types of programs. There were 30 two-way immersion programs in 1987 and 261 in 1999; most were supported by Title VII monies (Lindholm-Leary, 2001).

A large part of the BEA's inability to move toward a well-defined language policy was that law did not recommend a particular instructional approach; rather, it provided funding for development, training, and research of innovative approaches to the education of ELL students. While native language instruction was originally recommended, the BEA did not specify that it must be used (Wiese & Garcia, 1998). Since its inception, the primary aim of the BEA has been "providing meaningful and equitable access for English-language learners to the curriculum, rather than serving as an instrument of language policy for the nation through the development of their native languages" (August & Hakuta, 1997, p. 16). Echoing this, Wiese and Garcia (1998) argue that the BEA has aimed to address equal educational opportunity for language minority students and has not evolved as a language policy. Therefore, the BEA neither legislated for a particular language policy or instructional approach nor guaranteed the rights of ELL students based on language.

As a result, immigrant students and families have frequently turned to other courts. The U.S. Supreme Court's school desegregation decision, *Brown v. Board of Education*, the 1964 Civil Rights *Act* (Title VI), and the 1974 Equal Educational Opportunity Act (EEOA) have been used as a base to protect these students' rights. This protection has come through a safeguard of these students' other civil rights and their right to equal educational opportunities (Del Valle, 2003). In the prominent case of *Lau v. Nichols* (1974), Kinney Kinmon Lau and 12 Chinese American students on behalf of about 1,800 Chinese-speaking students filed a class-action suit against the San Francisco Unified School District stating that their children were not given equal educational opportunities because of the linguistic barriers they faced. In this landmark case, the San Francisco schools were found to be in violation of the rights of Chinese students under Title VI and EEOA. While lower courts disagreed with the parents, the Supreme Court overturned this ruling, finding "There is no equality of treatment merely by providing students with the same facilities, textbooks, teachers and curriculum; for students who do not understand English are effectively foreclosed from any meaningful education."

The legacy of Lau has created important contributions to the improvement of programs for ELL students, even if vague. Policy guidelines, which were followed by the Office of Civil Rights (OCR) were put together in the LAU remedies in 1975 for school districts' compliance with the Title VI requirements upheld in the *Lau* decision. These have required districts to have a program in place for ELL students and for these students to be identified and assessed. While Lau also did not specify any particular programs or polices for ELL students, it did create momentum for subsequent federal policies and court ruling to more specifically protect the rights of linguistically diverse students. Moreover, particulars were fully flushed out in *Castaneda v. Pickard (1981)*, a regional case, which offers a "test" to see if the needs of ELL students are being met by policies and programs. This case required that districts adhere to the following three areas:

1. *Theory:* The school must pursue a program based on an educational theory recognized as sound or, at least, as a legitimate experimental strategy.

2. *Practice:* The school must actually implement the program with instructional practices, resources, and personnel necessary to transfer theory into reality.

3. *Results:* The school must not persist in a program that fails to produce results.

In addition, in *Plyer vs. Doe (1982)*, the Supreme Court ruled that states cannot deny a free public education to immigrant children regardless of their immigrant status (documented or undocumented). While these requirements may not offer as strong an articulation of ELL students' rights as some may have hoped, they do protect ELL students from negligence and mistreatment and are an important foundation in ensuring effective programs for ELL students. Overall, the LAU remedies, the Bilingual Education Act, and Title VI have provided some protection for equal educational opportunities for linguistically diverse students at the federal level. They also provided federal funding that made possible the inception and growth of a number of bilingual programs in the United States (Hornberger, 2005; Ruiz, 2004; Wiley & Wright, 2004).

Similar to the Lau court case, the "Black English case" (1979) mandated measures to teach Standard English to children speaking Black English. This 1979 case, *Martin Luther King Junior Elementary School Children v. Ann Arbor School District*, "was as much about educating Black children as about Black English" (Smitherman, 1998, p. 163). The parents of a group of African American children alleged that the school was not equipping their students to succeed through a variety of ways, including preventing them from learning Standard English. The judge ruled that the school had not helped its teachers and personnel to respond to the linguistic needs of its African American children. As a result of the ruling, school districts have been required to respond to the needs of African American children by providing professional development to its staff and the recognition that Black English or Ebonics is a "systematic, rule-governed language system" in its own right. Black English has also been given legal standing in some districts, such as in Oakland, California.

Language Policy in Recent History

The mandates of bilingual and bidialectal education have been controversial. Critics have adopted different arguments, from the historically prevalent charge that it promotes social divisiveness to the more recent concerns that students will not learn English if they use their native language or dialect at school. Others have asserted that it simply does not work (Porter, 1990). When President Reagan took office in 1981, he made his views on bilingual education very clear, saying that he understood why teachers who spoke children's native languages were needed but also arguing that

> it is absolutely wrong and against American concepts to have a
> bilingual education program that is now openly, admittedly
> dedicated to preserving their native language and never getting
> them adequate in English so they can go out into the job market
> and participate. (quoted in Lyons, 1990, pp. 74–75)

The Reagan administration acted on these beliefs by reducing funding for the Bilingual Education Act by $23 million in 1982, a trend that continued until the 1990s. English as a Second Language (ESL) and transitional bilingual education to a lesser extent had been, and became even more so, the most favored approaches promoted by the mainstream media and the general public. Therefore the unstated federal policy goal has been to learn English as quickly as possible. Hornberger (1990) states that "there can be little doubt that the language-as-problem orientation has been the predominant one in the United States's public sphere" (p. 24). This was manifested most predominantly by the English Only movement that started in the 1980s, and which continues (McGroarty, 1991).

The proponents of English Only argue that to preserve the unity of the United States, English should become the official language. At the same time, there have been periods in the nation's history when administrations have leaned more toward a "language-as-a-resource" orientation, maintaining and supporting the teaching of languages other than English, such as Clinton's 1994 reauthorization of the BEA. The support or lack of support for this orientation at the federal level has depended on the particular administration in office (Wiley & Wright, 2004).

Similar to the last 200 years, this decade has witnessed the ambivalent rapport with language that the nation's press, politics, and people have been grappling with. In recent years the debate has escalated to a new level with English-only initiatives, such as the Unz Initiative in California. Proposition 227, a state-level proposal in California spearheaded by the millionaire businessman Ron Unz and passed by California voters in June 1998, outlawed bilingual education in the state of California. Proposition 227 brought all the debates on bilingual education under a magnifying lens. The English Only faction stressed that bilingual programs were not working and students were being ghettoized (although most ELLs were not in bilingual programs). Strong proponents of bilingual education such as Crawford (1999) have argued that the lack of large-scale political support has undermined its potential effectiveness. In bridging these two factions, Cummins (1999) states that "the challenge for opponents and advocates is to create an ideological space to collaborate in planning quality programs for bilingual students" (p. 223).

Although the change in policy with Proposition 227 has led to a dismantling of some bilingual programs, the parental waiver provisions of the law allowed some schools and districts to maintain their programs (Stritikus & Garcia, 2000). The aftermath of Proposition 227 demonstrates the difficulty of changing the linguistic practices of groups through legislation, a viewpoint commonly shared by researchers in the field of language education. After Proposition 227 was passed in California, similar laws were enacted in Arizona and Massachusetts, and currently 15 states have English-only laws.

Many linguists and educators regard the Ebonics debate in the same purview as bilingual education. The Oakland school board decision in 1996 to pass the Ebonics resolution was also a way for the school district to receive federal monies reserved for bilingual education and use them for a Standard English program. The board resolution stated that the district's purpose should be to facilitate the acquisition and mastery of English language skills, while respecting and embracing the legitimacy and richness of different language patterns. The rationale for the decision was that students could benefit from instruction which made use of their cultural and linguistic resources. In the same way as the Ann Arbor case two decades earlier, a large number of African American parents and students protested their children's poor academic performance, disproportionate placement in special education, and frequent suspensions. Like Proposition 227, the Oakland school board decision resulted in gross misrepresentations and biases by the media, the public, educators, and academics.

The latter half of the 1990s has also been marked by anti-minority and anti-immigration policies throughout the United States. Such is the case with California's Proposition 209, a law to repeal affirmative action, and California's Proposition 187, a law that attempted to restrict social services to undocumented immigrants. Ricento (1996) observes that the peak decades of immigration in the United States, 1901–1910 and 1981–1990, coincided with the most restrictive social and language policies. Others have noted that the current anti-immigrant sentiment should also be viewed in the same light (Beykont, 2002; Wiley & Lukes, 1996). The periods which have been the most language-restrictive in U.S. history have also been ones where there have been the largest number of immigrants that have been perceived as most "different" (Hornberger, 2005; Ricento, 2003).

Like bilingual education, the movement for equal access in education put into motion legally by *Brown vs. Board of Education* (1954) occurred in the same spirit as the civil rights movement and the development of the welfare state. Both were viewed as attempts to redress inequalities and to give issues of integration and cohesion top priority.

As Casanova (1991) states, "From its conception then, bilingual education was . . . heavily laced with a sense of social responsibility" (p. 170). In the last decade, there has been a shift away from viewing the federal government as the solution to social problems. This argument has been made most articulately with regards to welfare reform. As the nation has moved away from the concept of "big government," political leaders have increasingly called on individuals to accept responsibility for their social and economic position. This orientation has influenced linguistically diverse students. Political leaders have increasingly called on schools to reduce the number of programs which provide direct and special assistance to these students under the guise that such programs constitute a special service. Similar to supporters of Proposition 227 in California, others have made the argument to reduce or eliminate special programs such as bilingual education because they believe that focusing on English rather than students' native language will provide them greater social and economic advantage (Porter, 1990).

In 2002 during the Bush administration, Title VII (BEA) was replaced by Title III as part of a larger school reform measure in the United States known as the No Child Left Behind Act. Title III carried with it a new name, "Language Instruction for Limited English Proficient and Immigrant Students." The word "bilingual" had been deleted from all government offices and legislation, signaling a shift to an assimilationist, English-first orientation of the 2000–2008 Bush administration. Even though this new law is more supportive of programs that focus on learning English, it does not require English-only programs. Many have argued that there is still space in the new law for the creation of bilingual programs (Freeman, 2004; Hornberger, 2005). Wiley and Wright (2004) show that, paradoxically, the name change has come with double funding for ELL students.

It is important for teachers to have a grasp of the historical trends and policies that influence the environments of their linguistically diverse students. Teachers who are aware of such political and social movements can establish historically relevant relationships with their students and influence programmatic decisions at the school and district level. In the next section of this chapter, we summarize different programmatic options for schools. Central to these decisions is the role that English and the home language of students will play in instruction. Should students learn to read in their first language (L1) and then learn to read in their second language (L2)? Should recent immigrants be instructed in content area classes in their L1, so they do not fall behind in the critical areas of math, science, and social studies? Or will cultural and linguistically diverse students benefit from instruction provided solely in English? Across the nation, schools and districts struggle with these questions. As we explore the different programmatic options available to districts, we also delve deeper into the debate over bilingual education.

PROGRAMMATIC RESPONSES TO LINGUISTIC DIVERSITY

Instructional Programs

A variety of instructional programs have been devised and implemented over the last several decades to meet the educational needs of linguistically diverse students. We describe the five major program types that districts and schools have designed and implemented that were identified by August and Hakuta's (1997) comprehensive review of the research on linguistic minority students:

- **Submersion:** Students are placed in regular English-only classrooms and are given no special instructional support. (This approach is illegal in the United States as a result of Supreme Court decision in *Lau v. Nichols.* However, many ELL students find themselves in submersion-like settings.)

- **English as a Second Language (ESL):** No instruction is given in a student's primary language. ESL either is taught through pullout programs or is integrated with academic content throughout the day.

- **Transitional Bilingual Education (TBE):** Students receive some degree of instruction in their primary language for a period of time. However, the goal of the program is transition to English-only instruction as rapidly as possible, generally within 1–3 years.

- **Maintenance Bilingual Education (MBE):** Students receive instruction in their primary language and in English throughout the elementary school years (K-6) with the goal of developing academic proficiency in both languages.

- **Dual Language Programs:** Language majority and language minority students are instructed together in the same program with the goal of each group achieving bilingualism and biliteracy.

The five programs identified here are not an exhaustive list; they do not exist in pure forms; and districts mix and blend aspects of various programs. A variety of large- and small-scale studies have examined the effectiveness of these programs. The researchers of the studies have willingly and unwillingly become a part of the great debate about the effectiveness of bilingual education. It is difficult to determine the exact number of ELL students in each of these programs because of the lack of comprehensive national data. However, the majority of ELL students are instructed through ESL approaches using little to no native language instruction (Kindler, 2002).

The Bilingual Debate and the Research Context

As bilingual education continued to evolve throughout the 1960s and 1970s, there was a major split in public opinion regarding the program. Colin Baker (2001) explains that some citizens viewed bilingual education as failing to foster social integration and as a waste of public funds. Many opponents of bilingual education portrayed Latinos and supporters of bilingual education as using the latter for their own political gain (Baker, 2001). Critics of bilingual education have drawn from two major reviews of bilingual research (Baker & de Kanter, 1981; Rossel & Baker, 1996) to try to convince schools and districts to move away from bilingual education.

Rossel and Baker (1996) reviewed 72 "scientifically methodologically acceptable" studies. They concluded that bilingual education was not superior to ESL instruction, particularly in reading achievement. This study is widely cited by critics of bilingual education. Several researchers have noted that the review is plagued by many methodological issues. The Rossel and Baker (1996) review applied arbitrary and inconsistent criteria to establish methodologically acceptable studies and inaccurate and arbitrary labeling of programs (Cummins, 1999; Stritikus & Manyak, 2000). Colin Baker (2001) points out that the study had:

> a narrow range of expected outcomes for bilingual education in the [research] questions. Only English language and non-language subject areas were considered as the desirable outcome of schooling. Other outcomes such as self-esteem, employment, preservation of minority languages, and the value of different cultures were not considered. (p. 246)

Critics of bilingual education have drawn heavily from the work of Rossel and Baker (1996) and Baker and de Kanter (1983) to push educational policy. Advocates of bilingual education have drawn from a body of research that has reached opposite conclusions and supports the use of students' native language in instruction. Willig (1985) conducted a meta-analysis of 23 of the 28 studies reviewed by Baker and de Kanter (1983). *Meta-analysis* is a collection of systematic techniques for resolving apparent contradictions in research findings. Meta-analysis translates results from different studies to a common metric and statistically explores relationships between study characteristics and findings. Employing this technique, Greene (1998) found that an unbiased reading of the scholarly literature indicates that limited-English-proficient students taught using bilingual approaches perform significantly better than those students taught using English-only approaches. In a 2003 review of methodologically acceptable research studies, Slavin and Chueng found that bilingual approaches—particularly those that include reading instruction in the native language—are favorable to English-only approaches.

Beyond Research on Program Types

Research examining the success or failure of various program types has not completely addressed the central question of how best to educate culturally and linguistically diverse students. A body of research has reported detailed studies of what has worked in actual classrooms. Rather than focus on program models, this body of research has concentrated on the characteristics of schools and classrooms which contribute to successful educational practice for culturally and linguistically diverse students.

August and Hakuta (1997) provide a comprehensive review of optimal learning conditions which serve linguistically and culturally diverse student populations—conditions leading to high academic performance. Their review of some 33 studies indicates there is a set of generally agreed upon practices that foster academic success. These practices can exist across program types. August and Hakuta (1997) found that the following school and class-room characteristics were likely to lead to academic success:

> A supportive school-wide climate, school leadership, a customized
> learning environment, articulation and coordination within and
> between schools, use of native language and culture in instruction,
> a balanced curriculum that includes both basic and higher-order
> skills, explicit skill instruction, opportunities for student-directed
> instruction, use of instructional strategies that enhance
> understanding, opportunities for practice, systematic student
> assessment, staff development, and home and parent involvement.
> (August & Hakuta, 1997, p. 171)

These findings were confirmed in other more recent studies, such as Corallo and McDonald (2002) and Marzano (2003). Thus, culturally and linguistically diverse students can benefit greatly from cognitively challenging and student-centered instruction that makes use of cultural and linguistic resources of students.

Beyond Programs and Program Characteristics: Lived Reality of Today's Linguistically Diverse Students

Several studies of students' everyday experience provide a powerful but painful picture of how schools meet—or do not meet—the challenge of linguistic diversity. These studies are not meant as simple critique; they offer us understanding of how much further we need to go in meeting the challenge. Valdés (1998) conducted an important study analyzing the manner in which recent immigrant students are served by schools. Focusing on the way that four Latino students' initial experience with U.S. schooling shaped their future possibilities, Valdés found that school curriculum for these students focused on English-language instruction at the expense of access to engaging grade-level curriculum in key subject areas like science, social studies, and math. Valdés draws an important connection between the social position of cultural and linguistically diverse students and families in the broader society and the quality of education they receive. The students in Valdés's research found themselves in "ESL Ghettoes," which afforded little possibility for academic advancement.

In a study similar to Valdés's, Olsen (1997) studied the experiences of Latino and Asian immigrant students at Madison High School as they attempted to become "American." The teachers at Madison High believed that through hard work and perseverance all students—regardless of their linguistic and cultural background—could succeed. The teachers accepted, without question, the idea of the American meritocracy. Through careful interviews and observations, Olsen revealed the tensions and contradiction of this view. First, linguistically diverse students were segregated in the overall school context. They found themselves in low academic tracks with the most inexperienced teachers. Second, immigrant students felt extreme pressure to forgo defining elements of their own identities—their culture, their language, their dress, and their values. School for recent immigrant students was not a wondrous list of opportunities, but rather a process in which students found their place on the U.S. racial hierarchy.

Other researchers such as Toohey (2000) and Valenzuela (1999) have documented the powerful forces of racism, xenophobia, and pro-English mentality as factors that prevent educators from seeing linguistic diversity as an educational resource. To be sure, there are students who rise above these challenges, but unfortunately school practices and policies make this difficult.

The next section of this chapters offers a synopsis of classroom-level issues. It examines what types of knowledge and skills would help teachers who have English language learners in their classroom. The purpose of this section is to synthesize some of the important dimensions of second language acquisition for content area and second language (ESL and bilingual) teachers as well as to describe strategies to use in the classroom. We would also like to point out that much of the discussion in this section can also apply to teachers of bidialectals.

VIEWS ON LANGUAGE LEARNING AND TEACHING

This section provides a summary of what teachers of second language learners need to know in relation to language, language learners, and language learning and teaching.

Becoming proficient in a language or dialect can take on different meanings in various social, academic, and personal settings. In attempting to make students learning a second language or dialect successful in schools, scholars have observed that a distinction needs to be made between learning a language *socially* and *academically* (Cummins, 1981; Hakuta, Butler, & Witt, 2000–2001). Therefore, a critical goal for teachers should be to enable students to successfully use academic English (Bartolomé, 1998; Gibbons, 2002; Valdés, 2004). In discussing language learning and teaching, we focus most of our discussion on teaching academic English and the language needed for content areas.

Language

Wong Fillmore and Snow (2000) describe the most salient aspects of language that would be helpful for teachers of second language/dialects to know. Language is a complex system of communication that includes the following major subsystems: *pragmatics* (sociolinguistic rules governing language use, e.g., apologizing in a specific language and culture); *syntax* (rules of word order in a sentence); *semantics* (meanings of words and sentences); *morphology* (rules of word formation); and *phonology* (the sound system of a language). When people are using language, they must manipulate and coordinate all these subsystems together, as the following example illustrates. If a child in a classroom asks the following question, *What is photosynthesis?* the child would need to know the social convention of when and how to ask this question. The student would also need to know how to form a Wh- question and pronounce the words in a way that is intelligible to their audience.

In addition, the child presumably would need to learn the academic language needed to participate in a school-based discussion around photosynthesis. Moreover, certain students may not feel comfortable asking questions in a classroom, even when they are called on by the teacher. Therefore, a significant aspect of language to bear in mind is how it is inextricably linked to culture and identity. Teachers need to develop an awareness that students from diverse linguistically and culturally diverse backgrounds participate in different ways, especially in school settings that are often mainly tailored to mainstream Anglo structures and rules (Heath, 1983; Philips, 1993). For all people, language is linked closely to their identity and their way of life; learning a language often means negotiating part of one's identity in doing so (Cummins, 2000; Delpit, 1998; Norton-Peirce, 1995).

Language Learners

A number of learner characteristics can affect second language learning and success in an English-speaking school setting. Here, we focus on some of the most salient ones, such as age, the learner's first language, and motivation. Examples of others that can be considered are learning styles and aptitude. Although these tend to be described by researchers as individual learner characteristics, it is important to note that such characteristics are shaped by cultural and social contexts.

Age

There has been a push in the United States and in several other countries to start early schooling for children in a second/foreign language because younger learners are thought to be better language learners. Research indicates that younger children show advantages in terms of pronunciation and accent. Several researchers (Hyltenstam & Abrahamsson, 2001; Johnson & Newport, 1989; Patowski, 1980) also believe that there is a "critical period," a time when the brain is more predisposed to learn all the linguistic features of a language, not just phonological ones. This belief has been challenged by others (Snow & Hoefnagel-Hohle, 1978) who did not find an advantage to being younger; indeed, they found that adolescents and adults learn at a faster rate, especially in the early stages of language development. Even among scholars who have found the data on the critical period convincing (Hyltenstam & Abrahamsson, 2001), the recommendation has been that programmatic decisions should not be based on the age of learners. Rather, the research indicates that more attention should be paid to the quality of the programs and the quantity and quality of exposure to the second language rather than the age of students.

First Language

Research indicates that all second language learners, regardless of their first language, seem to progress through similar developmental stages of language learning in some areas. For example, researchers have found that there is a developmental sequence for learners of English as a second language in question formation, negation, and past tense formation (Lightbown & Spada, 1999). Learners go through pre-verbal negation (e.g., I no play), and are then able to insert the negative term with auxiliary verbs although not necessarily correctly (e.g., "I can't play," He don't play"), and last are able to produce negative sentences correctly (e.g., "She doesn't play").

Additionally, there are specific errors that we can now attribute to a learner's first language. For example, Spanish-speaking learners will stay in the pre-verbal negation stage (*I no like*) because of this structure's similarity to the Spanish language (*No quiero*). This example demonstrates that the popular belief that it is easier to learn a second language the more similar it is to the first language is not necessarily true. Actually, there can be a tendency to revert to the rules of the first language if they share many similarities. Thus, it is useful for teachers to learn about cross-linguistic similarities and differences in terms of different aspects of language, such as phonemes, spelling, writing systems, and sociolinguistic rules (Wong Fillmore & Snow, 2000).

Overall, whatever the learner's first language, students who are literate and have had prior formal schooling in their first language have been found to outperform students who have not had this experience (August & Hakuta, 1997; Collier, 1987; Cummins, 1984).

Motivation

The relationship between motivation and language learning is unclear. It is not known whether motivation leads to successful learning or vice versa. Norton-Peirce (1995) coined the term "investment" rather than motivation to describe the relationship between the learners and their environment. Investment is, therefore, defined as a characteristic that is dependent on this relationship. Certain contexts can be detrimental to a student's motivation, especially if the relationship between speakers of both languages is strained or clearly unequal in terms of power relations. In sum, it is critical for teachers to attempt to motivate students through engaging lessons and the relationships they create with them.

Language Learning and Teaching

Theories of Second Language Learning

While many theories have been advanced to explain second language learning, three main theories have had the most influence on second language students in schools. The three major theories are:

- Input hypothesis
- Interactionist theory
- Basic Interpersonal Communication Skills (B.I.C.S) and Cognitive Academic Language Proficiency (C.A.L.P)

We describe these theories in detail.

Input Hypothesis

The most influential set of hypotheses or single theory which has influenced teachers has been that of Stephen Krashen (1985). Krashen, with others, has advanced the following hypotheses: (1) Acquisition is the unconscious process of acquiring a language through interaction, while learning is the formal process of memorizing rules and structures of a language. He contends that language learning is most successful when built on the principle of acquisition through activities that are mostly communicative in nature. (2) Krashen proposes that language learning consists of particular sequences and stages, an example of which is given above in how negation develops for language learners. (3) For language acquisition to occur, learners must be offered comprehensible input (or i + 1), structures that are just beyond the learner's current level. This last part of Krashen's theory has been the most influential on classroom teaching. The recommendation for teachers is that input in the classroom can be made comprehensible through strategies such as creating visual cues and establishing background knowledge. Overall, Krashen's proposals suggest that language teaching be conducted in the most natural, communicative situations where learners are relaxed and teachers are not focusing on error correction.

Interactionist Theory

The second theory that is discussed in this section is the Interactionist theory (Lightbown & Spada, 1999), which has widely influenced and been influenced by research and teaching on immersion programs in Canada. The basic tenet of this theory is that both input and output are crucial for language learning. Teachers who draw on this theory create tasks where conversational interactions between speakers are central to the process of language learning. This process has been described as the *negotiation of meaning*, which in many ways is similar to the process between caretakers and children in first-language acquisition.

B.I.C.S. and C.A.L.P

The third theory that has most influenced the teaching of English in schools is one that focuses explicitly on language and content learning, and pertains to the distinction made between learning a language socially and academically. Learning another language academically is known to be a lengthy process that can take from 7 to 10 years (Cummins, 1984), as compared to conversational proficiency in a language, which can take from 1 to 5 years. Cummins distinguished these by coining the terms B.I.C.S. (Basic Interpersonal Conversational Skills) and C.A.L.P. (Cognitive Academic Language Proficiency). Academic language offers few clues for learners and is therefore much more difficult to learn, while B.I.C.S occurs "when there are contextual supports and props for language delivery" (Baker, 2001, p. 170). If we think of it, many of us might know how to converse with a speaker in our second or third language, but might have difficult listening to an academic lecture in that language or writing a technical report. This is especially true for students who start this process in the later grades (Collier, 1987; Cummins & Swain, 1986), for students who are not literate or academically skilled in their first language, and for many who come from war-torn countries.

At the same time, we must also bear in mind the limitations of B.I.C.S. and C.A.L.P. (Wiley, 1996). First, the strict dichotomy between the two is viewed by many as overly simplistic. In some cases, C.A.L.P. can be developed before B.I.C.S., as with individuals who can read but not converse in a second language. There is also danger in viewing B.I.C.S. as inferior to C.A.L.P. We know that oral conversation can be equally demanding in certain settings. Second, the notion of academic language is somewhat abstract. In a more recent re-working of this distinction, Cummins (2000) has attempted to define *academic proficiency* in more concrete terms: "the extent to which an individual has access to and command of the oral and written academic registers of schooling" (Cummins, 2000, p. 67). Other attempts to make this term more useful for teachers can be found in the national ESL standards (TESOL, 1997). Nonetheless, there is still considerable debate about how academic language should be defined (Valdés, 2004).

Instructional Methods and Approaches

The Input hypothesis and the Interactionist theories have provided a significant set of guidelines for creating optimal language learning environments. Their theories have influenced teachers and methods in some of the following ways: (1) making teachers think through how to make verbal input at a level that is a little bit beyond the level of the learner (e.g., using visuals, paraphrasing); (2) creating communicatively oriented activities (e.g., problem-solving activities) which are of a low-anxiety level; and (3) setting up tasks so that learners are forced to talk and listen to each other (e.g., through jigsaw activities). Krashen's work has been associated most closely with a method described as the Natural Approach (Krashen & Terrell, 1983), which integrates a number of these strategies.

The Interactionist theory, as indicated above, has been cited mostly in conjunction with immersion programs in Canada. In these programs, researchers have found that the most effective language learning situation is one that is content based or communicatively oriented (Lightbown & Spada, 1999). Therefore, as Cummins's work has suggested, instruction offered to language minority students in schools should be where language and content are jointly taught. The research and scholarship subsequent to that of Cummins has focused on the importance of learning academic language and content (Bartolomé, 1998; Gibbons, 2002; Valdés, 2004). Much of this research has shown how instruction for these students learning a second language must concentrate on acquiring academic language and subject-specific knowledge in several ways.

Students can attain subject-specific knowledge by using their primary language or with richer and more sustained collaborations between content area teachers and English language specialists so that pullout classes do not focus exclusively on decontextualized skills and language. In many cases content area teachers will need training in making language and content more accessible to ELL students. Content-Based-Instruction (CBI) (Snow, Met, & Genesee, 1989) can be used, in which language is taught in conjunction with the academic subject matter. One example of CBI is SDAIE: Specifically Designed Academic Instruction in English, which has often been referred to as Sheltered Instruction.

A comprehensive program of Sheltered Instruction that has gained much recognition is that of the Sheltered Instruction Observation Protocol, S.I.O.P. (Echevarria, Vogt, & Short, 2000). Another is C.A.L.L.A. (Cognitive Academic Language Learning Approach), which focuses on developing language, content, and learning strategies (Chamot & O'Malley, 1994). Another more recent method that is becoming widely adopted is Guided Language Acquisition Design (GLAD) (Brechtel, 2001). Many of these methods are used in a large number of school districts across the United States. The resource list at the end of the chapter provides more information for mainstream teachers, including additional references for these methods.

Instructional Strategies and Contexts for Learning

The methods described above that recommend an integration of language and content call for teachers to practice similar strategies to those described in the effective programs by August and Hakuta (1997), Corallo and McDonald (2002), and Marzano (2003). These strategies recommend a student-centered, meaning-based, context-rich classroom and cognitively demanding curriculum. Schleppegrell, Achugar, and Oteíza (2004) helpfully summarize these strategies:

> Typical recommendations for a CBI approach include a focus on disciplinary vocabulary and use of a variety of learning and teaching strategies, especially visual aids and graphic organizers to make meanings clear. . . . Teachers are encouraged to help students comprehend and use the language structures and discourse features found in different subjects and to facilitate students' practice with academic tasks such as listening to explanations, reading for information, participating in academic discussions, and writing reports. (p. 69)

A successful class for English language learners is one where often the following features are present: A high level of noise; students working in groups with hands-on materials; word walls, graphic organizers, displays of student work; teachers modeling strategies; assessment being used to drive instruction; and high expectations for all members of the classroom community. An example of teacher modeling is to provide students with explicit instruction in different learning strategies for gaining academic competence (Chamot & O'Malley, 1992). When asking students to write a summary, for example, teachers (even content teachers, such as social studies or science) cannot assume that students will know how to write a summary and must either model for them the necessary steps or collaborate with an English language specialist to accomplish the task. Setting up cooperative learning (Johnson, Johnson, & Holubec, 1986) or complex instruction groups (Cohen & Lotan, 1997) where students are given different roles in completing a project are examples of effective groupwork.

Teachers need to learn tools for authentic assessment (O'Malley & Valdez Peirce, 1996) in order to assess students in different ways and to use with standardized assessments. Along with the academic focus, teachers should work toward making the classroom a welcoming place for students and their families. Implicit rules should be made explicit. The cultural and linguistic resources that students bring to school (especially with the involvement of parents and community partners) should also be integrated and celebrated in the classroom.

Although many of the strategies and methods described above can be very helpful, teachers should realize that a number of scholars have challenged the assumption that these are sufficient to help second-language students succeed, especially in the higher grades and with their mainstream counterparts. Bartolomé (1998), Gibbons (2002), and Valdés (2004) stress the need to create events where students have to "address real or imaginary distant audiences with whom they can assume little shared knowledge" (Valdés, 2004, p.122), in order to make them "elaborate linguistic messages explicitly and precisely to minimize audience misinterpretation" (Bartolomé, 1998, p. 66). Schleppegrell, Achugar, and Oteíza (2004) discuss the need to delve deeply into disciplinary specific linguistic challenges, such as those found in social studies textbooks. Moreover, teachers should always remember that the education of linguistically diverse students is situated in larger issues about immigration, distribution of wealth and power, and the empowerment of students (Cahnmann & Varghese, 2006; Varghese & Stritikus, 2005). Thus, effective classroom strategies and climate must be situated in a supportive school and societal context.

CONCLUSION

This chapter stresses the social, political, and historical realities that shape the nature of schooling for linguistically diverse students. The first section examines linguistically diverse populations in the United States and considers how recent trends in immigration have influenced linguistic diversity in the United States. To understand the experiences of immigrant students in schools, we must look at the political and economic realities that drive and shape immigration. Immigration has changed the look and feel of schools in every state in the United States. The manner in which linguistically diverse students are received by schools is directly related to the manner in which immigrants are treated by society. At present, immigration presents a source of cheap labor that fuels aspects of the U.S. economy. Immigrant communities find themselves pinched by social and economic pressures. Thus, it is important for future teachers to consider the manner in which immigrant populations are viewed by their host countries.

The second section of this chapter considers important legal and historical milestones in the evolution of language education policy. Past and recent developments in language policy demonstrate the contradictory position of the United States toward linguistic diversity. While we frequently celebrate our status as a nation of immigrants or as a land of equality, language policy in the United States has continually attempted to suppress and minimize linguistic diversity. Linguistically diverse students in the United States have rarely seen their languages and cultures promoted at the federal and state levels. Teacher practice both influences and is influenced by language policy. In order for teachers to support and promote linguistic diversity, they need to understand how language policy shapes education (Varghese & Stritikus, 2005).

In the third section of this chapter, we reviewed the existing research regarding which programs best serve the needs of linguistically diverse students. Research supports the idea that students learn best in meaning-centered and intellectually rich environments and indicates that linguistically diverse students have the maximum potential to succeed when their language and culture are used and developed in instruction. Practice for immigrant students has not always lived up to this ideal. In the final section of this chapter, we provide practical knowledge required to meet the needs of their linguistically diverse students.

In nearly every classroom, linguistic diversity shapes the nature of teachers' work. Linguistic and cultural diversity is one of the nation's great assets, yet schooling for linguistically diverse students continues to be plagued by poor programs, limited resources, and lack of commitment. The success of our educational system will be judged on how well we meet the needs of the linguistically diverse population. Future teachers can play a significant role in opening the doors of opportunity for linguistically diverse students.

Questions and Activities

1. What did you learn about immigrant students and their schooling in this chapter? Imagine you are asked to provide a 30-minute workshop for the mainstream teachers and staff in your school. What concepts and principles would you incorporate in this workshop?

2. In what ways are the challenges facing English language learners, African American students, and indigenous students in schools similar and different? What types of practices and activities could teachers do in their classroom that would assist these groups of students?

3. What support is provided for English language learners in a local school, and how are these decisions made? Interview school staff and document their responses to these questions.

4. You are in charge of designing the best possible program in your school for English language learners. What features would be part of this program? Why? What aspects

of language and language learning would be useful for mainstream teachers to know? How can they incorporate this knowledge when teaching their subject matter? Parents and households as well as their relationships with schools are critical influences on the achievement of immigrant students. Interview one parent and if possible, one child, who has been identified as an ELL student. Document their social and educational experiences before and since coming to the United States.

Resources

August, D., & Hakuta, K. (Eds.). (1997). *Improving Schooling for Language Minority Students: A Research Agenda*. Washington, DC: National Academy Press.

Baugh, J. (1999). *Out of the Mouth of Slaves: African American Language Educational Malpractice*. New York: Oxford University Press.

Brechtel, M. (2001). *Bringing It All Together: Language and Literacy in the Multilingual Classroom*. San Diego: Dominie Press.

Chamot, A. U., & O'Malley, J. M. (1994). *The CALLA Handbook: How to Implement the Cognitive Academic Language Learning Approach*. Reading, MA: Addison-Wesley.

Davies Samway, K., & McKeon, D. (1999). *Myths and Realities: Best Practices for Language Minority Students*. Portsmouth, NH: Heinemann.

Echevarria, J., Vogt, M., & Short, D. J. (2000). *Making Content Comprehensible for English Language Learners: The SIOP Model*. Boston: Allyn & Bacon.

Gibbons, P. (2002). *Scaffolding Language, Scaffolding Learning: Teaching Second Language Learners in the Mainstream Classroom*. Portsmouth, NH: Heinemann.

Herrera, S. G., & Murphy, K. G. (2005). *Mastering ESL and Bilingual Methods*. Boston: Pearson, Allyn & Bacon.

Lightbown, P., & Spada, N. (1999). *How Languages Are Learned* (2nd ed.). New York: Oxford University Press.

Ovando, C., & Collier, V. P. (1985). *Bilingual and ESL Classrooms: Teaching in Multicultural Contexts*. New York: McGraw-Hill.

Peregoy, S. F., & Boyle, O. F. (2005). *Reading, Writing, and Learning in ESL: A Resource Book for K-12 Teachers* (4th ed.). Boston: Pearson Education, Inc.

Suarez-Orozco, C. E., & Suarez-Orozco, M. M. (2003). *Children of Immigration*. Cambridge, MA: Harvard University Press.

Teachers of English to Speakers of Other Languages (1997). *ESL Standards for Pre-K 12 Students*. Alexandria, VA: Author.

Wong-Fillmore, L., & Snow, C. (2000). *What Teachers Need to Know about Language*. Washington, DC: ERIC Clearinghouse on Languages and Linguistics.

Professional Associations

Teachers of English to Speakers of Other Languages, T.E.S.O.L.

National Association for Bilingual Education, N.A.B.E.

National Association for Multicultural Education, N.A.M.E.

Websites

American Educational Research Association: http://www.aera.net/

TESOL: www.tesol.org

NABE: www.nabe.org

National Clearinghouse for English Language Acquisition: www.ncbela.gwu.edu

Center for Applied Linguistics: www.cal.org

Center for Research on Education, Diversity, and Excellence: www.crede.ucsc.edu

Center on English Learning and Achievement: www.cela.albany.edu

References

August, D., & Hakuta, K. (Eds.). (1997). *Improving Schooling for Language Minority Students: A Research Agenda.* Washington, DC: National Academy Press.

Baker, C. (2001). *Foundations of Bilingual Education and Bilingualism.* Clevedon, UK: Multilingual Matters.

Baker, K., & de Kanter, A. (1981). *Effectiveness of Bilingual Education: A Review of the Literature.* Washington, DC: U.S. Department of Education.

Banks, C. A. M. (2005). *Improving Multicultural Education: Lessons from the Intergroup Education Movement.* New York: Teachers College Press.

Bartolomé, L. (1998). *The Misteaching of Academic Discourse: The Politics in the Language Classroom.* Boulder, CO: Westview Press.

Behdad, A. (1997). Nationalism and Immigration to the United States. *Diaspora, 6*(2), 155–176.

Beykont, Z. F. (2002). *English Only Laws in the U.S.* Retrieved November 1, 2005, from www.linguapax.org/congres/taller/taller1/Beykont.html.

Brown v. Board of Education, 327 U.S. 483 (1954).

Cahnmann, M., & Varghese, M. (2006). Critical Advocacy and Bilingual Education in the United States. *Linguistics and Education, 16*(1), 59–73.

Casanova, U. (1991). Bilingual Education: Politics or Pedagogy? In O. García (Ed.), *Bilingual Education: Focusschrift in Honor of Joshua A. Fishman on the Occasion of His 65th Birthday* (pp. 167–180). Philadelphia: John Benjamins.

Castaneda v. Pickard, 648 F.2d 989, 1007 5th Cir. 1981.

Castles, S. (2003). Towards a Sociology of Forced Migration and Social Transformation. *Sociology, 37*(1), 13–34.

Castles, S., & Davidson, A. (2000). *Citizenship and Migration: Globalization and the Politics of Belonging.* New York: Routledge.

Chamot, A. U., & O'Malley, J. M. (1994). *The CALLA Handbook: How to Implement the Cognitive Academic Language Learning Approach.* Reading, MA: Addison-Wesley.

Chomsky, N. (2000). (Edited by N. Mukherji, B. N. Patnaik, & R. K. Agnihotri). *The Architecture of Language.* Oxford: Oxford University Press.

Chung, H.C. (2000). English Language Learners of Vietnamese Background. In S. L. McKay and S. C. Wong (Eds.), *New Immigrants in the United States* (pp. 216–232). Cambridge, UK: Cambridge Press.

Cohen, E. G., & Lotan, R. A. (1997). *Working for Equity in Heterogeneous Classrooms: Sociological Theory in Practice.* New York: Teachers College Press.

Collier, V. P. (1987). Age and Rate of Acquisition of Second Language for Academic Purposes. *TESOL Quarterly, 21,* 617–641.

Corallo, C., & McDonald, D. H. (2002). *What Works with Low-Performing Schools: A Review of Research.* Charleston, WV: AEL, Regional Educational Laboratory, Region IV Comprehensive Center.

Crawford, J. (1999). *Bilingual Education: History, Politics, Theory, and Practice* (4th ed.). Los Angeles: Bilingual Education Services.

Cummins, J. (1981). The Role of Primary Language Development in Promoting Educational Success for Language Minority Students. In California State Department of Education (Ed.), *Schooling and Language Minority Students: A Theoretical Framework* (pp. 3–50). Los Angeles: California State University: Evaluation, Dissemination, and Assessment Center.

Cummins, J. (1984). *Bilingualism and Special Education: Issues in Assessment and Pedagogy.* Clevedon, UK: Multilingual Matters.

Cummins, J. (1999). Alternative Paradigms in Bilingual Education Research: Does Theory Have a Place? *Educational Researcher, 28,* 26–32.

Cummins, J. (2000). *Language, Power, and Pedagogy.* Clevedon: Multilingual Matters.

Cummins, J., & Swain, M. (1986). *Bilingualism in Education.* London: Longman.

Del Valle, S. (2003). *Language Rights and the Law in the United States: Finding Our Voices.* Clevedon, UK: Multilingual Matters.

Delpit, L. (1998). What Should Teachers Do? Ebonics and Culturally Responsive Instruction. In T. Perry & L. Delpit (Eds.), *The Real Ebonics Debate: Power, Language, and the Education of African-American Children* (pp. 17–28). Boston, MA: Beacon Press.

Echevarria, J., Vogt, M., & Short, D. J. (2000). *Making Content Comprehensible for English Language Learners: The SIOP Model.* Boston: Allyn & Bacon.

Freeman, R. D. (1998). *Bilingual Education and Social Change.* Clevedon, UK: Multilingual Matters.

Freeman, R. D. (2004). *Building on Community Bilingualism.* Philadelphia: Caslon Publishing.

Garcia, E. (1999). *Understanding and Meeting the Challenge of Student Cultural Diversity.* Boston, MA: Houghton Mifflin Company.

Gibbons, P. (2002). *Scaffolding Language, Scaffolding Learning: Teaching Second Language Learners in the Mainstream Classroom.* Portsmouth, NH: Heinemann.

Gordon, M. (1964). *Assimilation in American Life.* New York: Oxford University Press.

Greene, J. P. (1998). *A Meta-analysis of the Effectiveness of Bilingual Education.* The Tomas Rivera Policy Institute. Los Angeles: University of Southern California.

Hakuta, K., Butler, Y. G., & Witt, D. (2000–2001). How Long Does It Take English Learners to Attain Proficiency? Retrieved November 1, 2005, from http://www.stanford.edu/~hakuta.

Heath, S. B. (1983). *Ways with Words: Language, Life, and Work in Communities and Classrooms.* New York: Cambridge.

Hornberger, N. (1990). Bilingual Education and English-only: A Language Planning Framework. In C. B. Cazden & C. E. Snow (Eds.), *Annals of the American Academy of Political and Social Science:* Vol. 508. *English Plus: Issues in bilingual education.* (pp. 12–26). Newbury Park, CA: Sage.

Hornberger, N. H. (2005). Nichols to NCLB: Local and Global Perspectives on U.S. Language Education Policy. *Working Papers in Educational Linguistics 20*(2).

Hyltenstam, H., & Abrahamsson, N. (2001). Age and L2 Learning: The Hazards of Matching Practical "Implications" with Theoretical Facts. *TESOL Quarterly, 35*(1), 151–170.

Itzigsohn, J., Dore-Cabral, C. B., Hernandez-Medina, E., & Vazquez, O. (1999). Mapping Dominican Transnationalism: Narrow and Broad Transnational Practices. *Ethnic and Racial Studies, 22*(2), 316–339.

Jacobson, M.F. (1998) *Whiteness of a Different Color: European Immigrants and the Alchemy of Race.* Cambridge: Harvard University Press.

Johnson, D. W., Johnson, R. T., & Holubec, E. J. (1986). *Circles of Learning: Cooperation in the Classroom.* Edina, MN: Interaction Book.

Johnson, J., & Newport, E. (1989). Critical Period Effects in Second Language Learning: The Influence of Maturational State on the Acquisition of English as a Second Language. *Cognitive Psychology, 21,* 60–99.

Kindler, A. (2002). *Survey of the States' Limited English Proficient Students and Available Educational Programs and Services: 1999–2000 Summary Report.* Washington, DC: National Clearinghouse for English Language Acquisition and Language Instruction Educational Programs.

Krashen, S. (1985). The Input Hypothesis: Issues and Implications. New York: Longman.

Krashen, S. D., & Terrell, D. (1983). *The Natural Approach: Language Acquisition in the Classroom.* Hayward, CA: Alemany Press.

Krauss, M. (1998). The Condition of Native North American Languages: The Need for Realistic Assessment and Action. *International Journal of the Sociology of Language, 132,* 9–21.

Labov, W. (1972). The Logic of Standard English. In W. Labov (Ed.), *Language in the Inner City: Studies in Black English Vernacular* (pp. 201–240). Philadelphia: University of Pennsylvania Press.

Lau v. Nichols, 414 U.S. 563 (1974).

Lightbown, P., & Spada, N. (1999). *How Languages Are Learned* (2nd ed.). New York: Oxford University Press.

Lindholm-Leary, K. J. (2001). *Dual Language Education.* Clevedon, UK: Multilingual Matters.

López, M. G. (2000). The Language Situations of the Hmong, Khmer, and Laotian Communities in the United States. In S. L. McKay and S. C. Wong (Eds.), *New Immigrants in the United States* (232–262). Cambridge, UK: Cambridge Press.

Lucas, T. (1997). *Into, Through, and Beyond Secondary School: Critical Transitions for Immigrant Youths.* The National Center for Restructuring Education, Schools, and Teaching. Teachers College, NY: Columbia University.

Lyons, J. J. (1990). The Past and Future Directions of Federal Bilingual-Education Policy. In C. B. Cazden & C. E. Snow (Eds.), *Annals of the American Academy of Political and Social Science:* Volume 508. *English Plus: Issues in Bilingual Education* (pp. 66–80). Newbury Park, CA: Sage.

Mahler, S. J. (1998). Theoretical and Empirical Contributions Toward a Research Agenda for Transnationalism. In M. P. Smith, & L. E. Guarnizo (Eds.), *Transnationalism from below* (pp. 64–102). New Brumswick, NJ: Transaction Publishers.

Marzano, R. (2003). *What Works in Schools: Translating Research into Action.* Alexandria, VA: Association for Supervision and Curriculum Development.

McCarty, T. (2002). Comment: Bilingual/Bicultural Schooling and Indigenous Students: A Response to Eugene Garcia. *International Journal of the Sociology of Language, 155/156,* 161–174.

McGroarty, M. (1991). The Societal Context of Bilingual Education. *Educational Researcher, 21*(2), 7–9.

Meyer v. Nebraska, 262 U.S. 390 (1923).

National Center for Education Statistics [NCES]. (2002). *Public School Membership by Race/Ethnicity and State.* U.S. Department of Education: Washington. D.C.

Norton-Peirce, B. (1995). Social Identity, Investment, and Language Learning. *TESOL Quarterly, 29*(1), 9–31.

Olneck, M. R., & Lazerson, M. (1974). The School Achievement of Immigrant Children, 1900–1930. *History of Education Quarterly,* 14, 453–482.

Olsen, L. (1997). *Made in America: Immigrant Students in our Public Schools.* New York: The New York Press.

O'Malley, J. M., & Valdez Peirce, L. (1996). *Authentic Assessment for English Language Learners: Practical Approaches for Teachers.* New York: Addison-Wesley.

Patowski, M. (1980). The Sensitive Period for the Acquisition of Syntatx in a Second Language. *Language Learning, 30*(2), 449–472.

Perlmann, J. (1990). Historical Legacies: 1840–1920. In C. B. Cazden & C. E. Snow (Eds.), *Annals of the American Academy of Political and Social Science:* Vol. 508. *English Plus: Issues in Bilingual Education* (pp. 147–159). Newbury Park, CA: Sage.

Philips, S. U. (1993). *The Invisible Culture: Communication in the Classroom and Community on the Warm Springs Indian Reservation* (2nd ed.). New York: Free Press.

Plyer v. Doe, 457 U.S. 202, 210 (1982).

Portes, A. (1996). Global Villagers: The Rise of Transnational Communities. *The American Prospect, 25,* 74–77.

Portes, A. (1999). Towards a New World: The Origins and Effects of Transnational Activities. *Ethnic and Racial Studies, 22*(2), 463–477.

Portes, A., & Rumbaut, R. G. (1996). *Immigrant America: A Portrait.* Berkeley: University of California Press.

Portes, A., & Rumbaut, R. G. (2001). *Legacies: The Story of the Immigrant Second Generation.* Berkeley: University of California Press.

Porter, R. P. (1990). *Forked Tongue: The Politics of Bilingual Education.* New York: Basic Books.

Ricento, T. (1996). A Brief History of Language Restrictionism in the United States. In *Official English? No! TESOL's Recommendations for Countering the Official English Movement.* TESOL Sociopolitical Concerns Committee. Retrieved September 27, 1999, from http://www.ncbe.gwu.edu/miscpubs/tesol/official/restrictionism.htm.

Ricento, T. (2003). The Discursive Construction of Americanism. *Discourse and Society, 14*(5).

Rose, P. I. (1997). *They and We: Racial Ethnic Relations in the United States.* New York: McGraw-Hill.

Rossel, C., & Baker, K. (1996). The Effectiveness of Bilingual Education. *Research in the Teaching of English, 30,* 7–74.

Ruiz, R. (2004, April). From Language as a Problem to Language as an Asset: The Promise and Limitations of Lau. Paper presented at the Annual Conference of the American Educational Research Association, San Diego.

Rumbaut, R. (1997). *Children of Immigrants: The Adaptation Process of the Second Generation (Report to the Russell Sage Foundation).* New York: Russell Sage Foundation.

Rumberger, R. W., & Gandara, P. (2004). Seeking Equity in the Education of California's English Learners. *Teachers College Record, 106,* 2032–2056.

Schleppegrell, M. J., Achugar, M., & Oteíza, T. (2004). The Grammar of History: Enhancing Content-based Instruction Through a Functional Focus on Language. *TESOL Quarterly, 38*(1), 67–94.

Skutnabb-Kangas, T. (1988). Multilingualism and the Education of Minority Children. In T. Skutnabb-Kangas & J. Cummins (Eds.), *Minority Education: From Shame to Struggle* (pp. 9–44). Clevedon, UK: Multilingual Matters.

Slavin, R. E., & Cheung, A. (2003). Effective Reading Programs for English Language Learners: A Best-Evidence Synthesis. Baltimore, MD: Johns Hopkins University, Center for Research on the Education of Students Placed at Risk.

Smith, M. P., & Guarnizo, L. E. (Eds.) (1998). *Transnationalism from Below: Comparative Urban and Community Research.* New Brunswick, NJ: Transaction Publishers.

Smitherman, G. (1998). Black English/Ebonics: What It Be Like? In T. Perry & L. Delpit (Eds.), *The Real Ebonics Debate: Power, Language, and the Education of African-American Children* (pp. 29–37). Boston, MA: Beacon Press.

Smitherman, G. (2000). *Talkin that Talk: Language, Culture and Education in African America.* New York: Routledge.

Snow, C. & Hoefnagel-Höhle, M. (1978). The Critical Period for Language Acquisition: Evidence from Second Language Learning. *Child Development, 49*(4): 1114–1128.

Snow, M. A., Met, M., & Genesee, F. (1989). A Conceptual Framework for the Integration of Language and Content in Second/Foreign Language Instruction. *TESOL Quarterly, 23,* 201–219.

Stritikus, T. (2004, April). *Latino Immigrant Students: Transitions and Educational Challenges.* Paper presented at the Annual Meeting of the American Educational Research Association, San Diego, CA.

Stritikus, T., & Garcia, E. (2000). Education of Limited English Proficient Students in California Schools: An Assessment of the Influence of Proposition 227 on Selected Teachers and Classrooms. *The Bilingual Research Journal, 24*(1&2).

Stritikus, T., & Manyak, P. (2000). Creating Opportunities for the Academic Success of Linguistically Diverse Students: What Does the Research Say? In T. Bergeson (Ed.), *Educating Limited English Proficient Students in Washington State.* Olympia, WA: Office of Superintendent of Public Instruction.

Suarez-Orozco, C. E., & Suarez-Orozco, M. M. (2003). *Children of Immigration.* Cambridge, MA: Harvard University Press.

Suarez-Orozco, M. M. (1997). Globalization, Immigration, and Education: The Research Agenda. *Harvard Educational Review, 71*(3), 345–365.

TESOL (1997). *ESL Standards for Pre-K-12 Students.* Alexandria, VA: Author.

Toohey, K. (2000). *Learning English at School: Identity, Social Relations and Classroom Practice.* Clevedon, England: Multilingual Matters.

U.S. Census Bureau. (2001, March). Census Brief 2000. Retrieved November 15, 2004, from Population Division: http://www.census.gov/popest/national/.

Valdés, G. (1998). The World Outside and Inside Schools: Language and Immigrant Children. *Educational Researcher, 27*(6), 4–18.

Valdés, G. (2000). Bilingualism and Languages Use among Mexican Americans. In S. L. McKay and S. C. Wong, (Eds.), *New Immigrants in the United States* (pp. 99–136). Cambridge, UK: Cambridge Press.

Valdés, G. (2004). Between Support and Marginalization: The Development of Academic Language in Linguistic Minority Children. In J. Brutt-Griffler, & M. Varghese (Eds.), *Bilingualism and Language Pedagogy* (pp. 102–132). Clevedon, England: Multilingual Matters.

Valenzuela, A. (1999). *Subtractive Schooling: U.S.–Mexican Youth and the Politics of Caring.* New York: SUNY.

Varghese, M., & Stritikus, T. (2005). *"Nadie me dijó* [Nobody told me]": Language Policy Negotiation and Implications for Teacher Education. *Journal of Teacher Education, 56*(1).

Wiese, A., & García, E. E. (1998). The Bilingual Education Act: Language Minority Students and Equal Educational Opportunity. *The Bilingual Research Journal, 22*(1), 1–18.

Wiley, T. G. (1996). Language Planning and Policy. In S. L. McKay & N. H. Hornberger (Eds.), *Sociolinguistics and Language Teaching,* 103–148.

Wiley, T. G., & Lukes, M. (1996). English-only and Standard English Ideologies in the US. *TESOL Quarterly, 30*(3), 511–535.

Wiley, T. G., & Wright, W. E. (2004). Against the Undertow: Language-minority Education Policy and Politics in the "Age of Accountability." *Educational Policy, 18*(1), 142–168.

Willig, A. (1985). A Meta-analysis of Selected Studies on the Effectiveness of Bilingual Education. *Review of Educational Research, 55*(3), 269–317.

Wolfram, W., Adger, C. T., & Christian, D. (1998). *Dialects in Schools and Communities.* Mahwah, NJ: Lawrence Erlbaum Associates.

Wong Fillmore, L., & Snow, C. (2000). *What Teachers Need to Know about Language.* Washington, DC: ERIC Clearinghouse on Languages and Linguistics.

Wong, S. C., & López, M. G. (2000). English Language Learners of Chinese Background: A Portrait of Diversity. In S. L. McKay and S. C. Wong, (Eds.), *New Immigrants in the United States* (pp. 263–305). Cambridge, UK: Cambridge Press.

Multicultural classrooms and schools provide rich learning opportunities for students with disabilities as well as for gifted and talented students.

Exceptionality

Expanded rights for students with disabilities was one major consequence of the civil rights movement of the 1960s and 1970s. The Supreme Court's *Brown* decision, issued in 1954, established the principle that to segregate students solely because of their race is inherently unequal and unconstitutional. This decision, as well as other legal and social reforms of the 1960s, encouraged advocates for the rights of students with disabilities to push for expanded rights for them. If it was unconstitutional to segregate students because of their race, it was reasoned, segregating students because of their disabilities could also be challenged.

The advocates for the rights of students with disabilities experienced a major victory in 1975, when Congress enacted Public Law 94-142, the Education for All Handicapped Children Act. This act is unprecedented and revolutionary in its implications. It requires free public education for all children with disabilities, nondiscriminatory evaluation, and an individualized education program (IEP) for each student with a disability. The act also stipulates that each student with a disability should be educated in the least restricted environment. This last requirement has been one of the most controversial provisions of Public Law 94-142. Most students who are classified as having disabilities—about 85 percent—have mild disabilities.

Exceptionality intersects with factors such as gender and race or ethnicity in interesting and complex ways. Males and students of color are more frequently classified as special education students than are females and White mainstream students. Nearly twice as many males as females are classified as special education students. Consequently, males of color are the most likely group to be classified as mentally retarded or learning disabled. The higher proportion of males and students of color in special education programs is related to the fact that mental retardation is a socially constructed category (see Chapter 1).

Students with disabilities as well as gifted students are considered exceptional. Exceptional students are those who have learning or behavioral characteristics that differ substantially from most other students and that require special attention in instruction. Concern for U.S. students who are gifted and talented increased after the Soviet Union successfully launched *Sputnik* in 1957. A Gifted and Talented Children's Education Act was passed by Congress in 1978. However, the nation's concern for the gifted is ambivalent and controversial. In 1982, special funding for gifted education was consolidated with 29 other educational programs. The controversy over gifted education stems in part from the belief by many people that it is élitist. Others argue that gifted education is a way for powerful mainstream parents to acquire an excellent education for their children in the public schools. The fact that few students of color are classified as gifted is another source of controversy. Despite controversies that surround programs for gifted and talented youths, schools need to find creative and democratic ways to satisfy these students' needs.

This part describes the major issues, challenges, and promises that equal educational opportunities for exceptional students—those with disabilities and those who are intellectually gifted and talented.

CHAPTER 13

Educational Equality for Students with Disabilities

William L. Heward, Sara Ernsbarger Bicard, and Rodney A. Cavanaugh

Children differ from one another. Look in any classroom in any school and you will immediately notice differences in children's height, weight, style of dress, hair and skin color, and other physical characteristics. Look a bit closer and you will see some obvious differences in children's language and their academic and social skills. Closely observe the interactions among students, curriculum, and instruction, and you will begin to see how individual children respond differently to the curriculum content and to the instructional methods.

Children also differ from one another in ways that are usually not apparent to a casual observer. Differences in the educational opportunities children receive and the benefits they derive from their time in school are two examples. The educational implications of gender, race, social class, religion, ethnicity, and language diversity not only influence how children may respond to curriculum and instruction but also affect the structure and design of educational systems in general.

While diversity in social class, race, culture, and language differences increasingly characterizes U.S. classrooms, every classroom is also characterized by students' *skill diversity*. Some children learn quickly and easily apply what they learn to new situations. Other children need repeated practice to perform a simple task and then may have difficulty successfully completing the same task the next day. Some children begin a lesson with a large store of relevant experience and background knowledge; others come to the same lesson with little or no relevant prerequisite skills or knowledge. Some children are popular and have many friends. Others are ostracized because they have not learned how to be friendly.

The skill differences among most children are relatively small, allowing these children to benefit from the general education program offered by their schools. When the physical, social, and academic skills of children differ to such an extent that typical school curricula or teaching methods are neither appropriate nor effective, however, equitable access to and benefits from educational programs are at stake.

Like the others in this book, this chapter is not about surface or educationally irrelevant differences among children. Teachers must have the knowledge and skills to recognize and to be instructionally responsive to the diversity their students represent. This chapter extends the concept of diversity to include children with disabilities, and it lays the foundation for teachers to examine educational equity for learners with diverse skills.

This chapter briefly outlines the history of exclusion and educational inequality experienced by many students with disabilities in our nation's schools. It also examines the progress made during the past three decades, paying particular attention to the Individuals with Disabilities Education Act (IDEA), federal legislation that requires that all children, regardless of the type or severity of their disabilities, be provided with a free and appropriate public education. We look at the key features of this landmark law, the outcomes of its implementation, and the major barriers that continue to impede true educational equity for students with disabilities. But first, let us take a closer look at the concept of disability and examine when skill diversity necessitates special education.

WHO ARE STUDENTS WITH DISABILITIES?

A variety of related terms are used to refer to children with special learning needs. When the term *exceptional* is used to describe students, it includes both children who have difficulty learning and children whose performance is advanced. The performance of exceptional children differs from the norm (either above or below) to such an extent that individualized programs of special education are necessary to meet their diverse needs. *Exceptional* is an inclusive term that describes not only students with severe disabilities but also those who are gifted and talented. This chapter focuses on children with disabilities—those students for whom learning presents a significant challenge.

The term *disability* refers to the loss or reduced function of a certain body part or organ; *impairment* is often used synonymously with *disability*. A child with a disability cannot perform certain tasks (e.g., walking, speaking, seeing) in the same way in which nondisabled children do. A disability does not constitute a handicap, however, unless the disability leads to educational, personal, social, vocational, or other difficulties for the individual. For example, a child with one arm who can function in and out of school without special support or accommodations is not considered handicapped. *Handicap* refers to the challenges a person with a disability experiences when interacting with the physical or social environment. Some disabilities pose a handicap in some environments but not in others. The child with a prosthetic arm may be handicapped (i.e., disadvantaged) when competing with nondisabled classmates on the playground but experience no handicap in the classroom. Individuals with disabilities also experience handicaps that have nothing to do with their disabilities but instead are the result of negative attitudes and inappropriate behavior of others who needlessly restrict their access and ability to participate fully in school, work, or community activities.

Children who are not currently identified as handicapped but are considered to have a higher-than-normal chance of developing a disability are referred to as *at risk*. This term is used with infants and preschoolers who, because of difficulties experienced at birth or conditions in the home environment, may be expected to have developmental problems as they grow older. Some educators also use the term to refer to students who are having learning problems in the regular classroom and are therefore "at risk" of being identified as disabled and in need of special education services. Physicians also use the terms *at risk* or *high risk* to identify pregnancies in which there is a higher-than-usual probability of the baby being born with a physical or developmental disability.

A physical, behavioral, or cognitive disability is considered a handicap when it adversely affects a student's educational performance. Students with disabilities are entitled to special education because their physical or behavioral attributes conform to one or more of the following categories of disability:

- Mental retardation (developmental disabilities) (Beirne-Smith, Patton, & Smith, 2006)
- Learning disabilities (Mercer & Pullen, 2005)
- Emotional or behavioral disorders (Kauffman, 2005)
- Communication (speech and language) disorders (Anderson & Shames, 2006)
- Hearing impairments (Moores, 2001)
- Visual impairments (Barraga & Erin, 2001)
- Physical and health impairments (Best, Heller, & Bigge, 2005)
- Autism (Scheuermann & Webber, 2002)
- Traumatic brain injury (Hill, 1999)
- Multiple disabilities (Snell & Brown, 2006)

It is beyond the purpose and scope of this chapter to describe the defining characteristics and educational implications of each type of disability. Interested readers should refer to the sources identified in the References section to obtain information about each area.

Regardless of the terms used to refer to students who exhibit diversity in academic, vocational, and social skills, it is incorrect to believe that there are two distinct kinds of students—those who are exceptional and those who are typical. All children differ from one another to some extent. Exceptional students are those whose skill diversity is significant enough to require a specially designed program of instruction in order to achieve educational equality.

Students with disabilities are more like other students than they are different from them. All students are alike in that all students can benefit from an appropriate education, an education that enables students to do things they were previously unable to do and to do them with greater independence and enjoyment.

Is Disability a Social Construct?

The proposition that some (perhaps all) disabilities are social constructs merits attention in any discussion of educational equity for exceptional children (Danforth, 1995; Elkind, 1998; Smith, 1999; Smith & Mitchell, 2001). The issue is particularly relevant to a text about multicultural education (Huebner, 1994). The establishment of membership criteria in any group is, by definition, socially constructed because the criteria have been created by human beings (Banks, 2000). How educational communities respond to the cultural-, ethnic-, gender-, and class-specific attributes children bring to the classroom is more important than how they perceive the establishment of membership criteria for a particular group. Education's response to the diversity children represent will influence their achievement as well as the professional and societal judgments about that achievement.

Children who are poor or whose ethnicity is not White European American are generally underrepresented in programs for children who are gifted and talented and overrepresented in programs for children who experience learning difficulties (Artiles, Aguirre-Munoz, & Abedi, 1998; Daugherty, 2001; Ford, 1998; MacMillan & Reschly, 1998; Oswald & Coutinho, 2001; Patton, 1998). There is evidence that some children's so-called disabilities are primarily the result of culture, class, or gender influences that are at odds with the culture, class, or gender that has established a given category of disability and the assessment procedures used to make those determinations (Gollnick & Chinn, 2002; Langdon, Novak, & Quintanar, 2000). As is discussed later in this chapter, a significant focus of special education litigation and legislation has been directed on these inequities.

Deconstructing the traditional sociopolitical view of exceptionality, changing social group membership, or passing legislation will not, however, eliminate the real challenges students with disabilities experience in acquiring fundamental academic, self-help, personal-social, and vocational skills. While the criteria for determining the presence or absence of a disability may be hypothetical social constructions, the handicaps created by educational disabilities are not (Fuchs & Fuchs, 1995a; Sugai, 1998).

School-age learners with disabilities, those who have pronounced difficulty acquiring and generalizing new knowledge and skills, are real children, with real needs, in real classrooms. Be wary of the conception that disabilities are merely socially constructed phenomena, that all children who are identified as disabled would achieve success and behave well if others simply viewed them more positively. This romantic ideology is seldom, if ever, promoted by individuals with disabilities themselves or by their parents and families.

Our discussion of students with disabilities and of the role special education plays in addressing their needs assumes that a child's physical, behavioral, or cognitive skill diversity is influenced by, but also transcends, other variables such as ethnicity and social class. We also assume that the educational challenges students with disabilities experience represent real and significant barriers to their ability to experience independence and personal satisfaction across a wide range of life experiences and circumstances. Many factors will contribute to educational equality for children with disabilities. Among the most important of these factors is carefully planned and systematically delivered instruction with meaningful curricula and future-oriented learning objectives (Heward & Dardig, 2001).

How Many Students with Disabilities Are There?

It is impossible to know for certain how many students with disabilities there are in U.S. schools for many reasons, including the following:

- The use of different criteria by state and local school systems for identifying exceptional students
- The relative degree to which different school systems provide services that prevent at-risk students from becoming special education students

- The imprecise nature of assessment and the large part that subjective judgment plays in interpreting assessment data
- The fact that a student might be identified as disabled at one time and as not disabled (or included in another disability category) at another time.

The most complete and systematic information about the number of students with disabilities in the United States is found in the U.S. Department of Education's annual report to Congress on the education of children with disabilities. The most recent information available is for the 2003–2004 school year (U.S. Department of Education, 2004):

- More than 6.3 million children with disabilities, from birth to age 21, received special education services during the 2003–2004 school year.
- The number of children and youth who receive special education has increased every year since a national count was begun in 1976.
- New early-intervention programs have been major contributors to the increases since 1986. During 2003–2004, 679,212 preschoolers (ages three to five) and 272,082 infants and toddlers (birth through age two) were among those receiving special education.
- Children with disabilities in special education represent approximately 11 percent of the entire school-age population.
- The number of children who receive special education increases from age three through age nine. The number served decreases gradually with each successive year after age nine until age 17. After age 17, the number of students receiving special education decreases sharply.
- Of all school-age children receiving special education, 84 percent are reported under four disability categories: learning disabilities (47.2 percent), speech and language impairment (18.8 percent), mental retardation (9.6 percent), and emotional disturbance (8.1 percent) (see Table 13.1).
- The percentage of school-age students with learning disabilities receiving special education has grown dramatically since 1976 (from 23.8 percent to 47.2 percent), while the percentage of students with mental retardation has decreased by more than half (from 24.9 percent to 9.6 percent).
- About twice as many males as females receive special education.
- The vast majority—approximately 85 percent—of school-age children receiving special education have mild to moderate disabilities.

Classification of Students with Disabilities

The classification and labeling of exceptional students have been widely debated for many years. Some educators believe the classification and labeling of exceptional students serve only to stigmatize and exclude them from the mainstream of educational opportunities (Danforth & Rhodes, 1997; Kliewer & Biklen, 1996; Reschly, 1996). Others argue that a workable system of classification is necessary to obtain the special educational services and programs

Table 13.1   Number of Students Ages 6–21 Who Received Special Education Services Under the Federal Government's Disability Categories (2003–2004 school year)

Disability Category	Number	Percent of Total
Specific learning disabilities	2,816,361	47.2
Speech or language impairments	1,118,543	18.8
Mental retardation	570,643	9.6
Emotional disturbance	482,597	8.1
Other health impairments	449,093	7.5
Autism	140,473	2.3
Multiple disabilities	131,225	2.2
Hearing impairments	71,188	1.2
Orthopedic impairments	67,772	1.1
Developmental delay	65,878	1.1
Visual impairments	25,294	0.4
Traumatic brain injury	22,459	0.4
Deaf-blindness	1,603	<0.1
All disabilities	5,963,129	100.0

Source: From U.S. Office of Special Education. (2004). *Individuals with Disabilities Education Act (IDEA) Data* (Table AA3). Washington, DC: Author. Available at http://www.ideadata.org/PartBdata.asp.

that are prerequisite to educational equality for exceptional students (Kauffman, 1999; MacMillan, Gresham, Bocian, & Lambros, 1998). Like most complex questions, there are valid perspectives on both sides of the labeling issue, with political, ethical, and emotional concerns competing with educational, scientific, and fiscal considerations (Luckasson & Reeve, 2001). The most common arguments for and against the labeling of students with exceptional learning needs follow (Heward, 2006).

Possible Advantages of Labeling

- Labeling recognizes meaningful differences in learning or behavior and is a first and necessary step in responding responsibly to those differences.
- Labeling helps professionals communicate with one another and classify and assess research findings.
- Funding and resources for research and other programs are often based on specific categories of exceptionality.
- Labels allow disability-specific advocacy groups (e.g., parents of children with autism) to promote specific programs and to spur legislative action.

- Labeling helps make the special needs of exceptional children more visible to policy makers and the public.

Possible Disadvantages of Labeling

- Because labels usually focus on disability, impairment, and performance deficits, some people may think only in terms of what the individual cannot do instead of what he or she can do or might be able to learn to do.
- Labels may stigmatize the child and lead peers to reject or ridicule the labeled child.
- Labels may negatively impact the child's self-esteem.
- Labels may cause other people to react to and hold low expectations of a child based on the label, resulting in a self-fulfilling prophecy.
- Labels that describe a child's performance deficit often mistakenly acquire the role of explanatory constructs (e.g., "Brandy acts that way *because* she is emotionally disturbed").
- Labels suggest that learning problems are primarily the result of something wrong within the child, thereby reducing the systematic examination of and accountability for instructional variables as the cause of performance diversity. This is an especially damaging outcome when the label provides educators with a built-in excuse for ineffective instruction (e.g., "Chris hasn't learned to read because he's learning disabled").
- Special education labels have a certain permanence; once labeled, a child has difficulty ever achieving the status of simply being just another kid.
- Labels may provide a basis for keeping students out of the regular classroom.
- The classification of exceptional children is costly and requires the expenditure of much professional and student time that could be better spent in planning, delivering, and receiving instruction.

There are strong arguments both for and against the classification and labeling of exceptional students. Research conducted to assess the effects of labeling has been of little help, with most of the studies contributing inconclusive, often contradictory, evidence. Two important issues are how the use of categorical labels affects a child's access to special education services and the quality of instruction that he or she receives as a result of classification.

Eligibility for Special Education

Under current law, to receive an individualized program of special educational services to meet his or her needs, a student must first be identified as having a disability, that is, must be labeled and then, with few exceptions, further classified into one of the categories, such as learning disabilities or visual impairment. So, in practice, membership in a given disability category, and therefore exposure to the potential disadvantages that label carries with it, is a prerequisite to receiving the special education services necessary to achieve educational equality.

Kauffman (1999) points out the reality of labels as a necessary first step in serving students with important differences in behavior and learning: "Although universal interventions that apply equally to all, regardless of their behavioral characteristics or risks of developing disorders, can be implemented without labels and risk of stigma, no other interventions are possible without labels. Either all students are treated the same or some are treated differently. Any student who is treated differently is inevitably labeled" (p. 452).

Impact on Instruction

The classification of students according to the various categories of exceptionality is done largely under the presumption that students in each category share certain physical, behavioral, and learning characteristics that hold important implications for planning and delivering educational services. It is a mistake, however, to believe that once a child has been identified by a certain disability category his or her educational needs and the manner in which those needs should be met have also been identified. Although written more than three decades ago, the advice of Becker, Engelmann, and Thomas (1971) is still pertinent today: "For the most part the labels are not important. They rarely tell the teacher who can be taught in what way. One could put five or six labels on the same child and still not know what to teach him or how" (p. 436).

HISTORY OF EDUCATIONAL EQUALITY FOR STUDENTS WITH DISABILITIES

If a society can be judged by the way it treats people who are different, our educational system does not have a distinguished history. Students who are different, whether because of race, culture, language, gender, or disability, have often been denied equal access to educational opportunities. For many years, educational opportunity of any kind did not exist for many students with disabilities. Students with severe disabilities were completely excluded from public schools. Before 1970, many states had laws permitting local school districts to deny access to children whose physical or intellectual disability caused them, in the opinion of school officials, to be unable to benefit from instruction (Murdick, Gartin, & Crabtree, 2006).

Most students with disabilities were enrolled in school, but perhaps half of the nation's children with disabilities were denied an appropriate education through what H. R. Turnbull and A. P. Turnbull (2001) call "functional exclusion." The students were allowed to come to school but were not participating in an educational program designed to meet their special needs. Students with mild learning and behavior problems remained in the regular classroom but were given no special help. If they failed to make satisfactory progress in the curriculum, they were called "slow learners"; if they acted out in class, they were called "disciplinary problems" and were suspended from school.

For students who did receive a program of differentiated curriculum or instruction, special education usually meant a separate education in segregated classrooms and special schools isolated from the mainstream of education. These children were labeled *mentally retarded, crippled*, or *emotionally disturbed*. Special education often meant a classroom especially reserved for students who could not measure up in the regular classroom. The following passage exemplified what was too often a common occurrence:

> I accepted my first teaching position in a special education class in a basement room next door to the furnace. Of the fifteen "educable mentally retarded" children assigned to work with me, most were simply nonreaders from poor families. One child had been banished to my room because she posed a behavior problem to her fourth-grade teacher. My class and I were assigned a recess spot on the opposite side of the play yard, far away from the "normal" children. I was the only teacher who did not have a lunch break. I was required to eat with my "retarded" children while the other teachers were permitted to leave their students. (Aiello, 1976, p. 14)

As society's concepts of equality, freedom, and justice have expanded, education's response to students with disabilities has changed slowly but considerably over the past several decades. Educational opportunity has gradually shifted from a pattern of exclusion and isolation to one of integration and participation. But change has not come easily, nor has it occurred by chance. Judiciary and legislative authority has been necessary to begin to correct educational inequities for children with disabilities. Recent efforts to ensure educational equality for students with disabilities can be viewed as an outgrowth of the civil rights movement. All of the issues and events that helped shape society's attitudes during the 1950s and 1960s affected the development of special education for exceptional students, particularly the 1954 landmark case of *Brown* v. *Board of Education of Topeka*. This case challenged the practice, common at the time, of segregating schools according to the race of the children. The U.S. Supreme Court ruled that education must be available to all children on equal terms and that it is unconstitutional to operate segregated schools under the premise that they are separate but equal.

The *Brown* decision that public school education should be provided to African American and White children on equal terms initiated a period of intense questioning by parents of children with disabilities who wondered why the same principles of equal access to education did not also apply to their children. Numerous cases challenging the exclusion and isolation of children with disabilities by the schools were brought to court by parents and advocacy groups. At issue in these cases were numerous questions, including (1) the fairness of intelligence testing and the legitimacy of placing children in special education classes solely on the basis of those tests; (2) intelligence testing and other assessment instruments that were not administered in a child's native language or were otherwise culturally biased; and (3) arguments by schools that they could not afford to educate exceptional students. One of the most influential court cases in the development of educational equality for exceptional students was *Pennsylvania Association for Retarded Children* v. *Commonwealth of Pennsylvania* (1972). The association (PARC) brought the class-action suit to challenge a state law that enabled public schools to deny education to children they considered "unable to profit from public school attendance."

The attorneys and parents who represented PARC argued that it was neither rational nor necessary to assume that the children were uneducable. Because the state could neither prove that the children were uneducable nor demonstrate a rational basis for excluding them from public school programs, the court decided that the children were entitled to a free public education. Other court cases followed with similar rulings—children with disabilities, like all other people in the United States, are entitled to the same rights and protection under the law as guaranteed in the Fourteenth Amendment, which declares that people may not be deprived of their equality or liberty on the basis of any classification such as race, nationality, or religion. (For a summary of these court cases, see Heward, 2006.)

The term *progressive integration* (Reynolds, 1989) has been used to describe the history of special education and the gradual but unrelenting progress of ensuring equal educational opportunity for all children. Of the many court cases involving education for children with disabilities, no single case resulted in sweeping educational reform. With each instance of litigation, however, the assembly of what was to become the Individuals with Disabilities Education Act became more complete. Together, all of these developments contributed to the passage of a federal law concerning educational equality for students with disabilities.

THE INDIVIDUALS WITH DISABILITIES ACT: A LEGISLATIVE MANDATE FOR EDUCATIONAL EQUALITY FOR STUDENTS WITH DISABILITIES

In 1975 Congress passed the Education for All Handicapped Children Act (P.L. 94–142). When he reluctantly signed the act, President Gerald Ford expressed concern that the federal government was promising more than it could deliver. Shortly after its passage, P.L. 94–142 was called "blockbuster legislation" (Goodman, 1976) and hailed as the law that "will probably become known as having the greatest impact on education in history" (Stowell & Terry, 1977, p. 475). Since it became law in 1975, Congress has reauthorized and amended P.L. 94–142 five times, most recently in 2004. The 1990 amendments renamed the law the Individuals with Disabilities Education Act—often referred to by its acronym, IDEA.

IDEA is a landmark piece of legislation that has changed the face of education in the United States. IDEA has affected every school in the United States and has changed the roles of regular and special educators, school administrators, parents, and many other people involved in the educational process. Its passage marked the culmination of the efforts of a great many educators, parents, and legislators to bring together in one comprehensive bill this country's laws regarding the education of children with disabilities. The law reflects society's concern for treating people with disabilities as full citizens, with the same rights and privileges that all other citizens enjoy.

The purpose of IDEA is

1. (A) to ensure that all children with disabilities have available to them a free appropriate public education which emphasizes special education and related services designed to meet their unique needs and to prepare them for further

education, employment, and independent living; (B) to ensure that the rights of children with disabilities and parents of such children are protected; (C) to assist States, localities, educational service agencies, and Federal agencies to provide for the education of all children with disabilities.

2. to assist States in the implementation of a statewide, comprehensive, coordinated, multidisciplinary, interagency system of early intervention services for infants and toddlers with disabilities and their families;

3. to ensure that educators and parents have the necessary tools to improve educational results for children with disabilities by supporting system improvement activities; coordinated research and personnel preparation; coordinated technical assistance, dissemination, and support; and technology development and media services; and

4. to assess and assure the effectiveness of efforts to education children with disabilities (H.R. 1350, Sec 601 (d)).

Major Principles of the Individuals with Disabilities Education Act

IDEA is directed primarily at the states, which are responsible for providing education to their residents. The majority of the many rules and regulations defining how IDEA operates are related to six major principles that have remained unchanged since 1975 (Turnbull & Cilley, 1999; Turnbull & Turnbull, 2000).

Zero Reject

Schools must educate *all* children with disabilities. This principle applies regardless of the nature or severity of the disability; no child with disabilities may be excluded from a public education. This requirement of the law is based on the proposition that all children with disabilities can learn and benefit from an appropriate education and that schools, therefore, do not have the right to deny any child access to equal educational opportunity. The mandate to provide special education to all students with disabilities is absolute between the ages of six and seventeen. If a state provides educational services to children without disabilities between the ages three and five and 18 and 21, it must also educate all children with disabilities in those age groups. Each state education agency is responsible for locating, identifying, and evaluating all children, from birth to age 21, residing in the state who have disabilities or are suspected of having disabilities. This requirement is called the *child find system*.

Nondiscriminatory Identification and Evaluation

IDEA requires that students with disabilities be evaluated fairly. The school or parents can request that a child be evaluated for special education. Parents must be notified and consent to the evaluation. IDEA Improvement Act of 2004 (P.L. 108–446) mandates that the evaluation for special education must be completed within 60 days of receiving parental consent for the evaluation. Assessment must be nondiscriminatory. This requirement is particularly important because of the disproportionate number of children from non-White and non–English-speaking cultural groups who are identified as having disabilities, often solely on the basis of a score from standardized intelligence tests. The intelligence tests that have been used most often in the identification of students with learning problems were developed based on the performance of White, middle-class children. Because of their Anglocentric nature, the tests are often considered to be unfairly biased against children from diverse cultural groups who have had less of an opportunity to learn the knowledge sampled by the test items (Venn, 2004). IDEA states clearly that the results of one test cannot be used as the sole criterion for placement into a special education program. Ortiz and colleagues (Ortiz, 1997; Ortiz & Wilkinson, 1991) have developed a prereferral process for preventing inappropriate placements of culturally diverse students in special education.

In addition to nondiscriminatory assessment, testing must be multifactored to include as many tests and observational techniques as necessary to fairly and appropriately identify an individual child's strengths and weaknesses. A child who has been referred for a multifactored assessment for a learning disability, for example, must be evaluated by several individuals across several different social and academic areas. The school psychologist may administer several different tests in order to obtain reliable data about the child's ability and achievement levels. The school counselor may observe the child in various academic as well as nonacademic settings such as the playground and lunchroom. Observational data from the child's teachers and samples of the child's work should be compiled. A speech and language therapist, occupational therapist, rehabilitation counselor, or social worker may also be included in the assessment process. Parental input and the child's own perceptions of his or her needs complete a thorough and well-rounded multifactored assessment. The result of these efforts should be an accurate picture of the child's current levels of performance, with clear indications as to what type of educational program will be most appropriate.

Free, Appropriate Public Education

All children with disabilities, regardless of the type or severity of their disability, shall receive a free, appropriate public education. This education must be provided at public expense—that is, without cost to the child's parents. An *individualized education program* (IEP) must be developed and implemented for each child with a disability. The law is specific in identifying the kind of information an IEP must include and who is to be involved in its development. Each IEP must be created by an *IEP team* consisting of (at least) the child's parents (or guardians); at least one regular education teacher of the child; at least one special education teacher; a representative of the local school district who is qualified to provide or supervise specially designed instruction, is knowledgeable of the general curriculum and about the resources of the local education agencies; and, an individual who can interpret the instructional implications of evaluation results, other individuals who have knowledge of regarding the child (at discretion of the parent or the school); and whenever appropriate, the child. Many IEP teams also include professionals from various disciplines such as school psychology, physical therapy, and medicine. (For suggestions on how IEP teams can work effectively and involve parents and students with disabilities in the IEP process, see Al-Hassan & Gardner, 2002; Martin, Hughes, Huber Marshall, Jerman, & Maxson, 1999; Menlove, Hudson, & Suter, 2001; A. P. Turnbull & H. R. Turnbull, 2001.)

The IEP is the foundation of the special education and related services a child with a disability receives. A carefully and collaboratively prepared IEP specifies the skills the child needs to learn in relation to his or her present levels of performance, the procedures that will be used to occasion that learning, and the means of determining the extent to which learning has taken place (Bateman & Linden, 1998). Although IEP formats vary widely across school districts, and schools may go beyond the requirements of the law and include additional information, all IEPs must include the following seven components:

1. A statement of the child's present levels of academic and functional performance, including
   - How the child's disability affects the child's involvement and progress in the general curriculum;
   - For preschool children, as appropriate, how the disability affects the child's participation in appropriate activities; and
   - For children with disabilities who take alternate assessments aligned to alternate achievement standards, a description of benchmarks or short-term objectives;

2. A statement of measurable annual goals, including academic and functional goals, designed to
   - Meet the child's needs that result from the child's disability to enable the child to be involved in and make progress in the general curriculum; and
   - Meet each of the child's other educational needs that result from the child's disability;

3. A description of how the child's progress toward meeting the annual goals described in subclause (2) will be measured; and when periodic reports on the progress the child is making toward meeting the annual goals (such as through use of subquarterly or other periodic reports, concurrent with the issuance of report cards) will be provided;

4. A statement of the special education and related services and supplementary aids and services, based on peer-reviewed research to the extent practicable, to be provided to the child, or on behalf of the child, and a statement of the program modifications or support for school personnel that will be provided for the child
   - To advance appropriately toward attaining the annual goals;
   - To be involved in and progress in the general curriculum in accordance with subclause (1) and to participate in extracurricular and other nonacademic activities; and
   - To be educated and participate with other children with disabilities and nondisabled children in the activities described in this subparagraph;

5. An explanation of the extent, if any, to which the child will not participate with nondisabled children in the regular class and in the activities described in subclause (IV)(cc);

6. (a) A statement of any individual appropriate accommodations that are necessary to measure the academic achievement and functional performance of the child on state and district-wide assessments consistent with section 612(a)(16)(A); and (b) if the IEP team determines that the child shall take an alternate assessment on a particular state or districtwide assessment of student achievement, a statement of why—

   • The child cannot participate in the regular assessment; and

   • The particular alternate assessment selected is appropriate for the child;

7. The projected date for the beginning of the services and modifications described in subclause (4), and the anticipated frequency, location, and duration of those services and modifications. (Individuals with Disabilities Education Improvement Act of 2004, H. R. 1350, Sec 614 (d)(B))

Essentially, the IEP is a system for spelling out where the child is, where he or she should be going, how he or she will get there, how long it will take, and how to tell when he or she has arrived. Although the IEP is a written document signed by both school personnel and the child's parents, it is not a legally binding contract. That is, parents cannot take their child's teachers or the school to court if all goals and objectives stated in the IEP are not met. However, schools must be able to document that the services described in the IEP have been provided in a systematic effort to meet those goals (Huefner, 2000). IEPs must be reviewed by the IEP team at least annually.

The IEP process has been problematic since its inception (Huefner, 2000; Yell & Drasgow, 2000). Early on, it was coined as "probably the single most unpopular aspect of the law, not only because it requires a great deal of work, but also because the essence of the plan itself seems to have been lost in the mountains of paperwork" (Gallagher, 1984, p. 228). Properly including all of the mandated components in an IEP is no guarantee that the document will guide the student's learning and teacher's teaching in the classroom, as intended by IDEA. Although most educators agree with the idealized concept of the IEP, inspection and evaluation of IEPs often reveal inconsistency between what is written on the document and what students experience in the classroom (e.g., Bateman & Linden, 1998; Grigal, Test, Beattie, & Wood, 1997; Smith & Brownell, 1995).

Several tools have been developed that IEP teams can use to create IEPs that go beyond compliance with the law and actually serve as a meaningful guide for the "specially designed instruction" a student with disabilities needs (e.g., Gibb & Dyches, 2000; Hammer, 2004; Lignugaris/Kraft, Marchand-Martella, & Martella, 2001; Keys & Owens-Johnson, 2003; Lytle & Bordin, 2001; Menlove et al., 2001; Rock, 2000; Walsh, 2001; Wood, Karvonen, Test, Browder, & Algozinne, 2004). For example, *Choosing Outcomes and Accommodations for Children (COACH)* is a field-tested program that guides child-study teams through the assessment and planning stages of IEP development in a way that results in goals and objectives directly related to functional skills in integrated settings (Giangreco, Cloninger, & Iverson, 1998).

Least Restrictive Environment

IDEA mandates that students with disabilities be educated in the *least restrictive environment* (LRE). Specifically, the law states that:

> to the maximum extent appropriate, children with disabilities,
> including children in public or private institutions or other care
> facilities, [will be] educated with children who are not disabled,
> and that special classes, separate schooling or other removal of
> children with disabilities from the regular educational environment
> [may occur] only when the nature or severity of the disability is
> such that education in regular classes with the use of
> supplementary aids and services cannot be achieved satisfactorily.
> (20 U.S.C. Section 1412[a][5])

The LRE requirement has been one of the most controversial and least understood aspects of IDEA. During the first few years after its passage, some professionals and parents erroneously interpreted the law to mean that all children with disabilities, regardless of type or severity of their disabilities, had to be placed in regular classrooms. Instead, the LRE principle requires that each child with a disability be educated in a setting that most closely resembles a regular class placement in which his or her individual needs can be met. Although some people argue that any decision to place a child with a disability in a special class or school is inappropriate, most educators and parents realize that a regular classroom placement can be overly restrictive if the child's academic and social needs are not met. LRE is a relative concept; the least restrictive environment for one student with a disability would not necessarily be appropriate for another. Therefore, two students who have the same disability should not necessarily be placed in the same setting.

Children with disabilities need a wide range of special education and related services. Today, most schools provide a *continuum of services*—that is, a range of placement and service options to meet the individual needs of students with disabilities. The continuum can be symbolically depicted as a pyramid, with placements ranging from least restrictive (regular classroom placement) at the bottom to most restrictive (special schools, residential programs, and hospital or homebound programs) at the top (see Figure 13.1). The regular classroom is at the bottom of the pyramid and is widest to show that the greatest numbers of exceptional students are placed there. Moving up from the bottom of the pyramid, each successive placement option represents an environment in which increasingly more restrictive, specialized, and intensive instructional and related services can be offered. Typically, as the severity of a child's disability increases, so too does the need for more specialized services. As noted, however, the majority of students who receive special education services experience mild disabilities; hence, the pyramid grows smaller at the top to show that more restrictive settings are required for fewer students (see Table 13.2).

Placement of a student with disabilities should not be viewed as all-or-nothing at any one level on the continuum. The IEP team should consider the extent to which the student can effectively be integrated in each of three dimensions of school life—the general academic curriculum, extracurricular activities (e.g., clubs), and other school activities (e.g., recess,

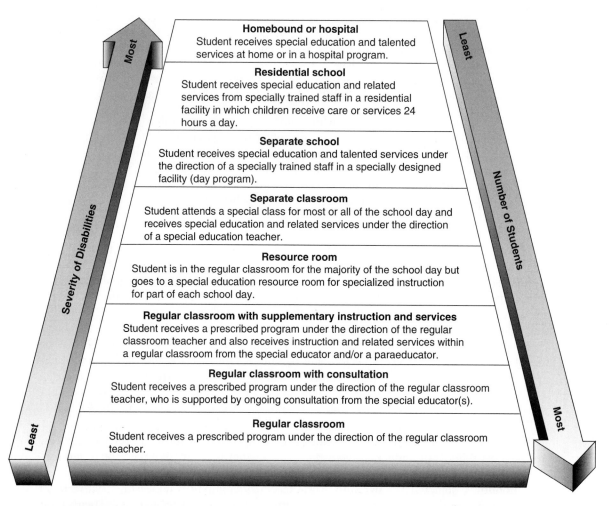

Figure 13.1 Continuum of Educational Placements for Students with Disabilities

Source: From W. L. Heward. (2006). *Exceptional Children: An Introduction to Special Education* (8th ed., p. 78). Upper Saddle River, NJ: Merrill/Prentice-Hall. Used by permission.

mealtimes). The LRE "provision allows for a 'mix and match' where total integration is appropriate under one dimension and partial integration is appropriate under another dimension" (Turnbull & Cilley, 1999, p. 41).

In addition, placement must not be regarded as permanent. The continuum concept is intended to be flexible, with students moving from one placement to another as dictated by their individual educational needs. The IEP team should periodically review the specific goals and objectives for each child—they are required to do so at least annually—

Table 13.2   Percentage of Students Ages 6 through 21 Served in Six Educational Environments (2003–2004 school year)

Disability Category	Regular Classroom	Resource Room	Separate Classroom	Separate School	Residential School	Homebound or Hospital
Specific learning disabilities	48.7	37.3	13.0	0.6	0.2	0.2
Speech or language impairments	88.2	6.8	4.6	0.3	<0.1	<0.1
Mental retardation	11.6	30.2	51.8	5.3	0.5	0.5
Emotional disturbance	30.3	22.5	30.2	12.0	3.7	1.2
Other health impairments	51.1	30.5	15.0	1.5	0.3	1.6
Multiple disabilities	12.1	17.2	45.8	20.3	2.4	2.2
Autism	26.8	17.7	43.9	10.2	1.1	0.4
Orthopedic impairments	46.7	20.9	26.2	3.6	0.8	1.8
Hearing impairments	44.9	19.1	22.2	6.9	6.6	0.2
Developmental delay	51.2	28.1	18.7	1.7	0.1	0.2
Visual impairments	54.6	16.9	15.7	5.9	6.3	0.6
Traumatic brain injury	34.6	29.9	27.1	5.9	0.9	1.5
Deaf-blindness	22.2	13.9	33.6	16.6	12.3	1.4
All disabilities	49.9	27.7	18.5	2.8	0.7	0.4

Source: From U.S. Department of Education. (2004). *Individuals with Disabilities Education Act (IDEA) Data* (Table AB2). Washington, DC: Author. Available at http://www.ideadata.org/PartBdata.asp.

and make new placement decisions if warranted. Note that in the first three placement options, students with disabilities spend the entire school day in regular classes with their nondisabled peers. Approximately three out of four students with disabilities receive at least part of their education in regular classrooms with their nondisabled peers (see Figure 13.2). Many of these students, however, spend a portion of each school day in a resource room, where they receive individualized instruction from a specially trained teacher. Approximately one of every five students with disabilities is educated in a separate classroom in a regular public school. Special schools and residential facilities provide the education for less than 4 percent of children with disabilities, usually students with the most severe disabilities.

Neither IDEA nor the regulations that accompany it specify exactly how a school district is to determine LRE. After reviewing the rulings on litigation in four LRE suits that have reached the U.S. courts of appeals, Yell (1995) concluded that the courts have held that IDEA does not require the placement of students with disabilities in the regular classroom but fully supports the continuum of services.

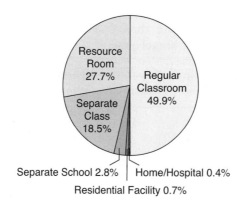

Figure 13.2 Percentage of All Students with Disabilities Ages 6 through 21 in Six Educational Placements

Note: Separate school includes both public and private separate school facilities. Residential school includes both public and private residential facilities.

Source: From U.S. Department of Education. (2004). *Twenty-sixth Annual Report to Congress on the Implementation of the Individuals with Disabilities Act* (Table AB2). Washington, DC: U.S. Government Printing Office.

Although the continuum-of-services model represents well-established practice in special education, it is not without controversy. A number of specific criticisms have been leveled at this approach to providing services to exceptional students. Some critics have argued that the continuum overly legitimizes the use of restrictive placements, implies that integration of persons with disabilities can take place only in least restrictive settings, and may infringe on the rights of people with disabilities to participate in their communities (e.g., Stainback & Stainback, 1996; Taylor, 1988).

The relative value of providing services to students with disabilities outside of the regular classroom, and especially in separate classrooms and schools, is a hotly contested issue (e.g., Fuchs & Fuchs, 1994, 2003; Giangreco, 2003; Kauffman & Hallahan, 1994; Mitchell, 2004a, 2004b; Sasso, 2001; Shanker, 1995; Schwartz, 2005; Taylor, 1995). Virtually all special educators, however, support the responsible inclusion of students with disabilities in which systematic modifications in curriculum and instruction provide the student with frequent and meaningful IEP goals (Kochar, West, & Taymans, 2000; Schwartz, 2000; Vaughn, Schumm, & Brick, 1998). Responsible inclusion models have been developed for children ranging in age from preschool (Sandall, Schwartz, & Joseph, 2000) through high school (Bauer & Brown, 2001) and for students whose disabilities range from mild (Hock, Schumaker, & Deshler, 1999) to severe (Fisher & Ryndak, 2001). Numerous strategies have been developed to help teachers, administrators, parents, and students work together to build inclusive classrooms and schools (Giangreco, Cloninger, Dennis, & Edelman, 2000; Lewis & Doorlag, 2006; Mastropieri & Scruggs, 2004; Salend, 2005; Snell & Janney, 2000; Thomas, Correa, & Morsink, 2001; Wood, 2006).

Due Process Safeguards

IDEA acknowledges that students with disabilities are people with important legal rights. The law makes it clear that school districts do not have absolute authority over exceptional students. Schools may not make decisions about the educational programs of children with disabilities in a unilateral or arbitrary manner.

Due process is a legal concept that is implemented through a series of procedural steps designed to ensure fairness of treatment among school systems, parents, and students. Specific due process safeguards were incorporated into IDEA because of past educational abuses of children with disabilities. In the past, special education placements were often permanent, void of periodic reviews, and made solely on the basis of teacher recommendations. Further, students with severe and profound disabilities were automatically excluded from public school programs and placed in residential programs, where the quality of instructional programs often was very poor. The fact that children from minority cultural groups were disproportionately placed into special education programs was another factor in mandating the due process procedures.

Key elements of due process as it relates to special education are the parents' right to the following:

- Be notified in writing before the school takes any action that may alter the child's program (testing, reevaluation, change in placement)
- Give or withhold permission to have their child tested for eligibility for special education services, reevaluated, or placed in a different classroom or program
- See all school records about their child
- Have a hearing before an impartial party (not an employee of the school district) to resolve disagreements with the school system
- Receive a written decision following any hearing
- Appeal the results of a due process hearing to the state department of education (school districts may also appeal)

A. P. Turnbull and H. R. Turnbull (2001), who are special educators and parents of a young man with disabilities, describe due process as the legal technique that seeks to achieve fair treatment, accountability, and a new and more equal "balance of power" between professionals, who have traditionally wielded power, and families, who have felt they could not affect their children's education.

Parent and Student Participation and Shared Decision Making

IDEA recognizes the benefits of active parent and student participation. Parents not only have a right to be involved in their child's education, but parents can also help professionals select appropriate instructional goals and provide information that will help teachers be more effective in working with their children. As noted, parents (and, whenever appropriate, students) are to take an active role as full members of the IEP team; their input and wishes must be considered in determining IEP goals and objectives, placement decisions, and related services needs (e.g., sign language interpreting, special transportation). Of course, parents cannot be forced to do so and may waive their right to participate.

Additional Features Introduced by the Individuals with Disabilities Education Improvement Act of 2004

The Individuals with Disabilities Education Improvement Act of 2004 (PL 108–446) retained the major principles and components of IDEA. However, it also entailed a number of changes that are likely to affect the field of special education for years to come.

Several of the changes are related to the workload and paperwork involved with IEPs. The new law allows states to choose to pilot plans to reduce paperwork without negatively affecting civil rights requirements or a child's right to a free appropriate education and to allow local school districts to develop comprehensive, multi-year IEPs which can be in effect for up to three years with parental consent. In addition, benchmarks and short-term objectives, statements specifying student achievements that will lead to accomplishing annual goals on the IEP, are now required in IEPs only for students with severe disabilities who will participate in the school district's alternative assessments related to alternate achievement standards.

Other changes in the IDEA Improvement Act of 2004 can be categorized as attempts to align special education with the No Child Left Behind Act (NCLB). One of the key goals of the NCLB legislation is that "highly qualified" teachers will teach all children. IDEA Improvement Act of 2004 includes definitions of "highly qualified" special educators. The law stipulates basic requirements for being a "highly qualified" special educator as (1) hold full state certification as a special education teacher or (2) pass the state special education teacher licensing exam and as a result hold a license to teach in the state as a special education teacher. Additional licenses are required for special educators teaching two or more core subjects or teaching students working toward alternative achievement standards.

The new law allows local education agencies to use a "response-to-instruction" method of determining if a student has learning disabilities as an alternative to identifying a severe discrepancy between academic achievement and intellectual ability. The IDEA Improvement Act of 2004 states, "In determining whether a child has a specific learning disability, a local educational agency may use a process that determines if the child responds to scientific, research-based intervention as a part of the evaluation procedures (Sec 614 (b)(6)(B))." In emphasizing the response-to-instruction approach, the new law aligns itself with the NCLB Act by supporting research-based instruction in general education as a precursor to identification for learning disabilities (U.S. Department of Education, 2005).

Section 504 of the Rehabilitation Act of 1973

Another important law that extends civil rights to people with disabilities is Section 504 of the Rehabilitation Act of 1973. This regulation states, in part, that "no otherwise qualified handicapped individual shall, solely by reason of his handicap, be excluded from the participation in, be denied the benefits of, or be subjected to discrimination in any program or activity receiving federal financial assistance." This law, worded almost identically to the Civil Rights Act of 1964 (which prohibited discrimination based on race, color, or national origin), promises to expand opportunities to children and adults with disabilities in education, employment, and various other settings. It calls for provision of "auxiliary aides for students with impaired sensory, manual, or speaking skills"—for example, readers for students who are blind, interpreters for students who are deaf, and people to assist students with physical disabilities in moving from place to place. This requirement does not mean that schools, colleges, and employers must have *all* such aides available at *all* times; it simply mandates that no person with disabilities may be excluded from a program because of the lack of an appropriate aide.

Architectural accessibility for students, teachers, and other people with physical and sensory impairments is an important feature of Section 504; however, the law does not call for a completely barrier-free environment. Emphasis is on accessibility to programs, not on physical modification of all existing structures. If a chemistry class is required for a premedical program of study, for example, a college might make this program accessible to a student with physical disabilities by reassigning the class to an accessible location or by providing assistance to the student in traveling to an otherwise inaccessible location. All sections of all courses need not be made accessible, but a college should not segregate students with disabilities by assigning them all to a particular section, regardless of disability. Like the IDEA, Section 504 calls for nondiscriminatory placement in the "most integrated setting appropriate" and has served as the basis for many court cases over alleged discrimination against individuals with disabilities, particularly in their right to employment.

The Americans with Disabilities Act

The Americans with Disabilities Act (PL 101–336) was signed into law on July 26, 1990. Patterned after Section 504 of the Rehabilitation Act of 1973, the Americans with Disabilities Act (ADA) extends civil rights protection to persons with disabilities in private-sector employment, in all public services, and in public accommodations, transportation, and telecommunications. A person with a disability is defined in the ADA as a person (1) with a mental or physical impairment that substantially limits that person in a major life activity (e.g., walking, talking, working, self-care); (2) with a record of such an impairment (e.g., a person who no longer has heart disease but is discriminated against because of that history); or (3) who is regarded as having such an impairment (e.g., a person with significant facial disfiguration due to a burn who is not limited in any major life activity but is discriminated against). The major provisions of the ADA are as follows:

- Employers with fifteen or more employees may not refuse to hire or promote a person because of a disability if that person is qualified to perform the job. Also, the employer must make reasonable accommodations that will allow a person with a disability to perform essential functions of the job. Such modifications in job requirements or situation must be made if they will not impose undue hardship on the employer.

- All new vehicles purchased by public transit authorities must be accessible to people with disabilities. All rail stations must be made accessible, and at least one car per train in existing rail systems must be made accessible.

- It is illegal for public accommodations to exclude or refuse persons with disabilities. Public accommodations are everyday businesses and services, such as hotels, restaurants, grocery stores, parks, and so on. All new buildings must be made accessible, and existing facilities must remove barriers if the removal can be accomplished without much difficulty or expense.

- Companies offering telephone service to the general public must offer relay services to individuals who use telecommunications devices for the deaf (such as TDDs) 24 hours a day, seven days a week.

No Child Left Behind Act

Another landmark piece of federal legislation that affects students with disabilities is the Elementary and Secondary Education Act of 2001, which was later renamed the No Child Left Behind Act (NCLB). The intended purpose of NCLB is to "improve student achievement and change the culture of America's schools" (U.S. Department of Education, 2002c, p. ix). The ultimate goal of NCLB is for all children to be proficient in all subject matter by 2014 and to be taught by teachers who are highly qualified in their subjects. NCLB has four key principles: accountability for results, flexibility in schools' use of federal funds, more options for parents, and an emphasis on curriculum and instructional methods that have been demonstrated to work through rigorous scientific research.

Accountability

Although IDEA already mandates participation of students with disabilities in state- and district-wide assessments, NCLB requires annual tests in reading and math in third grade through eighth grade for all students (Ziegler, 2002). Test results must be disaggregated for students by poverty levels, race, ethnicities, disabilities, and limited English proficiency. Each school and children from each category must achieve state-determined pass rates, which will gradually rise. These "report cards" are intended to show not only how well students are doing on meeting standards but also the progress that disaggregated groups are making in closing achievement gaps. Districts and schools that do not make sufficient yearly progress toward state proficiency goals for their students are first targeted for assistance and subject later to corrective action and ultimately restructuring. Schools that meet or exceed objectives will be eligible for "academic achievement awards."

Flexibility and Local Control

States and school districts have increased flexibility under NCLB with how they spend federal education funds. Districts may transfer up to 50 percent of the federal formula grant funds they receive under the Improving Teacher Quality State Grants, Educational Technology, Innovative Programs, and Safe and Drug-Free School programs to any one of these programs or to their Title 1 program without separate approval.

Increased Parental Choice

NCLB gives parents of children in low-performing schools several options. Parents with children in schools that fail to meet state standards for two consecutive years may transfer their children to a better-performing public school, including public charter school, within their district. If they do so, the district must provide transportation. Students from low-income families in schools that fail to meet state standards for 3 years are eligible to receive sup-plemental educational services—including tutoring, after-school services, and summer school. NCLB also provides increased support to parents, educators, and communities to create new charter schools.

Focus on What Works

NCLB puts special emphasis on determining what education programs and practices have been clearly demonstrated to be effective through rigorous scientific research. "One major benefit of this approach would be reduced identification of children for special education ser-vices due to a lack of appropriate reading instruction in their early years" (U.S. Department of Education, 2002a). NCLB provides support for scientifically based reading instruction in preschool and the early grades through the Reading First grant program. Reading First is intended to help states, school districts, and schools ensure that every child can read at grade level or above by the end of third grade through the implementation of evidence-based instructional programs and materials, assessments, and professional development. Reading First defines evidence-based instructional programs as those programs that have foundations in research that uses rigorous, systematic, and empirical methods; adequately analyzes data to test the stated hypotheses and justify conclusions drawn; use valid and reliable measurements and observations; and have been rigorously, objectively, and scientifically reviewed and approved by independent experts (U.S. Department of Education, 2002b). Effective reading instruction is defined as focusing on the essential components of reading instruction—phonemic awareness, alphabetic principle (i.e., phonics), fluency with text, vocabulary, and compre-hension (National Reading Panel, 2000; National Research Council, 1998; U.S. Department of Education, 2002b).

EDUCATIONAL EQUALITY FOR STUDENTS WITH DISABILITIES: PROGRESS MADE BUT CHALLENGES REMAIN

What impact has IDEA had? The most obvious effect is that many more students with dis-abilities are receiving special education and related services than before the law's passage. But this is what the law requires and is only one aspect of its impact.

Educational equality for students with disabilities is also evidenced in the ways that today's schools function as complex human services agencies. Since the passage of IDEA, there has been a dramatic increase in the number of both special education teachers and sup-port staff. Providing the related services necessary to meet the diverse needs of students with disabilities requires that the number of nonclassroom professionals be nearly equal to that of special education teachers. School psychologists, social workers, speech and language therapists, occupational therapists, physical therapists, audiologists, recreational therapists, adaptive physical educators, vocational specialists, and mental health professionals all lend support and expertise to the education of learners with special needs.

Perhaps the law has had its most dramatic effect on students with severe disabilities, many of who had been completely denied the opportunity to benefit from an appropriate education. No longer can schools exclude students with disabilities on the premise that they are uneducable. IDEA is based on the presumption that all students can benefit from an appropriate education, and it states clearly that the local school has the responsibility to modify curriculum content and teaching methods according to the needs of each student. In essence, the law requires schools to adapt themselves to the needs of students rather than allowing schools to deny educational equality to students who do not fit the school. Most people would agree that IDEA has contributed positively to the education of students with disabilities, but significant barriers remain to full educational equality for exceptional students in the United States. We briefly examine five of these issues. If a truly appropriate educational opportunity is to be a reality for students with disabilities, U.S. schools must work hard to (1) bridge the research-to-practice gap with regard to effective instruction, (2) improve cooperation and collaboration between special and regular educators, (3) provide more and better early intervention programs for young children with disabilities, (4) increase the success of young adults with disabilities as they make the transition from school to adult life, and (5) ensure relevant, individualized education to students with disabilities from culturally and linguistically diverse backgrounds.

Effective Instruction

Educational equality for students with disabilities is required by IDEA. The letter of the law can be met by following the mandates for multifactored evaluations, IEPs, due process, and placements in the least restrictive environment. None of these mandated processes, however, teach. True educational equality for children with disabilities can be achieved only through effective instruction (Heward & Dardig, 2001).

Special education is not a slowed-down, watered-down version of general education. It is a systematic, purposeful approach to teaching students with disabilities the academic and social skills they will need to live independent, satisfying, and productive lives, and to do it more effectively and efficiently than could be accomplished by general education alone.

Effective teaching is much more than simply assigning something to learn. One role of all teachers, but especially special educators, is to ensure that the instruction they deliver is measurably effective in meeting the needs of their students. When this occurs, the education that students with disabilities receive will be truly special (Heward, 2003).

Special education can be nothing more, or less, than the quality of instruction provided by teachers. Teachers, of course, are ultimately responsible for providing effective instruction to exceptional students. With this responsibility come several obligations. Working collaboratively with their regular education colleagues and parents (Heron & Harris, 2001), special educators must (1) target instructional objectives that will improve the quality of students' lives in school, home, community, and workplace; (2) use research-validated methods of instruction (Gersten, 1998; Lovitt, 2000); (3) continually evaluate the effectiveness of instruction with direct measures of student performance (Greenwood & Maheady, 1997); and (4) change an instructional program when it does not promote achievement and success (Bushell & Baer, 1994).

Teachers must demand effectiveness from their instructional approaches. For many years, conventional wisdom has fostered the belief that it takes unending patience to teach children with disabilities. We believe this view is a disservice to students with special needs and to the educators—both special and general education teachers—whose job it is to teach them.

Teachers should not wait patiently for exceptional students to learn, attributing lack of progress to some inherent attribute or faulty process within the child, such as mental retardation, learning disability, attention-deficit disorder, or emotional disturbance. Instead, the teacher should use direct and frequent measures of the student's performance as the primary guide for modifying instruction in order to improve its effectiveness. This, we believe, is the real work of the educator (Heward, 2006).

Although IDEA does not state that the job of a teacher is to change behavior, that is what good teachers do. When a teacher helps a child who previously could not add, spell, compose, tie his or her shoes, apply for a job, or make a friend, behavior has been changed. Effective instruction does not change children's behavior by chance. Effective instruction is deliberate in its intent (Heward & Silvestri, 2005). Chance has no place in assuring children's equal opportunity to lead productive, independent, and satisfying lives.

In order to remove chance from the equation for children with disabilities, special education must bridge the research-to-practice gap regarding instructional practice in the classroom (Carnine, 1997; Gersten, 2001; Heward, 2003; Vaughn, Klingner, & Hughes, 2000). Contrary to the contentions of some people, special education research has produced a significant and reliable knowledge base about effective teaching practices (Lovitt, 2000; Spear-Swerling & Sternberg, 2001; Vaughn, Gersten, & Chard, 2000). No knowledgeable person will argue that research has discovered everything that is important to know about teaching exceptional students. There are many questions to be answered, the pursuit of which will no doubt lead to other questions yet to be asked.

While there is a significant gap between what is relatively well understood and what is poorly understood or not understood at all, the more distressing gap may be between what research has discovered about teaching and learning and what is practiced in many classrooms. For example, scientific research has helped us discover a great deal about the features of early reading instruction that can reduce the number of children who later develop reading problems (Kame'enui, Good, & Harn, 2005; National Reading Panel, 2000), how to enhance the success of students with learning disabilities in content-area classes (Deshler et al., 2001), how to teach students the skills they need to more effectively self-determine and self-manage their lives (Algozzine, et al., 2001) and the components of secondary special education programs that can increase students' success in making the transition from school to work (Kohler & Field, 2003), but the education that many students with disabilities receive does not reflect that knowledge (Moody, Vaughn, Hughes, & Fischer, 2000; Wagner, Blackorby, Cameto, & Newman, 1994; Wehby, Symons, Canale, & Go, 1998).

Regular and Special Education Partnership

Traditionally, regular and special education have been viewed as separate disciplines, each serving a different student population. Today, general and special education teachers are becoming partners in meeting the needs of all learners. The concept of "your kids" and "my kids" is gradually being replaced by that of "our kids."

Mainstreaming has traditionally been thought of as the process of integrating students with disabilities into regular schools and classes. Today, the term *inclusive education* is changing not only the language of special education reform but also its intent. Inclusive education can be successful only with full cooperation of and collaboration among those people responsible for the educational programs of students with disabilities (Bauer & Brown, 2001; Giangreco et al., 2000; Snell & Janney, 2000). Although IDEA does not specifically mention mainstreaming or inclusion, it creates a presumption in favor of the regular classroom by requiring that educational services be provided in the least restrictive environment, which in turn necessitates cooperation between general and special educators.

The effects of IDEA on general education are neither entirely clear nor without controversy. This dissonance is further complicated by the tone and content of many discussions about how special education can or should reform while ensuring that the best interests of students with disabilities are appropriately served (Fuchs & Fuchs, 1994, 1995a, 1995b; Taylor, 1995). What is clear, however, is that the entire educational community has the responsibility to do the best job it can in meeting the needs of children with diverse skills. In the final analysis, issues of labeling, classification, placement, and teaching assignments are secondary to the quality of instruction that takes place in the classroom (Heward & Dardig, 2001).

Improved collaboration between special education and general education is important not only for the six million students with disabilities in U.S. schools. In addition to the 10 to 12 percent of school-age children with disabilities who receive special education, it is estimated that another 10 to 20 percent of the student population have mild to moderate learning or behavior problems that interfere with their ability to progress and succeed in the general education program. Both special and regular educators must develop strategies for working together and sharing their skills and resources to prevent these millions of students, who are at risk, from becoming failures of our educational system.

Early Intervention

The years from birth to school age are critical to a child's learning and development. The typical child enters school with a large repertoire of intellectual, language, social, and physical skills on which to build. For many children with disabilities, unfortunately, the preschool years represent a long period of missed opportunities. Without systematic instruction, most young children with disabilities do not acquire many of the basic skills their nondisabled peers seemingly learn without effort. Parents concerned about their child's inability to reach important developmental milestones have often been told by professionals, "Don't worry. He'll probably grow out of it before too long." Many children with disabilities, as a result, fall further and further behind their nondisabled peers, and minor delays in development often become major delays by the time the child reaches school age.

Twenty-five years ago, there were very few early-intervention programs for children with disabilities from birth to school age; today, early childhood special education is the fastest-growing area in the field of education. As with special education of school-age exceptional students, federal legislation has played a major role in the development of early-intervention programs (Shonkoff & Meisels, 2000). By passing Public Law 99–457, the Education of the Handicapped Act Amendments of 1986, Congress reaffirmed the basic principles of the original PL 94–142 and added two major sections concerning early-intervention services.

Only about 70 percent of the preschoolers aged three to five with disabilities were being served under the incentive provisions of IDEA (which did not require states to provide a free public education to children with disabilities under age six). PL 99–457 requires each state to show evidence of serving all three- to five-year-old children with disabilities in order to receive any preschool funds. The second major change brought about by PL 99–457 is that incentive grants are available to states for developing systems of early identification and intervention for infants and toddlers with disabilities from birth to age two. The services must be planned by a multidisciplinary team that includes the child's parents and must be implemented according to an *individualized family services plan (IFSP)* that is similar in concept to the IEP for school-age students with disabilities.

Nearly every special educator today now realizes the critical importance of early intervention for both children who are at risk and those who have disabilities, and most also agree that the earlier intervention is begun, the better (Guralnick, 1997; Sandall, McLean, & Smith, 2000). Fortunately, many educators are working to develop the programs and services so desperately needed by the increasing numbers of babies and preschoolers who are at risk for developing disabilities due to poverty or prenatal exposure to drugs and alcohol (Carta, 2003; Howard, Williams, & McLaughlin, 1994). Early intervention is necessary to give these children a fighting chance to experience educational equality when they enter school.

Transition from School to Adult Life

If the degree of educational equality afforded to students who are exceptional is to be judged, as we think it should, by the extent to which students with disabilities can function independently in everyday environments, then we still have a long way to go. Follow-up studies of young adults who have graduated or left public school secondary special education programs have shown slightly improving results. For example, data from the National Longitudinal Transition Study-2 (NLTS2) (Wagner, Newman, Cameto, & Levine, 2005), an ongoing study of approximately 7,000 youths with disabilities after they left secondary special education programs since 2001, show that 70 percent of youths with disabilities have worked for pay at some time after being out of school for up to 2 years. Much of the work for those who do find jobs is part-time and at or above minimum wage. When adjusted for inflation and compared to pay received by youths with disabilities in the mid-1980s, the average hourly wage has not increased. The probability of a person with moderate or severe disabilities finding real work in the community is much lower. The NLTS-2 found extremely low full-time employment rates during the first few years after high school for young adults with orthopedic impairments (20 percent), mental retardation (24 percent), and multiple disabilities (27 percent).

Employment problems are not the only difficulties faced by adults with disabilities. If the degree of school exit status, postsecondary education, independent living, and socialization and other measures are aspects of successful adult adjustment, then youths with disabilities have become more successful adults over the years. However, much room for improvement remains. For example, the number of youths with disabilities completing school and participating in postsecondary education has increased 17 percent since the 1980s. Since 2001, a majority of youths with disabilities (70 percent) completed high school and approximately 32 percent of youths with disabilities have participated in postsecondary education. However, changes in independent living have not been noted. Since 2001, 81 percent of youths with disabilities live with parents or family, 15 percent live independently, 1 percent live in an institution or facility, and 3 percent had other living arrangements (Wagner et al., 2005).

Education cannot be held responsible for all the difficulties faced by adults with disabilities, but the results of this and other studies make it evident that many young people leave public school special education programs without the skills necessary to function in the community. Many youths with disabilities find all aspects of adult life a challenge (Knoll & Wheeler, 2001; Tymchuk, Lakin, & Luckasson, 2001). Many educators today see the development of special education programs that will effectively prepare exceptional students for adjustment and successful integration into the adult community as the ultimate measure of educational equality for students with disabilities (Test, Aspel, & Everson, 2006; Sitlington, Clark, & Kolstoe, 2000).

Special Education in a Diverse Society

Both special and general educators face major challenges in providing relevant, individualized education to students with disabilities from culturally diverse backgrounds (Correa & Heward, 2003). Many students with disabilities experience discrimination or inadequate educational programs because their race, ethnicity, social class, or gender is different from that of the majority. Students from culturally and linguistically diverse backgrounds are often under- or overrepresented in educational programs for exceptional children (Artiles, Aguirre-Munoz, & Abedi, 1998; Artiles & Zamora-Durán, 1997; Baca & Cervantes, 1998; Correa, Blanes-Reyes, & Rapport, 1995; Daugherty, 2001; Kauffman, Hallahan, & Ford, 1998; Oswald & Coutinho, 2001). For example, Native Americans are in classes for students with learning disabilities in disproportionately high numbers, whereas their representation in classes for students who are gifted is consistently low (Montgomery, 2001).

The 1997–1998 school year was the first time the federal government required states to report the race and ethnicity of students receiving special education. Those data showed disparities between the distribution of race/ethnicity within the general population and participation in special education, particularly for African American students. Those disparities remain evident in the most recent data. Although they constitute about 15 percent of the general school population, African American students make up 34.2 percent of students classified with mild mental retardation and 28.6 percent of students with severe emotional disturbance (U.S. Department of Education, 2004).

The fact that culturally diverse students are identified as having disabilities is not, in itself, a problem. All students with a disability that adversely affects their educational performance have the right to special education services, whatever their racial or cultural background. Disproportionate representation is problematic, however, if it means that children have been wrongly placed in special education, results in segregation and stigmatization, or in other instances students' disabilities are overlooked because of their membership in a racial or ethnic minority group and they are denied access to needed special education as result. Although a student's ethnicity or language should never be the basis for inclusion in or exclusion from special education programs, the disproportionate numbers of students from culturally and linguistically diverse backgrounds will require that educators attend to three important issues.

First, the adequacy of assessment and placement procedures must be assured. Multifactored assessments must be conducted in ways that will be appropriately sensitive to the student's culture and language to ensure that a special education placement is a function of the student's documented needs rather than of biased referral and assessment practices (Utley & Obiakor, 2001).

Second, providing appropriate support services that are responsive to the cultural and linguistic needs of the student may enhance the child's educational program. For example, bilingual aides, inservice training for teachers, and multicultural education for peers may be necessary to ensure that the child's education is meaningful and maximally beneficial.

Third, teachers and other school staff may need to learn about the values and standards of behavior present in the child's home. Since most teachers are White (Nieto, 2000; Pavri, 2001), learning not only to understand but also to respect and appreciate the child's culture as it is reflected in his or her home will be important to understanding the child's behavior in the classroom and in communicating with parents (Harry, Rueda, & Kalyanpur, 1999; Robins, Lindsey, Lindsey, & Terrell, 2002). Good intentions or token attempts at cultural sensitivity, of course, will do little to provide an appropriate IEP for students with disabilities from culturally diverse backgrounds. The instructional materials educators use and the methods they employ while teaching must be responsive to the differing cultural backgrounds of their students. For example, Gersten and Baker (2000) found that effective instruction for students who are not proficient in English is "more than just 'good teaching.' It is teaching that is tempered, tuned, and otherwise adjusted, to the correct 'path' at which English-language learners will best 'hear' the content (i.e., find it most meaningful)" (p. 461).

Does this mean that a teacher with students from four different cultural backgrounds needs four different methods of teaching? The answer is both "no" and "yes." For the first answer, it is our view that systematic instruction benefits children from all cultural backgrounds. When students with disabilities must also adjust to a new or different culture or language, it is especially important for the teacher to plan individualized activities, convey expectations clearly, observe and record behavior precisely, and give the child specific, immediate feedback during instruction. When coupled with a respectful attitude, these procedures will increase the motivation and achievement of most students.

Good teachers must also be responsive to changes (or lack of change) in individual students' performance. It thus can also be argued that the effective teacher needs as many different ways of teaching as there are students in the classroom. Cultural diversity adds another dimension to the many individual characteristics students present each day. While the basic methods of systematic instruction apply to all learners, teachers who will be most effective in helping children with disabilities from culturally diverse backgrounds achieve success in school will be those who are sensitive to and respectful of their students' heritage and values.

SUMMARY

The task of providing educational equality for students with markedly diverse skills is enormous. By embracing the challenge, U.S. schools have made a promise to exceptional students, to their parents, and to society. Progress has been made, but significant challenges must still be overcome if the promise is to be kept. The views of our society are changing and continue to be changed by people who believe that our past practice of excluding people with disabilities was primitive and unfair. As an institution, education reflects society's changing attitudes.

Common expressions of humanity and fair play dictate that all children are entitled to educational equality; but the history of exclusion and inequality for students with disabilities tells us that humanity and fair play have not driven a great deal of educational policy for children with disabilities in the absence of legislation or litigation. While much progress has been made in achieving educational equality for students with disabilities, much work remains to be done.

Educational equality for children with disabilities must ultimately be assessed by the effects of the schooling those children receive. If educational equality means simply having access to curriculum and instruction in schools and classrooms attended by students without disabilities, it has largely been attained. But equal access alone does not guarantee equal outcomes. Special education must ultimately be judged by the degree to which it is effective in helping individuals with disabilities to acquire, maintain, and generalize skills that will appreciably improve their lives. New skills are needed that will promote real participation and independence in the changing school, workplace, and community environments of the twenty-first century.

Providing educational equality for students with disabilities does not mean either ignoring a child's disability or pretending that it does not exist. Children with disabilities do have differences from children who do not have disabilities. But, as stated at the beginning of this chapter, students who are exceptional are more like than unlike other students. Every exceptional student must be treated first as an individual, not as a member of a labeled group or category.

There is a limit to how much educational equality can be legislated. In many cases, it is possible to meet the letter but not necessarily the spirit of the law. Treating every student with a disability as a student first and as an individual with a disability second may be the most important factor in providing true educational equality. This approach does not diminish the student's exceptionality, but instead it might give us a more objective and positive perspective that allows us to see a disability as a set of special needs. Viewing exceptional students as individuals tells us a great deal about how to help them achieve the educational equality they deserve.

Questions and Activities

1. Why are both children who are learning disabled and those who are gifted considered exceptional?

2. In what ways are students with disabilities similar to and different from other students?

3. What are the advantages and disadvantages of labeling and classifying students with disabilities? Be sure to consider the views of educators, parents, and students.

4. How did the civil rights movement influence the movement for educational equality for students with disabilities?

5. Interview a local special education school administrator to determine (a) how many students in the district receive special education services; (b) how many of these students are English-language learners, bilingual, males, females, and/or are students of color; (c) how many students are in each of the various categories of disability; and (d) how many students with disabilities receive some or all of their education in the regular classroom, the portion of the school day in which they are included in the regular classroom, and the curriculum areas or other school activities in which they participate in inclusive settings.

6. What is an IEP and how can it benefit students with disabling conditions? Visit a special education classroom and talk with the teacher about how an IEP might influence regular classroom teachers when students are mainstreamed.

7. How does the concept of least restrictive environment influence alternative placements for students with disabilities?

8. Do you think all students with disabilities should be educated in regular classrooms? Why or why not?

9. Why are collaboration and teaming between special educators and general classroom teachers so critical to the quality of education experienced by children with disabilities?

10. In your view, what is the most critical challenge currently facing the education of exceptional students? What suggestions would you make for meeting that challenge?

References

Aiello, B. (1976, April 25). Up from the Basement: A Teacher's Story. *New York Times*, p. 14.

Al-Hassan, S., & Gardner, R., III. (2002). Involving Immigrant Parents of Students with Disabilities in the Educational Process. *Teaching Exceptional Children, 35*(2), 12–16.

Algozzine, B., Browder, D., Karvonen, M., Test, D. W., & Wood, W. M. (2001). Effects of Interventions to Promote Self-determination for Individuals with Disabilities. *Review of Educational Research, 71,* 219–277.

Anderson, N. B., & Shames, G. H. (2006). *Human Communication Disorders: An Introduction* (7th ed.). Boston: Allyn & Bacon.

Artiles, A. J., Aguirre-Munoz, Z., & Abedi, J. (1998). Predicting Placement in Learning Disabilities Programs: Do Predictors Vary by Ethnic Group? *Exceptional Children, 64,* 543–559.

Artiles, A. J., & Zamora-Durán, G. (1997). *Reducing Disproportionate Representation of Culturally Diverse Students in Special and Gifted Education.* Reston, VA: Council for Exceptional Children.

Baca, L. M., & Cervantes, H. T. (1998). *The Bilingual Special Education Interface* (3rd ed.). Upper Saddle River, NJ: Merrill/Prentice-Hall.

Banks, J. A. (2000). *Cultural Diversity and Education: Foundations, Curriculum, and Teaching* (4th ed.). Boston: Allyn & Bacon.

Barraga, N. C., & Erin, J. N. (2001). *Visual Handicaps and Learning* (4th ed.). Austin, TX: PRO-ED.

Bateman, B. D., & Linden, M. L. (1998). *Better IEPs: How to Develop Legally Correct and Educationally Useful Programs* (3rd ed.). Longmont, CO: Sopris West.

Bauer, A. M., & Brown, G. M. (2001). *Adolescents and Inclusion: Transforming Secondary Schools.* Baltimore: Brookes.

Becker, W. C., Engelmann, S., & Thomas, D. R. (1971). *Teaching: A Course in Applied Psychology.* Chicago: Science Research Associates.

Beirne-Smith, M., Patton, J. R., & Kim, S. (2006). *Mental Retardation: An Introduction to Intellectual Disability* (7th ed.). Upper Saddle River, NJ: Merrill/Prentice-Hall.

Best, S. J., Heller, K. W., & Bigge, J. L., (2005). *Teaching Individuals with Physical or Multiple Disabilities* (5th ed.). Upper Saddle River, NJ: Merrill/Prentice-Hall.

Brown v. Board of Education of *Topeka.* 347 U.S. 483 (1954).

Bushell, D., Jr., & Baer, D. M. (1994). Measurably Superior Instruction Means Close, Continual Contact with the Relevant Outcome Data. Revolutionary! In R. Gardner III, D. M. Sainato, J. O. Cooper, T. E. Heron, W. L. Heward, J. Eshleman, & T. A. Grossi (Eds.), *Behavior Analysis in Education: Focus on Measurably Superior Instruction* (pp. 3–10). Pacific Grove, CA: Brooks/Cole.

Carnine, D. (1997). Bridging the Research to Practice Gap. *Exceptional Children, 63,* 513–521.

Carta, J. J. (2003). Perspectives on Educating Young Children Prenatally Exposed to Illegal Drugs. In W. L. Heward, *Exceptional Children: An Introduction to Special Education* (7th ed., pp. 168–169). Upper Saddle River, NJ: Merrill/Prentice-Hall.

Correa, V. I., Blanes-Reyes, M., & Rapport, M. (1995), Minority issues. In H. R. Turnbull & A. P. Turnbull (Eds.). *A compendium report to Congress.* Lawrence, KS: Beach Center.

Correa, V. I., & Heward, W. L. (2003). Special Education in a Culturally Diverse Society. In W. L. Heward, *Exceptional Children: An Introduction to Special Education* (7th ed., pp. 82–114). Upper Saddle River, NJ: Merrill/Prentice-Hall.

Danforth, S. (1995). Toward a Critical Theory Approach to Lives Considered Emotionally Disturbed. *Behavioral Disorders, 20*(2), 136–143.

Danforth, S., & Rhodes, W. C. (1997). On What Basis Hope? Modern Progress and Postmodern Possibilities. *Remedial and Special Education, 18,* 357–366.

Daugherty, D. (2001). *IDEA '97 and Disproportionate Placement.* Retrieved June 20, 2003, from http://www.naspcenter.org/teachers/IDEA_disp.html.

Deshler, D. D., Schumaker, J. B., Lenz, B. K., Bulgren, J. A., Hock, M. F., Knight, J., & Ehren, B. J. (2001). Ensuring Content-Area Learning by Secondary Students with Learning Disabilities. *Learning Disabilities Research and Practice, 16,* 96–108.

Elkind, D. (1998). Behavior Disorders: A Postmodern Perspective. *Behavioral Disorders, 23,* 153–159.

Fisher, D., & Ryndak, D. L. (Eds.). (2001). *The Foundations of Inclusive Education: A Compendium of Articles on Effective Strategies to Achieve Inclusive Education.* Baltimore: Association for Persons with Severe Handicaps.

Ford, D. Y. (1998). The Underrepresentation of Minority Students in Gifted Education: Problems and Promises in Recruitment and Retention. *Journal of Special Education, 32,* 4–14.

Fuchs, D., & Fuchs, L. S. (1994). Inclusive Schools Movement and the Radicalization of Special Education Reform. *Exceptional Children, 60,* 294–309.

Fuchs, D., & Fuchs, L. S. (1995a). What's "Special" about Special Education? *Phi Delta Kappan, 76*(7), 531–540.

Fuchs, D., & Fuchs, L. S. (1995b). Sometimes Separate Is Better. *Educational Leadership, 52*(4), 22–25.

Fuchs, D., & Fuchs, L. S. (2003). Inclusion versus Full Inclusion. In W. L. Heward, *Exceptional Children: An Introduction to Special Education* (7th ed., pp. 80–81). Upper Saddle River, NJ: Merrill/Prentice-Hall.

Gallagher, J. J. (1984). The Evolution of Special Education Concepts. In B. Blatt & R. J. Morris (Eds.), *Perspectives in Special Education: Personal Orientations* (pp. 210–232). Glenview, IL: Scott, Foresman.

Gersten, R. (1998). Recent Advances in Instructional Research for Students with Learning Disabilities: An Overview. *Learning Disabilities Research and Practice, 13,* 162–170.

Gersten, R. (2001). Sorting Out the Roles of Research in the Improvement of Practice. *Learning Disabilities Research and Practice, 16,* 45–50.

Gersten, R., & Baker, S. (2000). What We Know about Effective Instructional Practices for English-Language Learners. *Exceptional Children, 66,* 454–470.

Giangreco, M. F. (2003). Moving toward Inclusion. In W. L. Heward, *Exceptional Children: An Introduction to Special Education* (7th ed., pp. 78–79). Upper Saddle River, NJ: Merrill/Prentice-Hall.

Giangreco, M. F., Cloninger, C., Dennis, R., & Edelman, S. (2000). Problem-Solving Methods to Facilitate Inclusive Education. In J. S. Thousand, R. A. Villa, & A. I. Nevin (Eds.), *Restructuring for Caring and Effective Education: Piecing the Puzzle Together* (2nd ed., pp. 293–327). Baltimore: Brookes.

Giangreco, M. F., Cloninger, C. J., & Iverson, V. S. (1998). *Choosing Options and Accommodations for Children: A Guide to Educational Planning for Students with Disabilities* (2nd ed.). Baltimore: Brookes.

Gibb, G. S., & Dyches, T. T. (2000). *Guide to Writing Quality Individualized Education Programs.* Boston: Allyn & Bacon.

Gollnick, D. M., & Chinn, P. G. (2002). *Multicultural Education in a Pluralistic Society* (6th ed.). Upper Saddle River, NJ: Merrill/Prentice-Hall.

Goodman, L. V. (1976). A Bill of Rights for the Handicapped. *American Education, 12*(6), 6–8.

Greenwood, C. R., & Maheady, L. (1997). Measurable Change in Student Performance: Forgotten Standard in Teacher Preparation? *Teacher Education and Special Education, 20,* 265–275.

Grigal, M., Test, D. W., Beattie, J., & Wood, W. (1997). An Evaluation of Transition Components of Individualized Education Programs. *Exceptional Children, 63,* 357–372.

Guralnick, M. J. (1997). *The Effectiveness of Early Intervention.* Baltimore: Brookes.

Hammer, M. R. (2004). Using The Self-Advocacy Strategy to Increase Student Participation in IEP Conferences. *Intervention in School and Clinic, 39*, 295–300.

Harry, B., Rueda, R., & Kalyanpur, M. (1999). Cultural Reciprocity in Sociocultural Perspective: Adapting the Normalization Principle for Family Collaboration. *Exceptional Children, 66*,123–136.

Heron, T. E., & Harris, K. C. (2001). *The Educational Consultant: Helping Professionals, Parents, and Mainstreamed Students* (4th ed.). Austin, TX: PRO-ED.

Heward, W. L. (2006). *Exceptional Children: An Introduction to Special Education* (8th ed.). Upper Saddle River, NJ: Merrill/Prentice-Hall.

Heward, W. L. (2003). Ten Faulty Notions about Teaching and Learning That Hinder the Effectiveness of Special Education. *Journal of Special Education, 36*(4), 186–205.

Heward, W. L., & Dardig, J. C. (2001, Spring). What Matters Most in Special Education. *Education Connection*, pp. 41–44.

Heward, W. L., & Silvestri, S. M. (2005). The Neutralization of Special Education. In J. W. Jacobson, J. A. Mulick, & R. M. Foxx (Eds.), *Fads: Dubious and Improbable Treatments for Developmental Disabilities*. Hillsdale, NJ: Erlbaum.

Hill, J. L. (1999). *Meeting the Needs of Students with Special Physical and Health Care Needs*. Upper Saddle River, NJ: Merrill/Prentice-Hall.

Hock, M. F., Schumaker, J. B., & Deshler, D. D. (1999). Closing the Gap to Success in Secondary Schools: A Model for Cognitive Apprenticeship. In D. D. Deshler, J. B. Schumaker, K. R. Harris, & S. Graham (Eds.), *Teaching Every Adolescent Every Day: Learning in Diverse Middle and High School Classrooms* (pp. 1–51). Cambridge, MA: Brookline Books.

Howard, V. F., Williams, B. F., & McLaughlin, T. F. (1994). Children Prenatally Exposed to Alcohol and Cocaine: Behavioral Solutions. In R. Gardner III, D. M. Sainato, J. O. Cooper, T. E. Heron, W. L. Heward, J. Eshleman, & T. A. Grossi (Eds.), *Behavior Analysis in Education: Focus on Measurably Superior Instruction* (pp. 131–146). Pacific Grove, CA: Brooks/Cole.

Huebner, T. A. (1994). Understanding Multiculturalism. *Journal of Teacher Education, 45*(5), 375–377.

Huefner, D. S. (2000). The Risks and Opportunities of the IEP Requirements under IDEA '97. *Exceptional Children, 63*, 195–204.

Kame'enui, E. J., Good, R., III, & Harn, B. A. (2005). Beginning Reading Failure and the Quantification of Risk: Reading Behavior as the Supreme Index. In W. L. Heward, T. E. Heron, N. A. Neef, S. M. Peterson, D. M. Sainato, G. Cartledge, R. Gardner, III, L. D. Peterson, S. B. Hersh, & J. C. Dardig (Eds.), *Focus on Behavior Analysis in Education: Achievements, Challenges, and Opportunities* (pp. 69–89). Upper Saddle River, NJ: Merrill/Prentice Hall.

Kauffman, J. M. (1999). How We Prevent the Prevention of Emotional and Behavioral Disorders. *Exceptional Children, 65*, 448–468.

Kauffman, J. M. (2005). *Characteristics of Emotional and Behavioral Disorders of Children and Youth* (8th ed.). Upper Saddle River, NJ: Merrill/Prentice-Hall.

Kauffman, J. M., & Hallahan, D. K. (1994). *The Illusion of Full Inclusion: A Comprehensive Critique of a Current Special Education Bandwagon*. Austin, TX: PRO-ED.

Kauffman, J. M., Hallahan, D. P., & Ford, D. Y. (Guest Eds.). (1998). Special section: Disproportionate Representation of Minority Students in Special Education. *Journal of Special Education, 32*, 3–54.

Keyes, M. W., & Owens-Johnson, L. (2003). Developing Person-Centered IEPs. *Intervention in School and Clinic, 38,* 145–152.

Kliewer, C., & Biklen, D. (1996). Labeling: Who Wants to Be Retarded? In W. Stainback & S. Stainback (Eds.), *Controversial Issues Confronting Special Education: Divergent Perspectives* (pp. 83–95). Boston: Allyn & Bacon.

Knoll, J. A., & Wheeler, C. B. (2001). My Home: Developing Skills and Supports for Adult Living. In R. W. Flexer, T. J. Simmons, P. Luft, & R. M. Baer (Eds.), *Transition Planning for Secondary Students with Disabilities* (pp. 499–539). Upper Saddle River, NJ: Merrill/Prentice-Hall.

Kochar, C. A., West, L. L., & Taymans, J. M. (2000). *Successful Inclusion: Practical Strategies for a Shared Responsibility.* Upper Saddle River, NJ: Merrill/Prentice-Hall.

Kohler, P. D., & Field, S. (2003). Transition-Focused Education: Foundation for the Future. *Journal of Special Education, 37,* 174–183.

Langdon, H. W., Novak, J. M., & Quintanar, R. S. (2000). Setting the Teaching–Learning Wheel in Motion in Assessing Language Minority Students. *Multicultural Perspectives, 2*(2), 3–9.

Lewis, R. B., & Doorlag, D. H. (2006). *Teaching Special Education in General Education* (7th ed.). Upper Saddle River, NJ: Merrill/Prentice Hall.

Lignugaris/Kraft, B., Marchand-Martella, N., & Martella, R. C. (2001). Writing Better Goals and Short-Term Objectives or Benchmarks. *Teaching Exceptional Children, 34*(1), 52–58.

Lovitt, T. C. (2000). *Preventing School Failure: Tactics for Teaching Adolescents* (2nd ed.). Austin, TX: PRO-ED.

Luckasson, R., & Reeve, A. (2001). Naming, Defining, and Classifying in Mental Retardation. *Mental Retardation, 39,* 47–52.

Lytle, R. K., & Bordin, J. (2001). Enhancing the IEP Team: Strategies for Parents and Professionals. *Teaching Exceptional Children, 33*(5), 28–33.

MacMillan, D. L., Gresham, F. M., Bocian, K. M., & Lambros, K. M. (1998). Current Plight of Borderline Students: Where Do They Belong? *Education and Training in Mental Retardation and Developmental Disabilities, 33,* 83–94.

MacMillan, D. L., & Reschly, D. J. (1998). Overrepresentation of Minority Students: The Case for Greater Specificity or Reconsideration of the Variables Examined. *Journal of Special Education, 32,* 15–24.

Martin, J. E., Hughes, W., Huber Marshall, L., Jerman, P., & Maxson, L. L. (1999). *Choosing Personal Goals.* Longmont, CO: Sopris West.

Mastropieri, M. A., & Scruggs, T. E. (2004). *The Inclusive Classroom: Strategies for Effective Instruction* (2nd ed.). Upper Saddle River, NJ: Merrill/Prentice Hall.

Menlove, R. R., Hudson, P. J., & Suter, D. (2001). A Field of IEP Dreams: Increasing General Education Teacher Participation in the IEP Development Process. *Teaching Exceptional Children, 33*(5), 28–33.

Mercer, C. D., & Pullen, P. C. (2005). *Students with Learning Disabilities* (6th ed.). Upper Saddle River, NJ: Merrill/Prentice-Hall.

Mitchell, D. (Ed.). (2004a). *Special Educational Needs and Inclusive Education: Major Themes in Education.* London and New York: Routledge Falmer.

Mitchell, D. (Ed.). (2004b). *Contextualizing Inclusive Education: Evaluating Old and New International Paradigms.* London and New York: RoutledgeFalmer.

Montgomtery, W. (2001). Creating culturally response, inclusive classrooms. *Teaching Exceptional Children, 33*(4), 4–9.

Moody, S. W., Vaughn, S. Hughes, M. T., & Fischer, M. (2000). Reading Instruction in the Resource Room: Set Up for Failure. *Exceptional Children, 66,* 305–316.

Moores, D. F. (2001). *Educating the Deaf: Psychology, Principles, and Practices* (5th ed.). Boston: Houghton Mifflin.

Murdick, N., Gartin, B., & Crabtree, T. (2006). *Special Education Law* (2nd ed.). Upper Saddle River, NJ: Merrill/Prentice Hall.

National Reading Panel (2000). Teaching Children to Read: An Evidence-Based Assessment of the Scientific Research Literature on Reading and Its Implications for Reading Instruction. Reports of the Subgroups. http://www.nichd.hih.gov/publications/nrp/smallbook.htm.

National Research Council (1998). *Preventing Reading Difficulties in Young Children.* Washington, DC: National Academy Press.

Nieto, S. (2000). *Affirming Diversity: The Sociopolitical Context of Multicultural Education* (3rd ed.). New York: Longman.

O'Neil, J. (1995). Can Inclusion Work? A Conversation with Jim Kauffman and Mara Sapon-Sevin. *Educational Leadership, 52*(4), 7–11.

Ortiz, A. (1997). Learning Disabilities Occurring Concomitantly with Linguistic Differences. *Journal of Learning Disabilities, 30,* 321–333.

Ortiz, A. A., & Wilkinson, C. Y. (1991). Assessment and Intervention Model for the Bilingual Exceptional Student (AIM for the BEST). *Teacher Education and Special Education, 14,* 35–42.

Oswald, D. P., & Coutinho, M. J. (2001). Trends in Disproportionate Representation: Implications for Multicultural Education. In C. Utley & F. Obiakor (Eds.), *Special Education, Multicultural Education, and School Reform: Components of Quality Education for Learners with Mild Disabilities* (pp. 53–73). Springfield, IL: Thomas.

Patton, J. M. (1998). The Disproportionate Representation of African Americans in Special Education: Looking behind the Curtain for Understanding and Solutions. *The Journal of Special Education, 32,* 25–31.

Pavri, S. (2001). Developmental Delay or Cultural Differences? Developing Effective Child Find Practices for Young Children from Culturally and Linguistically Diverse Families. *Young Exceptional Children, 4,* 2–9.

Pennsylvania Association for Retarded Children v. Commonwealth of Pennsylvania, 343 F., Supp. 279 (1972).

Reschly, D. J. (1996). Identification and Assessment of Students with Disabilities. *Future of Children, 6*(1), 40–53.

Reynolds, M. C. (1989). An Historical Perspective: The Delivery of Special Education to Mildly Disabled and At-Risk Students. *Remedial and Special Education, 10,* 6–11.

Robins, K. N., Lindsey, R. B., Lindsey, D. B., & Terrell, R. D. (2002). *Culturally Proficient Instruction: A Guide for People Who Teach.* Thousand Oaks, CA: Corwin.

Rock, M. L. (2000). Parents as Equal Partners: Balancing the Scales in IEP Development. *Teaching Exceptional Children, 32*(6), 30–37.

Salend, S. J. (2005). *Creating Inclusive Classrooms: Effective and Reflective Practices* (5th ed.). Upper Saddle River, NJ: Merrill/Prentice-Hall.

Sandall, S., McLean, M. E., & Smith, B. J. (Eds.). (2000). *DEC Recommended Practices in Early Interventioan/Early Childhood Special Education.* Reston, VA: Council for Exceptional Children, Division for Early Childhood.

Sandall, S., Schwartz, I., & Joseph, G. (2000). A Building Blocks Model for Effective Instruction in Inclusive Early Childhood Settings. *Young Exceptional Children, 4*(3), 3–9.

Sasso, G. (2001). The Retreat from Inquiry and Knowledge in Special Education. *The Journal of Special Education, 34*, 178–193.

Scheuermann, B., & Webber, J. (2002). *Autism: Teaching Does Make a Difference.* Belmont, CA: Wadsworth.

Schwartz, I. (2000). Standing on the Shoulders of Giants: Looking ahead to Facilitating Membership and Relationships for Children with Disabilities. *Topics in Early Childhood Special Education, 20,* 123–128.

Schwartz, I. S. (2005). Inclusion and Applied Behavior Analysis: Mending Fences and Building Bridges. In W. L. Heward, T. E. Heron, N. A. Neef, S. M. Peterson, D. M. Sainato, G. Cartledge, R. Gardner, III, L. D. Peterson, S. B. Hersh, & J. C. Dardig (Eds.), *Focus on Behavior Analysis in Education: Achievements, Challenges, and Opportunities* (pp. 239-251). Upper Saddle River, NJ: Merrill/Prentice Hall.

Shanker, A. (1995). Full Inclusion Is Neither Free nor Appropriate. *Educational Leadership, 52*(4), 18–21.

Shonkoff, J. P., & Meisels, S. J. (Eds.). (2000). *Handbook of Early Childhood Intervention* (2nd ed.). New York: Cambridge University Press.

Sitlington, P. L., Clark, G. M., & Kolstoe, O. P. (2000). *Comprehensive Transition Education and Services for Adolescents with Disabilities* (3rd ed.). Needham Heights, MA: Allyn & Bacon.

Smith, P. (1999). Drawing New Maps: A Radical Cartography of Developmental Disabilities. *Review of Educational Research, 69*, 117–144.

Smith, S. W., & Brownell, M. T. (1995). Individualized Education Programs: From Intent to Acquiescence. *Focus on Exceptional Children, 28*(1), 1–12.

Snell, M. E., & Brown, F. (Eds.). (2006). *Instruction of Students with Severe Disabilities* (6th ed.). Upper Saddle River, NJ: Merrill/Prentice-Hall.

Snell, M. E., & Janney, R. E. (2000). *Practices for Inclusive Schools: Collaborative Teaming.* Baltimore: Brookes.

Spear-Swerling, L., & Sternberg, R. J. (2001). What Science Offers Teachers of Reading. *Learning Disabilities Research and Practice, 16*, 51–57.

Stainback, S., & Stainback, W. (Eds.). (1996). *Inclusion: A Guide for Educators* (2nd ed.). Baltimore: Brookes.

Stowell, L. J., & Terry, C. (1977). Mainstreaming: Present Shock. *Illinois Libraries, 59*, 475–477.

Sugai, G. (1998). Postmodernism and Emotional and Behavioral Disorders: Distraction or Advancement. *Behavioral Disorders, 23*, 171–177.

Taylor, S. J. (1988). Caught in the Continuum: A Critical Analysis of the Principle of Least Restrictive Environment. *The Journal of the Association for Persons with Severe Handicaps, 13*, 41–53.

Taylor, S. J. (1995). On Rhetoric: A Response to Fuchs and Fuchs. *Exceptional Children, 61*, 301–302.

Test, D. W., Aspel, N., & Everson, J. M. (2006). *Transition Methods for Youth with Disabilities.* Upper Saddle River, NJ: Merrill/Prentice Hall.

Thomas, C., Correa, V., & Morsink, C. (2001). *Interactive Teaming: Enhancing Programs for Students with Special Needs* (3rd ed.). Upper Saddle River, NJ: Merrill/Prentice-Hall.

Turnbull, A. P., & Turnbull, H. R. (2001). *Families, Professionals, and Exceptionality: A Special Partnership* (4th ed.). New York: Macmillan.

Turnbull, H. R., & Turnbull, A. P. (2000). *Free Appropriate Public Education: The Law and Children with Disabilities* (6th ed.). Denver, CO: Love.

Turnbull, R., & Cilley, M. (1999). *Explanations and Implications of the 1997 Amendments to IDEA.* Upper Saddle River, NJ: Merrill/Prentice-Hall.

Tymchuk, A. J., Lakin, K. C., & Luckasson, R. (2001). *The Forgotten Generation: The Status and Challenges of Adults with Mild Cognitive Limitations.* Baltimore: Brookes.

U.S. Department of Education. (2002a). *Executive Summary of No Child Left Behind.* Washington, DC: U.S. Government Printing Office.

U.S. Department of Education. (2002b). *Guidance for the Reading First Program.* Washington, DC: U.S. Government Printing Office.

U.S. Department of Education. (2002c). *No Child Left Behind: A Desktop Reference.* Washington, DC: U.S. Government Printing Office.

U.S. Department of Education. (2004). *Twenty-Sixth Annual Report to Congress on the Implementation of the Individuals with Disabilities Education Act.* Washington, DC: U.S. Government Printing Office.

U.S. Department of Education. (2005). *U.S. Department of Education's Commentary and Explanation about Proposed Regulations for IDEA 2004.* Washington, DC: U.S. Government Printing Office.

Utley, C. A., & Obiakor, F. E. (2001). Learning Problems or Learning Disabilities of Multicultural Learners: Contemporary Perspectives. In C. Utley & F. Obiakor (Eds.), *Special Education, Multicultural Education, and School Reform: Components of Quality Education for Learners with Mild Disabilities* (pp. 90–117). Springfield, IL: Thomas.

Vaughn, S., Gersten, R. L., & Chard, D. J. (2000). The Underlying Message in LD Intervention Research: Findings from Research Syntheses. *Exceptional Children, 67,* 99–114.

Vaughn, S., Klingner, J., & Hughes, M. (2000). Sustainability of Research-Based Practices. *Exceptional Children, 66,* 163–171.

Vaughn, S., Schumm, J. S., & Brick, J. B. (1998). Using a Rating Scale to Design and Evaluate Inclusion Programs. *Teaching Exceptional Children, 30*(4), 41–45.

Venn, J. J. (2004). *Assessing Students with Special Needs* (3rd ed.). Upper Saddle River, NJ: Merrill/Prentice-Hall.

Wagner, M., Blackorby, J., Cameto, R., & Newman, L. (1994). *What Makes a Difference? Influences on Postschool Outcomes of Youth with Disabilities.* Menlo Park, CA: SRI International.

Wagner, M., Newman, L., Cameto, R., & Levine, P. (2005). *Changes over Time in the Early Postschool Outcomes of Youth with Disabilities: A Report of Findings from the National Longitudinal Transition Study (NTLS) and the National Longitudinal Transition Study-2 (NLST2).* Menlo Park, CA: SRI International.

Walsh, J. M. (2001). Getting the "Big Picture" of IEP Goals and State Standards. *Teaching Exceptional Children, 33*(5), 18–26.

Wehby, J. H., Symons, F. J., Canale, J. A., & Go, F. J. (1998). Teaching Practices in Classrooms for Students with Emotional and Behavioral Disorders. *Behavioral Disorders, 24,* 51–56.

Wehman, P. (1998). *Developing Transition Plans*. Austin, TX: PRO-ED.

Wood, J. W. (2006). *Teaching Students in Inclusive Settings: Adapting and Accommodating Instruction* (5th ed.). Upper Saddle River, NJ: Merrill/Prentice-Hall.

Wood, W. M., Karvonen, M., Test, D. W., Browder, D., & Algozinne, B. (2004). Promoting Student Self-Determination Skills in IEP Planning. *Teaching Exceptional Children, 70,* 391–412.

Yell, M. L. (1995). Least Restrictive Environment, Inclusion, and Students with Disabilities: A Legal Analysis. *Journal of Special Education, 28,* 389–404.

Yell, M. L., & Drasgow, E. (2000). Litigating a Free Appropriate Public Education: The Lovaas Hearing and Cases. *Journal of Special Education, 33,* 205–214.

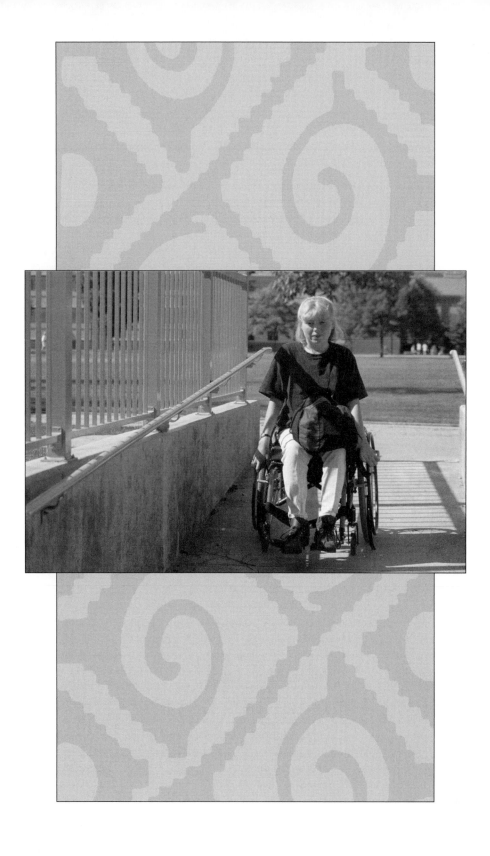

CHAPTER 14

School Inclusion and Multicultural Issues in Special Education

Luanna H. Meyer, Jill Bevan-Brown, Beth Harry, and Mara Sapon-Shevin

Before the passage of Public Law 94–142 by Congress in 1975, children with disabilities could be excluded from the public school system altogether if they were not performing academically at the level of their age-peers. If they did attend public school, there was no obligation for schools to adapt curricula and instruction to meet their educational needs so that they might ultimately graduate with qualifications for meaningful adult roles.

The advent of the legislation now known as the Individuals with Disabilities Education Improvement Act (IDEA 2004) changed the situation dramatically: This law requires that all children, regardless of the severity or extent of their disability, be provided with a free and appropriate education. Various due process protections are included in the law to ensure that schools not only cannot deny access but also must adapt curricula to meet diverse student needs, with no exceptions.

Throughout its history, special education has signified access to equality of educational opportunity as well as a commitment to meeting individualized student needs. Special education has also intersected with movements within general education—such as multicultural education—focused on pedagogical reform to address the diverse student population in today's schools. The relationship between special and general education is a complex one that can provide a measure of the extent to which our public education system is succeeding in its responsibility for equality of educational opportunity.

This chapter highlights this relationship and challenges the reader to acknowledge and promote future directions in both multicultural education and special education that do not compromise the fundamental responsibility to provide children with opportunity to learn. For some years now, researchers have investigated inequities inherent in the structure of special education services that demand increased consideration of the intersection of the study of disability and multiculturalism. Major journals such as *Teacher Education and Special Education* (Tyler & Smith, 2000), *The Journal of the Association for Persons with Severe Handicaps* (Park & Lian, 2001), and *Remedial and Special Education* (Torres-Velasquez, 2000) have published special issues on aspects of "ethics, power, and privilege" revealed by theoretical and empirical analysis of sociocultural perspectives in special education. Special education is a consequence of the inability and/or unwillingness of mainstream educational systems to accommodate diverse learners, and monocultural schools can utilize special education systems to maintain dominant cultural values and norms. We believe that the fields of multicultural education and special education have been conceptualized all too separately. As Patton and Townsend (1999) have said, the time is ripe for a critical analysis of special education and a shift away from a "search for deficits within the student and/or the family to a critique of educational processes and structures that result in unethical consequences for African American learners" (p. 284).

THE SPECIAL EDUCATION MANDATE TO EDUCATE ALL CHILDREN

Special education has come to occupy "the high ground of many contemporary educational debates," located at "the forefront of pedagogical innovation and judicial reform" (Richardson, 1994, p. 713). Following the passage of national legislation, special education rose to the challenge of developing diverse instructional strategies that resulted in significant educational achievement even in children once labeled "uneducable" (Horner, Meyer, & Fredericks, 1986). Furthermore, this evolution of effective specialized services in public education emerged at a time when general education continued, for the most part, to maintain the myth of homogeneity—a "one size fits all" approach. Special educators became the reformers, willing to address the complexities of educating children as they are, not as they are supposed to be. This is the generous and idealistic interpretation of the history of special education.

Special Education as Segregation from the Mainstream

There is another view, which Richardson (1994) describes as the consequence of the impact of compulsory education in linking three worlds of children—the typical, the delinquent, and the special. With the advent of compulsory education, students who had previously been excluded or absent voluntarily began to come to school. Richardson points to data from the state of California—a leader in the early special education movement before the passage of national legislation—that illustrates well the scenario that followed compulsory attendance requirements in general education. In 1947, a "separation of races" clause that had existed unchallenged since 1883 was under attack as the basis for segregating Mexican Americans in school. The California court ruled that because Mexican Americans were not one of the "great races of man" they could not be segregated. Richardson argues that this judicial decision became the impetus for the establishment of segregated, special education classes in California for students diagnosed as educably mentally retarded (EMR). At the same time, there was a dramatic increase in school use of long-term suspensions for behavior problems as the student population increased and became more diverse as a result of compulsory attendance requirements (*Divergent Youth*, 1963; Richardson, 1994). The original function of special education to provide programs for students with intellectual disabilities was also expanded to include a new category now known as emotional and behavioral disorders (EBD), rapidly populated by the same children previously excluded from school.

Special education in these early days was synonymous with special classes, which appeared to be the contemporary placement for many children who had previously been excluded from school. Thus, Richardson (1994) argues, special education emerged not primarily to meet individual needs but, instead, to provide a mechanism to continue to send some children to school elsewhere, apart from the mainstream. Dunn (1968) argued this same point in his influential article "Special Education for the Mildly Retarded: Is Much of It Justifiable?" He highlighted the disproportionate overrepresentation of children of color in segregated special classes and noted the increase of these segregated programs in the 1950s and 1960s, just as the *Brown* v. *Board of Education* decision was otherwise challenging racial segregation. Dunn also presented evidence that the special education classes were not so very special: Children in those segregated programs did less well academically than did similar children who had remained in general education without special education services. Special education was being used, Dunn charged, to achieve socially acceptable racial segregation. His scathing critique, widely discussed for many years, was accompanied by continued evidence that children of color were disproportionately represented in special education programs.

Mercer (1973) studied the phenomenon labeled the "six-hour retarded child" used to describe the irony of children who had been diagnosed as EMR in school while doing just fine outside the school day and in their communities. She argued that both school structure and the nature of diagnostic measures (such as IQ tests) used to identify mental retardation were culturally biased in favor of Anglo children and against children of color. Hence, Anglo children would be conservatively diagnosed as EMR by these biased measures, resulting in more accurate identification of those children in need of special education. In contrast, the majority of children of color labeled EMR through existing measures were not retarded at all but were mislabeled. To remediate this situation, Mercer (1979) developed and validated the System of Multicultural Pluralist Assessment (SOMPA), which became the model for culture-free cognitive assessment. Her pioneering work was also instrumental in the design of certain procedural safeguards incorporated into IDEA, with key provisions requiring nondiscriminatory assessment and the use of both intellectual and adaptive behavior evaluations to establish eligibility for special education services. Of course, a continuing dilemma for the diagnostic category of mild mental retardation was also an issue for categories such as learning disabilities and emotional disturbance: These are the "soft" disability categories for which diagnosis is primarily determined by professional judgment influenced heavily by existing classroom ecologies (Adelman & Taylor, 1993).

Special Education as Racial Discrimination

As attacks on the concept and practice of "educably mentally retarded" became more pronounced, a shift in the pattern of diagnosis occurred. The population of students labeled

EMR or "mildly mentally retarded" declined dramatically during the 1970s and 1980s, while the percentage of children labeled as learning disabled (LD) and emotionally/behaviorally disordered (EBD) grew proportionately. The historical overrepresentation of children of color in EMR classes expanded across similar patterns in LD and EBD programs (Argulewicz, 1983; Finn, 1982; MacMillan, Jones, & Meyers, 1976; Oswald, Coutinho, Best, & Singh, 1999; Tucker, 1980; Webb-Johnson, 1999). G. Smith's (1983) early observation that African Americans were overrepresented in EMR classes is mirrored by continued overrepresentation in the categories of mental retardation and emotional disturbance today (Artiles, Rueda, Salazar, & Higareda, 2005; Artiles, Trent, & Palmer, 2004; Hosp & Reschly, 2004; Skiba, et al. 2005).

Meier, Stewart, and England (1989) reported the results of a large-scale study conducted in nearly 200 school districts examining the effects of socioeconomic status and race on educational opportunities. They found widespread evidence of "second-generation discrimination," including various sorting practices resulting in overrepresentation of African American students in special education classrooms as well as in punishment and suspension statistics. In contrast, "a White student was 3.2 times more likely to be assigned to a gifted class than a black student" (Meier et al., 1989, p. 5). In their study of New York City referral patterns, Gottlieb, Alter, Gottlieb, and Wishner (1994) found that only 15 percent of LD students in a 1992 sample actually fit the criteria for this clinical disability, while the majority were poor children with low achievement and low scores on cognitive measures. What was happening, they argued, was that special education was being asked to accept "regular education fallout" (p. 458). They added, "The current state of urban education, so woefully underfunded relative to its needs, provides students little access to intensive resources outside of special education" (p. 459). Similarly, in a three-year ethnographic study of referral and placement practices in 12 elementary schools in Miami, Florida, Harry and Klingner (2006) found that inadequate opportunity to learn, arbitrary standards for referral, and pressure from high stakes testing to place low achievers in special education were key contributors to the overrepresentation of Black and Hispanic students in special education programs.

It has been argued that patterns of disproportionality result from the known overlap between race and poverty: If ethnic minorities are disportionately poor, they may be more likely to evidence learning needs associated with poverty (MacMillan & Reschly, 1998). If overrepresentation of ethnic minorities in special education statistics were actually a function of the impact of poverty, this finding would support interventions aimed at alleviating poverty rather than focusing on changing school practices (including the validity, reliability, and cultural appropriateness of the diagnosis and assessment process). To investigate this issue, Oswald, Coutinho, Best, and Singh (1999) analyzed extant data reported by nearly 4,500 U.S. school districts in 1992, and they reported that placement in special education was significantly influenced by ethnicity even after controlling for the effects of demographic variables. More recently, Skiba and his colleagues studied this relationship across school districts in one midwestern state; they found that poverty made a weak and inconsistent contribution to disproportionality, magnifying existing racial disparities (Skiba et al., 2005). Interestingly, they also found that the rates of suspension and expulsion consistently predicted the extent of disproportionality by race in special education placements, with the greatest disporportionality occurring for African

Americans and Native Americans in the service categories of mental retardation and emotional disturbance.

Whatever the relative contributions of discriminatory practices vs. poverty to the overrepresentation of minorities in special education, both factors must be addressed (Donovan & Cross, 2002; Fujiura & Yamaki, 2000). The National Academy of Sciences has implicated both school environments and community environments in this matter (Donovan & Cross, 2002). Data on detrimental environmental influences on the health and development of minority children who live in poverty are sobering, and we interpret these as further examples of structural discrimination in U.S. society.

Finding that ethnic minorities are disproportionately represented in special education even after controlling for the effects of demographic variables such as poverty requires that we revisit and reform discriminatory educational practices. Given that the vast majority of teachers and administrators in the U.S. educational system are White, evidence of widespread referral of ethnic minority children away from the mainstream (whether into special education or exclusion through suspension) represents a significant challenge to equality of educational opportunity. We concur with the conclusions reached by Artiles and his colleagues that "the presence of disproportionality should be taken as an opportunity for the examination of more complex issues that ultimately shape this problem" (Artiles et al., 2005, p. 299). Among these complex issues are the cultural perspectives and understandings of different cultural communities. Emerson, Robertson, and Wood (in press) in Britain report evidence of a relationship between particular cultural values and children's well-being, with factors such as religiosity, communal self-efficacy, and cultural views of mental illness positively associated with resilience to emotional and behavioral disorders among South Asian children, despite the presence of other negative socioeconomic indicators. Again, there is a strong case to be made for examination of the overlap between special education and multicultural education where the ultimate goal is support for a general education system that better provides for diversity.

Eliminating Racial Bias in Educational Practice

Oswald and his colleagues (1999) conclude that "further work is warranted to determine the impact of other factors not included in these models, such as educators who mistake cultural difference for cognitive or behavioral disabilities during the prereferral, referral, assessment, or eligibility process" (p. 203). Patton (1998) believes that the fundamental school structures of general and special education represent the dominant Anglo European culture such that our knowledge base and educational practices inevitably devalue the contributions of African Americans at all levels. He challenges the research community to adopt qualitatively different knowledge-producing approaches that are "culturally and interculturally competent" (p. 27). In Aotearoa New Zealand, similar concerns have been raised regarding the place of Maori in school and society, in a nation formally committed to Maori–Anglo biculturalism but reflecting predominantly Anglo cultural infrastructures. The call for culture-specific research approaches for indigenous people to counter traditional research methodologies, seen as disempowering non-European groups, focuses on "decolonizing methodologies" and the validation of Maori knowledge (Smith, 1999). The education of Maori children in New Zealand includes emphasis on the availability of immersion Kura Kaupapa Maori schools from early years through university level, in educational units and institutions where only Te Reo Maori is spoken. Tertiary degrees are taught entirely in the indigenous language and are based on indigenous Maori knowledge rather than on a translation of Western knowledge into Te Reo; since 2000, doctoral degree level Maori education has been available.

Artiles (1998) locates competence within one's culture and emphasizes that we must deepen our understanding about how teachers deal with student diversity in the classroom. The message of contemporary work on multicultural education is not primarily fixed on remediation of racial discrimination and adoption of unbiased educational practices in schools and classrooms, although this is a part of what needs to be done whenever such discrimination and bias exist. Current multicultural education theory and practice highlight pedagogy in cultural context and prescribe a future classroom and school in which culturally diverse learners will find educational practices that value and develop their individual behavioral styles and culture-specific knowledge base (Banks & Banks, 2007).

Hence, work by Cronin (1998), Townsend (1998), and Webb-Johnson (1999) that examines and intervenes with the clash in cultural repertoire between teacher and child represents an important step in resolving the place of African American and other ethnically diverse students in today's classrooms. But even more fundamental reform at the preservice teacher education level will be required if the result is to be an educational system that no longer discriminates by institutionalizing "dominant" Western cultural structures, values, and practices. Research by Artiles and Trent and their colleagues examines the process of learning to teach in culturally diverse schools (Artiles & McClafferty, 1998; Artiles & Trent, 1994, 1997; Trent, Artiles, & Englert, 1998). Their approach is data based, whereby strategies are ultimately informed by evidence regarding outcomes rather than by professional opinion about what teachers need to know and do.

Bevan-Brown's (1998a, 1999) Cultural Audit Process was designed for use by teachers in Aotearoa New Zealand, to ensure that their educational practices are culturally appropriate for Maori students. Bevan-Brown bases her definition of *cultural appropriateness* on existing tradition and entitlements (e.g., the Treaty of Waitangi between Maori and English, signed in the nineteenth century), comprising the criteria of partnership, participation, active protection, empowerment and *tino rangatiratanga*, equality and accessibility, and integration. The various components of programs and services offered at schools are to be measured against these criteria, and educators are challenged to describe specific actions (and action planning for vacant cells) to address each intersection on the framework. By aggregating individual teacher responses and structuring collaborative planning across teachers, teacher aides, and the principal within the school, a Maori cultural input action plan may be developed for the entire school, including specification of objectives, planned strategies to achieve objectives, and designation of who is responsible and by what target date. Ongoing research, with both the teacher and the school as units of analysis, provides a basis for evaluating the effectiveness of such proactive planning.

Based on these principles, Bevan-Brown (2001) developed a more generic checklist for ethnically appropriate evaluation and research in special education (see Table 14.1), now being used by some New Zealand educators from the dominant professional culture for the design and conduct of assessments, evaluation, and/or research involving learners from different cultures. Given the likelihood of differences in cultural and linguistic identities between the majority of children and their families on the one hand and the majority of educators, administrators, and researchers on the other (Tyler & Smith, 2000), formal prompts such as this could better promote systemic educational thinking and actions that are culturally appropriate (Bevan-Brown, 2006; Trent et al. 2002).

Table 14.1   A Checklist for Ethnically Appropriate Evaluation and Research in Special Education

The Right Person

- Is the interviewer from the same ethnic group as the person being questioned/receiving the special education service?

- If not, does the interviewer have the cross-cultural competence needed to interview people from a different culture and to accurately interpret the information given?

- Are the interviewer and the interviewee suitably matched (e.g., same gender, age, and socioeconomic status)?

- Where interviewers from the ethnic community are employed—has the method of recruitment been culturally appropriate? Have the interviewers received adequate training? Is involvement an empowering experience for the interviewers?

Asking the Right Questions

- Has the ethnic group's concept of special needs been incorporated into the evaluation/research?

- Have different cultural concepts, beliefs, values, attitudes, norms, customs, experiences, skills, knowledge, and practices been taken into account?

- Are culturally appropriate and relevant standards and measures used to evaluate special education services?

- Are differing language patterns, cognitive structures, and dialects taken into account?

- Is the evaluation/research important, relevant, empowering, and beneficial to the ethnic community concerned?

- Have both the service providers and the ethnic community been involved in formulating evaluation/research questions?

Of the Right People

- Has evaluation/research involved wide, in-depth consultation (e.g., have all relevant groups been included)?

- Has the ethnic community involved been consulted in the selection of appropriate interviewees?

In the Right Way

- Have culturally appropriate practices and protocols been incorporated into the evaluation/research process?

- Have approval and support of the evaluation/research been gained from the community concerrned or their representatives?

- Have culturally appropriate means been used and sufficient time allowed for rapport building prior to commencing interviews?

- Are culturally appropriate evaluation/research designs and methods used?

- Have interviewees been given the option of inviting family members or colleagues to support them in the interview situation?

(continued)

Table 14.1   (continued)

- Are interviews conducted in the first language of the people being interviewed?

- Where an interpreter is used, is this person appropriate, and have confidentiality and privacy concerns been addressed?

- Has jargon been avoided?

- When evaluation/research is complete, have appropriate means been used to share findings with interviewees and the ethnic community concerned?

At the Right Place and the Right Time

- Is the interview being conducted at a place that is both convenient and comfortable for the interviewee?

- Does the interview venue afford privacy?

- Is the interview being conducted at a time that is convenient to the interviewee?

Source: Bevan-Brown, J. (2001). Evaluating Special Education Services for Learners from Ethnically Diverse Groups: Getting It Right. *The Journal of the Association for Persons with Severe Handicaps, 26,* 138–147. Reprinted with permission of the author.

PARENT PARTICIPATION AND MULTICULTURAL SPECIAL EDUCATION

The importance of parental involvement is not unique to special education. However, parental involvement is particularly crucial for children with disabilities for two reasons. First, students with disabilities are more vulnerable because their performance and behavior may be misinterpreted through the use of inappropriate and incorrect assessments. Students with cognitive and language impairments may not be able to report negligent or abusive practices to their parents. Parental input is essential to ensure professional understanding of the student as well as to protect the student. Second, the historical fact that students with significant disabilities were traditionally excluded from schools necessitated greater specification of student rights and, consequently, of parental rights to ensure adequate provision of educational services to which a child is entitled.

For children of color, parental involvement becomes even more critical given the overrepresentation of these children in special education services and the likely negative impacts of poverty on minority families with children who have disabilities (Park, Turnbull, & Turnbull, 2002). Parental involvement can function as a protection against the misinterpretation of cultural behavioral differences by dominant-culture professionals. At the same time, low-income and ethnic minority parents are the least likely to participate in aspects of their children's schooling (Harry, 1992).

This section of the chapter analyzes how parental participation plays out for these families—or fails to work for them—in special education. Understanding why these parents are apparently disempowered by the special education system helps us develop alternative strategies enabling families to advocate effectively for their children's needs. The focus of the discussion is on families from diverse cultures who are expected to fit within a special education (and general education) structure designed to match dominant cultural values.

THE STRUCTURE OF PARENT PARTICIPATION IN THE CONTEXT OF SPECIAL EDUCATION

IDEA 2004 specifies a series of due process requirements for a parent–professional partnership that should be reflected in special education throughout the steps of referral, evaluation, placement, and instruction of a student with a disability (Turnbull, Turnbull, Erwin, & Soodak, 2005). Policy makers, practitioners, researchers, and theorists in special education attempted to implement an equitable parent–professional foundation for the prescription of services to meet children's individual needs with the best of intentions. Unfortunately, the designers of the special education model established a culturally biased structure that is firmly rooted in Western European cultural values. Many difficulties in implementing that model occur because the model is not always well suited to a multicultural population. Furthermore, the team of specialists involved at every stage of the special education process is most likely to be White and from a middle-class background, and thus culturally discontinuous with most of the people receiving special education services. The special education cultural tensions include the following:

1. The focus in special education on deficit behavior and on one person as the target of intervention is not a cultural universal.

For example, Pacific Nation and Native American peoples may find many principles and practices of IDEA culturally foreign, including the structure of the individualized education program (IEP) and the focus on the individual and his or her behaviors and skills in a formal, professional planning structure. In an interview with the parent of a child in Kohanga Reo, an immersion Maori preschool, a parent explains:

> After identifying the problem, the first step is always to talk about it, you know, and with Maori people they would rather communicate with their elders first, their whanau [family] . . . they would rather do that than have to be sitting in an office with these specialists who . . . it's frightening, it's daunting for parents to come into that situation. . . . The other thing too [is that] it's not appropriate to talk about yourself, not even your own problems as Maori people. The kumera doesn't go around talking about how sweet it is . . . that's why we do things in the whanau. (cited in Bevan-Brown, 1998b, p. 6)

2. The formal prescriptions for due process are grounded in Anglo legal traditions, so that written consent and legalistic entitlements actually disempower culturally diverse families.

IDEA 2004 requires that parents consent to the initial evaluation; if they disagree with the results of that evaluation, they may seek an independent evaluation that must be paid for by the district if the results do not concur. Parents must also formally participate in the annual IEP process and must sign their concurrence to the intervention plan developed for their child at the formal IEP meeting. At one level, these seem like reasonable due process guarantees that parental rights will be respected from referral to placement as well as throughout special education placement.

However, these very formalistic notions of legal accountability differ considerably from the interaction styles of most families. Research on such parent conferences reveals that it is not uncommon for professionals to hold low expectations of parent involvement at these meetings (Turnbull et al., 2005). Observations of meetings reveal that parents are not generally expected to participate actively and that the agenda is usually structured to relegate the parent to the position of passive recipient of professional opinions and signatory to their recommendations (Bennett, 1988; Harry, 1992; Mehan, Hartwick, & Meihls, 1986). Harry, Allen, and McLaughlin (1995) report the comments of an African American mother: "They lay it out [the IEP]. If you have a question, you can ask them. Then you sign it" (cited p. 372).

Maori parents would expect to bring the *whanau* (family) to such a meeting, and the *whanau* might comprise a group even larger than the professional team. Everyone in the *whanau* would be involved in setting goals, because intervention to meet the child's needs would also be seen as intervention with the entire whanau. In an interview with a parent at a Kura Kaupapa Maori, an immersion elementary school, one parent said:

> This was one of the main reasons why we came together . . . so that any issues arising came back and we could deal with them together. . . . We don't just look at the individual. It is the whanau katoa . . . we have specifics with culture, we have specifics with language. . . . [We need to] get services that look at us holistically, that look at whanau; . . . they look at these kids in isolation. (cited in Bevan-Brown, 1998c, pp. 3, 9, 10)

3. Further cultural discontinuities arise from the fact that the influence of culture is embedded in all aspects of special education service delivery. Specifically, we address here process factors such as communication style, goal setting, and psychological assessment.

The special education structure of written communication and formal face-to-face conferences assigns a passive role to parents unless they possess the professional language, cultural, and legalistic skills integral to the process. The distinct middle-class quality of these events is a source of discomfort for many low-income and working-class parents.

In her well-known guide for parents, Coyne Cutler (1993), herself a parent, exhorts parents to develop various skills to advocate for their children in the following ways: making effective telephone calls and writing formal letters to school principals and other professionals, reviewing school records, and keeping records themselves. The framework of productive assertiveness and confrontation in which these activities are suggested illustrates how difficult such advocacy would be for a parent whom professionals perceive as having low social status and less education, and whose literacy skills or experience with schools and bureaucracies are not adequate to these tasks.

Add to this the virtual certainty that the majority of the educational team (if not the entire team) will themselves be White and middle class, while most parents of children with disabilities are neither White nor middle class. Neither within nor outside these two sets of events is there any avenue for the voice of parents who do not use the language of the system. Logistical barriers to participation such as lack of transportation and child-care needs may be much more surmountable in comparison to the numerous barriers related to the structure and process of the special education system itself. Bennett (1988), for example, used ethnographic data with Caribbean Hispanic families to illustrate how school personnel determined what could be discussed at the IEP conference and, in so doing, effectively excluded a parent's concern with classroom climate as a factor in her child's education. Studies by Figler (1981), Harry (1992), Harry, Allen, and McLaughlin (1995), and Harry, Klingner, and Hart (2005) of the experiences of Puerto Rican and African American families offer vivid pictures of the progressive alienation of parents, who gradually withdrew from interaction with professional educators in the face of legal and formal diagnostic frameworks described here that were incompatible with the more personal and less technological cultural frameworks more familiar to the parents. These studies also identified a pattern of deferential parental behavior that masked the parents' real reactions to the process.

Dominant-culture professionals also often assume that the values driving their interventions and goal setting are universally applicable. Kalyanpur and Harry (1999) have argued that the principle of normalization, while a powerful tool for individualized planning for individuals with disabilities, is in itself culturally specific and is a frequent source of discontinuity for families from societies where equity and individualism are not highly valued. Geenen, Powers, and Lopez-Vasquez (2001), in a study of service providers' and culturally and linguistically diverse families' views of transition planning, found contrasting interpretations of "parent involvement." The service providers viewed European American families as much more involved in planning than the Hispanic and African American families. However, the latter two groups perceived themselves as highly involved in "launching" their youngsters into adulthood, but their family and community-based focus differed dramatically from the more formal and program-based goals envisioned by service providers.

With regard to psychological assessment, cognitive processes assumed to be universal that actually represent culture-specific behavior have become institutionalized in the diagnostic process. As a Maori mother explained:

> One of the big barriers . . . is those people who train up to be specialists [who] don't know anything about Te Reo [Maori language] and how the speaking of the language and the living of the language in Kohanga [immersion preschool] . . . this specialist would do these games and always ask the same question what isn't there. And I kept saying to her he doesn't understand what you're saying, he's come through Kohanga. We don't speak about what's not there, we speak about what is there, . . . it's the culture of the language, the structure of the language and how you implement it, the way you say things. Maori people do not ask what isn't there, what they ask is "What is in front of you, what you see, what you do know?" they don't ask you what don't you know. This is what I kept telling this specialist and she was really young and she just kept brushing me off; . . . it was culturally inappropriate for her to be asking questions like that.

Improving Practices in Supporting Parent Participation

Effective practices ensuring representation of family members of color will require strategies that begin with trust between parents and professionals. Such strategies are not likely to be illustrated solely through the more narrow framing of participation required by law, such as attendance at formal meetings and signatures at selected meetings arranged by professionals. Furthermore, where formal meetings are held, perhaps the structure and composition of the group meeting should shift toward including the child's family members—whoever the family feels is relevant to the educational process—rather than restricting attendance to selected "advocates."

We have also suggested elsewhere that ongoing communications between home and school could become a valued role performed by teacher aides who themselves come from the school community and thus are more likely to share cultural membership with the family (Meyer, 1998). Similarly, Evans, Okifuji, and Thomas (1995) describe the role of school partners who were paraprofessional staff hired by their urban school district to serve as mediators and go-betweens, to advocate for both parents and teachers, and to interpret each group's needs. This does not preclude the effectiveness of sensitive "border crossers," however, as illustrated by Harry's (1992) description of how a culturally sensitive American family liaison worker succeeded in increasing the participation of Puerto Rican parents. Because of her efforts to personalize and clarify the special education process for parents, families' perceptions of this service provider changed from "una Americana" ("an American woman") to "someone you can trust." However it is achieved, only ongoing communication between the family and the school will enable a true partnership to emerge.

The educational community must, however, address the cultural discontinuity between the teacher (most often White and middle class as well as English speaking) and the family (increasingly ethnically diverse and speaking a first language other than English). Harry (1992) and Harry, Grenot-Scheyer, and colleagues (1995) have reported on some strategies that professionals can and do use even where such cultural discontinuities exist in order to carry out exemplary parent–teacher conferences. Successful conferences are the result of sensitive responding of individual professionals or teams to the concerns expressed by parents during those meetings. Of course, truly exemplary conferences must be based on a systemic structure that incorporates parental participation, rather than relying on the goodwill and personality characteristics of individual professionals and the initiative of parents (Correa, 1987; Goldstein & Turnbull, 1982; Malmberg, 1984; Thompson, 1982). Turnbull, Turnbull, Erwin, and Soodak (2005) have delineated specific structures and strategies for successful parent–professional communication both within and outside of conferences. Several researchers have emphasized the need for increased use of qualitative methods that can use the voices of families from disenfranchised communities to instruct mainstream professionals (Sanchez, 1999; Skinner, Rodriguez, & Bailey, 1999). We also maintain that educators who choose to work in culturally diverse schools will have to make a commitment to multiculturalism themselves and develop a rich personal cultural repertoire that goes beyond the monocultural experiences with which they entered the educational profession—they will need to demonstrate what Lindsey, Robins, and Terrell (1999) labeled "culturally proficient leadership."

QUALITY INCLUSIVE SCHOOLING: BUILDING SCHOOL COMMUNITIES

IDEA has been a bold social experiment, signaling our acceptance of the responsibility to educate all children. Yet, while we adhere to the principles of compulsory education for all children, our ambivalence regarding its practice evidences itself in varied strategies for labeling and separating children who seem to fall outside the margins of a hypothetical mainstream that still fails to accommodate diversity. The persistent overrepresentation of children of color in special education is possible because disability itself can be a social judgment, most likely made about culturally diverse children and their families by the dominant school cultures.

As long as predominant models of special education involve segregation from the mainstream, special education can become a vehicle for legitimizing continued segregation of children whose behavior and learning differs from dominant cultural norms. The intentions of special education may be noble, but its practice can further delay the evolution of a public school system with the capacity to serve all children as they are. Students are diverse in many ways; no single response to that diversity is appropriate. Some differences can be celebrated, others redefined, others remediated. Each response to diversity has implications for how educational programs are organized and services delivered. Inclusive schools are purposely heterogeneous and attempt to meet individual educational needs within a shared, common social context, without the requirement or expectation that a child must go elsewhere for services (Meyer, 1997; Roach, 1994; Sapon-Shevin, 2001).

The movement for quality inclusive schooling in special education and general education began with a focus on enabling students with disabilities to attend their neighborhood schools and classrooms with their peers (Will, 1986). However, the inclusive schooling movement is now centered within the broader agenda of de-tracking and merging previously fragmented and categorical services for children (Cohen, 1994/1995; Meyer, 1997; Roach, 1994; Sapon-Shevin, 1994). From this broader perspective, inclusion entails a system that responds sensitively and constructively to racial, ethnic, religious, and all other student differences within a cohesive school community—accepting that children are different rather than expecting them to be the same (Ayres, 1993; Sapon-Shevin, 1999). Requiring schools to accommodate all children in the general education classroom is seen as the basis for creating multicultural schools to replace monocultural schools that exclude and separate children into groups of those who belong and those who do not. How we treat students with disabilities can, in practice, be how we treat children who are culturally different from the mainstream; and the messages schools give about who belongs in the mainstream classroom reveals our larger, lifelong agenda about who really belongs in our communities.

Ramsey's (1998) goals for teaching from a multicultural perspective represent the kinds of interpersonal and intrapersonal attitudes and behaviors also regarded as critical to quality inclusive schooling. These goals include teaching children to appreciate and value the contributions of others, to see themselves as members of a larger society, to respect different perspectives, and to accept responsibility for their social environment and society. Teaching children to be knowledgeable about difference, supportive of others, and active in changing structures that are oppressive to various groups can begin within inclusive classrooms. Effective strategies now exist for the inclusion of even those students with the most severe disabilities, and Fisher and Meyer (2002) have documented that quality inclusive programs are associated with significantly greater gains on measures of development and social competence in comparison to gains made by students educated in self-contained settings. We now have a rich database demonstrating the benefits to individual children (those with and without disabilities), professional school personnel, and the community as a function of the development of quality inclusive schooling (Meyer & Park, 1999).

Delivering Special Education within the Context of General Education

In inclusive schools, special services to meet the needs of individual children are delivered within the general education classroom and context. For example, Shakira may need speech therapy. Rather than sending her down the hall for a 15-minute pullout individual speech therapy session, the speech therapist plans with the general education classroom teacher how to meet Shakira's speech needs within the regular classroom. The speech therapist would most likely come into the classroom and work with Shakira and a small group of children—who can also be positive models for her and for the speech therapist, who might otherwise lose touch with how children Shakira's age actually do speak and converse. The speech therapist may also coach the teacher on how to work with Shakira during her usual reading group activities. Because Shakira is African American, the speech therapist must be sensitive to issues of her dialect of English as she plans what speech patterns do and do not require remediation. Shakira must be viewed as a person with multiple identities, and these identities must be dealt with in an integrated fashion within the classroom and social context (Vygotsky, 1978).

All individuals are multifaceted. Banks (see Chapter 1) emphasizes that all persons bring with them to any interaction a racial identity, an ethnic background, their age, their religion, their social class, as well as other group identities. Mee Wong is a 10-year-old girl. She is also Korean, lives in the city, has two working-class parents, and is a practicing Buddhist. Having a learning disability may be part of her identity, but it does not define who she is. All of her characteristics help define who she is and must be respected in the classroom. Having a learning disability should not preclude her from participation in the schooling experiences of her peer group (including attending the general education classroom) any more than being Buddhist should exclude her from interactions with her peers in the neighborhood. Grant and Sleeter (Chapter 3) explain that race, social class, and gender are used to construct major groups of people in society. Because all students are members of all three status groups, each group and the interactions among these groups affect students' perceptions and actions. When issues of disability are added to these categories, the number of interactions and spheres of influence increase exponentially. Adapting a Christmas craft activity for Joshua, who has cerebral palsy and uses a communication board, may not be an appropriate or adequate response to his individual identity when we know that Joshua is Jewish and does not celebrate Christmas. If we define Joshua according to only one dimension of his identity, we cannot meet his needs and treat him with respect. Shamika is African American, lives with her mother, and has difficulty reading. When she is given books at her level, we must be thoughtful about not limiting reading materials to books that portray only

European American, two-parent families. We should create classroom environments in which children are comfortable revealing all aspects of their backgrounds and experiences that matter to them.

Classrooms must support the diversity of students by responding to each of their identities and by not stereotyping students according to unidimensional and narrow notions of who they are. Social context is critical for virtually all learning, and a child's experiences are the foundation of mastery of everything new (Tharp & Gallimore, 1989; Vygotsky, 1978). Putting our educational theories about social contexts for learning into action requires that we model the realities of children's personal and social lives throughout their academic lives in the general education classroom.

Sapon-Shevin (1992; 1999; 2005a; 2005b) has detailed the ways in which teachers can structure their classrooms so that students learn about racial, cultural, family, gender, religious, and skill differences as part of the curriculum. This information need not be limited to learning facts about other groups but can be extended so that students are actively working to understand and combat prejudices and stereotypes they encounter in school and society. Work by Derman-Sparks and the ABC Task Force (1989) and by Cronin (1998) provide examples of how even very young children can be empowered through antibias curricula to challenge injustices and inequities in society. Inclusive classroom communities must also model social and academic interactions between and among children and adults that build capacities for lifelong competence in multicultural communities outside school. Cooperative learning strategies enable students to achieve academic mastery within the context of positive, collaborative social interactions that reflect student diversity. These alternatives to tracking and ability grouping can be adapted to enable the inclusion of the full range of differences in the classroom, and they can also send powerful messages about individual responsibility to work together in order to achieve goals (Meyer & Fisher, 1999; Sapon-Shevin, Ayres, & Duncan, 2002).

Meyer, Minondo, et al. (1998) describe the range of possible social relationships in children's lives, evident in their research, that can be fostered by educational practices and the organization of schooling. Their work highlights the importance of attention to the implementation of inclusive schooling, which is much more than the physical presence of students with disabilities in the classroom or even the provision of special education services within the general education environment. They found that when teachers communicated through actions and words that did not fully include children with disabilities, children mirrored those social patterns in their peer interactions. Thus, when the teacher always refers to "helping" the student with disabilities rather than working together, and fails to identify meaningful opportunities for academic participation for the student with disabilities, children without disabilities are most likely to see their peers with disabilities as students to be ignored, helped, or treated "specially," much as one would interact with a very young child or even a plaything (Evans, Salisbury, Palombaro, Berryman, & Hollowood, 1992). When classroom practices support full participation in the range of academic and social activities occurring in school, students with even the most severe disabilities experience social lives that include being part of the group in some contexts as well as enjoying regular and best friendships (Meyer, Minondo, et al., 1998; Schnorr, 1997). Figure 14.1 provides some examples of how teachers can assess their practices to support different social outcomes for children in inclusive classrooms.

Question to ask to assess informally the nature of children's social relationships:

Ghost / Guest: Does the child frequently get "passed over" as if he or she were not there (ghost)? Do staff talk about another placement as soon as there is a problem (guest)?

Inclusion Child: Does the teacher say "I have 27 students plus 2 included students"?

I'll Help: Do classmates use the words "work with" or "help" whenever they refer to time spent with the child?

Just Another Child: Is the child expected to participate in the class activity along with everyone else?

Regular Friend: Has the child ever been invited to a party by a classmate?

Best Friend: Does the child have one or more friends who call him or her on the telephone at home and/or visit after school or on weekends?

Figure 14.1   Six Frames of Friendship Characterizing a Student's Social Relationships at School

Source: L. H. Meyer, H. Park, M. Grenot-Scheyer, I. S. Schwartz, & B. Harry (Eds.) (1998). *Making Friends: The Influences of Culture and Development* (p. 216). Baltimore: Paul H. Brookes. Reprinted with permission of the publisher.

Inclusive Classrooms, Inclusive Pedagogy

An inclusive classroom requires not only that a full range of students be represented and respected within the classroom context but also that the teaching strategies respond to and include those differences. Narrow, inflexible teaching practices that assume all students learn best in the same way and bring the same experiences, background, learning style, and interests to the task are neither inclusive nor sensitive to student needs. Inclusive pedagogy can be described in terms of both the content of what is taught and the process.

Banks (Chapter 10) discusses the ways in which the "mainstream-centric curriculum" can be modified to incorporate multiple perspectives; he describes four levels of integration of multicultural content (see Chapter 10 for a more extensive discussion of these levels). In keeping with Banks's levels of integration, issues of ability/disability can be seen to have been incorporated into the practices of teaching and learning at each level as well, with substantial differences in the extent to which the status quo is accepted or challenged.

The *contributions* level focuses on heroes, holidays, and discrete cultural elements. This approach is reflected in having the class read a book about Helen Keller and then teaching a unit on blindness. Students may come to appreciate that persons who are blind can make important contributions, but this level does not challenge the more fundamental notions of segregation and exclusion of *most* people who are blind and who are not seen as making exemplary contributions.

At the *additive* level, teachers "put ethnic content into the curriculum without restructuring it" (Banks, 2001, p. 232). A special education parallel to the additive approach is to mainstream students with special education needs while leaving the curriculum of the classroom intact. Special activities may be implemented for the students with disabilities, but these activities are not integrated into the main life and curriculum of the classroom. Operationally, this level alone would result in an island in the mainstream, consisting of a special education student or small group working with a special educator (or teacher aide) on a separate activity while classmates are engaged in the larger-group, *real* academic activity. Early exemplars of integration differed from today's inclusive efforts in their fundamental practices of creating small tutorials within the general education classroom rather than modifying ongoing instructional activities to enable the student with disabilities to participate fully.

The *transformational* approach "changes the basic assumptions of the curriculum and enables students to view concepts, issues, events, and themes" from the perspectives of diverse ethnic and cultural groups (Banks, 2001, p. 233). This approach from an inclusive perspective involves not only having students with special needs become part of the classroom but also rethinking and reinventing the curriculum so that it is inclusive and multilevel. All students—across a diverse range of abilities and needs—would be engaged in educational experiences appropriate to their level but as part of a common topic, focus, and lesson (Putnam, 1998).

The *social action* approach "includes all the elements of the transformation approach but adds components that require students to make decisions and take actions related to the concept, issue, or problem studied in the unit" (Banks, 2001, p. 236). This requires both reshaping and reinventing the nature of general education classrooms and making them multilevel and inclusive as well as thinking about how schools and teaching can be part of a broader social goal of changing arbitrary and limiting notions of ability, expectations, and the need for segregation (Bigelow, Harvey, Karp, & Miller, 2001). This level has implications for school-based and systemwide decisions about outcomes evaluation, diplomas, testing of students, and curriculum design. Portfolio assessment of student outcomes—as opposed to using a uniform psychometric test—is one example of flexible educational practices that can better accommodate the richness of the repertoires of all students and their achievements (Kleinart, Kearns, & Kennedy, 1997).

Other examples of fundamental change at this level are the National Council of the Teachers of Mathematics (1993) standards that reconceptualize broader outcomes, such as critical thinking and problem solving. These goals relate meaningfully to the use of mathematics in life and can be readily adapted to represent the wide range of mathematics skill levels of students found in any given classroom. Thus, students with and without disabilities might be working on their problem-solving skills in mathematics, but each student would have an individually appropriate learner objective, and the instructional unit would be adapted to accommodate differences rather than assuming everyone is learning at the same level.

Inclusive Pedagogy

Inclusive pedagogy can be described as a set of teaching practices and structures that acknowledge student differences and are responsive to that diversity. Banks's (Chapter 10) transformation and social action levels represent inclusive pedagogy. Cooperative learning and other strategies to support multilevel instruction are examples of pedagogy that can be structured inclusively (Kagan, 1998; Putnam, 1998; Sapon-Shevin et al., 2002). In cooperative learning structures, students work together to achieve common goals. Social skills (listening, compromising, asking questions, encouraging) are taught both formally and informally, and the task is structured so that students must work together in order to achieve a successful outcome. A cooperatively structured math lesson, for example, may involve students generating and then solving their own multistep math problems. A student with a disability who cannot write could contribute to the task as the checker for the group, doing the problem on a calculator and confirming the group's answer. Tasks can be structured so that students generate problems related to their own lives and experiences. Because students are working together, student differences can contribute to successful task completion rather than being viewed as obstacles to some standard curriculum.

Multilevel instruction involves structuring lessons so that different modalities, different content areas, and different levels of performance can be accommodated within current educational practices (Putnam, 1998). A thematic unit on families could be constructed involving math activities (graphing family demographics), language (writing biographies of family members, taking oral histories), and exploration of music and arts activities related to different cultures. All students could be involved in reading, writing, and mathematics activities appropriate to their level and interests, so that even a student with the most profound disabilities could be meeting his or her educational objective in such a unit.

For example, a student with multiple disabilities might be working on operating a switch to activate a computer, small appliances, or a tape recorder. Depending on the student's communication goals, two needs could be met within the context of this hypothetical thematic unit on the family. First, the student could be telling a biography of a family member by listing some descriptive facts about a brother or sister—this might be part of a communication goal for that student involving describing important personal characteristics and using an augmentative communication system to write the list. Second, the student could be working on operating a switch to activate a tape recording of that list read out by a classmate. When it is the student's turn to read the biography to the class, he or she must operate the switch to start the recording and then again to stop it at the end. There are numerous examples of successfully including students with special needs through adaptations to good instruction and educational best practices for all students (Fisher, Bernazzani, & Meyer, 1998; Hedeen, Ayres, & Tate, 2001; Meyer, Williams, Harootunian, & Steinberg, 1995; Ryndak, Morrison, & Sommerstein, 1999; Salisbury, Palombaro, & Hollowood, 1993; Sapon-Shevin et al., 2002; Smith, 1997).

Inclusive School Supports and Teacher Education

Before the advent of quality inclusive schooling, the delivery of special education services occurred in separate schools, classrooms, and/or resource rooms. Both general and special educators were professionally prepared to teach their respective students in separate environments. Teacher education, curricula, classroom organization, instructional practices, and structures of educational teaming to support students have evolved for two parallel systems— one general and one special—over a period of decades. Winn and Blanton (1997) describe the major implications for changes in teacher education and school collaboration that will be needed if inclusive schools are to become a reality. Early movements toward the integration of students with disabilities into general education were characterized by attempts to transplant specialized special education approaches into the mainstream (Meyer & Park, 1999). In contrast, the contemporary inclusive schooling movement recognizes that fundamental school reform will be required for both special and general education—indeed, merger toward one unified system of education—if quality-inclusive schooling is to become a reality (Gartner & Lipsky, 1987; Meyer, 1997; Pugach & Johnson, 1995).

Goessling (1998) describes the changes that were required in thinking and practice by both general and special educators in 14 different elementary schools following the decision to provide special education services within K–8 classrooms. She contrasts the traditions (e.g., homogeneity vs. heterogeneity); language (e.g., scope and sequence vs. goals and objectives); rituals (e.g., report cards vs. IEPs); and symbols (e.g., worksheets vs. graphs of student performance) of general versus special education programs as background to the restructuring efforts undertaken by the 14 schools in her sample. For example, the traditional pullout system of service delivery in special education had been supplanted by a more collaborative consultation model, with all special education services provided within the context of general education activities and lessons. Her research report chronicles the "process of assimilation" for the special education teachers in particular as they moved from special education into general education. Their presence within the general education classroom had an impact on them as well as on the culture of general education itself:

> This research indicated that these fourteen teachers of students
> with severe disabilities were assimilated into the culture of general
> education and that their presence in general education could bring
> about changes within the culture of general education itself. . . .
> The presence of students with severe disabilities appeared to
> influence the push forward of school restructuring efforts and
> helped create schools that were less bureaucratic and more
> personalized and caring. . . . Perhaps there will be another study in
> a few years that does not discuss the cultural assimilation of special
> education teachers into general education, but rather the creation
> of a third school culture that incorporates the best of both.
> (Goessling, 1998, p. 249)

The model of the methods and resource (M&R) teachers develop as an alternative to the traditional special education teacher exemplifies specialized school support personnel who are staffed to assist the learning of all students, working in collaboration with the classroom teacher. Porter and Stone (1998) describe the role and responsibilities of the M&R teacher and the school-based student services team structure that evolved in New Brunswick, Canada, once the school district had made the commitment to quality inclusive schooling. School district officials recognized that significant restructuring of teachers' roles and responsibilities was needed to operationalize inclusion. This model does not involve placing students with disabilities into the mainstream without support services, nor does the model deny that some students do have disabilities that require significant services. The model does change the nature of those support services and creates a new "special education" support teacher role charged to work collaboratively with the classroom teacher to meet the diverse needs of all students—not only those with a disability label.

A major argument advanced in support of quality inclusive schooling is capacity building: Schools and teachers within those schools would be committed to and capable of delivering effective instruction to all children, not only to those judged to be typical or tracked according to various criteria (Byrnes & Kiger, 2005; Gartner & Lipsky, 1987; Roach, 1994; Sapon-Shevin, 1994). Yet the evidence is that today's teachers are not confident of their abilities to manage and accommodate the diverse range of student characteristics in their classrooms. Gottlieb et al. (1994) reported that 63 percent of the teachers who referred children out of the classroom to special education said they did not know what resources would enable them to teach those children within their classrooms. Only 16 percent believed they could be trained with the skills to enable them to teach children whom they had referred. Only 10 percent of the referring general education teachers could even describe a curricular adaptation they might make to accommodate the child. It is no wonder, then, that Gottlieb and his colleagues (1994) conclude that without "massive staff development efforts," the mainstreaming movement is unlikely to improve children's academic status (p. 462).

Similarly, in their 1994 study in New York City—again showing disproportionate referrals to special education for students whose needs were not much different from the needs of other students—referring classroom teachers had made only one attempt to address the learner's needs before seeking placement elsewhere. That one attempt did not involve making curricular adaptations, modifying instruction, or even seeking additional professional technical assistance from within their school or district; the teachers called the students' home and asked the parent to fix the problem! Given stressed economic circumstances and both cultural and language differences from that of the school professional staff, it is difficult to envision what parents would be expected to do to address the academic learning and behavioral difficulties their children were experiencing in school.

Who, then, will staff the quality inclusive schools and classrooms of the future? What are the implications of teaching staff in schools who were themselves prepared in teacher education programs tracked for either special or general education? We believe that just as cultural diversity demands preparation in multicultural education for all teachers, individual learning differences (including disabilities) and multiple intelligences (Gardner, 1993) demand the preparation of a new generation of teachers with a repertoire of values and strategies that match the demands of inclusive classrooms. The National Association of State Boards of Education (1992) recognized the implications of inclusion for teacher preparation programs and called for the development of new directions in teacher education consistent with the merger of general and special education. Historically, many preservice teacher education programs have included dual-certification options in both general and special education, but a truly merged program incorporating multicultural education as well as both special and general education preparation is still a rarity (Winn & Blanton, 1997).

An early example of a merged and unified inclusive teacher education program was implemented at Syracuse University in 1990 (Meyer, Mager, Yarger-Kane, Sarno, & Hext-Contreras, 1997). Its graduates are in strong demand, and graduate follow-up indicates that they enter the teaching profession with the commitment and professional repertoire for successful inclusion (Meyer et al., 1997). Ornelles and Goetz (2001) describe the University of Hawaii's post-baccalaureate program to recruit and train teachers with cultural competence who are better prepared to work with ethnically diverse students who have special needs (for other examples, see Blanton, Griffin, Winn, & Pugach, 1997). The Wingspread Conference coordinated by the Teacher Education Division of the Council for Exceptional Children (CEC) focused on the development of guiding principles and specific action steps if we are to prepare teachers to work with diverse learners (Dieker, Voltz, & Epanchin, 2002; see also CEC, 2001). Achieving quality inclusive schooling will require significant reform of teacher education at all levels, both preservice and inservice.

DIVERSITY AND CARING COMMUNITIES: OUTCOMES FOR THE SOCIAL GOOD

We believe that the existence and perpetuation of pullout solutions to student differences inevitably generates (and reflects) some perhaps unintended but nonetheless real negative side effects:

1. As long as the belief persists that general education classrooms are homogenous, the cycle of referral for differences will continue and will, ultimately, exceed the resources of marginalized systems.

Our current dual system of general and special education encourages the school to conceptualize homogeneous typical groupings as the only functional structures for teaching and learning. Language which implies that the optimal response to differences is to make them invisible is particularly problematic because it does not help teachers or students learn to be responsive and proactive when faced with differences and oppression (Sapon-Shevin, 2001). Systems that allow and even encourage narrowing of commitment and capacity to serve diverse needs, that expect children to fit curriculum rather than adapting schooling to meet children's needs, and that institutionalize the identification of difference through segregation and tracking will increasingly reduce tolerance for differences and restrict the range of those who are viewed as being typical and who are seen as belonging. This is particularly dysfunctional now, when new immigrant groups, increased poverty, and proportionately greater numbers of culturally and linguistically diverse students and families are facts of life in the

United States. The inevitable result will be an increasing cycle of referrals that will ultimately exceed the resources of the various special systems that are both marginalized and devalued by the mainstream society.

> **2.** In the long run, efforts to reduce class size and restrict general education enrollment to smaller groups of students ready to learn will fail. Instead, as children leave the mainstream, resources will follow, and the cycle will repeat.

Gottlieb and his colleagues (1994) note that the current system of special education reduces any need for the general education system to develop meaningful instructional and student support programs and services for children in the general education classrooms. Teachers seemed to believe that the only mechanism available to them to reduce class size and the instructional challenges confronting them in the short run was to fully access referrals to special education—which, in large urban areas, continued to mean placement in a separate educational environment. But as children do leave general education, resources must be provided to them at their new destination—and those resources must come from somewhere. Increasingly, resources have declined in general education as our many entitlement programs have increased. While the relationship may not be a simple one, we believe that declining resources will be spread ever more thinly—and, ultimately, that those resources will come from the same budget and require subsequent increases in class size in general education.

A major argument advanced by proponents of quality inclusive schooling is that our educational system cannot afford separate and fragmented systems. Children with disabilities must return to the general education classroom and attend school with their peers. But the resources supporting those children must return as well—and those resources must be restructured and capacities enhanced to better serve all children, both those with and without disabilities.

> **3.** When children with and without disabilities grow up in isolation from one another, everyone loses. Children will "do as I do, and not as I say." If we model segregation and rejection in a social system as central to our democratic institutions as the public schools, we will have a great deal to answer for when those exclusionary models play out in the domains of daily living.

When children with disabilities are segregated from their nondisabled peers, they lose the mainstream social context as a major teaching and learning environment. They become increasingly dependent on teacher-directed, highly structured learning and on adults in particular as the source of all new knowledge and support. On the other hand, they give up peer groups and participation in their neighborhood and community. Increasingly, as natural supports are thwarted from developing, persons with disabilities become more and more dependent on costly professional and paid services to fill the void.

More than 50 years ago, Adorno, Frenkel-Brunswik, Levinson, and Sanford (1950) advanced their theory that one's attitudes toward persons who are viewed as different is part of a consistent pattern that affects all aspects of the individual's behavior and beliefs. Their studies of racial prejudice and political conservatism were premised on the theory that cultural acceptance would be associated with democratic principles and that the promotion of cultural acceptance would thus have broad benefits for the social good. The movement for diversity in education makes a similar point while acknowledging the futility of ignoring the pluralism that now dominates the population of U.S. schoolchildren. Learning to accept individual differences and to celebrate diversity as an enriching experience are broad principles consistent with democratic values and the creation of caring schools that support children's growth and development.

In addition to multicultural education, various other general education reform movements emphasize the need for caring school communities. Berman (1990) builds a case for such school communities if we are to address the basic societal needs of our democracy for the "nurturing in young people of a sense of social responsibility and social efficacy" (p. 1); he notes with irony that "we teach reading, writing, and math by doing them, but we teach democracy by lecture" (p. 2). In her writings, Noddings (1992) has long emphasized that the creation of educational environments that support learning involves the creation of caring communities, where teachers supplement the emphasis on academic excellence with relational ethics and moral education. She emphasizes that teachers must model caring throughout their teaching and interactions with students, a concern that can be traced to John Dewey's writings. As Sapon-Shevin (2003; 2004; 2005a; 2005b) argues, it is only through inclusive schooling that we can create and maintain democratic societies as preparing citizens requires diverse school experiences.

Wells and Grain (1994) note that a thirty-year research literature on school desegregation has most often focused on the immediate effects of racial integration on individual students—their achievement, their self-esteem, and their intergroup relations. These researchers argue that another perspective focused on the life chances of African American students requires a longer-term outlook. According to a sociological perspective referred to as *perpetuation theory*, "the goal of desegregation is also to break the cycle of segregation and increase access to high status institutions and the powerful social networks within them" (p. 531). Clearly, action beyond the school gate is required so that educational reform occurs in the context of a major commitment to the wide-ranging societal changes necessary to improve the life chances of children with disabilities and from ethnic minorities (Bevan-Brown, 2006). In the interim, there is much our schools can do. What is the purpose of our educational system and public education in the United States? Is it exclusively intended to meet the needs of each individual child? We think not. At least in part, our educational system was conceptualized as a pathway to a democratic community and the betterment of all its citizenry. Our challenge is, of course, to examine the rhetoric and practices within education with the goal of reaching a better balance between meeting unique needs and building community.

Questions and Activities

1. Why, according to the authors, are students of color and low-income students overrepresented in special education classes and programs?

2. Why is it especially important for parents of color and low-income parents to be involved in special education programs for their children? What are some effective ways in which these parents can become involved in special education programs?

3. Why do parents, especially low-income parents and parents of color, often find it difficult to participate meaningfully in special education programs even though laws exist to ensure their participation?

4. The research and assessment work by Jane R. Mercer revealed that special education is a social construction. Special education can also be viewed as a cultural construction: Give specific examples from this chapter to show the impact of culture on perspectives of disability.

5. According to the authors, what are some of the major characteristics of quality *inclusive* schools? On what major assumptions and beliefs are they based? How do inclusive schools exemplify and foster the idea of "the school as a community" described by the authors?

6. What do the authors mean by "inclusive pedagogy"? Give specific examples of this concept.

7. The authors believe that special education students should be educated in the same schools and classrooms as general education students. What problems and opportunities does this practice pose for classroom teachers? What changes might need to occur within teacher education to prepare teachers for inclusive classrooms? What guidelines, tips, and insights do the authors provide that may help teachers deal with the challenges and problems posed by inclusive education?

8. The authors maintain that a commitment to the principles and practices of inclusive education not only will benefit special education students but also will lead to classrooms and schools that reflect diversity and can thus better serve all students with and without disabilities. How might fully inclusive schools prepare our children for fully inclusive communities?

References

Adelman, H. S., & Taylor, L. (1993). *Learning Problems and Learning Disabilities: Moving Forward.* Pacific Grove, CA: Brooks/Cole.

Adorno, T. W., Frenkel-Brunswik, E., Levinson, D. J., & Sanford, R. N. (1950). *The Authoritarian Personality* (Vols. 1 & 2). New York: Wiley.

Argulewicz, E. N. (1983). Effects of Ethnic Membership, Socioeconomic Status, and Home Language on LD, EMR, and EH Placements. *Learning Disabilities Quarterly, 6,* 195–200.

Artiles, A. J. (1998). The Dilemma of Difference: Enriching the Disproportionality Discourse with Theory and Context. *The Journal of Special Education, 32,* 32–36.

Artiles, A. J., & McClafferty, K. (1998). Learning to Teach Culturally Diverse Learners: Charting Change in Preservice Teachers' Thinking about Effective Teaching. *The Elementary School Journal, 98,* 189–220.

Artiles, A. J., Rueda, R., Salazar, R. & Higareda, I. (2005). Within Group Diversity in Minority Disproportionate Representation: English Language Learners in Urban School Districts. *Exceptional Children, 71,* 283–300.

Artiles, A. J., & Trent, S. C. (1994). Overrepresentation of Minority Students in Special Education: A Continuing Debate. *The Journal of Special Education, 27,* 410–437.

Artiles, A. J., & Trent, S. C. (1997). Forging a Research Program on Multicultural Preservice Teacher Education in Special Education: A Proposed Analytic Scheme. In J. W. Lloyd, E. J.

Kameenui, & D. Chard (Eds.), *Issues in Educating Students with Disabilities* (pp. 275–304). Mahwah, NJ: Erlbaum.

Artiles, A. J., Trent, S. C., & Palmer, J. (2004). Culturally Diverse Students in Special Education: Legacies and Prospects. In J. A. Banks & C. A. M. Banks (Eds.), *Handbook of Research in Multicultural Education* (2nd ed., pp. 716–735). San Francisco, CA: Jossey-Bass.

Ayres, B. J. (1993). *Equity, Excellence, and Diversity in the "Regular" Classroom.* Unpublished doctoral dissertation, Syracuse University, Syracuse, NY.

Banks, J. A. (2001). Approaches to Multicultural Curriculum Reform. In J. A. Banks & C. A. M. Banks (Eds.), *Multicultural Education: Issues and Perspectives* (4th ed., pp. 225–246). New York: Wiley.

Banks, J. A., & Banks, C. A. M. (Eds.). (2007). *Multicultural Education: Issues and Perspectives* (6th ed.). New York: Wiley.

Bennett, A. T. (1988). Gateways to Powerlessness: Incorporating Hispanic Deaf Children and Families into Formal Schooling. *Disability, Handicap, and Society, 3*(2), 119–151.

Berman, S. (1990). The Real Ropes Course: The Development of Social Consciousness. *ESR Journal: Educating for Social Responsibility, 1,* 1–18.

Bevan-Brown, J. (1998a). *A Cultural Audit for Teachers: Looking Out for Maori Learners with Special Needs. SET: Special Education 2000.* Wellington, New Zealand: New Zealand Council for Educational Research.

Bevan-Brown, J. (1998b). [Kohanga reo interview transcript, No. 3]. Unpublished raw data.

Bevan-Brown, J. (1998c). [Kura kaupapa Maori interview transcript, No. 1]. Unpublished raw data.

Bevan-Brown, J. (1999). Catering for Maori Learners with Special Needs. Paper presented at the 23rd Annual International Conference of the Association for Persons with Handicaps, Seattle.

Bevan-Brown, J. (2001). Evaluating Special Education Services for Learners from Ethnically Diverse Groups: Getting It Right. *Journal of the Association for Persons with Severe Handicaps, 26,* 138–147.

Bevan-Brown, J. (March–May 2006). Beyond Policy and Good Intentions. *International Journal of Inclusive Education, 10*(2–3), Part 1, 221–234.

Bigelow, B., Harvey, B., Karp, S., & Miller, L. (Eds.). (2001). *Rethinking our Classrooms: Teaching for Equity and Justice* (Vol. 2). Milwaukee, WI: Rethinking Schools.

Blanton, L. P., Griffin, C. C., Winn, J. A., & Pugach, M. C. (Eds.). (1997). *Teacher Education in Transition: Collaborative Programs to Prepare General and Special Educators.* Denver, CO: Love.

Byrnes, D. A., & Kiger, G. (Eds.). (2005). *Common Bonds: Anti-Bias Teaching in a Diverse Society* (3rd ed.). Olney, MD: Association for Childhood Education International.

Cohen, F. (1994/1995). Prom Pictures: A Principal Looks at Detracking. *Educational Leadership, 52*(4), 85–86.

Correa, V. I. (1987). Involving Culturally Diverse Families in the Educational Process. In S. H. Fradd & M. J. Weismantel (Eds.), *Meeting the Needs of Culturally and Linguistically Different Students: A Handbook for Educators* (pp. 130–144). Boston: College Hill.

Council for Exceptional Children (CEC). (2001). *What Every Special Educator Must Know: The Standards for the Preparation and Licensure of Special Educators.* Reston, VA: Author.

Coyne Cutler, B. (1993). *You, Your Child, and "Special" Education: A Guide to Making the System Work.* Baltimore: Brookes.

Cronin, S. (1998). Culturally Relevant Antibias Learning Communities: Teaching Umoja. In L. H. Meyer, H. S. Park, M. Grenot-Scheyer, I. S. Schwartz, & B. Harry (Eds.), *Making Friends: The Influences of Culture and Development* (pp. 341–351). Baltimore: Brookes.

Derman-Sparks, L., & ABC Task Force. (1989). *Anti-Bias Curriculum: Tools for Empowering Young Children*. Washington, DC: National Association for the Education of Young Children.

Dieker, L., Voltz, D., & Epanchin, B. (2002). Report of the Wingspread Conference: Preparing Teachers to Work with Diverse Learners. *Teacher Education and Special Education, 25,* 1–10.

Divergent Youth (Report of the Senate Fact Finding Committee on Education: Subcommittee on Special Education). (1963). Washington, DC: U.S. Government Printing Office.

Donovan, S., & Cross, C. (2002). *Minority Students in Special and Gifted Education.* National Academy of Sciences. Washington, DC: National Academy Press.

Dunn, L. (1968). Special Education for the Mildly Retarded: Is Much of It Justifiable? *Exceptional Children, 35,* 5–22.

Emerson, E., Robertson, J., & Wood, J. (in press). The Association between Area-Level Indicators of Social Deprivation and the Emotional and Behavioural Needs of Black and South Asian Children with Intellectual Disabilities in a Deprived Urban Environment. *Journal of Applied Research in Intellectual Disabilities,* in press.

Evans, I. M., Okifuji, A., & Thomas, A. D. (1995). Home–School Partnerships: Involving Families in the Educational Process. In I. M. Evans, T. Cicchelli, M. Cohen, & N. P. Shapiro (Eds.), *Staying in School: Partnerships for Educational Change* (pp. 23–40). Baltimore: Brookes.

Evans, I. M., Salisbury, C. L., Palombaro, M. M., Berryman, J., & Hollowood, T. M. (1992). Peer Interactions and Social Acceptance of Elementary-Age Children with Severe Disabilities in an Inclusive School. *Journal of the Association for Persons with Severe Handicaps, 17,* 205–212.

Figler, C. S. (1981). Puerto Rican Families with and without Handicapped Children. Paper presented at the Council for Exceptional Children Conference on the Exceptional Bilingual Child, New Orleans. (ERIC Document Reproduction Service No. ED 204 876.)

Finn, J. D. (1982). Patterns in Special Education Placement as Revealed by the OCR Surveys. In K. A. Heller, W. H. Holtzman, & S. Mesrick (Eds), *Placing Children in Special Education: A Strategy for Equity* (pp. 322–381). Washington, DC: National Academy Press.

Fisher, M., Bernazzani, J., & Meyer, L. H. (1998). Participatory Action Research: Supporting Social Relationships in the Cooperative Classroom. In J. Putnam (Ed.), *Cooperative Learning and Strategies for Inclusion: Celebrating Diversity in the Classroom* (2nd ed., pp. 137–165). Baltimore: Brookes.

Fisher, M., & Meyer, L. H. (2002). Development and Social Competence after Two Years for Students Enrolled in Inclusive and Self-Contained Educational Programs. *Research and Practice for Persons with Severe Disabilities, 27,* 165–174.

Fujiura, G. T., & Yamaki, K. (2000). Trends in Demography of Childhood Poverty and Disability. *Exceptional Children, 66,* 187–199.

Gardner, H. (1993). *Multiple Intelligences: The Theory in Practice.* New York: Basic Books.

Gartner, A., & Lipsky, D. K. (1987). Beyond Special Education: Toward a Quality System for All Students. *Harvard Educational Review, 57,* 367–395.

Geenen, S., Powers, L. E., & Lopez-Vasquez, A. (2001). Multicultural Aspects of Parent Involvement in Transition Planning. *Exceptional Children, 67,* 265–282.

Goessling, D. P. (1998). Inclusion and the Challenge of Assimilation for Teachers of Students with Severe Disabilities. *Journal of the Association for Persons with Severe Handicaps, 23,* 238–251.

Goldstein, S., & Turnbull, A. P. (1982). The Use of Two Strategies to Increase Parent Participation in IEP Conferences. *Exceptional Children, 48,* 360–361.

Gottlieb, J., Alter, M., Gottlieb, B. W., & Wishner, J. (1994). Special Education in Urban America: It's Not Justifiable for Many. *Journal of Special Education, 27,* 453–465.

Harry, B. (1992). *Cultural Diversity, Families, and the Special Education System: Communication for Empowerment.* New York: Teachers College Press.

Harry, B., Allen, N., & McLaughlin, M. (1995). Communication vs. Compliance: African American Parents' Involvement in Special Education. *Exceptional Children, 61,* 364–377.

Harry, B., Grenot-Scheyer, M., Smith-Lewis, M., Park, H.-S., Xin, F., & Schwartz, I. (1995). Developing Culturally Inclusive Services for Individuals with Severe Disabilities. *Journal of the Association for Persons with Severe Handicaps, 20,* 99–109.

Harry, B., & Klingner, J. (2005). African American Families under Fire: Ethnographic Views of Family Strengths. *Remedial and Special Education, 26*(2), 101–112.

Harry, B., & Klingner, J. (2006). *Why Are So Many Minority Students in Special Education? Understanding Race and Disability in Schools.* New York: Teachers College Press.

Hedeen, D. L., Ayres, B. J., & Tate, A. (2001). Getting Better, Happy Day, Problems Again! The Ups and Downs of Supporting a Student with Autism in Her Home School. In M. Grenot-Scheyer, M. Fisher, & D. Staub (Eds.), *At the End of the Day: Stories of Ordinary Lives of Children and Youth in Inclusive Schools and Communities* (pp. 47–72). Baltimore: Brookes.

Horner, R. H., Meyer, L. H., & Fredericks, H. D. B. (Eds.). (1986). *Education of Learners with Severe Handicaps: Exemplary Service Strategies.* Baltimore: Brookes.

Hosp, J. L., & Reschly, D. J. (2004). Disproportionate Representation of Minority Students in Special Education: Academic, Demographic, and Economic Predictors. *Exceptional Children, 70,* 185–199.

Kagan, S. (1998). New Cooperative Learning, Multiple Intelligences, and Inclusion. In J. W. Putnam (Ed.), *Cooperative Learning and Strategies for Inclusion* (2nd ed.). Baltimore: Brookes.

Kalyanpur, M., & Harry, B. (1999). *Culture in Special Education: Building Reciprocal Parent–Professional Relationships.* Baltimore: Brookes.

Kleinert, H. L., Kearns, J. F., & Kennedy, S. (1997). Accountability for All Students: Kentucky's Alternate Portfolio Assessment for Students with Moderate and Severe Cognitive Disabilities. *Journal of the Association for Persons with Severe Handicaps, 22,* 88–101.

Lindsey, R. B., Robins, K. N., & Terrell, R. D. (1999). *Cultural Proficiency: A Manual for School Leaders.* Thousand Oaks, CA: Corwin.

MacMillan, D. L., Jones, R. L., & Meyers, C. E. (1976). Mainstreaming the Mildly Retarded: Some Questions, Cautions and Guidelines. *Mental Retardation, 14,* 3–10.

MacMillan, D. L., & Reschly, D. J. (1998). Overrepresentation of Minority Students: The Case for Greater Specificity or Reconsideration of the Variables Examined. *The Journal of Special Education, 32,* 15–24.

Malmberg, P. A. (1984). *Development of Field Tested Special Education Placement Committee Parent Education Materials.* Unpublished doctoral dissertation, Virginia Polytechnic Institute and State University, Blacksburg.

Meier, K. J., Stewart, J., & England, R. E. (1989). *Race, Class, and Education: The Politics of Second-Generation Discrimination.* Madison: University of Wisconsin Press.

Mercer, J. R. (1973). *Labeling the Mentally Retarded: Clinical and Social System Perspectives on Mental Retardation.* Berkeley: University of California Press.

Mercer, J. R. (1979). *System of Multicultural Pluralistic Assessment: Technical Manual.* Cleveland, OH: The Psychological Corporation.

Meyer, L. H. (1997). Tinkering around the Edges? *Journal of the Association for Persons with Severe Handicaps, 22,* 80–82.

Meyer, L. H., & Fisher, M. (1999). Participatory Research on Strategies to Support Inclusion. In *SET 1999: Special Education.* Wellington, New Zealand: New Zealand Council for Educational Research.

Meyer, L. H., Mager, G. M., Yarger-Kane, G., Sarno, M., & Hext-Contreras, G. (1997). Syracuse University's Inclusive Elementary and Special Education Program. In L. P. Blanton, C. C. Griffin, J. A. Winn, & M. C. Pugach (Eds.), *Teacher Education in Transition: Collaborative Progams to Prepare General and Special Educators* (pp. 18–38). Denver, CO: Love.

Meyer, L. H., Minondo, S., Fisher, M., Larson, M. J., Dunmore, S., Black, J. W., & D'Aquanni, M. (1998). Frames of Friendship: Social Relationships among Adolescents with Diverse Abilities. In L. H. Meyer, H.-S. Park, M. Grenot-Scheyer, I. S. Schwartz, & B. Harry (Eds.), *Making Friends: The Influences of Culture and Development* (pp. 189–221). Baltimore: Brookes.

Meyer, L. H., & Park, H.-S. (1999). Contemporary Most Promising Practices for People with Disabilities. In J. S. Scotti & L. H. Meyer (Eds.), *Behavioral Intervention: Principles, Models, and Practices* (pp. 25–45). Baltimore: Brookes.

Meyer, L. H., Park, H. S., Grenot-Scheyer, M., Schwartz, I., & Harry, B. (1998). Participatory Research: New Approaches to the Research to Practice Dilemma. *Journal of the Association for Persons with Severe Handicaps, 23,* 165–177.

Meyer, L. H., Williams, D. R., Harootunian, B., & Steinberg, A. (1995). An Inclusion Model to Reduce At-Risk Status among Middle School Students: The Syracuse Experience. In I. M. Evans, T. Chicchelli, M. Cohen, & N. Shapiro (Eds.), *Staying in School: Partnerships for Educational Change* (pp. 83–110). Baltimore: Brookes.

National Association of State Boards of Education. (1992). *Winners All: A Call for Inclusive Schools.* Alexandria, VA: Author.

National Council of Teachers of Mathematics. (1993). *Curriculum and Evaluation Standards for School Mathematics.* Reston, VA: Author.

Noddlings, N. (1992). *The Challenge to Care in Schools: An Alternative Approach to Education.* New York: Teachers College Press.

Ornelles, C., & Goetz, L. (2001). Considerations for Changing Populations: Supporting Nontraditional Students in Acquiring Special Educators Licensure. *Journal of the Association for Persons with Severe Handicaps, 26,* 171–179.

Oswald, D. P., Coutinho, M. J., Best, A. M., & Singh, N. N. (1999). Ethnic Representation in Special Education: The Influence of School-Related Economic and Demographic Variables. *The Journal of Special Education, 32,* 194–206.

Park, H. S., & Lian, M-G. J. (Eds.). (2001). Culturally and Linguistically Diverse Learners: Issues and Practices [Special issue]. *The Journal of the Association for Persons with Severe Handicaps, 26*(3).

Park, J., Turnbull, A. P., & Turnbull, H. R. (2002). Impacts of Poverty on Quality of Life in Families of Children with Disabilities. *Exceptional Children, 68,* 151–170.

Patton, J. M. (1998). The Disproportionate Representation of African Americans in Special Education: Looking behind the Curtain for Understanding and Solutions. *The Journal of Special Education, 32,* 25–31.

Patton, J. M., & Townsend, B. (1999). Ethics, Power, and Privilege: Neglected Considerations in the Education of African American Learners with Special Needs. *Teacher Education and Special Education, 22,* 276–286.

Porter, G. L., & Stone, J. A. (1998). The Inclusive School Model: A Framework and Key Strategies for Success. In J. W. Putnam (Ed.), *Cooperative Learning and Strategies for Inclusion: Celebrating Diversity in the Classroom* (2nd ed., pp. 229–248). Baltimore: Brookes.

Pugach, M. C., & Johnson, L. J. (1995). *Collaborative Practitioners, Collaborative Schools.* Denver, CO: Love.

Putnam, J. (Ed.). (1998). *Cooperative Learning and Strategies for Inclusion: Celebrating Diversity in the Classroom* (2nd ed.). Baltimore: Brookes.

Ramsey, P. G. (1998). *Teaching and Learning in a Diverse World: Multicultural Education for Young Children* (2nd ed.). New York: Teachers College Press.

Richardson, J. G. (1994). Common, Delinquent, and Special: On the Formalization of Common Schooling in the American States. *American Educational Research Journal, 31,* 695–723.

Roach, V. (1994). The Superintendent's Role in Creating Inclusive Schools. *The School Administrator, 52*(4), 64–70.

Ryndak, D. L., Morrison, A. P., & Sommerstein, L. (1999). Literacy before and after Inclusion in General Education Settings: A Case Study. *Journal of the Association for Persons with Severe Handicaps, 24,* 5–22.

Salisbury, C. L., Palombaro, M. M., & Hollowood, T. M. (1993). On the Nature and Change of an Inclusive Elementary School. *Journal of the Association for Persons with Severe Handicaps, 18,* 75–84.

Sanchez, S. (1999). Learning from the Stories of Culturally and Linguistically Diverse Families and Communities. *Remedial and Special Education, 20,* 351–359.

Sapon-Shevin, M. (1992). Celebrating Diversity, Creating Community: Curriculum That Honors and Builds on Differences. In S. Stainback & W. Stainback (Eds.), *Curriculum Considerations in Inclusive Classrooms: Facilitating Learning for All Students* (pp. 19–36). Baltimore: Brookes.

Sapon-Shevin, M. (1994). *Playing Favorites: Gifted Education and the Disruption of Community.* Albany: State University of New York Press.

Sapon-Shevin, M. (1999). *Because We Can Change the World: A Practical Guide to Building Cooperative, Inclusive Classroom Communities.* Boston: Allyn & Bacon.

Sapon-Shevin, M. (2001). Making Inclusive Visible: Honoring the Process and the Struggle. *Democracy and Education, 14,* 24–27.

Sapon-Shevin, M. (2003). Inclusion: A Matter of Social Justice. *Educational Leadership, 61*(2), 25–29.

Sapon-Shevin, M. (2004). Thinking Inclusively about Inclusive Education. In K. Kesson & E. W. Ross (Eds.), *Defending Public Schools: Teaching for a Democratic Society* (Vol. 2, pp. 161–172). Westport, CT: Praeger.

Sapon-Shevin, M. (2005a). Ability Differences in the Classroom: Teaching and Learning in Inclusive Classrooms. In D. Byrnes & G. Kiger (Eds.), *Common Bonds: Anti-bias Teaching in a Diverse Society* (3rd ed., pp. 37–51). Olney, MD: Association for Childhood Education International.

Sapon-Shevin, M. (2005b). Teachable Moments for Social Justice. In B. Engel & A. C. Martin (Eds.), *Holding Values: What We Mean by Progressive Education* (pp. 93–97). Portsmouth, NH: Heinemann.

Sapon-Shevin, M., Ayres, B., & Duncan, J. (2002). Cooperative Learning and Inclusion. In J. Thousand, R. Villa, & A. Nevin (Eds.), *Creativity and Collaborative Learning: The Practical Guide to Empowering Students, Teachers and Families* (2nd ed., pp. 209–221). Baltimore: Brookes.

Schnorr, R. F. (1997). From Enrollment to Membership: "Belonging" in Middle and High School Classes. *Journal of the Association for Persons with Severe Handicaps, 22*, 1–15.

Skiba, R. J., Poloni-Staudinger, L., Simmons, A. B., Feggins-Azziz, L. R., & Chung, C. G. (2005). Unproven Links: Can Poverty Explain Ethnic Disproportionality in Special Education? *The Journal of Special Education, 39*, 130–144.

Skinner, D., Rodriguez, P., & Bailey, D. B., Jr. (1999). Qualitative Analysis of Latino Parents' Religious Interpretations of their Childrens' Disabilities. *Journal of Early Intervention, 22*, 271–285.

Smith, G. R. (1983). Desegregation and Assignment of Children to Classes for the Mentally Retarded and Learning Disabled. *Integrated Education, 21*, 208–211.

Smith, L. T. (1999). *Decolonizing Methodologies: Research and Indigenous Peoples.* London: Zed.

Smith, R. M. (1997). Varied Meanings and Practice: Teachers' Perspectives Regarding High School Inclusion. *Journal of the Association for Persons with Severe Handicaps, 22*, 235–244.

Tharp, R. G., & Gallimore, R. (1989). *Rousing Minds to Life: Teaching, Learning and Schooling in Social Context.* New York: Cambridge University Press.

Thompson, T. M. (1982). An Investigation and Comparison of Public School Personnel's Perception and Interpretation of P.L. 94–142. *Dissertation Abstracts International, 43*, 2840A.

Torres-Velasquez, D. (Ed.). (2000). Sociocultural Perspectives in Special Education [Special issue]. *Remedial and Special Education, 21*(2).

Townsend, B. L. (1998). Social Friendships and Networks among African American Children and Youth. In L. H. Meyer, H. S. Park, M. Grenot-Scheyer, I. S. Schwartz, & B. Harry (Eds.), *Making Friends: The Influences of Culture and Development* (pp. 225–241). Baltimore: Brookes.

Trent, S. C., Artiles, A. J., & Englert, C. S. (1998). From Deficit Thinking to Social Constructivism: A Review of Theory, Research, and Practice in Special Education. *Review of Research in Education, 23* (pp. 277–307). Washington, DC: American Educational Research Association.

Trent, S. C., Artiles, A. J., Fitchett-Bazemore, K., McDaniel, L., & Coleman-Sorrell, A. (2002). Addressing Theory, Ethics, Power, and Privilege in Inclusion Research and Practice. *Teacher Education and Special Education, 25*, 11–22.

Tucker, J. A. (1980). Ethnic Proportions in Classes for the Learning Disabled: Issues in Nonbiased Assessment. *Journal of Special Education, 14*, 93–105.

Turnbull, A. P., Turnbull, H. R., Erwin, E., & Soodak, L. (2005). *Families, Professionals, and Exceptionality: A Special Partnership* (5th ed.). Upper Saddle River, NJ: Prentice-Hall.

Tyler, N., & Smith, D. D. (2000). Preparation of Culturally and Linguistically Diverse Special Educators [Special issue]. *Teacher Education and Special Education, 23*(4).

U. S. Department of Education, Office of Civil Rights. (1994). *1992 Elementary and Secondary Civil Rights Compliance Report.* Washington, DC: U.S. Government Printing Office.

Vygotsky, L. S. (1978). *Mind in Society: The Development of Higher Psychological Processes* (M. Cole, V. John-Steiner, S. Scribner, & E. Souberman, Eds. and Trans.). Cambridge, MA: Harvard University Press.

Webb-Johnson, G. C. (1999). Cultural Contexts: Confronting the Overrepresentation of African American Learners in Special Education. In J. S. Scotti & L. H. Meyer (Eds.), *Behavioral Intervention: Principles, Models, and Practices* (pp. 449–464). Baltimore: Brookes.

Wells, A. S., & Crain, R. L. (1994). Perpetuation Theory and the Long-Term Effects of School Desegregation. *Review of Educational Research, 64,* 531–555.

Will, M. (1986). Educating Children with Learning Problems: A Shared Responsibility. *Exceptional Children, 52,* 411–415.

Winn, J., & Blanton, J. (1997). The Call for Collaboration in Teacher Education. In L. P. Blanton, C. C. Griffin, J. A. Winn, & M. C. Pugach (Eds.), *Teacher Education in Transition: Collaborative "Programs" to Prepare General and Special Educators* (pp. 1–17) Denver: Love Publishing.

CHAPTER 15

Recruiting and Retaining Gifted Students from Diverse Ethnic, Cultural, and Language Groups

Donna Y. Ford

One of the most persistent and pervasive problems in education is the underrepresentation of African American, Hispanic American, and Native American students in gifted education programs and services. Since at least the 1930s, reports and studies have revealed these culturally diverse students have always been inadequately represented in gifted education (Artiles, Trent, & Palmer, 2004; Donovan & Cross, 2002; Ford, 1998, 2004). Statistics show that these three groups are underrepresented by 50 to 70 percent (U.S. Department of Education, 1993; Elementary and Secondary Schools Civil Rights Survey, 1998; 2000). The percentages in Table 15.1

Table 15.1 Demographics of Gifted Education Programs in 1998 and 2000.

Race/Ethnicity	1998		2000	
	% School District	% Gifted & Talented	% School District	% Gifted & Talented
American Indian/Alaskan Native	1.1%	0.87	1.16	.91
Black	17.0%	8.40	16.99	8.23
Hispanic/Latino	14.3%	8.63	16.13	9.54
Asian/Pacific Islander	4.0%	6.57	4.14	7.00
White	63.7%	75.53	61.58	74.24
Total	100.00	100.00	100.00	100.00

Sources: Elementary and Secondary School Civil Rights Survey (1998 and 2000): www.demo.beyond2020.com/ocrpublic/eng. National Center for Education Statistics. (2001). *Common Core of Data (CCD), State Nonfiscal Survey of Public Elementary/Secondary Education, 1999–2000.* Washington, DC: U.S. Department of Education. Available online at: http://nces.ed.gov/ccd/pdf/stNfis99genr.pdf and http://nces.ed.gov/cc/pdf/stNfis00genr.pdf.

support the notion that "a mind is a terrible thing to waste," a statement popularized by the United Negro College Fund. These data also support the reality that a mind is a terrible thing to erase. In other words, many African American, Hispanic American, and Native American students are gifted but their gifts often go unidentified. Consequently, they are neither challenged nor given the opportunity to develop their gifts and talents, which atrophy. The No Child Left Behind Act of 2002 (Does the No Child Left Behind . . . 2002) recognized that gifted students are unlikely to develop without appropriate services:

> The term 'gifted and talented' . . . means students, children, or youth who give evidence of high achievement capacity in areas such as intellectual, creative, artistic, or leadership capacity, or in specific academic fields, and who need services or activities not ordinarily provided by the school in order to fully develop those capabilities. (Title IX, Part A, Section 9101(22) (p. 544)

ASSUMPTIONS OF THE CHAPTER

This chapter explores barriers to and recommendations for recruiting and retaining racial and ethnic minority students into gifted education programs. In particular, I present data on the underrepresentation of African American students in gifted education for at least two reasons: (1) between 1998 and 2000 African American students were the only group of color to become *more underrepresented* in gifted education, as noted in Figure 15.1 and (2) this group is more often the focus of litigation relative to inequities in gifted education (Office for Civil Rights, 2000). I recognize that Asian Americans are also racial and ethnic minority students. However, I have yet to find a report indicating that Asian American students are underrepresented in gifted education. Further, Asian Americans, unlike African American, Hispanic American, and Native American students, frequently experience positive stereotypes and many are high achieving. Consequently, they are not discussed in this chapter. By omitting Asian American students from this chapter, I am not ignoring the social injustices they have experienced and continue to experience in society and in the schools (Kitano & DiJosia, 2002; Pang et al., 2004).

This chapter is grounded in several assumptions and propositions. First, I propose that the majority of past and current efforts to redress the underrepresentation problem have been inadequate and misdirected, resulting in what may be the most segregated programs in our public schools. Second, gifted education is a need—not a privilege. By not being identified as gifted and receiving appropriate services and programming, gifted students from racial, ethnic, and language backgrounds are being denied an opportunity to reach their potential and promise. A third assumption and proposition is that no group has a monopoly on "giftedness." Giftedness exists in every cultural group and across all economic strata (USDE, 1993). Consequently, there should be little or no underrepresentation of racial and ethnic minority students in gifted education. A fourth assumption and proposition is that giftedness is a social construct; subjectivity guides definitions, assessments, and perceptions of giftedness (Pfeiffer, 2003; Sternberg, 1985). This subjectivity contributes to segregated gifted education programs in numerous and insidious ways. Sapon-Shevon (1996) states that "the ways in which gifted education is defined, constituted, and enacted lead directly to increased segregation, limited educational opportunities for the majority of students, and damage to children's social and political developments" (p. 196). Accordingly, educators must examine their views about the purposes of gifted education in particular as well as their perceptions of students from racially and ethnically diverse backgrounds.

The fifth guiding assumption is that all decisions made on behalf of students should be made with their best interests in mind. Education should be additive for students, not subtractive. We should be about the business of building on what students have when they enter our schools. Finally, I believe that efforts to recruit and retain racial and ethnic minority students in gifted education must be comprehensive, proactive, aggressive, and systematic. Educators, families, and children themselves need to work together to ensure that gifted education is desegregated (Harris, Brown, Ford, & Richardson, 2004). Gallagher's (2004) assertion seems apropos here:

> In another profession, the physician treating a patient will often
> start with the weakest treatment available and then progress to
> stronger treatments once the first attempt has seen little effect. We
> seem to have been following that approach in educating gifted
> students by prescribing a minimal treatment (one might even say
> a non-therapeutic dose) designed hopefully to do some good with
> out upsetting other people . . . as a profession, we need to come to
> some consensus that we need stronger treatments. (Gallagher,
> 2004, p. xxviii)

This chapter is divided into three major sections. The first section focuses on recruitment issues and barriers, the second section focuses on recruitment recommendations, and the third focuses on retention recommendations. The guiding questions of the chapter are: How can we recruit and retain more racial and ethnic minority students in gifted education? How can we have gifted education programs that are both excellent and equitable?

RECRUITMENT ISSUES AND BARRIERS

Most of the scholarship that explains underrepresentation focuses on recruitment. Specifically, it is assumed that racial and ethnic minority students are underrepresented because of problems associated with screening and identification instruments, specifically tests. Little attention has been given to retention, which is discussed later in this chapter.

The first step in addressing (or redressing) the underrepresentation of racial and ethnic minority students in gifted education is to focus on recruitment. Recruitment refers to screening, identification, and placement (or getting students into gifted education). Perceptions about racial and ethnic minority students combined with a lack of cultural understanding significantly undermine the ability of educators to recruit diverse students into gifted education and to retain them. Elsewhere, I have argued that a "cultural deficit" perspective pervades decisions made about and on behalf of African American, Hispanic

American, and Native American students (Ford, Harris, Tyson, & Frazier Trotman, 2002). This phenomenon is described below.

Deficit Thinking

> The more we retreat from the culture and the people, the less we learn about them. The less we know about them, the more uncomfortable we feel among them. The more uncomfortable we feel among them, the more inclined we are to withdraw. The more we withdraw from the people, the more faults we find with them. The less we know about their culture, the more we seem to dislike it. And the worst of it is that, in the end, we begin to believe the very lies we've invented to console ourselves. (Storti, 1989, pp. 32–34)

As stated earlier, a major premise of this chapter is that a deficit orientation held by educators hinders access to gifted programs for diverse students, as reflected in the above quote. This thinking hinders the ability and willingness of educators to recognize the strengths of students from diverse ethnic, racial, and language groups. Deficit thinking exists when educators interpret differences as deficits, dysfunctions, and disadvantages. Consequently, many diverse students quickly acquire the "at-risk" label and there is a focus on their shortcomings or weaknesses rather than their strengths. With deficit thinking, differences are interpreted negatively as if they are abnormal, substandard, or otherwise inferior. For example, when a student speaks nonstandard English and is making good grades in school, he may not be referred to screening and identification if the teacher neither understands nor appreciates nonstandard English. Likewise, if a student has excellent math skills but weak writing skills, she may not be perceived as gifted or intelligent. Every student has strengths and weaknesses. Educators need to move beyond a deficit orientation in order to recognize the strengths and potential of racial, ethnic, and language minorities.

Ideas about racial groups influence the development of definitions, policies, and practices designed to understand and deal with differences. For instance, Gould (1981/1995) and Menchaca (1997) noted that deficit thinking contributed to past (and, no doubt, current) beliefs about race, ethnicity and intelligence. Gould takes readers back two centuries to demonstrate how *a priori* assumptions and fears associated with different ethnic groups, particularly African Americans, led to conscious fraud: dishonest and prejudicial research methods, deliberate miscalculations, convenient omissions, and data misinterpretation among scientists studying intelligence. These early assumptions and practices gave way to the prevailing belief that human races could be ranked in a linear scale of mental worth, as evidenced by the research of Cyril Burt, Paul Broca, and Samuel Morten on craniometry (Gould, 1981/1995).

Later, as school districts faced increasing ethnic/racial diversity (often attributable to immigration), educators resorted to increased reliance on biased standardized tests (Armour-Thomas, 1992; Gould, 1981/1995; Helms, 1992; Menchaca, 1997). These tests almost guaranteed low test scores for immigrants and racial and ethnic minority groups who were unfamiliar with U.S. customs, traditions, values, norms, and language (Ford, 2004). These tests measured familiarity with mainstream American culture and English proficiency, not intelligence. According to Gould (1981/1995), intelligence tests provide limited information about racial and ethnic minority populations. The results from these tests often limited the educational opportunities of diverse students, who tended not to score high on them. Menchaca (1997) stated:

> Racial differences in intelligence, it was contended, are most
> validly explained by racial differences in innate, genetically
> determined abilities. What emerged from these findings regarding
> schooling were curricular modifications ensuring that the
> "intellectually inferior" and the social order would best be served
> by providing these students concrete, low-level, segregated
> instruction commensurate with their alleged diminished
> intellectual abilities. (p. 38)

The publication of *The Bell Curve* (Herrnstein & Murray, 1994) revived deficit thinking about diverse groups. Seeking to influence public and social policy, Herrnstein and Murray, like researchers of earlier centuries (such as Cyril Burt), interpreted—or misinterpreted and misrepresented—their data to confirm institutionalized prejudices. As Gould (1981/1995) noted, the hereditarian theory of IQ is a homegrown American product that persists in current practices of testing, sorting, and discarding. Issues associated with screening support this assertion.

Screening Issues and Barriers

To be considered for placement in gifted education, students often undergo screening in which they are administered assessments with predetermined criteria (e.g., cutoff scores). If students meet the initial screening requirements, they may be given additional assessments, which are used to make final placement decisions. In most schools, entering the screening pool is based on teacher referrals (Colangelo & Davis, 2003). This practice hinders the effective screening of racial and ethnic minority students because they are seldom referred by teachers for screening (Ford, 1996). Specifically, a Hispanic American student may meet the school district's criteria for giftedness but be overlooked because she has not been referred for screening. The teacher may not refer this student because of her biases and stereotypes about Hispanic Americans (deficit thinking), because the student's English skills are not strong, or because of many of the teacher's perceptual and attitudinal barriers. Intuitively, it makes sense that teacher referrals should be used as part of the screening or decision-making process. As the above example illustrates, however, this practice may negatively affect racial, ethnic, and language minority students.

Similarly, teachers and other adults (e.g., counselors, parents, community members) may be required to complete checklists on the referred students. If the checklists ignore cultural diversity—how giftedness manifests itself differently in various cultures—then gifted diverse students may receive low ratings that do not accurately capture their strengths, abilities, and potential. A framework proposed by Frasier et al. (1995) describes how the core attributes of giftedness vary by culture. They contended that educators should define and assess giftedness with each group's cultural differences in mind. As an illustration, one core characteristic of giftedness is a keen sense of humor. A common verbal game—or match—among low-income African Americans is "playing the dozens" or "signifying" (Lee, 1993; Majors, R., & Billson, J. M., 1992). African American students are exemplifying three characteristics of giftedness when playing the dozens—humor, creativiy, and verbal skills. Teachers may be offended by the students' humor, blinding them from seeing these core characteristics of giftedness.

One of the first signs of giftedness is strong verbal skills. However, if the student does not speak standard English (e.g., speaks Black English Vernacular or Ebonics) or has limited English proficiency, the teacher may not recognize the student's strong verbal skills. A third example relates to independence, which is another characteristic of giftedness. Racial and ethnic minority students who have communal values, such as interdependence and cooperation, may be social and prefer to work in groups rather than individually (Boykin, 1994; Ramírez & Castañeda, 1974; Shade, Kelly, & Oberg, 2001). Consequently, the teacher may not consider such students to be independent workers or thinkers.

Like tests, checklists can be problematic. In addition to referral/nominations forms and checklists being "culture-blind," they frequently focus on demonstrated ability and performance. As a result, they overlook students who are gifted but lack opportunities to demonstrate their intelligence and achievement. These "potentially gifted" students and/or gifted underachievers are those who live in poverty and/or are culturally different from mainstream students. A study by Smith, Constantino, and Krashen (1997) sheds light on this issue. These researchers compared the number of books in the homes and classrooms of three California communities. There was an average of 199 books in the homes of Beverly Hills children, four in the homes of Watts children, and 2.7 in the homes of Compton children. In terms of classrooms, there was an average of 392 books in Beverly Hills classrooms, 54 in Watts classrooms, and 47 in Compton classrooms. Essentially, because of exposure to books and educational opportunities, children from Beverly Hills homes and schools are more likely to demonstrate their giftedness (e.g., have a large vocabulary, be able to read at an early age) than are children from the other homes and schools. Many children in Compton and Watts are gifted but lack essential academic experiences and exposure to develop their abilities and potential.

In 1993, the U.S. Department of Education recognized that our schools are filled with potentially gifted students. To help educators improve the recruitment of diverse students into gifted education, the department issued the following definition of giftedness, one that relies heavily on the notion of talent development:

> Children and youth with outstanding talent perform or show the
> potential for performing at remarkably high levels of
> accomplishment when compared with others of their age,
> experience, or environment. These children and youth exhibit high
> performance capacity in intellectual, creative, and/or artistic areas,
> possess an unusual leadership capacity, or excel in specific academic
> fields. They require services or activities not ordinarily provided by

the schools. Outstanding talents are present in children and youth
from all cultural groups, across all economic strata, and in all areas
of human endeavor. (USDE, 1993, p. 3)

The percentage of school districts adopting this definition or some version of it is
unknown. The ramifications of not adopting the federal definition, or some version of it, are
clear—continued underrepresentation of students from racial, ethnic and language minorities in gifted education.

Identification/Assessment Issues and Barriers

Monolithic definitions of *giftedness* pose serious barriers to recruiting diverse students into
gifted education. Monolithic definitions ignore human differences in general and cultural
diversity in particular. They ignore the fact that what is valued as giftedness in one culture
may not be valued in another. For example, most European Americans highly value cognitive and academic ability over spatial, musical, interpersonal, and other abilities (Gardner,
1993) and tend to value academic knowledge and skills over tacit or practical knowledge and
skills (Sternberg, 1985). Conversely, navigational skills or hunting skills may be prized in
another culture. These differences raise the question: If a student is not gifted in the ways
that are valued by my culture, is she gifted? Based on current practice, most culturally
different students are not likely to be perceived as gifted.

Perceptions and definitions also influence the instruments or tests selected to assess giftedness. Dozens of intelligence and achievement tests exist. What determines which instrument
a school district selects? If we value verbal skills, we will select an instrument that assesses verbal skills. If we value logic and/or problem-solving skills, we will select an instrument that
assesses these skills. If we value creativity, the instrument we select will assess creativity. We
are not likely to choose an instrument that measures a construct or skill that we do not value.

Accordingly, many schools use intelligence and achievement tests—more than other
types of tests—to assess giftedness. Test scores play a dominant role in identification and
placement decisions. For example, a study by Van Tassel-Baska, Patton, and Prillaman (1989)
revealed that 88.5 percent of states rely primarily on standardized, norm-referenced tests to
identify gifted students, including those from economically and culturally diverse groups.
More than 90 percent of school districts use scores from these types of tests for labeling and
placement (Colangelo & Davis, 2003; Davis & Rimm, 2003). These tests measure verbal
skills, abstract thinking, math skills, and other skills considered indicative of giftedness (or
intelligence or achievement) by educators. Likewise, they ignore skills and abilities that may
be also valued by other groups (e.g., creativity, interpersonal skills, group problem-solving
skills, navigational skills, musical skills). Consequently, racial and ethnic minority students
are more likely than others to display characteristics that place them at a disadvantage in
testing situations (Helms, 1992; Office for Civil Rights, 2000). Monolithic definitions result
in the adoption of unidimensional, ethnocentric tests that contribute significantly to racially
homogeneous gifted education programs. These tests are more effective at identifying giftedness among middle-class White students than among racial and ethnic minority students,
particularly if these students are from low socioeconomic status (SES) backgrounds.

An additional concern related to tests is the extensive use of cutoff scores, referred to earlier. The most frequently used cutoff score for placement in gifted education is an IQ score of 130 or above, two standard deviations above the average IQ of 100 (Colangelo & Davis, 2003). Decades of data indicate that groups such as African Americans, Puerto Rican Americans, and Native Americans have mean tested IQ scores lower than White students, even at the highest economic levels. For the most part, the average tested IQ of African Americans is 83 to 87, compared to 97 to 100 for White students on traditional intelligence tests (see Helms, 1992; Kaufman, 1994). The same holds for children who live in poverty, regardless of racial background. Their average IQ is about 85. I have consulted with several psychologists who believe that because the "average" IQ score of African Americans is about 85, giftedness would mean an IQ of 115 or higher among this population. Sadly, those holding racist ideologies will attribute these differences to genetics and argue that giftedness (or intelligence) is primarily inherited. This position implies that the environment is less important than heredity in the development of talents and abilities. Such a view is counterproductive in education, which is supposed to build upon and improve the skills and abilities of students.

Conversely, those who recognize the influence of the environment and culture on performance attribute these different scores primarily to social, environmental and cultural factors. For instance, it has been demonstrated in numerous studies on "environmental racism" that poverty, exposure to lead, malnutrition, and poor educational experiences negatively affect test performance (Baugh, 1991; Bryant & Mohai, 1992; Bullard, 1993; Dwight, 1994; Ford, 2004; Grossman, 1991). Thus, cutoff scores cannot be selected arbitrarily and in a culture-blind fashion. If adopted at all, cutoff scores should be used with caution and should take into consideration the different mean scores of the various racial, ethnic, cultural, and language groups.

A final issue related to testing is interpreting results (see Kaufman, 1994). When other information is considered, it is possible to select and use a test that effectively assesses the strengths of racial, ethnic, and langauge minority students. However, perceptions can prevent a teacher, counselor, or psychologist from interpreting the results in a culturally fair way. What if a teacher, counselor, or psychologist interpreting the test results holds negative stereotypes about African Americans? What if the counselor holds stereotypes about groups who have limited English proficiency? What if a student from these two groups receives a very high IQ or achievement test score? How would this affect the psychologist's, teacher's, and counselor's interpretation of the results? Test interpretation is heavily subjective and interpretations are influenced by the quantity and quality of training to work with diverse cultural, ethnic, and language groups. Results from a "good" test can be poorly interpreted if the interpreter has little understanding of how culture influences test performance (Ford, 2004).

In a collaborative effort, the American Educational Research Association (AERA), the American Psychological Association (APA), and the National Council on Measurement in Education (NCME) (1999) addressed the myriad problems of interpreting test scores. They noted the harmful effects of misinterpreting test results, especially with racial and ethnic minority groups: "The ultimate responsibility for appropriate test use and interpretation lies predominantly with the test user. In assuming this responsibility, the user must become knowledgeable about a test's appropriate uses and the populations for which it is appropriate" (p. 112). They advise, as do others (e.g., National Council for Gifted Children, 1997), that test users collect extensive data on students to complement test restults and use a comprehensive approach in the assessment process (Armour-Thomas, 1992; Helms, 1992). Test users are encouraged to consider the validity of a given instrument or procedure as well as the cultural characteristics of the student when interpreting results (Office of Ethnic Minority Affairs, 1993; extensive information on equity and testing can be found at the National Center for Fair and Open Testing, www.fairtest.org).

In sum, the data collected on all students should be multidimensional—a variety of information collected from multiple sources. For example, data are needed from school personnel, family members, and community members. Data on intelligence, achievement, creativity, motivation, interests, and learning styles are essential when making decisions about students. In this era of high-stakes testing, educators should err on the side of having "too much" information rather than too little to make informed, educationally sound decisions.

The data collected should also be multimodal, that is, collected in a variety of ways. Information should be collected verbally (interviews, conversations) and nonverbally (e.g., observations, writing, performances), and both subjective and objective information should be gathered. Further, if the student speaks a first language other than English, educators should use an interpreter and use instruments translated into that student's primary or preferred language. Essentially, assessment should be made with the students' best interests in mind, and the principle of "do no harm" should prevail. As noted by Sandoval, Frisby, Geisinger, Scheuneman, and Grenier (1998): "In any testing situation, but particularly high stakes assessments, examinees must have an opportunity to demonstrate the competencies, knowledge, or attributes being measured" (p. 183). Few equitable opportunities exist when assessments are unidimensional, unimodal, and ethnocentric (colorblind or culture-blind) (Ford, Moore, & Milner, 2005). How can we make responsible and defensible decisions about culturally diverse students when assessments and interpretation of test results ignore or trivialize the impact of culture?

After screening, the next step is placement considerations. Like screening, placement considerations are complex and riddled with potential problems.

Placement Issues and Barriers

Giftedness is often equated with achievement or productivity. To most educators and laypersons alike, the notion of a "gifted underachiever" may seem paradoxical. However, any educator who has taught students identified as gifted knows that gifted students can and do underachieve—some are unmotivated and uninterested in school, some are procrastinators, others do not complete assignments or they do just enough to get by. In my work with gifted African American students, I have observed about 80 percent of them underachieving (Ford, 1996). Other researchers, such as Rimm (1995) and Silverman (1993), believe that at least 20 percent of gifted students underachieve, especially gifted females (Reis & Callahan, 1989).

One problem associated with placement, therefore, is the belief that gifted students should receive gifted education services *if* they are high achievers, hard workers, and motivated. That is, achievement must be manifested (e.g., high grade point average [GPA] or high achievement test scores). Gifted underachievers are not likely to be referred for or placed in gifted education. If placement occurs, it is often provisional for this group. For example, several school districts will remove students from a gifted program if their GPA falls below a designated level, they fail a course, or have poor attendance that is unexcused. This situation of students meeting gifted education criteria (e.g., high test scores) but underachieving often arises when testing has been unidimensional and unimodal—educators have focused solely on determining the students' IQ scores and with a narrow range of instruments. Conversely, if intelligence *and* achievement data were collected during screening, educators would know whether the student is: (1) gifted and achieving or (2) gifted and underachieving. And they could make placement decisions based on these data. For example, they could place gifted underachievers in gifted education classes and provide them with a tutor, study skills, language skills, or counseling (Ford, 1996). The objective would be to help gifted underachievers become achievers and experience success in gifted education classrooms.

Many racial, ethnic, and language minority groups are likely to be gifted underachievers or potentially gifted students (Ford, 1996). Some educators do not wish to place these students in gifted education programs because they believe that the level and pace of the schoolwork may frustrate students. In theory, the issue of underachievers being overwhelmed in gifted education programs may be a valid concern, depending on why the students are underachieving. In practice, it has harmed gifted students who are members of racial, ethnic, and language minority groups.

Instead of supporting diverse students and helping them to overcome their weaknesses and achievement barriers, educators have often chosen the option of least resistance under the guise of altruism. ("I don't want him to be frustrated." "She'll be unhappy." "He'll just fall further behind.") As we seek to prevent students from being frustrated, we should ask: What are we doing to help to alleviate their frustration? Tutoring, counseling, and other support systems (academic, vocational, social-emotional) are essential. When placement is combined with support, gifted underachieving students are more likely to be successful in gifted education programs.

As described below, recruiting students from diverse groups into gifted education programs is one thing; retaining them is another. What policies, practices, procedures, philosophies, and supports should be in place for diverse students to experience success and remain in gifted education?

RECRUITMENT RECOMMENDATIONS

Recruiting students from diverse groups into gifted education is the first half of resolving their underrepresentation in gifted education. As described below, recruitment should include a talent-development philosophy, changes in standardized tests and assessment practices, culturally sensitive tests, multicultural assessment preparation for professionals, and the effective development of policies and procedures.

Talent Development Philosophy

Educators who support a talent-development philosophy and culturally sensitive definitions of giftedness are more likely than others to have supports in place to assist students from diverse groups. For example, school districts would begin screening and placing students in gifted education at the preschool and primary levels. Currently, most gifted education programs begin in grades 2–4, which may be too late for potentially gifted students and those beginning to show signs of underachievement, commonly referred to as the second-grade syndrome. Abilities—gifts and talents—should be recognized and nurtured early (USDE, 1993), especially among students already at risk of being unrecognized as gifted.

Changes in Standardized Tests and Assessment Practices

Tests standardized on middle-class White populations are here to stay, despite the reality that they are another form of discrimination favoring the privileged (Sowell, 1993). However, educators concerned about improving the test performance of diverse students on these instruments have a number of options to consider. First and foremost, they should never select, use, and interpret tests that lack validity for students from racial, ethnic, and language minorities (Joint Standards, 1999). Second, they need to mesh the process of assessment with the cultural characteristics of the group being studied while recognizing that assessment is made culturally sensitive through a continuing and open-ended series of substantive and methodological insertions and adaptations (Suzuki, Meller, & Ponterotto, 1996). In essence, equitable and culturally sensitive assessment necessitates a combination of changed attitudes, accumulation of more knowledge, thoughtful practice, and development of keen insight into the dynamics of human behavior (Heubert & Hauser, 1999; Kornhaber, 2004; Sandoval et al., 1998). Tests should never be given so much power that other data are disregarded—tests simply assist educators in making *conditional probability statements* on the basis of the particular test (Kaufman, 1994; Sandoval et al., 1998).

Culturally Sensitive Tests

Tests vary in the amount of language used in the directions and in the items. When working with linguistically diverse groups, we must use caution when tests have a high linguistic and/or high cultural demand (Flanagan & Ortiz, 2001). Much data indicate that the results from such tests may underestimate what students from racial, ethnic, and language minorities can do or misjudge behaviors to be abnormal and in need of intervention when, in reality, they are normal within a different cultural context (Dana, 1993; Mercer, 1973; Naglieri & Ford, 2005). To address these issues, educators will need to include more culturally sensitive tests, such as nonverbal tests, in screening and identification procedures (Ford, 2004; Naglieri & Ford, 2003; 2005; Sandoval et al., 1998). To date, the most promising instruments for assessing the strengths of African American students are such nonverbal tests of intelligence as the Naglieri Non-Verbal Abilities Test and Raven's Matrix Analogies Tests, which are considered less culturally loaded than traditional tests (Flanagan & Ortiz, 2001; Kaufman, 1994; Saccuzzo, Johnson, & Guertin, 1994).

Contrary to popular misconceptions, nonverbal tests do not mean that students are nonverbal. Rather nonverbal tests measure abilities nonverbally; they rely less on language proficiency. Thus, the intelligence of students with limited English proficiency, bilingual students, and students who speak nonstandard English can be assessed with less reliance on language skills.

Relative to cultural loading, Jensen (1980) distinguished between culturally loaded and culturally reduced tests. Culturally reduced tests are often performance based and include abstract figural and nonverbal content; culturally loaded tests have printed instructions, require reading, have verbal content, and require written responses. Essentially, nonverbal tests decrease the confounding effects of language skills on test performance and consequently increase the chances of students from diverse groups being identified as gifted.

Other testing accommodations in the best interest of diverse students include using tests that have been translated into different languages, using interpreters and translators when students are not proficient in English, and having educators who are bilingual and bicultural administer the tests.

Multicultural Assessment Preparation

Finally, on the issue of testing, multicultural assessment preparation is essential for any educator who administers, interprets, and uses results based on tests with diverse students (AERA, APA, & NCME, 1999). As stated earlier, the test results are only as good as the test-taking situation, including the qualifications and competencies of the educator administering the test. Comas-Diaz (1996) has developed a list of cultural assessment variables with which educators should be familiar when making comprehensive assessments and interpreting results. These cultural assessment variables include information about the individual's heritage, religion, history of immigration, child-rearing practices, language skills, gender roles, and views about assimilation and about authority figures and family structure. The more information, the better.

Policies and Procedures

Students should be placed in gifted education based on multiple data, which are then used to create profiles of students' strengths and weaknesses. Consequently, recruitment becomes diagnostic and prescriptive, with the idea and ideal that strengths are used to place students in gifted education, and weaknesses are remediated rather than used as an excuse to avoid placement.

If teacher referral is the first step in the screening and placement process, and diverse students are underreferred and underidentified, then teachers are serving as gatekeepers and schools should reevaluate this practice. To qualify as a valid referral source, teachers require preparation in at least three areas: (1) gifted education; (2) urban and multicultural education; and (3) multicultural assessment (Ford & Frazier Trotman, 2001). Preparation in these areas prepares educators to be knowledgeable about gifted students from diverse groups, as well as the limitations of testing them.

RETENTION RECOMMENDATIONS

Half of our efforts to desegregate gifted education should focus on recruitment and half on retention. This section centers almost extensively on how multicultural education can be used to retain diverse students in gifted education. Just as important, teachers require substantive preparation in multicultural education to ensure that classrooms are culturally responsive and responsible (Ford & Harris, 1999; Ford & Frazier Trotman, 2001).

Multicultural Instruction

Boykin (1994), Saracho and Gerstl (1992), and Shade, Kelly, and Oberg (1997) are just a few of the scholars who have presented convincing research supporting the notion that culture influences learning styles and thinking styles. Due to space limitations, only Boykin's (1994) work will be discussed in this chapter. Before doing so, I want to add a word of caution. As noted by Irvine and York (2001), we must never adhere so strongly to generalizations or frameworks that they become stereotypes. Irvine and York point out that "negative teacher expectations can be fueled if teachers incorporate generalized and decontextualized observations about children of color without knowledge of the limitations of learning-styles labels" (p. 492). This model is presented with the understanding that although each of us belongs to several groups, we are nonetheless individuals first and foremost.

In his Afrocentric model, Boykin (1994) identified nine cultural styles commonly found among African Americans: spirituality, harmony, oral tradition, affective orientation, communalism, verve, movement, social time perspective, and expressive individualism. Movement refers to African Americans being tactile and kinesthetic learners who show a preference for being involved in learning experiences. They are active learners who are engaged when they are physically and psychologically involved. Otherwise, they may be easily distracted and go off-task. Harmony refers to an ability to read the environment well and to read nonverbal behaviors proficiently. Thus, students who feel unwelcome in their classes may become unmotivated and uninterested in learning. Communalism refers to a cooperative, interdependent style of living and learning in which competition—especially with friends—is devalued. Students with this learning preference may be unmotivated in highly individualistic and competitive classrooms, preferring instead to learn in groups.

Harmony and communalism may explain why an increasing number of African American students—especially middle school and high school students—are choosing not to be in gifted programs. They recognize that such programs are primarily composed of White students and express concerns about alienation and isolation (Ford, 1996). Further, communalism may result in some African American students shunning participation in gifted programs and equating high achievement with "acting White" (Fordham, 1988; Fordham & Ogbu, 1986). Educators who take the time to get to know racial, ethnic, and language minority students and their families can avoid what I refer to as "drive-by teaching"—driving into minority communities, teaching students who are strangers, working with families without building relationships and respect, and driving out of the community immediately after school. Drive-by teaching is counterproductive to students and the educational process in general. It does not give educators time to get to know and understand their students and fails to give students opportunities to get to know their teachers in meaningful ways.

Teachers should learn to modify their teaching styles to accommodate different learning styles. For example, to accommodate students' preference for communalism, teachers can use cooperative learning strategies and place students in groups (Cohen & Lotan, 2004). To accommodate the oral tradition as well as verve and movement, teachers can give students opportunities to write and perform skits, to make oral presentations, and to participate in debates. More examples of ways in which teachers can use culturally responsive teaching activities are described by Ford (1998), Shade et al. (1997), Gay (2000), and Lee (1993).

Multicultural Gifted Curriculum

In the area of retention, curricular considerations are also critical. How to teach and what to teach gifted students have been discussed extensively by other scholars (Maker & Nielson, 1996; Tomlinson, 1995; VanTassel-Baska & Stambaugh, 206). These strategies, such as curriculum compacting, independent study, acceleration, and grade skipping will not be discussed here because of space limitations. While these strategies are certainly appropriate for gifted students from diverse groups, an equally important but overlooked retention recommendation is the need to create culturally responsive and responsible learning environments (Gay, 2000) and to ensure that the curriculum for gifted students is multicultural.

Ford and Harris (1999) have created a framework that uses Bloom's (1985) taxonomy and Banks's (2002; Chapter 10, this volume) multicultural education model to assist educators in developing learning experiences that are multicultural and challenging. The result is a 24-cell matrix. The model is presented in Table 15.2. Four of the 24 levels in the model are described below (for a more complete discussion of the model, see Ford & Harris, 1998).

At the knowledge–contributions level, students are provided information and facts about cultural heroes, holidays, events, and artifacts. For example, students might be taught about Martin Luther King, Jr., and then asked to recall three facts about him on a test. They might be introduced to Cinco de Mayo and be required to recite the year when it became a holiday.

At the comprehension–transformation level, students are required to explain what they have been taught—but from the perspective of another group or individual. For instance, students might be asked to explain the events that led to slavery in the United States and then to discuss how enslaved persons might have felt about being held captive. They might discuss the Trail of Tears from the perspective of a Native American child living when this tragic event occurred.

At the analysis–social action level, students are asked to analyze an event from more than one point of view. Students might be asked to compare and contrast events during slavery with events associated with infractions of child labor laws today. Following these comparisons, students could be asked to develop a social action plan for eliminating illegal child labor.

At the evaluation–social action level, students might be asked to conduct a survey about prejudice in their local stores or businesses. This information could be given to store owners, along with a plan of action for change, such as developing a diversity-training program.

Table 15.2 Ford-Harris Multicultural Gifted Education Framework—Description of Levels

	Knowledge	Comprehension	Application	Analysis	Synthesis	Evaluation
Contributions	Students are taught and know facts about cultural artifacts, events, groups, and other cultural elements.	Students show an understanding of information about cultural artifacts, groups, etc.	Students are asked to and can apply information learned about cultural artifacts, events, etc.	Students are taught to and can analyze (e.g., compare and contrast) information about cultural artifacts, groups, etc.	Students are required to and can create a new product from the information on cultural artifacts, groups, etc.	Students are taught to and can evaluate facts and information based on cultural artifacts, groups, etc.
Additive	Students are taught and know concepts and themes about cultural groups.	Students are taught and can understand cultural concepts and themes.	Students are required to and can apply information learned about cultural concepts and themes.	Students are taught to and can analyze important cultural concepts and themes.	Students are asked to and can synthesize important information on cultural concepts and themes.	Students are taught to and can critique cultural concepts and themes.
Transformation	Students are given information on important cultural elements, groups, etc., and can understand this information from different perspectives.	Students are taught to understand and can demonstrate an understanding of important cultural concepts and themes from different perspectives.	Students are asked to and can apply their understanding of important concepts and themes from different perspectives.	Students are taught to and can examine important cultural concepts and themes from more than one perspective.	Students are required to and can create a product based on their new perspective or the perspective of another group.	Students are taught to and can evaluate or judge important cultural concepts and themes from different viewpoints (e.g., minority group).
Social action	Based on information about cultural artifacts, etc., students make recommendations for social action.	Based on their understanding of important concepts and themes, students make recommendations for social action.	Students are asked to and can apply their understanding of important social and cultural issues; they make recommendations for and take action on these issues.	Students are required to and can analyze social and cultural issues from different perspectives; they take action on these issues.	Students create a plan of action to address a social and cultural issue(s); they seek important social change.	Students critique important social and cultural issues, and seek to make national and/or international change.

Note: Actions taken on the social action level can range from immediate and small scale (e.g., classroom and school level) to moderate scale (e.g., community or regional level) to large scale (state, national, and international levels). Likewise, students can make recommendations for action or actually take social action.

Source: Ford & Harris, 1999. Adapted from Banks, Chapter 10, this volume; Bloom, 1956.

Multicultural education can engage students and give them opportunities to identify with, connect with, and relate to the curriculum. It consists of deliberate, ongoing, planned, and systematic opportunities to avoid drive-by teaching—to make learning meaningful and relevant to students, and to give minority students mirrors in order to see themselves reflected in the curriculum. Multicultural gifted education challenges students culturally, affectively, academically, and cognitively.

Multicultural Counseling

Fordham and Ogbu (1986), Fordham (1998), and Ford (1998) have conducted research examining the concerns that high-achieving, gifted African American students have about being academically successful. A common finding is that many of these students are accused of "acting White" by other African American students because of their academic success. Such accusations can be frustrating, overwhelming, and unmotivating for students. Should an anti-achievement ethic be present in schools, educators should provide students—the accused and the accusers—with social-emotional and psychological supports. The students accused of acting White will need assistance with coping skills, conflict resolution skills, and anger management. The accusers will need assistance examining the negative implications—the self-defeating thoughts and behaviors—of an anti-achievement ethic. Peer-group counseling is one potentially effective method for addressing these issues (Whiting, 2006).

Skills-Based Supports

Retention efforts must also address and rectify skill deficits. As stated earlier, many diverse students are gifted but need support to maintain an acceptable level of achievement. Supportive systems include test-taking skills, study skills, time-management skills, and organizational skills.

Ongoing Professional Development in Multicultural Education and Counseling

In order to implement the above recommendations, educators should participate in ongoing and formal preparation in multicultural education and counseling. Whether in the form of courses or workshops, such preparation should focus on educators becoming culturally competent in the following areas:

1. Understanding cultural diversity and its impact on (a) teaching, (b) learning, and (c) assessment.
2. Understanding the impact of biases and stereotypes on (a) teaching, (b) learning, and (c) assessment (e.g., referrals, testing, expectations).
3. Working effectively and proactively with (a) students from racial, ethnic, and language minorities, (b) their families, and (c) their community.
4. Creating multicultural (a) curricula and (b) instruction.
5. Creating culturally responsive (a) learning and (b) assessment environments.

SUMMARY AND CONCLUSIONS

Gifted students are gifted 24 hours of the day. Racial and ethnic minority students are racial and ethnic minorities 24 hours of the day.

In 1954 the U.S. Supreme Court ruled deliberate (*de jure*) school segregation unconstitutional. And more recently, we have such legislation as No Child Left Behind targeting the pervasive achievement gap. Yet, *de facto* segregation persists in schools and in gifted education programs. Educators should focus extensively, consistently, and systematically on the many factors that contribute to and exacerbate the underrepresentation of students from racial, ethnic, and language minorities in gifted education. I have argued that a deficit orientation among educators, based primarily on a lack of understanding of culture, permeates all areas of the recruitment and retention of certain diverse students in gifted education programs. Deficit thinking has no place in education. Instead, educators must acknowledge the realities of the diversity in the world, in the United States, and in schools, and seek to acquire and use the resources and preparation needed to become culturally responsive and responsible professionals. Culturally competent educators are advocates for students from diverse racial, ethnic, cultural, and language groups. The multicultural philosophy and preparation of educators will guide their referrals, instrument selection, test interpretation, and placement decisions—all of which are essential for recruiting and retaining diverse students into gifted education programs.

Questions and Activities

1. Why, according to the author, are ethnic minority and low-income students underrepresented in school programs for gifted and talented youths?

2. What does the author mean by "deficit orientation" among educators regarding the education of gifted and talented minority students? In her view, how does deficit thinking contribute to the underrepresentation of minority students in programs for gifted and talented students?

3. Why are many ethnic minority and low-income students likely to be gifted underachievers or potentially gifted students? Describe some specific actions that teachers can take to identify these students and to provide them the support they need to achieve at higher levels.

4. The author describes some ways in which culture influences learning and thinking. How might theories about culture and learning, such as those by Boykin and Shade and her colleagues, help teachers to better meet the needs of gifted talented and minority students? Do these theories have drawbacks and limitations? If so, what are they?

5. Visit a school in your community and interview teachers to determine: (1) the criteria used to identify students for gifted and talented programs; (2) the percentage of students from ethnic and language minority students who are in gifted and talented programs in the school; and (3) the steps that are taken by the school to recruit and retain students from low-income and minority groups into programs for gifted and talented students.

References

American Educational Research Association (AERA), American Psychological Association (APA), & National Council on Measurement in Education (NCME) (1999). *Standards for Educational and Psychological Testing.* Washington, DC: Author.

Armour-Thomas, E. (1992). Intellectual Assessment of Children from Culturally Diverse Backgrounds. *School Psychology Review, 21,* 552–565.

Artiles, A. J., Trent, S. C., & Palmer, J. D. (2004). Culturally Diverse Students in Special Education: Legacies and Prospects. In J. A. Banks & C. A. M. Banks (Eds.), *Handbook of Research on Multicultural Education* (2nd ed., pp. 716–735). San Francisco: Jossey-Bass.

Banks, J. A. (2002). *An Introduction to Multicultural Education* (3rd ed.). Boston: Allyn & Bacon.

Baugh, J. H. (1991). African Americans and the Environment: A Review Essay. *Policy Studies Journal, 19*(2), 182–191.

Bloom, B. (Ed.). (1956). *Taxonomy of Educational Objectives: The Classification of Educational Goals.* New York: McKay.

Boykin, A. W. (1994). Afrocultural Expression and Its Implications for Schooling. In E. R. Hollins, J. E. King, & W. C. Hayman (Eds.), *Teaching Diverse Populations: Formulating a Knowledge Base* (pp. 225–273). Albany: State University of New York Press.

Byrant, B., & Mohai, P. (Eds.). (1992). *Race and the Incidence of Environmental Hazards: A Time for Discourse.* Boulder, CO: Westview.

Bullard, R. D. (Ed.). (1993). *Confronting Environmental Racism: Voices from the Grassroots.* Boston: South End Press.

Cohen, E. G., & Lotan, R. A. (2004). Equity in Heterogeneous Classrooms. In J. A. Banks & C. A. M. Banks (Eds.), *Handbook of Research on Multicultural Education* (2nd ed., pp. 736–750). San Francisco: Jossey-Bass.

Colangelo, N., & Davis, G. A. (2003). *Handbook of Gifted Education* (3rd ed.). Boston: Allyn & Bacon.

Dana, R. H. (1993). *Multicultural Assessment Perspectives for Professional Psychology.* Boston: Allyn & Bacon.

Davis, G. A., & Rimm, S. B. (1903). *Education of the Gifted and Talented* (3rd ed.). Boston: Allyn & Bacon.

Does the No Child Left Behind Act 'Do' Anything for Gifted Students? Retrieved March 2, 2006 from, http://www.nagc.org/index.aspx?id=999.

Donovan, M. S., & Cross, C. T. (Eds.). (2002). *Minority Students in Special and Gifted Education.* Washington, DC: National Academy Press.

Dwight, H. (1994). Overcoming Racism in Environmental Decision Making. *Environment, 36,* 10–27.

Flanagan, D. P., & Ortiz, S. O. (2001). *Essentials of Cross-Battery Assessment.* Boston: Allyn and Bacon.

Ford, D. Y. (1996). *Reversing Underachievement among Gifted Black Students: Promising Practices and Programs.* New York: Teachers College Press.

Ford, D. Y. (1998). The Under-Representation of Minority Students in Gifted Education: Problems and Promises in Recruitment and Retention. *The Journal of Special Education, 32*(1), 4–14.

Ford, D. Y., & Frazier Trotman, M. (2001). Teachers of Gifted Students: Suggested Multicultural Characteristics and Competencies. *Roeper Review, 23*(4), 235–239.

Ford, D. Y. (2004). *Intelligence Testing and Cultural Diversity: Concerns, Cautions, and Considerations.* Storrs, CT: University of Connecticut, National Research Center on the Gifted and Talented.

Ford, D. Y., & Harris, J. J., III. (1999). *Multicultural Gifted Education.* New York: Teachers College Press.

Ford, D. Y., Harris, J. J., III, Tyson, C. A., & Frazier Trotman, M. (2002). Beyond Deficit Thinking: Providing Access for Gifted African American Students. *Roeper Review, 24*(2), 52–58.

Ford, D. Y., Moore III, J. L., & Milner, H. R. (2005). Beyond Cultureblindness: A Model of Culture with Implications for Gifted Education. *Roeper Review, 27*(2), 97–103.

Fordham, S. (1988). Racelessness as a Strategy in Black Students' School Success: Pragmatic Strategy or Pyrrhic Victory? *Harvard Educational Review, 58*, 54–84.

Fordham, S., & Ogbu, J. (1986). Black Students' School Success: Coping with the "Burden of 'Acting White,'" *The Urban Review, 18*, 176–203.

Frasier, M. M., Martin, D., Garcia, J., Finley, V. S., Frank, E., Krisel, S., & King, L. L. (1995). *A New Window for Looking at Gifted Children.* Storrs: University of Connecticut, National Research Center on the Gifted and Talented.

Gallagher, J. (2004). *Public Policy and Gifted Education.* Thousand Oaks, CA: Corwin Press and National Association for Gifted Children.

Gardner, H. (1993). *Frames of Mind: The Theory of Multiple Intelligences.* New York: Basic Books.

Gay, G. (2000). *Culturally Responsive Teaching: Theory, Research, and Practice.* New York: Teachers College Press.

Gould, S. J. (1995). *The Mismeasure of Man* (Rev. ed.). New York: Norton. (Original work published 1981).

Grossman, K. (1991). Environmental Racism. *Crisis, 98*(4), 14–17, 31–32.

Harris III, J. J., Brown, E. L., Ford, D. Y., & Richardson, J. W. (2004). American Americans and Multicultural Education: A Proposed Remedy for Disproportionate Special Education Placement and Underinclusion in Gifted Education. *Education and Urban Society, 36*, 304–341.

Helms, J. E. (1992). Why Is There No Study of Cultural Equivalence in Standardized Cognitive Ability Testing? *American Psychologist, 47*, 1083–1101.

Herrnstein, R. J., & Murray, C. (1994). *The Bell Curve: Intelligence and Class Structure in American Life.* New York: Free Press.

Heubert, J. P., & Hauser, R. M. (Eds.). (1999). *High Stakes: Testing for Tracking, Promotion, and Graduation.* Washington, DC: National Academy Press.

Irvine, J. J., & York, D. E. (2001). Learning Styles and Culturally Diverse Students: A Literature Review. In J. A. Banks & C. A. M. Banks (Eds.), *Handbook of Research on Multicultural Education* (pp. 484–497). San Francisco: Jossey-Bass.

Jensen, A. R. (1980). *Bias in Mental Testing.* New York: Free Press.

Kaufman, A. S. (1994). *Intelligent Testing with the WISC-III.* New York: Wiley.

Kitano, M. K., & DiJosia, M. (2002). Are Asian and Pacific Islanders Overrepresented in Programs for the Gifted and Talented? (When Who I Am Impacts How I Am Represented: Addressing Minority Student Issues in Different Contexts). *Roeper Review, 24*(2), 76–81.

Kornhaber, M. (2004). Assessment, Standards and Equity. In J. A. Banks & C. A. M. Banks (Eds.), *Handbook of Research on Multicultural Education* (2nd ed., pp. 91–109). San Francisco: Jossey-Bass.

Lee, C. (1993). *Signifying as a Scaffold for Literary Interpretation: The Pedagogical Implications of an African American Discourse Genre.* Urbana, IL: National Council of Teachers of English.

Majors, R., & Billson, J. M. (1992). *Cool Pose: The Dilemmas of Black Manhood in America*. New York: Touchstone.

Maker, J., & Nielson, A. B. (1996). *Curriculum Development and Teaching Strategies for Gifted Learners* (2nd ed.). Austin, TX: PRO-ED.

Menchaca, M. (1997). Early Racist Discourses: The Roots of Deficit Thinking. In R. Valencia (Ed.), *The Evolution of Deficit Thinking* (pp. 13–40). New York: Falmer.

Mercer, J. R. (1973). *Labeling the Mentally Retarded*. Berkeley: University of California Press.

Naglieri, J. A., & Ford, D. Y. (2003). Addressing Under-Representation of Gifted Minority Children Using the Naglieri Nonverbal Ability Test (NNAT). *Gifted Child Quarterly, 47*, 155–160.

Naglieri, J. A., & Ford, D. Y. (2005). Increasing Minority Children's Representation in Gifted Education: A Response to Lohman. *Gifted Child Quarterly, 49*(1), 29–36.

National Council for Gifted Children. (1997). Position Paper on Testing. Washington, DC: Author.

Office of Ethnic Minority Affairs. (1993). Guidelines for Providers of Psychological Services to Ethnic, Linguistic, and Culturally Diverse Populations. *American Psychologist, 48*, 45–48.

Office for Civil Rights. (2000). The Use of Tests as Part of High-Stakes Decision-Making for Students: A Resource Guide for Educators and Policy-Makers. Washington, DC: Author.

Pang, V. O., Kiang, P. N., & Pak, Y. K. (2004). Asian Pacific American Students: Challenging a Biased Educational System. In J. A. Banks & C. A. M. Banks (Eds.), *Handbook of Research on Multicultural Education* (2nd ed., pp. 542–563). San Francisco: Jossey-Bass.

Pfeiffer, S. I. (2003). Challenges and Opportunities for Students Who Are Gifted: What the Experts Say. *Gifted Child Quarterly, 47*(2), 161–169.

Ramírez, M., III, & Castañeda, A. (1974). *Cultural Democracy, Bicognitive Development, and Education*. New York: Academic Press.

Reis, S. M., & Callahan, C. M. (1989). Gifted Females—They've Come a Long Way—or Have They? *Journal for the Education of the Gifted, 12*, 99–117.

Rimm, S. B. (1995). *Why Bright Kids Get Poor Grades—and What You Can Do about It*. New York: Crown.

Saccuzzo, D. P., Johnson, N. E., & Guertin, T. L. (1994). *Identifying Underrepresented Disadvantaged Gifted and Talented Children: A Multifaceted Approach* (Vols. 1–2). San Diego: San Diego State University.

Sandoval, J., Frisby, C. L., Geisinger, K. F., Scheuneman, J. D. & Grenier, J. R. (1998). *Test Interpretation and Diversity: Achieving Equity in Assessment*. Washington, DC: American Psychological Association.

Sapon-Shevon, M. (1996). Beyond Gifted Education: Building a Shared Agenda for School Reform. *Journal for the Education of the Gifted, 19*, 194–214.

Saracho, O. N., & Gerstl, C. K. (1992). Learning Differences among At-Risk Minority Students. In H. C. Waxman, J. Walker de Felix, J. E. Anderson, & H. P. Baptiste (Eds.), *Students at Risk in At-Risk Schools: Improving Environments for Learning* (pp. 105–136). Newbury Park, CA: Corwin.

Shade, B. J., Kelly, C., & Oberg, M. (1997). *Creating Culturally Responsive Classrooms*. Washington, DC: American Psychological Association.

Silverman, L. K. (1993). *Counseling the Gifted and Talented*. Denver, CO: Love.

Smith, C., Constantino, R., & Krashen, S. (1997). Differences in Print Environment for Children in Beverly Hills, Compton, and Watts. *Emergency Librarian, 24*(4), 8–9.

Sowell, T. (1993). *Inside American Education: The Decline, the Deception, the Dogma*. New York: Free Press.

Sternberg, R. J. (1985). *Beyond IQ: A Triarchic Theory of Human Intelligence*. New York: Cambridge University Press.

Storti, C. (1989). *The Art of Crossing Cultures* (2nd ed.). Yarmouth, ME: Intercultural Press.

Suzuki, L. A., Meller, P. J., & Ponterotto, J. G. (Eds.). (1996). *Handbook of Multicultural Assessment: Clinical, Psychological, and Educational Adaptations*. San Francisco: Jossey-Bass.

Tomlinson, C. A. (1995). *How to Differentiate Instruction in Mixed-Ability Classrooms*. Alexandria, VA: Association for Supervision and Curriculum Development.

U.S. Department of Education (USDE). (1993). *National Excellence: A Case for Developing America's Talent*. Washington, DC: Author.

VanTassel-Baska, J. (1994). *Comprehensive Curriculum for Gifted Learners*. Boston: Allyn & Bacon.

VanTassel-Baska, J., Patton, J., & Prillaman, D. (1989). Disadvantaged Gifted Learners At-Risk for Educational Attention. *Focus on Exceptional Children, 22*, 1–16.

VanTassel-Baska, J. & Stambaugh, T. (2006). *Comprehensive Curriculum for Gifted Learners* (3rd ed.). Boston: Allyn and Bacon.

Whiting, G. 2006. Promoting a Scholar Identity in African American Males: Recommendations for Gifted Education. *Gifted Education Quarterly, 20*(3), 1–6.

Multicultural education provides a framework for conceptualizing and implementing school reform.

422

School Reform

Reforming schools so that all students have an equal opportunity to succeed requires a new vision of education and social actors who are willing to advocate for and participate in change. The two chapters in Part VI discuss effective ways to conceptualize and implement school reform within a multicultural framework. In Chapter 16, Sonia Nieto presents and analyzes five conditions that will promote student achievement within a multicultural perspective. According to Nieto, schools should (1) be antiracist and antibiased; (2) reflect an understanding and acceptance of all students as having talents and strengths that can enhance their education; (3) be considered within the parameters of critical pedagogy; (4) involve those people most intimately connected with teaching and learning; and (5) be based on high expectations and rigorous standards for all learners.

Cherry A. McGee Banks, in Chapter 17, discusses ways to involve parents in schools. She argues that parent involvement is an important factor in school reform and student achievement and that parents can be a cogent force in school reform. Parents, perhaps more than any other group, can mobilize the community to support school reform. Parents have first-hand knowledge about the school's effectiveness and can be vocal advocates for change. As consumers of educational services, parents can raise questions that are difficult for professional educators and administrators to raise, such as "What is the proportion of males in special education classes?" and "What is the ethnic breakdown of students enrolled in higher-level math and science classes?"

Banks argues that parents are more willing to work for school reform when they are involved in schools. They are more likely to become involved in schools when parent involvement opportunities reflect their varied interests, skills, and motivations. Banks suggests ways to expand traditional ideas about parent involvement and to increase the number and kinds of parents involved in schools.

CHAPTER 16

School Reform and Student Learning: A Multicultural Perspective

Sonia Nieto

Learning is at the heart of schooling. If this is the case, then it makes sense that student learning be a major focus of school reform efforts. This means that educational policies and practices need to be viewed in terms of how they affect the learning and academic achievement of students. But some school policies, especially as espoused in the reform movement that began with the publication of *A Nation at Risk* (National Commission on Excellence in Education, 1983) and that are now institutionalized through the No Child Left Behind federal legislation, as well as similar legislation in many states, pay scant attention to whether and to what extent students actually learn. These reform efforts often end up punishing schools, teachers, districts, and ultimately students who have not measured up to norms of success predetermined by politicians, policy makers, and others who know little about schools. Longer school days and years, strict retention policies, placement of schools "on probation," more high-stakes testing (that is, tests used as the sole or primary criterion for such crucial decisions as class placement and college admission), and less attention to pedagogy and curricula have been the result. Students who are most at risk of receiving an inadequate education are often the ones most jeopardized by such reform efforts.

This chapter begins with the assumption that student learning can be positively influenced by changes in school policies and practices that affirm students' identities and that are part of systemic school reform measures. Given the social nature of schooling, it is impossible to ascribe a fixed causal relationship between student learning and schooling. Many complex forces influence student learning, including personal, psychological, social, cultural, community, and institutional factors (Nieto, 2004). That is, we cannot simply say that eliminating tracking will help all students succeed or that native-language instruction will guarantee success for all language-minority students. Neither can we state unequivocally that culturally responsive pedagogy is always the answer. Although these changes may in fact substantially improve educational outcomes for many more students than are now achieving academic success, taken in isolation, they may fail to reflect the complex nature of student learning.

A comprehensive view of student learning that takes into account the myriad influences on achievement can help explain why some students succeed academically while others do not. For example, a number of years ago, my colleague Manuel Frau-Ramos and I did a study of Puerto Rican students who had dropped out of school in a particular city. We found that 68 percent of those who had never been in bilingual programs dropped out of school, while only 39 percent of those who had been in bilingual classrooms for at least part of their school experience dropped out (Frau-Ramos & Nieto, 1993). The difference in dropout rates was dramatic, but a 39 percent dropout rate is still unacceptably high. It suggests that other conditions also were involved. We found that these included the students' perceptions of fitting in and their previous educational preparation; teachers' limited knowledge of their students' backgrounds and their negative attitudes about diversity; school policies and practices that led some students to feel like outsiders; and the structural inequality, poverty, and racism that they lived with on a daily basis. In this case, although bilingual education was significant in mediating the school retention of some students, it was insufficient to ensure that all students would succeed academically.

Culturally responsive education, an approach based on using students' identities and backgrounds as meaningful sources of their education, can go a long way toward improving the education of students whose cultures have been maligned, denied, or omitted in school curricula (Au & Kawakami, 1994; Gay, 2000; Irvine, 2003; Ladson-Billings, 1994). This approach offers crucial insights for understanding the lack of achievement of students from culturally subordinated groups. However, by itself, culturally responsive pedagogy cannot guarantee that all students will learn. For example, if viewed simply as "cultural sensitivity" or as including a few activities in the curriculum, culturally responsive education offers little hope for substantive change. Moreover, there are cases in which culturally marginalized students have been successfully educated *in spite* of what might be considered culturally incompatible settings. As a case in point, Catholic schools might seem at first glance to be culturally inappropriate for some children because bilingual programs are seldom offered, classes are usually overcrowded, and formal environments stress individual excellence rather than cooperation. Yet many students of African American and Latino backgrounds who attend Catholic schools have been academically successful (Bryk, Lee, & Holland, 1993; Irvine & Foster, 1996).

In the case of Catholic schools, we need to look beyond just cultural responsiveness to explain student academic success. Because of generally limited resources, Catholic schools tend to offer *all* students a less differentiated curriculum, less tracking, and more academic classes, in addition to having clear, uncomplicated missions and strong social contracts (Bryk, Lee, & Holland, 1993; Irvine & Foster, 1996). What at first glance might appear to be incongruous in terms of cultural compatibility can nevertheless reflect high expectations for all students. This example illustrates the complex relationship of academic success to a multiplicity of conditions, and it again indicates that there is no one simple solution to academic failure.

In this chapter, I explore the meaning of school reform with a multicultural perspective and consider implications for student learning. I begin by defining school reform with a multicultural perspective, including how a school's policies and practices implicitly illustrate beliefs about who deserves the benefits of a high-quality education. That is, certain school policies and practices may exacerbate the pervasive structural inequalities that exist in society. I then describe a set of five interrelated conditions for successful school reform within a multicultural perspective. These conditions are intimately interconnected, but for the purpose of expediency, I explain the five conditions separately, with implications for increasing student achievement.

SCHOOL REFORM WITH A MULTICULTURAL PERSPECTIVE

Many people assume that multicultural education consists of little more than isolated lessons in sensitivity training or prejudice reduction, or separate units about cultural artifacts or ethnic holidays. Sometimes, it is used to mean education geared for inner-city schools or, more specifically, for African American students. If conceptualized in this limited way, multicultural education will have little influence on student learning. When conceptualized as broad-based school reform, however, multicultural education can have a major influence on how and to what extent students learn. When it focuses on conditions that can contribute to student underachievement, multicultural education allows educators to explore alternatives to systemic problems that may lead to academic failure and it fosters the design and implementation of productive learning environments, diverse instructional strategies, and a deeper awareness of how cultural and language differences can influence learning.

To approach school reform with a multicultural perspective, we need to begin with an understanding of multicultural education within its *sociopolitical context* (Nieto, 2004). A sociopolitical context underscores that education is part and parcel of larger societal and political forces, such as inequality based on stratification due to race, social class, gender, and other differences. Given this perspective, decisions concerning such practices as ability tracking, high-stakes testing, native-language instruction, retention, curriculum reform, and pedagogy are all influenced by broader social policies.

As Freire (1985) states, every educational decision, whether made at the classroom, city, state, or national level, is imbedded within a particular ideological framework. Such decisions can be as simple as whether a classroom should be arranged in rows with all students facing the teacher, or in tables with groups of students to encourage cooperative work, or in a variety of ways depending on the task at hand. Alternatively, these decisions can be as far-reaching as eliminating tracking in an entire school system, or teaching language-minority students by using both their native language and English, or by using English only. Within each educational decision are assumptions about the nature of learning, about what particular students are capable of achieving, about whose language is valued, and about who should be at the center of the educational process. Even seemingly innocent decisions carry an enormous amount of ideological and philosophical baggage, which is in turn communicated to students either directly or indirectly.

As stated more extensively elsewhere, I define multicultural education within a sociopolitical context as (Nieto, 2004):

> a process of comprehensive school reform and basic education for
> all students. It challenges and rejects racism and other forms of
> discrimination in schools and society and accepts and affirms the
> pluralism (ethnic, racial, linguistic, religious, economic, and gender,
> among others) that students, their communities, and teachers
> reflect. Multicultural education permeates the schools' curriculum
> and instructional strategies, as well as the interactions among

> teachers, students, and families, and the very way that schools conceptualize the nature of teaching and learning. Because it uses critical pedagogy as its underlying philosophy and focuses on knowledge, reflection, and action *(praxis)* as the basis for social change, multicultural education promotes democratic principles of social justice. (Nieto, 2004, p. 346)

This definition of multicultural education assumes a comprehensive school reform effort rather than superficial additions to the curriculum or one-shot treatments about diversity, such as workshops for teachers or assembly programs for students. As such, I use this definition as a lens to view conditions for systemic school reform that can improve the learning of all students.

CONDITIONS FOR SYSTEMIC SCHOOL REFORM WITH A MULTICULTURAL PERSPECTIVE

Failure to learn does not develop out of thin air; it is scrupulously created through policies, practices, attitudes, and beliefs. In a very concrete sense, the results of educational inequality explain by example what a society believes its young people are capable of achieving and what they deserve. For instance, offering only low-level courses in schools serving culturally diverse and poor youngsters is a clear message that the students are not expected to achieve to high levels; in like manner, considering students to be "at risk" simply because of their ethnicity, native language, family characteristics, or social class is another clear sign that some students have been defined by conventional wisdom as uneducable based simply on their identity.

As a result, we cannot think about education reform without taking into account both micro- and macro-level issues that may affect student learning. Micro-level issues include the cultures, languages, and experiences of students and their families and how these are considered in determining school policies and practices (Cummins, 1996; Nieto, 1999). Macro-level issues include the racial stratification that helps maintain inequality, and the resources and access to learning that schools provide or deny (Kozol, 2005; Orfield, 2001; Spring, 2002). In addition, how students and their families view their status in schools and society must be considered. Ogbu (1994), for instance, has argued that school performance gaps persist because of racial stratification and the unequal treatment of dominated groups, as well as the responses of dominated groups to these experiences.

Conditions such as inequitable school financing (National Center for Education Statistics, 2000), unrepresentative school governance (Meier & Stewart, 1991), and large class size (Mosteller, 1995) may play a powerful role in promoting student underachievement. For example, inequities in school financing have remained quite stable since Jonathan Kozol's (1991) landmark study of more than a decade ago (National Center for Educational Statistics, 2000). Yet reform strategies such as longer school days, more rigorous graduation standards, and increased standardized testing often do not take such issues into account. The evidence is growing, for example, that school size makes a difference in student learning and that it may also influence students' feelings of belonging, and thus their engagement with learning. One study, for example, concluded that elementary schools of fewer than 400 students tend to display stronger teacher collective responsibility for student learning and greater student achievement in math (Lee & Loeb, 2000). In fact, equalizing just two conditions of schooling—funding and class size—would probably result in an immediate and dramatic improvement in learning for students who have not received the benefits of these two conditions.

School reform strategies that do not acknowledge such macrolevel disparities are bound to be inadequate because they assume that schools provide all students with a level playing field. The conditions described below, while acknowledging these disparities, nevertheless provide hope for school systems where such changes as equitable funding or small class size may not occur in the near future. Rather than wait for these changes to happen, schools and teachers can begin to improve the conditions for successful student learning. Five such conditions are described below (these conditions are described in greater detail in Nieto, 1999). These conditions, along with changes in funding and resource allocation, would help create schools where all students have a better chance to learn.

School Reform Should Be Antiracist and Antibiased

An antiracist and antibiased perspective is at the core of multicultural education. This is crucial because too often people believe that multicultural education automatically takes care of racism, but this is far from the reality. In fact, multicultural education without an explicit antiracist focus may perpetuate the worst kinds of stereotypes if it focuses only on superficial aspects of culture and the addition of ethnic tidbits to the curriculum.

In contrast, being antiracist means paying attention to all areas in which some students may be favored over others, including the curriculum and pedagogy, sorting policies, and teachers' interactions and relationships with students and their communities. Schools committed to multicultural education with an antiracist perspective need to examine closely both school policies and the attitudes and behaviors of their staff to determine how these might be complicit in causing academic failure. The kind of expectations that teachers and schools have for students (Nieto, 2002/2003), whether native-language use is permitted or punished (Gebhard, Austin, Nieto, & Willett, 2002), how sorting takes place (Oakes, 2005), and how classroom organization, pedagogy, and curriculum may influence student learning (Bennett deMarrais & LeCompte, 1999) each need to be considered.

To become antiracist, schools also need to examine how the curriculum may perpetuate negative, distorted, or incomplete images of some groups while exalting others as the makers of all history. Unfortunately, many textbooks and children's books are still replete with racist and sexist images and with demeaning portrayals of people from low-income communities. Although the situation is improving, and the stereotypes that exist are not as blatant as they once were, there are still many inaccuracies and negative portrayals (Harris, 1997; Loewen, 1995, 2000; Willis, 1998).

In a related vein, most of the women and men presented as heroes or heroines in the standard curriculum—whether from dominant or nondominant cultures—are "safe"; that is, they do not pose a challenge to the status quo. Other people who have fought for social justice are omitted, presented as bizarre or insane, or made safe by downplaying their contributions. A now-classic article by Kozol (1975) graphically documents how schools bleed the life and soul out of even the most impassioned and courageous heroes, such as Helen Keller and Martin Luther King, Jr., in the process making them boring and less-than-believable caricatures. A powerful book by Kohl (2005) demonstrates how Rosa Parks, the mother of the civil rights movement, was made palatable to the mainstream by portraying her not as a staunch civil rights crusader who consciously battled racist segregation but rather as a tired woman who simply did not want to give up her seat on the bus (Kohl, 2005). Taking another example, few children learn about the slave revolt led by Nat Turner (Aptheker, 1943/1987), although most learn that "Abraham Lincoln freed the slaves all by himself." These are examples of at best misleading, and at worst racist, representations.

Through this kind of curriculum, students from dominant groups learn that they are the norm, and consequently they often assume that anyone different from them is culturally or intellectually disadvantaged. On the other hand, students from subordinated cultures may internalize the message that their cultures, families, languages, and experiences have low status, and they learn to feel inferior. The result may be what has been called "stereotype threat," or the impact on Blacks, other people of color, and women of their devaluation in schools and society (Steele, 1999; Aronson & Steele, 2005). All students suffer as a result of these messages, but students from dominated groups are the most negatively affected.

The issue of institutional power is also at play here. The conventional notion of racism is that it is an *individual* bias toward members of other groups. This perception conveniently skirts the issue of how institutions themselves, which are much more powerful than individuals, develop harmful policies and practices that victimize American Indians, African Americans, Latinos, poor European Americans, females, gays and lesbians, and other people from powerless groups. The major difference between *individual racism* and *institutional racism and bias* is the wielding of power, because it is primarily through the power of the people who control institutions such as schools that oppressive policies and practices are reinforced and legitimated (Tatum, 2003; Weinberg, 1990). That is, when racism is understood as a systemic problem, not just as an individual dislike for a particular group of people, we can better understand its negative and destructive effects.

I do not wish to minimize the powerful effect of individual prejudice and discrimination, which can be personally very painful, nor to suggest that individual discrimination occurs only in one direction, for example, from Whites to African Americans. No group monopolizes prejudice and discrimination; they occur in all directions, and even within groups. But interethnic hostility, personal prejudices, and individual biases, while certainly hurtful, do not have the long-range and life-limiting effects on entire groups of people that institutional racism and bias have. Testing practices, for example, may be institutionally discriminatory because they label students from culturally and socially dominated groups as inferior as a result of their performance on these tests (McNeil, 2000). Rather than critically examining the tests themselves, the underlying purpose of such tests, or their damaging effects, the students themselves are often blamed (Orfield & Kornhaber, 2001). In addition, the fact that textbook companies and other companies that develop tests earn huge profits from test construction and dissemination is often unmentioned, yet it, too, is a reality (Kohn, 2000).

An antiracist perspective is also apparent in schools when students are permitted, and even encouraged, to speak about their experiences with racism and other biases. Many White teachers feel great discomfort when racism is discussed in the classroom. They are uncomfortable for several reasons: their lack of experience in confronting such a potentially explosive issue, the conspiracy of silence about racism (as if not speaking about it will make it disappear), the guilt they may feel being a member of the group that has benefited from racism, the generally accepted assumption that we live in a colorblind society, or a combination of these reasons (Fine, 1991; Howard, 1999; Pollock, 2004; Sleeter, 1994; Tatum, 2003). Yet when students are given time and support for expressing their views, the result can be compelling because their experiences are legitimated and used in the service of their learning. For example, both Levin (2001) and Landsman (2001) have written eloquently about the impact of addressing issues of racism and discrimination in the classroom. In a related vein, Donaldson (1996) described how urban high school students used the racism they and their peers experienced in school as the content of a peer-education assembly program. The result was a critical examination of the impact that race can have on their education. Rather than shying away from such topics, these researchers found that directly confronting issues of bias can help students become more critical and reflective learners.

In my own research on the views of students concerning their education, they mentioned racism and other examples of discrimination on the part of fellow students and teachers (Nieto, 1994). Manuel, a Cape Verdean student who moved to the United States at age eleven, described how it felt to be the butt of jokes from his peers: "When American students see you, it's kinda hard [to] get along with them when you have a different culture, a different way of dressing and stuff like that. So kids really look at you and laugh, you know, at the beginning" (cited p. 414). Avi, a Jewish American young man, discussed a number of incidents of anti-Semitism, including one in which a student walked by him and whispered, "Are you ready for the Second Holocaust?" Other students talked about discrimination on the part of teachers. Marisol, a Puerto Rican student, and Vinh, who was Vietnamese, specifically mentioned language discrimination as a major problem. In Marisol's case, it happened when a teacher did not allow her to use Spanish in the classroom. For Vinh, it concerned teachers' attitudes about his language. He explained: "Some teachers don't understand about the language. So sometimes, my language, they say it sounds funny" (cited p. 414).

As these examples demonstrate, an antiracist perspective is essential in schools if all students are to be given equitable environments for learning. An antiracist perspective is a vital lens through which to analyze a school's policies and practices, including the curriculum, pedagogy, testing and tracking, discipline, faculty hiring, student retention, and attitudes about and interactions with parents.

School Reform Should Reflect an Understanding and Acceptance of All Students as Having Talents and Strengths That Can Enhance Their Education

Many educators believe that students from culturally subordinated groups have few experiential or cultural strengths that can benefit their education. A classic example comes from Ryan (1972), who coined the expression "blaming the victim" for the tendency to place responsibility on students and their families for their failure to achieve in school. These students, generally low-income children of all groups and children of color specifically, are often considered deficient or "culturally deprived," a patronizing term popularized in the 1960s (Reissman, 1962). But Ryan turned the perspective of "cultural deprivation" on its head when he wrote:

> We are dealing, it would seem, not so much with culturally
> deprived children as with culturally depriving schools. And the task
> to be accomplished is not to revise, amend, and repair deficient
> children, but to alter and transform the atmosphere and operations
> of the schools to which we commit these children. (p. 61)

Students may be thought of as culturally deprived simply because they speak a language other than English as their native language or because they have just one parent or live in poverty. Sometimes they are labeled in this way just because of their race or ethnicity. Rather than begin with this kind of deficit view, however, it makes sense to begin with a more positive and, in the end, more realistic and hopeful view of students and their families. Thus, school reform measures based on the assumption that children of all families bring cultural and community strengths to their education would go a long way toward providing more powerful learning environments for a greater number of youngsters. Gonzalez et al.'s (2005) research on incorporating "funds of knowledge" into the curriculum—that is, using the experiences and skills of all families to encourage student learning—is a more promising and productive way of approaching families than is the viewpoint that they have only deficits that must be repaired.

If we begin with the premise that children and their families have substantial talents that can inform student learning, a number of implications for improving schools follow. Instead of placing the blame for failure to learn solely on students, teachers need to become aware of how their own biases can act as barriers to student learning. Teachers also need to consider how their students best learn and how their own pedagogical practices need to change as a result. This implies that teachers need to learn culturally responsive ways of teaching all of their students (Irvine, 2003; Ladson-Billings, 2001).

Teachers also need to consider how the native language of students influences their academic achievement. For this to happen, they need to "unlearn" some of the conventional myths surrounding native-language use (Snow, 1997). For instance, it is common practice in schools to try to convince parents whose native language is other than English that they should speak only English with their children. This recommendation makes little sense for at least three reasons. First, these parents often speak little English themselves, and their children are thus provided with less than adequate models of English. Second, this practice often results in cutting off, rather than stimulating, communication between parents and children. Third, if young people are encouraged to learn English at the expense of their native language, rather than in conjunction with it, they may lose meaningful connections that help maintain close and loving relations with family members (Beykont, 2000).

A more reasonable recommendation, and one that would honor the contributions parents can make to their children's education, is to encourage rather than discourage them to speak their native language with their children, to speak it often, and to use it consistently. In schools, this means that students would not be punished for speaking their native languages; rather, they would be encouraged to do so, and to do so in the service of their learning (Reyes & Halcón, 2001). A rich communicative legacy, both in school and at home, could be the result.

Another example of failing to use student and community strengths can be found in the curriculum. Young children are frequently presented with images of community helpers who may be unrelated to their daily lives. A perspective that affirms the talents and experiences of students and their families can expand the people and roles included in the curriculum. Not only would children study those community helpers traditionally included, such as police officers, mail carriers, and teachers, but they could also learn about local merchants, community activists, and street vendors. These people are also community helpers, although they have not generally been sanctioned as such by the official curriculum.

A further consideration concerning the talents and strengths of students and their families is what Cummins (1996) has called the "relations of power" in schools. In proposing a shift from "coercive" to "collaborative" relations of power, Cummins argues that traditional teacher-centered transmission models can limit the potential for learning, especially among students from communities whose cultures and languages are devalued by the dominant canon. In a powerful study of urban high school students becoming critical researchers, Ernest Morrell (2004) documented how students' experiences, knowledge, and enthusiasm can help engage them in robust learning. He concluded that a significant outcome of the study was students' recognition that youth and urban issues were worthy of serious study and that research can have a social impact. These findings suggest that using students as collaborators in developing the curriculum can help promote student learning. By encouraging collaborative relations of power, schools can begin to recognize other sources of legitimate knowledge that have been overlooked. This practice can, in turn, positively affect the degree to which students learn.

School Reform Should Be Considered within the Parameters of Critical Pedagogy

According to Banks (2003), the main goal of a multicultural curriculum is to help students develop decision-making and social action skills. Consequently, when students learn to view situations and events from a variety of viewpoints, critical thinking, reflection, and action are promoted. The connection between critical pedagogy and a multicultural perspective is a promising avenue for expanding and informing both of these philosophical frameworks (Lee, Menkart, & Okazawa-Rey, 1998; Sleeter & Delgado Bernal, 2004). Critical pedagogy is an approach through which students and teachers are encouraged to view what they learn in a critical light, or, in the words of Freire (1970), by learning to read both "the word and the world." According to Freire, the opposite of a critical or empowering approach is "banking education," where students learn to regurgitate and passively accept the knowledge they are given. A critical education, on the other hand, expects students to seek their own answers, to be curious, and to question.

Many students do not have access to a wide range of viewpoints, but such access is essential if they are to develop the critical judgment and decision-making skills they will need to become productive members of a democratic society. Because a critical perspective values diverse viewpoints and encourages critical thinking, reflection, and action, students are empowered as learners because they are expected to become problem solvers. Critical pedagogy is based on using students' present reality as a foundation for their further learning, rather than on doing away with or belittling what they know and who they are. As a result, critical pedagogy acknowledges diversity of all kinds instead of suppressing or supplanting it.

Shor's (1992) pioneering analysis concerning critical pedagogy is instructive. He begins with the assumption that because no curriculum can be truly neutral, it is the responsibility of schools to present students with the broad range of information they will need to learn to read and write critically and in the service of social justice. Thus, critical pedagogy is not simply the transfer of knowledge from teacher to students, even though it may be knowledge that has heretofore not been made available to them. A critical perspective does not simply operate on the principle of substituting one truth for another; instead, students are encouraged to reflect on multiple and contradictory perspectives in order to understand reality more fully. For instance, learning about the internment of Americans of Japanese descent and Japanese residents in the United States during World War II is not in itself critical pedagogy; it only becomes so when students analyze different viewpoints and use them to understand the inconsistencies they uncover. They can then begin to understand the role played by racist hysteria, economic exploitation, and propaganda as catalysts for the internment, and they can judge this incident through the stated ideals of our nation.

Without a critical perspective, reality is often presented to students as if it were static, finished, and flat; underlying conflicts, problems, and inherent contradictions are omitted. As we have seen, textbooks in all subject areas generally exclude information about unpopular perspectives or the perspectives of disempowered groups in society. Few of the books to which students have access present the viewpoints of people who have built our country, from enslaved Africans to immigrant labor to other working-class people, even though they have been the backbone of society (Zinn, 2003).

Likewise, the immigrant experience, shared by many groups in the United States, is generally treated, if at all, as a romantic and successful odyssey instead of as a more complicated process that has been also a wrenching experience of loss. Moreover, the European immigrant experience is generally presented in our history books as the sole model for all immigrants, although the historical context, the racial politics and hostility, and the economic structures awaiting more recent immigrants are very different and more complicated than was true for the vast majority of Europeans who arrived during the late nineteenth and early twentieth centuries (Takaki, 1993).

Using critical pedagogy as a basis for school reform renders very different policies for schools than do traditional models of school reform. Even more important than just increasing curricular options, critical pedagogy helps to expand teachers' and schools' perspectives about students' knowledge and intellectual capabilities. In terms of students, using critical pedagogy helps them become agents of their own learning so they can use what they learn in productive and critical ways. The knowledge they learn can be used to explore the reasons for certain conditions in their lives and to design strategies for changing them.

A number of recorded accounts of critical pedagogy in classrooms are compelling examples of the positive and empowering influence that teachers' guidance can have on student learning. In a now-classic essay, Peterson (1991) wrote about how he used critical pedagogy to teach literacy, debunk myths, and provide a rich environment for learning in his fifth-grade classroom. He describes how class meetings became "problem-posing" exercises (Freire, 1970) as students listed the concerns or problems they wanted to discuss and then decided which one to tackle on a particular day. He described the five-step plan they used by listing a series of questions students needed to answer:

1. What is the problem?
2. Are you sure about it?
3. What can we do about it?
4. Try it.
5. How did it work? (p. 166)

Peterson (1991) does not propose this process as a panacea. Instead, he states, "While many of the problems poor and minority children and communities face cannot be easily or immediately 'solved,' a 'problem-posing' pedagogy can encourage a questioning of why things are the way they are and the identification of actions, no matter how small, to begin to address them" (p. 166).

More recently, Patty Bode, a gifted art teacher who incorporates a multicultural perspective in her teaching, reflected on her experience with a first-grade child who was concerned about unfair representation in some of the books she was reading. In "A Letter from Kaeli" (Nieto, 1999), Patty discussed how she had received in her mailbox at school the following letter, using invented spelling, from a first-grade student:

> Dear !!!!!! mis Boudie
> Ples! halp. my moom was spcing to me abut wite piple leving
> bran and blak piple out of books.
>   Love Kaeli
>
> [Dear Ms. Bode,
> Please help! My mom was speaking to me about White people
> leaving Brown and Black people out of books.
>   Love, Kaeli] (cited p. 125)

In the letter she sent to Kaeli as a response, Patty wrote, in part, "I am glad you asked for help. This is a problem that we need to help each other with. We need to ask our friends and teachers and families for help so we can work together. . . . I think we should work on this problem in art class" (cited p. 126). As a result, when Kaeli's class came to the art room, she read her letter aloud. She also showed her classmates the book that was the basis for her letter to Patty. It was a book about the human body that had been published fairly recently by a prominent publishing house. Out of the many illustrations in the book, Kaeli found only a small number of pictures of Brown and Black people. When the students discussed why this might be a problem, Patty recounted:

> In their first-grade voices and six-year-old vocabulary, they
> discussed "fair" and "unfair," "discrimination," "stereotypes," and
> more. Through their dialogue, they decided—without my
> prompting—that it was OK for some books to exclusively depict
> Black people or Brown people or White people or others if it was
> a story about a specific family or event. But books that claimed to
> be about the "HUMAN BODY" or about "PEOPLE OF THE
> WORLD" needed to be much more balanced to pass the
> scrupulous eye of this first-grade class. (cited p. 127)

After engaging in a number of art activities—color theory, self-portraits, face shapes—the students discussed terminology and why some terms for people of different ethnic, racial, and social groups might be more appropriate than others. As a result of this discussion, the students concluded that "using words like *Black* or *African American*, *White* or *European American*, *Latino* or *Hispanic*, and *Asian* or *Chinese-American* were important decisions that required lots of thinking" (cited p. 127). Patty also gave the students examples of various books for analysis. At this point, the students decided that the publishers should receive some letters of information from them and some of their artwork to display good examples of fair pictures. Erika, one of the first-grade students, wrote the following letter, again in invented spelling:

> Dear publisher,
>   Make your books faire! And if you don't me and my famyuliy
> will never by or read your unfaire books. we want fairenes.
>
> From, Erika
>
> [Make your books fair! And if you don't, me and my family will
> never buy or read your unfair books. We want fairness.] (cited p. 128)

In a moving description of the impact of this kind of pedagogy and curriculum on students, Patty went on to describe what happened when she prepared a bulletin board around the theme of diversity in textbook representation:

> I filled the walls of the art room with photographs of children's
> faces. I spent a great deal of time choosing images of children to
> reflect the enormous variety of ethnicity and race that our
> society holds. One European American boy looked at the photo
> display and said, "Ms. Bode, you left out the White people."
> (cited p. 127)

Patty asked him to count the number of people he thought were of different backgrounds (an activity through which he realized that this was not always easy to do), and, to his surprise, he discovered that the bulletin board actually included many Whites. When Patty asked him why he had thought that European Americans were missing from the display, he answered "Maybe it's 'cuz I'm used to seeing more of them" (cited p. 128).

Patty's reflection ended with the following words:

> This unit proved to be a good reminder to me that it is the
> responsibility of the entire community to work for social justice.
> One individual or one group should not be burdened to fight for
> their rights in solitude nor exempt from the responsibility of
> democracy. It requires careful observation, attentive listening, and
> critical thought to facilitate sociopolitical consciousness effectively
> within a first-grade classroom. (cited pp. 128–129)

Experiences such as Patty Bode's reinforce the idea that critical multicultural education should not be reserved for the college classroom or just for classes in history or English. Even an art class for six-year-olds is fertile ground for planting the seeds of critical thinking and social justice. Other accounts of critical pedagogy in action, written mostly by classroom teachers, are contained in publications by Rethinking Schools (Bigelow, Christensen, Karp, Miner, & Peterson, 1994; Bigelow, Harvey, Karp, & Miller, 2001) and Teaching for Change (Lee et al., 1998; Menkart et al., 2004). Book-length accounts of critical pedagogy (Cowhey, 2006; Vasquez, 2004) provide compelling evidence that using critical pedagogy with the youngest students, even pre-school children, is both worthwhile and effective. In all these inspiring accounts, which discuss specific curricular and pedagogical innovations, critical pedagogy is the force behind student learning.

The People Most Intimately Connected with Teaching and Involved in School Reform

Research on involvement by families, students, and teachers has consistently indicated that democratic participation by people closest to learners can dramatically improve student learning. This is especially true in urban schools and in schools that serve poor, African American, Latino, and immigrant students (Epstein, 2001; Olsen, Jaramillo, McCall-Perez, White, & Minicucci, 1999). Yet these are the people most often excluded from discussions and implementation of school reform measures.

Cummins (1996) reviewed programs that included student empowerment as a goal and concluded that students who are encouraged to develop a positive cultural identity through interactions with their teachers experience a sense of control over their own lives and develop the confidence and motivation to succeed academically. School reform measures that stress the meaningful involvement of teachers, families, and students look quite different from traditional approaches. They begin with the assumption that these groups have substantial and insightful perspectives about student learning. Rather than thinking of ways to bypass their ideas, school reformers actively seek the involvement of students, families, and teachers in developing, for instance, disciplinary policies, curriculum development, and decisions concerning tracking and the use of tests. Similarly, allowing time in the curriculum for students to engage in critical discussions about issues such as whose language is valued in schools can help to affirm the legitimacy of the discourse of all students.

At the same time, these kinds of discussions also acknowledge the need to learn and become comfortable with the discourse of the larger society (Delpit, 1995). In addition, involving families in curriculum development enriches the curriculum, affirms what families have to offer, and helps students overcome the shame they may feel about their cultures, languages, and values, an all-too-common attitude for students from culturally subordinated groups (Nieto, 2004; Olsen, 1997).

School Reform Needs to Be Based on High Expectations and Rigorous Standards for All Learners

Many students cope on a daily basis with complex and difficult problems, including poverty, violence, racism, abuse, families in distress, and lack of health care and proper housing. In addition to such situations, many students come to school with experiences and conditions that some teachers and schools consider as placing them at risk for learning, including speaking a language other than English or simply belonging to a particular racial or ethnic group. But beginning with this perspective leaves teachers and schools with little hope. Rather than viewing language and cultural differences as impediments to learning, they can be viewed as resources that students bring to their education. In this way, instead of using these differences as a rationalization for low expectations of what students are capable of learning, they can be used to promote student learning. In addition, in our society we have generally expected schools to provide an equal and equitable education for all students, not just for those who have no problems in their lives or who fit the image of successful students due to race, class, or language ability. The promise of an equal education for all students of all backgrounds in the United States has yet to be realized, as is evident from a number of classic critiques of the myth of our schools as "the great equalizer" (Bowles & Gintis, 1976; Katz, 1975; Spring,

1989). Nevertheless, the ideal of equitable educational opportunity is worth defending and vigorously putting into practice.

It is undeniably true that many students face unimaginably difficult problems, and the school cannot be expected to solve them all. Neither can we dismiss the heroic efforts of many teachers and schools who, with limited financial and other material resources, teach students who live in dire circumstances under what can best be described as challenging conditions. Nevertheless, the difficult conditions in which some students live need not be viewed as insurmountable barriers to their academic achievement. It is too often the case that society's low expectations of students, based on these situations, pose even greater obstacles to their learning. For example, if students do not speak English, teachers may assume that they cannot learn; or if they do not have consistent experiences with or access to libraries, museums, or other cultural institutions considered essential for preparing students for schools, teachers may assume that these children are not even, to use the language of current reform efforts, "ready to learn."

If we are serious about giving all students more options in life, particularly students from communities denied the necessary resources with which to access these options, then we need to begin with the assumption that these students are academically capable, both individually and as a group. Too many students have been dismissed as uneducable simply because they were not born with the material resources or family conditions considered essential for learning. The conventional attitude that students who do not arrive at school with such benefits are incapable of learning is further promoted by assertions of race-based genetic inferiority, an assumption that is unfortunately still too prevalent (Herrnstein & Murray, 1994).

Numerous examples of dramatic success in the face of adversity are powerful reminders that great potential exists in all students. Consider, for example, the case of Garfield High School in East Los Angeles, California. Here, the mostly Mexican American students taught by Jaime Escalante, the protagonist of the popular film *Stand and Deliver*, were tremendously successful in learning advanced mathematics. In fact, when they took the Advanced Placement (AP) calculus test, they did so well that the test-makers assumed they had cheated. As a result, they had to take it a second time, and this time their performance was even better.

The success of the Algebra Project in Cambridge, Massachusetts, is another example. In this project, young people who had previously been denied access to algebra because they were thought to be incapable of benefiting from it became high achievers in math. When they went on to high school, 39 percent of the first graduating class of the project were placed in honors geometry or honors algebra classes; in fact, none of the graduates was placed in a lower-level math course. The Algebra Project has now spread to other school systems throughout the United States (Moses & Cobb, 2002).

Although students' identities are often perceived to be handicaps to learning by an assimilationist society that encourages cultural and linguistic homogeneity, numerous success stories of students who use their cultural values and traditions as strengths have been reported in the educational research literature (Lomawaima, 2005; Igoa, 1995; McCarty, 2002; Nieto, 2004; Soto, 1997; Zentella, 1997). This result leads us to the inevitable conclusion that before fixing what they may consider to be problems in students, schools and society need to change their own perceptions of students and view them as capable learners.

CONCLUSION

There is no simple formula for increasing student learning. A step-by-step blueprint for school reform is both unrealistic and inappropriate because each school differs from all others in its basic structure, goals, and human dimensions. Moreover, inequitable conditions such as school funding and the distribution of resources for learning also help explain why some students are successful and others are not. However, certain conditions can dramatically improve the learning of many students who are currently marginalized from the center of learning because of school policies and practices based on deficit models. If we begin with the assumptions that students cannot achieve at high levels, that their backgrounds are riddled with deficiencies, and that multicultural education is a frill that cannot help them to learn, we will end up with school reform strategies that have little hope for success.

This chapter presented and analyzed five conditions to promote student achievement within a multicultural perspective:

1. School reform should be antiracist and antibiased.
2. School reform should reflect an understanding and acceptance of all students as having talents and strengths that can enhance their education.
3. School reform should be considered within the parameters of critical pedagogy.
4. The people most intimately connected with teaching and learning (teachers, parents, and students themselves) need to be meaningfully involved in school reform.
5. School reform needs to be based on high expectations and rigorous standards for all learners.

This chapter is based on two related assumptions: (1) that students, families, and teachers bring strengths and talents to teaching and learning, and (2) that a comprehensive and critical approach to multicultural education can provide an important framework for rethinking school reform. Given these assumptions, we have a much more promising scenario for effective learning and for the possibility that schools can become places of hope and affirmation for students of all backgrounds and situations.

Questions and Activities

1. What does the author mean by "culturally responsive education"? Why does she think it is important? According to the author, is culturally responsive education sufficient to guarantee academic success for students of color and low-income students? Why or why not?

2. What does it mean to say that multicultural education takes place within a sociopolitical context? What social, political, and economic factors must be considered when multicultural education is being implemented? How can a consideration of sociopolitical factors help multicultural school reform to be more effective?

3. What five conditions does the author believe are needed to improve students' academic achievement? How are these factors interrelated?

4. How does the author distinguish *individual* and *institutional racism?* Why does she think this distinction is important? Give examples of each type of racism from your personal experiences and observations.

5. What is an antiracist perspective? Why does the author believe that an antiracist perspective is essential for the implementation of multicultural education? Give specific examples of antiracist teaching and educational practices with which you are familiar.

6. The author briefly describes Moll's concept of incorporating community knowledge into the curriculum. How does this concept help teachers to implement "culturally sensitive" teaching?

7. What is critical pedagogy? How, according to the author, can it be used to enrich and strengthen multicultural education?

8. What positive contributions can parents and students make to creating an effective multicultural school? Give specific examples.

References

Aptheker, H. (1987). *American Negro Slave Revolts.* New York: International Publishers. (Original work published 1943.)

Aronson, J., & Steele, C. M. (2005). Stereotypes and the Fragility of Academic Competence, Motivation, and Self-concept. In A. J. Elliott & C. S. Dweck (Eds.). *Handbook of Competence and Motivation* (pp. 436–456). New York: The Guilford Press.

Au, K. A., & Kawakami, A. J. (1994). Cultural Congruence in Instruction. In E. R. Hollins, J. E. King, & W. C. Hayman (Eds.), *Teaching Diverse Populations: Formulating a Knowledge Base* (pp. 5–24). New York: State University of New York Press.

Banks, J. A. (2003). *Teaching Strategies for Ethnic Studies* (7th ed.). Boston: Allyn & Bacon.

Bennett deMarrais, K., & LeCompte, M. G. (1999). *The Way Schools Work: A Sociological Analysis of Education* (3rd ed.). New York: Longman.

Beykont, Z. (Ed.). (2000). *Lifting Every Voice: Pedagogy and Politics of Bilingual Education.* Cambridge, MA: Harvard Educational Publishing Group.

Bigelow, B., Christensen, L., Karp, S., Miner, B., & Peterson, B. (Eds.). (1994). *Rethinking Our Classrooms: Teaching for Equity and Justice* (Vol. 1). Milwaukee, WI: Rethinking Schools.

Bigelow, B., Harvey, B., Karp, S., & Miller, L. (Eds.). (2001). *Rethinking Our Classrooms: Teaching for Equity and Justice* (Vol. 2). Milwaukee, WI: Rethinking Schools.

Bowles, S., & Gintis, H. (1976). *Schooling in Capitalist America: Educational Reform and the Contradictions of Economic Life.* New York: Basic Books.

Bryk, A. S., Lee, V. E., & Holland, P. B. (1993). *Catholic Schools and the Common Good.* Cambridge, MA: Harvard Educational Review.

Cowhey, M. (2006). *Black Ants and Buddhists.* Portland, ME: Stenhouse Publishers.

Cummins, J. (1996). *Negotiating Identities: Education for Empowerment in a Diverse Society.* Ontario, CA: California Association for Bilingual Education.

Delpit, L. (1995). *Other People's Children: Cultural Conflict in the Classroom.* New York: New Press.

Donaldson, K. (1996). *Through Students' Eyes*. New York: Bergin & Garvey.

Epstein, J. L. (2001). *School, Family, and Community Partnerships: Preparing Educators and Improving Schools*. Boulder, CO: Westview.

Fine, M. (1991). *Framing Dropouts: Notes on the Politics of an Urban Public High School*. Albany: State University of New York Press.

Frau-Ramos, M., & Nieto, S. (1993). "I Was an Outsider": An Exploratory Study of Dropping Out among Puerto Rican Youths in Holyoke, Massachusetts. In R. Rivera & S. Nieto (Eds.), *The Education of Latino Students in Massachusetts: Issues, Research, and Policy Implications* (pp. 147–169). Boston: Gastón Institute.

Freire, P. (1970). *Pedagogy of the Oppressed*. New York: Seabury.

Freire, P. (1985). *The Politics of Education: Culture, Power, and Liberation*. South Hadley, MA: Bergin & Garvey.

Gay, G. (2000). *Culturally Responsive Teaching: Theory, Research, and Practice*. New York: Teachers College Press.

Gebhard, M., Austin, T., Nieto, S., & Willett, J. (2002). "You Can't Step on Someone Else's Words": Preparing All Teachers to Teach Language Minority Students. In Z. Beykont (Ed.), *The Power of Culture: Teaching across Language Difference* (pp. 219–243). Cambridge, MA: Harvard Educational Publishing Group.

Gonzalez, N., Moll, L. C., & Amanti, C. (Eds.) (2005). *Funds of Knowledge: Theorizing Practices in Households and Classrooms*. Mahwah, NJ: Lawrence.

Harris, V. J. (Ed.). (1997). *Using Multiethnic Literature in the K–8 Classroom*. Norwood, MA: Christopher-Gordon.

Herrnstein, R. J., & Murray, C. (1994). *The Bell Curve: Intelligence and Class Structure in American Life*. New York: Free Press.

Howard, G. (1999). *We Can't Teach What We Don't Know: White Teachers, Multiracial Schools*. New York: Teachers College Press.

Igoa, C. (1995). *The Inner World of the Immigrant Child*. Mahwah NJ: Erlbaum.

Irvine, J. J. (2003). *Educating Teachers for Diversity: Seeing with a Cultural Eye*. New York: Teachers College Press.

Irvine, J. J., & Foster, M. (Eds.). (1996). *Growing up African American in Catholic Schools*. New York: Teachers College Press.

Katz, M. B. (1975). *Class, Bureaucracy, and the Schools: The Illusion of Educational Change in America*. New York: Praeger.

Kohl, H. (2005). *She Would Not Be Moved: How We Tell the Story of Rosa Parks and the Montgomery Bus Boycott*. New York: New Press.

Kohn, A. (2000). *The Case against Standardized Testing: Raising the Scores, Ruining the Schools*. Portsmouth, NH: Heinemann.

Kozol, J. (1975, December). Great Men and Women (Tailored for School Use). *Learning Magazine*, pp. 16–20.

Kozol, J. (1991). *Savage Inequalities: Children in America's Schools*. New York: Crown.

Kozol, J. (2005). *The Shame of the Nation: The Restoration of Apartheid Schooling in America*. New York: Crown Publishers.

Ladson-Billings, G. (1994). *The Dreamkeepers: Successful Teachers of African American Children*. San Francisco: Jossey-Bass.

Ladson-Billings, G. (2001). *Crossing over to Canaan: The Journey of New Teachers in Diverse Classrooms.* San Francisco: Jossey-Bass.

Landsman, J. (2001). *A White Teacher Talks about Race.* Lanham, MD: Scarecrow.

Lee, E., Menkart, D., & Okazawa-Rey, M. (1998). *Beyond Heroes and Holidays: A Practical Guide to K–12 Anti-Racist, Multicultural Education and Staff Development.* Washington, DC: Teaching for Change.

Lee, V. E., & Loeb, S. (2000). School Size in Chicago Elementary Schools: Effects on Teachers' Attitudes and Students' Achievement. *American Educational Research Journal, 37,* 3–31.

Levin, M. (2001) *"Teach Me!" Kids Will Learn When Oppression Is the Lesson.* Lanham, MD: Rowman & Littlefield.

Loewen, J. W. (1995). *Lies My Teacher Taught Me: Everything Your American History Textbook Got Wrong.* New York: Free Press.

Loewen, J. W. (2000). *Lies across America: What Our Historic Sites Got Wrong.* New York: New Press.

Lomawaima, K. T. (2005). Educating Native Americans. In J. A. Banks & C. A. M. Banks (Eds.) *Handbook of Research on Multicultural Education.* (2nd ed., pp. 441–461). San Francisco: Jossey-Bass Publishers.

McCarty, T. L. (2002). *A Place to Be Navajo: Rough Rock and the Struggle for Self-Determination in Indigenous Schooling.* Mahwah, NJ: Erlbaum.

McNeil, L. (2000). *Contradictions of School Reform: Educational Costs of Standardized Testing.* New York: Routledge.

Meier, K. J., & Stewart, J., Jr. (1991). *The Politics of Hispanic Education: Un Paso Pálante y Dos Pátras.* Albany: State University of New York Press.

Menkart, D., Murray, A. D., & View, J. (2004). *Putting the Movement Back into Civil Rights Teaching.* Washington, DC: Teaching for Change.

Morrell, E. (2004). *Becoming Critical Researchers: Literacy and Empowerment for Urban Youth.* New York: Peter Lang.

Moses, R. P., & Cobb, C. E. (2002). *Radical Equations: Math Literacy and Civil Rights.* Boston: Beacon.

Mosteller, F. (1995). The Tennessee Study of Class Size in the Early School Grades. *The Future of Children, 5*(2), 113–127.

National Center for Education Statistics. (2000). *Trends in Disparities in School District Level Expenditures per Pupil.* Washington, DC: U.S. Department of Education, Office of Educational Research and Improvement.

National Commission on Excellence in Education. (1983). *A Nation at Risk: The Imperative for Educational Reform.* Washington, DC: Author.

Nieto, S. (1994). Lessons from Students on Creating a Chance to Dream. *Harvard Educational Review, 64*(4), 392–426.

Nieto, S. (1999). *The Light in Their Eyes: Creating Multicultural Learning Communities.* New York: Teachers College Press.

Nieto, S. (2002/2003). Profoundly Multicultural Questions. *Educational Leadership, 60*(4), 6–10.

Nieto, S. (2004). *Affirming Diversity: The Sociopolitical Context of Multicultural Education* (4th ed.). Boston: Allyn & Bacon.

Oakes, J. (2005). *Keeping Track: How Schools Structure Inequality.* (2nd ed.). New Haven: Yale University Press.

Ogbu, J. U. (1994). Racial Stratification and Education in the United States: Why Inequality Persists. *Teachers College Record, 96*(2), 264–298.

Olsen, L. (1997). *Made in America: Immigrant Students in Our Public Schools.* New York: New Press.

Olsen, L., Jaramillo, A., McCall-Perez, Z., White, J., & Minicucci, C. (1999). *Igniting Change for Immigrant Students: Portraits of Three High Schools.* Oakland, CA: California Tomorrow.

Orfield, G. (2001). *Schools More Separate: Consequences of a Decade of Resegregation.* Cambridge, MA: Harvard Civil Rights Project.

Orfield, G., & Kornhaber, M. L. (Eds.). (2001). *Raising Standards or Raising Barriers? Inequality and High-Stakes Testing in Public Education.* New York: Century Foundation Press.

Peterson, R. E. (1991). Teaching How to Read the World and Change It: Critical Pedagogy in the Intermediate Grades. In C. E. Walsh (Ed.), *Literacy as Praxis: Culture, Language, and Pedagogy* (pp. 156–182). Norwood, NJ: Ablex.

Pollock, M. (2004). *Colormute: Race Talk Dilemmas in an American School.* Princeton, NJ: Princeton University Press.

Reissman, F. (1962). *The Culturally Deprived Child.* New York: Harper & Row.

Reyes, M. de la Luz, & Halcón, J. J. (Eds.) (2001). *The Best for Our Children: Critical Perspectives on Literacy for Latino Students.* New York: Teachers College Press.

Ryan, W. (1972). *Blaming the Victim.* New York: Vintage.

Shor, I. (1992). *Empowering Education: Critical Teaching for Social Change.* Chicago: University of Chicago Press.

Sleeter, C. E. (1994). White Racism. *Multicultural Education, 1*(4), 5–8, 39.

Sleeter, C. E., & Delgado Bernal, D. (2004). Critical Pedagogy, Critical Race Theory, and Antiracist Education: Implications for Multicultural Education. In J. A. Banks & C. A. M. Banks (Eds). *Handbook of Research on Multicultural Education* (2nd ed., pp. 240–258). San Francisco: Jossey-Bass Publishers.

Snow, C. (1997). The Myths around Bilingual Education. *NABE News, 21*(2), 29.

Soto, L. D. (1997). *Language, Culture, and Power: Bilingual Families and the Struggle for Quality Education.* Albany: State University of New York Press.

Spring, J. (1989). *The Sorting Machine Revisited: National Educational Policy Since 1945.* White Plains, NY: Longman.

Spring, J. (2002). *American Education* (10th ed.). Boston: McGraw-Hill.

Steele, C. M. (1999). Thin Ice: "Stereotype Threat" and Black College Students. *The Atlantic Monthly, 284*(2), 44–54.

Takaki, R. (1993). *A Different Mirror: A History of Multicultural America.* Boston: Little, Brown.

Tatum, B. D. (2003). *"Why Are All the Black Kids Sitting Together in the Cafeteria?" and Other Conversations about Race* (Rev. ed.). New York: Basic Books.

Vasquez, V. M. (2004). Negotiating Critical Literacies with Young Children.

Weinberg, M. (1990). *Racism in the United States: A Comprehensive Classified Bibliography.* Westport, CT: Greenwood.

Willis, A. (Ed.). (1998). *Teaching and Using Multicultural Literature in Grades 9–12: Moving beyond the Canon.* Norwood, MA: Christopher-Gordon.

Zentella, A. C. (1997). *Growing up Bilingual: Puerto Rican Children in New York.* Malden, MA: Blackwell.

Zinn, H. (2003). *A People's History of the United States: 1492–Present* (Rev. ed.). New York: HarperCollins.

CHAPTER 17

Communities, Families, and Educators Working Together for School Improvement

Cherry A. McGee Banks

The diversity of parent and community groups, with their different concerns and issues, illustrates one of the important complexities of parent and community involvement in schools (De Carvalho, 2001). That complexity, which may be reflected in different interaction styles, expectations, and concerns, complicates but does not negate the need for parent and community involvement in schools (DeSteno, 2000). Educators lose an important voice for school improvement when parents and community groups are not involved in schools. They can give teachers unique and important views of their students as well as help the school garner resources that are available in the community.

In a comprehensive review of research on parent involvement, Henderson and Berla (1994) found compelling evidence that parent involvement improves student achievement. Parent involvement is also associated with improvements in students' attendance and social behavior. However, to capitalize on the benefits of parent and community involvement, strategies must be broadly conceptualized. Parents should be given an opportunity to contribute to school improvement by working in different settings and at different levels of the educational process (Hidalgo, et al., 2004; Mannan & Blackwell, 1992). For example, some parents may want to focus their energies on working with their own children at home. Other parents may want to work on decision-making committees. Still others may be able to provide in-class assistance to teachers. Joyce L. Epstein (2002) and her colleagues have identified six different types of involvement: (1) parenting, (2) communicating, (3) volunteering, (4) learning at home, (5) decision making, and (6) collaborating with the community. Though very different, each type of involvement provides opportunities for parents to have a positive influence on their students' school experience.

Parents, other family members, and community groups can also work with teachers to reform schools. Many tasks involved in restructuring schools, such as setting goals and allocating resources, are best achieved through a collaborative problem-solving structure that includes parents, educators, and family and community members (Mannan & Blackwell, 1992).

Family and community members can form what Goodlad (1984) calls "the necessary coalition of contributing groups" (p. 293). Educational reform needs their support, influence, and activism. Schools are highly dependent on and vulnerable to citizens who can support or impede change. Family members and community leaders can validate the need for educational reform and can provide an appropriate forum for exploring the importance of education. They can also extend the discussion on school improvement issues beyond formal educational networks and can help generate support for schools in the community at large. Family members and community leaders can help provide the rationale, motivation, and social action necessary for educational reform.

WHY IS PARENT AND FAMILY INVOLVEMENT IN SCHOOLS IMPORTANT?

Parent involvement is important because it acknowledges the importance of parents in the lives of their children, recognizes the diversity of values and perspectives within the community, provides a vehicle for building a collaborative problem-solving structure, and increases the opportunity for all students to learn in school. Parents, however, are not the only adults who support and contribute to the care of children.

When parents struggle with poverty, incarceration, substance abuse, mental illness, and other challenges, grandparents and other relatives often become the children's primary caregivers (McCallion, Janicki, & Kolomer, 2005). In 2000, 4.5 million children under 18 lived in grandparent-headed households. There was a 29.7 percent increase from 1990 in the number of grandchildren in grandparent-headed households. Neither of the parents was present in one-third of these families.

The trend of grandparents caring for grandchildren is continuing, and grandparent-headed households are one of the fastest growing demographic groups in the United States. In 2001, about 9 percent of all U.S. children lived with at least one grandparent. Almost 1.4 million of the children were living with a grandparent with no parent present (Kreider and Fields, 2005). About half of the grandparent caregivers were two-grandparent families. Grandmothers headed the other 45 percent of the families (Kleiner, Hertzog, & Targ, 2005). Some of the grandparents were elderly with a number of health complications, but in 1997 55 percent were under 55 years old and 19 percent were younger than 45 (Casper & Bryson, 1998) of grandparents caring for grandchildren in all ethnic and income groups. In 2000, about one-third of the children living in their grandparents' homes do not have parents living with them (U.S. Bureau of the Census, 2000).

Students, parents, and teachers all benefit when parents and family members are involved in schools (Comer, Ben-Avie, Haynes, & Joyner, 1999). When parents help their children at home, the children perform better in school (Booth & Dunn, 1996).

Parent involvement allows parents and teachers to reinforce skills and provides an environment that has consistent learning expectations and standards. Parents also become more knowledgeable about their child's school, its policies, and the school staff when they are involved in schools. Perhaps most important, parent involvement provides an opportunity for parents and children to spend time together. During that time, parents can communicate a high value for education, the importance of effort in achievement, and a high positive regard for their children.

Parents and family members are often children's first and most important teachers. Students come to school with knowledge, values, and beliefs they have learned from their parents and in their communities. Parents directly or indirectly help shape their children's value system, orientation toward learning, and view of the world (Stratton, 1995). Most parents want their children to succeed in school. Schools can capitalize on the high value most parents put on education by working to create a school environment that respects the students' home and community (Hidalgo, Sau-Fong, & Epstein, 2004). When schools are in conflict with their students' home and community, they can alienate students from their families and communities.

To create harmonious relations among the school, home, and community, parents need information about the school. They need to know what the school expects their children to learn, how they will be taught, and the required books and materials their children will use in school. Most important, parents need to know how teachers assess students and how they can support their children's achievement. Teachers need to understand their students' community and home life. Teachers also need to know about their students' parents, homes, and communities. It would be helpful for teachers to have a clear understanding of the educational expectations parents have for their children, the languages spoken at home, the family's values and norms, and how children are taught in their homes and communities.

Teachers and principals who know parents treat them with greater respect and show more positive attitudes toward their children (Berger, 2003). Teachers generally see involved parents as concerned individuals who support the school. Parents who are not involved in schools are frequently seen as parents who do not value education.

While it is important for parents and teachers to have open lines of communication, good communication does not necessarily eliminate tensions between home and school. Tensions can, for example, occur when teachers are required to teach something that parents think is inappropriate for their student. In years past, sex education has been a topic of concern for some parents. Today, concerns are often centered on science curricula and evolution versus intelligent design. Intelligent design is a concept that explains that an intelligent cause—not natural selection—best explains certain features of the universe and living things. Some parents have strongly expressed their concerns about teaching intelligent design in science classes alongside evolution, while others have argued very strongly that intelligent design belongs in the science curriculum (Milner & Maestro, 2002). In situations such as this, teachers should respectfully listen to parents' concerns and then explain the school's rules and regulations regarding the issue. If the parents pursue the matter, tell them whom to contact to express their concerns.

HISTORICAL OVERVIEW

While parent involvement in education is not new, its importance and purpose have varied over time. In the early part of the nation's history, families were often solely responsible for educating children. Children learned values and skills by working with their families in their communities.

When formal systems of education were established, parents continued to influence their children's education. During the colonial period, schools were viewed as an extension of the home. Parental and community values and expectations were reinforced in the school. Teachers generally came from the community and often personally knew their students' parents and shared their values.

At the beginning of the twentieth century, when large numbers of immigrants came to the United States, schools became a major vehicle for assimilating immigrant children into U.S. society (Banks, 2003). In general, immigrant parents were not welcomed in schools. Children of immigrants were taught that their parents' ways of speaking, behaving, and thinking were inferior to those of mainstream Americans. In his study of the sociology of teaching, Waller (1932/1965) concluded that parents and teachers lived in a state of mutual distrust and even hostility. There were, however, some notable exceptions.

One such exception was Benjamin Franklin High School (BFHS) in East Harlem, New York. Leonard Covello, principal at BFHS, instituted a program of intergroup education at Franklin in the 1930s. Parents were welcome at Franklin, and teachers encouraged students to appreciate their parents' language, values, and customs. Community groups were also actively involved at BFHS. Covello saw parent and community involvement as a way to promote democratic values, reduce prejudice, and increase cross-cultural understanding and appreciation (Banks, 2005).

As society changed and education became more removed from the direct influence of parents, responsibility for transmitting knowledge from generation to generation was transferred from the home and community to the school. Formal education was seen as a job for trained professionals. Schools became autonomous institutions staffed by people who were often strangers in their students' home communities. Teachers did not necessarily live in their students' neighborhoods, know the students' parents, or share their values. Schools were given more and more duties that traditionally had been the responsibility of the home and community. Schools operated under the assumption of *in loco parentis*, and educators were asked to assume the role of both teacher and substitute parent.

In a pluralist society, what the school teaches as well as whom and how the school teaches can create tensions between parents and schools. Issues ranging from what the school teaches about the role of women in our society to mainstreaming students with disabilities point to the need for teachers, parents, and community leaders to work together (Schneider & Coleman, 1996). However, parents, community leaders, and teachers do not always agree on meaningful ways to cooperate and partner in the educational process (Cibulka & Kritek, 1996).

THE CHANGING FACE OF THE FAMILY

Parent/family diversity mirrors student diversity. As the student population becomes more diverse, parent/family diversity also increases. Involving parents in schools means that teachers have to be prepared to work with a range of parents, including single parents, parents with special needs, low-income parents, parents with disabilities, and parents who do not speak English as their first language. Working with parents from diverse backgrounds requires sensitivity to and an understanding of their circumstances and worldviews (Chavkin & Gonzalez, 1995; Kagan, 1995; Pena, 2000; Schneider & Coleman, 1996).

It is especially important that teachers be sensitive to and understand the changing nature of the ethnic and racial makeup of their students and their students' parents. The ethnic landscape of U.S. schools includes an increasing number of Arab, Jewish, Eastern European, and African students (McFalls, 2003). African Americans constituted 8 percent of the nation's total foreign-born population in 1999. In 2000, about 80 percent of the African American foreign-born population came from Latin America, and about 63 percent of that number came from the Caribbean (U.S. Bureau of the Census, 2000). For many of these individuals, their ethnic identity has primacy over their racial identity. Such individuals, for example, would identify themselves as Cuban Americans or Puerto Ricans, not as Blacks or Whites. Their phenotype, however, might conflict with physical characteristics that traditionally have been used to identify races in the United States. For example, a Cuban American with brown skin may consider himself White.

The lines between racial groups are becoming blurred. A growing number of students and parents are members of more than one racial group. Even though marriage between people from different races is still an exception rather than the rule, more and more people are marrying interracially. As a result, the number of students with parents or grandparents of different races is increasing. In 2000, about 2.4 percent of the U.S. population, or about 6.8 million people, identified with two or more races (U.S. Census Bureau, 2000). While this is a relatively small percentage of the U.S. population, the percentage of people who are multiracial is more salient when geographic regions and subgroups within the population are examined. For example, children are more likely to be multiracial than adults, and racial groups that have small populations tend to include higher percentages of multiracial people. Additionally, urban areas tend to have higher rates of interracial marriage than rural areas. In 2000, about 1.9 percent of U.S. adults identified themselves as multiracial compared to 4.0 percent of children.

Among all the racial groups, American Indians were the most likely to marry someone outside their racial group (Pollard & O'Hare, 1999). Data from the 2000 census indicate that approximately 40 percent of American Indians are multiracial. Asians also tend to marry at a high rate outside their racial group; consequently, a growing number of Asians are multiracial. The 2000 census indicates that about 14 percent of Asians report that they are multiracial, compared to 5 percent of Blacks and 3 percent of Whites (Lee, 2001). About 52 percent of the total number of the multiracial Asians are Asian and White. Historically this population has been referred to as Amerasians and associated with the interracial marriages of service personnel stationed in Asian countries after WWII and the Vietnam War. Today the term "Hapa," a Hawaiian term meaning half White and half Hawaiian, is frequently used to refer to Asians of mixed-race ancestry (Krebs, 2000).

The increase in interracial marriage has resulted in an increase of interracial children. Between 1977 and 1997, the number of babies born to interracial couples increased from less than 2 percent of the total births to about 5 percent. In 1997, interracial births were the third-largest racial or ethnic category of U.S. births. In California, the number of interracial births surpassed Asian, Black, and American Indian births. Of all the ethnic and racial groups, interracial births were highest for American Indians. Approximately 50 percent of American Indians born in 1997 were biracial. About 20 percent of births to Asian women and 5 percent of births to African American women were biracial (Pollard & O'Hare, 1999). Also adding to the increasing number of interracial families are the growing number of children adopted from other countries. Foreign-born children, usually Asian, are being adopted by American families, usually White families, in growing numbers. In 2000, immigration visas were issued to 5,053 orphans from China, 4,269 orphans from Russia, and 1,794 orphans from South Korea. The vast majority of the adoptees are girls (Lee, 2001).

Diversity in parent and community groups can be a tremendous asset to the school. However, it can also be a source of potential conflicts and tensions. Some parents are particularly difficult to involve in their children's education. They resist becoming involved for several reasons (Harry, 1992; Walker, 1996). In a national survey, parents indicated that a lack of time was the primary reason they were not involved in their children's schools (Clark, 1995). The pressures to earn a living and take care of a home and children can result in a great deal of stress. At the end of the day, some parents just want to rest. Other parents do not believe they have the necessary educational background to be involved in their children's school. They feel intimidated by educators and believe that education should be left to teachers. Still others feel alienated from their children's schools because of negative experiences they had in school or because they believe the school does not support their values (Berger, 2003; Clark, 1995; Rasinski, 1990).

Three groups of parents are frequently underrepresented in school activities: parents with special needs, single parents, and low-income parents. These are not the only groups that are underrepresented in school activities; however, their experiences and needs illustrate particular problem areas. The specific groups of parents discussed should not be viewed as an indication that only parents from these groups are difficult to involve in schools or that all parents from these groups resist participation in schools. Parents from all groups share many of the concerns discussed below. Moreover, there are examples of parents from each of the groups discussed below who are actively involved in schools.

Parents with Special Needs

Parents with special needs include a wide range of individuals. They are found in all ethnic, racial, and income groups. Chronically unemployed parents, parents with long-term illnesses, abusive parents, and parents with substance abuse problems are examples of parents with special needs. Abusive parents require special attention from the school. Most schools have policies on how to treat suspected cases of child neglect and abuse. The policies should be written and available to all school personnel. All states require schools to report suspected cases of child abuse.

Although parents with special needs frequently have serious problems that the school cannot address, teachers should not ignore the importance of understanding their students' home environments. Knowing the difficulties students are coping with at home can help teachers create school environments that are supportive (Swadener & Niles, 1991). Schools can help compensate for the difficult circumstances students experience at home. The school, for some students, is the only place during the day where they are nurtured.

Working with special-needs families requires district or building support in identifying places for family referrals and support for students and teachers. Some schools hire outreach community service workers to provide these kinds of services. Although some special-needs parents may resist the school's help, they need to know that their problems can negatively affect their children's success in school. Referring these parents to places where they can receive help can show students who are in difficult home environments that they are not alone. Most parents want to feel that they are valued and adequate human beings and that they can help their children succeed. When they are willing to be involved in school, they do not want to be humiliated (Berger, 2003).

Some parents with special needs will be able to be actively involved in schools, but many will be unable to sustain ongoing involvement. An important goal for working with parents with special needs is to keep lines of communication open. To the extent possible try to get to know the parents. Do not accept a stereotypical view of them without ever talking to them. Encourage parents to become involved whenever and however they feel they are able to participate. Your goal should be to develop a clear understanding of your student's home environment so that you can provide appropriate intervention at school.

Members of the community who are involved in school may be willing to serve as intermediaries between the school and uninvolved parents and in some cases as surrogate parents. In an ethnography of an inner-city neighborhood, Shariff (1988) found that adults shared goods and services and provided support for each other. Educators can build on the sense of extended family and fictive kinship that may exist in some neighborhoods to connect with community support groups for students whose parents cannot be involved in school.

Working with students whose parents have special needs is complicated and challenging. However, regardless of the circumstances students confront at home, teachers have a responsibility to help them perform at their highest level at school. Schools with large numbers of parents with special needs require experienced and highly qualified teachers who have district and school support to help them meet the additional challenges that they will face. Traditionally, however, these schools have many teachers who are relatively new to the field and are not certified in the areas in which they teach (Darling-Hammond, 2004).

Single Parents

One of the most significant social changes in the United States in the last 30 years is the increase in the percentage of children living with one parent. In 2003, 32 percent of U.S. households with children under 18 were headed by a single parent. The number of single-parent families is particularly significant in the African American community. In 2003, 62 percent of African American families with children under eighteen were headed by one parent (U.S. Census Bureau, 2003). Almost 27 percent of White and 35 percent of Hispanic families with children under 18 were headed by one parent (U.S. Census Bureau, 1998). Most children who live with one parent are from divorced homes or are the children of unwed mothers. In 2003, approximately 50 percent of all new marriages in the United States ended in divorce (National Vital Statistical Reports, 2004). First marriages that end in divorce last an average of seven to eight years. In 2000, only 51.7 percent of U.S. households contained a married couple. This was down from 55 percent in 1990, 60.8 percent in 1980, 70.5 percent in 1970, and 78 percent in 1950 (U.S. Census, 2000).

Single-parent families have many of the same hopes, joys, and concerns about their children's education as two-parent families. However, because these parents have a lower rate of attendance at school functions, they are frequently viewed as not supporting their children's education. When teachers respond sensitively to their needs and limitations, they can be enthusiastic partners with teachers. Four suggestions for working with single parents are listed below. Many of these suggestions apply to other groups of parents as well.

1. Provide flexible times for conferences, such as early mornings, evenings, and weekends.
2. Provide baby-sitting service when activities are held at the school.

3. Work out procedures for acknowledging and communicating with noncustodial parents. For instance, under what circumstances are noncustodial parents informed about their children's grades, school behavior, or attendance? Problems can occur when information is inappropriately given to or withheld from a noncustodial parent.

4. Use the parent's correct surname. Students will sometimes have different names from their parents.

Low-Income Parents

The poverty rate in the United States was 12.7 percent in 2004, with 37 million people living in poverty. The number of people living below the poverty line increased by 1.1 million from 2003 to 2004. The poverty rate for children under 18 years old was 17.8 percent in 2004. The poverty level is an official governmental estimate of the income necessary to maintain a minimally acceptable standard of living. Poverty rates vary by family type. Households headed by single women have the highest poverty rate, at 28.6 percent. The poverty rate for married couples is 5.7 percent (Proctor & Dalaker, 2002). A family of four in 2000 with a total income less than $18,104 was considered to be living below the poverty line (Proctor & Dalaker, 2002).

Even though the number of individuals of color in the highest income brackets has more than doubled since 1980, race continues to be a salient factor in poverty. The poverty rate in 2002 was 8 percent for non-Hispanic Whites, 23.9 percent for African Americans, and 10 percent for Asians and Pacific Islanders. Most minorities earn less than Whites. However, Asians males earn more than all other groups. In 2004, their median income was $46,888 per year, compared to $45,573 per year for non-Hispanic White males, $26,749 for Hispanics, and $32,686 for Blacks (Fronczek, 2005).

Low-income parents are often among the strongest supporters of education, because they often see it as a means to a better life for their children. However, their definition and understanding of "support for education" may be different from that of the school staff. Additionally, they are often limited in their ability to buy materials and to make financial commitments that can enable their children to participate in activities such as field trips or extracurricular programs. Schools can provide workbooks and other study materials for use at home as well as transportation for school activities and conferences. The school can also support low-income parents by establishing community service programs. For example, students can help clean up neighborhoods and distribute information on available social services. The schools can provide desk space for voter registration and other services.

Perhaps the most important way for schools to work with low-income parents is to recognize that they can contribute a great deal to their children's education. Even though their contributions may not be in the manner traditionally associated with parent involvement, they can be very beneficial to teachers and students. The positive values and attitudes parents communicate to their children and their strong desire for their children to get a good education in order to have a better chance in life than they had are important forms of support for the school.

TEACHER CONCERNS WITH PARENT AND FAMILY INVOLVEMENT

Even though teachers often say they want to involve parents, they may be suspicious of parents and are not sure what parents expect from them. Some teachers think parents may disrupt their routine, may not have the necessary skills to work with students, may be inconvenient to have in the classroom, and may be interested only in helping their own child, not the total class. Even teachers who would like to involve parents may not be sure that they have the time, skill, or knowledge to involve parents in the school. Many teachers believe that they already have too much to do and that working with parents would make their already-overburdened jobs impossible.

Many of these concerns derive from a limited view of the possibilities for parent involvement. Frequently, when parents and teachers think of parent involvement, they think it means doing something for the school generally at the school or having the school teach parents how to become better parents. In today's ever-changing society, a traditional view of parent involvement inhibits rather than encourages parents and teachers to work together. Traditional ideas about parent involvement have a built-in gender and social-class bias and can be a barrier to many men and low-income parents. Moreover, they tend to focus on parents, not on community groups. With a national focus on education, more and more community groups are interested in working with schools. It is not uncommon for schools to have corporate or community sponsors. While these are generally supportive and cooperative relationships, they can be time consuming and present new challenges for schools. More consideration will need to be given to how to work effectively with community groups. Educators will need to think carefully about how to involve these groups in schools, their expectations for the relationship, and how the goals they established will be evaluated.

When parent involvement is viewed as a means of getting support for the school, parents are encouraged to bake cookies, raise money, or work at the school as unpaid classroom, playground, library, or office helpers. This form of parent involvement is generally directed to mothers who do not work outside the home. However, the number of mothers available for this form of involvement is decreasing. In 2003, 63 percent of women with children under six years old worked outside the home (Bureau of Labor Statistics, 2003).

The parent-as-helper idea is geared toward parents who have the skills, time, and resources to become school helpers. Not all parents want to or feel they can or should do things for the school. Whether parents are willing to come to school is largely dependent on the parent's attitude toward school. This attitude results in part from the parent's own school experiences.

Cultural perspectives also play an important role in the traditional approach to parent involvement. Bullivant (1993) points out the importance of understanding a social group's cultural program. To be effective, strategies for parent and community involvement should reflect what Bullivant calls the core of the social group's cultural program, which consists of the knowledge and conceptions embodied in the group's behaviors and artifacts and the values subscribed to by the group.

When teachers do not understand a group's cultural program, they may conceptualize parent involvement as a means to help deficient parents become better parents (Linn, 1990). This view of parent involvement is often directed toward culturally different and low-income parents (Jennings, 1990). Teachers are presented as more skilled in parenting than parents. Instead of helping parents and teachers work cooperatively, this attitude can create barriers by suggesting that parents are the cause of their children's failure in school. Parents and teachers may even become rivals for the child's affection (Lightfoot, 1978).

Involvement efforts based on "the parent in need of parenting skills" assume that there is one appropriate way to parent and that parents want to learn it. Both "the parent as helper" and "the parent in need of parenting skills" are conceptualizations derived from questionable assumptions about the character of contemporary parents and reflect a limited cultural perspective.

STEPS TO INCREASE PARENT AND FAMILY INVOLVEMENT

Teachers are a key ingredient in parent and family involvement. They play multiple roles, including facilitator, communicator, and resource developer. Their success in implementing an effective parent/community involvement program is linked to their skill in communicating and working with parents and community groups. Teacher attitudes are also very important. Parents are supportive of the teachers they believe like their children and want their children to succeed. Teachers who have a negative attitude toward students will likely have a similar attitude toward the students' parents. Teachers tend to relate to their students as representatives of their parents' perceived status in society. Teachers use such characteristics as class, race, gender, and ethnicity to determine students' prescribed social category. Being aware of this tendency can help teachers guard against it.

There are five steps you can take to increase parent/community involvement in your classroom: (1) establish two-way communication, (2) enlist support from staff and students, (3) enlist support from the community, (4) develop resource materials for home use, and (5) broaden the activities included in parent involvement.

Establish Two-Way Communication between the School and the Home

Establishing two-way communication between the school and the home is an important step in involving parents (Decker & Majerczyk, 2000). Most parents are willing to become involved in their children's education if they understand what you are trying to accomplish and how they can help. Teachers should be prepared to engage in outreach to parents and not to wait for them to become involved. Actively solicit information from parents on their thoughts about classroom goals and activities. When you talk with parents and community members, be an active listener. Listen for their feelings as well as for specific information. Listed next are seven ways you can establish and maintain two-way communication with parents and community members.

1. If possible, have an open-door policy in your classroom. Let parents know they are welcome to assist in your classroom. When parents visit, make sure they have something to do.

2. Send written information home about school assignments and goals so that parents are aware of what is going on in the classroom. Encourage parents to send notes to you if they have questions or concerns.

3. Talk to parents by phone. Let parents know when they can reach you by phone. Call parents periodically and let them know when things are going well. Have something specific to talk about. Leave some time for the parent to ask questions or make comments.

4. Report problems to parents, such as failing grades and behavior problems, before it is too late for them to take remedial action. Let parents know what improvements you expect from their children and how they can help.

5. Get to know your students' community. Take time to shop in their neighborhoods. Visit community centers and attend religious services. Let parents know when you will be in the community and that you are interested in talking to them.

6. If you teach in an elementary school, try to have at least two in-person conferences a year with parents. When possible, include the student in at least part of the conference. Be prepared to explain your curriculum to parents and have books and materials that students use available for them to examine. Let the parents know in specific terms how their children are doing in class. Find out how parents feel about their children's levels of achievement, and let them know what you think about their children's achievement levels. Give the parents some suggestions on what their children can do to improve and how they can help.

7. Solicit information from parents about their views on education. Identify their educational goals for their children, ways they would like to support their children's education, and their concerns about the school. There are a number of ways to get information from parents, including sending a questionnaire home and asking parents to complete it and return it to you, conducting a telephone survey, and asking your students to interview their parents. Don't forget high-tech solutions for staying in touch with parents. These include school web pages, homework hotlines, e-mail correspondence, videotaped events, and televised meetings. Be sure to work with local libraries to make sure that parents who do not own computers will be able to use computers in the library to access the information.

Enlist Support from Other Staff Members and Students

Teachers need support from staff, students, the principal, and district-level administrators to design, implement, and enhance their parent-involvement activities (Kirschenbaum, 2001). Teachers generally have some flexibility in their classrooms, but are not always able to determine other important factors that influence their ability to have a strong parent-involvement program. For example, when teachers are consulted about the type and amount of supplies purchased for their classroom, they should be able to decide whether they want to have enough supplies to be able to send paper, pencils, and other materials home for parents to use with their children. If the school cannot provide extra supplies for teachers to send home with students, community groups may be able to provide them. Also, if teachers are allowed to modify their schedules, they can find free time to telephone parents, write notes, and hold morning or evening conferences with parents. Additionally, school climate influences parent involvement. Parents will not have positive feelings about schools where they do not believe they are welcome. School climate, however is not determined by the teacher alone. It is influenced by a broad range of individuals, including students, teachers, the principal, and the school secretary. The support of all these individuals is necessary to create a positive school environment.

Your students can help solicit support for parent and community involvement from school staff and other students. Take your class on a tour of the school. Ask the students to think about how their parents would feel if they came to the school. Two obvious questions for students are: Is there a place for visitors to sit? Are there signs welcoming visitors and inviting them to the school office? Ask your students to list things they could do to make the school a friendlier place for parents.

Invite your principal to come to your classroom and discuss the list with your students. Divide the class into small groups and have them discuss how they would like their parents to become involved in their education. Ask them to talk to their parents and get their views. Have each group write a report on how parents can be involved in their children's education. Each group could make presentations to students in the other classrooms in the building on how they would like to increase parent involvement in their school. They could also publish a newsletter on parent involvement in schools. The newsletter could be sent to the students, parents, and other schools in the district.

If funds or other forms of support are needed from the district office for parent-involvement activities, have the students draw up a petition requesting funding and solicit signatures from teachers, students, and parents. When all the signatures are gathered, they can be delivered to an appropriate district administrator. The petition could also be used to inform community groups about school issues and solicit their support.

Building principals and district administrators can give teachers the support they need to do the following:

1. Help create and maintain a climate for positive parent/community involvement. This can include supporting flexible hours for teachers who need to be out of the classroom to develop materials or to work with parents. Teachers can be given time out of the classroom without negatively affecting students. Time can be gleaned from the secondary teacher's schedule by combining homerooms one day a week, by team-teaching a class, or by combining different sections of a class for activities such as chapter tests. At the elementary school level, team teaching, released time during periods when students are normally out of the classroom for specialized subjects such as music and art, or having the principal substitute in the classroom are ways to provide flexible hours for teachers.

2. Set up a parent room. The parent room could be used for a number of functions, including serving as a community drop-in center where parents could meet other parents for a cup of coffee or as a place for parents to work on school activities without infringing on the teachers' lounge. It could also be used as a waiting room for parents who need to see a student or a member of the school staff.

3. Host parent nights during which parents can learn more about the school, the curriculum, and the staff.

4. Send a personal note to students and to their parents when students make the honor roll or do something else noteworthy. Some schools give parents bumper stickers announcing their student's achievements.

5. Develop and distribute a handbook that contains the names and phone numbers of students, PTA or other parent-group contacts, and staff. Be sure to get parents' permission before publishing phone numbers, addresses, and other personal information.

6. Ask the school secretary to make sure visitors are welcomed when they come to the school and are given directions as needed.

7. Encourage students to greet visitors and help them find their way around the building.

Enlist Support from the Community

To enlist support from the community, you need to know something about the people, organizations, and issues in the community. The following are some questions you should be able to answer.

1. Are there any drama, musical, dance, or art groups in the community?

2. Is there a senior-citizen group, a public library, or a cooperative extension service in the community?

3. Are employment services such as the state employment security department available in the community?

4. Are civil rights organizations such as the Urban League, Anti-Defamation League, or National Association for the Advancement of Colored People (NAACP) active in the community?

5. What is the procedure for referring people to the Salvation Army, Goodwill, or the state department of public assistance for emergency assistance for housing, food, and clothing?

6. Does the community have a mental health center, family counseling center, or crisis clinic?

7. Are programs and activities for youth—such as Boys and Girls Clubs, Campfire U.S.A., Boy Scouts, Girl Scouts, YMCA, and YWCA—available for your students?

As you learn about the community, you can begin to develop a list of community resources and contacts that can provide support to families, work with your students, and provide locations for students to perform community service projects. Collecting information about your students' community and developing community contacts should be viewed as a long-term project. You can collect information as your schedule permits and organize it in a notebook. This process can be shortened if several teachers work together. Each teacher could concentrate on a different part of the community and share information and contacts.

Community groups can provide support in several ways. They can develop big sister and big brother programs for students, provide quiet places for students to study after school and on weekends, donate educational supplies, help raise funds for field trips, set up mentor programs, and tutor students.

Community-based institutions and groups can also provide opportunities for students to participate in community-based learning programs. Community-based learning programs provide an opportunity for students to move beyond the textbook and experience real life. They give students an opportunity to see how knowledge is integrated when it is applied to the real world. It puts students in touch with a variety of people and lets them see how people cope with their environment. Community-based learning also enhances career development. It can help students learn about themselves, gain confidence, and better understand their strengths and weaknesses. Students can learn to plan, make decisions, negotiate, and evaluate their plans. Here are some examples of community work students can do:

- Paint an apartment for an ill neighbor
- Clean alleys and backyards for the elderly
- Write letters for people who are ill
- Read to people who are unable to read
- Prepare an empty lot as a play area for young children
- Plant a vegetable garden for the needy
- Collect and recycle newspapers

Develop Learning Resources for Parents to Use at Home

Many of the learning materials teachers use with students at school can be used by parents at home to help students improve their skills. The materials should be in a format suitable for students to take home and should provide clear directions for at-home completion. Parents could let the teacher know how they liked the material by writing a note, giving their child a verbal message for the teacher, or by calling the school. Clark (1995) has written a series of math home-involvement activities for kindergarten through eighth grade. The activities are included in a booklet and are designed to help students increase their math skills. Parents are able to use the creative activities to reinforce the skills their children learn at school. These kinds of materials are convenient for both parents and teachers to use.

It is important for teachers to have resources available for parents to use. This lets parents know that they can help increase their children's learning and that teachers want their help. Simply telling parents they should work with their children is not sufficient. Parents need specific suggestions. Once parents get an idea of what you want them to do, some will develop their own materials. Other parents will be able to purchase materials or check them out from the library. You can suggest specific books, games, and other materials for parents to purchase and let them know where these learning materials are available.

Some parents will not have the financial resources, time, or educational background to develop or purchase learning materials. With your principal's help or help from community groups, you can set up a learning center for parents. The learning center could contain paper, pencils, books, games, a portable typewriter, a portable computer, and other appropriate resources. The learning center could also have audiocassettes on such topics as instructional techniques, classroom rules, educational goals for the year, and readings from books. Parents and students could check materials out of the learning center for use at home.

Broaden the Conception of Parent and Community Involvement

Many barriers to parent/community involvement can be eliminated by broadly conceptualizing parent/community involvement. Parents can play many roles, depending on their interests, skills, and resources. It is important to have a variety of roles for parents so that more parents will have an opportunity to be involved in the school. It is also important to make sure that some roles can be performed at home as well as at school. Below are four ways parents and community members can be involved in schools. Some of the roles can be implemented by the classroom teacher. Others need support and resources from building principals or central office administrators.

Parents Working with Their Own Children

Working with their own children is one of the most important roles parents can play in the educational process. Parents can help their children develop a positive self-concept and a positive attitude toward school as well as a better understanding of how their effort affects achievement. Most parents want their children to do well in school and are willing to do whatever they can to help them succeed. Teachers can increase the support they receive from their students' homes by giving parents a better understanding of what is going on in the classroom, by letting parents know what is expected in the classroom, and by suggesting ways in which they can support their children's learning. Teachers can work with parents to support the educational process in these three ways:

1. Involve parents in monitoring homework by asking them to sign homework papers.
2. Ask parents to sign a certificate congratulating students for good attendance.
3. Give students extra points if their parents do things such as sign their report card, attend conferences, or read to them.

Some parents want a more active partnership with the school. These parents want to help teach their children. Below are three ways you can help parents work with their children to increase their learning:

1. Encourage parents to share hobbies and games, discuss news and television programs, and talk about school problems and events with their children.
2. Send information home on the importance of reading to children and include a reading list. A one-page sheet could be sent home stating, "One of the best ways to help children become better readers is to read to them. Reading aloud is most helpful when you discuss the stories, learn to identify letters and words, and talk about the meaning of the words. Encourage leisure reading. Reading achievement is related to the amount of reading kids do. It increases vocabulary and reading fluency." Then list several books available from the school library for students to check out and take home.
3. Supply parents with materials they can use to work with their children on skill development. Students can help make math games, crossword puzzles, and other

materials that parents can use with them at home. Parents should also be encouraged to take their children to the local library where they can get their own library card.

Professional Support Person for Instruction

Many parents and community members have skills that can be shared with the school. They are willing to work with students as well as teachers. These people are often ignored in parent- and community-involvement programs. A parent or community member who is a college professor could be asked to talk to teachers about a topic that interests him or her or to participate in an inservice workshop. A bilingual parent or community member could be asked to help tutor foreign-language students or to share books or magazines written in his or her language with the class. Parents who enjoy reading or art could be asked to help staff a humanities enrichment course before or after school or to recommend materials for such a course. Parents and community members who perform these kinds of duties could also serve as role models for your students and would demonstrate the importance of education in the community. Review the list below and think of how you could involve parents and community members in your classroom. Parents and community members can do the following:

- Serve as instructional assistants
- Use carpentry skills to build things for the school
- Tutor during school hours or after school
- Develop or identify student materials or community resources
- Share their expertise with students or staff
- Expand enrichment programs offered before, after, or during school, such as a program on great books or art appreciation
- Sew costumes for school plays
- Videotape or photograph school plays or activities
- Type and edit a newsletter

General Volunteers

Some parents are willing to volunteer their time, but they do not want to do a job that requires specific skills. When thinking of activities for general volunteers, be sure to include activities that can be performed at the school as well as ones that can be performed at home. Some possible activities include:

- Working on the playground as a support person
- Working in the classroom as a support person
- Working at home preparing cutouts and other materials that will be used in class
- Telephoning other parents to schedule conferences

Decision Makers

Some parents are interested in participating in decision making in the school. They want to help set school policy, select curriculum materials, review budgets, or interview prospective staff members. Roles for these parents and community members include school board, committee, and site council members. Serving on a site council is an excellent way for parents to participate in decision making. Site councils are designed to increase parent involvement in schools, empower classroom teachers, and allow decisions to be made at the school level.

The Comer (1995; Comer et al., 1999) model is an effective way to involve parents, classroom teachers, and other educators in decision making. Comer (1997) believes schools can be more effective when they are restructured in ways that encourage and support cooperation among parents and educators. Comer did much of his pioneering work on parent involvement and restructuring schools in Prince George's County, Maryland. There he implemented two committees—the School Planning and Management Team (SPMT) and the Student Staff Services Team (SSST).

The SPMT included the school principal, classroom teachers, parents, and support staff. Consensus was used to reach decisions. The committee also had a no-fault policy, which encouraged parents not to blame the school and educators not to blame parents. The SPMT provided a structure for parents and educators to create a common vision for their school; reduce fragmentation; and develop activities, curriculum, and in-service programs. It also developed a comprehensive school plan, designed a schoolwide calendar of events, and monitored and evaluated student progress. The SPMT met at least once a month. Subcommittees of the SPMT met more frequently.

The second committee that Comer implemented was the SSST, which included the school principal, guidance counselor, classroom teachers, and support staff, including psychologists, health aides, and other appropriate personnel. Teachers and parents were encouraged to join this group if they had concerns they believed should be addressed. The SSST brought school personnel together to discuss individual student concerns. It also brought coherence and order to the services that students receive.

SUMMARY

Parent and community involvement is a dynamic process that encourages, supports, and provides opportunities for teachers, parents, and community members to work together to improve student learning. Parent and community involvement is also an important component of school reform and multicultural education. Parents and community groups help provide the rationale, motivation, and social action necessary for educational reform.

Everyone can benefit from parent/community involvement. Students tend to perform better in school and have more people supporting their learning. Parents know more about what is going on at school, have more opportunities to communicate with their children's teachers, and are able to help their children increase their learning. Teachers gain a partner in education. Teachers learn more about their students through their parent and community contacts and are able to use that information to help increase their students' performance.

Even though research has consistently demonstrated that students have an advantage in school when their parents support and encourage educational activities, not all parents know how they can support their children's education or feel they have the time, energy, or other resources to be involved in schools. Some parents have a particularly difficult time supporting their children's education. Three such groups are parents who have low incomes, single parents, and parents with special needs. Parents from these groups are often dismissed as unsupportive of education. However, they want their children to do well in school and are willing to work with the school when the school reaches out to them and responds to their needs.

To establish an effective parent/community involvement program, you should establish two-way communication with parents and community groups, enlist support from the community, and have resources available for parents to use in working with their children. Expanding how parent/community involvement is conceptualized can increase the number of parents and community members able to participate. Parents can play many roles. Ways to involve parents and community members include parents working with their own children, parents and community members sharing their professional skills with the school, parents and community groups volunteering in the school, and parents and community members working with educators to make decisions about school reform.

Questions and Activities

1. Compare the role of parents in schools during the colonial period and now. Identify and discuss changes that have occurred and changes you would like to see occur in parent involvement.

2. Consider this statement: Regardless of the circumstances students experience at home, teachers have a responsibility to help them perform at their highest level at school. Do you agree? Why or why not?

3. Interview a parent of a bilingual, ethnic minority, religious minority, or low-income student to learn more about the parent's views on schools and the educational goals for his or her children. This information cannot be generalized to all members of these groups, but it can be an important departure point for learning more about diverse groups within our society.

4. Consider this statement: All parents want their children to succeed in school. Do you agree? Why or why not?

5. Interview a classroom teacher and an administrator to determine his or her views on parent/community involvement.

6. Write a brief paper on your personal views of the benefits and drawbacks of parent/community involvement.

7. Form a group with two other members of your class or workshop. One person in the group will be a teacher, the other a parent, and the third an observer. The teacher and the parent will role-play a teacher–parent conference. Afterward, discuss how it felt to be a parent and a teacher. What can be done to make the parent and teacher feel more comfortable? Was the information shared at the conference helpful? The observer can share his or her view of the parent and teacher interaction. Then change roles and repeat the process.

References

Banks, C. A. M. (2005). *Improving Multicultural Education: Lessons from the Intergroup Education Movement.* New York: Teachers College Press.

Banks, J. A. (2003). *Teaching Strategies for Ethnic Studies* (7th ed.). Boston: Allyn & Bacon.

Berger, E. H. (2003). *Parents as Partners in Education: Families and Schools Working Together* (7th ed.). New York: Macmillan.

Booth, A., & Dunn, J. F. (Eds.). (1996). *Family–School Links: How Do They Affect Educational Outcomes?* Mahwah, NJ: Erlbaum.

Bullivant, B. M. (1993). Culture: Its Nature and Meaning for Educators. In J. A. Banks & C. A. M. Banks, *Multicultural Education: Issues and Perspectives* (2nd ed., pp. 29–47). Boston: Allyn & Bacon.

Bureau of Labor Statistics. (March, 2003). *Current Population Survey.* Bureau of Labor Statistics. Washington, DC: U.S. Department of Labor.

Casper, L. M., & Bryson, K. R. (1998). *Co-Resident Grandparents and Their Grandchildren: Grandparent Maintained Families.* Washington, DC: U.S. Census Bureau.

Chavkin, N. F., & Gonzalez, D. L. (1995). *Forging Partnerships between Mexican American Parents and the Schools.* Charleston, WV: Clearinghouse on Rural Education and Small Schools, Appalachia Educational Laboratory.

Cibulka, J. A., & Kritek, W. J. (Eds.). (1996). *Coordination among Schools, Families, and Communities: Prospects for Educational Reform.* Albany: State University of New York Press.

Clark, C. S. (1995). Parents and Schools. *CQ-Researcher, 5*(3), 51–69.

Comer, J. P. (1995). *School Power: Implication of an Intervention Project.* New York: Free Press.

Comer, J. P. (1997). *Waiting for a Miracle: Why Schools Can't Solve Our Problems—and How We Can.* New York: Dutton.

Comer, J. P., Ben-Avie, M., Haynes, N. M., & Joyner, E. T. (1999). *Child by Child: The Comer Process for Change in Education.* New York: Teachers College Press.

Darling-Hammond, L. (2004). What Happens to a Dream Deferred? The Continuing Quest for Equal Educational Opportunity. In J. A. Banks and Cherry A. McGee Banks, *Handbook of Research on Multicultural Education* (2nd. ed., pp. 525–547). San Francisco: Jossey-Bass.

De Carvalho, M. E. P. (2001). *Rethinking Family–School Relations.* Mahwah, NJ: Erlbaum.

Decker, J., & Majerczyk, D. (2000). *Increasing Parent Involvement through Effective Home/School Communication.* Chicago: Saint Xavier University. (ERIC Document Reproduction Service No. ED 439790)

DeSteno, N. (2000). Parent Involvement in the Classroom: The Fine Line. *Young Children, 55*(3), 13–17.

Epstein. J., Sanders, M. G., Simon, B. S., Salinas, K. C., Jansorn, N. R., & Van Voorhis, F. L. (2002). *School, Family, and Community Partnerships: Your Handbook for Action.* Thousand Oaks, CA: Corwin Press.

Fronczek, P. (2005). *Income, Earnings, and Poverty from the 2004 American Community Survey.* Washington, DC: U.S. Census Bureau.

Goodlad, J. I. (1984). *A Place Called School: Prospects for the Future.* New York: McGraw-Hill.

Harry, B. (1992). Restructuring the Participation of African-American Parents in Special Education. *Exceptional Children, 59*(2), 123–131.

Henderson, A. T., & Berla, N. (Eds.). (1994). *A New Generation of Evidence: The Family Is Critical to Student Achievement*. Washington, DC: National Committee for Citizens in Education.

Hidalgo, N. M., Sau-Fong, S., & Epstein, J. L. (2004). Research on Families, Schools, and Communities: A Multicultural Perspective. In J. A. Banks & C. A. M. Banks (Eds.), *Handbook of Research on Multicultural Education* (2nd ed., pp. 631–655). San Francisco: Jossey-Bass.

Jennings, L. (1990, August 1). Parents as Partners. *Education Week*, 23, 35.

Kagan, S. L. (1995). *Meeting Family and Community Needs: The Three C's of Early Childhood Education*. Paper presented at the Australia and New Zealand Conference on the First Years of School, Tasmania, and Australia.

Kirschenbaum, H. (2001). Educating Professionals for School, Family, and Community Partnerships. In D. B. Hiatt-Michael (Ed.). *Promising Practices for Family Involvement in Schools*. Greenwich, CT: Information Age.

Kleiner, H. S., Hertzog, J., & Targ, D.B., (2005). *Grandparents Acting as Parents*. Washington, DC: Grandparents United [http://www.uwex.edu/ces/gprg/article.html].

Krebs, N. B. (2000). For Students with Multicultural Heritage. *Multicultural Education*, 8(2), 25–27.

Kreider, R. M., & Fields, J. (2005, July). *Living Arrangements of Children: 2001. Current Population Reports*. Washington, DC: U.S. Census Bureau.

Lee, S. M. (2001). *Using the New Racial Categories in the 2000 Census: A Kids' Count/PRB Report on Census 2000*. Baltimore, MD: The Annie E. Casey Foundation.

Lightfoot, S. L. (1978). *Worlds Apart: Relationships between Families and Schools*. New York: Basic Books.

Linn, E. (1990). Parent Involvement Programs: A Review of Selected Models. *Equity Coalition*, 1(2), 10–15.

McCallion, P., Janicki, M. P., & Kolomer, S. R. (2005). Controlled Evaluation of Support Groups for Grandparent Caregivers of Children with Developmental Disabilities and Delays. *American Journal of Mental Retardation*. 109(5), 532–361.

McFalls, J. A., Jr. (2003) Population: A Lively Introduction, 4th ed. *Population Reference Bulletin*. 58(4), 1–44. Washington, DC: Population Reference Bureau.

Mannan, G., & Blackwell, J. (1992). Parent Involvement: Barriers and Opportunities. *Urban Review*, 24(1), 219–226.

Milner, R., & Maestro, V. (Eds.) (2002). Intelligent design? *Natural History Magazine*.

National Vital Statistical Reports. (2004). Births, Marriages, Divorces, and Deaths: Provisional Data for 2003. *National Vital Statistics Reports*, 52(22). Washington, DC: Center for Disease Control and Prevention.

Hidalgo, N. M., Sau-Fong S., & Epstein, J. L. (2004). Research on Families, Schools, and Communities: A Multicultural Perspective. In J. A. Banks and C. A. M. Banks. *Handbook of Research on Multicultural Education* (pp. 631–655). San Francisco: Josey-Bass.

Pena, D. C. (2000). Parent Involvement: Influencing Factors and Implications. *Journal of Educational Research*, 94(1), 42–54.

Pollard, K. M., & O'Hare, W. P. (1999). America's Racial and Ethnic Minorities. *Population Reference Bulletin*, 54(3), 1–48. Washington, DC: Population Reference Bureau.

Proctor, B. D., & Dalaker, J. (2002). *Poverty in the United States: 2001*. Washington, DC: U.S. Government Printing Office.

Rasinski, T. (1990). Reading and the Empowerment of Parents. *Reading Teacher*, 42, 226–231.

Schneider, B., & Coleman, J. S. (Eds.). (1996). *Parents, Their Children, and Schools*. Boulder, CO: Westview.

Shariff, J. W. (1998). Free Enterprise and the Ghetto Family. In J. S. Wurzel (Ed.), *Toward Multiculturalism: A Reader in Multicultural Education* (pp. 30–54). Yarmouth, ME: Intercultural Press.

Stratton, J. (1995). *How Students Have Changed: A Call to Action for Our Children's Future*. Arlington, VA: American Association of School Administration.

Swadener, B. B., & Niles, K. (1991). Children and Families "At Promise": Making Home–School–Community Connections. *Democracy and Education, 6*, 13–18.

U.S. Census Bureau. (2003). Annual Social and Economic Supplement: *2003 Current Population Survey, Current Population Reports*, Series P20-553. Washington, DC: U.S. Government Printing Office.

U.S. Census Bureau. (1998). *Statistical Abstract of the United States* (118th ed.). Washington, DC: U.S. Government Printing Office.

U.S. Census Bureau. (2000). *Statistical Abstract of the United States, 2000* (120th ed.). Washington, DC: U.S. Government Printing Office.

Walker, V. S. (1996). *Their Highest Potential: An African American School Community in the Segregated South*. Chapel Hill: University of North Carolina Press.

Waller, W. (1965). *The Sociology of Teaching*. Hoboken: Wiley. (Original work published 1932.)

Winter, G. (2002, December 28). Rigorous School Tests Grow, but Big Study Doubts Value. *New York Times*, p. A1.

Internet Resources for Information on Parent Involvement

1. Center on School, Family, and Community Partnerships:
    [http://csos.jhu.edu/p2000/center.htm]

2. National Coalition for Parent Involvement in Education:
    [http://www.ncpie.org/]

3. National Parent Information Network:
    [http://npin.org/]

4. Parents as Teachers National Center:
    [http://www.parentsasteachers.org/]

5. Partnership for Family Involvement in Education:
    [http://www.ed.gov/pubs/whoweare/index.html]

APPENDIX

Multicultural Resources

Issues and Concepts

Banks, J. A. (Ed.). (2004). *Diversity and Citizenship Education: Global Perspectives.* San Francisco: Jossey-Bass.

Banks, C. A. M. (2005). *Improving Multicultural Education: Lessons from the Intergroup Education Movement.* New York: Teachers College Press.

Banks, J. A. (2006). *Cultural Diversity and Education: Foundations, Curriculum, and Teaching* (5th ed.). Boston: Allyn & Bacon.

Banks, J. A. (Ed.). (1996). *Multicultural Education, Transformative Knowledge, and Action: Historical and Contemporary Perspectives.* New York: Teachers College Press.

Banks, J. A. (2006). *Race, Culture, and Education: The Selected Works of James A. Banks.* New York & London: Routledge.

Banks, J. A., & Banks, C. A. M. (Eds.). (2004). *Handbook of Research on Multicultural Education* (2nd ed.). San Francisco: Jossey-Bass.

Cochran-Smith, M. (2004). *Walking the Road: Race, Diversity, and Social Justice In Teacher Education.* New York: Teachers College Press.

Gay, G. (2000). *Culturally Responsive Teaching: Theory, Research, and Practice.* New York: Teachers College Press.

Howard, G. (2006). *We Can't Teach What We Don't Know: White Teachers, Multiracial Schools* (2nd ed.). New York: Teachers College Press.

Ladson-Billings, G., & Gillborn, D. (Eds.). (2004). *The RoutledgeFalmer Reader in Multicultural Education.* New York & London: Routledge.

Leonardo, Z. (Ed.). (2005). *Critical Pedagogy and Race.* Malden, MA: Blackwell.

Nieto, S. (1999). *The Light in Their Eyes: Creating Multicultural Learning Communities.* New York: Teachers College Press.

Noguera, P. A. (2003). *City Schools and the American Dream: Reclaiming the Promise of Public Education.* New York: Teachers College Press.

Sleeter, C. E. (2005). *Un-Standardizing Curriculum: Multicultural Teaching in the Standards-Based Classroom.* New York: Teachers College Press.

Social Class

Anyon, J. (2005). *Radical Possibilities: Public Policy, Urban Education, and a New Social Movement.* New York & London: Routledge.

Collins, C., Leondar-Wright, B., & Sklar, H. (1999). *Shifting Fortunes: The Perils of the Growing American Wealth Gap.* Boston: United for a Fair Economy.

Conley, D. (1999). *Being Black, Living in the Red: Race, Wealth, and Social Policy in America.* Berkeley: University of California Press.

Gans, H. (1995). *The War against the Poor: The Underclass and Antipoverty Policy.* New York: Basic Books.

Hernandez, D. J. (Ed.). (1999). *Children of Immigrants: Health, Adjustment, and Public Assistance.* Washington, DC: National Academy Press.

Kozol, J. (2005). *The Shame of the Nation: The Restoration of Apartheid Schooling in America.* New York: Crown.

Lareau, A. (2003). *Unequal Childhoods: Class, Race, and Family Life.* Berkeley: University of California Press.

Lucas, S. R. (1999). *Tracking Inequality: Stratification and Mobility in American High Schools.* New York: Teachers College Press.

Oakes, J. (2005). *Keeping Track: How Schools Structure Inequality* (2nd ed.). New Haven, CT: Yale University Press.

Quint, S. (1994). *Schooling Homeless Children: A Working Model for America's Public Schools.* New York: Teachers College Press.

Religion

Barbour, I. G. (2002). *Nature, Human Nature, and God.* Minneapolis, MN: Fortress Press.

Bowie, F. (2006). *Anthropology of Religion: An Introduction.* Oxford: Blackwell.

Bowker, J. (1997). *World Religions: The Great Faiths Explored and Explained.* New York: DK Publishing.

Carpenter, J. A. (1999). *Revive Us Again: The Reawakening of American Fundamentalism.* New York: Oxford University Press.

Corbett, J. M. (2000). *Religion in America* (4th ed.). Upper Saddle River, NJ: Prentice-Hall.

Coward, H. (Ed.). (2000). *Experiencing Scripture in World Religions.* Maryknoll, NY: Orbis Books.

Doniger, W. (1999). *Merriam-Webster's Encyclopedia of World Religions.* Springfield, MA: Merriam-Webster.

Eck, D. L. (2001). *A New Religious America: How a "Christian Country" Has Become the World's Most Religiously Diverse Nation.* New York: Harper.

Finke, R. (2005). *The Churching of America, 1776–2005: Winners and Losers in Our Religious Economy.* New Brunswick, NJ: Rutgers University Press.

Lippy, C. H. (2000). *Pluralism Comes of Age: American Religious Culture in the Twentieth Century.* Armonk, NY: Sharpe.

Neusner, J. (Ed.). (2003). *World Religions in America: An introduction.* Louisville, KY: Westminster John Knox Press.

Odell-Scott, D. (Ed.). (2000). *Democracy and Religion: Free Exercise and Diverse Visions.* Kent, OH: Kent State University Press.

Urofsky, M. I. (2002). *Religious Freedom: Rights and Liberties under the Law.* Santa Barbara, CA: ABC-CLIO.

Yoo, D. K. (Ed.). (1999). *New Spiritual Homes: Religion and Asian Americans.* Honolulu: University Press of Hawaii.

Young, W. A. (2005). *The World's Religions: Worldviews and Contemporary Issues.* Upper Saddle River, NJ: Pearson Prentice Hall.

Gender

Anzaldua, G. E., & Keating, A. (Eds.). (2002). *This Bridge We Call Home: Visions of Transformation.* New York: Routledge.

Boyd, H., & Allen, R. L. (Eds.). (1995). *Brotherman: The Odyssey of Black Men in America-An Anthology.* New York: Ballantine.

Collins, P. H. (2000). *Black Feminist Thought: Knowledge, Consciousness, and the Politics of Empowerment* (2nd ed.). New York: Routledge.

Eagly, A. H., Beall, A. E., & Sternberg, R. J. (Eds.) (2005). *The Psychology of Gender* (2nd ed.). New York: Guilford.

Ferguson, A. A. (2001). *Bad Boys: Public Schools in the Making of Black Masculinity.* Ann Arbor: The University of Michigan Press.

Guy-Sheftall, B. (Ed.). (1995). *Words of Fire: An Anthology of African American Feminist Thought.* New York: New Press.

Hernandez, D., & Rehman, B. (Eds.). (2002). *Colonize This: Young Women of Color on Today's Feminism.* New York: Seal Press.

Hune, S., & Nomura, G. (Eds.). (2003). *Asian/Pacific Islander American Women: A Historical Anthology.* New York: New York University Press.

Jones-Royster, B., & Mann-Simpkins, A. M. (Eds.). (2005). *Calling Cards: Theory and Practice in the Study of Race, Gender, and Culture.* Albany: State University of New York Press.

Kimmel, M. S. (2003). *The Gendered Society* (2nd ed.). New York: Oxford University Press.

Ling, P. & Monteith, S. (Eds.). (2004). *Gender and the Civil Rights Movement.* New Brunswick, NJ: Rutgers University Press.

Mankiller, W., Mink, G., Navarro, M., Smith, B., & Steinem, G. (Eds.). (1998). *The Reader's Companion to U.S. Women's History.* Boston: Houghton Mifflin.

Moghadam, V. M. (2005). *Globalizing Women: Transnational Feminist Networks.* Baltimore, MD: Johns Hopkins University Press.

Morales, A. L. (1998). *Remedios: Stories of Earth and Iron from the History of Puertoriquenas.* Boston: Beacon.

Moya, P. (2002). *Learning from Experience: Minority Identities, Multicultural Struggles.* Berkeley: University of California Press.

Nouraie-Simone, F. (Ed.). (2005). *On Shifting Ground: Muslim Women in the Global Era.* New York: Feminist Press.

Pollack, W. (1998). *Real Boys: Rescuing Our Sons from the Myths of Boyhood.* New York: Holt.

Sarasohn, E. S. (Ed.). (1998). *Issei Women: Echoes from Another Frontier.* Palo Alto, CA: Pacific Books.

Schiff, K. G. (2006). *Lighting the Way: Nine Women Who Changed Modern America.* New York: Miramax Books/Hyperion.

Wharton, A. S. (2005). *The Sociology of Gender: An Introduction to Theory and Research.* Malden, MA: Blackwell.

Zinn, M. B., Hondagneu-Sotelo, P., & Messner, M. A. (Eds.). (2000). *Gender through the Prism of Difference.* Boston: Allyn and Bacon.

Race, Ethnicity, and Language

Banks, J. A. (2003). *Teaching Strategies for Ethnic Studies* (7th ed.). Boston: Allyn & Bacon.

Banks, J. A., & Banks, C. A. M. (Eds.). (2004). *Handbook of Research on Multicultural Education* (2nd ed.). San Francisco: Jossey-Bass.

Crawford, J. (1999). *Bilingual Education: History, Politics, Theory, and Practice* (4th ed.). Los Angeles: Bilingual Educational Services.

Delpit, L., & Dowdy, J. K. (Eds.). (2002). *The Skin That We Speak: Thoughts on Language and Culture in the Classroom.* New York: New Press.

Garcia, E. (2005). *Teaching and Learning in Two Languages: Bilingualism and Schooling in the United States.* New York: Teachers College Press.

Ladson-Billings, G. (2005). *Beyond the Big House: African American Educators on Teacher Education.* New York: Teachers College Press.

Moreno, J. F. (Ed.). (1999). *The Elusive Quest for Equality: 150 Years of Chicano/Chicana Education*. Cambridge, MA: Harvard Educational Review.

Ovando, C. J., & Collier, V. P. (1998). *Bilingual and ESL Classrooms: Teaching in a Multicultural Context* (2nd ed.). Boston: McGraw-Hill.

Pollock, M. (2004). *Colormute: Race Talk Dilemmas in an American School*. Princeton, NJ: Princeton University Press.

Smitherman, G. (2000). *Talkin That Talk: Language, Culture and Education in African America*. New York: Routledge.

Stephan, S., & Vogt, W. P. (Eds.). (2004). *Education Programs for Improving Intergroup Relations: Theory, Research, and Practice*. New York: Teachers College Press.

Suárez-Orozco, M. M., Suárez-Orozco, C., & Qin, D. B. (Eds.). (2005). *The New Immigration: An Interdisciplinary Reader*. New York & London: Routledge.

Valdés, G. (2001). *Learning and Not Learning English: Latino Students in American Schools*. New York: Teachers College Press.

Exceptionality

Artiles, A. J., & Trent, S. C. (2000). Representation of Culturally/Linguistically Diverse Students. In C. R. Reynolds & E. Fletcher-Jantzen (Eds.), *Encyclopedia of Special Education* (2nd ed., Vol. 1, pp. 513–517). New York: Wiley.

Artiles, A. J., Trent, S. C., & Palmer, J. D. (2004). Culturally Diverse Students in Special Education: Legacies and Prospects. In J. A. Banks & C. A. M. Banks (Eds.). *Handbook of Research on Multicultural Education* (2nd ed., pp. 716–735). San Francisco: Jossey-Bass.

Baca, L. M., & Cervantes, H. T. (1997). *The Bilingual Special Education Interface*. Englewood Cliffs, NJ: Prentice-Hall.

Bauer, A. M., & Brown, G. M. (2001). *Adolescents and Inclusion: Transforming Secondary Schools*. Baltimore: Brookes.

Billingsley, B. S. (2005). *Cultivating and Keeping Committed Special Education Teachers: What Principals and District Leaders Can Do*. Thousand Oaks, CA: Corwin Press.

Burkhardt, S. A., Obiakor, F. E., & Rotatori, A. F. (Eds.). (2004). *Current Perspectives on Learning Disabilities*. Boston: JAI.

Carrasquillo, A. L., & Rodriguez, V. (1995). *Language Minority Students in the Mainstream Classroom*. Bristol, PA: Taylor & Francis.

Cummins, J. (1984). *Bilingualism and Special Education: Issues in Assessment and Pedagogy*. Bristol, PA: Taylor & Francis.

Davis, G. A., & Rimm, S. B. (2004). *Education of the Gifted and Talented*. Boston: Pearson.

Ford, D. Y., & Harris, J. J., III. (1999). *Multicultural Gifted Education*. New York: Teachers College Press.

Grossman, H. (1994). *Special Education in a Diverse Society*. Boston: Allyn & Bacon.

Heward, W. L. (2003). *Exceptional Children: An Introduction to Special Education* (7th ed.). Upper Saddle River, NJ: Prentice-Hall/Merrill.

Lombardi, T. P. (Ed.). (1999). *Inclusion: Policy and Practice*. Bloomington, IN: Phi Delta Kappa.

Mercer, C. D., & Mercer, A. R. (1998). *Teaching Students with Learning Problems* (5th ed.). Upper Saddle River, NJ: Prentice-Hall/Merrill.

Meyer, L. H., Park, H., Grenot-Scheyer, M., Schwartz, I., & Harry, B. (Eds.). (1998). *Making Friends: The Influences of Culture and Development*. Baltimore: Brookes.

Purcell, J. H., & Eckert, R. D. (Ed.). (2006). *Designing Services and Programs for High-Ability Learners: A Guidebook for Gifted Education*. Thousand Oaks, CA: Corwin Sage.

Sapon-Shevin, M. (1999). *Because We Can Change the World: A Practical Guide to Building Cooperative, Inclusive Classroom Communities*. Boston: Allyn & Bacon.

Shapiro, A. (Ed.). (1999). *Everybody Belongs: Changing Negative Attitudes toward Classmates with Disabilities.* New York: Garland.

Shelton, C. F., & Pollingue, A. B. (2000). *The Exceptional Teacher's Handbook: The First-Year Special Education Teacher's Guide for Success.* Thousand Oaks, CA: Corwin Press.

School Reform

Au, K. (2006). *Multicultural Issues and Literacy Achievement.* Mahwah, NJ: Earlbaum Associates.

Banks, J. A., Cookson, P., Gay, G., Hawley, W. D., Irvine, J. J., Nieto, S., Schofield, J. W., & Stephan, W. G. (2001). *Diversity within Unity: Essential Principles for Teaching and Learning in a Multicultural Society.* Seattle: Center for Multicultural Education, University of Washington.

Carter, P. L. (2005). *Keepin' It Real: School Success Beyond Black and White.* New York: Oxford University Press.

Cohen, E. G., & Lotan, R. A. (Eds.). (1997). *Working for Equity in Heterogeneous Classrooms: Sociological Theory in Practice.* New York: Teachers College Press.

Comer, J. P. (2004). *Leave No Child Behind: Preparing Today's Youth for Tomorrow's World.* New Haven, CT: Yale University Press.

Darling-Hammond, L. (1997). *The Right to Learn: A Blueprint for Creating Schools That Work.* San Francisco: Jossey-Bass.

Gonzáles, N., Moll, L. C., & Amanti, C. (Eds.). (2005). *Funds of Knowledge: Theorizing Principles in Households, Communities, and Classrooms.* Mahwah, NJ: Earlbaum Associates.

Gordon, E. W., Bridglall, B. L., & Meroe, A. S. (Eds.). (2005). *Supplementary Education: The Hidden Curriculum of High Academic Achievement.* Lanham, MA: Rowman & Littlefield.

King, J. E. (Ed.). (2005). *Black Education: A Transformative Research and Action Agenda for the New Century.* Mahwah, NJ: Erlbaum Associates.

Lipman, P. (2004). *High Stakes Education: Inequality, Globalization, and Urban School Reform.* New York & London: RoutlegeFalmer.

Meier, D., & Kohn, A. (Eds.). (2004). *Many Children Left Behind: How the No Child Left Behind Act is Damaging Our Children and Our Schools.* Boston: Beacon.

Glossary

African Americans U.S. residents and citizens who have an African biological and cultural heritage and identity. This term is used synonymously and interchangeably with Blacks and Black Americans. These terms are used to describe both a racial and a cultural group. The U.S. Census indicated that as of July 1, 2004, there were an estimated 39.2 million African Americans in the United States.

The number of African Americans increased by 33 percent between 1980 and 2000 to about 13.4 percent of the U.S. population in 2004. The U.S. Census Bureau (2000) projects that African Americans will make up 14.7 percent of the nation's population by 2050; they were slightly outnumbered by Hispanic Americans in 2000. Today, African Americans make up 13.4 percent of the U.S. population, while Hispanics make up 13.7 percent. An excellent one-volume encyclopedia on African Americans is *Africana: The Encyclopedia of the African and African American Experience* (Appiah & Gates, 1999).

Afrocentric curriculum A curriculum approach in which concepts, issues, problems, and phenomena are viewed from the perspectives of Africans and African Americans. This curriculum is based on the assumption that students learn best when they view situations and events from their own cultural perspectives (Asante, 1998).

American Indian See Native Americans.

Anglo Americans Americans whose biological and cultural heritage originated in England, or Americans with other biological and cultural heritages who have assimilated into the dominant or mainstream culture in the United States. This term is often used to describe the mainstream U.S. culture or to describe most White Americans.

Antiracist education A term used frequently in the United Kingdom and Canada to describe a process used by teachers and other educators to eliminate institutionalized racism from the schools and society and to help individuals to develop nonracist attitudes. When antiracist educational reform is implemented, curriculum materials, grouping practices, hiring policies, teacher attitudes and expectations, and school policy and practices are examined and steps are taken to eliminate racism from these school variables. A related educational reform movement in the United States that focuses more on individuals than on institutions is known as prejudice reduction (Stephan & Vogt, 2004).

Asian Americans and Pacific Islanders Americans who have a biological and cultural heritage that originated on the continent of Asia or in the Pacific region. The largest groups of Asian Americans in the United States

471

in 2000 were (in descending order) Chinese, Filipinos, Asian Indians, Vietnamese, Koreans, and Japanese. Other groups include Laotians, Thai, Hmong, Taiwanese, Cambodians, Pakistanis, and Indonesians. Asians are the fastest-growing ethnic group in the United States. They increased 194 percent between 1980 and 2000. There were about 13.1 million Asian Americans in the United States in 2004. The U.S. Census projects that Asians will make up 9.3 percent of the nation's population by 2050 (Pollard & O'Hare, 1999; Population Reference Bureau, 2003; U.S. Census Bureau, 2000, 2002).

Cultural assimilation A phenomenon that takes place when one ethnic or cultural group acquires the behavior, values, perspectives, ethos, and characteristics of another ethnic group and sheds its own cultural characteristics. (For a further discussion of assimilation of ethnic groups in the United States since the 1960s, see Alba & Nee, 2003).

Culture The ideations, symbols, behaviors, values, and beliefs that are shared by a human group. Culture can also be defined as a group's program for survival and adaptation to its environment. Pluralistic nation-states such as the United States, Canada, and Australia are made up of an overarching culture, called a macroculture, that all individuals and groups within the nation share. These nation-states also have many smaller cultures, called microcultures, that differ in many ways from the macroculture or that contain cultural components manifested differently than in the macroculture. (See Chapters 1 and 2 for further discussions of culture.)

Disability The physical or mental characteristics of an individual that prevent or limit him or her from performing specific tasks.

Discrimination The differential treatment of individuals or groups based on categories such as race, ethnicity, gender, sexual orientation, social class, or exceptionality.

Ethnic group A microcultural group or collectivity that shares a common history and culture, values, behaviors, and other characteristics that cause members of the group to have a shared identity. A sense of peoplehood is one of the most important characteristics of an ethnic group. An ethnic group also shares economic and political interests. Cultural characteristics, rather than biological traits, are the essential attributes of an ethnic group. An ethnic group is not the same as a racial group. Some ethnic groups, such as Puerto Ricans in the United States, are made up of individuals who belong to several different racial groups. White Anglo-Saxon Protestants, Italian Americans, and Irish Americans are examples of ethnic groups. Individual members of an ethnic group vary considerably in the extent to which they identify with the group. Some individuals have a very strong identification with their particular ethnic group, whereas other members of the group have a very weak identification with it.

Ethnic minority group An ethnic group with several distinguishing characteristics. An ethnic minority group has distinguishing cultural characteristics, racial characteristics, or both, which enable members of other groups to identify its members easily. Some ethnic minority groups, such as Jewish Americans, have unique cultural characteristics. African Americans have unique cultural and physical characteristics. The unique attributes of ethnic minority groups make them convenient targets of racism and discrimination. Ethnic minority groups are usually a numerical minority within their societies. However, the Blacks in South Africa, who are a numerical majority in their nation-state, were often considered a sociological minority group by social scientists because they had little political power until the constitution of the Republic of South Africa was established in 1996 (Moodley & Adam, 2004).

Ethnic studies The scientific and humanistic analysis of behavior influenced by variables related to ethnicity and ethnic group membership. This term is often used to refer to special school, university, and college courses and programs that focus on specific racial and ethnic groups. However, any aspects of a course or program that includes a study of variables related to ethnicity can accurately be referred to as ethnic studies. In other words, ethnic studies can be integrated within the boundaries of mainstream courses and curricula.

Eurocentric curriculum A curriculum in which concepts, events, and situations are viewed primarily from the perspectives of European nations and cultures and in which Western civilization is emphasized. This approach is based on the assumption that Europeans have made the most important contributions to the development of the United States and the world. Curriculum theorists who endorse this approach are referred to as Eurocentrists or Western traditionalists.

European Americans See Anglo Americans.

Exceptional Term used to describe students who have learning or behavioral characteristics that differ substantially from those of most other students and that require special attention in instruction. Students who are intellectually gifted or talented as well as those who have disabilities are considered exceptional.

Gender A category consisting of behaviors that result from the social, cultural, and psychological factors associated with masculinity and femininity within a society. Appropriate male and female roles result from the socialization of the individual within a group.

Gender identity An individual's view of the gender to which he or she belongs and his or her shared sense of group attachment to other males or females.

Global education A curriculum reform movement concerned with issues and problems related to the survival of human beings in the world community. International studies is a part of global education, but the focus of global education is the interdependence of human beings and their common fate, regardless of the national boundaries within which they live. Many teachers confuse global education and international studies with ethnic studies, which deal with ethnic groups within a particular national boundary, such as the United States.

Handicapism The unequal treatment of people who are disabled and related attitudes and beliefs that reinforce and justify discrimination against people with disabilities. The term handicapped is considered negative by some people. They prefer the term disabled. "People with disabilities" is considered a more sensitive phrase than disabled people because the word "people" is used first and given emphasis.

Hispanic Americans Americans who share a culture, heritage, and language that originated in Spain. Most of the Hispanics living in the United States have cultural origins in Latin America. Many Hispanics in the United States prefer to use the word *Latino* rather than *Hispanic*, as do the editors of this book. However, Hispanic is the term used by the U.S. Census. Most Hispanics in the United States speak Spanish and are mestizos. A mestizo is a person of mixed biological heritage. Most Hispanics in the United States have an Indian as well as a Spanish heritage. Many of them also have an African biological and cultural heritage.

The largest groups of Hispanics in the United States are Mexican Americans (Chicanos), Puerto Ricans, and Cubans. According to the U.S. Census, as of July 1, 2003, there were an estimated 39.9 million Hispanics in the United States, which was about 13.7 percent of the U.S. population. In 2000, there were 20.6 million Mexican Americans, 3.4 million Puerto Ricans in the mainland United States, 1.2 million Cubans, and 10 million Hispanics from other nations (U.S. Census Bureau, 2000, 2002, 2003).

Hispanics are one of the nation's fastest-growing ethnic groups of color. They increased 142 percent between 1980 and 2000, from 14.6 to 35.3 million. The nation's total population increased 24 percent between 1980 and 2000 (Pollard & O'Hare, 1999; U.S. Census Bureau, 2002). The U.S. Census Bureau (2000) projects that Hispanics will make up 24.3 percent of the nation's population in 2050.

It is misleading to view Hispanics as one ethnic group. Some Hispanics believe that the word Hispanics can help to unify the various Latino groups and thus increase their political power. The primary identity of most Hispanics in the United States, however, is with their particular group, such as Mexican American, Puerto Rican American, or Cuban American.

Mainstream American A U.S. citizen who shares most of the characteristics of the dominant ethnic and cultural group in the nation. Such an individual is usually White Anglo-Saxon Protestant and belongs to the middle class or a higher social-class status.

Mainstream-centric curriculum A curriculum that presents events, concepts, issues, and problems primarily or exclusively from the points of view and perspectives of the mainstream society and the dominant ethnic and cultural group in the United States—White Anglo-Saxon Protestants. The mainstream-centric curriculum is also usually presented from the perspectives of Anglo males.

Mainstreaming The process that involves placing students with disabilities into the regular classroom for instruction. They might be integrated into the regular classroom for part or all of the school day. This practice was initiated in response to Public Law 94–142 (passed by Congress in 1975), which requires that students with disabilities be educated in the least restricted environment.

Multicultural education A reform movement designed to change the total educational environment so that students from diverse racial and ethnic groups, both gender groups, exceptional students, and students from each social-class group will experience equal educational opportunities in schools, colleges, and universities. A major assumption of multicultural education is that some students, because of their particular racial, ethnic, gender, and cultural characteristics, have a better chance of succeeding in educational institutions as they are currently structured than do students who belong to other groups or who have different cultural and gender characteristics. See Chapter 1 in the *Handbook for Research on Multicultural Education* (Banks & Banks, 2004) for a further discussion of multicultural education.

Multiculturalism A philosophical position and movement that assumes that the gender, ethnic, racial, and cultural diversity of a pluralistic society should be reflected in all of the institutionalized structures of educational institutions, including the staff, the norms and values, the curriculum, and the student body.

Native Americans U.S. citizens who trace their biological and cultural heritage to the original inhabitants in the land that now makes up the United States. The term Native American is sometimes used synonymously with American Indian. There were about 2.5 million Native Americans (including American Indians, Eskimos, and Aleuts) in the United States in 2000. In 2002, six of the ten largest tribes the Cherokee, Navajo, Latin American Indian, Choctaw, Chippewa, and Sioux—had a population of more than 100,000 persons. The two largest tribes were the Cherokee (730,000) and the Navajo (298,000) (Banks, 2003; U.S. Census, 2002).

People of color Groups in the United States and other nations who have experienced discrimination historically because of their unique biological characteristics that enabled potential discriminators to identify them easily. African Americans, Asian Americans, and Hispanics in the United States are among the groups referred to as people of color. Most members of these groups still experience forms of discrimination today.

Positionality An idea that emerged out of feminist scholarship stating that variables such as an individual's gender, class, and race are markers of her or his relational position within a social and economic context and influence the knowledge that she or he produces. Consequently, valid knowledge requires an acknowledgment of the knower's position within a specific context (See Chapter 7).

Prejudice A set of rigid and unfavorable attitudes toward a particular individual or group that is formed without consideration of facts. Prejudice is a set of attitudes that often leads to discrimination, the differential treatment of particular individuals and groups.

Race A term that refers to the attempt by physical anthropologists to divide human groups according to their physical traits and characteristics. This has proven to be very difficult because human groups in modern societies are highly mixed physically. Consequently, different and often conflicting race typologies exist. An excellent book on race is *Whiteness of a Different Color: European Immigrants and the Alchemy of Race* (Jacobson, 1999).

Racism A belief that human groups can be validly grouped according to their biological traits and that these identifiable groups inherit certain mental, personality, and cultural characteristics that determine their behavior. Racism, however, is not merely a set of beliefs but is practiced when a group has the power to enforce laws, institutions, and norms, based on its beliefs, that oppress and dehumanize another group. An informative reference on racism is *Racism: A Short History* (Fredrickson, 2002).

Religion A set of beliefs and values, especially about explanations that concern the cause and nature of the universe, to which an individual or group has a strong loyalty and attachment. A religion usually has a moral code, rituals, and institutions that reinforce and propagate its beliefs.

Sex The biological factors that distinguish males and females, such as chromosomal, hormonal, anatomical, and physiological characteristics.

Sexism Social, political, and economic structures that advantage one sex group over the other. Stereotypes and misconceptions about the biological characteristics of each sex group reinforce and support sex discrimination. In most societies, women have been the major victims of sexism. However, males are also victimized by sexist beliefs and practices.

Social class A collectivity of people who have a similar socioeconomic status based on such criteria as income, occupation, education, values, behaviors, and life chances. Lower class, working class, middle class, and upper class are common designations of social class in the United States.

References

Alba, R. D., & Nee, V. (2003). *Remaking the American Mainstream: Assimilation and Contemporary Immigration*. Cambridge, MA: Harvard University Press.

Appiah, K. A., & Gates, H. L., Jr. (Eds.). (1999). *Africana: The Encyclopedia of the African and African American Experience*. New York: Perseus.

Asante, M. K. (1998). *The Afrocentric Idea* (rev. ed.). Philadelphia: Temple University Press.

Banks, J. A. (2003). *Teaching Strategies for Ethnic Studies* (7th ed.). Boston: Allyn & Bacon.

Banks, J. A., & Banks, C. A. M. (Eds.). (2004). *Handbook of Research on Multicultural Education* (2nd ed.). San Francisco: Jossey-Bass.

Fredrickson, G. M. (2002). *Racism: A Short History*. Princeton, NJ: Princeton University Press.

Jacobson, M. F. (1999). *Whiteness of a Different Color: European Immigrants and the Alchemy of Race*. Cambridge, MA: Harvard University Press.

Moodley, K. A., & Adam, H. (2004). Citizenship Education and Political Literacy in South Africa. In J. A. Banks (Ed.), *Diversity and Citizenship Education: Global Perspectives* (pp. 159–183). San Francisco: Jossey-Bass.

Pollard, K. M., & O'Hare, W. P. (1999). America's Racial and Ethnic Minorities. *Population Bulletin*, 54(3), 1–48. Washington, DC: Population Reference Bureau.

Population Reference Bureau. (2003). *A First Look at Asian Americans in the Census*. Retrieved June 12, 2003, from http://www.prb.org/pdf/asianamericans.pdf.

Stephan, W., & Vogt, W. P. (Eds.). (2004). *Education Programs for Improving Intergroup Relations: Theory, Research, and Practice*. New York: Teachers College Press.

U.S. Census Bureau. (2000). *Resident Population by Race and Hispanic Origin—Status Projections: 2005 to 2050*. Retrieved June 12, 2003, from http://www.census.gov/population/www/projections/natsum-T3.html.

U.S. Census Bureau. (2002). USA Statistics in Brief—Population and Vital Statistics. Retrieved June 12, 2003, from http://www.census.gov/statab/www/poppart.html.

Contributors

Cherry A. McGee Banks is professor and interim director, education program, University of Washington, Bothell. Her latest book is *Improving Multicultural Education: Lessons From the Intergroup Education Movement.* She is associate editor of the *Handbook of Research on Multicultural Education*, co-editor of *Multicultural Education: Issues and Perspectives*, and co-author of *Teaching Strategies for the Social Studies.* In 1997, she received the Distinguished Teaching Award from the University of Washington, Bothell, and was named a Worthington Distinguished Professor in 2000.

James A. Banks is Kerry and Linda Killinger Professor of Diversity Studies and director of the Center for Multicultural Education at the University of Washington, Seattle. His books include *Educating Citizens in a Multicultural Society; Cultural Diversity and Education: Foundations, Curriculum and Teaching; Diversity and Citizenship Education: Global Perspectives; Race, Culture, and Education: The Selected Works of James A. Banks;* and *Handbook of Research on Multicultural Education.* Professor Banks is a past president of the American Educational Research Association (AERA) and the National Council for the Social Studies (NCSS). He is a member of the National Academy of Education and holds honorary Doctorates of Humane Letters from six colleges and universities.

Jill Bevan-Brown is an associate professor in inclusive education at Massey University College of Education, New Zealand. Being of Maori heritage (the indigenous people of New Zealand), she has a particular interest in the special education needs of Maori children and has concentrated her writing and research efforts in this area. She has published a cultural self-review workbook which is widely used in New Zealand schools. Dr. Bevan-Brown is a member of national advisory committees on autism and gifted education and has had responsibility for the Maori component of two government-commissioned, national research projects evaluating special education and gifted education policies and provisions. At present she is directing an evaluation of a national intersectoral training program for professionals who work with families and young children who have severe and challenging behaviors.

Sara Ernsbarger Bicard received her Ph.D. in special education from The Ohio State University in 2002. She is currently an assistant professor of education at Mercy College in New York, where she teaches special education and literacy courses. Prior to working in higher education, Dr. Bicard taught behavior management classes for foster parents and was a special education teacher for adolescents with learning disabilities. Dr. Ernsbarger's research interests include effective and efficient instructional strategies and methods to help struggling readers acquire and generalize reading skills.

Johnnella E. Butler is provost and vice president for academic affairs and professor of comparative women's studies at Spelman College. A specialist in African American literature, American ethnic literature and criticism, and multicultural studies, she is known for her work in advancing diversity in the undergraduate curriculum and in graduate education. Formerly associate dean and associate vice provost in the graduate school at the University of Washington, Dr. Butler is editor and lead contributor of *Color Line to Borderlands: Ethnic Studies and the Matrix of Higher Education*, co-editor of the *Encyclopedia of American Studies*, and author of the essay, "African American Literature and Realist Theory: Seeking the 'true-true'" in *Identity Politics Reconsidered* (2005, Mohanty, Alcoff, Moya, and Hames-Garcia, eds).

Rodney A. Cavanaugh is a professor of special education at Plattsburgh State University of New York where he teaches courses in curriculum and instructional methods, research design, and classroom management and supervises field practica. For 15 years prior to beginning his career in higher education, Dr. Cavanaugh was a public school teacher of adolescents with learning and behavior disorders. His current research interests include effective teaching strategies for learners with disabilities and teacher-as-researcher models in teacher education. The Carnegie Foundation for the Advancement of Teaching named Dr. Cavanaugh the 1995 New York State Professor of the Year.

Frederick Erickson is the George F. Kneller Professor of Anthropology of Education at the University of California, Los Angeles, where he teaches in the Graduate School of Education and Information Studies. His publications include *The Counselor as Gatekeeper: Social Interaction in Interviews*; *Talk and Social Theory* (winner of the American Educational Research Association's Outstanding Book Award for 2005); and a chapter on qualitative research methods in the *Handbook of Research on Teaching* (3rd ed.). He is a past president of the Council on Anthropology and Education of the American Anthropological Association. He received the council's George and Louise Spindler Award for

outstanding scholarly contributions to educational anthropology in 1991. He is a past editor of the *Anthropology and Education Quarterly*. In 1998–99 he was a Spencer Fellow at the Center for Advanced Study in the Behavioral Sciences. He will return there as a Fellow in 2006–2007.

Donna Y. Ford is Betts Chair of Education and Human Development and Education, and professor in the special education program at Vanderbilt University. She has written four books on multicultural education and gifted education and numerous articles on topics in these fields. Professor Ford consults with school districts nationally on recruiting and retaining culturally diverse students in gifted education, creating culturally responsive learning environments, and improving achievement among culturally diverse students. She has received several awards for her research and serves on numerous education boards and professional committees.

Carl A. Grant is Hoefs-Bascom Professor of Teacher Education in the Department of Curriculum and Instruction at the University Wisconsin–Madison. He has written or edited 25 books or monographs in multicultural education and/or teacher education. He has also written more than 135 articles, chapters in books, and reviews. Several of his writings and programs that he directed have received awards. He is a former classroom teacher and administrator. He served as president of the National Association for Multicultural Education (NAME) from 1993 to 1999; editor of *Review of Educational Research* (RER) from 1996 to 1999; a member of the National Research Council Committee on Assessment and Teacher Quality (1999–2001); and is currently the chair of American Educational Research Association (AERA) Publication Committee.

Beth Harry is professor of special education at the University of Miami, Florida. Her research and teaching focus on the impact of culture and social status on the experiences of families of children with disabilities and on the disproportionate placement of ethnic minorities in special education. Her book, *Why Are So Many Minority Students in Special Education? Understanding Race and Disability in Schools*, presents an ethnographic study of the processes that contribute to disproportionality. Dr. Harry has been a recipient of a Fulbright senior scholar research award to study the situation of immigrant students of color in Spain. She entered the field of special education as a parent of a child with cerebral palsy and received her Ph.D. from Syracuse University in 1989.

William L. Heward is professor emeritus of special education at The Ohio State University, where he taught for 30 years. The author of more than 140 professional publications, Dr. Heward's texts include *Applied Behavior Analysis* (2nd ed.) and *Exceptional Children: An Introduction to Special Education* (8th ed.), which has been used at more than 400 colleges and universities in the United States and translated into Chinese, Japanese, Korean, and Spanish. Professor Heward's research interests focus on increasing the effectiveness of group instruction, improving the academic success of students with disabilities in general education classrooms, and promoting the generalization and maintenance of newly learned skills.

Gloria Ladson-Billings is the Kellner Family Professor of Urban Education in the Department of Curriculum and Instruction and faculty affiliate in the Department of Educational Policy Studies at the University of Wisconsin–Madison. She is the author of *The Dreamkeepers: Successful Teachers of African American Children; Crossing over to Canaan: The Journey of New Teachers in Diverse Classrooms; Beyond the Big House: African American Educators on Teacher Education;* and more than 50 journal articles and book chapters. She is the former editor of the *American Educational Research Journal* and a member of several editorial boards. She is a past president of the American Educational Research Association (AERA), has been a fellow at the Center for Advanced Study in the Behavioral Sciences, and is a member of the National Academy of Education. She is the co-editor of *Education Research in the Public Interest: Social Justice, Action, and Policy.*

Charles H. Lippy is the LeRoy A. Martin Distinguished Professor of Religious Studies at the University of Tennessee at Chattanooga. His most recent books include *Being Religious, American Style: A History of Popular Religiosity in the United States; Pluralism Comes of Age: American Religious Culture in the Twentieth Century;* and *Do Real Men Pray: Images of the Christian Man and Male Spirituality in White Protestant America.* He is

co-editor of the *Encyclopedia of the American Religious Experience,* the second edition of the *Encyclopedia of Religion in the South,* and the forthcoming four-volume *Encyclopedia of American Religion.*

Luanna H. Meyer is professor of education (research), Victoria University, New Zealand, where she has responsibility for providing research leadership in the College of Education. Previously, she held positions at Massey University in New Zealand, Syracuse University, the University of Minnesota, and the University of Hawaii. She is internationally known for her work in special and inclusive education and has published more than 200 books, journal articles, and book chapters. She has been an invited speaker in several countries and more than 30 U.S. states. She is currently engaged in research investigating how teachers teach culturally diverse students, effective inventions for problem behavior, effective professional development for teachers, and how assessment practices impact student motivation and behavior.

Sonia Nieto is professor emerita of language, literacy, and culture at the University of Massachusetts, Amherst. She has researched and written widely on multicultural teacher education, Latino education, and the education of students of linguistically and culturally diverse backgrounds. Her books include *Affirming Diversity: The Sociopolitical Context of Multicultural Education* (4th ed., 2004); *The Light in Their Eyes* (1999); *What Keeps Teachers Going?* (2003); and two edited books, *Puerto Rican Students in U.S. Schools* (2000) and *Why We Teach* (2005). She serves on various national advisory boards that focus on educational equity and social justice, and she has received many awards for her community service, advocacy, and scholarly activities.

Caroline Hodges Persell is professor of sociology at New York University. A past vice president of the American Sociological Association, she has received grants from the Carnegie Academy for the Scholarship of Teaching and Learning, the National Science Foundation, the Danforth Foundation, the Fund for the Improvement of Post-Secondary Education, and the U.S. Office of Education. Besides scores of articles in scholarly journals, her books include *How Sampling Works* (with Richard Maisel); *Understanding Society: An Introduction to Sociology; Preparing for Power: America's*

Elite Boarding Schools (with Peter W. Cookson, Jr.); and *Education and Inequality*. She has received teaching awards from the American Sociological Association and New York University.

Deirdre Raynor is an assistant professor in the Interdisciplinary Arts and Sciences Program at the University of Washington, Tacoma. She also serves as the faculty coordinator of the Ethnic, Gender, and Labor Studies Concentration in Interdisciplinary Arts and Sciences. Professor Raynor teaches courses in American ethnic literature with an emphasis on literature by women from diverse racial and ethnic backgrounds and African American female and male authors. She has written and published articles on Julia C. Collins, Ann Petry, Edward Christopher Williams, and the Harlem Renaissance. She is currently editing a book on race, pedagogy, and the curriculum tentatively titled *Navigating the Frontlines of Academia: The Dialogic of Race in the Humanities*.

David Sadker is a professor at the American University and with his late wife Myra Sadker has written extensively on the impact of gender in schools. The Sadkers' book, *Failing at Fairness: How Our Schools Cheat Girls*, was published by Touchstone Press in 1995, and their introductory teacher education textbook, *Teachers, Schools and Society* is now in its 7th edition. His new co-authored text is *Teachers, Schools, and Society: A Brief Introduction to Education*, and he is co-editor of *Gender in the Classroom: Foundations, Skills, Methods and Strategies across the Curriculum*.

Mara Sapon-Shevin is professor of inclusive education in the Teaching and Leadership Department of the School of Education at Syracuse University. She teaches in the university's Inclusive Elementary and Special Education Teacher Education Program, which prepares teachers for inclusive, heterogeneous classrooms. Mara is active in promoting social justice education in schools and consults on a national and international basis. Her DVD, ". . . And Nobody Said Anything: Uncomfortable Conversations about Diversity," is being used in higher education to help faculty examine their own classroom practices relative to diversity. Her most recent book is *Because We Can Change the World: A Practical Guide for Building Cooperative, Inclusive Classroom Communities*. She is cur-

rently writing a book on the imperative of inclusive education for a democratic future.

Janet Ward Schofield is professor of psychology and a senior scientist at the Learning Research and Development Center at the University of Pittsburgh. Her book *Black and White in School: Trust, Tension or Tolerance?* was awarded the Society for the Psychological Study of Social Issues Gordon Allport Intergroup Relations Prize. She is a contributing author of the *Handbook of Research on Multicultural Education*, a former member of the governing body of the American Psychological Association, and a member of the board on International Comparative Studies in Education at the National Research Council. She is the author of *Computers and Classroom Culture* and *Bringing the Internet to School: Lessons from an Urban District*.

Christine E. Sleeter is professor emerita of teacher education and multicultural education at California State University, Monterey Bay. She consults nationally and internationally in multicultural education and multicultural teacher education. She currently serves as vice president of Division K (Teaching and Teacher Education) of the American Educational Research Association. Dr. Sleeter has received several awards for her work, most recently the California State University Monterey Bay President's Medal. She has published numerous books and articles in multicultural education. Her most recent books include *Un-Standardizing Curriculum*; *Culture, Difference and Power*; and *Turning on Learning* (with Carl Grant).

Tom Stritikus is assistant professor in the College of Education, University of Washington. He earned his Ph.D. in 2000 from the University of California, Berkeley. He is author of *Immigrant Children and the Politics of English-Only*, published by LFB Scholarly Publishing and edited by Professors Marcelo and Carola Suárez-Orozco. His teaching and research focus on policy and practice issues for culturally and linguistically diverse students. He has published articles in the *Bilingual Research Journal*, *Teachers College Record*, *Educational Policy*, and the *Journal of Language, Identity, and Education*.

Mary Kay Thompson Tetreault is provost emerita at Portland State University. Her research interests center around feminist pedagogy, diversifying universities, and the epistemology of knowing and learning. She is completing a manuscript on privilege and diversity in the academy, which will be published in 2006 by Routledge. She is the author (with Frances Maher) of *The Feminist Classroom* (2nd ed., Rowman & Littlefield) and also co-authored (with Maher) "Learning in the Dark: How Assumptions of Whiteness Shape Classroom Knowledge," published in the *Harvard Educational Review*.

Manka M. Varghese received her Ph.D. in 2000 in educational linguistics from the University of Pennsylvania, after having taught EFL and ESL for 10 years. She is currently an assistant professor at the University of Washington. Her areas of research and teaching include language teacher education and teacher identity, with a particular emphasis on anti-oppressive education. She is co-editor of *Bilingualism and Language Pedagogy*, and has authored various articles appearing in *TESOL Quarterly*, *Linguistics and Education*, and the *Journal of Teacher Education*.

Karen Zittleman is an adjunct professor at American University and co-author of *Teachers, Schools, and Society: A Brief Introduction to Education*. Her articles have appeared in the *Journal of Teacher Education*, *Educational Leadership*, *Phi Delta Kappan*, *Principal* and other professional journals. Karen is a contributing author to *Gender in the Classroom: Foundations, Skills, Methods and Strategies Across the Curriculum* and wrote *Making Public Schools Great for Every Girl and Boy*, a guide for promoting equity in math and science instruction. Professor Zittleman's research and teaching interests focus on educational equity, foundations of education, teacher preparation, and spirituality in education.

Index